T0214233

Lecture Notes of the Institute for Computer Sciences, Social Informatics and Telecommunications Engineering 388

More information about this series at http://www.springer.com/series/8197

Weina Fu · Yuan Xu · Shui-Hua Wang ·
Yudong Zhang (Eds.)

Multimedia Technology and Enhanced Learning

Third EAI International Conference, ICMTEL 2021
Virtual Event, April 8–9, 2021
Proceedings, Part II

 Springer

Editors
Weina Fu (iD)
Hunan Normal University
Changsha, China

Yuan Xu (iD)
University of Jinan
Jinan, China

Shui-Hua Wang (iD)
University of Leicester
Leicester, UK

Yudong Zhang (iD)
University of Leicester
Leicester, UK

ISSN 1867-8211   ISSN 1867-822X (electronic)
Lecture Notes of the Institute for Computer Sciences, Social Informatics
and Telecommunications Engineering
ISBN 978-3-030-82564-5   ISBN 978-3-030-82565-2 (eBook)
https://doi.org/10.1007/978-3-030-82565-2

This Springer imprint is published by the registered company Springer Nature Switzerland AG
The registered company address is: Gewerbestrasse 11, 6330 Cham, Switzerland

Preface

We are delighted to introduce the proceedings of the Third European Alliance for Innovation (EAI) International Conference on Multimedia Technology and Enhanced Learning (ICMTEL 2021). This conference has brought together researchers, developers, and practitioners from around the world who are leveraging and developing multimedia technologies and related enhanced learning methods. The theme of ICMTEL 2021 was "the state of the art and future perspectives of multimedia technologies and enhanced learning".

The technical program of ICMTEL 2021 consisted of 97 full papers, including 2 invited papers, in oral presentation sessions at the main conference tracks. Track 1 – state-of-the-art techniques for multimedia and Track 2 – multimedia-based applications with machine learning methods. The technical program also featured three keynote speeches and four technical workshops. The three keynote speeches were given by Manu Malek from Stevens Institute of Technology, USA, Ng Yin Kwee from Nanyang Technological University, Singapore, and Shuai Liu from Hunan Normal University, China. The five workshops organized were "Deep Learning Techniques for Online Social Network Analysis", which aimed to present novel solutions for problems of online social networks with deep learning methods; "Networking Representations of Data, Images, and Systems", which aimed to provide structure, thinking, and technologies of networking representations for image-based systems; "Intelligent Application in Education", which aimed to focus on the intelligent educational system with multimedia analysis; "Information Fusion and Their Applications", which aimed to analyze how to construct the information fusion system for multimodal multimedia data and the industrial application of the multimodal systems; and "AI-based Data Processing, Intelligent Control, and Their Applications", which aimed to discuss research on the dynamic system of multimedia data processing.

Coordination with the steering chairs, Imrich Chlamtac, Deshuang Huang and Chunming Li, was essential for the success of the conference. We sincerely appreciate their constant support and guidance. It was also a great pleasure to work with such an excellent Organizing Committee team for their hard work in organizing and supporting the conference. In particular, we are grateful to the Technical Program Committee, led by our TPC chair, Shi-Hua Wang, who completed the peer-review process of technical papers and put together a high-quality technical program. We are also grateful to the conference manager, Natasha Onofrei, for her support and all the authors who submitted their papers to the ICMTEL 2021 conference and workshops.

We strongly believe that ICMTEL provides a good forum for all researchers, developers, and practitioners to discuss all science and technology aspects that are relevant to multimedia and enhanced learning. We also expect that future ICMTEL conferences will be as successful and stimulating as ICMTEL 2021, as indicated by the contributions presented in this volume.

Shuai Liu

Conference Organization

Steering Committee

Chair

Imrich Chlamtac   University of Trento, Italy

Co-chairs

Deshuang Huang   Tongji University, China
Chunming Li   University of Electronic Science and Technology
       of China, China

Organizing Committee

General Chair

Yu-Dong Zhang   University of Leicester, UK

General Co-chair

Shuai Liu   Hunan Normal University, China

Technical Program Committee Chairs

Shui-Hua Wang   Loughborough University, UK
Ruidan Su   Shanghai Advanced Research Institute, China

Technical Program Committee Co-chairs

Vishnu Varthanan   Kalasalingam Academy of Research and Education,
  Govindaraj   India
Xianwei Jiang   Nanjing Normal University of Special Education,
       China
Zhuqing Jiao   Changzhou University, China
Siamak Khatibi   Blekinge Institute of Technology, Sweden
Raymond F. Muzic, Jr.   Case Western Reserve University, USA
Pengjiqng Qian   Jiangnan University, China
Yuan Xu   University of Jinan, China

Special Issue Chair

Zheng Zhang   Harbin Institute of Technology, China

Workshops Chair and Co-chairs

Zhuqing Jiao	Changzhou University, China
Xinhua Mao	Nanjing University of Aeronautics and Astronautics, China
Shuhui Bi	University of Jinan, China

Panel Chairs

Arun Kumar Sangaiah	Vellore Institute of Technology, India
Yin Zhang	University of Electronic Science and Technology of China, China
T. S. Pradeep Kumar	Vellore Institute of Technology, India

Session Chairs

Xujing Yao	University of Leicester, UK
Yan Yan	University of Leicester, UK
Wei Wang	University of Leicester, UK
Xinyu Liu	Hunan Normal University, China

Publications Chair

Shuai Liu	Hunan Normal University, China

Tutorials Chair

Zhengchao Dong	Columbia University, USA

Web Chair

Lijia Deng	University of Leicester, UK

Publicity and Social Media Chair

Qinghua Zhou	University of Leicester, UK

Local Chair

Yu Xiang	University of Leicester, UK

Technical Program

Ali Saberi	Iranian Researchers Network, Iran
Aijun Liu	Xidian University, China
Amin Taheri-Garavand	Lorestan University, Iran
Chenxi Huang	Xiamen University, China
Dang Thanh	Hue Industrial College, Vietnam
David Guttery	University of Leicester, UK
Jun Dai	California State University, USA
Kaijian Xia	Soochow University, China

Mengjun Xie	University of Tennessee at Chattanooga, USA
Nianyin Zeng	Xiamen University, China
Pengjiang Qian	Jiangnan University, China
Praveen Agarwal	Harish-Chandra Research Institute, India
Ravipudi Venkata Rao	S. V. National Institute of Technology, India
Rossi Kamal	Xaria ICT, Bangladesh
Seifedine Kadry	Beirut Arab University, Lebanon
Shui-Hua Wang	University of Leicester, UK
Shuai Liu	Hunan Normal University, China
Sunil Kumar	National Institute of Technology, China
Xianwei Jiang	Nanjing Normal University of Special Education, India
Yizhang Jiang	Jiangnan University, China
Jie Zhang	Newcastle University, UK
Yuan Zhang	Nanjing University, China
Yu-Dong Zhang	University of Leicester, UK
Yuriy Shmaliy	Universidad de Guanajuato, Mexico
Zhimin Chen	Shanghai Dianji University, China
Zhou Zhang	New York City College of Technology, USA

Contents – Part II

Intelligent Application in Education

A Simple and Efficient Key Frame Recognition Algorithm for Sign
Language Video 3
   Zhaosong Zhu, ShengWei Zhang, and YunLei Zhou

Research on Dynamic Sign Language Recognition Based on Key Frame
Weighted of DTW 11
   ShengWei Zhang, ZhaoSong Zhu, and RongXin Zhu

An Optimized Seven-Layer Convolutional Neural Network with Data
Augmentation for Classification of Chinese Fingerspelling Sign Language ... 21
   Yalan Gao, Rongxin Zhu, Ruina Gao, Yuxiang Weng, and Xianwei Jiang

Similar Gesture Recognition via an Optimized Convolutional Neural
Network and Adam Optimizer 43
   Ya Gao, Chenchong Jia, Yifei Qiao, Xi Huang, Juan Lei,
   and Xianwei Jiang

Development and Creation of Open Online Course Resources
in Tourism Colleges from the Perspective of School-Enterprise
Collaborative Education 62
   Rui Jiang and Hua Jiang

Research on the Application of MOOC in O2O Teaching Model Innovation
of Aesthetic Education in Higher Vocational Colleges 71
   Gege Ma

Design of Hospital Remote Consultation and Teaching System Based
on Deep Learning 79
   Ying Bao

A Feasibility Analysis Model for Developing Wushu Sanda Courses
in Universities Based on Deep Learning...................... 92
   Dong-Dong Liu

Performance Evaluation Model of Wushu Sanda Athletes Based on Visual
Signal Processing 103
   Dong-dong Liu

Online Matching Method of News Communication Innovative Teaching
Mode Driven by Artificial Intelligence....................... 117
   Jia Qian and Li-li Wang

Motion Recognition System of Table Tennis Players Based
on MEMS Sensor   128
   Wei Tang and Chonggao Chen

Open Sharing of Digital Education Training Resources Based
on Machine Learning.   142
   Jichao Yan and Jingya Zheng

Design of Basketball Shot Track Recognition
System Based on Machine Vision   152
   Chonggao Chen and Wei Tang

Design and Implementation of Mobile Learning System Based
on Wireless Communication Technology   165
   Hui-jun Wang and Ang Li

Mining Recessive Teaching Resources of University Information
Based on Machine Learning.   178
   Zheng Jingya and Jichao Yan

Networked Teaching System of College Basketball Course Based
on Virtual Reality   189
   Er-wei Liu

Research on Remote Online Teaching Assistant System Based
on Human-Computer Interaction   203
   Zijin Xiao, Ying Li, and Hai Zhou

Towards the Automatic Generation of Pedagogical Conversational
Agents from Lecture Slides   216
   Matthias Wölfel

Research on the Fusion Pattern Recognition System Based on the Concept
of Production Education Integration and Application of Generative
Countermeasure Network   230
   Conggang Lv

Design of Multimedia Learning Resource Recommendation System
Based on Recurrent Neural Network   243
   Zijin Xiao, Ying Li, and Hai Zhou

Human/Medical Based Data Processing and Systems

Research on Constructing Regional Telemedicine Imaging Diagnosis
Center Based on Ctirix Technology.   257
   Jinshun Ding, Yu Ren, Kefeng Xu, and Yixin Wang

Research on Multi-agency Data Fusion Mode Under Regional
Medical Integration   267
   Yixin Wang, Weiqing Fang, Wei Zhu, and Jinshun Ding

Research on Brain Image Segmentation Based on FCM
Algorithm Optimization   278
   Xinlei Chen, Dongming Zhao, Wei Zhong, and Jiufeng Ye

Facial Expression Recognition via ResNet-18   290
   Bin Li, Runda Li, and Dimas Lima

Comparison of AWS and AZURE for COVID-19 Information Retrieval   304
   Hemil Patel, Roopakala Mankaveettil, Reshmi Kanakuzhiyil Rajan,
   Nagamaisamma Challa, Rajeshwar Maryala, Saitheja Parsha,
   and Pavan Kumar Bayyarapu

Expression Recognition Algorithm Based on Infrared Image   321
   Ying Cui and Shi Qiu

The Study About the Emotional State and Physical Activity of Adolescents
During the COVID-19 Epidemic   331
   Runda Li, Yutong Wu, Wenxuan Zhanggu, Chihao Xu, Yuhan Gu,
   Shihan Yao, Hangxiao Li, Yuwei Shi, Yaojun Yang, Zhuoyang Zhen,
   Baijun Zhang, Chengyu Ye, Zimeng Li, Shumeng Shi, Xinyan Wang,
   Jingyang Chen, and Jiaxi Lei

Remote Consultation Information Mobile Phone Intelligent Display System
Under Augmented Reality and Human-Computer Interaction   338
   Ying Bao

Design of Real Information Collection Model of Physical Fitness
for the Elderly Based on Internet of Things Technology   349
   Wei-Ping Cao and Yu-Shuo Tan

Track and Field Head Posture Error Correction System Based on Deep
Reinforcement Learning   362
   Liu Er-wei

Visual Imaging Method of 3D Virtual Scene Based on VR Technology   373
   Zhao Bing and Zhou Qian

Human Centered Computing in Digital Persona Generation   385
   Nisha Ramachandra, Manish Ahuja, Raghotham M. Rao,
   and Neville Dubash

Content-Based Image Retrieval Using Local Derivative Laplacian
Co-occurrence Pattern   402
   Prashant Srivastava, Manish Khare, and Ashish Khare

Multi-spectral Image Filtering Algorithm Based on Convolutional
Neural Network   413
   Dan Luo and Rong Hu

Interactive Virtual Reality Indoor Space Roaming System Based
on 3D Vision   425
   Jing He

Multi-viewpoint Rendering Optimization of Indoor Scene
Based on Binocular Vision.   436
   He Jing

A New Confidence Propagation Algorithm for Regional Image Based
on Deep Learning   448
   Jia Qian, Li-li Wang, and Hai-yue Huang

Feature Extraction Method of EEG Signal Based on
Synchroextracting Transform   462
   Lin Han, Liang Lu, Haoran Dong, Shuangbo Xie, Gang Yu, Tao Shen,
   Mingxu Sun, Tianyi Wang, and Xuqun Pei

Human Cross-Border Alarm Detection Method Based on OpenPose   469
   Hang Yu, Qinjun Zhao, Yong Zhang, and Shengjun Shi

Design and Implementation of Disconnector Condition Monitoring System
Based on Attitude Sensor.   476
   Yueyu Du and Shubo Qiu

Author Index   483

Contents – Part I

AI-based Data Processing, Intelligent Control and Their Applications

Research on Multithreaded Data Scheduling Control Method for Power
Communication Based on Wireless Sensor   3
    Zhou Qian and Zhao Bing

Recognition Method of Metal Material Pitting Defect Based on Visual
Signal Processing   14
    Ying Zhao and Li Zhang

Research on Detection Method of Internal Defects of Metal Materials Based
on Computer Vision   27
    Li Zhang and Ying Zhao

Error Correction Method for Rotating Axis of Large Rotating Machinery
Based on Machine Vision   39
    Yu-Shuo Tan, Wen-Bin Zhang, Jing Wang, Han Han, and Wei-Ping Cao

Simulation Study on Tensile Mechanical Properties of Graphene Based
on Long and Short-Term Memory Neural Network   51
    Li Ang and Wang Hui-jun

Design of Distributed Hybrid Pipeline Multimedia Aided
Scheduling System   64
    Guang Xie and Yuxia Pan

Intelligent Scheduling of Distributed Displacement Pipeline Based
on Hybrid Discrete Drosophila Optimization Algorithm   77
    Pan Yuxia and Xie Guang

Research on Grid Planning Method of Distribution Network Based
on Artificial Intelligence Technology   91
    Fu Guan-hua, Chen Da-xing, Sun Yang, Xia Jia, Wang Fei-feng,
    and Zhu Lian-huan

Intelligent Monitoring Method for Backstage Data Security of Tourism
Information Promotion Platform Based on Cloud Computing   103
    Yiqiong Ding and Guozhi Lin

Research on Industrial Product Modeling Design Method Based
on Deep Learning   115
    Guozhi Lin and Yiqiong Ding

A Frequency Conversion Circuit for Piezoelectric Vibrating
Energy Harvesting.   128
   Xingjun Gao, Zijian Li, Yongbin Li, and Qiang Zhou

An Adaptive Optimization Strict Reverse Navigation Algorithm for Ship
Fine Alignment Process   137
   Junwei Wang, Xiyuan Chen, Xin Shao, and Zhen Ma

Research on Load Feature Extraction Method of Typical Users Based
on Deep Learning   145
   Zhu Lian-huan, Wei Wei, Zhu Wei-yang, Ding Can-song, Shen Kai,
   and Fu Guan-hua

Enterprise Financial Risk Early Warning System Based on Catastrophe
Progression Method.   157
   Bo Hou and Chang-song Ma

Research on Transportation Route Planning Method of Regional Logistics
Network Based on Transfer Learning.   170
   Bo Hou and Chang-song Ma

Simultaneous Localization of Multiple Defects in Software Testing Based
on Reinforcement Learning   180
   Jiajuan Fang and Yanjing Lu

Design of Embedded Network Human Machine Interface Based
on VR Technology   191
   Yi Huang and Yubin Wang

Design of Information Security System Based on JSP Technology
and Reinforcement Model   202
   Yubin Wang and Yiping Li

Sliding Mode Adaptive Control for Sensorless Permanent Magnet
Synchronous Motor.   214
   Lei Wang, Tongwei Liang, and Shengjun Wen

An Improved Detection Method of Safety Helmet Wearing Based
on CenterNet   223
   Bo Wang, Yong Zhang, Qinjun Zhao, and Shengjun Shi

Information Techniques for Social/Natural Application

Influence Maximization Based on True Threshold in Social Networks   235
   Wei Hao, Qianyi Zhan, and Yuan Liu

An Exemplar-Based Clustering Model with Loose Constraints
in Social Network   248
   Bi Anqi and Ying Wenhao

Personal Name Disambiguation for Chinese Documents
in Online Medium.   255
   Chao Fan and Yu Li

Research on Behavior Characteristics of Festival Tourists in Jianye District
of Nanjing Based on Big Data   265
   Yueli Ni, Yijuan Ge, and Xiaoling Zhang

Application of GNSS Virtual Reference Station in Poyang Lake Area   273
   Zhigang Wang, Hang Guo, Hepeng Wang, Min Yu, and Xindong Chen

Cruise Tourism Prosperity Index Based on Principal Component Analysis . . .   281
   Fangqing Sheng, Yang Zhang, Hua Jiang, and Gege Ma

Interactive Evolution Model of Industrial Cluster and Regional Innovation
Based on LSTM   288
   Le Tong and Fen Wang

Design of Hotel Marketing Information Management Model Based
on Deep Learning   298
   Lei Tong and Fen Wang

Design of Intelligent Dispatching System for Logistics Distribution
Vehicles Based on Transfer Learning.   311
   Li Yu and Yuanyuan Guan

Design of Supply Chain Resource Distribution Allocation Model Based
on Deep Learning   321
   Yuanyuan Guan and Li Yu

Arabic Question-Answering System Using Search Engine Techniques   333
   *Manal Alamir, Sadeem Alharth, Shahad Alqurashi, and Tahani
Alqurashi*

Adaptive Encryption Model of Internet Public Opinion Information Based
on Big Data   344
   Yanjing Lu and Jiajuan Fang

Intelligent Classification System of Financial Statistics Information Based
on Recurrent Neural Network.   354
   Conggang Lv

Design and Implementation of Financial Management Analysis Based
on Big Data Platform of Psychiatric Hospital   368
    Meiying Su and Xinlei Chen

Study of Measurement and Inverse Prediction Methods of Heat Storage
Efficiency for the Wood Heating Floor   377
    Guangyue Du

Apple Classification Based on Information Fusion of Internal
and External Qualities   388
    Xue Li, Liyao Ma, Shuhui Bi, and Tao Shen

Apple Defect Detection Method Based on Convolutional Neural Network . . .   398
    Zheng Xu, Tao Shen, Shuhui Bi, and Qinjun Zhao

Information Fusion and Their Applications

Lidar/IMU Integrated Navigation and Positioning Method   407
    Zhigang Wang, Jiehua Liao, Hang Guo, and Min Yu

Indoor Positioning and Navigation Methods Based on Mobile
Phone Camera   414
    Min Yu, Jiaohao Yu, Hailei Li, Huixia Li, and Hang Guo

PD Controller of a Lower Limb Exoskeleton Robot Based on Sliding Mode
RBF Neural Network.   427
    Aihui Wang, Wei Li, and Jun yu

Verification of Deformation Measurement Method Based on FBG Sensor . . .   437
    Zhen Ma, Xiyuan Chen, and Junwei Wang

Air Alignment Method of Guided Projectile Based on INS/BDS   442
    Shiqi Li and Xiyuan Chen

Motion Constraint Aided Underwater Integrated Navigation Method Based
on Improved Adaptive Filtering   452
    Siyi Zhang and Xiyuan Chen

High-Precision Calibration and Error Estimation of RLG SINS.   460
    Yikun Geng and Xiyuan Chen

Design of an Interactive LiDAR-Vision Integrated Navigation System   470
    Jidong Feng, Wanfeng Ma, Tongqian Liu, and Yuan Xu

Research on Residential Power Consumption Behavior Based on Typical
Load Pattern.   476
    Anmeng Mao, Jia Qiao, and Yong Zhang

A Comparative Study of REST with SOAP   485
  Usman Riaz, Samir Hussain, and Hemil Patel

Matrix Profile Evolution: An Initial Overview   492
  Bin Sun, Liyao Ma, Renkang Geng, and Yuan Xu

LS-SVM/Federated EKF Based on the Distributed INS/UWB Integrated
2D Localization   502
  Fukun Li, Shuhui Bi, Meng Wang, Liyao Ma, and Bo Zhang

LiDAR Map Construction Using Improved R-T-S Smoothing Assisted
Extended Kalman Filter   510
  Bo Zhang, Meng Wang, Shuhui Bi, and Fukun Li

Path Planning Method for Unmanned Surface Vehicle Based on RRT*
and DWA   518
  Xiaotian Zhang and Xiyuan Chen

A Novel Brain-Like Navigation Based on Dynamic Attention with
Modified Unet   528
  Yu Zhang and Xiyuan Chen

Feature Extraction of Network Temporal and Spatial Distribution Based
on Data Stream Clustering   541
  Hu Rong and Luo Dan

Design of Advance Security Early Warning System for Network Data
Based on Artificial Intelligence   553
  Ya-fei Wang and Wei- na He

Research on Network Information Security Risk Assessment Based
on Artificial Intelligence   566
  Ya-fei Wang and Wei-na He

Research on Normalized Network Information Storage Method Based
on Deep Reinforcement Learning   579
  Qiang Wang and Lai-feng Tang

Research on the Method of Eliminating Duplicated Encrypted Data
in Cloud Storage Based on Generated Countermeasure Network   590
  Lai-feng Tang and Qiang Wang

Author Index   603

Intelligent Application in Education

A Simple and Efficient Key Frame Recognition Algorithm for Sign Language Video

Zhaosong Zhu, ShengWei Zhang, and YunLei Zhou(✉)

Nanjing Normal University of Special Education, Nanjing 210038, China

Abstract. Sign language is an important means of social communication for hearing-impaired people, and most developed countries have established their own hand language banks. Under the guidance of the National Language Commission, China has created a national sign language corpus, which is mainly composed of video. For the database, one of the most important work is to establish the index of retrieval. For sign language videos, the most important index is the hand shape displayed in the video key frame. In this paper, a simple and efficient key frame extraction algorithm is proposed based on the video library with good consistency, namely the sign language video library, to create a fast and efficient index. At the same time, it can be used as a reference for similar video libraries.

Keywords: Classification of videos · Classification of sign language · Key frame extraction · Chinese Sign Language

1 Introduction

It is an important work in the development of national language to establish a national corpus of sign language and carry out the standardization of sign language. China created its national sign language corpus in 2016. It now contains more than 60,000 sign language videos. It can be searched through the website of Nanjing Normal University for Special Education. Current retrieval methods mainly rely on Pinyin and Chinese strokes, as well as hand-shape image indexing. The indexing mainly depends on manual division, which has the disadvantages of high cost, low efficiency, high error and so on. Moreover, from the linguistic point of view, the generation of sign language video needs to rely on its own information, and cannot be disturbed by normal natural language. Therefore, the use of computers from the perspective of video itself, from the perspective of linguistics, is a very important means.

The key frame recognition technology of sign language based on graphics is a challenging subject. In a video of sign language movements, not every frame has a semantic effect on the expression. As a person who uses sign language, he will take the initiative to emphasize his sign language semantics. So there is a pause in sign language presentation, and this pause is what he emphasizes. The relatively still image produced in this pause process can be used as the key frame of sign language video. Graphics obtained

W. Fu et al. (Eds.): ICMTEL 2021, LNICST 388, pp. 3–10, 2021.
https://doi.org/10.1007/978-3-030-82565-2_1

from this key frame can be directly used as an index, or classified to generate a secondary index.

Video key frame extraction methods are generally divided into four categories. The first category is to extract key frames according to the content of the image. The content of the video is the embodiment of the image features, and the corresponding content variation degree is the standard for selecting key frames. The second category is the motion analysis in the image. According to the optical flow field of the image, the optical flow diagram is calculated and the minimum frame is taken as the key frame. The third type is the key frame detection based on the trajectory curve density feature. The density of the trajectory density curve is used to distinguish the key frame and the non-key frame. The fourth class is a popular clustering method, which needs to set the number of clusters in advance, and then group the similar pins into one category, with each category being a key frame.

The second type of algorithm requires a large amount of computation and takes a long time, while the third type of algorithm will produce a large deviation trajectory due to inaccurate positioning. The fourth type of algorithm needs to establish clustering, which has a lot of redundancy and a high computational load. Their advantages and disadvantages are shown in the Table 1.

Table 1. The advantages and disadvantages of the four algorithms

Common key frame extraction algorithms	Advantages	Disadvantages
Based on image content [1, 2]	The feature of the bottom layer of the image can be fused	The image depth feature cannot be utilized
Based on optical flow field [3, 4]	Better expression of global movement	The image depth feature cannot be utilized
Based on curve density [5]	It can better reflect the motion trajectory	Inaccurate positioning, large deviation
Based on cluster analysis [6, 7]	Popular big data processing methods	Not being able to determine the number of clusters is prone to redundancy

The video content in the video library of sign language has good consistency, including similar background, similar light and clothes with less color difference. Therefore, it is not necessary to use a high amount of computation in the process of extracting key frames. It is only necessary to extract a small number of key frames based on content and carry out screening.

2   Key Frame Selection Process Design

This algorithm is mainly divided into the following steps: Step 1, serialization of images. Step 2, grayscale of the image. Step 3, removal of the image background, Refer to the background image provided. Step 4. difference processing with adjacent frames. Step 5, find out the minimum frame between two maximum frames, which is the key frame. Step 6 is optional. According to the actual demand, find the best frame in the neighborhood of the smallest frame that meets the actual demand.

2.1 Serialization of Images

Complete conversion of images to frames without redundant processing. This is a relatively large amount of data, but it reduces the computation. As shown in the figure, at 25 frames per second, the three-second video is split into 75 frames, while the one-minute video has about 1,500 frames. In order to keep the video consistent and not make redundant cuts. A sequence $(I_1\text{-}I_n)$ of images is formed shown in Fig. 1.

Fig. 1. Serialized picture of sign language video

2.2 Grayscale of the Image

According to the standard graying formula (1) proposed in literature [8], the color space of each image I_i is reduced from three dimensions to one dimension gray-scale image G_i, and the gray order is normalized to a range between 0 and 255. See Fig. 2 for the gray scale image.

$$gray = 0.299 \times R + 0.587 \times G + 0.114 \times B \tag{1}$$

2.3 Removal of the Image Background

Select the standardized reference image. Under normal circumstances, the first frame of image G_{first} can be used as the reference image. However, considering that the sign language presenter will have slight deviation in the process of expression, the last frame of image G_{last} also needs to be referred. The average value of the two can be taken, $G_{ref} = (G_{first} + G_{last})/2$, to generate the standard as shown in the Fig. 3(a).

Please note that if the video is longer, scenes change under the condition of larger, G_{first} and G_{last} can be replaced with $KEY_{previous}$ and KEY_{next}, This is easy to understand, the video sequence is contiguous, so the reference image of the current key frame can be selected from the previous and the next key frame. This is done only if the previous key frame and the next key frame have been found.

Fig. 2. A sequence of images after graying

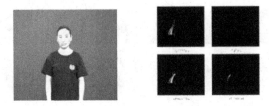

Fig. 3. a $G_{first} + G_{last}$. b. $R_i = G_i - G_{i-1} - G_{ref}$

2.4   Difference Processing of Frames

The difference processing can be carried out with the adjacent frames, and with the before and after frames, $R_i = G_i - G_{i-1} - G_{ref}$, and the obtained part is the part formed by the gesture in the motion.

Because of the difference between the two values, there are fewer pixels, and the negative pixels are automatically set to 0, so it is more difficult to see as shown in Fig. 3(b).

2.5   Find Out the Minimum Frame Between Two Maximum Frames

All the gray-scale values of the pixels are summed up, $SUM\_GRAY_i = SUM(R_i)$, draw the line chart (Fig. 4), find the extreme value point. The frame where the extreme point is located is the time sequence region that varies greatly in the video. The middle point of the extreme point may be the image emphasized by the gesture pause, which is the key frame that the video is looking for. As shown in the figure, the extreme points are frame 17 (Fig. 5(a), value: 118745) and frame 44 (Fig. 5(b), value: 127596). This indicates that these two frames have the greatest changes, and the 30th frame (Fig. 5(c)) between them has a minimum value of 71, which is optional as a key frame.

2.6   Find the Best Frame in the Neighborhood of the Smallest Frame (Optional)

In some cases, minimum frames may not be sufficient for key frame processing. For example, it does not have clear edges and corners, which is not convenient for subsequent

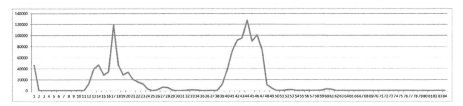

Fig. 4. A line diagram of a grayscale summation sequence

Fig. 5. a Frame 17. b. frame 44. c. frame30

image feature collection. Therefore, it is necessary to search in the area near the minimum frame. This requires defining a search area that is the neighborhood of the minima frame. The neighborhood distance formula (2) is as follows:

$$d = a*diff_{NO.} + b*diff_{vlaue} \qquad (2)$$

Where, parameters a and b are weights, $diff_{NO.}$ is the difference of sequence number, and $diff_{value}$ is the difference of values between two frames. The ratio of a and b can be adjusted to meet actual needs. This process results in a region, as shown in Fig. 6.

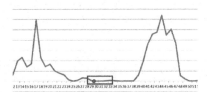

Fig. 6. The neighborhood of the minimum frame

3 Extract Key Frames from Long Videos for Verification

The selected video is an alphabet video, showing the 26 letters of English and the three initials unique to Chinese. It lasts for 1 min and 16 s, 25 frames per second, and produces a total of 1900 frames of images.

Due to the large amount of data, three segments of data (Fig. 7, Fig. 8, Fig. 9) were randomly selected to verify whether the key frame was selected properly:

In Fig. 7, the maximum frame is Frame 26 and Frame 69, the minimum frame is Frame 47, and the neighborhood is 41–53.

Fig. 7. The first data sequence.

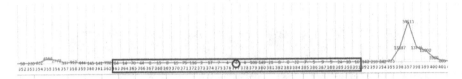

Fig. 8. The second data sequence

In Fig. 8, the maximum frame is 355 and 397, the minimum frame is 377, and the neighborhood is 363–391.

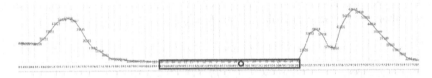

Fig. 9. The third data sequence

In Fig. 9, the maximum frame is frame 872 and frame 919, the minimum frame is frame 893, and the neighborhood is frame 887–909.

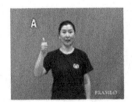

Fig. 10. The key frame found from three sequence data

The minima is found between the two maxima, resulting in three sequence images, as shown in Fig. 10.

From the results obtained, the edges of the image frames obtained by this algorithm are clear and the features are obvious, which can meet the requirements of some algorithms, such as Canny [9, 10] and SURF [11] algorithms. The key frame acquisition of sign language video is basically realized.

4 Conclusion

In this paper, a simple recognition method belonging to the key frame is essentially the application of the first derivative. When the difference between a frame sequence and its front pin is large, the frame is considered to be in motion change. And the minimum value between the two moving frames, that's the stressed and paused frame that the sign language shows. These frames play a key role in video classification retrieval and sign language recognition.

In addition, the algorithm that is not necessarily complex will have higher efficiency. If the curve density method and cluster analysis method are adopted, a large amount of data and operations will be generated, which is not a small cost for the whole sign language video library.

Therefore, in the practical application, we should analyze the specific situation and adopt the appropriate method, just like the difference method used in this paper to find the key frame for the image with good consistency, which is effective.

Acknowledgement. This work was supported by The Ministry of Education has approved a key project in the 13th Five-Year Plan for Education Science in 2017: "Research on Higher Education Teaching Support for the Disabled in the Context of Big Data". (No. DIA170367), The Major Programs of Natural Science Foundation of the Jiangsu Higher Education Institutions of China (No. 19KJA310002.) and The Natural Science Foundation of the Jiangsu Higher Education Institutions of China (No. 17KJD520006).

References

1. Cao, J., et al.: A key frame selection algorithm based on sliding window and image features. In: 2016 International Conference on Parallel and Distributed Systems (ICPADS), pp. 956–962. IEEE, Wuhan, China (2016)
2. Chen, L., Wang, Y.: Automatic key frame extraction in continuous videos from construction monitoring by using color, texture, and gradient features. Autom. Constr. **81**, 355–368 (2017)
3. Ioannidis, A., Chasanis, V., Likas, A.: Weighted multiview key-frame extraction. Pattern Recogn. Lett. **72**, 52–61 (2016)
4. Devanne, M., et al.: 3-D human action recognition by shape analysis of motion trajectories on Riemannian manifold. IEEE Trans. Cybern. **45**(7), 1340–1352 (2015)
5. Guo, X.P., Huang, Y.Y., Hu, Z.J.: Research on recognition algorithm of continuous sign language statement based on Key frame. Comput. Sci. **44**(2), 188–193 (2017). (in Chinese)
6. Nasreen, A., et al.: Key frame extraction and foreground modeling using K-means clustering. In: 2015 7th International Conference on Computational Intelligence, Communication Systems and Networks (CICSyN), vol. 34, pp. 141–145. IEEE, USA, (2015)
7. Gharbi, H., et al.: Key frames extraction using graph modularity clustering for efficient video summarization. In: IEEE International Conference on Acoustics, pp. 1502–1506. IEEE, USA (2017)
8. Rubner, Y.I., Tomasi, C., Guibas, L.J.: Mover's distance as a metric for image retrieval. Int. J. Comput. Vision **40**(2), 99–121 (2000)
9. Canny, J.: A computational approach to edge detection. IEEE Trans. Pattern Anal. Image Understand. **18**(6), 679–698 (1986)

10. Wang, X., Liu, X., Guan, Y.: Image edge detection algorithm based on improved Canny operator. Comput. Eng. **34**(14), 196–198 (2012). (in Chinese)
11. Bay, H., Tuytelaars, T., Cool, L.V.: SURF: speeded up robust features. In: Proceedings of the 9th European Conference on Computer Vision, pp. 404–417. Springer-Verlag, Berlin, Germany (2006)

Research on Dynamic Sign Language Recognition Based on Key Frame Weighted of DTW

ShengWei Zhang, ZhaoSong Zhu$^{(\boxtimes)}$, and RongXin Zhu

Nanjing Normal University of Special Education, Nanjing 210038, China
zzs@njts.edu.cn

Abstract. Dynamic sign language can be described by its trajectory and key hand types. Most of the commonly used sign language can be recognized by trajectory curve matching. Therefore, In this paper, a new dynamic sign language recognition method is proposed, which uses trajectory and key hand type to extract features, adopts a key frame weighted DTW (dynamic time warping) algorithm to implement hierarchical matching strategy, and gradually matches sign language gestures from two levels of trajectory and key hand type, so as to effectively improve the accuracy and efficiency of sign language recognition.

Keywords: Sign language recognition · Key frames · Dynamic time warping

1 Introduction

As a special gesture, sign language is a way for deaf mutes to communicate by gesture instead of sound language. According to the latest statistics released by the Ministry of health, there are 20.57 million deaf people in China, accounting for 1.67% of the total population in China [1]. Due to the limitation of physiological factors, it is difficult for the deaf to speak. Therefore, sign language is the mother tongue of most deaf people and is the main tool for deaf people to express their thoughts and feelings, obtain information and participate in social life. However, there are few healthy people who are proficient in sign language. Apart from those engaged in special education, most of them do not understand sign language and have no intention to learn sign language. This has caused great obstacles to the communication between deaf and healthy people.

At present, there are few professional sign language training institutions and sign language translators, which are far from meeting the market demand. In order to further promote the barrier free construction of information exchange and shorten the communication distance between deaf mute and healthy people, it is particularly important to study sign language recognition technology. Sign language recognition is to obtain the sign language data of the deaf through the computer acquisition equipment, use machine learning algorithm, combined with context knowledge, to obtain the meaning of sign language, and then translate it into speech, and convey it to normal people who do not

© ICST Institute for Computer Sciences, Social Informatics and Telecommunications Engineering 2021
Published by Springer Nature Switzerland AG 2021. All Rights Reserved
W. Fu et al. (Eds.): ICMTEL 2021, LNICST 388, pp. 11–20, 2021.
https://doi.org/10.1007/978-3-030-82565-2_2

understand sign language. Sign language recognition technology can not only let us enter the deaf's silent world, but also make the deaf people understand the modern society more comprehensively. So as to further enhance the communication between the deaf and healthy people, and realize barrier free communication.

2 Literature Review

The research on sign language recognition can be traced back to the 1980s. According to the different acquisition methods of gesture data, sign language recognition technology can be divided into two types based on data glove and computer vision.

2.1 Sign Language Recognition Based on Data Glove

Early computer computing power is weak, but computer vision technology needs a lot of complex computing. In contrast, data glove can use sensors to obtain real-time and accurate gesture data, so in the early sign language recognition, the use of data glove has become the mainstream. Some data gloves can not only provide information on the position of the hand, but also record the force applied on each finger [2]. Han proposed a cheap data glove with high recognition accuracy [3]; Hernandez-Rebollar et al. Developed a data glove based method to recognize 26 American Sign Language (ASL), In 2004, a system capable of recognizing 176 asls was developed, with a recognition accuracy of 95% [4]; Kevin and Kim also used data gloves for gesture recognition [5]; In China, Gao Wen et al. Used a number of data gloves, combined with artificial neural network (ANN) and HMM model to train gesture, realized the recognition of isolated words, the recognition rate was more than 90%, and then realized the continuous Chinese sign language recognition system of more than 5000 words [6].

Although the use of data gloves can quickly and accurately get hand features, even subtle movements can be recognized, so it can get a higher recognition accuracy. However, the use of data gloves is complex and expensive, and does not conform to the natural human-computer interaction habits, which is not conducive to further promotion and use, so it can only be used in the laboratory or in specific occasions.

2.2 Sign Language Recognition Based on Computer Vision

Compared with data glove, computer vision technology has many advantages, such as interactive mode more in line with natural habits, cheap equipment and easy to promote. It can be divided into three types: monocular camera, multi camera and somatosensory camera.

Monocular Camera. Monocular means that the input device has only one two-dimensional camera. Camera can collect sign language data more naturally, but tracking and segmenting hand region from complex background is a challenge. The common processing method is to color mark the hand of sign language speaker. Deng et al. Simplified gesture segmentation with color gloves and used parallel HMM for recognition, and the recognition rate of 192 American sign language words reached 93.3% [7]; Manar et al. Used recurrent neural networks (RNN) to recognize Arabic static sign language, and sign language users wore gloves with highlighted marks, and the recognition rate reached 95.11% [8]. Pattern recognition is also used to recognize gesture regions, but the real-time performance is often poor. Ong et al. Used the boosted cascade classifier in the gray image to detect and track the hand [9]. Zhang Guoliang and others use color gloves to simplify gesture segmentation and use continuous hidden Markov model (CHMM) for recognition, with an average recognition rate of 92.5% [10].

Because the monocular camera can only obtain two-dimensional image information, it can not achieve accurate positioning, so it is difficult to adapt to the complex changes of hands in three-dimensional space, and hand marking is still not in line with natural human-computer interaction. Therefore, researchers try to use multi camera to capture images of different dimensions to make up for this defect.

Multi Camera. Multi camera refers to the use of two or more two-dimensional cameras to obtain two-dimensional image information from different angles, so as to obtain the accurate data of hand in three-dimensional space. Volger et al. Used three orthogonal cameras to locate the arm and estimate the shape and 3D motion parameters of the hand [11, 12]; Utsumi et al. Studied a gesture recognition system using four cameras [13]; Argyro et al. proposed a gesture tracking method based on two video streams with different angles to generate 3D data [14]. They mark the position of the hand in each video stream, and then match the information of the two parts with the angle calibration calculation, so as to obtain the three-dimensional data of the hand position. These methods require high performance of the computer, so it is difficult to process them in real time if their computing power is not strong. Moreover, there are many noises in the depth information estimated by this method. In addition, the use of multi camera, each need to calibrate, the use of inconvenience.

Somatosensory Camera. In recent years, due to the emergence of somatosensory cameras, gesture recognition based on 3D data has made great progress. In the aspect of gesture recognition using a somatosensory camera, Jang et al. Proposed a system based on Kinect to obtain depth information to recognize gesture, and used continuous adaptive mean shift algorithm, CAMSHIFT) to use depth probability and update depth histogram for hand tracking [15]; Chai et al. used Kinect to obtain 3D features of gestures and realized recognition through 3D trajectory matching of hands, with an average recognition rate of 83.51% [16]; Marin used Kinect to locate the hand area, then used leap motion to get the fine information of the hand, and then used support vector machine (SVM), SVM is used as a classifier to recognize gesture, and the recognition rate reaches 91.28% [17]. At present, using Kinect to obtain in-depth information to identify sign language has become the mainstream [18], but there are relatively few domestic related research results, and there are still some problems to be solved in current sign language recognition. For example, how to ensure the stability of hand region segmentation and sign language feature description due to the difference of body and action habits of different sign language speakers? In addition, dynamic sign language is a kind of sign language which is represented by the combination of several changing gestures, which has a large amount of data. For sign language recognition, how to ensure the recognition accuracy and meet the real-time requirements has always been a hot topic for researchers.

3   Key Frame Weighted of DTW Method

The Kinect camera is used as the data acquisition device, and the 3D bone data stream provided by Kinect camera is used for gesture recognition. Kinect provides 30 frames per second depth image and three-dimensional coordinates of 20 human joint points, including the joint point information of left and right hands. The skeleton flow data provided by Kinect was preprocessed. The process of gesture recognition includes four main parts: data acquisition, data preprocessing, data feature extraction and recognition output. After data preprocessing, the original feature data of gesture tracking trajectory is obtained, and the feature extraction of trajectory is carried out, and the hierarchical matching strategy is adopted for sign language recognition.

Kalman filter is used to correct the data returned by Kinect to eliminate singular points and ensure the accuracy and consistency of the trajectory. The hand position data points detected in each frame can be connected to get the gesture trajectory curve. Key frame is a key action in sign language. Through observation and personal experience, it is found that most sign language users will stop for a while to show their emphasis on the key action. In the trajectory curve, that is, near the time when the key frame appears, the data points are particularly dense. Based on this, a key frame extraction algorithm based on track point density is proposed. Firstly, the density set $crow(P)$ of a point P on the trajectory curve ρ was defined as Eq. (1).

$$crow(P) = \{X_i | \forall X_i \in \rho, \delta(P, X_i) \leq \Delta\} \tag{1}$$

$\delta(P, X_i)$ is the Euclidean distance between P and X_i, and Δ is the threshold. However, for the point P on the trajectory curve of sign language, we hope that it is not only close to X_i in space distance, but also adjacent in time. The definition of Eq. (1) ignores the change of time. For example, the positions of the start and end gestures are very close, but the time is quite different. However, according to the definition of Eq. (1), it is obvious that the point of ending gesture will be classified into the density set of the initial gesture, which will cause errors. Therefore, it is necessary to add a time limit when counting the density set of a point on the trajectory curve, that is, data points X_i and X_{i+1} must be adjacent in time. The number of data points in the density set is the point density of P. For a specific sign language, if it is completed by both hands, we need to calculate the point density of the left hand and the right hand trajectory curve respectively, and add them as the overall curve point density of the sign language. For example, for the gesture of sign language word "husband", the point density curve can be obtained from the trajectory curve (see Fig. 1).

The abscissa represents the time, and the ordinate represents the point density value of the corresponding time. The mean filter with width and length of 5 is used to smooth it (see Fig. 2).

There are three obvious peaks which marked by red circles. Check the key frame images corresponding to these three peaks, and the results are shown in Fig. 3. Except that the last frame is the termination gesture, the remaining two frames are consistent with our expected keyframes. At the same time, the "husband" sign language made by another sign language is processed the same way, and the same keyframes is obtained. Therefore, it is feasible to detect key frames by using point density. However, in fact,

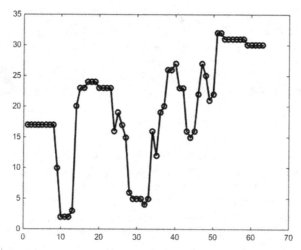

Fig. 1. The point density curve of sign language word "husband"

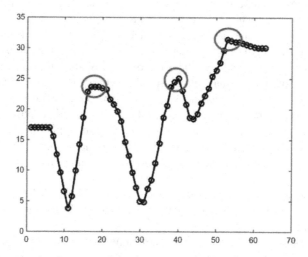

Fig. 2. The point density curve of sign language word 'husband' through mean filtering

most sign languages do not have such distinctive features, and can not easily get key frames from point density images.

Then, the point density curve can be segmented into several continuous and equal width windows. In each window, the maximum point density value is found. If the value is greater than the given threshold, the frame to which it belongs is taken as the candidate key frame. It can be seen that the selection of window size and threshold are two key factors affecting the candidate keyframes. If the window width is too small, there will be too many candidate frames, which will lead to too long time to filter the final key frame; if the window width is too large, the candidate frames will be too few, which will lead to missing key frames. Generally speaking, for most sign language, the number of key

Fig. 3. Keyframes of the sign language word "husband"

frames of a gesture will not exceed 6. When the number of candidate frames is two to three times of the number of key frames, it is more appropriate. In the candidate frames, the final key frame can be determined quickly by using the frame subtraction method. The threshold and the threshold Δ in Eq. (1) are defined in an adaptive way.

After the position of the key frame is determined, the trajectory can be matched one level. Trajectory is a typical time series. DTW algorithm is recommended to measure the similarity of time series. DTW distance can find the best alignment and matching relationship between time series by stretching and bending them, so as to measure the similarity of different length time series. Given two time series: $T = \{t_1, t_2, \ldots, t_m\}$ and $R = \{r_1, r_2, \ldots, r_n\}$. The DTW method finds an optimal bending path in the time series T and R, and takes the cumulative distance of this path as the distance between T and R. Even if the length of time series T and R is not equal, the similarity between them can be calculated in this way. The traditional DTW algorithm does not consider the characteristics of sign language itself. In other words, there are two kinds of data points in sign language time series, one is the transition point, the other is the key frame point where the key frame is located. Obviously, their semantic contributions to sign language are different, and they have the same status in the traditional DTW distance, which is obviously unreasonable. Therefore, a key frame weighted DTW algorithm is proposed to improve the accuracy of traditional DTW algorithm for sign language trajectory matching.

Suppose there are two sign language trajectory curves P and Q, P contains m frame of data points, Q contains n frame of data points, then $P = \{p_1, p_2, \ldots, p_m\}$, $Q = \{q_1, q_2, \ldots, q_n\}$.

The distance from point X of curve a to keyframe point was defined as Eq. (2).

$$\delta_{KP}(i) = min\{|i - x|, x \in K_P\} \tag{2}$$

The distance δ_{KQ} from point q_j of curve Q to keyframe point was defined as Eq. (3).

$$\delta_{KQ}(j) = min\{|j - x|, x \in K_Q\} \tag{3}$$

Then the cumulative cost matrix $D(i, j)$ was defined as Eq. (4).

$$D(i,j) = \left(\left|\delta_{KP}(i) - \delta_{KQ}(j)\right| + 1 \times P(i,j)\right) + min \begin{cases} D(i-1,j) \\ D(i-1,j-1) \\ D(i,j-1) \end{cases} \tag{4}$$

Here $P(i, j)$ is the distance from p_i to q_j For point p_i on curve P and point q_j on curve Q, if $\delta_{KP}(i) = \delta_{KQ}(j)$, then there are two cases. One is that point p_i and point q_j approach key points from the same direction, which indicates that they have the same distance from their respective keyframes, and they should have higher weights, so their corresponding coefficients are smaller; the other case is that point p_i and point q_j approach the key points from left and right respectively, although their values are lower The coefficients are still small, but the coefficients corresponding to other matching points on this matching path will increase, which also ensures the constraint of key frames.

Before measuring the similarity of tracks, we should normalize the trajectory curves, and deal with them both in space and time, so as to eliminate the different effects caused by the differences of sign language users. At the same time, it should be noted that some sign language can be completed by both hands at the same time, and some sign language can be completed with one hand. Therefore, the trajectory curve of gesture is to distinguish left and right hands. For those two hand sign language, the curves of left and right hand should be calculated respectively, and the DTW distance between the left and right curves should be taken as the final matching result. Moreover, there is no difference between the left and right hands in the semantic contribution of sign language, which is equally important.

If the ratio of the DTW distance of the most similar sign language to the sign language to be recognized is less than a certain threshold value, then the recognition can be finished. Otherwise, the first five sign language categories with the smallest distance are returned. In these five categories, the key hand type is used to do the second level matching. The key hand type is also a time series, but the number of elements in the sequence is small, which is less than five. It is easy to use DTW to calculate the distance for such a sequence.

4 Experimental Results and Discussions

This paper compares the time performance of traditional DTW distance, FastDTW distance and our improved DTW distance. As shown in Fig. 4. The abscissa is the length of the two time series, and the ordinate is the time required to match (in MS). The experimental data are randomly generated three-dimensional data, and the length of the two time series is equal. Keyframe points are randomly generated one or two points per 100 points. The experiment was repeated 1000 times and the average value was taken.

As can be seen from Fig. 4, with the increase of the length of time series, the matching time increases in a quadratic way, and the time performance is very poor. Although the matching time of the proposed algorithm is quadratic, the matching time is less than that of the FastDTW distance when the length of the time series is less than 576 because of the global constraint. Although the time of FastDTW distance matching is increasing, it needs to be refined from coarse-grained path, so its advantage is not obvious when the length of time series is short. However, due to the need of backtracking, its performance is not as good as the algorithm in this paper.

The video duration of a sign language word is generally about 2–6 s. The sampling frequency of Kinect camera is 30 frames/s, so a video has 60–180 frames of images, so the length of time series is between 60–180. Figure 4 shows the time performance of traditional DTW distance, FastDTW distance and the improved DTW distance when the time series length is less than 200. As can be seen from the figure, the time required by the algorithm in this paper is the lowest. Most of the matching time is within 1 ms.

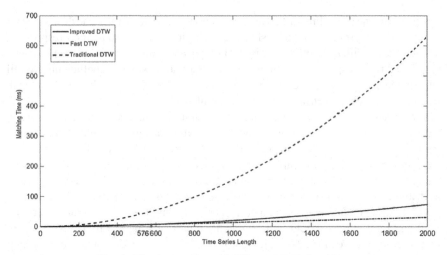

Fig. 4. Time comparison of different DTW algorithms

For 60 sign language templates, all matching needs less than 60 ms. Therefore, when the number of sign language templates is less than a few hundred, real-time recognition can be realized.

Table 1 shows the recognition accuracy of different sign language users when only one level matching and two level matching are added. It can be seen that on the basis of trajectory recognition, adding hand information for matching can effectively improve the accuracy of sign language recognition, which basically reaches more than 90% recognition rate, which verifies the effectiveness of the algorithm in this paper.

Table 1. Sign language recognition accuracy

Sign language tester	1	2	3	4	5
First level matching	0.8343	0.8667	0.8835	0.8967	0.9010
Two level matching	0.9010	0.9265	0.9310	0.9335	0.9668

5 Conclusion

In this paper, a new method of dynamic sign language recognition is proposed, which uses trajectory and key hand to extract features, adopts a key frame weighted DTW (dynamic time warping) algorithm to implement hierarchical matching strategy, due to fully considering the characteristics of dynamic sign language itself, In order to effectively improve the accuracy and efficiency of sign language recognition, sign language gestures are matched step by step from the two levels of trajectory and key hand type.

However, when deaf people play sign language, it is often accompanied by facial expression and lip movement. Recognition of facial expression and lip movement can better understand the emotion expressed by sign language. In addition, there are many other deep learning network structures at present [19]. For example, the deep network based on attention model is one of the most important core technologies in deep learning technology, and the future research goal is sign language recognition based on attention mechanism.

Acknowledgement. The work described in this paper was fully supported by a grant from the National Philosophy and Social Sciences Foundation of China (No.20BTQ065) and The Natural Science Foundation of the Jiangsu Higher Education Institutions of China (No. 16KJB520026).

References

1. http://www.cdpf.org.cn/sjzx/cjrgk/201206/t20120626_387581.shtml
2. Tarchanidis, K.N., Lygouras, J.N.: Data glove with a force sensor. IEEE Trans. Instrum. Meas. **52**(3), 984–989 (2003)
3. Han, Y.: A low-cost visual motion data glove as an input device to interpret human hand gestures. IEEE Trans. Consumer Electron. **56**(2), 501–509 (2010)
4. Hernandez-Rebollar, J.L., Kyriakopoulos, N., Lindeman, R.W.: A new instrumented approach for translating American Sign Language into sound and text. In: Proceedings of the Sixth IEEE International Conference on Automatic Face and Gesture Recognition, pp. 547–552. IEEE (2004)
5. Kim, J.H., Thang, N.D., Kim, T.S.: 3-D hand motion tracking and gesture recognition using a data glove. In: IEEE International Symposium on Industrial Electronics, 2009. ISIE 2009, pp. 1013–1018. IEEE (2009)
6. Gao, W., et al.: A Chinese sign language recognition system based on SOFM/SRN/HMM. Pattern Recogn. **37**(12), 2389–2402 (2004)
7. Deng, J., Tsui, H.T.: A Two-step Approach based on PaHMM for the Recognition of ASL. ACCV (2002)
8. Maraqa, M., Al-Zboun, F., Dhyabat, M., Zitar, R.A.: Recognition of Arabic sign language (ArSL) using recurrent neural networks. J. Intell. Learn. Syst. Appl. **2012**(4), 41–52 (2012)
9. Ong, E.J., Bowden, R.: A boosted classifier tree for hand shape detection. In: Proceedings of the Sixth IEEE International Conference on Automatic Face and Gesture Recognition, pp. 889–894. IEEE (2004)
10. Liangguo, Z., et al.: A medium vocabulary Chinese sign language visual recognition system. Comput. Res. Dev. **43**(3), 476–482 (2015)
11. Vogler, C., Metaxas, D.: Toward scalability in ASL recognition: breaking down signs into phonemes. Gesture-based Communication in Human-Computer Interaction, pp. 211–224. Springer Berlin Heidelberg (1999)
12. Vogler, C., Metaxas, D.: Parallel hidden Markov models for American sign language recognition. In: The Proceedings of the Seventh IEEE International Conference on Computer Vision, vol. 1, pp. 116–122. IEEE (1999)
13. Utsumi, A., et al.: Hand gesture recognition system using multiple cameras. In: Proceedings of the 13th International Conference on Pattern Recognition, vol. 1, pp. 667–671. IEEE (1996)
14. Argyros, A., Lourakis, M.I.A.: Binocular hand tracking and reconstruction based on 2D shape matching. In: 18th International Conference on Pattern Recognition, 2006. ICPR 2006, vol. 1, pp. 207–210. IEEE (2006)
15. Jang, Y.: Gesture recognition using depth-based hand tracking for contactless controller application. In: 2012 IEEE International Conference on Consumer Electronics (ICCE), pp. 297–298 (2012)

16. Chai, X., et al.: Sign language recognition and translation with Kinect. In: IEEE Conf. on AFGR (2013)
17. Marin, G., Dominio, F., Zanuttigh, P.: Hand gesture recognition with jointly calibrated leap motion and depth sensor. Multimedia Tools Appl. **75**(22), 14991–15015 (2015). https://doi.org/10.1007/s11042-015-2451-6
18. Raheja, J.L., et al.: Robust gesture recognition using Kinect: a comparison between DTW and HMM. Optik **126**(11), 1098–1104 (2015)
19. Jiang, X., Satapathy, S.C., Yang, L., Wang, S.-H., Zhang, Y.-D.: A survey on artificial intelligence in Chinese sign language recognition. Arab. J. Sci. Eng. **45**(12), 9859–9894 (2020). https://doi.org/10.1007/s13369-020-04758-2

An Optimized Seven-Layer Convolutional Neural Network with Data Augmentation for Classification of Chinese Fingerspelling Sign Language

Yalan Gao, Rongxin Zhu, Ruina Gao, Yuxiang Weng, and Xianwei Jiang$^{(\boxtimes)}$

Nanjing Normal University of Special Education, Nanjing 210038, China
jxw@njts.edu.cn

Abstract. Sign language recognition especially finger language recognition facilitates the life of deaf people in China. It overcomes many difficulties and provides convenience for deaf people's life. In this paper, we used the advanced convolutional neural network to extract the different characteristics of the input. We created an optimized seven-layer CNN, including five convolution layers for feature extraction and two fully connected layers for classification to enhance the original signal function and reduce noise after operation. Some advanced techniques such as batch normalization, ReLu and dropout were employed to optimize the neural network. Meanwhile, we adopted data augmentation technology, which not only expanded the data set and improve the performance of machine learning algorithm, but also avoided the over-fitting problem. The experimental results show that the average recognition accuracy reaches $91.99 \pm 1.21\%$, which indicate an excellent property.

Keywords: Convolutional neural network · Data augmentation · Chinese fingerspelling sing language · Batch normalization · ReLU · Maximum pooling · Dropout

1 Introduction

Sign language is a language for people with hearing and speech impairments to communicate with each other. People with hearing disabilities often combine gestures, body movements, and facial expressions to express themselves. Due to the convenience of fingerspelling sign language recognition, fingerspelling sign language recognition has attracted more and more attention and research. Fingerspelling language, an abbreviation for finger language, was developed specifically for the deaf and mute in China. It is a symbolic spelling of letters in which the syllables of words are typed in the order of the Pinyin Chinese system. It is worth mentioning that China is a vast country, and the same meaning is often confused with different sign language meanings due to different expressions in different regions. For this reason, a sign language containing only 30 letters is more accurate [1] and easier to recognize when facial expressions are not included. Images of letters for Chinese fingerspelling sign language are shown in Fig. 1.

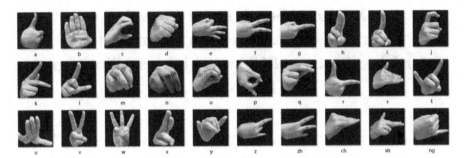

Fig. 1. Alphabets in sign language

Expression is the instinct and nature of human beings, and communication is equally important for deaf people. Like our Chinese language, sign language is the mother tongue of the deaf, and its use is becoming more and more popular nowadays. However, it is not easy for non-professionals to learn sign language, so it is difficult for people who have not mastered sign language to communicate with deaf and dumb people. We can choose to communicate with deaf people by means of sign language interpreters. However, this method is extremely inconvenient and expensive. In order to enable deaf people to communicate with normal people, we need a cheaper and more convenient solution. For a long time, scientists have been trying to find a way to make it easier for deaf and normal people to communicate with each other. A turning point in this field is the finger language recognition system. This system is designed to recognize the gestures of a deaf person and translate them into the local language using text or speech. This technology has had a positive effect on the social status of deaf people, allowing them to better adapt to society and enjoy normal civil rights to a greater extent than the average person.

Finger language recognition can be divided into wearable device recognition, touch technology recognition and computer vision recognition. The development of finger language recognition technology dates back to 1993, and gesture recognition technology has been adapted to speech and character recognition technology, Darrell and Pentland applied the dynamic time warp (DTW) of speech recognition to dynamic gesture recognition [2]; Rung-hui Liang et al. used gloves to collect raw data on 51 basic positions, including six directions and 8 The average recognition rate of consecutive sentences composed of these gestures was 80.4% [3]; Jiangqin Wu et al. combined a neural network with a learning decision tree to develop a recognition model and constructed a Chinese finger spelling gesture recognition system using a data glove [4]; later, Rung-hui Liang et al. used gloves to collect raw data for 51 basic positions, including six directions and eight movements, and then they simulated a dictionary system capable of recognizing 250 Taiwanese symbols using hidden Markov models (HMMs). The average recognition rate of consecutive sentences composed of these gestures was 80.4% [5]; Chuanbo Weng et al. used Bayesian gesture segmentation to model skin color and then combined it with skin color, Motion, and gesture recognition of contour shape information greatly improved segmentation accuracy [6]. The DWT algorithm builds a reference model by extracting the signal feature parameters of the reference model and storing them in the database of the reference model, builds a test model by extracting the signal feature parameters of the gestures to be recognized, and then adds the total distance between the frame vectors of the reference model and the test model to obtain the computational result showing that the shorter the total distance, the higher the similarity. Finally, the smallest distance is selected as the matching result. Although this recognition algorithm is relatively simple and efficient, it is computationally intensive, takes up a large memory space, and has a long response time. The hidden Markov model-based approach is superior to time series modeling, but it requires independent sequences of gesture movements, which are often interdependent. In addition, once the models of these traditional mechanical learning methods are trained during the training phase, they do not change throughout the recognition process.

We proposed this algorithm based on the foundations of many predecessors. Ameen et al. propose a model for ASL letter recognition using CNNs [7]. Mohanty et al. proposed a different deep learning framework for recognizing static gestures with CNNs on complex backgrounds and under different lighting conditions, and obtained good recognition results [8]. The advanced deep learning techniques and advances in convolutional neural networks (CNNs), in particular, CNNs, which have completely surpassed traditional gesture recognition methods. They can achieve maximum performance without the need to manually design features.

The purpose of this article is to implement an optimized 7-layer convolutional neural network and add data augmentation to improve the accuracy of Chinese fingerspelling sign language recognition. We also improve the validity of the test data by combining pooling, batch normalization, and dropout techniques to overcome the inefficiency of pre-training and improve CNN accuracy and usability. The rest of this article is arranged as follows: Sect. 2 describes the data set, Sect. 3 specifically introduces the Chinese fingerspelling sign language recognition methods used in this article, Sect. 4 describes the experiment process, Sect. 5 provides discussions, and observations and acknowledgements are given in the last section.

2 Dataset

2.1 Data Collection and Image Preprocessing

We used a camera to shoot Chinese finger gesture images and established a related gesture data set, which contained 44 samples (each sample covers 26 basic letters and 4 tongue sounds, commonly used pronunciations, words, a total of 30 categories) 1,320 sheets 1080 × 1080 pixels photos. Then Photoshop CS was used to reduce noise and keep the hand-shaped area, then adjusted the size of the picture to 256 × 256, and finally saved it in tif format to ensure that basically no image information is lost. (See Fig. 2).

During the shooting, we fully considered the differences in sign language gestures used by individuals to make the captured images more convincing. (See Fig. 3).

2.2 Data Preprocessing

Through the above operations, the preprocessed images have the same size and background, and have no effects on the test results. At the same time, according to experimental requirements, we extract 80% of each type of sign language image as training samples, and the remaining images are used as experimental samples. (See Table 1).

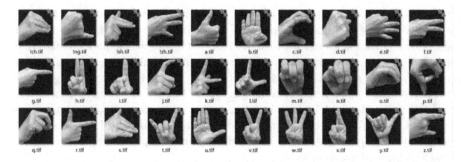

Fig. 2. Thirty classification source images of a sample

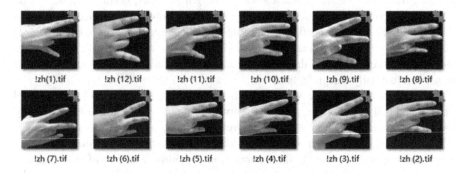

Fig. 3. Different people's sign language gestures about 'zh'

Table 1. Distribution of data integration

Type of data	Basic letters	Retroflex consonant	Total
Training set	915	140	1055
Test set	229	36	265
Total	1144	176	1320

3 Methodology

In this algorithm, the data augmentation technology is firstly used to increase the data scale and improve the reliability and accuracy of the experimental data. We mainly use convolutional neural network for image processing, including 5 convolutional layers for function extraction and 2 full connection layers to extract different features and reduce noise after operation. The use of batch normalization, ReLU, dropout and other advanced technologies to optimize the neural network not only provides convenience for our calculation but also improves the performance of the convolutional neural network.

3.1 Convolutional Layer

Convolutional neural network (CNN) is a kind of feedforward neural network with deep structure, which contains convolution computation and has the ability of representational learning. It can carry out large-scale image processing and is often used to analyze visual images. The convolutional layer is a part of the convolutional neural network, and it is the core of the convolutional neural network.

In a convolutional neural network, each convolutional layer is composed of several convolution units. The purpose of convolution operation is to extract different features of the input. The first layer of convolution may only be able to extract the edge of low-level features, while through multi-layer convolution, more complex features can be iteratively extracted from low-level features [9].

An important feature of convolution operation is that the original signal features are enhanced and noise is reduced after operation. The convolution algorithm is as follows:

Assuming that the size of the input image is 5×5 (a grid and a pixel), we had a convolutional neuron. The sliding window goes 2×2 and the step size is 2. When sliding the window, we found that one pixel cannot be obtained, so we added another layer of filling value to obtain all the pixels.

Our convolutional neuron started with a 3×3 matrix, and then selected a 3×3 matrix in the image to perform inner product calculation with the convolutional neuron. The result was obtained by adding 1 after the convolution operation [10, 11]. (see Fig. 4).

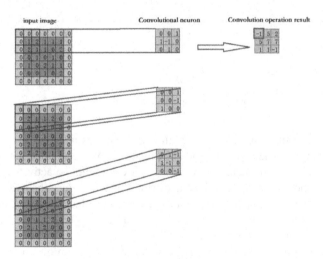

Fig. 4. The process of convolutional neuron network

The derivation formula of convolution layer output is as follows:

$$O = \frac{P - H + 2E}{S} + 1 \tag{1}$$

Where, the size of the input image is $P \times P$, the size of the convolution kernel is $H \times H$, the step size is S, the filling pixel is E. From the formula, we can also deduce that the size of our output feature graph is 3×3, that is, the green matrix in Fig. 4.

3.2 ReLU Function

ReLU
Rectified Linear Unit (ReLU), also known as modified linear element, is essentially a linear function and is a commonly used activation function in artificial neural networks. Its expression is as follows:

$$ReLU(x) = \begin{cases} 0, x \le 0 \\ x, x > 0 \end{cases} \tag{2}$$

The image of the ReLU function is shown in Fig. 5:

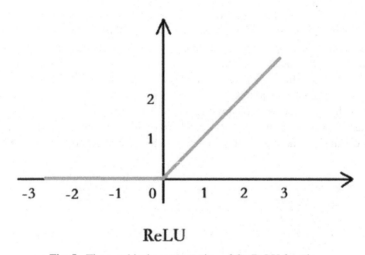

ReLU

Fig. 5. The graphical representation of the ReLU function

As can be seen from the figure, when the input value is negative, the output value is 0, while the input value is integer, the output value is A. We can understand from the perspective of the neurons, neurons in negative cases will not be activated, only under the condition of positive neurons can be activated, this will reduce the network density, thus simplifies the calculation process, and improve calculation efficiency and better training data fitting, in CNN, when the model increased the n layer, theoretically ReLU neuron activation rate would be reduced [12].

The ReLU function uses bionics to debug the activity of neurons, using linear correction and regularization. Typically, about 50 percent of neurons in a neural network using modified linear units are active. Moreover, the ReLU function avoids the problem of gradient explosion and gradient disappearance and can stabilize the convergence rate.

LReLU
With Leaky Rectified Linear Unit (LReLU), when X is negative, there will be no output of all zero. The formula is as follows:

$$LReLu(x) = \begin{cases} x, \ x \ge 0 \\ ax, \ x < 0 \end{cases} (a \ is \ usually \ 0.01) \tag{3}$$

The function image is shown in Fig. 6.

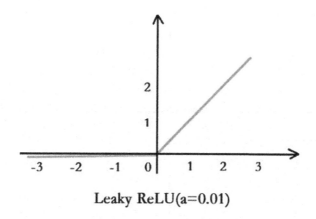

Fig. 6. The graphical representation of the LReLU function

ReLU is vulnerable in training, because it turns all input negative to 0. When the setting values are large, it will easily lead to the inactivation of neurons, and will not be activated in any form or way, resulting in the death of neurons. LReLU alleviates the problem of neuronal death. When the input is less than 0, it can maintain a certain output without causing permanent inactivation of neurons.

RReLU

Randomized Leaky Rectified Linear Unit (RReLU) functions with Leaky are an improvement on Leaky ReLU.

The formula is as follows:

$$RReLU(x) = \begin{cases} x, & x \geq 0 \\ ax, & x < 0, a \in [0, 1) \end{cases} \tag{4}$$

During model training, a is an arbitrary value, but during model testing, a becomes a fixed value. Compared with LReLU, the a in RReLU is a random variable derived from the probability model of continuous uniform distribution U (l, u). Theoretically, we could get the function image in Fig. 7:

Since a generates random allocation randomly in the U probability model, RReLU is more effective in the confrontation with overfitting.

3.3 Pooling Layer

Pooling layer is the network layer structure of convolutional neural network different from traditional neural network. Pooling layer is generally located behind the convolutional layer, as shown in Fig. 8.

The network model structure using pooling layer can speed up computer calculation and effectively prevent the occurrence of overfitting problem. Currently, almost all the mainstream convolutional neural network models include the pooling layer [13].

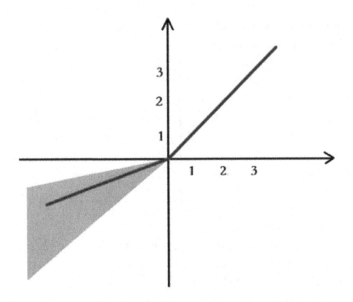

Randomized ReLU

Fig. 7. The graphical representation of the RReLU function

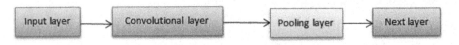

Fig. 8. Pooling layer connection location

Giving a feature mapping group $X \in R^{A \times B}$ and input it into the pooling layer 1^P. Here, the feature map X^d in this group can be subdivided into several sub-regions $R^d_{\alpha, \beta}$ and $1 \leq \alpha \leq A$, $1 \leq \beta \leq B$. In the algorithm of the seven-layer convolutional neural network in this paper, the convolution operation often appeared the problem of over-fitting and heavy computation. In order to solve these problems, a pooling operation was added after the convolution operation to reduce the number of parameters corresponding to the features [14]. In the pooling layer, the calculation method is not the weighted sum of the corresponding nodes, but the simpler operation of maximum or average value. The pooling layer that uses the maximum value operation is called the Max pooling layer, and the pooling layer that uses the average value operation is called the Average pooling layer. The maximum pooling has a good inhibitory effect on the estimated mean deviation caused by parameter errors of the convolutional layer, and the average pooling can reduce the estimated error caused by the limited size of adjacent areas. Currently, the maximum pooling layer is most commonly used [15]. Figure 9 and Fig. 10 respectively shows the calculation methods of maximum pooling and average pooling.

Two common methods of pooling are as follows:

Max pooling refers to taking out the max value of all neurons in the corresponding area, which can be expressed as:

$$Y^d_{\alpha,\beta} = \max(X_i), \ i \in R^d_{\alpha,\beta} \tag{5}$$

In the above formula, X_i is the activation value of each neuron in region $R^d_{\alpha,\beta}$.

Average pooling refers to the calculation of the average value of all neurons in the region as output, which is expressed as:

$$Y^d_{\alpha,\beta} = \frac{1}{R^d_{\alpha,\beta}} \sum_{i \in R^d_{\alpha,\beta}} X_i \tag{6}$$

Calculation method of maximum pooling and average pooling:

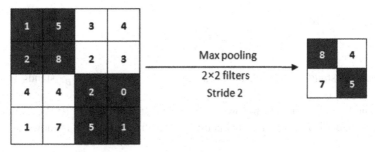

Fig. 9. Max pooling operation

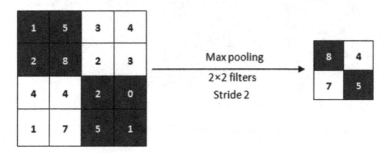

Fig. 10. Average pooling operation

Pooling can not only bring a larger view of the network architecture, but also maintain the invariability of some small local morphological changes in the image, and effectively reduce the number of neurons [16].

3.4 Batch Normalization

Batch normalization (BN) is often used to optimize the deep neural network. The method cannot merely improve the training speed, but also relax the requirement of parameter adjustment to some extent. In addition, it provides a regularization effect similar to dropout, preventing model overfitting [15]. The operation process of BN is as follows:

Batch mean (u is the batch size):

$$\mu_B = \frac{1}{\mu} \sum_{i=1}^{\mu} X_i \tag{7}$$

Batch variance:

$$\sigma_{B^2} = \frac{1}{\mu} \sum_{i=1}^{u} (X_i - \mu_B)^2 \tag{8}$$

The normalized:

$$\widehat{x_i} = \frac{x_i - \mu}{\sqrt{\sigma^2 + \gamma}} \tag{9}$$

Scaling and shifting:

$$Y_i \leftarrow \gamma \widehat{x_i} + \beta = BN_{\gamma,\beta}(X_i) \tag{10}$$

Where, μ_B stands for batch mean, u stands for batch size, σ_{B^2} stands for batch variance, and $\widehat{X_i}$ stands for normalized operation.

BN handles each data and follows the normal distribution of N (0, 1), reducing the changes in the distribution of internal neurons. The structure of BN is shown in Fig. 11.

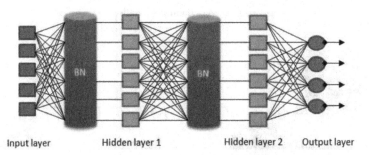

Input layer   Hidden layer 1   Hidden layer 2   Output layer

Fig. 11. Batch normalization

The deep learning network model can perform target recognition well. It is based on the assumption that the training set data and the test set data are independently and equally distributed. In the traditional training method, the data distribution of each batch is different, so the training is difficult, and the model is usually converged by reducing the learning rate. The deep learning network model is constantly changing, so the input value of each layer will have some deviation, which will affect the test accuracy [17]. In the use of BN, a relatively high learning rate can be selected to accelerate model convergence, improve training efficiency and enhance usability. Meanwhile, it can also standardize the process, thus eliminating dropout, simplifying network structure and improving utilization efficiency.

3.5 Dropout

Over-fitting problems often occur when training neural networks, which are specifically reflected in the following aspects: the loss function on the test data is relatively large, the prediction accuracy is low, and on the contrary, the prediction accuracy is high. When encountering over-fitting problems, the obtained model is almost unusable, but dropout can effectively alleviate the over-fitting problem [17, 18].

The dropout was proposed by Hinton in 2012 and its principle is simple: in a training iteration, neurons in each layer (total X) are randomly eliminated with probability Y, and the remaining $(1 - Y) \times X$ neurons are used to train the data in this iteration. In general, the effect is best when $Y = 0.5$. Half of the neurons are discarded during training, and only half of the remaining neurons can be activated, and the randomly generated network structure is the most diverse.

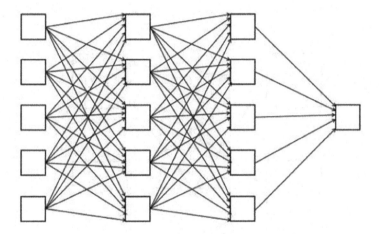

Fig. 12. The general neural network

As shown in the above figures, Fig. 12 is a general neural network, and Fig. 13 is a dropout neural network. We can conclude that the neural network is simplified after the application of this technology, easier to train, and can effectively prevent the occurrence of overfitting.

3.6 Fully Connected Layer

In the convolutional neural network, one or more fully connected layers are connected after multiple convolutional and pooling layers. Each node of the full connection layer is connected with all the nodes of the upper layer (as shown in Fig. 14), which is used to synthesize the features extracted from the front edge, so the weight parameters of the layer are the most. After the current convolutional layer has captured enough features to recognize the image, the next step is how to classify them. Fully connected layer in

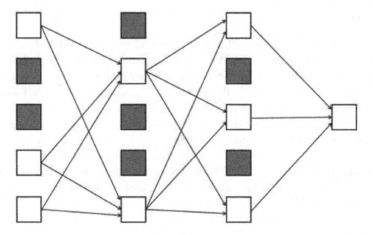

Fig. 13. The dropout neural network

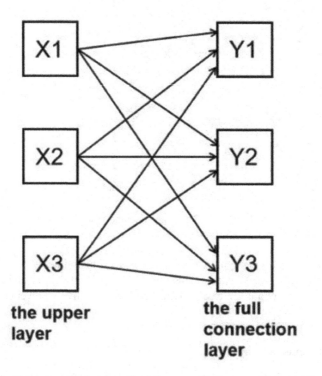

Fig. 14. The connection between the full connection layer and the upper layer

the whole convolution neural network is similar to "classifier", which is mainly used for classification, mapping distributed features to the sample label space.

Each output of the fully connected layer can be viewed as each node of the previous layer multiplied by a weight coefficient X and adding a bias value Y. For example, if there are $30 \times 2 \times 2$ neuron nodes in the input and 400 nodes in the output, a total of $30 \times 2 \times 2 \times 400 = 48000$ weight parameters X and 400 bias parameters Y.

In order to improve the performance of the convolutional neural network, we added the ReLU function to the excitation function of each neuron in the fully connected layer. The output value of the last fully connected layer was passed to an output, which can be classified by softmax regression. This layer is called softmax layer.

3.7 Data Augmentation

Large amounts of data can improve the performance of machine learning algorithms and avoid overfitting problems. Xiang Yu et al. created a new data augmentation framework called SCDA (Scaling and Contrast limited adaptive histogram equalization Data Augmentation) for accurate classification of breast abnormalities based on ResNet-50 [19]. For detection of COVID-19, Motamed Saman et al. proposed a new GAN architecture by using the data augmentation technology for augmentation of chest X-rays for semi-supervised detection of pneumonia and COVID-19 using generative models [20]. Our data set is going to include the different conditions, such as different orientation, position, scale, brightness, and so on. However, in the actual collection of data, the number of data sets we collect is limited, that is to say, collecting large amount of sample data is a challenging task. By performing data augmentation, we can solve the problem of sample data and prevent neural networks from learning unrelated characteristics and fundamentally improve overall performance [21].

In a convolutional neural network, if it can accurately classify objects under different circumstances, it means that the neural network is stable. CNN has invariance to shift, viewpoint, size and lighting and this is essentially a prerequisite for data augmentation. Data augmentation is an effective technique to improve the accuracy of image classifiers and can also help CNN learn more powerful functions. In this article, we use the following six methods for data augmentation.

PCA Color Augmentation
PCA color augmentation is mainly used to adjust the brightness, saturation and contrast of the image. In order to maintain the validity of the artificial image, the first step is to calculate the main component analysis (PCA) of the training dataset to restore the color of its distribution spindle [22]. Then, the artificial images are created by constantly adjusting multiples of the principal components of the data set. Figure 15 shows the contrast before and after the PCA color augmentation.

Affine Transform
The affine transformation (AFT) is a clutter operation that randomly changes the pixel position of an image. The affine transformation of an image $f(p, q)$ of size $N \times N$ pixels is calculated by (p', q') function is represented as follows:

$$\begin{bmatrix} p' \\ q' \end{bmatrix} = AFT\{(p, q), N\} = \begin{bmatrix} x + hp \\ y = kq \end{bmatrix}(mod\ N) \tag{11}$$

Where "mod" represents the modal operation, x and y are two random numbers between 1 and N, and h, k is selected by their relative prime number relative to N. This

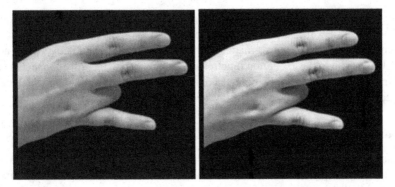

Fig. 15. The picture adds color augmentation before and after contrast

choice of h and k causes the AFT to map (p, q) to the unique pixels in the conversion coordinates. If h and k are not relative prime numbers, AFT maps different pixels to the same pixel in the transformed coordinates. After AFT, the total energy of the input image remains the same [23].

Noise Injection
The core of noise injection is to randomly disturb each pixel RGB of the image by adding the random value matrix sampled from the Gaussian distribution, so as to produce some new noise polluted images. At the same time, it can also help CNN learn more powerful functions [24].

Scaling
The scaling method includes scaling inward and outward. When zoomed out, the final image size is larger than the original image size. Similarity, when scaled inward, the final image size will be smaller than the image size. Most image frames cut out a section from a new image that is equal in size to the original image. The Fig. 16 shows the contrast of image zoomed in.

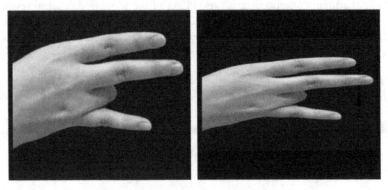

Fig. 16. The contrast of image zoomed in

Random Shift

Random shift only involves moving images in the X or Y direction (or both). In the following example, we assume that the image has a black background outside its boundaries and is shifted appropriately. This enhancement is useful because most objects can be located almost anywhere in the image. This forces your convolutional neural network to see all corners. The Fig. 17 shows the effect of rotating 90 degrees counterclockwise.

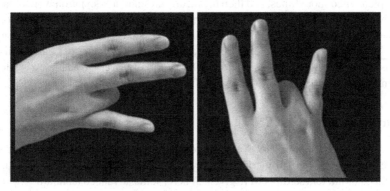

Fig. 17. The contrast of image shift

Gamma Correction

Gamma correction is used to correct the nonlinear photoelectric conversion characteristics of sensors in electronic devices such as cameras, which edits the gamma curve of an image to make nonlinear tonal edits to the image [25]. Gamma represents a diagonal line between the output value of the image and the input value and the gamma value is usually 2.3. In this paper, we produce a number of different brightness images by constantly adjusting the gamma value. The gamma correction curve is shown in Fig. 18.

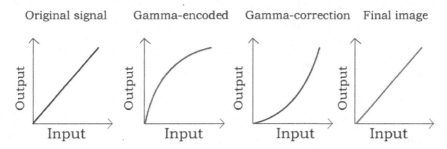

Fig. 18. The process of gamma correction of images

4   Experiment Results

4.1   Experiment Setting

Our experiment was run on the personal computer with windows 7 system, whose configuration is as follows: 3.2GHz Intel(R) Core (TM) i5 CPU, 16 GB RAM and NVIDA GeForce Graphics Processor. To overcome the issue of randomness, the training and test were implemented more times, and then the mean and standard deviation were obtained. The main parameters of training option are provided as follows: Adam (Adaptive momentum) algorithm is selected as training algorithm, MaxEpochs equals 30, InitialLearnRate is 0.01, MiniBatchSize is set to 256, LearnRateSchedule is piecewise, LearnRateDropFactor is set to 0.1 and L2Regularization is 0.005. Finally, average accuracy is adopted to evaluate the identification.

4.2   Structure of Proposed CNN

An optimized seven-layer CNN was created, including five convolutional layers for feature extraction and two fully-connected layers for classification. As shown in Table 2, the detailed parameters settings were given. Where, some advanced techniques i.e. batch normalization, ReLU and pooling were applied to improve the performance. Meanwhile, the dropout rate was set to 0.4. In addition, softmax function was employed.

Table 2.   Details of each layer in our CNN

Index	Layer	Filter/pool size	Filters	Stride
	Input	$256 \times 256 \times 3$		
1	Conv_BN_ReLU_1 (Pool)	7/3	32	3
2	Conv_BN_ReLU_2 (Pool)	3/3	64	3
3	Conv_BN_ReLU_3 (Pool)	3/3	128	1
4	Conv_BN_ReLU_4 (Pool)	3/3	256	3
5	Conv_BN_ReLU_5 (Pool)	3/3	512	1
6	FCL_1(Dropout = 0.4)			
7	FCL_2(Softmax)			

4.3   Statistical Analysis

As shown in Table 3, this table provides 10 runs results of our method. The average accuracy of identification reaches $91.99 \pm 1.21\%$, which is bolded in the column. Meanwhile, the highest accuracy achieves 93.36%, and the accuracy values of nine runs exceed 90%. Therefore, it can be considered that our method owns satisfactory effectiveness and stability.

Table 3. Ten runs of our method

Run	Our method
1	91.41
2	90.23
3	91.41
4	92.58
5	89.84
6	92.58
7	93.36
8	92.97
9	92.58
10	92.97
Average	**91.99 ± 1.21**

5   Discussions

5.1   Comparison to Pooling Method

Two common pooling methods i.e. maximum pooling and average pooling were tested in the experiment. Meanwhile, the parameter settings were unchanged. As shown in Table 4, comparison of average pooling and maximum pooling are listed in 10 runs. For a vivid comparison, the results are represented in Fig. 19. It can be seen that maximum pooling is obviously better than average pooling in term of average accuracy. Maximum pooling achieves the highest accuracy of 93.36% while average pooling gains the value of 92.58% in the highest accuracy. Moreover, the accuracy value of maximum pooling in each run is significantly greater than or equal to that of average pooling.

5.2   Effect of Data Augmentation

To verity the effectiveness of data augmentation (DA) in training, the same experiments were executed between using DA and without DA. The effect of data augmentation is indicated in Fig. 20. Average accuracy of method with DA reaches 91.99 ± 1.21%, which can increase about 2.9% than the accuracy of method without DA. Obviously, the data augmentation technique can generate more images to expand the dataset, which provides sufficient data and enhances the performance of identification. Furthermore, DA technology also cuts issue of over-fitting.

5.3   Comparison to State-of-the-Art Approaches

Our proposed method "CNN7-DA" was compared with five state-of-the-art approaches i.e. GLCM-MGSVM [26], HMI-RBF-SVM [27], CNN6-LReLU [28], WE-kSVM [29]

Table 4. Comparison of average pooling and maximum pooling

Run	Average pooling	Maximum pooling
1	89.06	91.41
2	90.23	90.23
3	89.45	91.41
4	88.28	92.58
5	89.84	89.84
6	91.02	92.58
7	89.45	93.36
8	90.23	92.97
9	90.63	92.58
10	92.58	92.97
Average	90.08 ± 1.18	91.99 ± 1.21

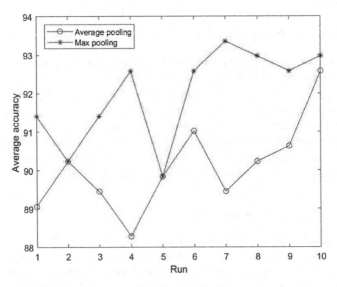

Fig. 19. Comparison of average pooling and maximum pooling

and AlexNet-TL [30] in the experiment. The average accuracy of GLCM-MGSVM, HMI-RBF-SVM, CNN6-LReLU, WE-kSVM and AlexNet-TL are 85.30%, 86.47%, 88.10%, 89.4% and 89.48%, respectively, which are denoted in Fig. 21. We can observe that proposed "CNN7-DA" obtains relatively better performance among six algorithms.

Two attributes are summarized to explain the reason why our method is superior. First and foremost, an optimized seven layers CNN was employed, which composed

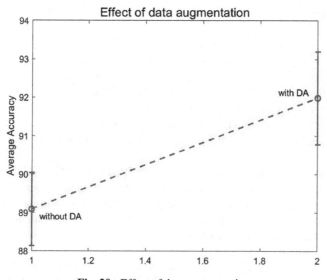

Fig. 20. Effect of data augmentation

BN, ReLU, pooling and dropout techniques into an advanced block. CNN can gain learnable weights through iteration and extract features automatically. Advanced block can overcome issue of over-fitting and improve performance. Secondly, application of DA extends image dataset and provides sufficiency of date, thus deep neural network generality can be enhanced.

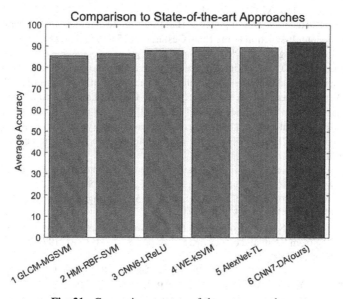

Fig. 21. Comparison to state-of-the-art approaches

6   Conclusions

In this study, a novel seven-layer CNN with advanced techniques block was proposed to identify Chinese fingerspelling sign language. Batch normalization and ReLU techniques are employed to accelerate convergence of learn and eliminate gradient disappearance. Pooling and dropout techniques are adapted to reduce dimensionality and overcome overfitting. Data augmentation technique provides sufficiency of image data. Our method achieves average accuracy of $91.99 \pm 1.21\%$, which is superior to five state-of-the-art approaches. The mainly explanation is indicated in Sect. 5.3 Comparison to state-of-the-art approaches.

In the future, we will try different levels of convolutional neural networks and try other training algorithms to further optimize parameters to improve overall performance. Meanwhile, we will try to verify our study in other application of recognition, for instance, Lip language recognition, movement recognition, rehabilitation gesture recognition, etc. are all potential areas.

Acknowledgements. This work was supported by National Philosophy and Social Sciences Foundation (20BTQ065), Natural Science Foundation of Jiangsu Higher Education Institutions of China (19KJA310002), The Philosophy and Social Science Research Foundation Project of Universities of Jiangsu Province (2017SJB0668).

References

1. Jiang, X., Satapathy, S.C., Yang, L., Wang, S.-H., Zhang, Y.-D.: A survey on artificial intelligence in Chinese sign language recognition. Arab. J. Sci. Eng. **45**(12), 9859–9894 (2020). https://doi.org/10.1007/s13369-020-04758-2
2. Premaratne, P.: Historical Development of Hand Gesture Recognition. In: Premaratne, P. (ed.) Human Computer Interaction Using Hand Gestures, pp. 5–29. Springer Singapore, Singapore (2014). https://doi.org/10.1007/978-981-4585-69-9_2
3. Liang, R.H., Ming, O.: A real-time continuous gesture recognition system for sign language. In: IEEE International Conference on Automatic Face & Gesture Recognition (1998)
4. Wu, J., Wen, G., Cheng, X.: A system recognizing Chinese finger-spelling alphabets based on data-glove input. Pattern Recogn. Artif. Intell. (1999)
5. Liang, R.-H.: A real-time continuous gesture recognition system for sign language. In: Proceedings of The Third IEEE International Conference on Automatic Face and Gesture Recognition (1998)
6. Weng, C., Li, Y., Zhang, M., Guo, K., Tang, X., Pan, Z.: Robust Hand Posture Recognition Integrating Multi-cue Hand Tracking. In: Zhang, X., Zhong, S., Pan, Z., Wong, K., Yun, R. (eds.) Edutainment 2010. LNCS, vol. 6249, pp. 497–508. Springer, Heidelberg (2010). https://doi.org/10.1007/978-3-642-14533-9_51
7. Ameen, S., Vadera, S.: A convolutional neural network to classify American sign language fingerspelling from depth and colour images. Expert Syst. **34**(3), e12197 (2017). https://doi.org/10.1111/exsy.12197
8. Mohanty, A., Rambhatla, S., Sahay, R.: Deep Gesture: Static Hand Gesture Recognition Using CNN. In: Raman, B., Kumar, S., Roy, P.P., Sen, D. (eds.) Proceedings of International Conference on Computer Vision and Image Processing, pp. 449–461. Springer Singapore, Singapore (2017). https://doi.org/10.1007/978-981-10-2107-7_41

9. Sun, J., He, X., Tan, W., Wu, X., Lu, H.: Recognition of crop seedling and weed recognition based on dilated convolution and global pooling in CNN. Trans. Chin. Soc. Agric. Eng. **34**(11), 159–165 (2018)

10. Yu, H., Ding, L., Shi, H., Hanchao, Y., Huang, T.S.: Computed tomography super-resolution using convolutional neural networks. In: IEEE International Conference on Image Processing (ICIP) (2017)

11. Wang, Shui-Hua., Hong, J., Yang, M.: Sensorineural hearing loss identification via nine-layer convolutional neural network with batch normalization and dropout. Multimedia Tools Appl. **79**(21–22), 15135–15150 (2018). https://doi.org/10.1007/s11042-018-6798-3

12. Banerjee, C., Mukherjee, T., Pasiliao, E.: An empirical study on generalizations of the ReLU activation function. In: The 2019 ACM Southeast Conference (2019)

13. Wang, Y., Liu, Z., Mu, X., Gao, S.: Modeling and verification of contact line transient temperature difference based on lifting or lowering the pantograph electric contacts. Chin. J. Sci. Instrum. **35**(12), 2663–2672 (2014)

14. Ying-bing, L.: Research on computer technology of remote supervisory and management system. In: Conference and Technology of West China (2010)

15. Li, D., Deng, L., Cai, Z.: Research on image classification method based on convolutional neural network. Neural Comput. Appl. **33**, 8157–8167 (2020). https://doi.org/10.1007/s00 521-020-04930-7

16. Wang, S.-H., Lv, Y.-D., Sui, Y., Liu, S., Wang, S.-J., Zhang, Y.-D.: Alcoholism detection by data augmentation and convolutional neural network with stochastic pooling. J. Med. Syst. **42**(1), 1–11 (2017). https://doi.org/10.1007/s10916-017-0845-x

17. Wei, Z., Yang, J., Min, S.: A method of underwater acoustic signal classification based on deep neural network. In: 2018 5th International Conference on Information Science and Control Engineering (ICISCE) (2019)

18. Shen, X., Tian, X., Liu, T., Xu, F. Tao, D.: Continuous dropout. IEEE Trans. Neural Netw. Learn. Syst. 1–12 (2017)

19. Yu, X., Kang, C., Guttery, D., Kadry, S., Chen, Y., Zhang, Yu-Dong.: ResNet-SCDA-50 for breast abnormality classification. IEEE/ACM Trans. Comput. Biol. Bioinform. **18**(1), 94–102 (2021). https://doi.org/10.1109/TCBB.2020.2986544

20. Motamed, S., Rogalla, P., Khalvati, F.: Data Augmentation using Generative Adversarial Networks (GANs) for GAN-based Detection of Pneumonia and COVID-19 in Chest X-ray Images (2020)

21. Eckert, D., Vesal, S., Ritschl, L., Kappler, S., Maier, A.: Deep Learning-based Denoising of Mammographic Images using Physics-driven Data Augmentation. Presented at the (2020). https://doi.org/10.1007/978-3-658-29267-6_21

22. Vasconcelos, C.N., Vasconcelos, B.N.: Convolutional Neural Network Committees for Melanoma Classification with Classical and Expert Knowledge Based Image Transforms Data Augmentation (2017)

23. Singh, P., Yadav, A.K., Singh, K.: Color image encryption using affine transform in fractional Hartley domain. Opt. Appl. 47(3) (2017)

24. Igl, M., Ciosek, K., Li, Y., Tschiatschek, S., Hofmann, K.: Generalization in Reinforcement Learning with Selective Noise Injection and Information Bottleneck (2019)

25. Wang, Shui-Hua., et al.: Multiple sclerosis identification by 14-layer convolutional neural network with batch normalization, dropout, and stochastic pooling. Front. Neurosci. **12**, 818 (2018)

26. Jiang, X.: Isolated Chinese sign language recognition using gray-level co-occurrence matrix and parameter-optimized medium Gaussian support vector machine. Front. Intell. Comput.: Theory Appl. **1014**, 182–193 (2019)

27. Ya, G., et al.: Chinese Fingerspelling Recognition via Hu Moment Invariant and RBF Support Vector Machine. In: Zhang, Y.-D., Wang, S.-H., Liu, S. (eds.) ICMTEL 2020. LNICSSITE, vol. 327, pp. 382–392. Springer, Cham (2020). https://doi.org/10.1007/978-3-030-51103-6_34

28. Jiang, X., Zhang, Y.-D.: Chinese sign language fingerspelling via six-layer convolutional neural network with leaky rectified linear units for therapy and rehabilitation. J. Med. Imag. Health Inform. **9**(9), 2031–2090 (2019)

29. Zhu, Z., Zhang, M., Jiang, X.: Fingerspelling identification for Chinese sign language via wavelet entropy and kernel support vector machine. Intell. Data Eng. Anal. **1177**, 539–549 (2020)

30. Jiang, X., Hu, B., Chandra Satapathy, S., Wang, S.-H., Zhang, Y.-D.: Fingerspelling identification for Chinese sign language via AlexNet-based transfer learning and Adam optimizer. Sci. Program. 2020, 1–10 (2020)

Similar Gesture Recognition via an Optimized Convolutional Neural Network and Adam Optimizer

Ya Gao, Chenchong Jia, Yifei Qiao, Xi Huang, Juan Lei, and Xianwei Jiang[✉]

School of Mathematics and Information Science, Nanjing Normal University of Special Education, Nanjing 210038, China
jxw@njts.edu.cn

Abstract. The recognition significance of similar sign language (or confusing gesture) in sign language recognition is highlighted, and the goal is to realize the recognition of such gesture and sign language based on deep learning with an optimized convolutional neural network and the Adam optimizer. The convolutional layer and the pooling layer are connected alternately. The locally connected image data and parameter features are used to extract the shared pooling layer, and the image resolution reduction of image data sampling and the reducibility of iterative training are used to achieve the extraction precision requirements of feature points. In addition, the information transfer between layers is realized through convolution, the introduction of pooling layer and RELU activation function to realize nonlinear mapping and reduce the data dimension. We also use the batch normalization method for faster convergence and dropout method to reduce overfitting. Ten experiments were carried out on a nine-layer "CNN-BN-ReLU-AP-DO" method, with an average accuracy of $97.50 \pm 1.65\%$. The overall accuracy is relatively high, and gesture recognition can be conducted effectively.

Keywords: Gesture recognition · CNN · Batch normalization · Dropout · Adam · Data augmentation

1 Introduction

As the development of artificial intelligence, human-computer interaction is becoming more and more popular. The main media to study human-computer interaction are different Convolutional Neural networks (CNN) or different machine learning methods. As a natural way of communication between people, gesture has gradually become a new way of human-computer interaction. More and more people are joining the field of human-computer interaction. In the field of human-computer interaction, gestures are usually used to convey some simple instructions. Using gestures to operate a computer is usually imperative, but this is not what people use gestures for. Gesture can be divided into dynamic gesture and static gesture. As a transient state of dynamic gesture, static

W. Fu et al. (Eds.): ICMTEL 2021, LNICST 388, pp. 43–61, 2021.
https://doi.org/10.1007/978-3-030-82565-2_4

gesture is of great significance for understanding dynamic gesture. In the research process of gesture recognition, the traditional method is to segment gestures from pictures and classify them under different rules and algorithms. However, the hand is a non-rigid object with abundant changes. The changes of different environments and spaces and the deviations of gestures of individual movement make gesture recognition more difficult.

At present, gesture recognition has been widely studied, including based on neural network, vision, variable target classification task, Kinect gesture recognition technology and so on. JongShill Lee, et al. from Inda University in South Korea and Korea Polytechnic University used entropy analysis to segment the gesture region from the background complex video stream and conduct gesture recognition [1]. They detected the contour of the gesture region with chain code method, and finally calculated the distance from the center of mass of the gesture region to the contour boundary. The system can recognize 6 gestures, with an average recognition rate of over 95%, and the recognition rate of 6 individuals for each gesture reaches an average of 90%–100% [2]. Beijing Jiaotong University Li Jiang, et al. on the basis of data glove, analysis the geometric relationships between a hand shape, set up the model of virtual hand, by the data glove data interface to get the knuckles of the flex point of view, establish gestures standard sample library, and puts forward the gesture recognition method based on BP neural network, with gesture training standard sample, make it have the function that identify gestures, and by using VC+ + programming to realize BP neural network, using Matlab to prove the validity of the results (see Fig. 1) [3].

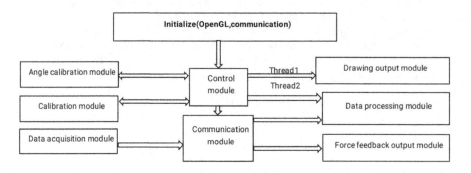

Data glove composition and working principle block diagram

Fig. 1. The structure and work principle of data glove

There are three methods for gesture recognition: template matching, neural network and hidden Markov model [4]. A gesture is a motion of the body that contains information. Neural network gesture recognition requires a certain learning stage, and in the process of processing, there may be serious shortcomings such as large number of middle layer neurons, too long learning time, and too wide range of combining coefficients. The gesture recognition based on vision uses camera to collect the sequence of gesture image, and recognizes the gesture through image processing and analysis. This method is simple to input, low to the equipment requirements, but the recognition rate is low.

Variable target based gesture recognition can improve the efficiency of gesture recognition without increasing the amount of computation, but it has many parameters and a large amount of computation. Kinect-based gesture recognition technology is highly dependent on machine learning, which makes it easier to recognize new gestures, but more difficult to establish the system.

However, in the process of sign language recognition, we found that some single samples have low ROC values. For instance, some ROC values are between 0.76 and 0.82. Meanwhile, based on actual experience, these gestures are easy to confuse due to their similarities, such as Y and T, N and M, SH and NG, etc. Therefore, similar gesture recognition is proposed as research content, and related experiments and tests have been carried out.

In this paper, a gesture recognition algorithm using convolutional neural network is proposed, which avoids complex preprocessing of gestures and can directly input the original gesture images. With the characteristics of local perception region, hierarchical structure, feature extraction and classification process, convolutional neural network has been widely applied in the field of image recognition. Moreover, it has high accuracy, low complexity, good robustness, and overcomes many inherent shortcomings of traditional algorithms.

2 Dataset

In order to analyze the different and similar sign language and gesture pairs scientifically, we need to analyze the sign language images. To this end, we quoted the relevant sign language self-built data set [5], and used image processing techniques to highlight gesture features, thereby making our data richer, more accurate, and more comprehensive. At the same time, the use of image processing technology reduces the uncertainty and contingency of experimental data. In order to complete this research, it is necessary to process the data in the data set more carefully, putting together images that represent the same meaning (see Fig. 2).

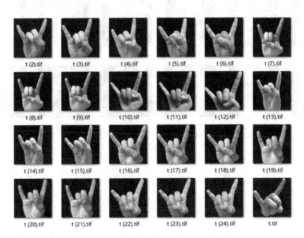

Fig. 2. The images representing the same pronunciation are put together

The data set sample used this time are the most similar and most confusing samples selected from 26 basic letters and 4 words with the pronunciation of rolling voice, and a total of six categories. The image size is 256 × 256. At the same time, the background color is uniformly set to RGB (0, 0, 0) to facilitate the realization of the training of the convolutional neural network in the following experiments.

Due to the high degree of similarity and small difference between different sign language pictures, in order to improve the accuracy of the experiment, in the stage of data screening feature samples, the following principles need to be followed [6]:

1. The sample selected from the data set needs to represent the characteristic hand shape of a specific sign language word, which is a basic requirement;
2. The samples selected from the data set are as different as possible from each other;
3. The selected samples from the data set need to include the past situation from different perspectives to reduce the influence of external factors;

Based on the above sample selection principle, in the existing sign language data set, we created a set of smaller data sets for analysis based on the sign language hand type with the smaller Roc value, which included samples of NG, SH, M, N, Y and T (see Fig. 3).

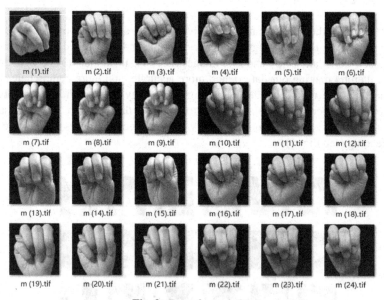

Fig. 3. Part of sample M

3 Methodology

3.1 Convolutional Layer

The convolutional layer and the pooling layer are alternately connected. The convolutional layer makes use of the local connectivity and parameter sharing of image data for feature extraction, while the pooling layer makes use of the reducibility of sampling of image data for image resolution reduction, and repeated iterative training achieves the precision requirements of feature point extraction.

The convolutional layer is the core layer of the convolutional neural network. In the multi-layer neural network architecture, the input of neurons in the latter layer is extracted from the important feature points in the local image area of the former layer, and the full connection layer in the latter performs combination matching of features, and performs classification or other tasks [7].

Convolutional layer is a process in which several feature maps are obtained through convolution calculation of data through filter to extract features from input data. Convolutional layer by using network and local connection and convolution kernel parameters share the way connected with the previous layer, a matrix that input data is local element contact more closely, distant element correlation is weak, so each neuron need only perceive the local area of the input data, perception of each local area will be connected to the next layer, this is the local connection of convolution layer; Convolution kernel sharing means that every pixel value on the characteristic surface shares the convolution kernel, which can reduce the network parameters and reduce the risk of overfitting [8]. The convolutional layer mainly has two key operations: local association and window sliding. Local association is to place each neuron as a convolution kernel; Window sliding is to set the size of filter, quantity, step length of window sliding and filling value of changing the size of feature map to carry out convolution operation on local data. The convolution operation is shown in Fig. 4. Parameter sharing is realized in all neurons of feature map, which greatly reduces the number of weights, improves the learning efficiency, and is very helpful for network training [9]. Suppose that a given two-dimensional image I (a,b), called "input", convolved with the kernel function K (p,q) is

$$S(a, b) = (I*K)(a, b) = \sum_p \sum_q I(p, q)K(a - p, b - q) \tag{1}$$

Where (p, q) represents the size of kernel. As the convolution is commutative, the formula is equivalent to

$$S(a, b) = (I*K)(a, b) = \sum_p \sum_q I(a - p, b - q)K(p, q) \tag{2}$$

3.2 Pooling Layer

The deep neural network realizes the information transfer between layers mainly through convolution, and introduces pooling layer to reduce the data dimension. The activation function realizes the nonlinear mapping. Pooling layer is equivalent to a filter, which

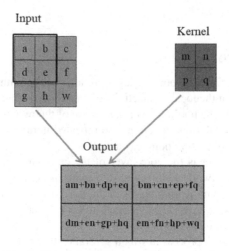

Fig. 4. Illustration of the convolution operation

is used to remove a lot of redundant information in the feature map obtained by convolutional layer and activation layer and to screen out the most representative feature information. The function of pooling layer is to gradually reduce the spatial size of the data body, so as to reduce the number of parameters in the network, reduce the consumption of computing resources, and effectively control the overfitting. The pooling layer mainly contains two parameters, namely the step size and the size of the pooling core. The pooling kernel processes the input feature graph in the way of sliding window, and the corresponding key features are obtained through the calculation of different pooling functions. Different pooling functions mean different pooling methods.

Maximum pooling core average pooling is the most common pooling method. The maximum pooling layer only retains the maximum value in the pooling box, so the most representative information in the feature diagram can be extracted effectively [10]. Averaging pooling can calculate the mean of all the values in the pooling box, so that all the information in the feature graph can be averaged, without losing too much key information. Figure 5 shows an example of a maximum pool and an average pool.

Given the pool area R, the activation set M contained in R is

$$M = \{m_i | i \in R\} \tag{3}$$

Then the max pooling P_m can be expressed as

$$P_m = \max(M_R) \tag{4}$$

Another pool strategy, the average pooling P_a is defined as:

$$P_a = \frac{\sum M_R}{|M_R|} \tag{5}$$

Where M_R is the number of elements in the set M.

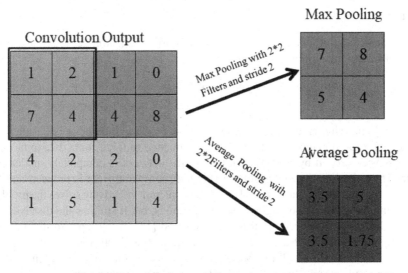

Fig. 5. Examples of max pooling and average pooling

Pooling helps the input representation to be approximately constant and reduces the computational burden. But both the max pooling and the average pooling have their own disadvantages. The former is easy to over fit training data and can only reduce the estimated average offset due to convolutional layer parameter errors and cannot be generalized to the test set. The latter may reduce the intense activation when many elements in the pool area are close to zero, and it only reduces the error estimated variance due to the size of the finite field.

In order to overcome the shortcomings of the maximum pool method and the average pool method, we introduce the Stochastic Pooling (SP). Stochastic Pooling replaces the traditional deterministic pooling operation with a random process, which is activated by randomly selecting a value in each pooling region according to the polynomial distribution given by the activity of the pooling region. To be more specific, firstly, the probability p of each region is calculated through the activation within the planning region. The specific formula is as follows:

$$p_i = \frac{b_i}{\sum b_k}, \quad k \in R_j \tag{6}$$

Where R_j is the pooling area, it is easy to sees that the greater the element value in each pooling domain is, the greater the probability P is. Then, a value in the pooling domain is randomly selected as the final value according to the probability value. Due to the randomness of Stochastic Pooling, it retains the advantages of max pooling and average pooling to a large extent, and can avoid the fitting of convolutional neural network [11].

3.3 ReLU

ReLU is an activation function commonly used in artificial neural networks, and it is a linear correction function. It is defined as:

$$f(x) = \begin{cases} x \text{ if } x > 0, \\ 0 \text{ if } x \leq 0, \end{cases} \tag{7}$$

If the input value is less than or equal to 0, then the output value is 0, otherwise the original value remains unchanged. This is a method to force some data to be zero, but it has been proved by practice that the trained network is completely moderately sparse. Thus, the interdependent relationship between parameters is reduced and the occurrence of overfitting is alleviated [12]. ReLU function effectively solves the problem of gradient disappearance of sigmoid series functions, but it still has the disadvantage of mean deviation. When $x < 0$, it is hard saturated [13]. If the input results fall into this region, the gradient of the neuron will always be 0 and will not activate any data again, that is, the neuron will die, which directly leads to the non-convergence of the calculation results. And the output of the ReLU function is 0 when $x < 0$, making the overall output mean greater than 0, which cannot alleviate the mean deviation problem.

Leaky ReLU (LReLU) is a variant of ReLU. Its proposal is to solve the Dead ReLU problem, where ReLU sets all negative values to zero and LReLU gives all negative values a non-zero slope. It is defined as:

$$y_i = \begin{cases} x_i \text{ if } x_i \geq 0, \\ \frac{x_i}{\alpha_i} \text{ if } x_i < 0, \end{cases} \tag{8}$$

Where α_i is a fixed parameter in $(1, +\infty)$. However, in some experiments, we found that LReLU had no significant influence on accuracy.

Parametric ReLU (PReLU) function is a modified version of LReLU function, which is unsaturated and can alleviate mean shift and neuronal death, and is defined as follows:

$$f(x) = \begin{cases} x \text{ if } x > 0, \\ \alpha x \text{ if } x \leq 0, \end{cases} \tag{9}$$

Compared with ReLU function, when x is less than or equal to 0, the slope coefficient α of PReLU function can be determined according to the data, or it can learn parameters from the data adaptively, instead of being fixed, and the output mean approaches 0. Moreover, the function is not hard saturated at this time, so the convergence speed of PReLU function is faster and there is no problem of neuron death. PReLU can be used for back propagation training and can be optimized in parallel with other layers [14].

Randomized Leaky ReLU (RReLU) is another improvement on LReLU. In RReLU, the negative slope is random in training and fixed in later tests. The highlight of RReLU is that α_{ji} is a value randomly selected from a uniform distribution U(I, U) during the training. Formally, we can get the following results:

$$y_{ji} = \begin{cases} x_{ji} \text{ if } x_{ji} \geq 0, \\ \alpha_{ji} x_{ji} \text{ if } x_{ji} < 0, \end{cases} \tag{10}$$

Where $\alpha_{ji} \sim U(l, u)$, $l < u$ and $l, u \in [0, 1)$.

The core idea of RReLU is that, during training, α is a random value from a Gaussian distribution U (l,u), which is then modified during testing. In the testing stage, take the average value of α_{ji} during the training process. PReLu is a bit of a regularization.

3.4 Batch Normalization

Batch Normalization is a very simple but easy-to-use practical technique that can reduce the problem of internal covariate shift and speed up training convergence. For deep neural networks, even if the output data of the previous layer has been "whitened", the update of various model parameters during training will still easily cause the hidden layer input distribution of the corresponding layer in the network to shift or Changes cause instability of calculated values. This instability due to drift and change usually makes it difficult for us to train an effective depth model. Batch Normalization adjusts the activation value of a number of training examples by selecting several min-batch data sets in each selected training data set. After activation, the input value of any neuron in each layer of the neural network will be forced back to the standard normal distribution with mean of 0 and a variance of 1, which effectively reduces the influence of the instability of the calculated value.

In order to improve the accuracy of network training to a certain extent and prevent the decrease of network expression ability during network training, the selection of min-batch data set in Batch Normalization training and inference should consider the distribution ratio of all training data, so that the neural network The prediction effect will be better, and the training accuracy of the network will be improved to a certain extent. After adopting Batch Normalization, the model parameter gradient will be less affected by the changes of various model parameters during the training update process, which speeds up the convergence speed [15].

3.5 Dropout

Dropout is a commonly used method to suppress over-fitting in deep learning. The method is to randomly delete a part of neurons during the neural network learning process. During training, a part of neurons are randomly selected and their output is set to 0. These neurons will not transmit signals to the outside [16]. Figure ab is a schematic diagram of Dropout, on the left is the complete neural network, and on the right is the network structure after applying Dropout. After applying Dropout, the marked neurons will be deleted from the network so that they will not transmit signals to the subsequent layers. Randomly identified neurons are discarded in the learning process, so the model does not rely too much on certain neurons, which can inhibit overfitting to a certain extent.

Dropout temporarily discards a part of neurons and their connections. Randomly discarding neurons can prevent overfitting, while connecting different network architectures exponentially and efficiently. The probability of neurons being discarded is $1 - p$, which reduces co-adaptation between neurons. The hidden layer usually discards neurons with a probability of 0.5. Use the complete network (the output weight of each node is p) to approximate the sample average of all 2^n dropout neurons. Dropout significantly reduces overfitting, and at the same time improves the learning speed of the algorithm by avoiding training nodes on the training data.

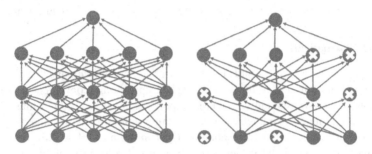

Fig. 6. Ordinary neural networks (left). Neural network with dropout (right)

When predicting the scene, the Dropout diagram in Fig. 6 will forward all neuron signals, which may lead to a new problem: because some neurons are randomly discarded during training, the total size of the output data will be reduced. For example: the calculation of its norm will be smaller than when Dropout is not used, but the neurons are not discarded during prediction, which will result in a different distribution of data during training and prediction. There are two ways to solve this problem:

1. During training, a part of neurons are randomly discarded in proportion, and their signals are not transmitted backward; during prediction, the signals of all neurons are transmitted backward, but the value on each neuron is multiplied by.
2. A part of neurons are randomly discarded in proportion during training, and their signals are not transmitted backward, but the values on those neurons that are reserved are divided by the signals of all neurons are transmitted backward during prediction, without any processing.

3.6 Data Augmentation

In order to better analyze sign language images, that is, to more accurately identify and distinguish similar sign languages, we validated some DA techniques, such as PCA color augmentation, affine transform, noise injection, scaling, random shift and gamma correction. Each part is explained in detail:

PCA Color Enhancement: First calculate the mean and standard deviation according to the three color channels of RGB, and then calculate the covariance matrix on the entire training set, perform eigen decomposition, and obtain eigenvectors and eigenvalues for PCA Data augmentation [17];

Affine Transformation: Also known as affine mapping, it means that in geometry, a vector space undergoes a linear transformation and is connected to a translation to transform it into another vector space [18]. Affine transformation can maintain the "flatness" of the image, including rotation, scaling, translation, and miscutting operations. Generally speaking, the affine transformation matrix is a matrix of 23, the elements in the third column play the role of translation, the numbers in the first two columns are scaled on the diagonal, and the rest are rotation or crosscutting. Affine transformation is a linear transformation from two-dimensional coordinates (x,y) to two-dimensional coordinates (α,β). The mathematical expression is as follows:

$$\begin{cases} \alpha = a_1 x + b_1 y + c_1 \\ \beta = a_2 + b_2 y + c_2 \end{cases} \tag{11}$$

The corresponding homogeneous coordinate system is as follows:

$$\begin{bmatrix} \alpha \\ \beta \\ 1 \end{bmatrix} = \begin{bmatrix} a_1 & b_1 & c_1 \\ a_2 & b_2 & c_2 \\ 0 & 0 & 1 \end{bmatrix} \begin{bmatrix} x \\ y \\ 1 \end{bmatrix} \tag{12}$$

Affine transformation maintains the "flatness" (straight lines are still straight lines after affine transformation) and "parallelism" (the relative positional relationship between straight lines remains unchanged, and parallel lines remain unchanged after affine transformation. It is a parallel line, and the position order of the points on the line will not change). Three pairs of non-collinear corresponding points determine a unique affine transformation.

Noise Injection: There are many kinds of noise injection in the neural network, such as input layer, hidden layer, weight, output layer, etc. Here only the input layer x and output layer y are used as examples.

In fact, injecting noise into the input layer can actually be regarded as a means of data set enhancement, which is essentially regularization. The reason is that the neural network is not robust to noise, so it has to be mixed with noise and then trained to improve robustness [19].

Injecting noise into the output layer is actually modeling label noise. The label of most data sets always has a certain error rate. For example, assume that the error rate E, as the number of classes k, this time is smoothed to 0, 1 is a flat slide to $1 - E$, the positive integer of the k-th output softmax.

Zoom: The image can be zoomed outward or inward. When zooming out, the final image size will be larger than the original image size. Most image frames cut out a part from the new image whose size is equal to the original image. We will deal with inward scaling in the next section because it reduces the size of the image and forces us to make assumptions about content that is beyond the boundary.

Gamma Correction: In the process of image formation, there are many factors that affect the clarity of the image. Gamma correction can help us improve the quality of the output image, so that we can distinguish more accurately when recognizing similar sign languages. The following will explain the reasons why gamma correction can improve the quality of the output image [20]. At the same time, we will also explain the importance of image quality in recognizing sign language.

Gamma correction is ignored in many graphics books. The results of lighting and shading calculations are directly output to the screen without modification, so the resulting image may not be what we expect. In fact, computer monitors (CRT and now LCD monitors) react nonlinearly to pixel brightness. For example, without using gamma correction, a gray value of 0.5 is not half of the brightness of 1.0, and its brightness is darker than half of 1.0. The nonlinear relationship of display brightness can usually be fitted using an exponential function. Perceived brightness (P) is proportional to the index of pixel brightness (l), and this index is called gamma r. For display devices, usually the value of r is between 2.0 and 2.4. This value can be accurately determined through display calibration. We can correct this problem through gamma correction. Gamma correction compensates for the non-linear response of the display to the brightness value by performing an exponential operation on the brightness value of the pixel, so that the display result looks linear. When rendering, we first ignore the problem that the brightness response of the display is non-linear. Before the result is written into the frame buffer object, we use gamma correction to correct this problem, thereby improving image quality.

As we all know, the quality of a picture will greatly affect the human visual experience. Similarly, in the process of sign language recognition, the quality of the picture will also have a great impact on the result of sign language recognition. In particular, for some similar pictures, different test results are likely to be produced due to subtle differences in picture quality. So here we introduce Gamma correction to improve the accuracy of sign language recognition by improving the quality of the picture.

3.7 Train Algorithms

ADAM (The Adaptive Momentum) Algorithm: Set a global learning rate ρ(recommend default $\rho = 0.001$), moment estimated exponential decay rate $^c\beta_1$ and $^c\beta_2$ ($^c\beta_1$ and $^c\beta_2$ in the interval [0,1) the recommended default were 0.9 and 0.990), initialization parameters for K, a small constant created for numerical stability (recommended) by default K − 1), the first and second moment variables s and r with an initial value of 0, and a time step counter t (initialized t = 0). Then there is the main body of the algorithm, which loops through the following steps and will not stop until the conditions for stopping are reached.

(1) Take out the small batch of data $\{X_1, X_2, X_3, X_4 \ldots \ldots X_m\}$ The target corresponding to the data is t represented by y_i.
(2) Calculate the gradient based on the small batch data according to the following formula:

$$g \leftarrow \frac{1}{m} \vee_\omega \sum_i L\big(f(x_i; \omega), y_i\big) \tag{13}$$

(3) Refresh time step:

$$t \leftarrow t + 1 \tag{14}$$

(4) Update the first-order partial moment estimation:

$$s \leftarrow \rho_1 s + (1 - \rho_1)g \tag{15}$$

(5) Update the second-order partial moment estimation:

$$r \leftarrow \rho_2 r + (1 - \rho_2)g \odot g \qquad (16)$$

(6) Correct the deviation of the first-order moment:

$$\tilde{s} \leftarrow \frac{s}{1 - \rho_1^t} \qquad (17)$$

(7) Correct the deviation of the second moment:

$$\tilde{r} \leftarrow \frac{s}{1 - \rho_2^t} \qquad (18)$$

(8) Calculate the update amount of parameters:

$$\Delta\omega = -\sigma\frac{\tilde{s}}{\sqrt{\tilde{r} + \delta}} \qquad (19)$$

(9) According to the $\Delta\omega$ updated parameters:

$$\omega \leftarrow \omega + \Delta\omega \qquad (20)$$

In Adam, momentum is directly incorporated into the estimation of the first moment of the gradient (exponentially weighted). The most intuitive way to add momentum to RMS Prop is to apply momentum to the scaled gradient. There is no clear theoretical motivation for the use of momentum combined with scaling. Secondly, Adam includes offset correction, which corrects the estimation of the first moment (momentum term) and (non-central) second moment initialized from the origin.

Stochastic Gradient Descent With Momentum (SGDM): The momentum gradient descent method is an improved version of the gradient descent method. Generally speaking, the optimization effect is better than the gradient descent method. The core of the momentum gradient descent method is the exponentially weighted average of a series of gradients.

For example, the gradient sequence obtained in 100 gradient descent is

$$\left\{ \nabla W_1, \nabla W_2 \ldots \ldots \nabla W_{99}, \nabla W_{100} \right\}$$

Then the momentum gradients corresponding to them are respectively

$$V_{\nabla W_0} = 0$$
$$V_{\nabla W_1} = \beta V_{\nabla W_0} + (1 - \beta)\nabla W_1$$
$$V_{\nabla W_2} = \beta V_{\nabla W_1} + (1 - \beta)\nabla W_2$$

$$\cdot$$

(21)

$$\cdot$$

$$\cdot$$

$$V_{\nabla W_{100}} = \beta V_{\nabla W_{99}} + (1 - \beta)\nabla W_{100}$$

The gradient after exponential weighted average is used to replace the original gradient for parameter update, because each gradient after exponential weighted average contains the information of the previous gradient.

RMS Prop: RMS prop is similar to first update vector of Adadelta,

$$E\left[g^2\right]_{i+1} = 0.9E\left[g^2\right]_i - 0.1g_i^2$$

(22)

The update rules of RMS prop are as follows:

$$\theta_{i+1} = \theta_i - \frac{\alpha}{\sqrt{E[g^2]_i + \epsilon}} \frac{\partial}{\partial \theta_i} L(\theta_i : (y_i, \hat{y}_i))$$

(23)

In RMS prop, the learning rate is divided by the exponential decay average of the squared gradient.

Stochastic gradient descent updates the parameters of each training sample, and updates each time, and the execution speed is faster. But the problem is that due to frequent updates and fluctuations, it will eventually converge to a minimum and there will be frequent overshoot due to fluctuations. Dam algorithm can calculate the adaptive learning rate of each parameter. This method not only stores the exponential decay average of AdaDelta's previous squared gradient, but also maintains the exponential decay average of the previous gradient M(t), which is similar to momentum. In practical application, Adam method is more effective than other adaptive learning rate algorithms, and can correct the problems existing in other optimization techniques.

4   Experiment Results

4.1   Structure of Proposed CNN

A customized 9-layer CNN model was built, which included seven convolutional layer blocks and two fully connected layer blocks. In each convolutional layer block, advanced techniques such as batch normalization, ReLU and average pooling were employed. The details of hyperparameters were listed in Table 1. Meanwhile, the value of pooling size was set as 3 × 3, stride and padding were defined as 2 and 1, respectively. All settings were based on fine-tuned method. Dropout technique was applied before first fully connected layer (FCL1). The dropout rate was set to 0.4. Furthermore, softmax function was adopted after second fully connected layer (FCL2). By this way, the size of output is shrunk layer by layer. At the same time, the features of each layer are automatically extracted.

Table 1. Conv layers' hyperparameters

Index	Block	Filter size	Filter number	Stride	Padding
1	Conv1_BN_ReLU	3	8	2	1
2	Conv2_BN_ReLU_Pool	3	8	2	1
3	Conv3_BN_ReLU	3	16	1	1
4	Conv4_BN_ReLU_Pool	3	16	1	1
5	Conv5_BN_ReLU	3	32	1	1
6	Conv6_BN_ReLU_Pool	3	32	1	1
7	Conv7_BN_ReLU	3	64	1	1
8	FCL1_Dropout				
9	FCL2_Softmax				

4.2 Statistical Analysis

Our 9-layer CNN with "BN-ReLU-AP-DO" was tested. Experiments ran ten times. As shown in Table 2, the average accuracy is $97.50 \pm 1.65\%$. It can be seen that two runs achieve 100% accuracy and the overall accuracy rate is relatively high, which is benefit from less categories of classification, advanced techniques and data augmentation.

Table 2. Ten runs of our method

Run	Our method
1	95.83
2	100
3	95.83
4	97.92
5	97.92
6	95.83
7	100
8	97.92
9	95.83
10	97.92
Average	**97.50 ± 1.65**

5   Discussions

5.1   Effect of Batch Normalization and Dropout Layers

To validate the effect of batch normalization (BN) and dropout techniques, we compared CNN using BN and CNN without BN, furthermore, we compared CNN using dropout and CNN without dropout. As shown in Fig. 7, it was found that the accuracy decreased to 18.75% when we removed BN layers from neural network. This is a huge drop, which indicated that BN layer played a significant role in our method. Meanwhile, dropout technique can help to increase 1.67%, which denoted that dropout has a positive effect but is not obvious.

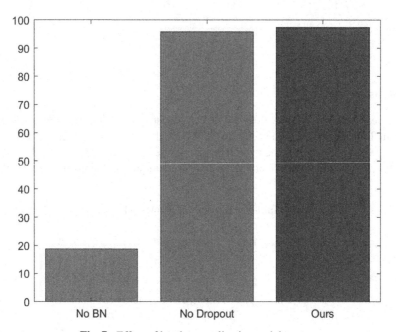

Fig. 7. Effect of batch normalization and dropout

5.2   Effect of Data Augmentation

We executed the same validation between with DA and without DA to confirm the effect of data augmentation. As listed in Table 3, not using DA will decrease the accuracy by 4.58%. Thus, data augmentation can provide sufficient image data and improve performance. We will test more DA techniques in the future than in this experiment.

5.3   Training Algorithms Comparison

In this experiment, three training algorithms i.e. Adam, RMSProp and SGDM were compared. The results were represented in Fig. 8. The means and standard deviation of

Table 3. Comparison of with DA and without DA

	With DA	Without DA
Average	97.50 ± 1.65	92.92 ± 1.07

Adam, RMSProp and SGDM are 97.50 ± 1.65%, 90.63 ± 1.77% and 91.25 ± 1.32%, respectively. It can be observed that Adam algorithm is significantly better than other two training algorithms.

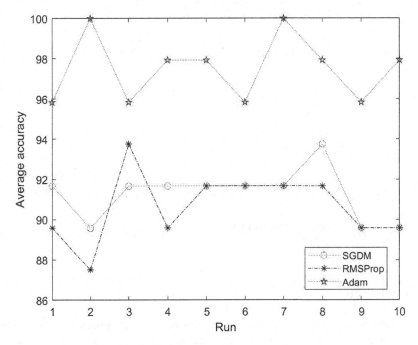

Fig. 8. Training algorithms comparison

5.4 Comparison to State-of-the-Art Approaches

In the experiment, we compared customized 9-layer CNN-BN-ReLU-AP-DO method with other three traditional machine learning approaches i.e. Decision Tree, KNN and SVM. The comparison can be observed in Fig. 9. In these four state-of-the-art approaches, average accuracy of Decision Tree, KNN, Quadratic SVM and CNN9 (ours) are 64.7%, 82.9%, 83.7% and 97.5%, respectively. Obviously, our method is superior to other state-of-the-art approaches.

The reason why we got the best performance in four approaches can be focus on three points. First, the introduction of BN can solve the issue of internal covariate shift and enhance performance. Second, dropout technique and DA can help to overcome overfitting. Finally, Adam algorithm is benefit to accelerate learning speed and improve effectiveness.

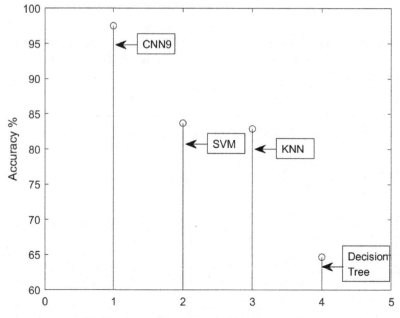

Fig. 9. Comparison to state-of-the-art approaches

6   Conclusions

A novel nine-layer "CNN-BN-ReLU-AP-DO" method was proposed for six-category similar gesture recognition. We trained this nine-layer CNN by Adam method, which achieves $97.50 \pm 1.65\%$ accuracy and is superior to other state-of-the-art approaches. Besides, we compared our method to CNN without BN and CNN without dropout. The results showed that BN technique played a major role and dropout provided a positive effect. Furthermore, data augmentation was proved to be beneficial for small dataset. Finally, different training algorithms were executed, It was found Adam is superior to RMSProp and SGDM.

In the future, we shall try other deep neural networks with different structures and optimize their hyperparameters [21]. Beside, we will transfer the mature method to other application field, such as facial expression recognition and lip language recognition.

Acknowledgements. This work was supported by Natural Science Foundation of Jiangsu Higher Education Institutions of China (19KJA310002), The Philosophy and Social Science Research Foundation Project of Universities of Jiangsu Province (2017SJB0668).

References

1. Lee, J.S., Lee, Y.J., Lee, E.H..: Hand region extraction and gesture recognition from video stream with complex background through entropy analysis. In: Proceedings of the 26th Annual International Conference of the IEEE EMBS, pp. 1–10 (2004)
2. Wu, X., Zhang, Q., Xu, Y.: A review of the development of gesture recognition research. Electron. Sci. Technol. **26**(6), 71–174 (2013). https://doi.org/10.3969/j.issn.1007-7820.2013. 06.053
3. Jiang, L., Ruan, Q.: Research on gesture recognition technology based on neural network. J. Beijing Jiaotong Univ. **30**(6), 32–36 (2006). https://doi.org/10.3969/j.issn.1673-0291.2006. 05.008
4. Feng, Z., Jiang, Y.: A review of gesture recognition research. J. Univ. Jinan (Sci. Technol.) **4**, 336–341 (2013)
5. Gao, Y., Jia, C., Chen, H., Jiang, X.: Chinese fingerspelling sign language recognition using a nine-layer convolutional neural network. EAI Endorsed Trans. e-Learn. **7**(20), e2 (2021)
6. Liu J, Zhao H. School of mechanical and electrical engineering and automation. J. Autom. EI CSCD, 31 (2020)
7. Zhang, Y., Li, L.: Realization of face feature point recognition based on cascaded convolutional neural network. J. Lanzhou Univ. Technol. **3**, 105–109 (2020)
8. Long, Y., Li, Y., Tao, W., et al.: Text sentiment analysis based on cascade convolution and attention mechanism. J. Taiyuan Normal Univ.: Nat. Sci. **2**, 30–36 (2020)
9. Jiang, X., Chang, L., Zhang, Y.D.: Classification of Alzheimer's disease via eight-layer convolutional neural network with batch normalization and dropout techniques. J. Med. Imaging Health Inform. **10**(5), 1040–1048 (2020)
10. Xiao, J., Tian, H., Zou, W.: Stereo matching based on convolution neural network. Inform. Technol. Inform. **38**(8), 0815017 (2018)
11. Yuan, M., Zhou, C., Huang, H., et al.: Survey on convolutional neural network pooling methods. Softw. Eng. Appl. **5**, 360–372 (2020)
12. Wang, S.Y., Teng, G.W.: Optimization design of ReLU activation function in convolutional neural network. Inform. Commun. **1673**(1131), 42–43 (2018)
13. M GCMMD: Noisy activation functions. arXiv preprint arXiv 1603:00391 (2016)
14. Jiang, A., Wang, W.: Research on optimization of ReLU activation function. Transducer Microsyst. Technol. **2**, 50–52 (2018)
15. Liu, J., Zhao, H., Luo, X., Xu, Y.: Research progress of deep learning batch normalization and its related algorithms. Acta Autom. Sinica **46**(6), 1090–1120 (2020)
16. Han, M.: Research and implementation of dropout method based on selective area drop, 003028, https://doi.org/10.27005/d.cnki.gdzku (2020)
17. Xie, F., Gong, J., Wang, Y.: Facial expression recognition method based on skin color enhancement and block PCA. J. Nanjing Normal Univ. (Eng. Technol. Ed.) **02**, 49–56 (2017)
18. Cai, L., Ye, Y., Gao, X., Li, Z., Zhang, C.: An improved visual SLAM based on affine transformation for ORB feature extraction. Optik **227**, 165421 (2021). https://doi.org/10. 1016/j.ijleo.2020.165421
19. Wang, Y., Biyun, X., Kwak, M., Zeng, X.: A noise injection strategy for graph autoencoder training. Neural Comput. Appl. **33**(10), 4807–4814 (2020). https://doi.org/10.1007/s00521- 020-05283-x
20. Zhang, X., Zuo, C., Shen, D.: Gamma nonlinear error correction method based on deep learning. G01B11/25, 1–10.
21. Jiang, X., Satapathy, S.C., Yang, L., Wang, S.-H., Zhang, Y.-D.: A survey on artificial intelligence in Chinese sign language recognition. Arab. J. Sci. Eng. **45**(12), 9859–9894 (2020). https://doi.org/10.1007/s13369-020-04758-2

Development and Creation of Open Online Course Resources in Tourism Colleges from the Perspective of School-Enterprise Collaborative Education

Rui Jiang[1] and Hua Jiang[2(✉)]

[1] Jiangsu Maritime Institute, Nanjing 211170, Jiangsu, China
[2] Nanjing Institute of Tourism & Hospitality, Nanjing 211100, Jiangsu, China

Abstract. The mode of teaching and learning in the "Internet+" era is undergoing changes. In order to adapt to the development of the times, the state has promulgated corresponding informatization policies to promote the reform of college education and teaching methods. Both online learning and hybrid learning play an important role in college education and teaching, and online open course resources are indispensable to hybrid teaching and online teaching. From the perspective of school-enterprise collaborative education, the article takes "Front Office Service and Management", an Excellent Open Online Course of China, as an example, and elaborates on online course team establishment, principles of development of online course resources, content selection, resource type creation, and creation experience summary, shedding light on how to develop and improve open online course resources in tourism colleges.

Keywords: School-enterprise collaborative education · Open online course · Resource development and creation

1 Introduction

In June 2016, the Ministry of Education of the People's Republic of China issued the "Guiding Opinions on Deepening Education and Teaching Reform in Universities under the Central Government", requiring the colleges affiliated to the Ministry of Education to vigorously step up efforts to create open online courses, and provided funding and policy support. In 2017, accreditation of the first group of "Excellent Open Online Courses of China" was commenced and 490 Excellent Open Online Courses of China were officially launched [1, 2]. In the "Internet+ education" environment, teaching has become inseparable from the Internet, with online learning and mobile learning becoming important ways of learning. In recent years, through continuous reflection on online education, more and more experts and scholars at home and abroad believe that the hybrid learning model combining online learning and face-to-face learning will become inevitable in future education. Hybrid teaching can effectively make up for the advantages and disadvantages of traditional teaching and online teaching models in their full sense, and

W. Fu et al. (Eds.): ICMTEL 2021, LNICST 388, pp. 62–70, 2021.
https://doi.org/10.1007/978-3-030-82565-2_5

result in optimal allocation and integration of educational resources. Due to organic combination of the two models, building of new types of teacher-student relationship and deepening of the concept of multi-method interactive learning have become important trends. However, high-quality online course resources are a basic condition for hybrid teaching. Therefore, in line with the course creation concept of school-enterprise collaborative education, we urgently need to solve this issue: How can tourism colleges bring enterprises into play, and, in light of courses' characteristics and students' characteristics and from the perspective of meeting the needs of online teaching and hybrid teaching, reasonably build an online course resource framework, elaborately design the content of online courses, and develop and create online course resources with the enterprises so as to contribute to O2O (online to offline) school-enterprise hybrid teaching and improve the efficiency and quality of tourism education?

The members of the "Front Office Service and Management" course team adhere to the course creation concept of school-enterprise collaborative education [3]. In 2017, the "Front Office Service and Management", an Excellent Open Online Course of Jiangsu Province, was officially launched. With the course, non-student learners can learn online, receive guidance and get answers to their questions free of charge; in addition, the course provides strong support for implementation of hybrid teaching by teachers in the school. After launched, the course has been highly spoken of by the students, other tourism colleges and experts. It was accredited by the Ministry of Education as an Excellent Open Online Course of China. So far, the course has been delivered for 7 semesters, and the number of students choosing the course has reached 22,876. With timely and accurate online guidance, the course focuses on sharing and application, and strives to share high-quality teaching resources with non-student learners [4].

2   Establishment of an Online Course Team

The creation of an online course should be undertaken by school teachers with support from teachers from the enterprise. There should be members who understand the course and those who are proficient in Internet technology [5]. At the same time, the student team can also play a role, helping the teachers organize, upload and supplement resources. The online course leader needs to determine 3–5 core members from the school as the main teachers of the course, and the number of teachers from the enterprise can be increased according to the needs of the course content. If the development period granted by the superior is relatively short, in order to ensure the quality of the course, the course team can be expanded. The course leader needs to know the professional expertise of existing professional teachers and teachers from the enterprise, and then perform ability matching and screening according to the needs of the course content.

3   Development and Creation of Online Course Resources

3.1   Basic Principles

Student-Centered
The course team needs to design and develop online course resources from the perspective of students, including the determination of teaching goals, the design of teaching

content, the organization of teaching activities, and the formation of teaching evaluations. Teaching should be carried out in line with how students think.

Alignment of the Course with Professional Standards
The course team needs to adhere to the concept of school-enterprise collaborative education, align the course with professional standards, cause the course to embody the "Four New" and integrate industrial culture into the course. The content of online courses should fully reflect the work development requirements of professional positions in enterprises, cover the new knowledge, new technologies, new processes and new methods in the industry and enterprises in a timely manner, and introduce the work specifications and standards of well-known international and domestic enterprises so as to broaden students' professional vision, enable students to learn knowledge and improve abilities in school which meet the requirements of front-line technical work for production and management work, and fully reflect the characteristics of the times.

Problem-Oriented
The design of the teaching content and teaching activities in the course should be, if possible, guided by the actual problems encountered at work in the enterprises. Through problems which are increasingly difficult, the students are guided to learn and think and try to figure out how to solve real problems facing the enterprises. In this way, the learners' interest in learning is simulated.

Task-Driven
Knowledge is applied by completing the actual work tasks of the enterprise, and the corresponding learning tasks are created according to the work tasks of the enterprise, and become increasingly difficult as the students learn more complicated knowledge. In the process of completing different levels of tasks, students can not only solve problems but also gain satisfaction and self-confidence from learning; therefore, their interest in learning is further stimulated [6].

3.2 Selection of Course Content

"Front Office Service and Management" is a professional core course that combines theory and practice. It teaches both theoretical knowledge and useful practices. The types of resources are also rich and diverse. Following the four principles of course resource design, the course team and the hotel front office staff select the online course content by taking into account the characteristics of the course, the students' academic performance and the typical tasks of each position in the front office.

Front-End Analysis of the Course
The course team needs to clarify the course's positioning, understand its status and role in the talent training program, clarify the teaching objectives of the course, and set specific quality objectives, knowledge objectives and ability objectives of the course. At the same time, it is also necessary to analyze the online course's main target audience. Generally, online courses have a wide audience. Therefore, the content design of the course should take into account the learning needs of learners at different levels. It is

recommended that course content with different levels of difficulty be designed so that students can selectively learn based on their own learning goals and needs to improve learning efficiency and satisfaction.

Analysis of Typical Work Tasks

Based on the characteristics of the "Front Office Service and Management" course and the analysis of students' academic performance, to give full play to the advantages of teachers from the enterprise, the school and the enterprise jointly analyzed the abilities required for each position in the hotel's front office, jointly determined the typical work tasks of each position in the front office based on professional abilities' characteristics and professional job skill standards, eventually selected 22 typical work tasks as the knowledge taught in the first stage of the front office open online course, and built a preliminary course content framework.

3.3   Creation of Course Resource Types

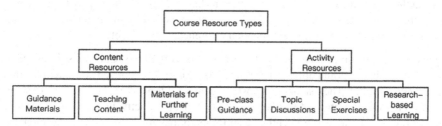

Fig. 1. The course resource framework

The course resource framework can be divided into two parts: content resources and activity resources (Fig. 1). The content resources mainly include guidance materials, teaching content, and materials for further learning. The activity resources mainly include pre-class guidance, topic discussions, special exercises and research-based learning [7]. According to the course content, and in light of the design modules of the online teaching platform, the school and the enterprise have designed the following resource framework for the online course "Front Office Service and Management":

Design of Content Resources

Guidance materials: Guidance materials mainly include two parts: basic information on the course and common problems, so that students can know the basic information on the course and how to solve the problems encountered in the learning process. The course introduction includes course name, start time, class schedule, course overview, teaching objectives, course outline, preparatory knowledge, reference materials, instructors, and assessment standards; common problems are the common problems that may be encountered when taking the course, which are usually problems concerning types of learning method, and generally do not involve specific learning content, such as resource release time, completion deadline, what to do if a unit test is missed, whether a certificate will be issued, and how to ask questions. Generally the questions and answers are shown in the course introduction page.

Teaching content: teaching resources provided around the knowledge that needs to be mastered in the class, such as teaching videos, teaching courseware, teaching pictures, lectures given by enterprise experts, display of student works and test question databases.

Materials for further learning: content which is related to the content taught in the class and intended to expand the knowledge so as to meet the needs of different types of learners, mainly including reading materials, online materials, business cases, professional English, and supporting textbooks.

Design of Activity Resources

Pre-class guidance mainly aims to enable students to know the content of the course to be studied and the requirements and prepare for study in advance. A course announcement can be made. For the online course on front office, a welcome letter and the teaching plan for this semester are released before the start of the course, and learners receive learning guidance, reminders, etc. during the learning process. We can also provide a pre-class guide at the beginning of each unit to let students know the main knowledge to be learned in the project and clarify the learning tasks, important and difficult knowledge, do's and don'ts, learning suggestions, recommended reference materials, etc.

Topic discussions are discussions on the key points, difficulties, questions, knowledge tested in examinations and other issues related to the current chapter. The content for this part is more flexible. The teacher can post 2 meaningful topics for classroom discussion based on the main content of the unit to guide students to actively share opinions and suggestions, stimulate learners' enthusiasm for learning, and increase their participation in learning [8]; the teacher can also post a thread for topic discussion based on more advanced knowledge related to this unit for students who have the ability to engage in more in-depth learning and thinking; at the same time, there shall be a teacher Q&A area, in which students can ask questions about what they feel uncertain at any time, and the teacher should answer all of such questions online as soon as possible. Meanwhile, students' questions should be sorted out and common questions should be further explained in classroom teaching. In addition, students can also encourage the teacher or provide the teacher with pertinent suggestions through course evaluations so that course teaching can be further improved in the future.

Special exercises mainly include targeted exercises on newly learned knowledge. Pre-class test, in-class questioning, unit test, homework, social practice, online final test, etc. are options available. Pre-class tests enable students to know their weaknesses in learning; in-class questioning, that is, questions will pop up when students watch the video, tests the efficiency of students' learning; unit tests test their understanding and mastery of new knowledge; through homework, social practice, etc., students apply the knowledge learned to solve practical problems so as to "do during learn" and "learn by doing" [9]. Online final test comprehensively tests the students' mastery of the main knowledge taught in the course; at the same time, the teacher performs a corresponding data analysis based on the test results and reflects on the problems existing in the online teaching process.

Research-based learning mainly means that, focusing on one theme, students engage in inquiry-based learning in groups. In the course, group work is assigned to each group (composed of at least 2 persons), and students are required to apply the learned knowledge to the actual work scenarios in enterprises, write a scenario simulation script, perform it and submit it. At the same time, each person is required to evaluate and score at least 6 groups of students. Research-based learning activities can strengthen communication and learning among peers, enhance their learning interest, improve learning efficiency, and reduce the loneliness in the learning process [10].

4   Discussion

4.1   Adhere to the Concept of School-Enterprise Collaborative Education

The teaching goal of the front office course is to enable students to master the knowledge and skills required by various positions in the front office of a hotel and be competent for all tasks in the front office of a hotel. Therefore, the active involvement of enterprises can make the courses more standardized and professional. In the creation of the resources of the Excellent Open Online Course of China "Front Office Service and Management", the course team has always adhered to the concept of school-enterprise collaborative education, which is mainly reflected in the joint front-end analysis of the course, the selection of course content, and the designated course syllabus; the school and the enterprise have jointly developed video resources for the course; course theories are mainly taught by the school teachers, and skill operation videos are mainly completed by the front office staff of the enterprise; the school and the enterprise have jointly developed more advanced course-related resources, such as case database and teaching materials.

4.2   Create Three-dimensional Supporting Resources

To create a good online course, we must do a good job in creating supporting resources for the course, so that the content-based resources for the course can be hierarchical, and the activity resources can be interactive and challenging. In addition to basic course materials accumulated over the years, the front office online course is also equipped with teaching cases and key textbooks jointly compiled by the school and the enterprise. At the same time, there are high-quality courses and bilingual courses. In addition, according to the results of a questionnaire survey conducted by the course team, the most popular new form of media for teaching among students is WeChat official accounts, followed by all kinds of mobile phone APPs, short video platforms, microlectures, and communities (QQ groups). Therefore, in the future, the courses will be available on more new forms of media, bringing more diverse online and offline teaching resources for many learners (Fig. 2).

4.3   Enhance Learner Stickiness

The course leader should follow up with the production progress according to the online release schedule, especially the coordination of shooting of teachers from the enterprise.

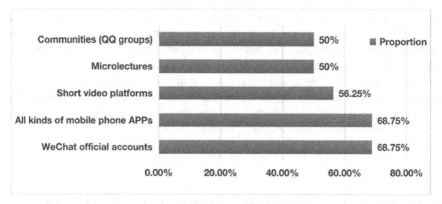

Fig. 2. New forms of media for teaching which are popular among students (students can choose more than one option)

Teachers need to complete detailed teaching design before recording a course video, write a micro-course shooting script and create a PPT file. The shooting script contains the course shooting ideas and course content, and the script for each knowledge point needs to be revised many times. A knowledge lecture video is not a condensation of an actual classroom lesson, but must be refined and designed in a way that meets the learning and psychological characteristics of the students, so that it can be in-depth and vivid, and can "stick" to the students [11]. Enterprise personnel can be invited to participate directly in the teaching. Their explanation of real enterprise projects can bring the classroom and the enterprise closer. PPT files should be illustrated and be concisely worded.

4.4 Create Fragmented Knowledge Points

According to research, when using the Internet and pockets of time to learn, most people pay attention to new content for no more than 15 min. Therefore, it is recommended that teachers control the duration of a knowledge point within 15 min (preferably 8–10 min) [12]. The average speech speed of general teachers is 200 Chinese characters/minute; thus, within 15 min, the number of Chinese characters in the speech should be controlled within 3,500 Chinese characters wherever possible. This requires us to split a completed knowledge system into several knowledge points, that is, fragmentation. Although the content of the course is divided into details, it is still a complete knowledge system after being integrated. Each video is short, and the content is the essence [13].

4.5 Continuous Update through School-Enterprise Collaboration

Generally, a MOOC requires about 600 min of videos, which need to be made gradually and cannot be completed at once [14]. In the first stage, the main unit knowledge points of the course should be identified first, and then the school should discuss with the enterprise how to further optimize the course knowledge system. When it comes to online course resources, more isn't necessarily better; instead, the resources must be necessary and sufficient. It is recommended that resources be used while being created rather than after completion; more expensive resources are not necessarily better, and the key is to be recognized by learners. According to the development and service requirements for the open online courses of China for the next five years, the front office course team needs to continuously improve and upgrade the existing online course resources, such as gradually increasing the content on operation of the enterprise Opera PMS system, and gradually increasing professional English terminology and bilingual teaching videos; the school and the enterprise should work together to continuously update course resources, that is, in the process of continuous deepening of the integration of industry and education, new progress in position research, new experience in practice development, and new changes in social needs are incorporated into online course resources in a timely manner through school-enterprise collaborative teaching and research to continuously improve the course, bring learners cutting-edge information on the industry and broaden learners' professional vision [15].

The development and creation of open online course resources are a long-term process of continuous improvement. From the perspective of school-enterprise collaborative education, tourism colleges should stick to the main principle of "school-enterprise collaboration", give full play to the advantages of tourism enterprises, bring in enterprises' work standards, teachers, teaching resources, working environment, etc., and create and share course resources with the enterprises and peer institutions so as to continuously improve the quality and visibility of the courses.

Acknowledgment. Projects supported by funds: Research and Practices on O2O Hybrid Teaching in Tourism Schools from the Perspective of School-Enterprise Cooperation for Education (WLRCS2019-065), funded by the 2019 "Dual-qualification" Teachers Program of the Ministry of Culture and Tourism of China "Research and Practices on O2O Hybrid Teaching of Core Professional Courses on Hotel Management Based on Online Open Courses" (2019JSJG469), a Higher Education Reform Research Project of Jiangsu Province in 2019.

References

1. (J.G.T.H. (2018) No. 44) Notice of the General Office of the Ministry of Education on Accreditation of Excellent Open Online Courses of China in 2018 [E B/OL]. http://www.moe.gov.cn/srcsite/A08/s5664/s7209/s6872/201807/t20180725_343681.html
2. Wu, Y.: An Introduction to the First Group of "Excellent Open Online Courses of China" [EB/OL]. http://www.moe.gov.cn/jyb_xwfb/xw_fbh/moe_2069/xwfbh_2018n/xwfb_20180115/wzsl/
3. Shi, W., Hao, T.: In-depth Integration of Industry and Education and School-Enterprise Cooperation for Education – Interpretation of the Plan for Implementation of the National Vocational Education Reform. Chin. Vocation. Tech. Educ. **03**, 93–97 (2019)
4. Ministry of Education of the People's Republic of China. Guidelines on Enhancing the Development, Application and Management of Open Online Courses of Higher Education Institutions. J.G.H. [2015] No. 3. 2015-04-28
5. Cheng, S., Xu, C.: Exploration and practice on open online courses – taking "Java language programming" for example. Adult Educ. **38**(06), 35–40 (2018)

6. Ping, Z., Gu, X., Kuang, L.: The construction of open online courses and the reform of the blended teaching model – taking "embedded Linux application and development" as an example. J. Xingtai Polytech. Coll. **36**(5), 5–12 (2019)
7. Li, Q.: Research on the Development and Application of Online Open Course Resources in Instructional System Design – From the Perspective of First Principle of Instruction. Nanning Normal University (2019)
8. Wu, Q., Zhao, X., Chen, Z.: A study on hybrid teaching models based on the development of online open courses – with "introduction to automobile service engineering" taken as an example. Times Agric. Mach. **46**(3), 69–72 (2019)
9. Bai, L., Hu, Y., Zheng, L.: A blended teaching model based on learning behavior analysis. Comput. Eng. Sci. 40(01) (2018)
10. Wang, W., Yang, W., Deng, X., Li, Y.: Principles and idea thinking of online course design. Modern Distance Educ. **05**, 54–60 (2016)
11. Lin, W.: A discussion on the principles and three key issues of micro-course teaching design. China Educ. Info **06**, 26–30 (2016)
12. Wang, Y.: A Study on Principles and Guidelines for Designing and Developing Instructional Videos of Online Courses. Shanghai International Studies University (2018)
13. Tan, Y., Sun, J., Zhu, L.: The research on digital resources construction specification about online open courses. New West (Theoretical Version) **7**(03), 120–121 (2015)
14. Ma, Q.: Design and development of MOOC video resources for "computer application basics" taught in higher vocational schools. J. Jinan Vocation. Coll. **04**, 63–65 (2018)
15. Kong, Y.: Construction of "dual-subject and integrated" educational mode in higher vocational school and enterprise. J. Hubei Open Univ. 33(12) (2020)

Research on the Application of MOOC in O2O Teaching Model Innovation of Aesthetic Education in Higher Vocational Colleges

Gege Ma[⊠]

Jiangsu Maritime Institute, Nanjing 211100, Jiangsu, China

Abstract. The rapid development of Internet technology has promoted the era of education informatization, and the construction of an O2O teaching model with online teaching and offline communication is a central link in the reform of aesthetic education in higher vocational colleges. As a representative of the education model in the new era, the emergence of MOOCs has greatly promoted the development of online and offline hybrid teaching models. This article will discuss MOOC's O2O teaching in aesthetic education in higher vocational colleges from four aspects: research background, current application status of MOOC in aesthetic education, implementation strategies of effective application of MOOC teaching under O2O mode, and improvement of the guarantee mechanism of MOOC teaching quality Application in model innovation.

Keywords: O2O teaching model · Aesthetic education · MOOC · Implementation strategy · Guarantee mechanism

1 Research Background

The "Outline of the National Medium and Long-term Education Reform and Development Plan" promulgated by the Ministry of Education in July 2010 clearly pointed out: "Information technology has a revolutionary impact on education development and must be highly valued." In May 2012, the "Ten-Year Development Plan for Educational Informatization" issued by the Ministry of Education emphasized: "Using educational informatization to drive the modernization of education, solve the problems that restrict the development of education in our country, and promote the innovation and reform of education is to accelerate the development of education A major strategic choice to become a powerful country in education" [1]. With the development of the "Internet+" action plan in the field of higher education, the application of O2O teaching mode in aesthetic education has become more and more popular. Online to Offline is abbreviated as "O2O". The O2O teaching model is based on the modernization of educational technology. The new e-commerce concept is borrowed from the teaching method reform practice, and the Internet technology is used to realize the learning and communication between teachers and students on the online teaching platform. "Online teaching, offline communication" two-way interactive education model, [2] and MOOC is a key part of this innovative teaching model.

W. Fu et al. (Eds.): ICMTEL 2021, LNICST 388, pp. 71–78, 2021.
https://doi.org/10.1007/978-3-030-82565-2_6

2 Educational Advantages Under the Background of MOOC

From a social perspective, the significance of using MOOC is that it cannot only impart knowledge, but more importantly, it can convey good learning concepts to people. Learning is not exclusive to students, nor can it be done only in school. MOOC can break through the limitations of time and space. No matter what occupation you are or where you live, you can become a learner, and solve the problem of educational imbalance caused by lack of resources in remote areas. Such a form helps to let the ideas of "lifelong learning" and "learning for all" take root in the hearts of the people, and promote the formation of a good learning atmosphere in society. Therefore, it is necessary to actively promote the development of MOOC.

From the school's point of view, a complete classroom system mainly includes three stages: before class, during class, and after class. The traditional teaching mode mainly focuses on the in-class stage. Teachers teach in the role of the leader in the classroom to invisibly split the entire teaching process, reducing the time for effective learning [3, 4]. The use of MOOCs can just solve this drawback. A pre-study session is added before the class, and the resources taken by the teacher in advance are used to allow students to complete the learning. Teaching tasks are completed in the classroom, teachers become the guides who provide help, and students become the leaders of learning, acquiring the knowledge they want and building a knowledge system are the real protagonists of the classroom. Aesthetic education courses are different from other disciplines. They belong to the category of art and are highly subjective. They pay more attention to the role of communication in learning. Traditional classroom teaching is often completed by a teacher from professor, answering questions to final evaluation, which is prone to problems such as single knowledge structure and too subjective evaluation. The use of MOOCs can allow students to get in touch with more outstanding experts and scholars in the industry through the Internet, and the learning angles are more diversified.

3 The Application Status of MOOC in Aesthetic Education

Since the first year of MOOC in 2012, the MOOC storm that originated in the United States has affected all parts of the world [5]. The world's most famous MOOC platforms include Edx, Coursera and Udacity in the United States, which are known as the "three giants of MOOC". These platforms classify courses according to subjects and languages, and can be used by learners from countries and regions around the world. In China, Internet education began to sprout from the 1990s when computers and the Internet were not popularized. In 1996, Tsinghua University first proposed the development of modern distance education, and in 1998 launched online postgraduate advanced courses [6]. With the introduction of a series of development policies, a good development environment has been created for Internet education. At the same time, Internet investment institutions have joined Internet education to promote the development of the industry, such as China University MOOC, Chaoxing Erya General Course, NetEase Open Course, etc. The platform was born under this background.

In recent years, the types of courses related to aesthetic education on the MOOC platform have become more and more abundant, and most of them can be provided to the public for free. The large-scale and openness of the MOOC integrates the high-quality teaching resources of aesthetic education in major universities at home and abroad to the greatest extent, and has great teaching advantages compared with traditional classroom teaching. At the same time that schools at all levels and types in our country are actively reforming online courses in response to national policies, it is not difficult to find that there are still some problems that cannot be ignored in MOOC development. The author selects the two platforms "Chinese College Student MOOC" and "Superstar Erya", which are frequently used in teaching, as the research objects, and conducts statistical research on the aesthetic education courses on the platforms. It is found that most of the two major online education platforms currently have aesthetic education. The setting of courses is relatively simple, mainly based on theoretical forms such as introduction to art and art appreciation, and very few practical courses of basic art technology training are carried out for students. In addition, their common attribute is to allow learners to use online education resources for autonomous learning. Although it has changed the passive learning model of traditional teaching classrooms with "teachers" as the main body and improved the learners' subjective initiative, this learning method also has a certain drawback, such as the lack of teacher-student interaction, which makes learners blind in online learning. At the same time, there is a certain contradiction between the high registration rate and low completion rate of some aesthetic education courses.

4   Implementation Strategies for Effective Application of MOOC Teaching Under O2O Mode

4.1   Hierarchical Teaching, Teaching Students in Accordance with Their Aptitude

The school's aesthetic education curriculum emphasizes universality. It is mainly a compulsory course for students from all majors in the school to strengthen college students' art education and strengthen their cultural and artistic literacy. Through a systematic overview of the basic knowledge and basic principles of art theory, students can master the essence of art, Classification and creation, etc., so as to improve students' aesthetic accomplishment. However, the current art education in higher vocational colleges lacks top-level design, and there are no unified curriculum standard and teaching materials. The teaching is often based on the teacher's own professional expertise. The teaching content is mostly based on professional skills or theoretical knowledge. Aesthetic education courses in the sense. In addition, the solidification of the fault phenomenon in aesthetic education in our country has caused most students to have a weak artistic foundation, and only a few groups have certain art learning experiences. Therefore, judging from the courses provided by schools in the past, the group of students that can really serve is very limited [7].

The above phenomenon inspires teachers to pay attention to the effective implementation of hierarchical teaching in the design of MOOC, so as to teach students in accordance with their aptitude. Although there are many teaching resources related to aesthetic education on the Internet, not all resources meet the learning needs of students. Because different students have different levels of learning ability and artistic literacy, there are also certain differences in their acumen to art skills learning and art appreciation in aesthetic education courses. If the content of the lessons in the learning process goes against the basis of the subjects themselves, it will not only waste a lot of learners' time, but also easily affect the learning efficiency and increase the learning burden. Therefore, it is recommended that teachers be able to formulate a systematic and complete evaluation plan for the subjects in the context of big data before the curriculum is set. Fangxian conducts scientific and effective evaluation, and organizes students into three different levels of learning groups of junior, middle, and senior according to the test situation, and prepares teaching materials of different difficulties according to the level.

4.2 Online and Offline, Dual Teachers Complement Each Other

In furthering the work of school aesthetic education, it is particularly important to speed up the construction of a curriculum system that meets the requirements. The core of the construction of a scientific and systematic curriculum system should be to improve the national quality and cultivate students' innovative spirit and practical ability. The O2O teaching model optimizes the flipped classrooms that have been put into use. It solves the problems of online communication between teachers and students and between students and students, and solves the problems of personalized interactions, and improves the lack of interaction in online education such as flipped classrooms [8]. But the O2O teaching model has just entered the field of aesthetic education, and has not completely replaced traditional online teaching. Therefore, the O2O teaching model is innovated, and the aesthetic education curriculum system integrating the "three classrooms" is constructed, that is, the online basic theory teaching is recognized as the first classroom, which mainly includes understanding course information, watching teaching videos, participating in online interaction, etc.; The offline skills teaching and on-campus practical activities are recognized as the second classroom, which mainly includes flipped classrooms, classroom teaching and explanation, skills exercises and practice, etc.; offline off-campus practical activities are recognized as the third classroom, mainly including practical performances, art venues internships, etc.. Form an internal cycle of online and offline aesthetic education, and realize a teaching linkage system that supports practice with theory and then feeds theory with practice.

Art theory courses can be set up in the form of MOOCs, using mature online teaching platforms to build online courses for students to flexibly complete online learning in their spare time. The learners are restricted to complete all the video and material learning in accordance with the requirements of the online course, and pass the classroom test and final assessment before they can receive theoretical credits. Online theoretical teaching transforms teachers' classroom "lectures" into online "guided learning", and students change from "passive learning" in the classroom to "active exploration" online. In the early stage of online course construction, art teachers complete the formation of the production team and collect and organize the teaching content according to the course standards. Then, contact the shooting company to complete the shooting of all the teaching videos, and use the rich audio, video and animation techniques in the post-editing to build digital teaching resources that meet the needs of students and fit the network teaching situation, so that students can't get enough Users can get a real-life experience like in a concert hall or art gallery. At the same time, the online learning platform provides a reasonable and effective communication mechanism for teachers and students, so that the problems encountered by students in the learning process can be solved in a timely manner. On the one hand, the construction of art online courses has changed the shortcomings of traditional teaching methods, and on the other hand, it has solved the complicated problems of naming, reviewing test papers, and calculating results caused by the large number of students in general art courses. The online theoretical courses set up chapters on art, music, film and television, drama, Chinese opera, and fine arts, changing the single knowledge structure that most vocational colleges specify a certain art category to teach in a professional unit, from the students' evaluation and After class feedback, it can be seen that this comprehensive art knowledge framework meets the students' demands for art knowledge learning, and also lays a theoretical foundation for the in-depth study of art practice skills of later students.

For the learning and internalization of any knowledge, external factors are the conditions and internal factors are the key. It is one-sided to focus on the teaching of static knowledge in the classroom. Practical learning is an important aspect of the aesthetic education teaching process, which is completed by the second and third classrooms. It is recommended that schools offer art practice courses in the form of optional courses. According to the teacher's situation, 8–12 public art practice courses are opened every semester for students to choose based on their interests. Students must complete at least one elective task of the course and pass the assessment during the university. Get practical credits. Practical optional courses also use the MOOC platform. In the teaching preparation stage, teachers first upload the important and difficult points of the artistic skills that each lesson needs to master on the platform, so that students can make full use of the role of pre-class preview. During the class, offline teaching is the main form. Under the teacher's on-site demonstration and guidance, students can practice repeatedly, correct mistakes, and explain common problems that students are likely to encounter in the practice of artistic skills. After class, teachers publish training assignments and extracurricular resources on the platform, allowing students to practice and apply the motor skills they have learned in social practice and club practice.

4.3 Process Evaluation, Focusing on Individuality

Objective and fair teaching evaluation is a necessary condition for innovative O2O aesthetic education curriculum system. According to the characteristics of the teaching mode and the learning rules of art subjects, it is possible to consider changing the assessment criteria of students' academic performance from the previous "normal performance (30%) + final assessment (70%)" form to a process evaluation method. A mature online teaching platform can monitor the entire process of students' online learning. Teachers can log in to the background to control the length of time the students watch videos, the number of discussions and interactions, the completion of usual homework, and the final assessment results. Through the comprehensive performance of students in the whole learning process, the procedural evaluation results of students' theoretical academic performance are completed. Because the learning of artistic practical skills is related to many factors such as artistic talents, personal expertise and learning experience, students will have large individual differences in the process of artistic practice, so the assessment methods cannot use the same standard to judge the practice level of all students. The grading will focus on the students' personal attitudes, efforts and space for progress during the learning process, and will not compare with the excellent practical skills of others, and fully protect the self-esteem and enthusiasm of students [9].

Since the MOOC adopts online learning and all teaching activities are carried out on the Internet, integrity issues such as "whether the homework is completed by the student" will inevitably become a hot topic in MOOC teaching [10]. Since all teaching links on the MOOC platform rely on limited teachers in the teaching team to monitor, MOOC's innovation in monitoring technology is necessary, adding new technologies such as face recognition, and identifying students in an intelligent way Whether to complete the homework and test independently, and record the cheating student's score as invalid before the final evaluation, which can improve the efficiency of the teacher's process evaluation. In addition, for students who lack learning motivation, some reward mechanisms can be adopted in the evaluation process. Set up a scoreboard on the homepage of the platform. When learners complete video learning, quizzes or participate in interaction, they can get corresponding points. In the assessment of final scholarships, certain preferential policies can be given based on the points in the learning platform. You can also set up a work display wall on the homepage of the platform to display the reports of outstanding learning teams on the homepage of the course. This will not only improve students' sense of honor and self-confidence, but also set a good example for other students.

5   Improve the Guarantee Mechanism of MOOC Teaching Quality

5.1   The Role Positioning of Online and Offline Compound Teachers

As a front-line art teacher, on the one hand, we still have the identity and role of the traditional "offline teacher", face-to-face communication and interaction with students in the classroom, and use basic teaching skills such as singing, playing, jumping, drawing, and writing in art teaching. Guide students to experience artistic activities such as appreciation, creation and performance. On the other hand, we should also strive to become online teachers, get rid of the limitations of traditional art classroom teaching, and carry out teaching activities related to information education technology by paying attention to, understanding and applying art teaching resources on the Internet; design, produce and teach by ourselves Related MOOC videos; use the teaching platform to guide students in online teaching interaction, and use information technology to optimize the traditional art classroom. Schools should take practical and effective measures to actively encourage teachers to participate in various forms of MOOC training, from MOOC topic selection and curriculum content planning to resource integration and course recording, and finally provide comprehensive training for students on how to answer questions online [11]. Further promote teachers to move closer to the new teaching platform, and rationally complete the dual teaching tasks from "online" to "offline".

5.2   Exploration of Aesthetic Education Resource Sharing in the Big Data Era

The introduction of a mixed teaching model in the aesthetic education system of higher vocational colleges has extended the time for students to study in class. Students can use fragmented time to carry out independent learning and solve the problem of insufficient time in traditional classroom teaching. At the same time, it also expands the learning space of students, providing students with a variety of teaching information such as videos, animations, images and courseware. With the rapid development of information technology and the Internet, the construction of informationizational education has put forward higher requirements for the integration of educational resources, and the storage of individual decentralized educational resources must be limited in the future development of art education. It is necessary for various colleges and universities to jointly discuss and formulate curriculum standards to regulate the quality of MOOC based on the actual learning situation of students and the actual development of aesthetic education in my country, and to monitor the quality of teaching. At the same time, it will further rely on NAS (Network Attached Storage) to build a shared resource library of aesthetic education in the school. Teachers will automatically synchronize the high-quality art education resources collected by individuals to the network storage, benefiting more art front-line art teachers. At the beginning, small-scale sharing in the teaching and research room was the main focus. In the future, it will be more ideal to gradually realize the sharing of resources across the school, so that more teachers and students can find effective resources for themselves in this rich educational resource library.

6 Summary

In summary, MOOC is a key product in the development of the "Internet+ Education" era. In the construction of the O2O teaching model of aesthetic education in higher vocational colleges, teachers should reasonably use MOOC to realize the advantages of teaching in accordance with their aptitude, complementary teaching, and multiple evaluations, and actively face the problems that still exist in the development of MOOC in aesthetic education teaching in higher vocational colleges. Strengthen the construction and improvement of the MOOC platform, raise teachers' awareness of innovative teaching concepts, improve the quality assurance mechanism of MOOC classrooms, and further optimize and innovate MOOC teaching, so that MOOC teaching is truly equivalent to aesthetic education courses in higher vocational colleges Fusion.

Acknowledgment. The work is supported by the Special project of ideological and political education of Jiangsu Province Social Science Application Research Excellent Project (No. 20SZC-077).

References

1. Li, Z.: Research on improving the teaching effectiveness of vocational education under the concept of wisdom education. Vocat. Educ. Forum **12**, 53–56 (2018)
2. Haijun, L.: Construct an effective and interactive O2O teaching model. Teach. Manage. **03**, 49–51 (2018)
3. Zhifang, L.: Reform and innovation of college piano flipped classroom based on MOOC technology. House Drama **06**, 31–32 (2021)

4. Xiaowen, W., Yuan, W.: The types of colleges and the number of general art courses. Art Technol. **08**, 230–231 (2018)
5. Xiu, W., Yulu, W.: A brief talk on the development of general art courses in colleges and universities under the Internet+ mode. Art Crit. **01**, 168–171 (2019)
6. Meini, S.: On the modern transformation of university art education under the background of Internet+. Educ. Teach. Forum **22**, 65–67 (2019)
7. Mengchen, L.: Research on the application of O2O teaching mode in college basketball elective courses. Mudanjiang Normal University (2019)
8. Wencai, Z., Minxue, H.: The nature and model construction of O2O teaching mode applied to physical education. Teach. Manage. **03**, 86–88 (2020)
9. Xiaoyao, H.: Research on music courses in "China University MOOC" (Part 2). Music. Instrum. **08**, 33–37 (2020)
10. Jingmei, L.: Analyze the measures of music teaching reform in colleges and universities under the background of "MO Class." North. Music **23**, 205–207 (2020)
11. Fei, H.: Exploration and practice of teaching mode reform in art colleges under the background of "Internet+." Mod. Vocat. Educ. **09**, 206–207 (2021)

Design of Hospital Remote Consultation and Teaching System Based on Deep Learning

Ying Bao[✉]

The First Affiliated Hospital of Soochow University, Suzhou 215000, China
baoying2172@tom.com

Abstract. The application of deep learning technology makes the hospital's remote consultation and teaching system more humane. Therefore, this research designed a hospital remote consultation and teaching system based on deep learning technology. First of all, through the analysis of the problems of system construction, clear system design objectives. With the support of the system hardware, the deep learning process is used to realize the functions of case collection, remote consultation, doctor recommendation, remote education and training, and case sharing. Using experiments to analyze the actual application performance of the hospital remote consultation and teaching system based on deep learning, and comparing it with the traditional system, it verifies that the system in this paper is more effective.

Keywords: Deep learning · Hospital · Remote consultation · Teaching system

1 Introduction

In order to meet the growing health needs of the people and the new requirements of economic and social development for the development of health services, the State Council issued the "Twelfth Five-Year Plan for the Development of Health Services". By 2015, a basic medical and health system covering urban and rural residents will be initially established, So that all residents can enjoy basic medical insurance and basic public health services. The accessibility, service quality, service efficiency and public satisfaction of medical and health services have been significantly improved, the burden of individual medical expenses has been significantly reduced, and the allocation of health resources between regions The difference in health status between the population and the population continues to shrink, and basically realize that all people have medical treatment [1].

Therefore, it is necessary to strengthen the construction of medical and health personnel team. We should give full play to the backbone role of urban hospitals in the diagnosis and treatment of critical emergency and difficult diseases, medical education and scientific research, guidance and training of grass-roots health personnel. The training of primary health personnel usually adopts on-the-spot learning. Due to the limitation of

W. Fu et al. (Eds.): ICMTEL 2021, LNICST 388, pp. 79–91, 2021.
https://doi.org/10.1007/978-3-030-82565-2_7

operating room space and the strict requirements of clean operating room, a large number of interns, interns and medical students are kept out of the operating room [2]. In order to better meet the needs of clinical teaching, improve the quantity and quality of surgical teaching, at the same time, ensure the high cleanliness of operating room and reduce the pollution of aseptic area by surgical observers, many hospitals need to build operation teaching and remote consultation system to provide students, medical experts and medical personnel with medical image quality details, discussion and analysis of operation process, Postoperative treatment, teaching observation, case study and other functions [3].

Under the above background, this study designed a hospital remote consultation and teaching system based on deep learning. Firstly, through the analysis of the problems of system construction, the system design goal was made clear. Then, with the support of system hardware, the functions of case collection, remote consultation, consultation doctor recommendation, remote education training and case sharing were realized, so as to make the hospital remote Cheng consultation and teaching system is more humanized and more timely.

2 Current Situation Analysis and Problems

2.1 Traditional Model

The traditional mode of medical operation observation and teaching is mainly to organize personnel to study in the operating room, or to video the operation situation as teaching. This model has many shortcomings.

(1) Due to the space limitations of the operating room, the number of visitors and observations that can be accommodated is small, and the efficiency of teaching and research is low.
(2) Due to the messy personnel, it will cause air pollution in the operating room and even affect the attention of the operating physician.
(3) Cannot connect with modern minimally invasive equipment.
(4) For the operation records of major operations and special operations, because the on-site video crews do not understand the key points that researchers or students want to pay attention to, some parts of the field of view and the depth of the field of view will be insufficient.
(5) Due to the poor shielding of the camera, when the radiographic equipment, chainsaw and other equipment are turned on during the operation, they will be severely disturbed, resulting in poor recording effect or inability to record.

2.2 Understanding of Operation Teaching in Hospital

Some hospitals recognized the value of surgical teaching, but because the equipment was not advanced enough and the companies that implemented the surgical teaching did not know enough about the surgical teaching, they replaced the surgical teaching system with a security system, but they couldn't meet the requirements of the surgical teaching system. Video clarity and software features. Up to now, some companies are still using security monitoring and video conferencing equipment to make surgical teaching systems for hospitals in order to make huge profits [4].

3 Construction Objectives

As an important task of many hospitals, clinical teaching is responsible for training medical staff. The training method is usually on-site observation. However, due to the limitations of on-site conditions or surgical equipment, the space for on-site surgical observation is narrow and the participants are limited. At the same time, it also brings unnecessary trouble to the normal treatment of patients, and the effect is not ideal [5]. In order to improve the quality of the operation and reduce the infection rate of the operation, the operating room of the hospital has formulated the control index for the number of observations in the operating room to strictly control the number of people entering the operating room. This has resulted in a greatly reduced opportunity for interns to learn and observe operations, which is not conducive to improving interns Quality of learning.

The rapid development of video communication technology brings new opportunities for the realization of remote visual teaching in hospitals. The hospital can build a high-quality hospital clinical network teaching system, thus the operation teaching and remote consultation system was born. Through the system, the video and audio digital coding and broadcasting teaching system can observe the operation process through the large screen outside the operating room for real-time teaching and consultation, which not only reduces the cross infection in the operating room, but also ensures the aseptic requirements in the operating room, and also expands the scope of surgical teaching, so as to get rid of the limitations of traditional teaching mode in time, space and number of people [6]. The hospital remote consultation and teaching system also realizes that one instructor can guide the teaching of multiple operating rooms, avoid the waste of teaching resources, and realize the sharing of teaching. Each teaching system can observe the video images of one or more operations at the same time. In the application of telemedicine consultation, doctors can complete the medical diagnosis directly through the video communication system without spending too much time on the road, and can also carry out remote multi-party consultation according to the patient's condition.

Construct the hospital's surgical teaching and remote consultation system to achieve the following goals:

(1) The operating room is equipped with video and audio pickup equipment to pick up the surgical field video signal and the voice signal of the instructor during the operation and transmit it to the surgical video demonstration classroom. The video quality is high and the voice is clear and clear.

(2) The operating room is equipped with a camera control system, which is used to remotely adjust the camera position and parameters, so as to avoid the phenomenon of white and distorted image produced by the camera under the high intensity light of shadowless lamp, and ensure high image quality, high definition and high color restoration.

(3)   The operating room realizes panoramic monitoring, with good image quality, and adjustable pan-tilt angle and lens focal length. Multi-screen monitoring, full-screen monitoring and control can be carried out through the network in the office of the chief nurse and the sub-head nurses.

(4)   In the central control room or in the classroom, the operating room camera can be remotely controlled in all directions to achieve video shooting without blind spots.

(5)   It can realize two-way voice intercom in operating room, demonstration room and central control room, realize multi screen preview and any full screen preview, and monitor any audio signal.

(6)   The functions of operation teaching, academic exchange and video storage are realized through the network. All video images (endoscope, microscope, endoscope, monitor, field camera, panoramic camera, etc.) can be transmitted and stored through the network, and any video image can be transmitted and stored at the same time to achieve audio and video synchronization.

(7)   The most advanced H.264 compression algorithm is used for network transmission, storage and playback. The definition reaches Fullhd level and HD DVD image quality is achieved to meet the requirements of medical operation. For example, pancreas and fat can be clearly distinguished by color. The bitstream transmitted and stored in the network shall not be less than 3mbps or higher than 10Mbps, and can be adjusted within this range to save bandwidth under the condition of ensuring picture quality.

(8)   The data after the operation storage video can be carved into HD DVD discs, which is convenient for storage and carrying.

(9)   Two-way audio and video intercom can be carried out during surgical teaching and academic exchanges to achieve clear voice, low delay, no echo, and clear and smooth video.

(10) Realize surgical teaching and academic exchange through the network in demonstration classrooms, operating rooms, conference rooms, leadership offices, medical offices, academic lecture halls, and multi-function halls. The video playback resolution is required to reach the FULLHD level and the effect to reach HD. DVD picture quality, high color reproduction. Each demand site can broadcast live, on-demand, intercom, and manage video and audio according to access rights. The two-way intercom communication function can be carried out everywhere, and the intercom equipment must support the video function, so that audio and video two-way intercom can be carried out when possible.

(11) In any network access point in the hospital, the authority can be assigned to manage the audio and video live broadcast, on-demand, intercom and other aspects of the operation process. In the case of a dedicated network, the remote operation observation, operation guidance, remote teaching, remote consultation and so on can be realized.

4 System Hardware Design

4.1 Development Environment

The development environment of this system is as follows:

1. Development tool: MyEclipse2019;
2. Development language: Java;
3. Database server: sQLServer 2008R2.

Software deployment environment:

1. PC operating system: Windows 10;
2. Server operating system: Windows Server 2008 R2;
3. Database server: sQLServer 2008 R2.

Hardware server environment:

1. Central processing unit: Inter(R) Xeon(R)CPU E5–2620 v3 @2.40 GHz 2.40 GHz;
2. Memory capacity: 32.O GB (31.9 GB Available);
3. Hard disk capacity: ITB.

4.2 Database Installation and Configuration

The database used by this system is Microsoft sQL Server 2008. The database installation file can be downloaded from the official Microsoft website of sQL Server 2008 Standard Edition (32-bit). Due to the huge database content and various functions, including: database engine, Analysis Services, OLAP, Integration Services, Notification Services, it is necessary to install sQL server Management Studio Express to coordinate and manage the database. When installing the database, set the account and password, and set the database remote access port [7].

After the database installation is completed, first open SQL Server 2008 to enter the main interface of the software normally; then create a new database designed by the system, configure the main and foreign keys, and generate the database relationship diagram; finally, add test data in the corresponding table, such as the province of the patient, the city of the patient, the county of the patient, the hospital information, doctor information, test user, etc.

4.3 Operating Environment Configuration

After the database installation, the software development environment needs to be configured. Because the system uses Java language for program development, JDK, JRE and Tomcat need to be installed and configured. JDK can be installed by downloading jdk-8ul ll-windows-i586.exe from the Java official website. Because JDK comes with JRE, you only need to download the JDK installation program. Tomcat can also download apache-tomcat-8.5.8.exe from its official website. After the installation, you need to configure the environment variables in the system computer → properties → advanced system settings → advanced → environment variables.

5 System Software Design

5.1 Medical Record Collection

The collection of medical records includes text data and image data. The text data mainly contains basic personal information, descriptions of main symptoms, disease history, and laboratory test results. The system provides manual entry of medical records. Basic-level doctors enter the patient's medical record and preliminary diagnosis information into the patient's current medical record. The medical record data is stored in the system database.

In the process of image data acquisition, the hospital PACS system is generally limited to the outside world, and even some primary medical institutions do not have PACS system [8]. The consultation center is equipped with medical special film scanner, which can convert the ordinary film of CT examination, B-ultrasound examination and radiology examination into DICOM3.0 standard digital image, and automatically store it in the database. The consultation system accesses the database to obtain the digital image data of patients. The paper materials were processed by conventional scanners and converted into pictures, and saved to the database of consultation system in JPEG format.

5.2 Remote Consultation

Based on the process of deep learning, through multiple input, training, learning, output, feedback and input, this study completed the design of consultation, information consultation, video consultation, consultation doctor recommendation, distance education training and medical record sharing. Among them, the number of iterations of deep learning is 1000.

5.2.1 Consultation

Consultation is one of the non real time consultation. Grassroots doctors send the content of the disease to be consulted to the consultation experts, who will reply after receiving the consultation message. Only consultation experts can be selected for consultation and consultation, not doctors [9]. The operation process of consultation and consultation is as follows:

(1) Basic-level doctors log in to the system and select consultation for specific patients;
(2) Fill in the details of the consultation and choose the consultation expert to consult;
(3) The expert log in to the system, check the questioning task, reply according to the question, and submit the questioning report;
(4) The primary doctors check the consultation report and the consultation is over.

5.2.2 Information Consultation

Information inquiry is also non real-time consultation, not limited by time. After the primary doctors submit the patient's medical records, the consultation type is data inquiry, and the specific consultation doctor is selected and submitted. After the management end of triage platform is approved, the consultant doctors diagnose the relevant diseases according to the text, data and images provided by the medical records, and finally fill in the consultation report and submit it. The grassroots doctors check the consultation report and give the final consultation conclusion. The process of data consultation is consistent with that of video consultation.

5.2.3 Video Consultation

The video consultation is a real-time consultation, and the basic-level doctors first submit the patient's medical records, and select the type of consultation as video consultation, and then choose the consultation doctor. After receiving the video consultation application, the consultation doctor will be managed by the triage station to review and arrange the consultation doctor and consultation time. The consultation doctor will have a video call with the grassroots doctors within the specified time and communicate with the grassroots doctors and patients in a "face-to-face" manner. In addition, the consultation doctors can view the consultation materials submitted by the primary doctors, which contain the patient's condition information, which is convenient for expert doctors and primary doctors to discuss the disease face-to-face, so as to give a better treatment plan for the patient's condition. After the real-time diagnosis is completed, the consulting doctor fills in the consultation report and submits it to the primary doctors, and finally the primary doctors issue the consultation conclusion [10].

The status of video consultation includes eight states: to be reviewed, to be consulted, to be consulted, to be reported, to be concluded, to be completed, to be approved, and to be closed. The status of data consultation includes six kinds: to be reviewed, to be consulted, to be reported, to be concluded, to be completed, and not to be approved. The operation of triage desk administrator includes the audit and management of consultation status.

The specific process of video consultation is as follows:

(1) Consultation of primary doctors: patients are treated at the primary level doctors, new patients are added to the primary doctors, and personal information is input and saved, including name, gender, age, ID card number, home address and so on. Then the patient's information is kept in the system. Then primary doctors select specific patients, add consultation application, select consultation type and consultation doctor, fill in consultation application information (including patient's symptoms, past medical history, upload medical records and submit consultation application). After consultation application, the consultation management center can see the consultation application form.

(2) Consultation management review: After logging in to the consultation management backstage, you can see all the consultation application forms and detailed information of the application form, check whether the content of the consultation application is complete and in compliance with the specifications, if the consultation application meets the requirements, the review will be passed, if the consultation application If it does not meet the requirements, the review will fail. After the consultation is approved, the consultation administrator sends a message to

the superior doctor selected in the consultation application to confirm whether the superior doctor has time for the consultation. If there is time, the superior doctor will be arranged for consultation; if the superior doctor refuses the consultation, the consultation management center will reject the consultation application and reschedule the doctor.

(3) Consultation of superior doctors: after logging in to the platform with their own account, the superior doctors can view their consultation application on the platform, and then conduct video consultation with primary doctors. In combination with the patient's medical record content and the patient's "meeting" in the video, the superior doctor can diagnose and treat the patient. After the video consultation, the superior doctor will fill in the consultation report and submit it.

(4) Primary doctors fill in the consultation conclusion. After the superior doctor submits the consultation report, the primary doctors can see that the consultation report has been submitted on their own platform. The primary doctors can view the consultation report, and combine the specific discussion of the patient's condition during the consultation process to give the patient's final treatment plan. The doctor finally fills in the consultation conclusion and submits it, and the consultation ends.

5.3 Recommended by Consultant

In the consultation module, after the primary doctors in the lower-level hospital fill in the patient's medical record, the next step is to select the consultation doctor. The system recommends a list of consultation doctors for the primary doctors according to

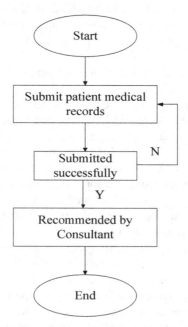

Fig. 1. Consultation doctor recommendation process

the department and the patient's medical record text selected by the primary doctors, and select a consultation doctor from the list, aAnd then submit the consultation application. Figure 1 is a flowchart of the consultation doctor recommendation.

5.4 Distance Education and Training

Distance education training includes knowledge lecture learning, medical history data learning, and knowledge lecture learning. The process is shown in Fig. 2.

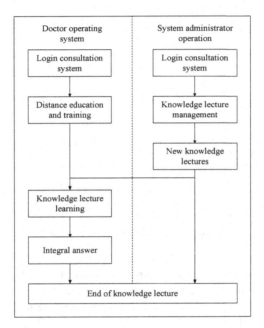

Fig. 2. Business process of knowledge lecture

Figure 2 shows the business operation flow of knowledge lecture. The administrator of the system background management end logs in and adds knowledge lectures. After the doctor logs in to the system, he or she can view the classification of knowledge lectures and learn in the distance education training module. Knowledge lectures are usually equipped with exercises, which can be scored after learning.

The remote consultation system includes three subsystems: system background management, triage table management and organization management. The operation permissions of the three subsystems are as follows: the operation permissions of the background management end of the system are the addition, modification and deletion of special lectures, lecturers and special categories; the permissions of the triage management end are the view of special lectures, lecturers and special categories; the operation permissions of the organization management end do not have the function of special lectures.

5.5 Medical Record Sharing

The business operation process of medical record learning is shown in Fig. 3.

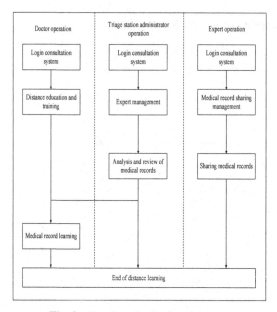

Fig. 3. Case learning business process

After consulting experts log in the system, they can add new medical record sharing in the medical record sharing management module. After the triage terminal administrator approves, the doctor can view the new medical record sharing in the system, so as to learn the medical record.

6 Experiment Analysis

6.1 Experiment Preparation

In order to better reflect the application effectiveness of remote consultation and teaching system, the black box method is used to test the experiment. According to the different functions of each module in the system design, the system as a whole is tested in detail, and the actual situation is simulated during the test to detect whether the modules of the system can meet the requirements of remote consultation. During the test, the system is regarded as a box, ignoring the situation inside the box, only verifying whether the function and interface of the program meet the requirements, and testing whether the remote consultation system can receive and transmit data information correctly.

The main content of the system function test includes the following parts: whether the system can log in normally, whether it can identify illegal accounts and report errors; whether the permissions of the system are normal, whether it can enter different interfaces according to different identities of users; whether the system is normal Application, arrangement and diagnosis; whether the information can be released normally; whether the overall function realized by the system meets the demand.

Test requirements: after the doctor user logs in to the system and selects view arrangement, the system can enter the view arrangement interface, view the consultation arrangement, click to fill in the diagnosis report to enter the diagnosis report filling interface, which can diagnose the patients.

Test result: After the doctor user logs in to the system, selects to view the schedule, the system can correctly query the consultation schedule of the current user by the consulting doctor; click the scheduled information, the user can correctly query the patient information; click to fill in the diagnosis report, the system can be correct Display the diagnosis report filling interface; when the doctor fills in, click save, the database can store the diagnosis report data normally. The lower-level hospital logs into the system and selects to view the report. The system can correctly query the diagnostic report information and display the diagnostic report.

Test conclusion: the diagnostic function enables doctors to fill in diagnosis reports, save data and share cases as teaching materials.

In order to highlight the performance of this system, it is compared with the remote consultation and teaching system based on neural network.

6.2 Comparison of Experimental Results

The response time of the system is tested. During the test, there are 50 pieces of data in the system. The test results are shown in Table 1.

Table 1. Comparison of experimental results

Test operation	Average response time of neural network system(ms)	Average response time of deep learning system(ms)
User login system	48	45
Lower level hospitals submit applications	54	48
Higher-level hospital inquiry application	66	46
Arrangement submitted by superior hospital	49	42
Doctor check arrangement	67	40
Doctors submit diagnostic reports	62	46
View the diagnosis report in the lower-level hospital	79	48
Hospital releases information	53	41

Through the above test, it can be seen that the system in this paper has a faster response speed when in use, and the system can quickly complete the data interaction of the above functions, which can meet the needs in actual work.

However, due to the limitation of test conditions, this system has not been used on site, and multi-user concurrent testing has not been carried out. In this regard, it needs to be strengthened and improved. And for the data query process of the system, when the amount of data reaches hundreds of thousands or even millions, the time complexity will increase, and the system itself does not have the ability to actively query and can only query passively. Therefore, more effective algorithms are needed to perform database query operations, such as using deep learning technology for data mining in the case of big data, to deal with higher challenges.

7 Conclusion

The hospital's remote consultation and teaching system not only meets the needs of patients to seek medical treatment in different regions, but also promotes the intelligent development of the medical industry, and at the same time solves the problems of limited operating space and the number of visitors, and the risk of cross-infection. The video of the operation process is used as an important data archive, which can be used for medical record archiving, scientific research and teaching, or medical dispute verification data. Therefore, this paper designs a hospital remote consultation and teaching system based on deep learning. On the basis of analyzing the problems of the system construction and clarifying the system design objectives, with the support of the system hardware, the deep learning process is used to realize the functions of case collection, remote consultation, doctor recommendation, remote education and training, and case sharing. In the experimental part, through the comparison with the traditional system, the system is more effective.

References

1. Liu, J., Liang, B., Liu, F.: Integration of remote image consultation system based on public cloud technology. China Digital Med. **13**(07), 118–120 (2018)
2. Yu, G., et al.: Research and test of a telemedicine software based on cloud platform and big data. China Medical Equipment **15**(11), 114–117 (2018)
3. Liu, S., et al.: Introduction of key problems in long-distance learning and training. Mobile Netw. Appl. **24**(1), 1–4 (2019)
4. Liu, S., et al. (eds.). E-Learning, E-Education, and Online Training, pp. 1–374. Springer International Publishing (2018)
5. Fu, W., Liu, S., Gautam, S.: Optimization of big data scheduling in social networks. Entropy **21**(9), 902–918 (2019)
6. Gao, J.: Building of multipath remote consultation platform based on medical alliance. J. Med. Intell. **20**(19), 204–205 (2018)
7. Zhou, F., et al.: Study and design of image transmission and remote consultation system based on cloud service. J. Med. Intell. **41**(04), 66–69 (2020)
8. Liu, H., et al.: The establishment and prospect of traditional Chinese medicine teleconsultation platform applying "Internet plus." Chin. J. Health Inform. Manage. **16**(04), 458–461 (2019)

9. Gu, H., et al.: Study on the construction of regional remote consultation service platform in China. Chin. J. Health Pol. **12**(07), 65–69 (2019)

10. Chen, B., et al.: Application effect of establishing remote consultation in basic hospital. Chin. Community Doctors **36**(18), 184–185 (2020)

A Feasibility Analysis Model for Developing Wushu Sanda Courses in Universities Based on Deep Learning

Dong-Dong Liu[✉]

Weifang University, Weifang 261061, China

Abstract. The current feasibility analysis of specific courses, expert analysis or single item analysis is usually used, and the results are relatively one-sided, so it is difficult to achieve a comprehensive feasibility analysis. Therefore, this paper designs the feasibility analysis model of Wushu Sanda course in universities based on deep learning. First of all, the relationship between curriculum system and training objectives is analyzed, and the relationship matrix between curriculum and objectives is established. Then according to the relationship between training objectives, the importance of the course is analyzed. After that, the training objective factors in the course are analyzed to realize the course process data. At last, use deep learning technology to analyze the marginal characteristics of data, and get the feasibility results of the course. The experiment is designed to analyze the feasibility of Wushu Sanda course in a university. The experimental results show that the model can analyze the feasibility of the course, and get the data for reference to meet the design requirements.

Keywords: Curriculum feasibility · Deep learning · Training target relationship · Marginal characteristics

1 Introduction

With the deepening of education reform, new courses have been continuously added to the original courses. Whether the added courses can achieve the training goals and the impact on other courses is one of the factors that need to be considered in the process of analyzing the feasibility of the new course [1, 2]. A strategic analysis of the Wushu Sanda courses in universities will help to discover the problems in the courses, and put forward solutions based on the existing problems, and provide certain practical guidance for the implementation and reform of the courses. Therefore, it is very important to study the feasibility of developing Wushu Sanda courses in universities.

At present, most of the domestic and foreign studies on the feasibility analysis of courses use expert evaluation methods, and most of the studies are conducted on the factors that experts need to consider, and there is a lack of research on the feasibility analysis using mathematical models. However, in related studies, there have also been methods of using analytic hierarchy process, Delphi technology and other aspects to

© ICST Institute for Computer Sciences, Social Informatics and Telecommunications Engineering 2021
Published by Springer Nature Switzerland AG 2021. All Rights Reserved
W. Fu et al. (Eds.): ICMTEL 2021, LNICST 388, pp. 92–102, 2021.
https://doi.org/10.1007/978-3-030-82565-2_8

analyze the single factor of the course, but it is difficult to realize the overall feasibility reference [3]. In addition, reference [4] proposed a feasibility analysis method based on the HACCP system for the management of experimental courses in universities, and explored the application of HACCP management concepts in the management of experimental courses in universities. Through combing and risk analysis of the experimental course development process, seven key control points are determined, including the submission and review of experimental projects, the condition evaluation of the experimental site, and the storage and acquisition of experimental consumables. Establish critical limits, monitoring systems, corrective measures, confirm procedures and records for critical control points in accordance with HACCP principles, and implement corresponding measures to achieve effective management and control of experimental courses. The experimental results show that this method can accurately analyze the feasibility of the management of experimental courses, but it has the problems of complicated analysis process and long analysis time. Reference [5] puts forward the feasibility analysis method of flipped classroom of clothing materials based on "rain class + SPOC". This method analyzes the feasibility of the application of flipped classroom teaching mode of "rain class + SPOC" in the teaching of clothing materials in higher vocational universities from the operability, teaching advantages and the advantages of process learning evaluation of the flipped classroom teaching mode of "rain class + SPOC". In practical application, this method also has the problem of long analysis time.

Aiming at the problems of traditional methods, this paper integrates deep learning technology into the course feasibility analysis model, and designs a feasibility analysis model for colleges and universities to develop Wushu Sanda courses based on deep learning. In the feasibility analysis of the course, it is relatively difficult because of the many factors involved and the complicated calculation. However, in the deep learning theory, the use of computer operations can achieve multi-factor analysis, the use of deep learning technology to analyze the marginal characteristics of the course data, and quickly obtain the feasibility analysis results of the course, thereby solving the traditional method of complex analysis process and analysis time longer question.

2 Feasibility Analysis Model Design of Wushu Sanda Course in Universities

2.1 Curriculum System and Operation of Training Objectives

The training goal is the soul and core of the curriculum system, which determines all other aspects of the system. Curriculum system is an organic whole of a series of courses to achieve the training objectives [6–8]. In other words, the training objectives must be supported and guaranteed by certain courses, and certain courses must be based on certain training objectives. Therefore, the optimization analysis of curriculum system must first be the interaction analysis between curriculum and objectives, so as to determine the degree of curriculum support for objectives and obtain the basis for optimizing the curriculum system. Then, the degree of realization of training objectives can be determined by calculating the number of courses supporting the objectives and the degree of support [9].

In the specific analysis, first, the cultivated target is decomposed into n sub-targets, namely $Z_1, Z_2, ..., Z_n$, in an orderly manner according to the logical relationship of self-existence. Then according to the analytic hierarchy process, according to the determined priority of the sub-objectives, the corresponding weight $w_1, w_2, ..., w_n$ is determined. At the same time, determine m alternative courses, namely $x_1, x_2, ..., x_m$, and establish a matrix table corresponding to the course department, as shown in Table 1.

Table 1. Matrix of the relationship between curriculum and objectives

P		General objective Z					
		Z_1	Z_2	...	Z_j	...	Z_n
Curriculum X	X_1	p_{11}	p_{12}	...	p_{1j}	...	p_{1n}
	X_2	p_{21}	p_{22}	...	p_{2j}	...	p_{2n}
	...	...	...	...	...	...	...
	X_i	p_{i1}	p_{i2}	...	p_{ij}	...	p_{in}
	...	...	...	...	...	...	...
	X_m	p_{m1}	p_{m2}	...	p_{mj}	...	p_{mn}

In Table 1, p_{ij} represents the degree of support for the j sub-goal in the i course. According to the value, it can have a key supporting role, an important supporting role, a general supporting role, and a small supporting role for the goal according to the value.

In order to facilitate quantitative analysis, the above four levels are assigned 1, 0.5, 0.25 and 0 respectively according to the effect of the course on the objectives, and the results are filled into the above matrix to obtain the quantitative data matrix ($m \times n$) of the relationship between the curriculum and the goal. Each row of the matrix indicates which sub goals a course supports and how much support it has. So far, the support degree of each alternative course to the sub objectives has been clarified, but how much support to the overall goal needs to be further analyzed. Therefore, the direct contribution index H of the course to the goal is introduced, which represents the direct contribution or support function of a course to the overall goal, which is obtained by weighted summation of the support degree of the course to the sub objectives:

$$H(i) = p_{ij} \times w_j \qquad (1)$$

In formula (1), w_j represents the weight of sub goal j, p_{ij} represents the support degree of sub goal j in the i course, and $H(i)$ represents the direct contribution index to the overall goal in the i course. The higher the contribution index, the greater the contribution of the course to the goal, which reflects the feasibility index of curriculum development to a certain extent.

2.2 Course Importance

For the feasibility of a course, it is necessary to consider the feasibility of participating in the course arrangement and the importance of the course [10]. In this paper, consider seven representative factors, including the nature of the program, the number of weeks, the type of classroom, the number of classes, the workload of teachers and the scheduling time mode, which are represented by $C_1......C_7$. If the number of factors to be considered is set as k, then the factors to be considered are C_k, $\sum\limits_{i=k}^{k} = 1$. Let M_k be the specific value of the k influencing factor. The obtained course priority formula is as follows:

$$PCF = \sum_{k=1}^{i} C_k \times M_k \tag{2}$$

It can be seen from formula (2) that the factors affecting the value of PCF include the size of weight and the specific value. How to determine the weight and value of each influencing factor is very important to the calculation of curriculum priority. According to the analysis of priority factors, the organization hierarchy is constructed, as shown in Fig. 1.

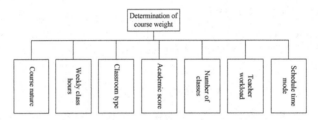

Fig. 1. Course weight hierarchy diagram

The construction of judgment matrix is the most important part of AHP, which can be divided into two steps: selecting experts and constructing judgment matrix. In the process of selecting experts, the subject structure and professional structure of experts play a decisive role in the construction of judgment matrix. In order to ensure that the construction of judgment matrix is reasonable, a total of 10 experts from computer, education and curriculum scheduling experience are selected to construct the judgment matrix. The construction of judgment matrix is actually a process of asking experts to compare all the factors shown in Fig. 1. If there is n factor in the hierarchy, $n(n-1)/2$ comparison is required, and there are 7 factors in the second layer of Fig. 1, so 21 comparisons are required.

In order to show the result of the comparison, the analytic hierarchy process puts forward a scale of relative importance. The comparison of the relative importance of two elements can be changed to get a measure. In order to illustrate the problem, there is now a factor n that has an impact on the target. Use a_{ij} to represent the relative importance ratio of B_i and B_j to the target under the influencing factors. The definition of a_{ij} can be divided into many kinds. In this article, the proportion scale is set to equal importance when the scale is 1, 3 is set to be slightly important, 5 is obviously important, 7 is really important, 9 is absolutely important, and the degree of adjacent The intermediate values including 2, 4, 6, and 8 can be represented by a matrix $A = \left(a_{ij}\right)_{n \times n}$, which is called a judgment matrix, as follows:

$$A = \begin{bmatrix} 1 & 3 & 1/3 & 7 & 1/2 & 6 & 5 \\ 1/3 & 1 & 1/5 & 6 & 1/4 & 4 & 1/2 \\ 3 & 5 & 1 & 9 & 2 & 7 & 6 \\ 1/7 & 1/6 & 1/9 & 1 & 1/8 & 1/3 & 1/4 \\ 2 & 4 & 2 & 8 & 1 & 5 & 4 \\ 1/6 & 1/4 & 1/7 & 3 & 1/5 & 1 & 1/3 \\ 1/5 & 2 & 1/6 & 4 & 1/4 & 3 & 1 \end{bmatrix} \tag{3}$$

In formula (3), A is reciprocal matrix, $a_{ii} = 1$, $a_{ij} = 1/a_{ji}, i, j = 1, 2, ..., n$. The value in the second column of the first row represents the influencing factors V1 course nature and V2 week class hours, and compares the impact of the evaluation target course scheduling effect. The result 3 represents that experts believe that the nature of the course is slightly more important than the weekly class hours, and so on to obtain the importance of the course, and arrange courses according to the importance of the course.

2.3 Curriculum Factor Analysis

p observable random vector $X = (x_1, x_2, ..., x_p)'$ is set up, which is decomposed into k dimensional $(k < p)$ common factor and a special factor of p dimension, and it is written as:

$$X_{p \times 1} = A f_{k \times 1} + \varepsilon_{p \times 1} \tag{4}$$

In formula (4), $X = (x_1, x_2, ..., x_p)'$ represents the observable random vector in the course, $f = (f_1, f_2, ..., f_k)$ represents the common factor vector, $\varepsilon = (\varepsilon_1, \varepsilon_2, ..., \varepsilon_p)'$ represents the special factor vector, and $A = (a_{ij})_{p \times k}$ represents the factor loading matrix. Given an observation data matrix X of p dimensional related variables $x_1, x_2, ..., x_p$, the purpose of factor analysis is to use a few common factors to describe the covariance structure among p related variables.

In order to establish the structure of factor analysis, it is necessary to estimate the factor load matrix $A = (a_{ij})_{p \times k}$ and the special variance matrix $D = diag(\sigma_1^2, \sigma_2^2, ..., \sigma_p^2)$. There are many methods for parameter estimation, among which the most common method is the principal component method. Using the principal component method, let the eigenvalues of the covariance matrix of sample X be marked as: $\lambda_1 \geq \lambda_2 \geq ...... \lambda_p \geq 0$, and the corresponding orthogonal unit eigenvector is: $\gamma_1, \gamma_2, ..., \gamma_p$. here, the smaller number of factors k is selected, and the cumulative contribution rate $\sum_{i=1}^{k} \lambda_i / \sum_{i=1}^{p} \lambda_i$ reaches a higher percentage.

Based on this, the factor analysis method can be used to analyze the variables of the course, and the situation of the course can be digitized.

2.4 Analysis of Marginal Characteristics of Deep Learning

In this paper, the LDA Algorithm in deep learning is used to analyze the above data. In this paper, the LDA Algorithm in deep learning is used to make each type of data obey the prior assumption of Gaussian distribution, but the actual data does not always meet this characteristic, and thus can not well describe the distinction between classes as shown in Fig. 2.

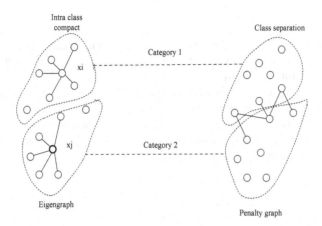

Fig. 2. Eigengraph and penalty graph of marginal embedding graph

In Fig. 2, the eigengraph describes the proximity relationship between points of the same kind. Each sample is connected with $k1$ nearest neighbor in the same kind of sample. The penalty graph describes the proximity of boundary points between classes, and different class point pairs are connected with each other. In class compactness can be described by eigengraph:

$$\tilde{s}_c = \sum_{\substack{i \in N_{k_1}^+ (j) \, or \, j \in N_{k_1}^+ (i)}}^{n} \left\| \omega^T x_i - \omega^T x_j \right\|^2 = 2\omega^T X \left(D^c - W^c \right) X^T \omega \tag{5}$$

In formula (5), $W^c = [0,1]$, $N_{k_1}^+ (j)$ represents the k_1 sample index sets that will be nearest neighbors in the class of sample x_j. Where ω represents the weight vector under the feature transformation.. The separation between classes can be described by (6). The concept of deep learning comes from the research of artificial neural network, and the multi-layer perceptron with multiple hidden layers is a deep structure model. Deep learning structure combines low-level features to form a more abstract high-level representation to discover the distributed feature representation of data. In the use of deep learning operation, need to consider the automatic decoder, including the parameter $\omega = [\omega_{eno}, \omega_{deo}]$, where ω_{eno} represents the encoding parameter, ω_{deo} represents the decoding parameter, and the encoding part realizes the mapping $\phi(\cdot|\omega_{eno})$ from the sample space to the feature space. The optimal parameters need to satisfy the objective cost function under the minimization formula:

$$\omega_{eno}^* = \arg\min_{\omega} JMF$$

$$= \arg\min_{\omega_{eno}} \frac{\phi_{\omega_{eno}}^T(X)(D^c - W^c)\phi_{\omega_{eno}}(X)}{\phi_{\omega_{eno}}^T(X)(D^\rho - W^\rho)\phi_{\omega_{eno}}(X)} \tag{6}$$

In formula (6), $\phi_{\omega_{eno}}(\cdot)$ represents the mapping from the sample space to the feature space. Since deep learning models have flexible function representation capabilities, they often result in overfitting training, and the generalization performance of the algorithm will be poor. To this end, it is necessary to further adopt regularization methods in the objective function. The method to obtain the internal structure distribution of the data is to minimize the reconstruction error, and the decoding part of the automatic encoding network naturally forms the reconstruction function $\vartheta(\cdot|\omega_{dec})$. The regularization defined by the unsupervised data is defined as follows:

$$R = \frac{1}{n}\sum_{i=1}^n \left\| x_i - \vartheta\left(\phi_{w_{deo}}(x_i|\omega_{enc})\right)\right\|_2^2 \tag{7}$$

In formula (7), $\|\;\|_2$ is the 2-norm of the vector. At the same time, it needs to be regularized. This article uses the attenuation of network weight and bias to regularize:

$$Dec = \|\omega_{eno}\|_2^2 \tag{8}$$

In this case, the target is transformed into the following formula:

$$E = JMF + \alpha R + \beta Dec \tag{9}$$

In formula (9), both α and β are regularization coefficients, which are used for feature extraction to obtain the optimal network weights

$$W^* = \arg\min_{\omega} E = \arg\min_{\omega} JMF + \alpha R + \beta Dec \tag{10}$$

After obtaining the optimized network weights, higher accuracy can be obtained in the calculation, so as to obtain the feasibility analysis results.

3 Experimental Demonstration Analysis

In order to verify the analysis ability of the feasibility analysis model of Wushu Sanda course in universities based on deep learning, the following experiments are designed to analyze the feasibility of Wushu Sanda course in a university.

3.1 Experimental Computing Equipment

Due to the large amount of data when using the model for analysis, the PC is used for relevant calculation in this paper. The configuration of PC host participating in the experimental calculation is shown in Table 2.

Table 2. Experimental PC configuration table

Equipment name	Usage amount	Device model	Device parameters
Motherboard	1	B360M MORTAR	CPU interface LGA1151, display interface DVI + HDMI + DP
CPU	1	I5-10600K	CUP main frequency 4.7GHz
Graphics card	1	RX560 4GB D5 Warrior	Graphics card memory 4GB, air cooling
RAM	2	3200 vest	Single memory capacity 8GB, memory frequency 3200 MHz
Hard disk	1	WD 1TB	Hard drive capacity 1TB, Hard disk revolutions 7200 revolutions

3.2 Experimental Calculation Process

First of all, it is decomposed according to the training objectives that the target course needs to achieve, decomposed into five sub-goals: Z_1, Z_2, Z_3, Z_4, and Z_5. At the same time, the target weight value is determined according to the above formula (1). In the experiment of this article, the determined value of the target weight is: $w_1 = 0.4$, $w_2 = 0.8$, $w_3 = 0.6$, $w_4 = 0.2$, $w_5 = 0.1$. At the same time, the candidate courses are determined. In this experiment, according to the course structure of the university, the candidate courses are $X_1, X_2, X_3, X_4, X_5, X_6$. Establish the target relationship matrix under the course, assign values to it, and get the data in Table 3.

Table 3. The target relationship matrix of the experimental course

P		Main target Z				
		Z_1	Z_2	Z_3	Z_4	Z_5
CourseX	X_1	1	0.4	0	0	0.24
	X_2	0.22	0.25	0	0.21	1
	X_3	0	0.24	0	0.5	0.24
	X_4	0.25	0.24	0.5	0	0
	X_5	1	0	0.15	1	0.25
	X_6	0.24	0.25	0	0	0.15

Use MATLAB software to program the acquired data to obtain analysis data that can be used by the LDA algorithm, and obtain the factor load table under the maximum variance rotation, as shown in Table 4.

Table 4. Maximum variance rotation factor loading table

Evaluation index	Factor1	Factor2	Factor3	Factor4	Factor5
X_1	0.07181	−0.1845	0.77216	0.14183	-0.1874
X_2	−0.05562	−0.01849	0.12741	0.22312	0.18274
X_3	0.31513	0.24521	−0.3181	0.22647	0.31826
X_4	−0.1962	−0.7415	−0.3015	0.22174	0.18612
X_5	0.45371	0.35826	−0.17651	0.18431	0.22185
X_6	−0.07132	0.22743	0.51241	0.71542	−0.1748

After obtaining the maximum variance of the rotation factor load, it is subjected to 3000 iterations of experiments. In the experiment, after 8 iterations of the LDA algorithm, the value of the log-likelihood function will reach stability, as can be seen from Fig. 3. Among them, the convergence speed is faster.

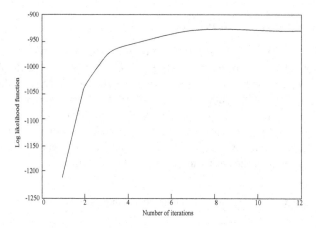

Fig. 3. Change of logarithm likelihood value of LDA Algorithm in the process of iteration

Through factor analysis of the original data, the potential variables are obtained, and the common factor comparison in Table 3 is basically consistent. The H value and T value of $H = 0.37$ and $T = 0.1746$ obtained by the model are smaller, which proves that the martial arts Sanda course Applied in the experiment has less direct contribution to the overall goal and less support for other courses. However, the numerical value also shows that the course is feasible. The course is suitable for elective courses, but not suitable for normal compulsory courses. According to the obtained H and T, complete the feasibility analysis of the course.

In order to verify the application effect of this method in the feasibility analysis of Wushu Sanda course in universities, taking the feasibility analysis time as the experimental index, the methods of reference [4], reference [5] and this method are compared, and the comparison results are shown in Fig. 4.

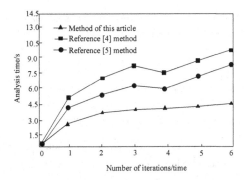

Fig. 4. Comparison of feasibility analysis time of different methods

Analysis of Fig. 4 shows that the time of feasibility analysis of Wushu Sanda course in universities is always less than 4.5 s, which is significantly lower than the traditional method, indicating that this method can realize the feasibility analysis of Wushu Sanda course in universities in a short time, and the analysis efficiency is higher.

4 Conclusion

In this paper, the deep learning technology is used to extract the influencing factors in the course, so as to realize the design of the course feasibility analysis model. The experimental results show that the analysis time of the method in this paper is shorter, which shows that the method is more efficient and effectively solves the problem of longer analysis time of traditional methods. However, the model can only give the relevant reference data and the feasibility of the course, and can not specifically allocate the curriculum itself. In the future research, according to the relevant parameters of the curriculum feasibility, the neural network technology can be used to help the calculation of curriculum allocation.

References

1. Wang, M.: A probe into mixed teaching mode reform of system engineering course. Logist. Technol. **37**(11), 138–141 (2018)
2. Zheng, L., Zhou, Z., Hu, Y., Cai, J.: A course pass rate prediction method based on large data of MOOC learning behavior. Comput. Eng. Sci. **40**(z1), 81–88 (2018)
3. Zhao, J., Liu, N.: Research on practice system of innovative entrepreneurship education for computer specialty in applied undergraduate colleges. Microcomput. Appl. **34**(12), 30–32 (2018)
4. Xie, S., Zhong, R., Zhu, J., et al.: Feasibility analysis and research on the management of experimental courses in colleges and universities based on the HACCP system. Light Ind. Sci. Technol. **259**(06), 156–157 (2020)
5. Pan, Z.: Research on the feasibility of the clothing material flipping class based on "Rain Class + SPOC." Light Text. Ind. Technol. **221**(08), 141–142 (2020)

6. Yang, X., Feng, S.: Cultivation models of innovative postgraduates based on CDIO notion under background of "Double First-Class" construction. Heilongjiang Res. High. Educ. **8**, 6–10 (2018)
7. Liu, S., et al.: Introduction of key problems in long-distance learning and training. Mobile Netw. Appl. **24**(1), 1–4 (2019)
8. Weina, F., Liu, S., Srivastava, G.: Optimization of big data scheduling in social networks. Entropy **21**(9), 902–918 (2019)
9. Liu, S., et al. (Eds.). E-Learning, E-Education, and Online Training. Springer International Publishing, pp. 1–374 (2018)
10. Zuo, G., Zhang, J., Su, X., Wang, H., et al.: Research on teaching quality evaluation of modern apprenticeship course based on SDAE deep learning framework. Intel. Comput. Appl. **6**(12), 165–167 (2020)

Performance Evaluation Model of Wushu Sanda Athletes Based on Visual Signal Processing

Dong-dong Liu[✉]

Weifang University, Weifang 261061, China

Abstract. In order to improve the accuracy of the performance evaluation of Wushu Sanda athletes, the performance evaluation model of Wushu Sanda athletes was designed based on visual signal processing. First, extract the contours of Wushu Sanda athletes, then collect the performance information of Wushu Sanda athletes, and finally complete the performance evaluation through the establishment of the performance evaluation index of Wushu Sanda athletes and the index processing. Experimental results show that the evaluation model designed in this study not only improves the accuracy of evaluation, but also has a higher evaluation efficiency.

Keywords: Visual signal processing · Wushu Sanda athletes · Performance evaluation · Contour extraction · Information collection

1 Introduction

Wushu Sanda is an important part of modern competitive sports. How to improve the athletes' competitive ability in such events is very important [1–3]. The expressiveness evaluation of Wushu Sanda athletes has a certain promotion effect on improving the athletes' competitive level. Through expressiveness evaluation, it is found that the strengths and weaknesses of athletes in training are the topics of general concern in training practice [4, 5]. Therefore, in order to improve the athlete's competitive level, it is necessary to design a performance evaluation model for Wushu Sanda athletes.

In this context, some scholars put forward the evaluation method of basketball players' competitive performance ability based on the hybrid model. This method follows the idea of analytic hierarchy process, constructs the evaluation index system of competitive performance ability, and establishes the hybrid evaluation model based on AHP-FCE to scientifically evaluate and analyze the basketball players' competitive performance ability. The experimental results show that this method can fully reflect the competitive ability of basketball players, but the evaluation time is long. Some scholars put forward the comprehensive quality evaluation method of cyclists Based on support vector machine, and selected 16 influencing factors of 225 cyclists' body shape, body function, sports ability and special ability as three methods to optimize the parameters of the network model. The experimental results show that the accuracy of this method is high, but the evaluation time is long.

Published by Springer Nature Switzerland AG 2021. All Rights Reserved
W. Fu et al. (Eds.): ICMTEL 2021, LNICST 388, pp. 103–116, 2021.
https://doi.org/10.1007/978-3-030-82565-2_9

Visual signal processing is an information processing department based on visual processing. It is the most natural, convenient, convenient and effective way to realize human-computer interaction. It can be used in almost any scene in the field of signal processing, which helps reduce human labor intensity and improve information processing efficiency. Therefore, the visual signal processing technology is applied to the performance evaluation of Wushu Sanda athletes. Aiming at the problems of traditional methods, this paper designs a performance evaluation model of Wushu Sanda athletes based on visual signal processing. The sports contours of Wushu Sanda athletes are extracted through visual signal processing, and the performance information of Wushu Sanda athletes is collected through visual signal processing. Finally, the performance evaluation is completed through the establishment of the performance evaluation index of Wushu Sanda athletes and the index processing. The experimental results show that the evaluation model designed in this study not only improves the accuracy of evaluation, but also has higher evaluation efficiency, which effectively improves the problems existing in traditional methods.

2   Construction of Evaluation Model of Wushu Sanda Athletes' Performance

2.1   Contour Extraction of Sanda Athletes

Before evaluating the performance of Wushu Sanda athletes, it is necessary to extract the contour data of Wushu Sanda athletes based on visual signal processing. In the process of contour extraction, the saliency of a single pixel does not provide meaningful guidance for the position of the contour, and the salient area composed of salient points is likely to correspond to the perceptual target in the image, which can be used for contour extraction based on the deformation template.

In the calculation of salient regions, the most primitive method is to divide the image into fixed rectangular regions, calculate the saliency values in each region, and select the regions with the highest values as salient regions [6, 7]. The disadvantage of this method is that it is easy to divide the perceptual object into several parts, and lose the matching and recognition meaning as a whole. Some researchers divide the image into overlapping rectangular or circular windows, and the size of the window is adjustable. The significance value of the area covered by each window is taken as the factor to compare the regional significance. The advantage of this method is that it can divide the salient region according to the actual size of the target, especially for a specific task, the given shape of the region is equivalent to providing a shape prior for finding the salient target, which can effectively improve the efficiency of target detection. However, the disadvantage of this method is that the overlapping of regions will lead to the repetition of saliency calculation and greatly increase the amount of calculation. In addition, another method is to use the segmentation algorithm to divide the image into several regions and calculate the saliency value of each region. This method avoids the increase of workload caused by repeated calculation. At the same time, the segmentation algorithm can guarantee the perceptual attributes of the region roughly, that is, the pixels in the region have the same or similar visual features, which is very helpful for extracting the perceptual object contour. Natural images are rich in brightness and texture changes, and the shape of the target is completely unknown, so we choose to use segmentation method to help build templates [8–10]. The expression is as follows:

$$\bar{S} = \frac{1}{n} \sum_{i=1}^{n} \bar{S}_{Ai} \tag{1}$$

In the formula (1), $\bar{S}$ represents the segmentation value, $\bar{S}_{Ai}$ represents the mean value of the regional average significant value, and n represents the number of general regions.

When the overall brightness of the target in it is dark, it is likely to be ignored or divided into non-significant areas. In order to avoid this situation, add position information to the template, assume that the target is located in the middle of the image, and define the connected area whose point coordinates are mostly in the middle of the image as the target area. In order to make the resulting template smoother, reduce the impact of repeated changes in local gray levels on the movement of the model, and obtain a template that stably predicts the direction of the curve's movement, the resulting template can be removed from isolated points and areas with smaller areas, and fill holes in the target area. And use median filter for smoothing operation, the expression is:

$$F = M(K) - k\frac{e}{m} \tag{2}$$

In formula (2), k represents the image force coefficient, m represents the parameter when the curve passes through the edge, e represents the external constraint coefficient, and M represents the background parameter.

On this basis, for closed contour extraction, curvature is an important invariant of the curve, which can remain unchanged in the translation and rotation of the image:

$$M(K) = (b - a)|Kn(s)| + a \tag{3}$$

In formula (3), K represents the image force coefficient, b represents a continuous monotonous non-decreasing function, and a represents the magnitude parameter of the external force.

This traditional method only uses the low-level feature of the image gray level, which is very sensitive to noise. It may take the small texture with great difference in gray level as the real edge. Moreover, this definition method loses the rich regional and structural information in the image, which can make the results of edge extraction process more robust and provide more reliable input for more advanced visual tasks.

Therefore, the following calculation method is adopted for further processing

$$\begin{cases} E_{snake} = E_{int}(v(s)) + E_{ev}(v(s)) \\ E_{im}(v(s)) = \int_0^1 \frac{1}{2}\left(\alpha|v'(s)| + \beta|v''(s)|\right)ds \\ E_{ext} = \int_0^{} M(K)\vec{n}(s) - k\frac{\nabla E_{SBP}}{\nabla E_{SBP}}d \end{cases} \tag{4}$$

In formula (4), E_{SBP} represents the image energy term, α represents the variance, and E_{int} represents the scalar function of the image surface.

The above process takes into account the changes of the dual features of grayscale and texture near the edge, can provide a clear and concise input image for contour extraction, and effectively improve the accuracy of the active contour model for contour extraction.

2.2 Information Extraction of Wushu Sanda Athletes' Expressive Force

The Fourier transform is used to achieve target detection through frequency filtering. The meaning of the frequency component is the change in the value (color, brightness, etc.) between adjacent pixels, which means that the faster the image changes in space, the corresponding in the frequency domain. The greater the value. The Fourier transform of an image is a method of observing the characteristics of the image from the grayscale distribution to the frequency distribution. The frequency of the image is an index that characterizes the intensity of the gray-scale change in the image, and it is also the gradient of the gray-scale in the plane space. According to the characteristics of high frequency reflecting the details and low frequency reflecting the general situation of the scene, the edge with strong transformation of visual attributes is a region with dramatic changes in the spectrum, and the corresponding frequency value is higher. In general, there are differences between foreground objects and background images in the regions with high visual saliency. This difference is mainly manifested in the large change of gray gradient. Therefore, in the frequency spectrum after Fourier transform, the abrupt part of the image is represented by high-frequency component, which includes not only image contour features, but also noise and interference. In addition, in some cases, the change of the image inside the salient region is relatively gentle. The low-frequency component of the spectrum is used to obtain the image. The low-frequency component determines the overall image of the image, including the contour information of the object.

The discrete two-dimensional Fourier transform formula of the image is as follows:

$$F(u, v) = \frac{1}{N}\left(-j2\pi\left(\frac{mu}{N} + \frac{nv}{N}\right)\right) \tag{5}$$

In formula (5), $F(u, v)$ represents the gray value of the image.

Since most of the energy in the image is concentrated on low-frequency components, the amplitude values of the four corners of the spectrogram are relatively large. However, in the actual image spectrum analysis process, because the low-frequency components are small and scattered in the four corners, it is not conducive to analyze them. At this time, the coordinates of the spectrogram can be shifted according to the periodicity and conjugate symmetry of the image spectrum. Therefore, the following formula is used to concentrate all the low-frequency components in the center of the spectrogram, while the high-frequency components are scattered around:

$$A(f) = |F(u, v)| = \sqrt{R(u, v)^2 + I(u, v)^2} \tag{6}$$

For image $f(x, y)$, if there are r_k kinds of gray values in the image, then the probability density function is as follows:

$$P(r_i) = \frac{N_r}{N}(i = 0, 1, 2..., k - 1) \tag{7}$$

$$\sum_{i=0}^{k-1} P(r_i) = 1 \tag{8}$$

In the above formula, r_i represents the number of pixels, and N is the total number of pixels.

On this basis, the gray histogram method is used to segment the image:

1) The number of pixels on each gray level;
2) The dynamic range of image grayscale;
3) The overall brightness and contrast of the image.

Histogram is a very useful decision and evaluation tool in image processing. The commonly used histogram operation methods include: image brightness adjustment, contrast adjustment, gray level correction and dynamic range adjustment. Infrared image is different from visible light image in imaging, and its spatial resolution and contrast are worse than that of visible image:

1) The overall gray scale of the image is excessively smooth, and most pixels are concentrated in some adjacent gray scale ranges;
2) There are obvious peaks and valleys in the gray histogram, among which there are more single peaks or double peaks.

Each image has a unique histogram. If the interior of the foreground object has a uniform gray value, and the background is evenly distributed on another gray value, and the difference between the two gray levels is far, then the gray histogram of the image presents a bimodal state. One peak corresponds to the center gray level of the target, and the other peak corresponds to the center gray level of the background. The valley point between the two peaks corresponds to the gray level of the boundary, and the gray value of the valley point is often used as the threshold value in image segmentation. However, the actual infrared image background is complex and changeable, which makes the valley or peak in the gray histogram not obvious, so the bimodal method is difficult to play its advantages. To solve this problem, the basic idea of the method is to calculate a certain gray level in the histogram, which divides the histogram into left and right parts, and makes the distance between the gray mean of these two parts and the overall gray mean value of the image maximum, then the gray level is the segmentation threshold. The expression is as follows:

$$N = \sum_{i=0}^{L-1} n_l \tag{9}$$

In formula (9), L represents the gray level.

In this way, the image segmentation is completed through the above process.

On this basis, a region with significant visual difference is generated. The Fourier spectrum shape of each image in the same image is similar, and the frequency range is similar. In visual selective attention, similar redundant information is allocated less computing resources, and more attention resources are allocated for information unique to each image. Finding out the unique information of each image is the key to discovering visually significant areas. Its expression is:

$$E_{L,ab} = \sqrt{(L_2 - L_1)^2 + (a_2 - a_1)^2 + (b_2 - b_1)^2} \tag{10}$$

In formula (10), L_2, L_1, a_2, a_1, b_2 and b_1 represent image parameters respectively.

In this way, the performance information extraction of Wushu Sanda athletes is completed through the above process, which provides a basis for the performance evaluation of Wushu Sanda athletes.

2.3   Construction of the Evaluation System of Wushu Sanda Athletes' Performance

The power transaction evaluation model is divided into the target layer, the criterion layer and the scheme layer. The corresponding three parts are the evaluation object, the evaluation module and the evaluation element. Among them, the indicators in the evaluation module are sub-indices, and the indicators in the evaluation elements are Sun indicators. The overall evaluation model framework is shown in Fig. 1.

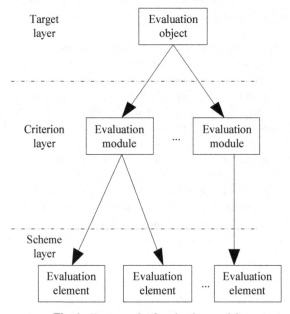

Fig. 1. Framework of evaluation model

Figure 2 shows the construction process of the comprehensive evaluation index system.

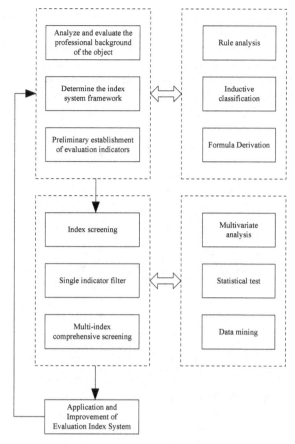

Fig. 2. Construction process of comprehensive evaluation index system

Analyzing the above figure, it can be seen that in qualitative analysis and calculation, the professional background of the evaluation object is analyzed through the methods of rule analysis, inductive classification and formula derivation to determine the index system, and the evaluation index is initially established.

The index system includes physical fitness and skills of athletes. These two parts include several elements, each of which can be decomposed into many specific indicators. In order to establish a perfect evaluation system of athletes' core competitive ability, it must include three parts: evaluation index, index weight and evaluation standard.

The methods and procedures for establishing indicators are as follows. For the selection of an effective indicator system, the following steps are generally followed:

(1) The determination of primary selection index must be supported by theoretical logic analysis;
(2) The primary selection indexes should be screened by the experience of relevant experts (the first round of screening);

(3) The second round of statistical screening (commonly used stepwise regression analysis or principal component analysis) was carried out on the measurement results of the final indicators (expert screening results indicators). According to this method, the establishment of the index system of this study has gone through three procedures: primary selection, expert evaluation and statistical optimization. The confirmation flow chart of indicator system is shown in Fig. 3.

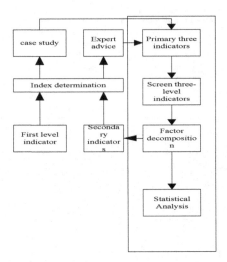

Fig. 3. Confirmation flow chart of indicator system

(1) Through the primary selection of indicators to determine the first level indicators. The first step is to decompose the first level evaluation index according to the objective and quantitative factors. The first level index should be determined according to the main requirements of Sanda competition for athletes' physical skills, and at the same time, it should also consider the principle requirements of establishing evaluation index system, as well as the situation of evaluation organization and implementation. According to the above discussion on the theoretical basis of the core competitive ability of athletes, this study designed four first-class indicators: body shape, body function, sports quality and technical quality.

(2) Decompose secondary indicators. In accordance with the principles of design indicators and the usual mode of establishing an indicator system, the indicators that can be set for each layer are listed item by item and level by level according to the first-level indicators determined above. The listed indicators are mainly based on their own evaluation requirements and management experience, and then refer to the collected evaluation indicator system. The above-identified first-level indicators are decomposed one by one, and a total of 16 second-level indicators have been established, as shown in Table 1.

Table 1. Evaluation index of core competitive ability of Sanda Athletes

Serial number	Primary indicators	Secondary indicators
1	Body shape	Length
		Dimension
		Fullness
		Body type
2	Body function	Circulation function
		Respiratory function
		Nerve function
3	Athleticism	Speed
		Power
		Endurance
		Flexible
		Sensitive
		Coordination
4	Technical quality	Technical quality
		Stability

In the comprehensive evaluation, in order to accurately and reasonably reflect the different importance of each evaluation index in the evaluation system, it is very important to work out the "weight" of each index as accurately as possible.

This study uses the index ranking method in the expert consultation method to determine the weight of the first-level indicators. The steps are:

According to their own opinions, the four first-class indexes of body shape, physical function, sports quality and technical quality, which reflect the core competitive ability of Sanda athletes, are asked to rank their importance according to their own opinions. The most important number is 1, the second is 2, and so on.

According to the above selected evaluation indicators, understand the relationship between each evaluation index, and establish a hierarchical structure model. According to the relationship between the indicators, the evaluation index is constructed as an evaluation index set composed of a target layer and multiple index layers. The judgment matrix is constructed by 1–9 scale method, as shown in Table 2.

Use the least square method to sort the indicators, the calculation formula is:

$$\varphi = \frac{q}{\prod\limits_{i} q}/t \tag{11}$$

Table 2. 9-scale method content

Serial number	Scale	Meaning
1	1	The two indicators are equally important
2	3	One indicator is slightly more important than the other
3	5	One indicator is obviously more important than the other
4	7	One indicator is more important than the other
5	9	One indicator is more important than the other
6	2, 4, 6, 8	The median value of the above two adjacent judgments

In formula (11), φ represents the number of indicators at this level, $\prod_i q$ represents the number of indicators evaluated, q represents the relative importance of indicators, and t represents the comprehensive weight of the underlying indicators.

However, the score of each single index only reflects the level of an athlete's ability in a certain aspect. If we want to make a comprehensive evaluation of the core competitive ability of the athletes, we must calculate the comprehensive score according to the weight of each index on the basis of the single score evaluation, and then evaluate it. The formula of comprehensive score is as follows:

$$Y_d = \sum_{i=1}^{n} Y_i W_i \tag{12}$$

In formula (12), Y_i represents the standard score of each sub-indicator, and W_i represents the weight of each sub-indicator.

The comprehensive score only reflects the overall development level and situation of the core competitive ability of athletes. Although the individual scores can reflect the differences of all aspects of athletes' abilities to a certain extent, they can not reflect this imbalance quantitatively. In order to evaluate the core competitive ability of athletes objectively and concretely, and reflect the balance degree of all aspects of athletes' ability development quantitatively, it is necessary to introduce discrete score to evaluate. The calculation method of reflecting the balance index is as follows:

$$S \cdot D = \sqrt{\sum_{i=1}^{n} (Y_i - Y_j)^2 / n} \tag{13}$$

In formula (13), $S \cdot D$ is the discrete score; Y_j is the mean score, that is, the average of the standard scores of each indicator. The calculation formula is:

$$Y_j = \left(\sum_{i=1}^{n} Y_i \right) / n \tag{14}$$

Through the single scoring table and the comprehensive score of the core competitive ability of athletes, we can directly determine the score of each index of athletes.

Therefore, an evaluation model is proposed based on the completion of evaluation index construction. The calculation process of the model is shown in Fig. 4.

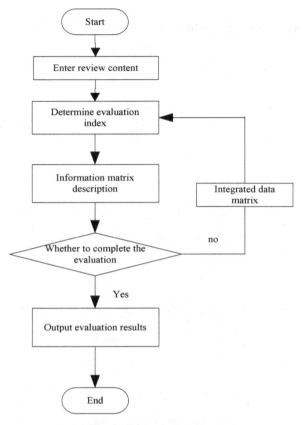

Fig. 4. Evaluation process

On this basis, normalization was carried out:

$$C = R_c/f \tag{15}$$

In formula (15), C represents a specific index, R_x represents the R value of the index, and f represents the weight coefficient.

In this way, through the above process, the performance evaluation of Wushu Sanda athletes based on visual signal processing is completed.

3 Experimental Comparison

In order to verify the effectiveness of the performance evaluation model of Wushu Sanda athletes based on visual signal processing designed in this study, the following experiments are designed. In order to ensure the rigor of the experiment, the traditional model is compared with the model in this paper, and the evaluation time and evaluation error of the two models are compared.

3.1 Comparison of Evaluation Time

The traditional model and the model in this paper are used to evaluate the performance of athletes. The evaluation time is shown in Fig. 5.

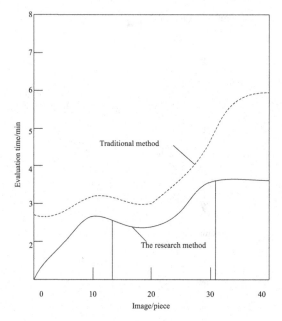

Fig. 5. Comparison of evaluation time

Analyzing Fig. 5, it can be seen that in the process of target evaluation, the performance evaluation model of Wushu Sanda athletes based on visual signal processing takes less time than the traditional model, which proves that the model can quickly evaluate the target.

3.2 Comparison of Evaluation Errors

Comparing the evaluation error of the traditional model and this model, the comparison result is shown in Fig. 6.

According to Fig. 6, the maximum evaluation error of the model in this paper is only 20%, while the maximum evaluation error of the traditional model is 98%. It can be seen from Fig. 6 that the evaluation error of the traditional model is relatively high, which is much higher than the performance evaluation model of Wushu Sanda athletes based on visual signal processing in this study.

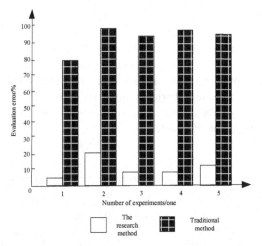

Fig. 6. Comparison of evaluation errors

3.3   Comparison of Rationality of Evaluation Results

The traditional model and this model are used to compare the performance evaluation results of the athletes with the human subjective evaluation results. The comparison results are shown in Table 3. The 5 athletes are divided equally, and the evaluation results are expressed by specific scores, specifically 0–100 points. The higher the score, the higher the evaluation of the athlete's performance.

Table 3. Comparison of rationality of evaluation results

Athlete number	Human subjective evaluation results	Paper model	Traditional model
1	87	87	75
2	75	74	70
3	69	69	73
4	90	89	80
5	73	73	67

Analyzing the data in Table 3, can see that there is no significant gap between the evaluation results obtained by this model and the human subjective evaluation results, and the equal splits of 1, 3, and 5 of the remote mobilization are completely consistent. The experiment shows that this model is highly consistent with the human subjective perception results. It shows that the evaluation results of this model are more reliable.

In summary, the evaluation model designed in this study has shorter evaluation time and lower evaluation error than the traditional model, which proves the effectiveness of the model.

4 Conclusion

This study designed a performance evaluation model for Wushu Sanda athletes based on the process of visual signal processing, and verified the effectiveness of the model through experiments. However, due to the limitation of the research time, the evaluation model of this study still has certain shortcomings. For this reason, in the follow-up study, the method of this study will be further optimized to continuously improve the accuracy of the performance evaluation of athletes.

References

1. Shi, H., Sun, G., Wang, Y., et al.: Adaptive image-based visual servoing with temporary loss of the visual signal. IEEE Trans. Industr. Inf. **15**(4), 1956–1965 (2019)
2. Peng, X.B., Abbeel, P., Levine, S., et al.: DeepMimic: example-guided deep reinforcement learning of physics-based character skills. ACM Trans. Graph. **37**(4), 1–14 (2018)
3. Dretsch, M.N., Fauth, J., Moya, M.M., et al.: Modest utility of brief oculomotor test for concussion screening in military mixed-martial arts training. Brain Inj. **33**(14), 1646–1651 (2019)
4. Sirisena, D., Leong, C.R., See, P., et al.: Popliteal artery entrapment syndrome in a Singaporean mixed martial arts fighter. Singapore Med. J. **59**(2), 114–115 (2018)
5. Bezodis, I.N., Cowburn, J., Brazil, A., et al.: A biomechanical comparison of initial sprint acceleration performance and technique in an elite athlete with cerebral palsy and able-bodied sprinters. Sports Biomech. **19**(2), 189–200 (2020)
6. Liu, S., Li, Z., Zhang, Y., et al.: Introduction of key problems in long-distance learning and training. Mob. Netw. Appl. **24**(1), 1–4 (2019)
7. Fu, W., Liu, S., Srivastava, G.: Optimization of big data scheduling in social networks. Entropy **21**(9), 902–918 (2019)
8. Liu, S., Liu, D., Srivastava, G., et al.: Overview and methods of correlation filter algorithms in object tracking. Compl. Intell. Syst. (3) (2020)
9. Boraita, A., Miriam, V., Sánchez-Testal, M.D., Diaz-Gonzalez, L., et al.: Apparent ventricular dysfunction in elite young athletes: another form of cardiac adaptation of the athlete's heart. J. Am. Soc. Echocardiogr. **32**(8), 987–996 (2019)
10. Hams, A.H., Evans, K., Adams, R., et al.: Throwing performance in water polo is related to in-water shoulder proprioception. J. Sports Sci. **37**(22), 1–8 (2019)

Online Matching Method of News Communication Innovative Teaching Mode Driven by Artificial Intelligence

Jia Qian[1(✉)] and Li-li Wang[2]

[1] Press Department, Anhui University of Arts, Hefei 230002, China
[2] Anhui University of Arts, Hefei 230002, China

Abstract. In order to improve the quality of training news communication talents, optimize the teaching mode of news communication innovation, combine with artificial intelligence technology, innovate the content of news communication, deeply analyze the types of students' learning characteristics, and match the different students' online learning content and methods according to the teaching content and the training needs of professional talents, so as to improve the teaching effect of news communication innovation, and provide a mixed teaching mode of online and offline news communication that can be discussed or criticized.

Keywords: Artificial intelligence · News communication · Innovative teaching · Online matching

1 Introduction

Artificial intelligence, also known as intelligent machinery and machine intelligence, refers to the intelligence displayed by machines made by human beings. Generally, artificial intelligence refers to the technology of presenting human intelligence through ordinary computer programs. The research of artificial intelligence is highly technical and professional, each branch of the field is in-depth and different, so it involves a wide range [1]. With the extensive application of artificial intelligence, the current teaching mode has been greatly changed. In the teaching process of news communication innovation, it emphasizes the combination of online teaching and offline teaching, so as to realize the complementary advantages and deep dialogue between the two teaching forms, so as to make up for the many shortcomings faced by the single offline teaching [2]. At present, a large number of tools have been applied to artificial intelligence, including search, mathematical optimization, logic deduction and so on. In the news communication innovation teaching mode online is also gradually exploring [3]. For journalism and communication courses, the emphasis on the importance and urgency of mixed teaching is fundamentally determined by the current overall goal of training journalism and communication personnel [4, 5]. In order to cultivate high quality, all-media, compound, expert and outstanding journalism and communication talents and promote the curriculum construction, the teaching reform of journalism and communication courses has continued to explore new teaching concepts and models, while the massive Internet resources and technical support system in the new media era have pushed the construction of online and offline hybrid courses to the forefront of the teaching reform [6, 7]. Based on this, combined with artificial intelligence - driven theory, the online matching method of news communication innovation teaching mode is studied.

2   News Communication Innovation Teaching Mode Online Matching Content Innovation

In the reform of journalism teaching, teachers' teaching content should match students' learning foundation and learning potential to meet the needs of the new situation [8, 9]. Teaching should focus on the students' nearest development area, provide students with appropriate difficult content, mobilize students' enthusiasm and bring into play their potential, go beyond their nearest development area and reach the level that can be achieved by overcoming their difficulties [10, 11]. The difficulty of teaching content should not be too simple or too abstruse. The depth of teaching content should meet the requirements of the students' nearest development area and match the nearest development area [12, 13]. The teaching content must have certain experience or the elementary knowledge to take the study cushion, also must have certain intelligence development as the foundation. Match the teaching content with the recent development area, pay attention to match the interest of knowledge with students' interest, match the content of knowledge with students' learning motivation, match the value of knowledge with students' needs [14, 15]. Teachers use language, sound, text, symbols, pictures, tables, animation, video and body movements and other information factors to convey knowledge or method information to the students' hearing and vision [16, 17]. Teaching combination surface is the field or interface that teachers and students contact or influence each other in information exchange or teaching function [18]. The information channel of the combination of teaching and learning mainly includes the channel that teachers transfer knowledge or method information to students, the channel that students transfer feedback information to teachers and the channel that students communicate with each other. In order to realize the information channel matching of teaching combination, the online matching content of news communication innovation teaching mode is optimized based on this. The specific content is shown in Table 1:

The greatest advantage of online journalism courses is that students can watch them over and over again, and can control the learning process according to their own learning progress. In teaching activities, teachers and students are the two basic components of the teaching system, which respectively assume the functions of teaching and learning [19]. Teaching and learning are not separate. We should attach importance to both teaching and learning [20]. Therefore, in the teaching process, we should make full use of the respective roles of teachers and students, rationally allocate teaching functions, assign the

Table 1. Matching content of news communication innovation teaching model

Pattern structure	On the construction of innovative teaching mode of news communication		
Teaching	Teaching concept	Teaching design	Teaching objectives
Pattern elements	Flipped: flipped classroom	Live: live interaction	Practical training: practical training
Pattern principle	Students as the main body	Organic dialogue between online and offline	Strengthen the improvement of comprehensive quality
Mixed connotation	Teacher student interaction	Internal and external interaction	Interaction between knowledge and Practice
Mixed targets	Innovation of teaching form	Reconstruction of content system	Knowledge and ability integration
Mixed path	Learning process reengineering	Design of SPOC system	Theme practice plan
Interactive logic	To provide the overall guiding ideology for teaching design and teaching objectives	Provide support management scheme for teaching idea and teaching goal	To provide feedback and evaluation basis for teaching concept and teaching design

functions of support and guidance to teachers, and assign the functions of participation, conversation, reflection and transformation to students [21]. To achieve the best teaching effect, we should pay attention to the matching between the teacher's leading role and the student's leading role, neither neglecting the teacher's leading role nor neglecting the student's leading role. But must realize teacher's leading role and student's main body role matching.

3   Teaching Characteristics of News Communication Talents Driven by Artificial Intelligence

Any method of teaching and learning itself can not be considered as good or bad in isolation, the key lies in whether a certain way is in line with the specific education situation, education content, education object and so on, and obtain good education effect. Given sufficient time to study and appropriate teaching, almost all students can achieve mastery of almost all of the learning content [22]. Proper teaching, in fact, is the teaching that matches students' learning. Matching teachers' teaching methods with students' learning methods helps students to understand the knowledge most easily. Must realize teacher's teaching method and student's study method match. Teaching matching refers to the mutual adaptation, cooperation and coordination between the teaching of teachers and the learning of students [23]. It can optimize the teaching of teachers and the learning of students. Teaching matching should be carried out from three aspects: teaching content, teaching mode and teaching method, that is, the matching of teaching content and students' nearest development area, the matching of teachers' leading role and students' main role, the matching of teaching method and learning method. In addition, attention should be paid to the matching of information channels and teaching aids with students' operation level [24].

AI -based online learning is more like a one-on-one learning process, unaffected by the environment and the progress of other students, allowing students to focus their attention more easily [25]. According to the actual situation of the students, the teacher makes a detailed study plan. The students use their spare time to finish the online study according to the study plan. Because the students are self-taught, so online learning management and monitoring is particularly important. Knowledge unit learning has been completed online, classroom online and offline is mainly to allow students to complete the comprehensive practice. The best difficulty and complexity of setting up practical projects is slightly higher than the comprehensive strength of online teaching courses in journalism and communication. Form a corresponding strategic structure around this key point, and then integrate the other elements into this key point to design a complete set of teaching matching strategies [26, 27]. According to this classification method, four types of teaching matching strategies can be summed up, which are: methodological teaching matching strategy, content-based teaching matching strategy, mode teaching matching strategy and task-based teaching matching strategy, as shown in Table 2.

Table 2. Teaching strategies of news communication

Teaching matching strategy	Feature description
Method type	Taking method as the center, the framework of teaching strategy is constructed. There are many teaching methods in the teaching process. According to these methods, teachers can choose the appropriate teaching content presentation and learning activities
Content type	The framework of teaching strategy is constructed with the teaching content as the center. This type of strategy is to organize teaching activities according to the attributes of teaching content and internal logical relations
Mode type	The teaching strategy is designed with the activity mode of teaching and learning between teachers and students as the center
Task based	Taking teaching task as the center, design teaching strategy on the basis of creating teaching situation

Because of the different definition of learning style, many different learning style models have been formed, and corresponding learning style measuring tools have been designed according to the models, in order to measure learners' learning style types more effectively [28]. From the four dimensions of information perception, input, processing and understanding, learning styles can be divided into four types: perceptual, visual and verbal, active and meditative A learning style model is created to provide the basis for learning style analysis in the blended learning environment, as shown in Table 3.

Table 3. Types of learning characteristics of journalism and communication talents

Theoretical basis	Types of learning styles	Learning style measurement tool
Theoretical basis	Assimilator Adaptive type composite Divergent type	Adult learning style scale (LSD)
Types of learning styles	Perceptual/intuitive Visual/verbal Active and meditative Sequential/integrated	Learning style index (CILS)
Learning style measurement tool	Introvert/extrovert Feeling/intuition Thinking/emotion Judgment/perception	MBT learning style scale (mbtd)
Perceptual learning style theory and cognitive learning style theory	Visual type. Auditory type. Kinesthetic type. Tactile. Group type. Personal type	Perceived learning style preference survey (plspq)

Although the knowledge and skills a student learns are limited by his own ability, the influence of the student's learning style on his academic performance cannot be ignored. Learning pattern matching based on the above features can further improve the matching accuracy.

4   Optimization of Teaching Mode Matching of News Communication

The teaching matching strategies are: methodological teaching matching strategy, content-based teaching matching strategy, mode teaching matching strategy and task-based teaching matching strategy. Teaching Matching Strategies for Different Learning Styles Based on Methodology and Content [29]. Method-based teaching matching strategy is designed from the perspective of learning tools, while content-based teaching strategy is designed from the perspective of learning resources [30]. At present, in the process of educational informatization, various means of informatization emerge in endlessly and develop faster and faster. Compared with the traditional methods, the designed optimization method of news communication teaching mode matching will be applied to the information technology means of education. Eight kinds of technical means, such as courseware, video, micro class, simulation software, mind map, news communication online teaching course, MOOCS, mobile platform and so on, are selected and compared according to the applicability of each stage of the course, as shown in Table 4:

Table 4. Intensity of information teaching matching

Information means	Teaching link/matching strength	Content matching
Courseware	Preview before class (in class) lecture in class (strong) review after class (weak) practice training (weak)	Lecturing content (offline learning cooperating with teacher's explanation) preview content (online cooperating with teaching resources) summative content (online cooperating with teaching resources) operational content (online cooperating with theoretical guidance)
Online course	Preview before class (strong) lecture in class (weak) review after class (strong) practice training (weak)	Lecturing content (offline teaching with teacher's guidance) preview content (independent completion of knowledge points) summary content (independent completion of teaching summary) operational content (online theoretical guidance)
MOOC	Preview before class (strong) lecture in class (strong) review after class (strong) practical training (weak)	Lecturing content (offline teaching with teacher's guidance) preview content (independent completion of knowledge points) summary content (independent completion of teaching summary) operational content (online theoretical guidance)
Mobile platform	Preview before class (strong) lecture in class (strong) review after class (strong) practical training (weak)	Teaching content (online interaction means) preview content (online interaction means) summative content (online interaction means) operational content (online interaction means)

Through carding the characteristics of curriculum, different types of curriculum have been formed, and the teaching methods of these courses are also different. According to the characteristics of information technology means, according to the different types of courses to complete the matching and classification of these means, China's university financial media laboratory compared with foreign universities, although there is still a certain gap, but has been groping forward. Based on this, a joint teaching innovation platform of news communication based on artificial intelligence is put forward, and a platform of innovation and practice communication is established. The platform is a practical teaching platform integrating production, learning and research, forming a relatively complete practical education and teaching system, and exploring the teaching matching mode of new media planning visual art design + news communication driven by artificial intelligence in practice. In combination with the theoretical logic and knowledge structure of traditional journalism and communication, integrate art design, visual communication, cross-media narrative and other practical teaching frameworks, and make full use of the cross-media practice creation module and audio-visual creation module to carry out the matching of news communication innovation teaching. The specific structure of the platform is shown in Fig. 1:

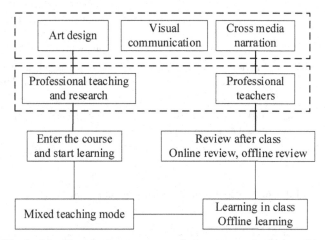

Fig. 1. Matching platform structure of news communication teaching

Based on the platform structure of Fig. 1, the online teaching of news communication specialty can improve the accuracy of teaching matching and guarantee the teaching quality. In the teaching process, the ability of media planning, for many major projects to create a unique cross-media products, enriched the content of the project, enhance the students' cross-media planning ability. Based on the characteristics of active learner and meditative learner, the teaching matching strategy designed in this study is divided into two dimensions: learning resources and learning tools, and different types of students are properly matched as shown in Tables 5, 6 and 7:

Based on the contents of Tables 5, 6 and 7, the online matching of teaching mode for students majoring in journalism and communication with different characteristics can be more accurate for teaching according to the learning characteristics of different students and improve the teaching quality.

Table 5. Online matching strategies for active/meditative students

	Active	Contemplative
Learning characteristics	Prefer to process information in an active experiment; like to study in a collective discussion way	Meditative learners like to think first and then do in the learning process, and tend to think independently before carrying out learning tasks, and summarize the acquired knowledge into their own problem-solving methods
Learn about sourcing	Providing practical learning resources	Provide sample activity results, activity task list and information retrieval tools
Learning tools	Task list of course discussion area, QQ group and Wechat group	Search engine, learning guide

Table 6. Perceptual/intuitive online matching strategies

	Perceptual	Intuitive
Learning characteristics	Perceptual learners like to learn facts, are willing to learn courses closely related to real life, have patience in dealing with detailed learning contents, and prefer to memorize declarative knowledge	Like theoretical knowledge: good at finding possibilities, willing to innovate, thinking jump; do not like repeated memory; good at learning new concepts, like abstract and mathematical reasoning knowledge
Learn about sourcing	Text video source	Cone map, concept map
Learning tools	Active task list web search engine	Web search engine, learning guide

Table 7. Sequential/integrated online matching strategies for students

	Sequential	Integrated
Learning characteristics	I am used to using linear steps to carry out learning. I like to learn conceptual knowledge step by step in the order of syllabus and content organization	Comprehensive learners have strong divergent thinking, their learning path has a certain jump, like to ball mill the relationship between things, through insight to learn and internalize new knowledge, this type of students are good at understanding the relationship between the knowledge points as a whole, and grasp the overall framework of the knowledge learned
Learn about sourcing	Color and font size chart and video resources for marking key concepts	Voice prompt audio resources
Learning tools	Simulation object, network search engine	QQ group, Wechat group, course discussion area

5 Conclusions

On-line matching of teaching means that teachers and students can adapt to each other, cooperate with each other and coordinate with each other in the process of teaching. Teaching matching should be carried out from three aspects: teaching content, teaching mode and teaching method, that is, the matching of teaching content and students' nearest development area, the matching of teachers' leading role and students' main role, the matching of teaching method and learning method. In addition, we should also pay attention to the matching of the information channel of the teaching combination surface and the matching of the teaching assistant equipment with the students' operation level.

References

1. Liu, Y.: Optimization of architectural art teaching model based on Naive Bayesian classification algorithm and fuzzy model. J. Intell. Fuzzy Syst. **36**(3), 1–12 (2020)
2. Myronchuk, O.Y., Shpylka, A.A., Zhuk, S.Y.: Two-stage method for joint estimation of information symbols and channel frequency response in OFDM communication systems. Radioelectron. Commun. Syst. **63**(8), 418–429 (2020)
3. Liu, Y., Zhou, S., Zhang, H.: Second screening use and its effect on political involvement in China: an integrated communication mediation model. Comput. Hum. Behav. **105**(Apr.), 106201.1–106201.8 (2020)
4. Kang, Z.: Transparent intersatellite optical wireless communication link with double sideband-suppressed carrier modulation and coherent homodyne detection. Appl. Opt. **57**(31), 9464–9470 (2018)

5. Pawar, P., Trivedi, A.: Interference-aware channel assignment and power allocation for device-to-device communication underlaying cellular network. AEU – Int. J. Electron. Commun. **112**(4), 152928 (2019)
6. Huang, Y., Sinclair, R.R., et al.: Does talking the talk matter? Effects of supervisor safety communication and safety climate on long-haul truckers' safety performance. Accid. Anal. Prev. **117**(Aug.), 357–367 (2018)
7. Ma, H., Teng, J., Hu, T., et al.: Co-communication protocol of underwater sensor networks with quantum and acoustic communication capabilities. Wirel. Pers. Commun. **113**(1), 337–347 (2020)
8. Fu, W., Liu, S., Srivastava, G.: Optimization of big data scheduling in social networks. Entropy **21**(9), 902 (2019)
9. Zuo, J., Yang, R., Luo, S., et al.: Training sequence design of TDS-OFDM signal in joint radar and communication system. Math. Probl. Eng. **2019**(3), 1–10 (2019)
10. Liu, S., Li, Z., Zhang, Y., et al.: Introduction of key problems in long-distance learning and training. Mob. Netw. Appl. **24**(1), 1–4 (2019)
11. Li, M.: Example-based learning using heuristic orthogonal matching pursuit teaching mechanism with auxiliary coefficient representation for the problem of de-fencing and its affiliated applications. Appl. Intell. **48**(9), 2884–2893 (2018)
12. Liu, S., Bai, W., Zeng, N., et al.: A fast fractal based compression for MRI images. IEEE Access **7**(99), 62412–62420 (2019)
13. Shi, Y., Yang, X.: A personalized matching system for management teaching resources based on collaborative filtering algorithm. Int. J. Emerg. Technol. Learn. (iJET) **15**(13), 207 (2020)
14. Martins, T.G.D.S., Martins, T.G.D.S., Schor, P.: Use of a versatile, inexpensive ophthalmoscopy teaching model in veterinary medical student education increases ophthalmoscopy proficiency. J. Vet. Med. Educ. **47**(3), 1–8 (2020)
15. Boothby, J., Gropelli, T., Succheralli, L.: An innovative teaching model using intraprofessional simulations. Nurs. Educ. Perspect. **40**(3), 1–7 (2019)
16. Huimin, F.: Research on the hybrid teaching model of ideological and political course based on MOOC platform. Guide Sci. Educ. **000**(010), 78–80 (2019)
17. Jing, Z.: The cultivation of ICC based on Chinese traditional culture—design and application of blended teaching model for language and culture course. J. Beijing Inst. Graph. Commun. **15**(12), 59–64 (2019)
18. Changsen, N., Nan, X.U.: Problems in wide area and intelligent cultivation: an overview of the study of journalism and communication in 2018. J. Chang'an Univ. (Soc. Sci. Ed.) **12**(12), 58–62 (2019)
19. Lihua, Z., Shicha, L.: "Sense of being" in synchronicity: interpersonal communication and everyday life mediated by live video streaming. Journal. Commun. Rev. **72**(4), 64–77 (2019)
20. Jesús, D., Matamoros, C.: Communication and public health challenges in Europe. Spec. Journal. Sources Media Cover. Times Anti-Vaccine Lobby **14**(12), 69–72 (2019)
21. Nkoala, S.B.: Student perceptions of multilingualism and the culture of communication in journalism studies in higher education. Read. Writ. **11**(1), 78–85 (2020)
22. King, T.: Practical R for mass communication and journalism. J. R. Stat. Soc. Ser. A **183**(12), 121–130 (2020)
23. Yan, Z.: Dilemma between "teaching" and "research" in journalism and communication. Media Observer **14**(23), 96–103 (2019)
24. He, J., Baxter, S., et al.: The practical implementation of artificial intelligence technologies in medicine. Nat. Med. **14**(12), 78–85 (2019)
25. Licato, J., Zhang, Z.: Correction to: evaluating representational systems in artificial intelligence. Artif. Intell. Rev. **52**(4), 11–18 (2019)
26. Topol, E.J., High-performance medicine: the convergence of human and artificial intelligence. Nat. Med. **25**(1), 44–56 (2019)

27. Roman, D., Bülow, K.J., Boor, P.: Multistain segmentation of renal histology: first steps toward artificial intelligence–augmented digital nephropathology. Kidney Int. **99**(1), 17–19 (2021)
28. Akhlaghi, Y.G., Aslansefat, K., Zhao, X., et al.: Hourly performance forecast of a dew point cooler using explainable artificial intelligence and evolutionary optimisations by 2050. Appl. Energy **281**(12), 85–94 (2021)
29. Ha, H.K.: Editorial for "deep-learning-based artificial intelligence for PI-RADS classification to assist multiparametric prostate MRI interpretation: a development study": editorial. J. Magn. Reson. Imaging **4**, 56–62 (2020)
30. Shimada, Y., Tanimoto, T., Nishimori, M., et al.: Incidental cerebral aneurysms detected by a computer-assisted detection system based on artificial intelligence: a case series. Medicine **99**(43), 215–221 (2020)

Motion Recognition System of Table Tennis Players Based on MEMS Sensor

Wei Tang$^{(\boxtimes)}$ and Chonggao Chen

Huali College Guangdong University of Technology, Guangzhou 511325, China

Abstract. In order to improve the accuracy of table tennis players' movement recognition, a movement recognition system based on MEMS sensor is designed. The hardware part chooses MEMS sensor chip as the core processing chip, and designs the connection circuit of sensor. In the software part, the overlapped motion recognition signals are filtered, the network camera with certain parameters is used to obtain the motion parameters, and the recognition process is constructed. Simulation results show that the system has a high recognition accuracy of up to 99.9%, which has a certain application prospect.

Keywords: MEMS sensor · Table tennis player · Movement recognition · Noise data

1 Introduction

With the further development of computer graphics, computer vision and motion capture technology, the application of advanced optical motion capture system has far exceeded the early design. It can capture more detailed motion with more tracking points and higher speed. However, due to its limited camera coverage, complex tracking scheme and high price, it is difficult for ordinary users and small companies to use. For this reason, there are mechanical capture system, electromagnetic capture system and acoustic capture system.

The goal of motion recognition is to enable the robot vision system to see and distinguish different human movements like the human eye and brain, and complete the marking of unknown action types. Nowadays, it has been widely applied to the field of motion recognition of athletes. For example, someone has designed a real-time collection system of motion attitude data through the combination of FPGA and ARM, and designed a Kalman filter to eliminate the random noise in the collected data signal so as to achieve the detection of related movements [2]. Also, someone has studied the Dynamic Time Warping (DTW) algorithm, based on the spatial characteristic data collected from the basic technical movements of excellent table tennis players and young table tennis players of the national team, constructed a basic ball movement model of table tennis players of the national team by taking the loop ball with the backhand pull as an example, so as to analyze and identify the ball strokes of young table tennis players [3]. In order to accurately identify the movements of table tennis players and lay

© ICST Institute for Computer Sciences, Social Informatics and Telecommunications Engineering 2021
Published by Springer Nature Switzerland AG 2021. All Rights Reserved
W. Fu et al. (Eds.): ICMTEL 2021, LNICST 388, pp. 128–141, 2021.
https://doi.org/10.1007/978-3-030-82565-2_11

a good foundation for the next training and analysis, this paper studies the movement recognition system of table tennis players based on MEMS sensor. In the hardware part, MEMS sensor chip is selected as the core processing chip, and the sensor connection circuit is designed. In the software part, the overlapped motion recognition signals are filtered, and the motion parameters are obtained by using the network camera with certain parameters, and the recognition process is constructed, hoping to improve the table tennis players' action recognition level, and improve the table tennis players' action skills and efficiency.

2 Hardware Design of Athlete Movement Recognition System

2.1 Select MEMS Sensor Chip

The selection of the sensor chip determines the sampling rate of the high-speed sampling system. On the basis of satisfying the sampling rate of the system, the vertical resolution of the AD chip is also a parameter to be carefully considered, but the resolution is not directly proportional to the accuracy, and the high-resolution AD chip cannot provide high-precision sampling [4–6]. Because the sampling rate of this system reaches about ten MHz to thirty MHz, after comprehensive consideration, it is decided to adopt a AD9280 high-speed ADC chip provided by ADI Company. Its internal schematic diagram is shown in Fig. 1:

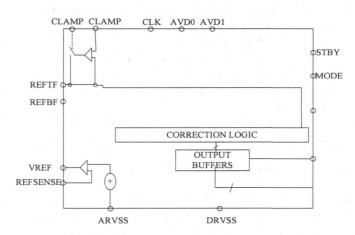

Fig. 1. Inner structure of sensor chip

The chip has a maximum sampling rate of 32 MSPS to support multiple sampling requirements, uses a vertical resolution of 8 bits, and combines bio-nano sensors. Single power supply is used to ensure low power consumption. Using its internal "embedded clamp" function, the integrated reference power supply circuit and sample and hold circuit. The error of differential nonlinearity (DNL) is controlled at 0.2 LSB, the IF subsampling is kept at 13 SMHZ, the reference voltage in the adjustable chip is used and the output mode of the three-state gate is adopted.

FPGA is a typical representative of programmable devices, which is based on PAL, GAL, CPLD and other programmable devices. Its level interface is quite rich, and it is easy to implement different kinds of protocols. In this system, the FPGA is required to complete the related logic control circuit functions, and at the same time to complete the task of storing a large number of collected data (the system intends to use SDRAM for data storage). Therefore, the choice of FPGA chip needs to include rich interface and logic resources, and can achieve the design requirements of SDRAM controller [7–9]. Therefore, after comprehensive consideration, it has been decided to adopt the EP4CE6F17C8 chip of Altera's Cyclone IV series as follows:

(1) It has as many as 6272 logical components/units, 392 LAB (Logic Macro Cell, programmable logical array)/CLB (Configurable Logic Block, configure logical modules), has very rich connection resources, and it runs very fast, up to 260 MHz.
(2) It is embedded with RAM up to 276480 bits, the main component of which is the M4K block of 4 KBit, and each block is very fast, up to 250 MHz. And configuration is flexible, each M4K module can be configured for a variety of memory, such as single-port or dual-port RAM, ROM and FIFO and so on.
(3) It has as many as 15 18 * 18 bit hardware multipliers built into it, runs at speeds up to several hundred MHz, and has selectable I/O registers.
(4) Two phase-locked loops (PLL) and 10 global clock networks shall be connected to facilitate the application and management of clock control. Provides a number of dedicated clock input pins.
(5) Capable of supporting multilevel single-ended I/O standards: 1.5 V, 1.8 V, 2.5 V and 3.3 V. High speed ports supporting various I/O standards, and providing up to 200 MHz DDR2 SDRAM interface, as well as 167 MHz QDRII SRAM and DDR SDRAM, this design uses these ports of FPGA to design SDRAM controller.

The system adopts HY57V2562GTR SDRAM chip, whose capacity is 256 Mbit, which can meet the requirements of the system, and its characteristics are: 256 Mbit (16M * 16 bit) storage capacity, 16blt bus. 8192 refresh cycle/64 ms. Power supply voltage, VDD = 3.3 V, VDDQ = 3.3 V. The 4M bit * 4banks* 16 I/O SDRAM functional module diagram is shown in Fig. 2:

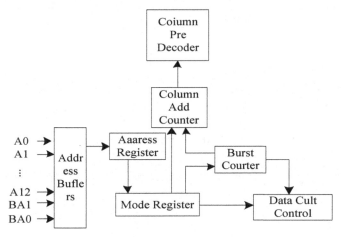

Fig. 2. Functional module diagram

As shown in Fig. 2, the hardware connection circuit is designed according to the functional module diagram shown in the diagram.

2.2 Design Hardware Connection Circuit

Under the control of the hardware card, there are many kinds of redundant resource outputs for the information of table tennis players, so when designing the hardware connection circuit, an output circuit is designed to realize the fault-tolerant function of hardware structure to data [10–12]. Set the voltage of the whole circuit to be between 3.3 V and 8 V. Set the resistance with low impedance and 10 Ω on the branch with few hardware components. Output a driving load at the same time. The output circuit is shown in Fig. 3.

Under the control of the output circuit structure shown in Fig. 3, the control processor in the control card is connected with pin 6, and the movement information of the table tennis player enters into the processing unit of the core through the pin 2. After being processed by the hardware core, the movement information is output through the pin 5. Control core processing board through the FGPA bus connection memory storage circuit, in the memory with the function of control, realize the external expansion of hardware circuit [13–15]. On the other side of the line bus, asynchronous serial interface is adopted, and the CPU processing board and the memory circuit are rationally arranged. Combined with RS422 standard four-wire system to regulate the movement data of athletes. Using the function of UART module integrated by processor and bridge chip, the level conversion form in circuit is set.

The hardware circuit of the system adopts an integral power module for power supply. Under the control of the storage circuit and the output circuit, the power supply demand of the hardware is divided into two parts. The first part supplies power to the integral hardware circuit, and the second part supplies power to the chip processor in the CPU board. A voltage converter is placed on the connecting line between the integral power supply and the hardware chip. In order to satisfy the stability between the hardware

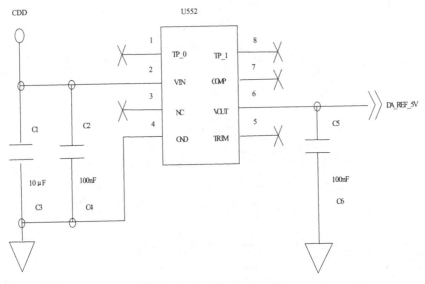

Fig. 3. Output circuit structure

components and the circuit, the voltage regulator is selected as the three-terminal voltage regulator of model AM S1084-3.3V [16–18].

3   Software Design of Athlete Movement Recognition System

3.1   Processing Overlapping Action Recognition Signals

The signals emitted by the single- chip microcomputer are generally in the form of a single channel. It is assumed that there are six commonly used digital modulation signals and noises in the time-frequency overlapping signals received by the single- chip microcomputer. The mathematical expressions are as follows:

$$r(t) = \sum_{i=1}^{6} s(t) + n(t) \tag{1}$$

Among them, $n(t)$ means Gaussian white noise, $s(t)$ means singlechip signal. The above generated overlapping signals are processed by sparse filtering with $n(t)$ numerically equal signals as overlapping signals, and the independent expression of overlapping signals can be recorded as shown in Fig. 2:

$$
\begin{cases}
s(t)_1 = \sum_k \sqrt{E} a_k P(t - kT_e) \\
s(t)_2 = \sum_k \sqrt{E}(a_k + jb_1)P(t - kT_e) \\
s(t)_3 = \sum_k \sqrt{E}P(t - kT_e)f_0 \\
s(t)_4 = \sum_k \sqrt{E}P(t - kT_e)
\end{cases}
\tag{2}
$$

In formula (2), a_k represents the code element sequence, E signal energy, f_0 represents the initial phase of the carrier, T_e represents the code element width, and $P(t)$ represents the raised cosine pulse shaping function. According to the above sparse signal energy cumulants, the higher-order cyclic cumulants of the sum of several independent cyclostationary signals are equal to the sum of the higher-order cyclic cumulants of several signals. Assuming that the overlapping signals are independent, we can obtain:

$$
C^a_{k,r}(\tau_1, \tau_1, ..., \tau_{k-1}) = \sum_{i=1}^{M} C^a_s + C^a_N
\tag{3}
$$

In formula (3), a denotes the cyclic frequency of the signal of the SCM, k denotes the cyclic cumulant, τ denotes the sparse filter parameter, and thus, if the cyclic frequency of several signals is known to be unequal and irreducible [19–21], the cyclic cumulant of several signals can be obtained respectively by calculating the cyclic cumulant of the received signals at different cyclic frequencies. Therefore, the feature parameters are set to highlight the difference of overlapping signal recognition. If the control delay parameter is 0, the first-order cyclic cumulant expression can be expressed as follows (4):

$$
C^a_{r,10} = \frac{\sqrt{E}}{T_e} \int_{-\infty}^{\infty} P(t)dt
\tag{4}
$$

The characteristic parameters of the signals BPSK, QPSK, 8PSK and 16QAM are obtained by integrating the above overlapped signal characteristics using the formula of formula (4) first order cyclic cumulants as the calculation formula of the characteristic parameters. From the above analysis, it can be seen that only the first-order cyclic cumulants of 2FSK signals in the overlapped signals have values at the cyclic frequency, and the first-order cyclic cumulants of other signals are zero [22–25]. Therefore, the first order cyclic cumulants are used as the characteristic parameters to identify the 2FSK signals and the BPSK, QPSK, 8PSK and 16QAM signals. The feature is highlighted as a discrete spectral line on the frequency axis, and the 2FSK signal is identified by detecting the discrete spectral line. The signal selectivity of the cyclic cumulants results in the recognition process shown in Fig. 4:

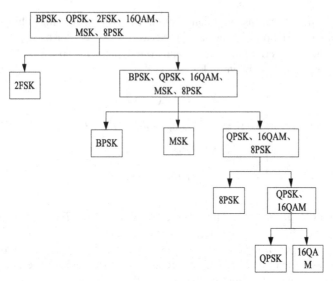

Fig. 4. Overlapping signal screening process

In the screening process shown in Fig. 4, in the background of Gaussian noise, the first order cyclic cumulant is used to eliminate the overlapping cumulant generated within the signal. After the overlapping signal is processed by sparse filtering, a software with recognition function is designed to finally complete the design of the motion recognition system.

3.2 Implementation of Software Action Recognition

In the application of motion recognition in real scene, it is necessary to use visual sensors to collect visual information. In view of the development trend of simple equipment and low cost in robot vision in the future [26–28], the TMV T828 (MINI) network camera, which is widely used at present, is selected to collect the imaging information of the actual scene, and its parameters are: USB2.0 interface, CMOS photosensitivity, and image imaging resolution 2048 × 1536. Based on the T828 (MINI) webcam, the application software system firstly utilizes the VideoCapture class in the OpenCV library as the video capture module to obtain the video equipment [29–31], and initializes the relevant parameters and sets the video object. The implementation process can be expressed as follows:

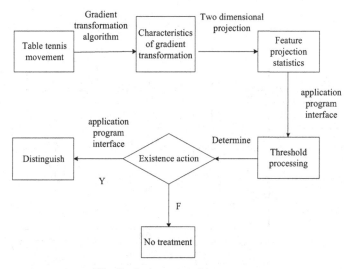

Fig. 5. Action recognition process

Under the realization flow shown in Fig. 5, the design of motion recognition system is finally realized.

4 Simulation Experiment

4.1 Construction of Development Environment

According to the non- functional requirements of the overall design of the identification system, the system uses ARM9 as the processor and reasonable peripheral hardware equipment, chooses Wince as the operating system of energy consumption acquisition software, and describes the structure of the action data acquisition system by modules according to the process.

Leads to 4 TTL serial port, 10 PIN JTAG interface and so on. GPRS interface module is used to transfer data to the server, RS485 and RS232 interface is used to collect data, NANDFLSAH is used to store energy consumption data, JTAG interface is used to debug hardware devices and bootloader burning. To take full advantage of the 2440's support for SD card startup, the produced superboot and object files are placed into the SD card for easier and faster installation or operation of various embedded systems (Windows CE 6/Linux, etc.). The S3C2440 itself has a total of 4 serial ports UARTO, 1, 2, 3, of which UARTO and 1 are a five-wire functional serial port and the other two are three-wire serial ports. All of these are greatly convenient for the use of embedded software system development. System hardware devices are shown in Fig. 6:

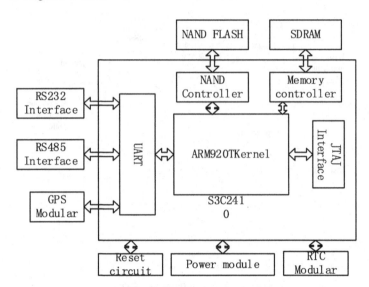

Fig. 6. Test environment

The data acquisition system takes S3C2410A as the processor, and communicates with the instrument through RS-485, RS-232 interface. When collecting RS-232 and RS-485 at the same time, the converter should be used. The converter can convert the single-ended RS-232 signal to the balanced differential RS-485 signal. The data is stored in NAND FLASH after the energy consumption equipment is collected, and finally the data is uploaded to the data center through the Ethernet interface. The real-time clock battery of the collector provides precise time for the equipment, and ensures the accuracy of the acquisition time (the real-time clock chip uses the crystal oscillator with high precision as the clock source). Insert the SD card into the card seat and use the SD card to flush the Wince operating system. Connect the LCD interface to the display screen, connect the 5 V power supply, and open the switch to start the operating system.

RS485 to TTL module metering equipment connected to the acquisition equipment, to achieve remote data communication with the measuring device. The controller communicates with the external measuring device through TTL serial port, sends instructions to the external measuring device, sets the relevant parameters of the external measuring device and collects the relevant measuring data. The serial port of TTL level is connected with the external measuring device through RS485/TTL converter to realize the mutual conversion of the standard serial interface. The RS485/TTL converter is compatible with the RS-232, RS-485 standard and can convert a single-ended RS-232 signal into a balanced differential RS-485 signal and transmit the collected data to the upper computer through the Ethernet interface. Set the pin description for the serial port, as shown in Table 1:

Table 1. Pin interface description

Pin	Definition	Explain			
		JTT-A-TTL	JTT-A-USB	JTT-A-232	JTT-A-485
1	GND	URAT input, TTL level	D−	Ground	A
2	RX/B/D−			Rx, 232 level	
3	TX/A/D+	URAT output, TTL level	D+	Tx, 232 level	B
4	VCC			DC5-7V	

After setting the pins, debug the serial port state and select the "Device Application" template. Then click the VS2008 menu tool "Connect to Device" and press F5 to start debugging. Finally, choose "Windows CE Devices" to start deployment, to this system after the completion of the hardware and software debug development environment setup. Then experiments are carried out by using the recognition system in document [2], document [3] and the recognition system designed in this paper to compare the performance of the three data acquisition systems.

4.2   Analysis of Experimental Results

Based on the above experimental preparation, 30 test users on the iPad are used as the load users of the identification system, and each five users are used as a test group to measure the response time results of the three action recognition systems under different number of user loads. The response time results are shown in Fig. 7:

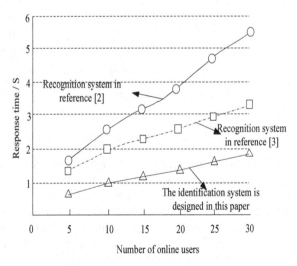

Fig. 7. Three identification system response times

The result of response time shown in Fig. 7 shows that the response time of the three identification systems gradually increases as the number of users accessing the action recognition system increases. When the number of online users is 30, the identification system in Document [2] has the longest response time and the final response time is about 5.5 s, and the identification system in Document [3] has the shortest response time. Under the control of the same number of online users, the final response time is about 3.3 s, while the identification system designed in this paper has the smallest response time and the value of response time is about 1.9 s. Compared with the above two identification systems, the final response time of the identification system designed in this paper is the shortest.

Keep the above experimental environment unchanged, select 10 of the 30 iPads used for the test, control the iPad to receive 50 identification resource data, when the visual image in the iPad is normal, test the number of packet loss, calculate and summarize the packet loss rate results. The packet loss rate results of the three identification systems are shown in Table 2:

Table 2. Results of packet loss rate of three identification systems

Test iPad serial number	Packet loss rate/%		
	Document [2] identification system	Document [3] identification system	Design system
1	0.78	0.50	0.15
2	0.75	0.47	0.19
3	0.74	0.45	0.18
4	0.74	0.47	0.23
5	0.73	0.49	0.17
6	0.80	0.45	0.25
7	0.79	0.48	0.24
8	0.78	0.49	0.18
9	0.77	0.46	0.21
10	0.78	0.50	0.21

Control three athletes' action recognition systems to recognize the same athletes' movements, count and calculate the packet loss rate. From the data in Table 2, we can see that the data of packet loss rate of the athletes' action recognition system used in Document [2] is the highest, the data of packet loss rate produced by each iPad is about 0.76%, the data of packet loss rate produced by the athletes' action recognition system used in Document [3] is less, the average packet loss rate is about 0.47%, and the data of packet loss rate produced by the recognition system designed in this paper is about 0.20. Compared with the above two resource recognition systems, the data of packet loss rate produced by the resource recognition system designed in this paper is the smallest, and the movements received by athletes are more complete in the actual process of movement recognition.

Assuming that the categories of athlete movements to be identified in the three recognition systems are Categories 1, 2, 3, 4, 5 and 6, and 50 sets of movement information are prepared for each movement information type, if the identified identifiers are the same as the identifiers in the movement information, it is a successful recognition process. Under the control of the three movement recognition systems, the accuracy rates of movement recognition for different categories of athletes are calculated and counted as shown in Table 3:

Table 3. Accuracy results of three recognition systems

Categories of information	Accuracy of action recognition/%		
	Document [2] identification system	Document [3] identification system	Design system
Category 1	79.4	88.6	96.2
Category 2	76.6	89.1	99.9
Category 3	77.7	85.2	96.6
Category 4	76.1	85.6	98.6
Category 5	79.5	87.3	98.7
Category 6	78.2	89.7	96.6
Mean value	77.91	87.58	97.76

As can be seen from Table 3, the three recognition systems show different recognition accuracy for the same number and types of athletes, and the average accuracy of the above table can be seen, the recognition accuracy of the recognition system in [2] literature is about 77.91%, and the recognition accuracy is low. When the recognition system in document [3] is used in practice, the final recognition accuracy is about 87.58%, and the accuracy is high. The final recognition accuracy of the system is about 97.76%. Compared with the above two systems, the accuracy of the system is the largest and the recognition is the most accurate.

5 Concluding Remarks

Motion recognition is an important guarantee for the friendly interaction between robot and AI, and it is also a research hotspot in robot vision, AI and robot technology. In this paper, the problem of low accuracy in current motion recognition is analyzed, and a motion recognition system based on MEMS sensor is designed to recognize the motion of table tennis players accurately. The simulation results show that the shortest recognition response time of the system is about 1.9 s, the packet loss rate is about 0.20, and the recognition accuracy is up to 97.76%. However, due to time constraints, the system still has some shortcomings, which will be the focus of the next step.

References

1. Liu, S., Sun, G., Fu, W.: e-Learning, e-Education, and Online Training. Springer, Cham (2020). https://doi.org/10.1007/978-3-030-63955-6
2. Chen, J., Chen, H., Wang, J., et al.: Design of data acquisition and trajectory recognition system based on MEMS sensor. Chin. J. Electron Devices **42**(02), 463–468 (2019)
3. Feng, Z., Xiao, Y., Cao, Z., et al.: Rationality evaluation of young table tennis players' striking action based on DTW: taking the backhand topspin loop for example. J. Shanghai Univ. Sport **44**(06), 76–84 (2020)
4. Liu, S., Bai, W., Zeng, N., et al.: A fast fractal based compression for MRI images. IEEE Access **7**, 62412–62420 (2019)
5. Liu, S., Li, Z., Zhang, Y., et al.: Introduction of key problems in long-distance learning and training. Mob. Netw. Appl. **24**(1), 1–4 (2019)
6. Xie, G., Liu, Y., Lu, Y., et al.: Human behavior recognition based on time-domain features of MEMS inertial sensors. Piezoelectr. Acoustooptics **41**(02), 221–224 (2019)
7. Jun, J., Wang, X., Xu, Y., et al.: Study on a MEMS sensor with embedded state machines and its application in body position detecting. Chin. High Technol. Lett. **28**(03), 244–250 (2018)
8. Zhang, M., Huang, Y., Gao, Q., et al.: Brain plasticity of table tennis athletes based on dynamic amplitude of low-frequency fluctuation method. J. Shanghai Univ. Sport **44**(06), 62–69 (2020)
9. Li, B., Jin, P., Wu, Z., et al.: Design of ping-pong recognition based on S_Kohonen neural network. J. Huazhong Univ. Sci. Technol. (Nat. Sci. Ed.) **48**(03), 52–56 (2020)
10. Zhao, Y., Lan, Y., Qu, X.: Design of personnel positioning system in coal mine underground based on MEMS sensor. Ind. Mine Autom. **44**(08), 87–91 (2018)
11. Xie, G., Huang, X., Li, Y., et al.: Review of research on step detection algorithm with MEMS-based acceleration sensor. Appl. Res. Comput. **35**(12), 3526–3532 (2018)
12. Cui, J., Cao, H., Zhu, J., et al.: Human gait monitoring system based on MEMS tilt sensors and thin film pressure sensors. China Meas. Test. Technol. **44**(08), 70–75 (2018)
13. Yang, Y., Zhang, L., Qi, Y., et al.: Intravascular ultrasound image recognition based on residual network. Comput. Simul. **37**(04), 269–273 (2020)
14. Cem, D., O'Connor, N.E.: Temporal segmentation and recognition of team activities in sports. Mach. Vis. Appl. **29**(5), 891–913 (2018)
15. Li, Y.M., Li, B., Wang, X.X., et al.: Application of energy cost in evaluating energy expenditure in multi-ball practice with table tennis players. Zhongguo ying yong sheng li xue za zhi = Zhongguo yingyong shenglixue zazhi = Chin. J. Appl. Physiol. **35**(4), 331–335 (2019)
16. Zemková, E., Muyor, J.M., Jeleň, M.: Association of trunk rotational velocity with spine mobility and curvatures in para table tennis players. Int. J. Sports Med. **39**(14), 1055–1062 (2018)
17. Ukhov, I., Bjurgert, J., Auer, M., et al.: Online problem gambling: a comparison of casino players and sports bettors via predictive modeling using behavioral tracking data. J. Gambl. Stud. 1–21 (2020)
18. Yüksel, M.F., Sevindi, T.: Examination of performance levels of wheelchair basketball players playing in different leagues. Sports **6**(1), 18 (2018)
19. Zhou, Y., Chen, C.T., Muggleton, N.G.: The effects of visual training on sports skill in volleyball players - ScienceDirect. Progr. Brain Res. **253**, 201–227 (2020)
20. Heo, G., Ha, J.E.: Analysis of table tennis swing using action recognition. J. Inst. Control **21**(1), 40–45 (2015)
21. Xu, B., Ye, H., Zheng, Y., et al.: Dense dilated network for video action recognition. IEEE Trans. Image Process. **28**(10), 4941–4953 (2019)
22. Hu, G., Cui, B., Yu, S.: Joint learning in the spatio-temporal and frequency domains for skeleton-based action recognition. IEEE Trans. Multimedia **22**(9), 2207–2220 (2020)

23. Ryu, J.H., Seo, J.O., Jebelli, H., et al.: Automated action recognition using an accelerometer-embedded wristband-type activity tracker. J. Constr. Eng. Manag. **145**(1), 04018114.1–04018114.14 (2019)
24. Sun, Y.-H., Zhou, J.-Q., Zhang, X.-F.: Human motion pattern recognition based on acceleration sensor. Comput. Syst. Appl. **29**(06), 196–203 (2020)
25. Liu, D., Ji, Y., Ye, M., et al.: An improved attention-based spatiotemporal-stream model for action recognition in videos. IEEE Access (99), 1 (2020)
26. Chen, H., Liu, W., et al.: Fast retinomorphic event-driven representations for video gameplay and action recognition. IEEE Trans. Comput. Imaging **6**, 276–290 (2019)
27. Li, B., Jin, P., Wu, Z.: Design of ping-pong recognition based on S_Kohonen neural network. J. Huazhong Univ. Sci. Technol. (Nat. Sci.) 2020(3), 52–56 (2020)
28. Sun, X.: Research of human motion recognition based on long short-term memory. Wuxian Hulian Keji **164**(16), 23–24+41 (2019)
29. Li, X., Yang, J., Yang, J., et al.: Action recognition algorithm based on depth motion maps and regularized representation. J. Electron. Meas. Instrum. **32**(01), 119–128 (2018)
30. Sun, Y.-H., Zhou, J.-Q., Zhang, X.-F.: Human motion pattern recognition based on acceleration sensor. Comput. Syst. Appl. **29**(06), 196–203 (2020)
31. Liu, T., Li, Y., Liang, Z.: Human action recognition based on multi-perspective depth motion maps. J. Image Graph. **24**(03), 80–89 (2019)

Open Sharing of Digital Education Training Resources Based on Machine Learning

Jichao Yan[✉] and Jingya Zheng

Zhengzhou Technical College, Zhengzhou 450121, China

Abstract. In order to solve the problem of poor security caused by data explosion in the traditional open sharing method of digital education training resources, this paper proposes a machine learning based open sharing method. Based on the national general control protocol standard, a control protocol of education and training resource sharing service based on GCCP gateway is constructed. With the support of the control protocol, support vector machine is designed by using machine learning ability, support vector machine is used to process resource data, and resource classification is realized. With the support of cloud computing mode, resource is open and shared. Experimental results show that the proposed open sharing method based on machine learning has short response time and low memory leak probability, and the security of the method is improved.

Keywords: Machine learning · Digitization · Education practice · Resource sharing

1 Introduction

Entering the 21st century, China's higher education has achieved unprecedented rapid development, entering a new era of transformation from elite education to popular education [1]. Colleges and universities have increasingly become the gathering center of a large number of talents and resources in the region, and become the main driving force and source of regional rapid and coordinated development. However, in the great development of higher education, there is a serious shortage of educational resources, especially high-quality ones [2]. The contradiction between people's demand for educational resources and insufficient supply of educational resources stands out. In this context, to promote the sharing of educational resources has become a strategic choice for deepening the sustainable development of higher education. In recent years, great achievements have been made in the construction of higher education resources sharing, but due to many reasons such as technology, demand, funds, management and system, the effect of digital education resources sharing among colleges and universities is not good, and there is still a big gap between the practical results of sharing and people's original ideas, which needs to be improved day by day [3].

The development and progress of modern network and computer technology provide the means to realize the sharing of higher education resources. In recent years, cloud

W. Fu et al. (Eds.): ICMTEL 2021, LNICST 388, pp. 142–151, 2021.
https://doi.org/10.1007/978-3-030-82565-2_12

computing is becoming more and more familiar with the people, is the current hot topic, has received extensive attention [4]. Cloud computing is regarded as the next revolution in science and technology. It is not only the development of technology, but also represents a service concept and service model. It will fundamentally change the way we work and the business model. Cloud computing technology has been initially applied in some fields and industries with its powerful functions. The popularity of network technology in various fields provides a convenient way for the sharing and exchange of information and knowledge. The Internet has become a public communication platform, in which network-based learning content can be provided by almost any media [4]. The ubiquitous 4×4 framework is the traditional teaching activity It is an important embodiment of the movement. As an extension of traditional classroom teaching, modern distance network education has developed rapidly. Online vocational skills education, distance education and online classroom have gradually become the mainstream of education at home and abroad [6, 7]. In this case, the opening and sharing of digital education and training resources is very urgent.

Digital network sharing education, as an important material means to solve the problem of educational equity and balance, is an important basis for building a learning society and realizing lifelong vocational skills education. At present, the integration development between education training and computer is still not mature enough, and there is a great room for progress. At present, the common sharing methods are the Web-based resource sharing method and the SSM -based framework sharing method [8]. These two methods need longer response time when they perform shared tasks in the face of today's data explosion. Memory leaks are easy to occur and the security needs to be further improved. Therefore, an open sharing method of digital education training resources based on machine learning is proposed to solve the problems mentioned above. It is main significance is as follows: using machine learning ability to design support vector machine, using support vector machine to process resource data, to achieve resource classification. Under the support of cloud computing mode, resources are open and shared. Its main contribution lies in the optimization of response time and memory leakage probability, which improves the security of the method.

2 Design of Open Sharing Method of Digital Education Training Resources Based on Machine Learning

2.1 Building Training Resource Sharing and Collaborative Service Control Protocol

The control protocol of digital education and training resource sharing and collaborative service is realized by common control equipment to realize intelligent interconnection, resource sharing and collaborative service of digital education and training resource [9].

According to the national standard -GB/T 29265, the general control protocol is a kind of protocol which is suitable for intelligent interconnection, resource sharing and collaborative service among shared resources. The GCCP protocol hierarchy is shown in Fig. 1.

GCCP processing unit has the general control function of sharing education and training resources, and it also handles the transmission of shared application data in the network. Point-to-point, point-to-multipoint transmission of shared data is accomplished by the physical, data link, and network layers of the GCCP protocol layer [10]. The network protocol conforming to the national standard carries the cooperation service among physical layer, data link layer and network layer of education and training resource sharing. In the general control GCCP network of digital education and training resource sharing, all protocols involved in realizing the interaction are shown in Fig. 1, which is completed by device A and device B.

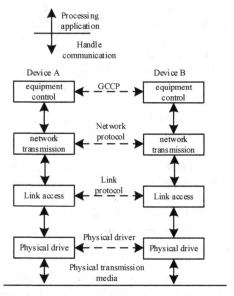

Fig. 1. Protocols for GCCP interaction design

The GCCP network is composed of general equipments, controllers, configurators, gateways and other core components. Among them, the general equipment is generally the general control equipment of the network sharing resource platform; the controller is the equipment in the sharing resource platform that operates and controls the general network equipment, such as the centralized controller and the intelligent control terminal; the configurator is mainly responsible for completing the configuration of other equipment in the sharing resource platform network, which assigns the network ID and device ID to other equipment; the gateway is mainly responsible for connecting two different networks, realizing the intelligent interconnection, resource sharing and collaborative service of the equipment in different networks; and the core component can connect the IGRS IP main network and the GCCP network, or connect the two GCCP shared networks. In a shared resource platform network, all devices are functionally configured with a single configurator, and each device in the network is configured with a separate network ID and device ID by the configurator. The network ID is composed of two octets, which are used to distinguish the different network resources of the shared resource platform. It is managed by the core component- configurator. All devices have the same network ID. The device ID consists of two octets to distinguish between different network devices. Its working ID is assigned by the component- configurator, and all devices in the same network environment have different device IDs. The usage assignments for the network ID and device ID are shown in Table 1.

Table 1. Distribution of ID usage

Network ID	Purpose	Device ID	Purpose
0x0000	Unknown network ID, used before the configurator assigns the network ID, or for other purposes	0x0000	Unknown network ID, used before the configurator assigns the network ID, or for other purposes
0x001–0xFEFF	Network ID	0x0001–0x0EFF	General device ID, assigned to general equipment
0 xFF00–0xFFFF	Retain	0 x0F00–0x0FFF	Controller ID, assigned to the controller for use

The file request device issues a "file transfer request" for the transfer of resource files in the shared resource platform, and the device holding the shared resource realizes the transfer of shared file data. The request device for sharing file data can request the holding device to transfer the file from any point. During the file transfer, it can start, pause or stop the file transfer according to the actual situation. The concrete work process by the file request device through the file total length and already obtained the file data quantity to judge whether the file transfers completes. As shown in Fig. 2, the specific transfer of a file's data is shown.

In the process of file transfer, the data attribute is mainly used to describe the transfer device, device status, device list, user-defined and other files.

2.2   Shared Information Classification Based on Machine Learning

Machine learning is a kind of learning method in which a machine can avoid contacting its internal complex logic and relationship by memorizing learning data. Through this learning method, a classifier, i.e. a support vector machine, can process the shared information, classify it reasonably, and transmit it in segments according to the classification results, so as to ensure the efficiency and security of transmission. Assuming that the resource sample has only two classes A and B, there is a linear function:

$$f(x) = \omega x + b \tag{1}$$

If the threshold value is 0, the samples a and B can be separated. When $f(x) > 0$ the threshold value is set as A, when $f(x) < 0$ the category is determined as B, then $f(x)$ it belongs to the discrimination function of the sample. In order to judge whether a

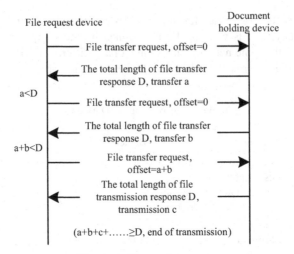

Fig. 2. A file transfer process

linear function is good or bad, the concept of classification interval is introduced. The so-called classification interval is the geometric distance between sample classes. Then, the best classification effect is to maximize the classification interval.

To make the classification more accurate, consider maximizing the distance from the hyperplane to the nearest point. The greater the distance, the less prone the classification is to error. Suppose you have found a hyperplane T_0 whose distance from the sample A is greater than that from the sample B. Thus the point closest to the hyperplane is the point of the sample B. Obviously, this distance is not the largest. The largest case is that the distance L_x from the hyperplane T_0 to the nearest point on b the distance L_y from the hyperplane T_0. The sample closest to the hyperplane is x, and the sample closest to the sample B. If the hyperplane is optimal, the condition must be satisfied: the distance from x should be equal to the distance from y. In order to understand the distance between classes more vividly, two new sums of hyperplanes T_1 and T_2 parallel to hyperplanes T_0. T_0 are introduced to cut the samples X and Y of the nearest two samples. Then the interval between T_1 and T_2 is called the interval between the sample classes, that is, the classification interval. The question then becomes how to maximize the distance between the sums T_1 and T_2.

Let's say that the vector x_i of a sample y_i is labeled minus 1 and plus 1, and the sample class y_i is labeled minus 1 or plus 1 in a binary linear space. Then the sample can be recorded as:

$$K_i(x_i, y_i) \tag{2}$$

For hyperplanes, the distance from this sample to the hyperplane is defined as:

$$\eta_i = y_i(\omega x_i + b) \tag{3}$$

The classification interval is maximized when the η_i calculated value is maximum. At this point the classification is complete.

2.3 Achieve Resource Open Cloud Sharing

According to the classified data, the cloud sharing mode is used to realize the open sharing of resources. Due to the size of the network and resource constraints needed, cloud computing is mainly promoted and implemented by several large companies, and most of it is used for commercial purposes, and only a few education projects are still in place. Therefore, if we directly adopt the cloud computing solution provided by the existing service providers, although the short-term cost is low and the implementation is simple, the migration of the original educational resources and the processing of the original computing capacity of the colleges and universities will become a major problem, which will cause a huge waste of resources. If these issues are not considered, reinvent the wheel to invest in cloud computing sharing systems, the initial construction costs are very expensive, the average small and medium -sized institutions can not afford. In this way, the advantages of cloud computing in the field of education can not be reflected, it is difficult to promote the application. Based on the comprehensive analysis, it is a feasible choice to deploy the cloud after reforming the existing education network. The current feasible measures are to transform the original campus network architecture, optimize and upgrade the cloud architecture, and build a cloud environment.

Concretely, it is to transform the B/S or C/S model into cloud, encapsulate or transform the existing education and training resources in a service-oriented way, and centralize the scattered servers and computing resources. Then use the virtualization technology to form the digital educational resources pool on the Internet. Provide different terminal interface, originally only through the fat client access to the Internet resources in the cloud computing environment can access resources through a variety of thin client.

In order to realize the sharing of educational practical training resources, we should not only use our own resources, but also broaden our view from the field of education to the whole society. With the enhancement of people's lifelong learning consciousness, the demand for digital educational resources is also increasing. The original distance network education is based on academic education, distance education system through learning and access to resources. However, as a student finishes a course, he can no longer obtain resources from the distance education system for the course, which is detrimental to autonomous learning and lifelong learning.

By sharing the cloud computing model, social students can also easily access learning resources through simple verification. Since the Digital Education Resources Cloud is jointly constructed by all the educators and shared by their contributions, some of the resources provided by the community students can be used for free and for a fee. Billing modules can be added to cloud application deployments. In this way, social learners can also use digital educational resources on demand. So the school resources as a part of the whole social resources, through further improving the openness to society this one way to improve the efficiency of running schools. To benefit more people.

3 Experimental Study on Open Sharing Method of Digital Education Training Resources Based on Machine Learning

In order to verify and evaluate the proposed open sharing method of digital education training resources, the experimental study will extract data from two open, real and widely used datasets. The dataset used in the experiment was extracted through the Java-based PcapParser program, and the sharing method was developed on the basis of the open-source Java machine learning tool Weka 3.8. The experiment was performed on an Intel Core i5-3470 3.20 GHz 8 GB Windows system (64-bit).

3.1 Experimental Data Set

The two open, real and widely used datasets used in the experiment are WITS and MAWI. The details of the two datasets are as follows:

The WITS dataset is the WAND Research Group of the Department of Computer Science at the University of Waikato, which collects and collects Internet resource data logs in New Zealand using the WITS project. The data of Waikato VIII is captured from the border network of Waikato University by the software of DAG3 card and WDCap, and is anonymously processed and truncated by the software of Crypto-Pan. A detailed description of the selected traffic dataset is shown in Table 2.

Table 2. WITS information resources dataset details

Interception date	Duration/h	Number of messages/million	Total/MB	Capture size/MB
0122	24	331	198107	25631
0241	12	135	80553	10400
0314	24	360	219693	27943
0452	24	266	163200	20511
0546	24	266	162967	20354
0635	12	120	76741	9243

MAWI traffic dataset is the network traffic dataset that the MAWI working group captures and collates from WIDE network. The MAWI project team persists in capturing network traffic from WIDE network for a certain time every day. The IP addresses of the traffic in the dataset are anonymously processed, and each packet contains only 50 bytes of application-layer payload. The details of the data intercepted in the experiment are shown in Table 3.

First of all, the PcapParser program based on Java is used to process the two traffic datasets, extract the sample data respectively, and annotate the instance of the dataset using the open source nDPI deep packet detection tool.

3.2 Shared Response Time Experiment and Analysis

In order to evaluate the performance of the proposed open resource sharing method, two other open resource sharing methods are selected to carry out experiments under the same experimental conditions. One is based on the web, the other is based on the SSM framework. The experimental results are shown in Fig. 3.

Table 3. MAWI traffic dataset details

Interception date	Duration/S	Number of messages/million	Capture size/MB
0124	3598.32	275	14452.21
0236	3600.03	368	2055.52
0341	3600.4	364	21041.86
0425	3600.35	384	21669.36
0529	3600.21	391	22100.32
0632	3599.9	412	24625.77

Compared with the results in the graph, it can be seen that in the experimental results of the sharing method based on the web, the sharing response time changes irregularly with the increase of the data amount, and most of them are at or above 20 ms; in the experimental results of the sharing method based on the SSM, the sharing time increases gradually with the increase of the data amount, and exceeds 20 ms when the data amount reaches 200 MB; in the experimental results of the sharing method based on the machine learning, the response time is always at a lower level with the increase of the data amount, and does not exceed 20 ms. To sum up, the designed open sharing method of digital education training resources based on machine learning has faster response time.

3.3   Memory Leak Probability Experiment and Analysis

In the memory leak probability experiment, LeakCanary, a memory leak analysis tool, is used to analyze the memory leak when the computer executes the shared task, and calculate the memory leak probability. Memory leak is an object reference error in the platform, which leads to the object occupying heap resources can not be reclaimed, and memory space is wasted seriously.

Use the LeakCanary tool to automate the detection of memory leaks in shared methods, introduce a dependency library in build.gr adle, initialize global configuration, install an application called Leaks locally after initialization to log information, and if memory leaks are detected, locate the error message and send it to the notification, and log it in Leaks. After a complete task is completed, calculate the probability of memory leaks. The experimental results are shown in Table 4.

From the data in the table, we can see that the memory leak probability of the resource sharing method based on machine learning is much lower than that of the other two methods. According to the results of the shared response time experiment, the designed open sharing method of digital education training resources based on machine learning has shorter response time, lower memory leakage probability and higher overall security.

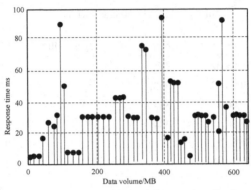

(a) Experimental results of a web-based resource-sharing approach

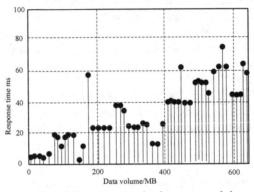

(b) Experimental results of the resource-sharing approach based on the SSM framework

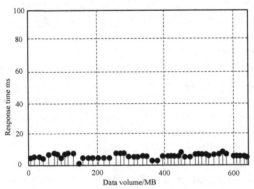

(c) Experimental results of a resource-sharing approach based on machine learning

Fig. 3. Shared response time experimental results for different sharing methods

Table 4. Experimental results of memory leak probability for different shared methods

Shared resource size/M	Sharing method based on web	Sharing method based on SSM framework	Sharing method based on machine learning
500	9.93%	9.24%	0.52%
1024	19.24%	15.62%	1.26%
5012	33.69%	29.45%	2.31%
10240	41.42%	36.22%	5.62%
20480	56.35%	47.85%	9.41%

4   Closing Remarks

In this paper, an open sharing method of digital education training resources based on machine learning is studied and designed. After the design is completed, several comparative experiments are designed. However, due to the limitation of personal ability and time, there are some deficiencies in the research, and the efficient computing ability of cloud computing has not been fully exerted.

References

1. Zhong, W., Li, Z.: Research on network education system based on learning machine. J. Commun. **39**(01), 135–140 (2018)
2. Yang, W.: Simulation of remote sharing method of database information under architecture of the Internet of Things. Comput. Simul. **35**(04), 457–461 (2018)
3. Sun, Y., Zhao, S., Zhang, F., et al.: A comparative study on the security mechanism of open & sharing government date information in China America and Britain. Library Inf. Serv. **62**(21), 5–14 (2018)
4. Li, J.: Research on method of information organizing and data sharing model of characteristic cultural resources: taking the project of the ancient dwellings digital memory of world Hakka City as example. Libr. J. **12**(05), 39–44 (2018)
5. Zhang, N., Chen, B., Yang, Y., et al.: Optimization technology of optical fiber communication network based on service classification. J. Phys.: Conf. Ser. **1746**(1), 012085 (6pp) (2021)
6. Schwartz, L.N., Shaffer, J.D., Bukhman, G.: The origins of the 4 × 4 framework for noncommunicable disease at the World Health Organization. SSM Popul. Health **13**(8490), 100731 (2021)
7. Fu, W., Liu, S., Srivastava, G.: Optimization of big data scheduling in social networks. Entropy **21**(9), 902 (2019)
8. Liu, S., Li, Z., Zhang, Y., et al.: Introduction of key problems in long-distance learning and training. Mobile Netw. Appl. **24**(1), 1–4 (2019)
9. Liu, S., Liu, D., Srivastava, G., Połap, D., Woźniak, M.: Overview and methods of correlation filter algorithms in object tracking. Complex Intell. Syst. 1–23 (2020). https://doi.org/10.1007/s40747-020-00161-4
10. Meng, X., Ma, C., Yang, C.: Survey on machine learning for database systems. J. Comput. Res. Dev. **56**(09), 1803–1820 (2019)

Design of Basketball Shot Track Recognition System Based on Machine Vision

Chonggao Chen(⊠) and Wei Tang

Huali College Guangdong University of Technology, Guangzhou 511325, China

Abstract. Aiming at the positioning of the existing shooting track, which leads to the deviation of basketball shooting track, in order to maintain the basketball shooting track accurately, a basketball shooting track recognition system based on machine vision is designed. The ARM processor is used as the core application terminal of the identification component, and the high-precision orientation module and power supply conversion module are combined to build the hardware environment. Based on this, a machine vision technology model is established. Through defining the format of machine datagram, the subprogram of tilt angle sensor is optimized, and the software execution environment is realized. Experimental results show that, compared with the traditional recognition system, the physical distance between the starting position and the terminating position of the shot is greatly reduced, which can effectively solve the problem of basketball trajectory deviation caused by inaccurate shooting and meet the practical application requirements of precise maintenance of basketball trajectory.

Keywords: Machine vision · Shot trajectory · Recognition system · End user · Peripheral structure · Power supply transformation · Machine data · Tilt sensor

1 Introduction

Machine vision is a branch of artificial intelligence that is developing rapidly. Simply put, machine vision is the use of machines instead of the human eye to do measurement and judgment. Tools Options Options Page. Machine vision system converts the captured object into image signal by machine vision product (namely image acquisition device, divided into CMOS and CCD), transmits it to the special image processing system, obtains the shape information of the captured object, and transforms it into digital signal according to the information of pixel distribution, brightness and color, et al. [1]. The image system carries out various operations to extract the feature of the object, and then controls the equipment action on the spot according to the result of discrimination. Machine vision is a comprehensive technology, including image processing, mechanical engineering, control, electrical lighting, optical imaging, sensors, analog and digital video technology, computer software and hardware (image enhancement and analysis algorithms, image cards, I/O cards, et al.). The typical machine vision application system includes image capture, light source system, image digitization module, digital image

W. Fu et al. (Eds.): ICMTEL 2021, LNICST 388, pp. 152–164, 2021.
https://doi.org/10.1007/978-3-030-82565-2_13

processing module, intelligent decision module and mechanical control module. The most basic characteristic of machine vision system is to improve the flexibility and automation of production. Machine vision is often used to replace artificial vision in some dangerous working environment which is not suitable for manual work or where artificial vision is difficult to meet the requirements [2]. At the same time, the machine vision inspection method can greatly improve the production efficiency and automation degree in the large batch and repetitive industrial production process.

At present, machine vision technology has become mature, and the cost of using machine language to locate has gradually become suitable for general application equipment. At the same time, a large number of new technologies have emerged, making the accuracy of localization more and more high, which has been able to fully meet the needs of basketball shot trajectory recognition and achieve the goal of path automation supervision [3]. This paper introduces the research status of machine vision at home and abroad, demonstrates the feasibility of using this method for high precision positioning, and introduces the development history, composition range, positioning accuracy, main functions and influence significance of machine vision. While studying the development environment of the identification system and the application conditions of the simulation software, the experience and skills related to the practical engineering are analyzed, including the isometric cabling, the impedance cabling, the coordinate measurement method of the center point, the calibration method of the reference azimuth, etc., and the feasibility of the algorithm for track recognition is verified by the actual data [4].

2 Hardware Design of Basketball Shot Track Recognition System

2.1 ARM Processor

The core of end-user device is ARM processor. If it is only used for arithmetic processing and signal control, FPGA can be used to get higher processing speed. But it is more suitable to use S3C2440 ARM processor for cost consideration. The S3C2440 processor is an ARM processor produced by Samsung [5]. The processor is a 32-bit low-power processor based on ARM920T. Different from the traditional MCU, S3C2440 adopts the Harvard architecture which is separated by data bus and address bus. It has powerful computing ability, up to 400 MHz main frequency speed, and has a memory management unit. It can carry many operating systems and has rich on-chip peripheral resources, as shown in Fig. 1.

Selecting this SCM as the hardware core of a terminal device has the following advantages:

(1) The S3C2440, as an ARM processor that has been available for several years, its price has become reasonable [6], and it still has strong computing power and high performance-to-price ratio. It is widely used, and has a large number of development materials and secondary development kits, which can greatly shorten the time needed for product development.

(2) S3C2440 has the function of 1VIIVIU, and can be equipped with LINUX, WINCE and other operating systems [7]. Especially in the application of LINUX, S3C2440 has rich and extensive application. Many development kits are written under the

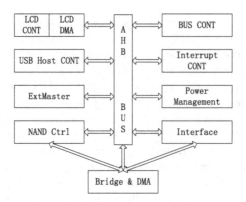

Fig. 1. S3C2440 peripherals for an ARM processor

platform of LINUX. Many difference algorithms of satellite positioning, path recognition algorithms and so on can find reference code in its application and shorten the development cycle of software.

(3) The S3C2440 has a large number of on-chip peripherals, such as analog-to-digital conversion, real-time clock, LCD control, various communication interfaces, and a large number of input-output interfaces, further reducing the cost, hardware volume and complexity of the equipment [8].

2.2 High-Precision Orientation Module

The high precision positioning and orientation module is the most important part of the hardware for basketball shot trajectory recognition. The performance of the module is directly related to the quality of the application equipment. This module selects the GT-1612-MTBD module of Gotop (as shown in Fig. 2), which is based on the MT3333 positioning chip of Media Tek and can be switched to GPS single mode, GPS double mode and Beidou single mode positioning mode [9].

The module has the following advantages:

(1) It is small in size and only 16 mm × 12 mm × 2.6 mm in size;
(2) Low power consumption, less than 160 mW;
(3) High reception sensitivity as low as 165 dBm;
(4) The positioning accuracy is high, which can reach 5 m even in the absence of a ground enhancement station.

According to the chip information of the chip, the wiring of the printed circuit board from the antenna port to the pin needs to use 50 Ω impedance line. The module communicates with ARM chip through serial port, and the 3 pin also outputs millimeter pulse, which can be used in other modules.

Hidden Markov model is the main method of dynamic trajectory recognition. Hidden Markov Model is very successful in node recognition, and there are many similarities between dynamic trajectory and node signal in space-time. So Hidden Markov Model is

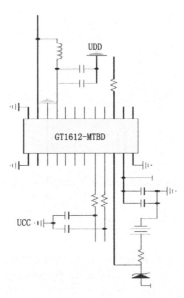

Fig. 2. High-precision orientation module

introduced into dynamic trajectory recognition. Hidden Markov model is a dual Markov stochastic process, which is developed on the basis of Markov chain. The hidden Markov model consists of two stochastic processes, one is the basic stochastic process, that is, the Markov chain describing the state transition, and the other is the general stochastic process describing the statistical relationship between the state and the observed value [10].

2.3   Power Conversion Module

Power supply conversion module is mainly composed of main power supply circuit and secondary power supply circuit. First of all, we must determine the coverage of the basketball shooting trajectory, that is, the implementation center and its boundary of each action, and define the range of shooting action approximately as a circle. Secondly, the position of the basketball can be obtained by satellite positioning, and the movement of the ball can be used to judge the direction of the shooting. Then the angle of the shot to the track center can be calculated by the movement of the ball to determine which basket the basketball is moving. According to the track of the basketball, judge the stage of the ball: the basketball is approaching to a certain area of the basket, the ball is moving in the basket, the basketball is gradually away from a free basket, the basketball is entering the preset frame. Finally, through the analysis of the stage characteristics of basketball, the recognition of the trajectory of shooting is realized.

Usually, only some parts of each image are interested in the captured trajectory sequence image, so we must segment it from the image in order to study it. Dynamic segmentation is the basis of the whole dynamic trajectory recognition system, and its segmentation effect directly affects the tracking of shooting behavior, feature extraction

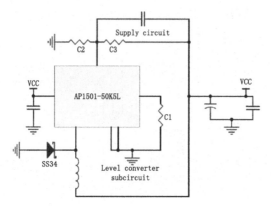

Fig. 3. Power supply switching circuit

and system recognition rate. Combining the advantages and disadvantages of the existing mature segmentation methods, a combined trajectory segmentation method is proposed. Firstly, the candidate regions are segmented from the trajectory images by motion detection method. In order to reduce the interference of shooting behavior near a given node in the candidate region, texture detection is introduced to remove the interference in the original shooting environment.

3 Software Design of Basketball Shot Track Recognition System

3.1 Machine Vision Technology

Using machine vision technology alone, the accuracy can only reach the meter level, and basketball shooting trajectory positioning is affected by many factors, which will cause errors, in addition to known satellite clock difference and receiver clock difference, there are satellite orbit errors, ionospheric effects, tropospheric effects, multi-path effects, changes in the antenna phase center and the combined errors of the receiver [11], the orbit error of satellite and the influence of troposphere and troposphere have the greatest impact on the accuracy of shooting trajectory. So the accuracy of shooting trajectory identification cannot be satisfied by machine vision alone.

Although the mathematical model of machine vision is simple, the amount of data is small, and the concept of innumerable datum ages, but the recognition base station and the end user must observe the same basketball shooting behavior. Although distance difference pairs do not need to observe exactly the same basketball shooting trajectory, the data age is only 30 s, and the data model is complex and the data is large [12]. The local difference model of single trajectory recognition base station is simple in structure, but the coverage is small, the difference precision will decrease with the increase of base station distance. The local difference of multiple base stations improves the reliability, improves the influence of distance on the accuracy, and enlarges the coverage, but the coverage is still limited and the model is not perfect. Wide-area difference can almost cover the whole system, and it has high precision, good reliability, precision is not affected by base station distance, but the system structure is complex and expensive.

In many machine vision technology, there is a called RTK positioning technology has been widely used, this system is also using this differential positioning technology for high-precision positioning. RTK is a real-time dynamic differential measurement technique, which uses the real-time dynamic positioning technique based on the carrier phase observation [13]. It can measure the 3D positioning results of the observation station in the specified coordinate system quickly, and the accuracy can reach centimeter level. RTK technology is also used in the GPS high-precision positioning at the earliest. Because the high-precision positioning technology must observe the carrier phase, RTK technology is also widely used in the BD high-precision positioning.

Suppose β represents the angle between the original position of the basketball and the position where the basketball terminates, $\bar{p}$ represents the mean value of the shooting behavior in the track to be identified, and λ represents the given identification coefficient, and the above physical quantities are combined. The application expression of machine vision technology may be defined as follows:

$$\varphi = \frac{\tan \beta^{-1} \frac{|Y_b - Y_a|}{|X_b - X_a|}}{\lambda \cdot \bar{p}} \tag{1}$$

Among them, $\tan \beta$ represents the tangent value of angle β, X_a, Y_a represents the transverse and longitudinal coordinate value of shot node a, X_b, Y_b represents the transverse and longitudinal coordinate value of shot node b.

3.2 Machine Datagram Format

With the further development of machine vision technology, and the coverage of ground base station and mobile base station is more and more wide, the technology of ground base station and mobile base station have appeared [14]. When the precision of ground reference station is high enough and the coverage is wide enough, sometimes it is not necessary to receive the satellite signal. Only by the identification signal of the reference station and the position information of some reference points, there is enough data information to ensure the accuracy of basketball shooting location. When the positioning requirements are not so high, even mobile base stations can be used to carry out rough positioning, the same can meet certain positioning needs [15–18]. The machine datagram is encoded in RTCM 3.1 frame structure, and the definition is shown in Table 1.

The RTCM3.1 frame structure includes 8-bit boot word, 6-bit reserved word, 0–1023 byte message data and 24-bit CRC check. The 8-bit guide is a fixed value, that is, 11010011;The reserved word is usually all 0 because it is undefined; The 10-bit message length represents the byte length of the datagram; Variable length message data is some defined message, such as RTCM1004 number, 1005 message; The 24-bit CRC check code is generated by the CRC algorithm through the data in front of it, which is used for verify the transmission [19].

In the research of trajectory processing theory, there are two kinds of motion detection methods: one is the calculation of motion vector field based on block matching or optical flow method, and the other is the detection of change between frames of sequential images. But it is not suitable to deal with fast moving objects because of its

Table 1. RTCM 3.1 frame structure encoding contents

Item	Head knot	Tail node
Guide word	8-digit number 11010011	10-digit number 1101001100
Preserve words	6-digit number all are 0	8-digit number all are 1
Message length	10-digit number message length in bytes	10-digit number message length in nodes
Variable length message data	0–1023 byte specific content of the message	0–511 byte specific contents of identification documents
CRC Checksum …	24-digit number based on previous data generation	12-digit number based on previous data generation

complexity and time consuming [20–22]. The second kind of inter-frame change detection method is simple and fast, which is more suitable for the applications with high real-time requirements. According to the actual situation of this subject, it is decided to use the second type of inter-frame change detection method to detect motion. Inter-frame change detection can be divided into frame difference method and background subtraction method.

Frame difference method is the simplest and most rapid motion detection method in video image sequence processing. The basic principle of the algorithm is that two consecutive adjacent frames in the trajectory image sequence are differentiated and denoised to segment moving objects. When moving objects appear in video image sequence, there will be a big difference between two adjacent frames [23]. Two frames of difference can remove the unchanged pixels, and then the moving objects can be obtained. The advantages of frame difference method are simple implementation, low program complexity, fast calculation speed, strong adaptability to dynamic environment and strong stability. Of course, the frame difference method also has some shortcomings: for example, when the gray value of some areas inside the moving object changes flat, the moving target extracted by the frame difference method is not complete, which will affect the following feature extraction and recognition.

Background subtraction is essentially a special frame-difference method. The biggest difference between the frame difference method and the frame difference method is the different reference background image [24, 25]. The frame difference method uses the previous frame of the current frame as the reference background image, while the background subtraction method uses the fixed or real-time updated image as the reference background image. The principle and algorithm design of background subtraction method are simple, and the information of moving target can be obtained more accurately than frame difference method [26]. But at the same time, the background subtraction method is also sensitive to the background environment, and it is easy to be affected by the changes of weather, light and other conditions. But at the same time, the background subtraction method is also sensitive to the background environment, and it is easy to be affected by the changes of weather, light and other conditions.

3.3 Dip Sensor Subroutine

Software Adopts Structured Design, Divides Software into Modules by Realization Functions, and Handles Various Processes in a Timely Manner by Interrupts and Inquiries. Using Mature Instance Programs, Library Functions, and Development Kits for Secondary Development reduces the difficulty in program development, makes code easier to understand and transplant, facilitates debugging, shortens the software development cycle, and improves efficiency [27–29]. The specific functions of the software include real-time acquisition of high-precision positioning and orientation information, reading of data from external tilt sensors, acquisition of application information of identification components; and receiving differential data and alarm information through wireless networks, sending high-precision position and azimuth data, shot trajectory information and configuration terminal parameters to the monitoring center; Display and play the alarm information, the basketball shot track recognition and processing [30]. Field configuration parameters and online upgrade system. The inclination sensor subroutine mainly collects the angle data of basketball shot track recognition sensor in real time, and saves the angle data to internal memory. Its application flow is shown in Fig. 3.

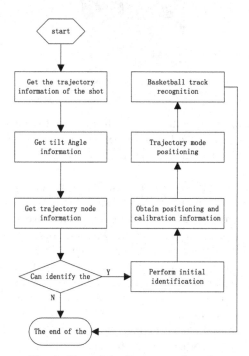

Fig. 4. Flow of the dip sensor subroutine

At this point, the software and hardware execution environment is built, and the smooth application of basketball shooting track recognition system is realized with the support of machine vision principle.

4　Data Comparison and Analysis

In order to verify the practical application value of basketball shot track recognition system based on machine vision, the following comparative experiments are designed. All participants were asked to make the standard shooting action shown in Fig. 4, fixed the position of the basket, so that all participants in turn to shoot into it, recording in the process, the specific changes in the experimental indicators.

Fig. 5. Standard shooting

DUI can be used to describe the actual deformation of human joints. In general, the larger the value of DUI is, the larger the deformation of human joints is, and vice versa. The following table records the specific changes of DUI in experimental group and control group (Fig. 5).

Table 2 shows that with the extension of the experimental time, the DUI index of the experimental group appears the trend of rising first and then stabilizing, and the global maximum value reaches 29.4%, and the limit value level can maintain a stable state of 40 min. After the small stable state, the DUI index of the control group began to rise continuously, and the global maximum value reached 52.7, which increased 22.7% compared with the extreme value of the experimental group. Based on the application of machine vision basketball shooting track recognition system, the rising trend of DUI index value has been suppressed to a certain extent, which can effectively control the point shape variables of human joints.

Show Starting Shot Position in v_0, Ending Shot Position in v_n, and Physical Distance Between v_0 and v_n in v, and recorded the specific changes of each index in the experimental group and the control group during the experimental time of 120 min respectively. The experimental details are shown in Table 3.

Table 2. DUI comparison of indicators

Experimental time/(min)	DUI indicators/(%)	
	Experimental group	Control group
10	30.6	51.2
20	30.5	51.2
30	30.3	51.2
40	30.2	51.3
50	30.1	51.4
60	29.8	51.5
70	29.7	51.8
80	29.5	52.0
90	29.4	52.1
100	29.4	52.3
110	29.4	52.5
120	29.4	52.7

Table 3 shows that with the prolongation of the experiment time, the initial shooting position and the stop shooting position of the experimental group changed obviously, and the real value of the physical difference between them was relatively low, and the maximum value of the whole experiment was only 1.3 m. Although there was no obvious change in the starting position and the ending position of shooting in the control group, the actual value of the physical difference between the two was relatively high. The maximum value of the whole experiment was 2.8 m, which was 1.5 m higher than the extreme value of the experimental group.

On this basis, taking the recognition accuracy as the test index, a comparative experiment is carried out by manual and the proposed method, and the experimental results are shown in Fig. 6.

According to the analysis of Fig. 6, when the recognition time is 20 min, the accuracy rate of the manual method reaches 90%, and the accuracy rate of the proposed system is about 95%; with the increase of recognition time, the accuracy rate of the manual method continues to decline; when the recognition time is 110 min, the accuracy rate of the proposed system is about 95% The accuracy of the proposed method is still as high as 90%, which is significantly higher than that of the manual method, indicating that the proposed system has high accuracy.

Table 3. Comparison of Physical Spacing of Shooting Position

Experimental time/(min)	Physical spacing of shooting position in experimental group/(m)		
	v_0	v_n	v
10	0	1.2	1.2
20	0.2	1.1	0.9
30	0	1.0	1.0
40	0	1.2	1.2
50	0.1	1.1	1.0
60	0	1.3	1.3
70	0.2	1.3	1.1
80	0.1	1.3	1.2
90	0.3	1.2	0.9
100	0	1.1	1.1
110	0.3	1.2	0.9
120	0.1	1.3	1.2
Experimental time/(min)	Physical spacing of shooting positions in control group/(m)		
	v_0	v_n	v
10	0.3	2.8	2.5
20	0.1	2.9	2.8
30	0	2.5	2.5
40	0	2.8	2.8
50	0.1	2.8	2.7
60	0.2	2.6	2.4
70	0.1	2.7	2.6
80	0	2.8	2.8
90	0.2	2.5	2.3
100	0.1	2.7	2.6
110	0.1	2.6	2.5
120	0	2.7	2.7

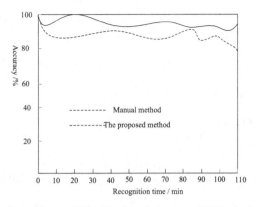

Fig. 6. Comparison of Identification Accuracy of Different Methods

5 Conclusion

To sum up, with the application of basketball shooting trajectory recognition system based on machine vision, the physical distance between the starting shooting position and the ending shooting position does show an obvious downward trend, which can meet the practical application needs of reducing the basketball trajectory offset, but there is still room for prompt. The future research direction is to shorten the basketball trajectory offset and reduce the basketball trajectory offset Less basketball shooting deviation times.

References

1. Chen, H., Cha, H., Liu, L., et al.: Vessel traffic pattern extraction based on automatic iden-tification system data and Hough transformation. J. Comput. Appl. **38**(11), 286–289+295 (2018)
2. Qin, H., Yang, Q.: Action recognition using spatio-temporal co-occurrence features and improved VLAD. J. Comput.-Aided Des. Comput. Graph. **10**, 1759–1767 (2019)
3. Ding, D., Shu, Y., Xie, C., et al.: Application of machine vision in the recognition of motion trajectory for shoe machine. Mach. Des. Manuf. **324**(2), 257–259 (2018)
4. Chen, H., Xu, Q., Huang, R., et al.: User identification across social networks based on user trajectory. J. Electron. Inf. Technol. **40**(11), 223–229 (2018)
5. Dong, W., Yu, H., Zhou, Y., et al.: Automatic Identification System (AIS) trajectory data compression algorithm of a fishing vessel based on improved sliding window. J. Dalian Fisheries Univ. **35**(3), 462–468 (2020)
6. Zhu, Z., Han, S., Guo, Z., et al.: Long baseline location algorithm based on beacon drift error recognition. Syst. Eng. Electron. **41**(1), 162–169 (2019)
7. Huang, Y.: Solution for detecting buried pipe network with data fusion of multi-sensors. J. Chin. Comput. Syst. **40**(4), 908–912 (2019)
8. Chen, J., Chen, H., Wang, J., et al.: Design of data acquisition and trajectory recognition system based on MEMS sensor. Chin. J. Electron Devices **42**(2), 463–468 (2019)
9. Feng, H., Bai, F., Xu, Y.: Urban traffic perception and critical node identification of road network based on trajectory Big Data. J. Transp. Syst. Eng. Inf. Technol. **18**(3), 42–47 (2018)

10. Yan, X., Liu, X., Liu, Y., et al.: Identification and evaluation of urban traffic congestion based on the big data of floating vehicles and grid modeling. J. Beijing Jiaotong Univ. **43**(1), 109–118 (2019)
11. Liu, S., Liu, D., Srivastava, G., Połap, D., Woźniak, M.: Overview and methods of correlation filter algorithms in object tracking. Complex Intell. Syst. 1–23 (2020). https://doi.org/10.1007/s40747-020-00161-4
12. Liu, S., Lu, M., Li, H., et al.: Prediction of gene expression patterns with generalized linear regression model. Front. Genet. **10**, 120 (2019)
13. Liu, S., Bai, W., Zeng, N., et al.: A fast fractal based compression for MRI images. IEEE Access **7**, 62412–62420 (2019)
14. Yoon, Y., Hwang, H., Choi, Y., et al.: Analyzing basketball movements and pass relationships using realtime object tracking techniques based on deep learning. IEEE Access **7**, 56564–56576 (2019)
15. Fechter, T., Baltas, D.: One shot learning for deformable medical image registration and periodic motion tracking. IEEE Trans. Med. Imaging **39**, 2506–2517 (2020)
16. Leigh, S.: Cardiorespiratory fitness alleviates the effect of fatigue on basketball free throw shooting performance. ISBS Proc. Archive **37**(1), 53 (2019)
17. Karunasekera, H., Wang, H., Zhang, H.: Multiple object tracking with attention to appearance, structure, motion and size. IEEE Access **7**, 104423–104434 (2019)
18. Hyönä, J., Li, J., Oksama, L.: Eye behavior during multiple object tracking and multiple identity tracking. Vision **3**(3), 35 (2019)
19. Edele, A., Jansen, M., Schachner, M.K., et al.: School track and ethnic classroom composition relate to the mainstream identity of adolescents with immigrant background in Germany, but not their ethnic identity. Int. J. Psychol. **55**, 754–768 (2020)
20. Hyn, J., Oksama, L., Rantanen, E.: Tracking the identity of moving words: stimulus complexity and familiarity affects tracking accuracy. Appl. Cogn. Psychol. **34**(1), 63–76 (2019)
21. Wu, F., Li, X., Xu, L., et al.: An anonymous and identity-trackable data transmission scheme for smart grid under smart city notion. Ann. Telecommun. - annales des télécommunications **75**(3), 33–42 (2020)
22. Belan, P.A., Macedo, R.A.G.D., Alves, W.A.L., et al.: Machine vision system for quality inspection of beans. Int. J. Adv. Manuf. Technol. **111**(11), 1–15 (2020)
23. Xu, S., Peng, B., Wu, H., et al.: An automatic machine vision-guided system for the propagation of potato test-tube plantlets. J. Robot. **2020**(10), 1–11 (2020)
24. Zhang, Y., Soon, H.G., Ye, D., et al.: Powder-bed fusion process monitoring by machine vision with hybrid convolutional neural networks. IEEE Trans. Ind. Inf. **16**(9), 5769–5779 (2020)
25. Chen, Y., Hou, C., Tang, Y., et al.: Citrus tree segmentation from UAV images based on monocular machine vision in a natural orchard environment. Sensors **19**(24), 5558 (2019)
26. Doan, M., Carpenter, A.E.: Leveraging machine vision in cell-based diagnostics to do more with less. Nat. Mater. **18**(5), 414–418 (2019)
27. Lauzon-Gauthier, J., Duchesne, C., Tessier, J.: A machine vision sensor for quality control of green anode paste material. JOM **72**(1), 287–295 (2020)
28. Penumuru, D.P., Muthuswamy, S., Karumbu, P.: Identification and classification of materials using machine vision and machine learning in the context of industry 4.0. J. Intell. Manuf. **31**(5), 1229–1241 (2020)
29. Link, C.: Telecentric blue light lenses: promising advantages for machine vision. Inf. Display **37**(1), 56–69 (2021)
30. Li, C., Chen, H., Li, X., et al.: A review for cervical histopathology image analysis using machine vision approaches. Artif. Intell. Rev. **53**(1), 56–69 (2020)

Design and Implementation of Mobile Learning System Based on Wireless Communication Technology

Hui-jun Wang[1][(✉)] and Ang Li[2]

[1] Xinhua College of Ningxia University, Yinchuan 750021, China
wanghuijun78523@yeah.net
[2] Basic Education School, Zhuhai College of Jilin University, Zhuhai 519041, China

Abstract. Due to the lack of comprehensive definition of learning resources in traditional mobile learning systems, the transmission efficiency of learning resource packets is poor. Therefore, a mobile learning system based on wireless communication technology is proposed. In terms of hardware, it adopts SOA technology framework, optimizes the overall system architecture, adds wireless communication environment middleware, and optimizes the system communication interface and resource reading channel. In software aspect, MySQL database is established to store learning resources, and load balance control theory is used to improve the storage density of resource information. The experimental results show that the design system improves the data throughput, reduces the data transmission delay, and the actual application effect is better.

Keywords: Wireless communication · Mobile learning · Hardware design · Software design

1 Introduction

At present, all kinds of scientific knowledge show explosive growth at the speed of exponential level. Therefore, learning through traditional education methods cannot meet the demand for knowledge at this stage. In such an environment, mobile learning with wireless communication technology as the main transmission carrier emerges as the times require. Mobile learning is a kind of learning method that breaks the geographical restrictions and makes full use of mobile terminal equipment and wireless network communication technology. Nowadays, domestic research on mobile learning is relatively perfect. Tsinghua University and Beijing Normal University, with the support of the Ministry of education, have carried out mobile learning application research projects and developed relevant mobile learning platforms running an open operating system, with perfect user interface and powerful expansibility, can easily install and uninstall application software. Through 4G, 5G and intelligent mobile terminal devices, rich multimedia content teaching has become a reality.

© ICST Institute for Computer Sciences, Social Informatics and Telecommunications Engineering 2021
Published by Springer Nature Switzerland AG 2021. All Rights Reserved
W. Fu et al. (Eds.): ICMTEL 2021, LNICST 388, pp. 165–177, 2021.
https://doi.org/10.1007/978-3-030-82565-2_14

Wireless communication technology is developing rapidly. The current mainstream standards are 4G and 5G mobile communication technologies, which can be used to simultaneously transmit images, audio, video and other content. Mobile terminal equipment has also changed from a functional mobile terminal device to a smart mobile terminal. Equipment, its processing capacity, storage capacity, etc. are greatly improved. Based on the above theory, this paper designs a mobile learning system based on wireless communication technology.

2 Design Method of Mobile Learning System Based on Wireless Communication Technology

2.1 Mobile Learning System Hardware Design

2.1.1 Design the Overall Architecture of the Mobile Learning System

Optimize the system architecture, adopt SOA as the core technical framework, use service middleware as the operating support, base on the basic database, and use the basic service as the center of the system architecture. The overall architecture is divided into application layers from top to bottom. Service system layer, middle component layer, basic resource layer. Use the basic resource layer to provide various resources for system development, including basic data and information database, control basic data not to be affected by development, describe learning resources in the form of words, programs, graphics, block diagrams, files, etc., so that basic data Different forms are stored in the resource layer [1]. In the middle component layer, the component interface standard specification is defined, the computing component and the presentation component are integrated through the multi-layer message bus, and the component entity and runtime state are managed through the lightweight component integration framework, so that the information between the components is balanced. Functions interact to provide core services required at runtime, including user management, security operations, etc. The middle component layer is divided into message middleware and integrated components. Through integrated components, component operation management, component access, environmental information integration and component registration are realized, and the development, operation and wireless communication of components are shielded, which provides efficient communication and comprehensive integration for upper network communication. Network communication realizes functions such as message transmission and time unification, as well as special protocol conversion, general information transmission and communication agent [2]. Use the service system layer to provide services for the application layer, and finally use the application layer as a service consumer in the system architecture to provide support for the development of supporting tools, and display information processing products to the operator, integrate interface components, including various business displays, Non-real-time information display, real-time information display. The overall architecture of the learning system is shown in Fig. 1.

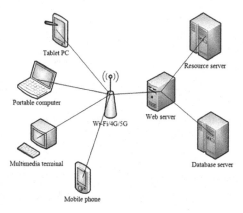

Fig. 1. Overall architecture diagram of the learning system

As shown in Fig. 1 above, the client of mobile learning system mainly runs various kinds of mobile terminal devices, such as mobile phones and tablet computers. Each learner has his own mobile terminal equipment. After inputting identity information in the client program, the learner connects to the server through wireless communication network for verification. After passing the verification, the client program can be used to request the required learning resources or interactive activities. The server side of the mobile learning system is mainly responsible for verifying learner information, managing learning resources and processing interactive information. The server-side program is developed by using the structure mode, and is deployed and run by Apache tomcat, and the storage of user information and learning resource information is realized [3].

So far, the overall architecture of the learning system is designed.

2.1.2   Design the Functional Structure of the Mobile Learning System

The functions are distributed on the client and server. The user establishes a connection with the middleware through COM/DCOM. The system receives the request through the web presentation layer, obtains learning resources from the database, processes the learner's request according to the coding business rules, exchanges with the data collector through the middleware, and returns the processing results to the web presentation layer, and finally sends the data to the database. The block is shown in Fig. 2:

The server side of the system provides support for the management of mobile learning course resources. It helps scholars enter their user name and password on the system login page to perform login operations. After successful login, they enter the main interface to help scholars to conduct courses for which they are responsible. The chapter catalog management can also manage the learning content of the existing chapters. Finally, you can upload the corresponding learning materials and reply to the inquiry questions sent by the learners from the client. The supporter module provides supporters with necessary support for the classification and management of mobile learning courses. Supporters enter the user name and password to log in. After the login is successful,

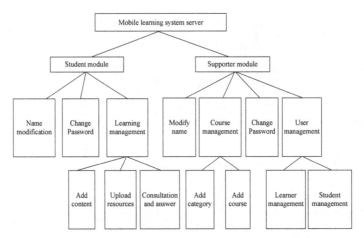

Fig. 2. Server-side functional structure of mobile learning system

they enter the main interface, create, modify or delete courses as needed, and perform courses classification, convenient for learners to search while studying. Supporters are also responsible for managing the related information of the assistant scholars, assigning the courses that the assistant scholars are responsible for, and dealing with the problems feedback from the learners. According to the analysis of the learner's role and behavior, the mobile learning system client program is designed into three modules: login module, online learning module, and support service module. The specific functions are shown in Fig. 3:

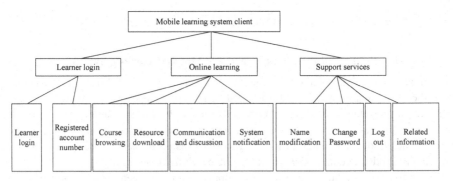

Fig. 3. Client function structure of mobile learning system

After login, the user can enter the next operation according to the user's name and user's needs. After entering the learning module in the main interface, learners can select the functions to be realized according to the menu icon, including course browsing, resource downloading, communication and discussion, and system notification. Course browsing allows learners to browse the course content online, download resources to provide auxiliary learning resources for learners, exchange and discussion provide support for learners' interactive activities, and system notification can send system notification information to learners. Learners can modify the user name and login password through the support service module, log off and return to the system login module, and view the relevant information of mobile learning system client.

So far, the functional structure of mobile learning system is designed.

2.1.3 Optimizing the Communication Interface of Mobile Learning System

In the middle component layer of the overall architecture, the host infrastructure middleware, which is a self-adapting communication environment, is used to optimize the network interface of electronic information and simplify the system communication process. In the underlying network communication, add self-adapting communication environment middleware, receive and process the target information of network transmission, give full play to the event-driven characteristics of network transmission, use the self-adapted communication environment to provide public interfaces, and process I/O events of network connections, So that the system communicates between interfaces through middleware [4]. The communication interface adopts the UDP protocol to collect data and monitor I/O events, so that the self-adapting communication environment uses the Wrapper Facade mode to receive real-time rebroadcast data. Call the registration object of the self-adapting communication environment middleware, set the multicast address and port number, make the registration object join different multicast addresses, keep the port number the same, and receive electronic information data. After the data is received, the network message is processed through the hook method, the network message protocol identification is analyzed, different types of messages are distinguished, and the electronic information data is finally updated. When there is a target message that has not been communicated for a long time in the network transmission, use the adaptive communication environment reactor to register I/O events to determine whether the message arrival time is overtime. When it is judged as a timeout event, it will be based on the last received position, automatically calculate the current position of the message, locate the target message, and transfer it to the network message interface after receiving it again to process the information data [5]. Optimize the communication circuit so that it can transmit video images and meet the volume limit of the inspection device. The optimized communication interface circuit is shown in Fig. 4.

The power supply voltage is transformed into a voltage suitable for the operation of the device, and the internal information of the mobile communication device is collected in real time. Its communication mode adopts multiple monitoring display, selects LAN to connect mobile terminal, establishes WiFi hotspot in the lower computer, establishes small LAN, and realizes multi terminal communication and other operations [6]. Then, the communication interface of the learning system is defined. Using programmable logic devices, it can store large capacity data. The pin definition of receiving interface is shown in Table 1.

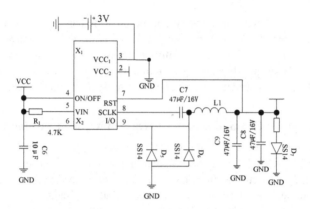

Fig. 4. Optimized communication interface circuit

Table 1. Definition of communication interface pins.

Pin number	Pin name	Features
2	MUTE	Backup data serialization signal output terminal
3	CD#	Backup data serialization signal input terminal
4	SDI#	The pin is grounded, and the output data serialization signal is enabled
6	AEC+	Detect serialized signal load
7	AEC−	High and low level conversion, directly output serialized signal
8	BYPASS	The pin is left floating to select the equalization effect of the output data serialization signal

As shown in Table 1 above, when the pin is at high level, the chip of backup memory works normally and directly outputs the backup data signal. When the pin is at low level, the chip is converted into a closed-loop feedback with series capacitors to eliminate the DC component of signal transmission and make the input signal enter into adaptive filtering. According to the signal difference regulated by the back-end DC recovery level, the gain and bandwidth of data backup memory are set to obtain AC coupled backup data input signal [7]. The optimized communication interface will provide a return loss for the network data, repair the distorted backup data transmission signal, and enable the mobile learning system to store multiple formats of backup data. In the storage process, the SD card storage mode of the lower computer is used to select the 4-bit data width, operate the communication interface, and set the read channel at the input end, as shown in Table 2:

According to the content of the above table, the learning resources are read, so that the optimization of the communication interface of the mobile learning system is realized, and the hardware design of the mobile learning system is completed.

Table 2. Learning resource reading channel settings.

Read signal	Description	Signal source
AWID/ARID	Identify the collected signal ID	Master/slave
AWLEN[7:0]/ARLEN[7:0]	Set the transmission length to 2, 4, 8, 16, and cyclically transmit data	Master/slave
WLAST/RLAST	Indicates the last transmitted data	Slave
BVALID	Respond to valid signals	Slave
WSTRB/RSTRB	Transmit unaligned data, 1 byte represents each bit	Master/slave
BREADY	Indicates that the inspection device can receive equipment acquisition signals	Master

2.2 Mobile Learning System Software Design

2.2.1 Design a Mobile Learning Resource Database

After the system hardware is designed, the system database is designed to record and store the mobile learning resources. Use the database relationship diagram to display the composition and internal connections of each entity data, use MySQL database to view each database table, and integrate with PHP/PERL and Apache, so that the database supports multi-threading and multiple connection methods [8]. Among them, MySQL database adopts the dual authorization mode of community edition and commercial edition to provide administrators with dynamic website technology. The main record data of the database is shown in Table 3.

Table 3. Learning system database.

Field name	Type of data	Data length	Field description
userId	varchar	11	Learner information form
Sett-status	varchar(50)	14	Help scholar information form
projectcode	varchar(50)	11	Course classification information table
areaname	varchar(50)	14	Course allocation information form
paymentplan	varchar(100)	64	Course information form
flowNum	varchar(255)	64	Course content information table
description	varchar(255)	11	Help scholar information form

As shown in Table 3, learners can access the databases within their authority on the premise of complying with GPL protocol. Using distributed technology, the MySQL database is customized and developed to support different requirements such as single point replication and cluster size, so as to meet the different needs of learners. MySQL database has better compatibility. The development of Linux+Apache+MySQL combination can realize the processing of tens of millions of data records [9]. Since learning resources are a key component, the learning resources stored in the database should be classified and standardized, and the following aspects are mainly defined: summary information mainly describes the identification and index of the resource; cycle information mainly describes the use cycle of the resource the content of the resource, such as the release time, effective time, and update status of the resource; the data information mainly describes the data format standard used in the learning resource, such as keywords, data types, and the language used; technical information mainly describes the technology of the resource attributes, such as resource format, production tools, usage guides, etc.; educational information mainly describes the pedagogical characteristics of the resource, such as the way the resource interacts, learning difficulty, and learning time; value information mainly describes the economic content of the resource For example, the copyright of the resource, the purchase price, etc.; the related information mainly describes the related information of the resource, such as the reference content of the resource, related resources, etc.; the annotation information mainly describes the review information of the resource, including the reviewer, the content of the annotation, the time of the annotation, etc.. Classification information mainly describes the classification of resources, such as keywords, tags, and languages of resources.

So far, the design of the learning resource database is completed.

2.2.2 Improve Storage Efficiency of Learning Resources

The load balance control theory is used to improve the storage density of learning resources in the database. According to the application environment of the learning system, a multi-user rule scheduling set is established to calculate the fitness function of resource information, which is regarded as the adaptive feature of resource information Set attributes are classified. The classification objective function x is as follows:

$$x = (t + 1)cTw\xi \tag{1}$$

In the formula, t is the storage overhead, c is the electronic information transmission threshold, T is the size of the information data rule set, W is the weight coefficient, and ξ is the transmission time length of the scheduling information [10]. For different types of resource information, storage nodes are set to maximize the information storage density, so that the storage space load is balanced, so as to meet the characteristic scheduling conditions. Distribute and output the scheduled resource information to obtain a feature subset of the redundant data, and then compress and process the redundant data, check the feature constraints of the remaining data, and obtain a large-scale storage distribution space structure. On this basis, according to the time sequence, the resource information is spatially reconstructed, the information data is distributed and reorganized according to the joint probability of the nearest neighbors, and the large-scale information flow is mapped to the phase space to obtain the optimal feature decomposition condition of the information. Finally, the feature set is output to realize the clustering processing of resource information, and several data blocks are obtained, and the data blocks are associated with the cache space area to improve the storage efficiency of learning resources.

So far, the software design of the mobile learning system is completed. Combining hardware and software design, complete the mobile learning system design based on wireless communication technology.

3   Experiment and Analysis

In contrast experiment, the designed system is taken as experimental group A, and two traditional systems are respectively taken as experimental group B and experimental group C. the transmission efficiency of the three groups of experimental learning resources is compared.

3.1   Experimental Preparation

Install JDK/JRE and install ADT plug-in in it. This plug-in provides learners with a powerful comprehensive environment for developing Android applications, using Java development language and SDK to develop mobile learning systems. The experimental data sets are text information learning resources, website learning resources, and multimedia learning resources. The college campus network is used as the test environment. The three groups of systems manage the learning resources in a unified manner. Students use mobile devices through unified dynamic users. Verify, access the access interfaces inside and outside the campus, share and download learning resources, the specific topology of the campus network of the college is shown in Fig. 5:

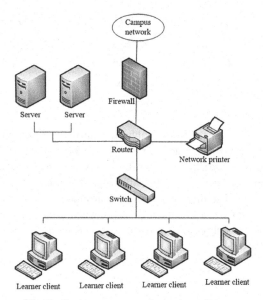

Fig. 5. System test network topology diagram

The experimental environment consists of two computers connected to the Internet through network equipment. One host runs WiniSCSI Target, which simulates iSCSI target, and acts as a storage device to send digital learning resources. The other host runs Windows iSCSI Initiator as a resource receiver. The connection mode is set to routing mode, the computer CPU is Intel F4600, the hard disk is SATA 500G, the memory is 2G, the main frequency is 5 GHz, and the access network download speed is 700 KB/s.

3.2   Experimental Result

3.2.1   The First Group of Experimental Results

Using iometer test tool, open the disk manager on the test host, get a new disk, that is, the learning resources accessed by the learner client, read data from the disk and write data to the disk. Change the size of the learning resource packet to control the data block of sharing request between 16 kb and 1024 KB. Test the throughput of the mobile learning system when the learning resources are read 100% on the disk. The experimental results are shown in Table 4.

Table 4. Comparison results of 100% read operations.

Shared data block size (KB)	Experimental group A throughput (MB/s)	Experimental group B throughput (MB/s)	Experimental group C throughput (MB/s)
16 KB	2.01	1.82	1.81
32 KB	4.73	4.08	3.95
64 KB	6.09	5.13	4.95
128 KB	7.45	6.57	6.29
256 KB	9.01	7.98	7.56
512 KB	9.67	8.56	8.16
1024 KB	10.53	8.63	8.26

According to the data in the above table, the throughput of experiment group A can reach 10 MB/s when 100% read operation is performed, while the throughput of experiment group B and experiment group C is only within 9 MB/s. Compared with the traditional system, this design system Throughput has improved. Convert file server virtualization to storage virtualization in disk linear mode, synthesize a logical disk in a linear manner, perform 100% write data, that is, when uploading learning resources, detect the throughput of the three systems in this case, and compare them. The test results are shown in Table 5.

Table 5. Comparison results of 100% write operations.

Shared data block size (KB)	Experimental group A throughput (MB/s)	Experimental group B throughput (MB/s)	Experimental group C throughput (MB/s)
16 KB	1.79	1.63	1.43
32 KB	4.02	3.82	3.67
64 KB	5.08	4.88	4.82
128 KB	6.35	5.87	5.63
256 KB	7.68	6.98	6.87
512 KB	8.63	7.62	7.58
1024 KB	8.78	7.82	7.62

It can be seen from the data in the above table that the throughput of group A is close to 9 mb/s, while that of group B and group C is only less than 8 MB/s. Finally, the storage virtualization in the disk linear mode is transformed into the virtualization in the slice mode. In the test, two hard disks are mapped to the learner's client, and a logical disk is synthesized according to the slice mode, so that the host can read and write at the same time, that is, upload and download learning resources at the same time. The comparative test results are shown in Table 6.

Table 6. Comparison results of simultaneous read and write operations.

Shared block size (KB)	Experimental group A throughput (MB/s)	Experimental group B throughput (MB/s)	Experimental group C throughput (MB/s)
16 KB	1.73	1.59	1.46
32 KB	3.79	3.48	3.23
64 KB	4.89	4.64	4.51
128 KB	6.07	5.78	5.54
256 KB	7.48	6.68	6.51
512 KB	8.25	7.48	7.39
1024 KB	8.35	7.52	7.41

According to the data in the table above, the data throughput of the three groups of systems decreased when reading and writing operations were performed simultaneously, but the data throughput of group A was still larger than that of group B and group C.

3.2.2 The Second Set of Experimental Results

On the basis of the first group of experiments, fixed transmission of a learning resource packet, the resource packet arrival rate of the three systems is 100%, recording the sending time and receiving time, and conducting many experiments to obtain the delay time of system transmission information. The comparison results are shown in Table 7:

Table 7. Comparison results of delay time.

Number of experiments	Group A delay (s)	Group B delay (s)	Group C delay (s)
1	0.48	1.02	1.13
2	0.42	1.09	1.12
3	0.43	0.99	1.08
4	0.39	0.98	1.18
5	0.51	1.01	1.15
6	0.47	0.96	1.14
7	0.46	1.03	1.11
8	0.44	0.99	1.09
9	0.41	0.95	1.03
10	0.44	1.04	1.15

According to the data in the table above, the delay time of transmitting learning resources in group A is far less than that in group B and group C, with an average delay of 0.46 s. The average delay of group B and group C is 1.01 s and 1.12 s respectively, and the delay time of group A is reduced by 0.55 s and 0.66 s respectively. To sum up, in the process of transmitting learning resources, the design system improves the data throughput, reduces the data delay, and the resource transmission efficiency is higher than the traditional system.

4   Conclusion

The mobile learning system designed this time uses wireless communication technology to improve the transmission efficiency of learning resources. However, this research still has certain shortcomings. In future research, we will better grasp the development trend of mobile devices and wireless communication technology, and create a mobile learning environment that makes learners more satisfied from the needs and usability of learners.

References

1. Guo, J., Fu, G., Xiang, Y.: Learning information retrieval system based on mobile software platform. Electron. Design Eng. **28**(19), 80–84 (2020)
2. Jiang, M.X., Zong, Y.Y.: Learning system of 3D animation automatic generation. Comput. Syst. Appl. **27**(8), 70–74 (2018)
3. Liu, Q., Ding, P., Huang, X., et al.: Research on personalized learning recommendation system based on test network. Mod. Educ. Technol. **28**(6), 11–16 (2018)

4. Yu, L.: Design of music distance education learning system based on computer. Tech. Autom. Appl. **38**(12), 64–68 (2019)
5. Zhao, H., Wang, J., Chen, Q., et al.: Application of active learning in recommendation system. Comput. Sci. **46**(z2), 153–158+184 (2019)
6. Wang, L., Zhano, W., Wei, J.: Empirical research on open learner model in adaptive learning system. J. Jilin Univ. (Inf. Sci. Edn.) **37**(5), 512–517 (2019)
7. Liu, S., Liu, D., Srivastava, G., Połap, D., Woźniak, M.: Overview and methods of correlation filter algorithms in object tracking. Complex Intell. Syst. 1 23 (2020). https://doi.org/10.1007/s40747-020-00161-4
8. Fu, W., Liu, S., Srivastava, G.: Optimization of big data scheduling in social networks. Entropy **21**(9), 902 (2019)
9. Liu, S., Li, Z., Zhang, Y., et al.: Introduction of key problems in long-distance learning and training. Mobile Netw. Appl. **24**(1), 1–4 (2019)
10. Nong, M.: Simulation of instant messaging digital push method for mobile learning terminal. Comput. Simul. **36**(4), 379–382 (2019)

Mining Recessive Teaching Resources of University Information Based on Machine Learning

Zheng Jingya[✉] and Jichao Yan

Zhengzhou Technical College, Zhengzhou 450121, China
zhengjingya222@yeah.net

Abstract. The accuracy of mining implicit teaching resources in traditional universities is low, so a method of mining implicit teaching resources in universities based on machine learning is designed. Firstly, it designs the process of data mining, define the problem, collect and preprocess the data, execute the mining algorithm and then explain and evaluate it. The classification method of data mining is optimized. In this paper, the classification technology is neural network, and the artificial neural network unit is built by biological neuron structure, and the classification is completed by biological transfer and activation function. Finally, the machine learning algorithm is improved, and the ight is updated by introducing momentum scalar factor. In the contrast experiment, it chooses the data set and train the parameters, design the process of data mining, and count the relevant parameters of the data set. The experiment results show that the accuracy of the designed method is 4.03% higher than that of the traditional method.

Keywords: Machine learning · Informatization teaching · Recessive resources

1 Introduction

With the advent of the information age, the application of information technology has been slowly penetrated into all areas of people's lives and quietly changing the way of people's lives. In this era of knowledge explosion, it is easy for people to get lost in the huge amount of information, it is difficult to find effective information, which requires people to have a higher information literacy [1, 2]. For a long time, the cultivation of college students' information literacy mainly relies on information technology courses. Hover, the lack of information technology curriculum hours has become a major problem in the cultivation of college students' information literacy, at the same time, it is not realistic to expand information technology curriculum hours in a short time. Therefore, looking for another way - information technology hidden curriculum, to cultivate college students' information literacy is particularly important.

At present, there are two main definitions of IT implicit curriculum: (1) IT implicit curriculum may be those that appear in the formal school teaching plan under the name of other courses, but in fact carry out IT education, including those that are not included in

W. Fu et al. (Eds.): ICMTEL 2021, LNICST 388, pp. 178–188, 2021.
https://doi.org/10.1007/978-3-030-82565-2_15

the formal teaching plan but are provided by the information environment construction of the school. (2) The hidden curriculum of information technology mainly refers to the non-public educational experience that is consciously or unconsciously conveyed or implied to students in the soft and hard environment of information technology education in the school context. It is irreplaceable and has the function of "teaching without teaching". It is an intangible asset of the school [3, 4]. In fact, the definition of these two courses is not contradictory. The former mainly discusses the process of information education inside and outside classroom teaching, while the latter focuses on the software and hardware environment of information technology. In the traditional process of mining the recessive resources of IT teaching in colleges and universities, the accuracy of the results is low, so a mining method based on machine learning is designed, it is innovation lies in the use of biological neuron structure to establish artificial neural network unit, and the use of biological transfer function and activation function to complete the classification. Its focus is to improve the machine learning algorithm and introduce momentum scalar factor. The final result is to modify the machine learning algorithm to ensure the effect of teaching resource mining.

2 Mining Recessive Teaching Resources of University Information Technology Based on Machine Learning

2.1 Design Data Mining Process

Data mining is a complete process, through continuous interaction with the user, the results of mining at different stages of continuous feedback is completed, the whole process is shown as follows (Fig. 1):

Problem definition: First, clear the actual work of data mining requirements; Second, to determine the available learning algorithm. Data preprocessing: generally includes eliminating noise, deriving calculation gap data, eliminating duplicate records and completing data type conversion. Mining algorithm execution: First, to determine the mining tasks; Second, to decide which algorithm to use [5, 6]. Interpretation and evaluation: Eliminate redundant or irrelevant patterns; for patterns that do not meet user requirements, you need to go back to the previous stage. The effectiveness of the data mining technology adopted and the quality and quantity of the data used for data mining are two main factors that affect the quality of data mining.

The core idea of this kind of method is to imitate some behavior activities of biology, and simulate these activities by computer program, mainly including neural network method class and genetic algorithm. Some researchers use genetic algorithm to optimize the search engine and resource scheduling, improve the search and sharing of network teaching resources, so that the majority of teachers and students in the teaching process to obtain quality teaching resources. In the application of RTVU pilot summing-up evaluation system, the fuzzy BP neural network method is used to develop the submodules of FBPNN learning, knowledge base and FBPNN reasoning machine. The fuzzy neural network module is responsible for knowledge acquisition, storage and solution.

Normalization of knowledge representation and expression transformation is the responsibility of the input/output schema transformation. In the evaluation application,

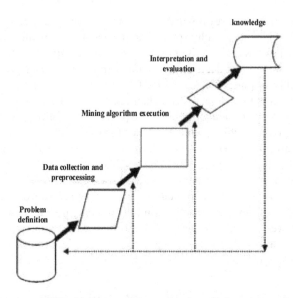

Fig. 1. Process diagram for data mining

it can better realize the summative evaluation of TV University, reduce the interference of artificial uncertainty factors, and enhance the scientific and standard [7–10]. Aiming at the advantages of neural network, the BP neural network is used in the teaching quality evaluation system of modern distance education to construct mathematical models, input different evaluation indexes, and output teaching effect, so as to evaluate teaching quality and teaching effect of modern distance education scientifically and accurately. In order to solve the problems in reality and highlight their own advantages, genetic algorithm and neural network are combined to form a novel evolutionary neural network research field, and many valuable conclusions and results are obtained.

2.2   Optimize Data Mining Classification Methods

Data mining includes a variety of analysis methods to mining data sets analysis, get patterns and apply them, of which classification is occupying a place, and classification methods have been well known. How to classify the data correctly will directly affect the accuracy of the mining results and the efficiency of mining patterns.

Applications of classification include a variety of problem areas, such as text, multimedia, social networking, and biological data. In addition, there may be different problems in many different scenarios. Classification is a fairly diverse topic, and its underlying algorithm relies heavily on data domains and problem scenarios. Classification algorithm is also one of the most important research fields. The overall goal of the data mining approach is to extract information from the information set and associate it with a comprehensive structure for future use.

Classification is a very important mining method in DM. It is a process of looking for classifiers. Objects in the dataset are assigned to different classes by some constraints.

It uses a given class tag to analyze the objects in the dataset, usually using a training set where all the objects are already associated with known class tags. The classification algorithm learns and builds a model from the training set, and then uses the model to classify new objects. In other words, it can say that classification is the process of summarizing data according to different classes. Classification techniques can handle a wider range of data and are becoming increasingly popular [11–15]. The basic principle of the artificial neural network is to imitate the structure and function of human brain, and the computer system is made up of several simple processing units connected in some way. Nerve cells constitute the basic unit of the nervous system, called biological neurons, neurons for short. Neurons consist mainly of three parts: (1) cell body, (2) axon, and (3) dendrite [16–19]. The following figure shows (Fig. 2):

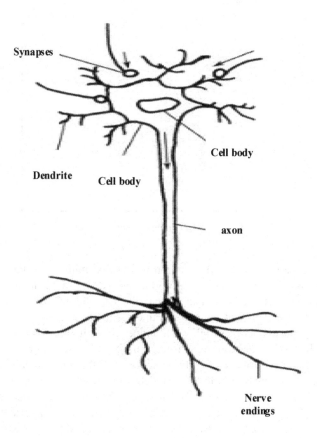

Fig. 2. Structure of biological neurons.

In the neuronal structure shown above, a neuron consists of a cell and its many processes. There is a nucleus in the cell, synaptic function is to transmit information. Several of the processes that introduce an input signal are called "dendrites," while only one of the outgoing processes is called an "axon." The process of neuron transmitting information can be regarded as a dynamic process of a nonlinear system with multiple inputs and single outputs [20–24]. The artificial neural network processing unit thus produced is shown in the following figure (Fig. 3):

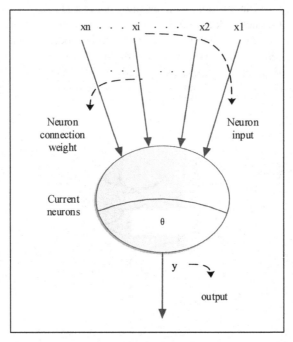

Fig. 3. Artificial neural network unit

Pictured above is a classic M-P neuron model that mimics the basic structure of biological neurons. Where,... is the input to a neuron, and for each neuron it receives input signals from multiple other neurons, and the synaptic intensities are expressed in real coefficients that represent the ighted values of the actions of each neuron on one another. The primary function of ights is to influence the input from a higher level, and the ights can be modified according to rules. All inputs to the neuron can be calculated using a summation formula, that is, the ighted sum of the input signals. The resulting value is compared to the threshold value to determine whether to output, and when the sum value is greater than the threshold value, the output signal is generated, otherwise no output [25–29]. It is the activation function of the processing unit, usually a nonlinear function, representing the threshold of the hidden layer neural node. To sum up [30], the input process of M-P neuron can be described as signal and its corresponding ighting coefficients afferent neuron processing unit, summing them up and substituting activation function to produce output and complete classification of data mining.

2.3 Improved Machine Learning Algorithm

In this paper, the design and improvement of machine learning algorithm is divided into two stages: feedforward stage and back-propagation stage. In the feedforward stage, input samples are imported from the input layer, processed layer by layer, and then transmitted to the output layer. When the actual output value of the output layer does not agree with the desired result, it is corrected by the back-propagation error. The back-propagation of error is to back-propagate the output error from the hidden layer to the input layer, and then distribute the error to all neurons passing through each layer to obtain the error signal of each layer. Then the error signal is used to correct the ight of each unit. When the output error is within the controllable range, that is, the error is less than a set threshold until the end of the cycle. In this paper, the momentum scalar factor is introduced, the ight is defined by the use of momentum term factor, and the batch learning technique is used to make the ight more accurate. The mathematical representation is as follows:

The training data X with P sample is given by the following formula:

$$X = \{x_p, d_p\} \quad p = 1, 2, ..., P \tag{1}$$

Where x_p is the input vector for the sample p with n feature (or dimension):

$$x = \{+1, x_1, x_2, ..., x_n\}^T \tag{2}$$

d_p is the vector to which it is associated with the expected output:

$$d = \{d_1, d_2, ..., d_k\}^T \tag{3}$$

In the feedforward stage, for neurons J in the hidden layer, compute (P, J) the dimension input matrix u:

$$u = XV \tag{4}$$

In the above expression,X is the matrix representing the $(P, n + 1)$ dimension training data, V is the dimension ight vector matrix $(n + 1, J)$ in the hidden layer. Two differentiable activation functions are used in the algorithm: hyperbolic tangent function and logistic model function. Output matrix y of hyperbolic tangent activation function in hidden layer:

$$y = \frac{2}{[1 + \exp(-u)] - 1} \tag{5}$$

Similarly, the signal matrix of the hidden layer is calculated as the product of the derivative output matrix and the ight. By using machine learning algorithm, the network ights are updated iteratively, and the LMS algorithm is used to find the corrected ights of each ight matrix. The correction ight vector is the correlation error signal of the input layer of the product matrix multiplied by a scalar selection learning rate. In order to accelerate the learning process, this paper introduces a momentum scalar factor. In order to use them in the adaptive process of network ights, the previous batch of network ights are saved separately, so the LMS algorithm and momentum factor are used to adjust the network ights.

3   Experiment

3.1   Experimental Environment Parameter Settings

In this chapter, it use TREC conference to provide four representative AD hoc information retrieval test datasets: diskl & 2, disk4 & 5, WT10G and GOV2. The size and type of these four resource datasets are different. For example, diskl & 2 and disk4 & 5 resource datasets mainly include many teaching platforms, the quality is relatively high, while WT10G and GOV2 datasets are obtained from the Internet through the crawler, the quality of its teaching resources cannot be guaranteed.

In this experiment, only the title field is used to construct the query for retrieval. In the process of indexing and query, only two simple pretreatments are carried out: (1) using the Porter word drying tool; and (2) using the standard discontinued word table in the InQuery system to remove discontinued words. The MAP values of 1000 teaching resources are used as evaluation criteria, which is the most commonly used evaluation index in TREC evaluation.

3.2   Parameter Training

From the above, this paper can see that there are some parameters to be adjusted in different feedback models. In order to find the best parameter setting, the comparison model and the model proposed in this paper are all obtained by parameter training. This method is a common method for establishing strong baselines in information retrieval field.

The entire excavation process is shown below (Fig. 4):

In order to verify the effectiveness of the improved method, some data samples from the UCI machine learning database are used in this paper. The following table shows the descriptive information for the experimental datasets used (Table 1):

The values of the fixed parameters used in the experiment are as follows: The momentum factor is used to accelerate the convergence of the cost function to the minimum, and η_0 is a value of 0.75 is good for convergence purposes. kw is A value of 0.1 is used to initialize the ight vector in the hidden layer, leaving it in a small range $[-0.1, +0.1]$. The K-multiple parameter refers to the cross-validation of 10 times during training.

In the experiment, 11 samples are set up, and 10 samples are used as training set and the other one is used as testing set. The average error percentage is obtained and compared with the results of traditional mining method.

3.3   Experimental Results and Analysis

Under the above experimental conditions, for all datasets trained in the MLP structure, the parameters are constant. Using the above resource dataset to train and study the mining method of this paper and the traditional mining method, the accuracy of the results are as follows (Table 2):

In this paper, the hidden resource mining method based on machine learning information teaching has higher classification accuracy than the traditional algorithm. In the experimental data set, this method and the traditional algorithm are used for training

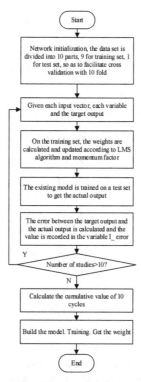

Fig. 4. Mining process

Table 1. Summary of experimental dataset information

Resource data set	Resource data scale	Number of attributes	Number of categories
Aural	160	5	3
Wine	280	8	5
Heart	297	13	5
Cancer	198	32	2
B can	232	19	2
Head	178	15	3
Arm	146	2	3
Craw	989	23	3
Liver	218	60	2
Vote	2533	21	6
Letter	378	35	4

Table 2. Comparison of accuracy of execution results

Resource data set	Accuracy of traditional mining method 1	Accuracy of traditional mining method 2	Accuracy rate of mining method in this paper
Aural	99.67	98.67	99.35
Wine	88.35	87.35	96.54
Heart	95.46	95.56	98.51
Cancer	100	100	100
B can	83.24	83.14	92.33
Head	100	100	100
Arm	87.65	87.35	94.34
Craw	98.35	98.15	98.35
Liver	62.45	62.45	77.35
Vote	97.33	97.23	97.68
Letter	91.23	91.13	95.63
Average value	91.25	91.15	95.28

and learning, respectively, so that the classifier can predict the results. Accuracy refers to the percentage of the ratio between the predicted value and the actual value (or the percentage of the ratio between the actual value and the predicted value, which is subject to the observation results and less than 1). In view of the current academic level, the teaching and research of hidden resources mining is difficult to achieve substantial upgrading, which is still the direction of follow-up action.

4   Closing Remarks

Under the impetus of global informationization, information technology has developed rapidly. Fully excavating and reasonably utilizing the recessive curriculum resources can enrich the curriculum resources and teaching contents, enhance the teaching vitality, and stimulate the students' interest and thirst for knowledge. In this context, under the guidance of the new curriculum reform theory, machine learning and data mining in the processing of mass data, make it easy to find useful information in a large number of data become a reality.

But there are still some deficiencies in this paper, the original data set in this paper is the standard operation order of order of magnitude to be unified between [0, 10], and then data mining work. Hover, there are some limitations, and the [0, 10] data range is not necessarily the most reasonable choice for different data sets. The scope of the specification should be different for different data sets, and this can be explored further.

References

1. Zhang, J.L.-L., Duan, Y.-F.: Analysis on the informatization teaching of specialized English in higher vocational colleges—taking the shipping management major as an example. J. Tianjin Vocat. Inst. **20**(10), 83–87 (2018)
2. Zhang, Z., Wu, F.-F.: Research on precision teaching model based on big data and data mining technology. Inf. Technol. Inf. **12**(10), 130–131,134 (2018)
3. Hong, Z.H.O.U.: Flipped-classroom-based implicit knowledge construction of business English. J. Shenyang Agric. Univ. (Social Science Edition) **20**(04), 463–467 (2018)
4. Wang, L.-P.: User implicit information requirement mining in reading promotion —based on censydiam model. Libr. Theory Pract. **234**(04), 75–79+103 (2019)
5. Tang, Q., Cheng, L., Zhang, L.: Rescheduling mode selection under recessive disturbance accumulation via machine learning. China Mech. Eng. **30**(04), 472–479 (2019)
6. Yi, I.: The impact of informal institutions on health resource allocation decision making— reflections on the implicit priority setting rules. Chinese Public Adm. **1**(03), 99–103 (2019)
7. Fu, W., Liu, S., Srivastava, G.: Optimization of big data scheduling in social networks. Entropy **21**(9), 902 (2019)
8. Liu, S., Li, Z., Zhang, Y., et al.: Introduction of key problems in long-distance learning and training. Mobile Netw. Appl. **24**(1), 1–4 (2019)
9. Liu, S., Liu, D., Srivastava, G., Połap, D., Woźniak, M.: Overview and methods of correlation filter algorithms in object tracking. Complex Intell. Syst. **1**, 23 (2020). https://doi.org/10.1007/s40747-020-00161-4
10. Li-you, W.A.N.G.: The design and implementation of big data platform of university smart campus. J. Hebei Norm. Univ. Natl. **162**(02), 94–99 (2020)
11. Ang, L.M., Ge, F.L., Seng, K.P.: Big educational data & analytics: survey, architecture and challenges. IEEE Access **8**(99):1–1 (2020)
12. Zhou, Y., Song, Z.: Effectiveness analysis of machine learning in education big data. J. Phys.: Conf. Ser. **1651**(1), 012105 (7pp) (2020)
13. Bulltail, G., Walter, M.T.: Impacts of coal resource development on surface water quality in a multi-jurisdictional watershed in the Western United States. J. Contemp. Water Res. Educ. **169**(1), 79–91 (2020)
14. Soini, K., Korhonen-Kurki, K., Asikainen, H.: Transactional learning and sustainability co-creation in a university - business collaboration. Int. J. Sustain. High. Educ. **20**(6), 965–984 (2019)
15. Hu, J., Huang, L., Sun, T., et al.: Proactive planning of bandwidth resource using simulation-based what-if predictions for Web services in the cloud. Front. Comp. Sci. **15**(1), 1–28 (2021)
16. Jones, L., Credo, J., Parnell, R., et al.: Dissolved uranium and arsenic in unregulated groundwater sources – western navajo nation. J. Contemp. Water Res. Educ. **169**(1), 27–43 (2020)
17. Hao, D., Tu, S., Zhang, C.: Experimental study on the effect of moisture content on bituminous coal porosity based on 3D reconstruction of computerized tomography. Nat. Resour. Res. **29**(3), 1657–1673 (2020)
18. Caron, J., Asselin, H., Beaudoin, J.M.: Attitudes and behaviors of mining sector employers towards the Indigenous workforce. Resour. Policy **61**(10), 108–117 (2019)
19. Wang, T., Zhang, H., Gamage, R.P., et al.: The evaluation criteria for rock brittleness based on double-body analysis under uniaxial compression. Geomech. Geophys. Geo-Energy Geo-Resourc. **6**(3), 1–19 (2020)
20. Hellqvist, M.: Teaching sustainability in geoscience field education at falun mine world heritage site in Sweden. Geoheritage **11**(4), 1785–1798 (2019)

21. Helal, S., Li, J., Liu, L., et al.: Identifying key factors of student academic performance by subgroup discovery. Int. J. Data Sci. Anal. **7**(3), 227–245 (2019)
22. Yu, J.: Analysis and design of course website for software testing based on SPOC. J. Phys. Conf. Ser. **1187**(5), 052015 (2019)
23. Turner, P.J., Thaler, A.D., Freitag, A., et al.: Deep-sea hydrothermal vent ecosystem principles: Identification of ecosystem processes, services and communication of value. Marine Pol. **101**, 118–124 (2019)
24. Patra, R., Saha, S.K.: A hybrid approach for automatic generation of named entity distractors for multiple choice questions. Educ. Inf. Technol. **24**(2), 973–993 (2019)
25. Lynch, S.: Education resources for the boiler supply chain. Eng. Syst. **36**(5APP.), 3–3 (2019)
26. Ma, T., Antoniou, C., Toledo, T.: Hybrid machine learning algorithm and statistical time series model for network-wide traffic forecast. Transp. Res. Part C Emerg. Technol. **2020**(111), 352–372 (2020)
27. Mu, A.Y.: A hybrid machine learning model with cost-function based outlier removal and its application on credit rating. J. Phys. Conf. Ser. **1584**(1), 012001 (2020)
28. Chefira, R., Rakrak, S.: Accuracy assessment of applied supervised machine learning models on usual data probability distributions. J. Phys.: Conf. Ser. **1743**(1), 012011 (13pp) (2021)
29. Gosal, A.S., Ziv, G.: Landscape aesthetics: spatial modelling and mapping using social media images and machine learning. Ecol. Ind. **117**(0), 106638 (2020)
30. Sengupta, P.P., Shrestha, S., Béatrice, B., et al.: Proposed requirements for cardiovascular imaging-related machine learning evaluation (PRIME): a checklist: reviewed by the American college of cardiology healthcare innovation council. JACC. Cardiovasc. Imaging **13**(9), 2017–2035 (2020)

Networked Teaching System of College Basketball Course Based on Virtual Reality

Er-wei Liu[✉]

School of Road Bridge and Architecture, Chongqing Vocational College of Transportation, Chongqing 402247, China

Abstract. Aiming at the poor performance of the traditional college basketball course networked teaching system, with the purpose of improving the performance of college basketball course networked teaching system, a virtual reality-based college basketball course networked teaching system is designed. Through the user registration module design, the question answering module design and the student user management module design, the hardware design of the system is completed, and the software design of the system is completed through the management of college basketball course resources and the design of the student basketball course homework management program. The design of the networked teaching system of the course. The test results show that the network teaching system of College Basketball Course Based on virtual reality has reached the design requirements and has higher performance.

Keywords: Virtual reality technology · Basketball course · Network teaching · System performance

1 Introduction

With the continuous development of network technology, the continuous development of information-based teaching equipment, teaching methods and teaching resources are becoming increasingly rich. The traditional teaching mode dominated by teachers can not adapt to the current teaching environment of higher education. It has become an inevitable requirement of education reform to widely apply information technology to the whole process of teaching and learning, so as to improve teaching quality and optimize talent training. The cultivation mode has positive significance [1–3]. In the information-based teaching environment, virtual reality technology based on information technology and personalized learning has emerged. After a period of practice and discussion, people have a clearer understanding of virtual reality technology. Virtual reality technology has not received much attention and in-depth practical research in Chinese physical education. Today when individualized teaching is advocated, research on the value and implementation strategies of virtual reality technology in the teaching of public physical education in colleges and universities is of great significance for deepening the reform of college physical education and improving teaching quality [4–6].

© ICST Institute for Computer Sciences, Social Informatics and Telecommunications Engineering 2021
Published by Springer Nature Switzerland AG 2021. All Rights Reserved
W. Fu et al. (Eds.): ICMTEL 2021, LNICST 388, pp. 189–202, 2021.
https://doi.org/10.1007/978-3-030-82565-2_16

With the continuous deepening of college physical education reform, coupled with the profound changes in college enrollment structure, the original physical education model no longer meets the requirements of higher education for talent training. The construction of new teaching mode has become an important link in the reform of physical education, which can promote the reform of physical education, improve the quality of classroom teaching and cultivate qualified talents needed by the society And so on. The essence of virtual reality technology is to use information technology and network technology to change the learning environment, make the learning process more personalized, give students more time and space for independent learning, promote classroom communication and interaction, and facilitate a good teacher-student relationship Construct. The efficient use of network resources is conducive to promoting teachers' development and expansion of curriculum resources [7].

The goal of training students in Colleges and universities is to cultivate labor skilled talents who meet the needs of economic and social development. From the perspective of employment, it puts forward more realistic and specific requirements for students' operational ability, physical quality and physical health. Therefore, in the process of practical teaching, higher education pays more attention to the training of students' hands-on ability and labor skills, and pays attention to cultivating students' will and quality of hard work. As far as public physical education is concerned, the tasks of the class also focus on quality training such as strength, so that students have a stronger physique and cultivate students' tenacious will.

Miller re et al. [8] described the functions of the applicant processing system designed for the virtual hotel chain. The system described in detail in the case includes a web form in which applicants can complete and submit work applications. The system also includes a desktop application for hotel managers and human resources departments to track applications and process job offers. The webform and desktop applications share a centralized database. This case is based on an actual system development project completed by a student for a real hotel chain. The materials in the case can be used for system analysis and design, database management, and web design courses. Teaching notes, including entity relationship diagrams, data dictionaries, data flow diagrams, job application forms, prototype screenshots and discussion questions are available on the JISE website.

Based on the above background, this article applies virtual reality technology to the design of the college basketball course networked teaching system. Through the user registration module design, the question answering module design and the student user management module design, the hardware design of the system is completed, and the college basketball course is managed. Resource and student basketball course homework management program design, completed the software design of the system, and completed the networked teaching system design of college basketball courses according to the hardware design and software design. And the effectiveness of the system is verified by simulation experiments.

2 Hardware Design of Network Teaching System for Basketball Course in Colleges

2.1 Design of User Registration Module

Student user registration is an important part of the college basketball course networked teaching system. Student users must register with their student ID to log in to the system. The student registration flowchart is shown in Fig. 1.

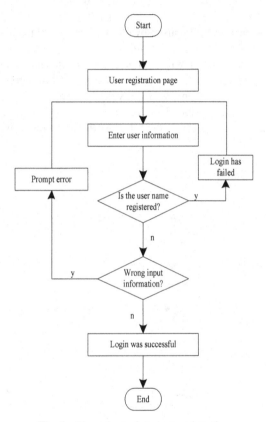

Fig. 1. Flow chart of student registration

After students enter the login page, click the "registration account" button on the page to register users.

The student's student ID is the only identifier that distinguishes the student. After entering the registration page, the student user needs to use the student ID as the user name to register. When submitting the information, the system will check whether the user name has been registered. If the user name is registered, it will prompt Registration failed, need to register again.

If the input information is wrong, such as the wrong e-mail address, a prompt will be given and can continue to register; if the registration is successful, will be prompted to register successfully. Click the login system connection to return to the system login page for user login.

2.2 Question Answering Module Design

The question and answer section provides a platform for students to communicate with teachers and students. Students who have questions during the course of learning basketball can use this board to ask questions and consult the teacher's answer. At the same time, they can check the questions raised by other students and the answers of teachers in this plate [9]. After the student user submits the relevant question information through the question page, the information will be submitted to the teacher background question answering management module. The teacher user can perform corresponding management operations on the question, and can review the questions raised by the student user. After the review is passed and responded, Students will be able to see the corresponding information in the question answering module, and the question answering flowchart is shown in Fig. 2.

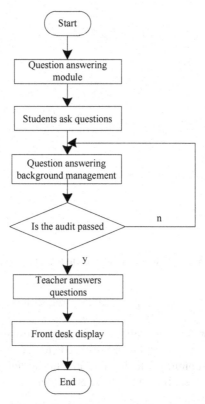

Fig. 2. Question answering flowchart

In the question answering module, student users can view, search and ask questions by category. The key operations are as follows:

Step1: View questions by category: In the Q&A module, student users can view all question information or view question information by real question type. The key operation for viewing by real question type is to pass the type_name of the real question type and receive the type_name value of the classification page.

Step 2: search question: in the question answering module, student users can search for relevant question titles through the search function, and set the record set first;

Step3: Asking questions: In the question answering module, student users can ask questions to the teacher by entering the subject, content and selecting the question type.

In the question information submitted by students, the hidden field passid is set to limit the display of question information in the question answering interface. By default, passid is 0, that is, the audit authority is 0 (failed). Only after the teacher user reviews and sets the permission to 1 (that is, passed), it can be displayed in the system question answering interface.

2.3 Design of Student User Management Module

In the student user management interface, teachers can operate as follows:

Step1: Student user search function: Teacher users can enter the name of the student user in the search bar of the student user management interface to search.

Step2: student user query function of each class: in the student user management module, the teacher user can query the information of all student users in each class in the list by viewing the class list and clicking the class list, and carry out corresponding management operation on the student user information. The main key technology to realize this function is to use the class name as the class_ The name field information is passed as a URL parameter, and the class is passed through the URL when the record set is established on the receiving page_ The name field information filters the database records and displays them.

Step3: Basic student user management operations: In the student user management interface, the teacher can add, update and delete student users accordingly. Since student users use their student ID as their user name when registering, they can distinguish different users. Therefore, in the update operation, the user name and student ID of the student user are set as "read-only" attributes.

Through the user registration module design, question answering module design and student user management module design, the hardware design of the system is realized.

3   Software Design of Network Teaching System for Basketball Course in Colleges

3.1   Management of College Basketball Curriculum Resources

Students choose courses including watching course videos, browsing course content, downloading courseware, etc. [10]. According to the constructivist learning view, students are the subject of cognition, that is, students can actively learn. Each student will build his own understanding of new knowledge based on his own original experience, and re-understand and re-understand new knowledge, coding. "Students should choose the curriculum resources uploaded by teachers with their own cognitive structure, so as to improve their learning efficiency". The process of course resource management is shown in Fig. 3. And for the sake of security, only the login users can use the teaching resources uploaded by teachers to learn.

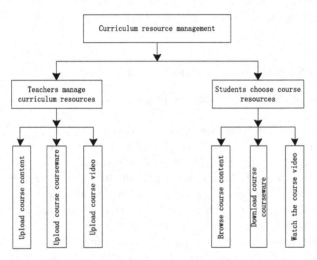

Fig. 3. Course resource management flowchart

Curriculum resource management includes two parts: teachers manage curriculum resources and students choose curriculum resources. Teacher resource management is to provide students with various curriculum resources through the system, including course video, course courseware, course schedule, course assignment, etc. According to the behavioral learning theory, the curriculum resources uploaded by teachers should create a positive learning atmosphere for students to maximize the positive behaviors of students and eliminate negative behaviors. The curriculum resources uploaded by teachers should follow the cognitive order of students, Sort from simple to difficult, shallow to deep. Curriculum resources should be combined with students' learning experience as much as possible to improve students' understanding of curriculum resources and improve students' autonomous learning ability.

3.2 Design of Homework Management Program for Students' Basketball Course

The homework management module mainly has the function of teachers assigning homework and the function of students completing homework. The teacher assignment process is shown in Fig. 4.

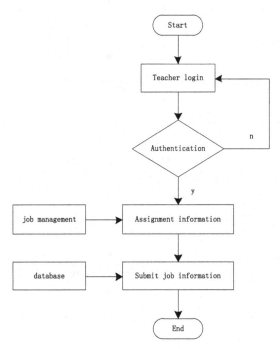

Fig. 4. Flow chart of teacher's assignment

The teacher assigns the course homework according to the selected course. Assignment of the homework includes two parts: filling in the overall information of the homework and the detailed information of the homework. The overall information of the assignment includes: the course ID of the assignment, the name of the assignment, the submission time and the deadline. The detailed information of the assignment is the topic design of the assignment. There are four kinds of homework questions: single choice questions, multiple choice questions, short answer questions and application questions. The information of single choice questions and multiple choice questions should include the content of the questions, options, question scores and standard answers, while the information of short answer questions and application questions should include the content of the questions, reference answers and question scores.

Figure 5 shows the process of students completing their homework.

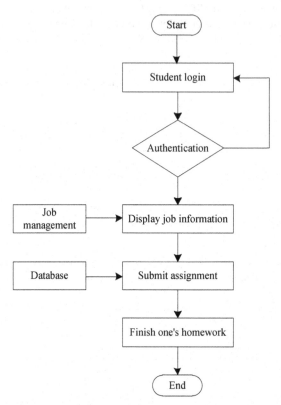

Fig. 5. Flow chart for students to complete homework

Operations on homework information should include selecting courses, viewing homework, completing homework, submitting homework, viewing corrections, etc. In the answer page, students need to complete the four types of questions respectively. Among them, single-choice questions can only choose only one item; multiple-choice questions need to choose at least two; application questions can view the files uploaded by the teacher or by themselves Upload files for teachers' reference. Marking homework belongs to the function of teacher users. According to the completion of homework, the teacher selects a student to grade. Among them, single-choice questions and multiple-choice questions have been automatically corrected by the system. The task for teachers to complete is to mark short answer questions and application questions. Teachers can grade according to the reference answers, and the score of teachers is less than the score of questions. For application questions, teachers can download the files uploaded by students for detailed evaluation.

4 System Test

A perfect college basketball course network teaching system, in order to make the system run normally, testing is an essential part. Although strict technical review has been adopted in the development process of the network teaching system of basketball course in Colleges and universities, it is inevitable to leave errors. If the errors and loopholes in the system are not found and corrected before they are put into operation, these loopholes and errors will directly affect the operation of the system. If the problems are corrected after they occur, the cost of manpower, material resources and so on will be required Greatly improved. Unit testing and functional testing are part of system testing. Unit testing is to let developers know that the code is executing correctly, and verifying whether the code performs its intended effect is the goal of functional testing. Unit tests are written from the perspective of the developer. The goal of each test is that the output we get is what we want when we enter it. What is written for the user is called a functional test. The purpose of the test is that the system runs to meet the user's requirements. The so-called software testing is mainly aimed at two aspects of function and performance. According to its process plan and related test tools, the results are analyzed and resolved accordingly. In summary, if want to improve software quality, many related software tests are indispensable.

4.1 Testing Environment

The test requirements of the system mainly include hardware requirements and software requirements. The specific configuration is as follows:

- Hardware requirements.

   Test terminal: Recommend Intel Pentium 4 or higher processor, 8 GB memory or more, hard disk 300G or more, support USB interface, support multiple network access methods.

- Software requirements.

   Test software: loaderunner.
   Test browser: IE, firefox.
   Test record: excel, Bugzilla.

4.2 System Performance Test

4.2.1 Concurrency Testing

The test scenario is shown in Table 1.

Step 1: first, log in to the system with the admin account;
Step 2: click "teacher management" on the function bar to enter the teacher management interface;
Step 3: click "new teacher" on the interface, and enter the teacher information "Zhang San, 45, male, 117124367@qq.com,13545075826";
Step 4: click Submit;
Step 5: click "log out" on the function bar to put forward the system.

The test results are shown in Tables 1, 2, 3 and 4 below.
1. The test data under simulated 200 users are shown in Table 1 below.

Table 1. Performance of 200 users under the same time

Test items	Pre test data	Data after test
IO Occupancy rate	0%	10%
Memory usage	100M	300M
Packet increase	1224	1224
Test average feedback time	3.1	3.1
Test maximum feedback time	4.5	4.5

2. Simulate the test data under 500 users, as shown in Table 2 below.

Table 2. The performance of 500 users online at the same time

Test items	Pre test data	Post test data
IO Occupancy rate	0%	50%
Memory usage	100M	469M
Packet increase	2235	2235
Test average feedback time	4.7	4.7
Maximum feedback time for testing	5.8	5.8

3. The test data under simulated 800 users is shown in Table 3 below.

Table 3. Performance of 800 users under the same time

Test items	Pre test data	Post-test data
IO Occupancy rate	0%	60%
Memory usage	100M	538M
Packet increase	3421	3421
Test average feedback time	4.9	4.9
Maximum feedback time for testing	5.3	5.3

4. Test data under simulated 1000 users is shown in Table 4 below.

Table 4. The performance of 1000 users online at the same time

Test items	Pre test data	Post-test data
IO Occupancy rate	0%	54%
Memory usage	100M	634M
Packet increase	45231	45231
Test average feedback time	6.0	6.0
Maximum feedback time for testing	8.2	8.2

4.2.2 Response Speed Test

In order to better test the performance of the system under high load, the system uses the Loader Runner tool to create multiple groups of different numbers of users to perform simultaneous operations and record the system's response time. The items tested in this test are: login to the system, online communication, and online teaching. The test results are shown in Tables 5, 6 and 7 below.

Table 5. Landing system test

Landing system test case			
Precondition	Normal login interface		
Test target	Understand the performance of the system under multi-user login at the same time		
Method	Use the LoadRunner tool to simulate multi-user login scenarios and execute test scripts		
Number of concurrent tests	Average time to complete business(s)	Maximum time spent on business completion(s)	Average use of network packets
30	1.045	2.345	67
60	4.231	6.892	68
200	5.123	9.352	100

Table 6. Online AC test

Online communication test cases			
Prerequisite	Normal login system		
Test objectives	Understand the performance of the system in simultaneous online communication with multiple users		
Method	Use the LoadRunner tool to simulate multi-user online communication scenarios and execute test scripts		
Number of concurrent tests	Average time to complete business (s)	Maximum time spent on business completion (s)	Average use of network packets
30	1.235	2.231	64
60	3.123	6.234	66
200	5.123	11.233	79

4.3 Test Conclusion

After the performance test of the network teaching system of College Basketball Course Based on virtual reality, the system has reached the standard of design requirements. Under the condition of less than 200 users, the system has stable speed and good perfor-

Table 7. Online teaching test

Online teaching test cases			
Prerequisite	Normal login system		
Test objectives	Normal login system		
Method	Use LoadRunner tools to simulate multi-user online teaching scenarios and execute test scripts		
Number of concurrent tests	Average time to complete business (s)	Maximum time-consuming business completion (s)	Average use of network packets
30	1.892	3.123	72
60	5.122	8.213	75
200	6.781	13.112	129

mance, but when more than 200 users are online at the same time, the system is inefficient and slow to respond. At present, the optimization is carried out in the following ways:

1. Database access performance optimization

Establishing, opening and closing links are commonly used by users to access database resources. In the process of these operations, information exchange is necessary to ensure that the database can pass the authentication. When users open and close such operations, hibernate can use the connection pool to change the impact of these operations on the system. The user's database connection is stored in the connection pool, and the user takes it out when needed, and puts it back when not needed, and then waits for the customer to use and request it again. However, the carrying capacity of the connection pool is also limited. If the connection pool is still required to be used when the connection pool is fully loaded, this will have a great impact on the function of the connection pool.

2. Connector optimization

In the Tomcat server, a thread needs to be opened for each request to serve it. When there are too many users, due to the limited number of threads, it is necessary to wait for the completion of other business processing before continuing to use the thread, which results in slow user response. In order to ensure that the system is connected quickly, it is necessary to first recommend a connection pool with sufficient number of connections. This pool can well support the requirement that the system is online with 1000 people at the same time. Therefore, the system defines the number of connection pools as 1000, which greatly exceeds The original 800, but from the test results, it does solve the current problem of connection thread tension.

5   Conclusion

This paper proposes a networked teaching system for college basketball courses based on virtual reality. Through the hardware design and software design of the college basketball course networked teaching system, the networked teaching of college basketball courses is realized. The test results show that the system has high performance.

References

1. Li Na, F., Ke, X., et al.: An effective combination analysis of PBL, PLTL and networked teaching mode in the teaching of gynaecology. China Continuing Med. Educ. **010**(017), 9–11 (2018)
2. Afsouran, N.R., Charkhabi, M., Siadat, S.A., et al.: Case-method teaching: advantages and disadvantages in organizational training. J. Manage. Dev. **37**(9–10), 711–720 (2018)
3. Mourtzis, D., Vlachou, E., Dimitrakopoulos, G., et al.: Cyber- physical systems and education 4.0 –the teaching factory 4.0 concept. Procedia Manuf. **23**, 129–134 (2018)
4. Steeves, V., Regan, P.M.: Teaching digital citizenship in the networked classroom. Int. J. Public Adm. Digital Age **5**(4), 33–49 (2018)
5. Mohialdeen, A.: Teacher development in technology-enhanced language teaching. In: Jeong-Bae, S. (ed.) Springer International, Switzerland (2018). https://doi.org/10.1007/978-3-319-75711-7. (xx + 233 pp[J]. System, 2019, 82:174-175)
6. Yingke, Z., Ping, H.: The evaluation system for young teachers' teaching quality. Sci. Educ. Lit. Collect. **000**(018), 25–26 (2018)
7. Polizzi, S.J., Michelle, H., Donna, B.W., et al.: The use of teacher leader roles in an online induction support system. Teach. Teach. Educ. **75**, 174–186 (2018)
8. Liu, S., Lu, M., Li, H., et al.: Prediction of gene expression patterns with generalized linear regression model. Front. Genet. **10**, 120 (2019)
9. Fu, W., Liu, S., Srivastava, G.: Optimization of big data scheduling in social networks. Entropy **21**(9), 902 (2019)
10. Liu, S., Li, Z., Zhang, Y., et al.: Introduction of key problems in long-distance learning and training. Mobile Networks Appl. **24**(1), 1–4 (2019)

Research on Remote Online Teaching Assistant System Based on Human-Computer Interaction

Zijin Xiao[✉], Ying Li, and Hai Zhou

College of Science, Engineering, Agriculture and Medicine, Gansu Radio and Television
University, Lanzhou 730030, China
fddsf222@aliyun.com

Abstract. In this study, human-computer interaction is applied to the design
of remote online teaching assistance system. The camera module consists of a
processor, a network camera and a microphone. The system software is composed of online examination module, course resource management module, online
question-answering module, client module, video teaching module and personal
information management module. Among them, the online examination module
is divided into question bank management, examination management and other
sub-functional modules; The course resource management module mainly completes the input and output of educational resources by uploading and downloading
learning materials. Online Q&A module is mainly divided into question database
management, question search and other sub-functional modules; The client module is mainly composed of Flash CS5; Video teaching module is mainly used to
realize remote video teaching.

Keywords: Human computer interaction · Distance learning · Network camera ·
Soap format · Educational resources

1 Introduction

Today's society has entered the information age, and the information society has put
forward new requirements for the training of high-level talents and high-quality talents.
And information technology provides opportunities for the development of education,
training of specialized talents and improving the quality of the labor force [1]. The
development of information technology has gradually changed the traditional classroom teaching methods, and multimedia teaching and distance teaching have also been
generally introduced into modern higher education.

Distance teaching provides students with individualized learning conditions and
diversified learning environment, so that students can study pertinently, give full play
to their strengths and improve their creativity while developing in an all-round way,
thus promoting the development of quality education [2]. With the popularization of
computer and the rapid development and application of computer network technology,
some universities and educational institutions at home and abroad have launched distance teaching on the network, which has pushed computer-aided teaching to a higher

W. Fu et al. (Eds.): ICMTEL 2021, LNICST 388, pp. 203–215, 2021.
https://doi.org/10.1007/978-3-030-82565-2_17

level. Distance teaching has the characteristics of wide opening, extension, flexibility and diversity. The extensive openness of distance education is the most basic feature different from traditional education. Distance teaching makes the educational resources can be effectively used and shared in the whole society. At the same time, because distance education effectively spreads the relevant teaching content and teaching concept in the whole society through various media, and is enriched and optimized again in each communication link, which makes the teaching content selectively spread and extend, which is conducive to the improvement of the quality of teaching resources.

With the development of computer and Internet technology, information technology support methods have also been continuously innovated and improved, which can adapt to more different application requirements and management requirements. The remote online teaching assistant system is an important means to realize remote teaching, so this research conducts in-depth research on the remote online teaching assistant system and applies human-computer interaction to the remote online teaching assistant system. In this study, the processor, network camera and microphone constitute the camera module of the system, so as to complete the construction of the hardware environment, and then the online examination module, course resource management module, online question-answering module, client module, video teaching module, personal information management module constitute the software environment of the system. The experimental results also prove that the system has the advantages of short average response time, strong database connectivity and high security.

2 Design of Distance Online Teaching Assistant System Based on Human Computer Interaction

2.1 Hardware Design

The hardware configuration of the system is camera module, which is composed of processor, network camera and microphone [4]. The specific technical data of the processor is shown in Table 1.

Table 1. Specific technical data of the processor

Serial number	Project	Data
1	Main frequency	1 GHz
2	Name	Intel Core i8
3	Memory	32 G
4	Hard disk	256 G

Network camera, also known as IP camera, is composed of network coding module and analog camera [5]. The network coding module encodes and compresses the analog video signal collected by the analog camera into digital signal, which can be directly connected to the network switching and routing equipment. An embedded chip is built into the network camera, and the embedded real-time operating system is used to control it. After being digitized, the video signal transmitted by the camera is compressed by an efficient compression chip and transmitted to the web server through the network bus [6]. Users on the network can directly use the browser to watch the camera images on the Web server, and authorized users can also control the actions of the camera's pan-tilt lens or operate the system configuration. Network cameras can realize monitoring more easily, especially remote monitoring, simpler construction and maintenance, better support for audio, better support for alarm linkage, more flexible video storage, higher-definition video effects and more perfect monitoring management [6]. In addition, IPC supports WIFI wireless access, 3G access, POE power supply (network power supply) and optical fiber access.

Microphones in the hardware environment are VHF segment microphones with frequencies ranging from 180 MHz to 280 MHz, which are subject to little environmental interference. In addition, VHF microphones adopt crystal frequency lock, so frequency conversion will not occur, and the receiving performance is relatively stable. The high frequency part of the microphone circuit adopts discrete processing, which makes it has the advantages of higher sensitivity and more stable performance. The audio processing part adopts 571 line.

2.2 Software Design

2.2.1 Design Online Examination Module

The online exam module is designed based on human-computer interaction. The online exam module is divided into four sub-function modules: question bank management, exam management, answer management and score management.

The main users of online examination are teachers and students [7]. The teacher establishes the corresponding test database according to the teaching plan, and updates and removes the test items according to the timeliness and popularity of the test questions. After students enter the online exam module, click start test. The module can randomly select the questions in the test database to generate the test papers randomly. Generally speaking, the examination time is 2 h.

The main function of the question bank management sub-module is to manage the question bank. In accordance with the requirements of the examination syllabus at the time, in combination with their own teaching plans and teaching arrangements, teachers set up examination questions of different difficulty in each teaching stage. Teachers can obtain excellent test resource resources through other media so as to better and more scientifically test the level of knowledge of students. In order to reduce the repetition of each set of test papers and do a good job of time management of test questions, the question bank must maintain a certain amount of test questions and update. The question bank management sub-module can remind teachers to manage the test question bank and update and revise the test questions in time. The questions in the test question bank mainly include multiple-choice questions and subjective questions. When the teacher enters the test question information, it will be entered together with the answer. It is convenient for students to check the correct answer to the question after checking the score, which is helpful for students to correct and summarize errors in a targeted manner.

The sub module of examination management will select 60 multiple-choice questions and 5 subjective questions from the question bank according to the frequency and difficulty of each test question, and the examination time is generally 2 h. The algorithm of examination management module follows two principles: random selection and time control under the premise of difficult and easy setting. The principle of random selection ensures the rationality and unpredictability of test paper preparation, which is conducive to comprehensive assessment of students' knowledge level from various aspects:

(1) Random principle: Each question will be marked with priority every time it is drawn. The system will combine the questions in a comprehensive consideration of the priority of the questions to realize the non-repetition of the test papers, avoid students from guessing the questions, and ensure the exam Fairness.

(2) Reasonable principle: in addition to priority identification, each topic also needs to have corresponding teaching chapters, corresponding grades, and estimated problem-solving time, so as to facilitate teachers to classify and select the difficulty degree of the test question resource pool during the test question extraction.

(3) Comprehensive principle: The test question bank contains multiple choice questions and subjective questions. Students only need to choose the correct answer from the test paper. There is no need to answer the process, which simplifies the examination process and is suitable for online examination. At the same time, taking into account the factors of examination time, the sum of the estimated time to solve the selected questions should not exceed 2 h in principle, and can be adjusted according to the degree of difficulty [8].

In addition, when uploading teaching resources, teachers need to give answers and some necessary calculation process of answers at the same time, so as to help students who participate in distance education to achieve 100 points after the test conveniently.

The main function of the score management sub-module is to manage test scores. After the student submits the test paper, the result of this test will be given. Score query is also indispensable as a key application after the exam. Query results needs to be quick and easy. Generally speaking, you need to enter the student's name to find out the corresponding results. This function should be open to groups that care about performance, such as teachers, students, and parents. Teachers can effectively formulate follow-up teaching plans by inquiring grades, helping students with poor academic performance to check for deficiencies, and at the same time help students with excellent grades to further improve. Parents learn about their children's learning situation by inquiring about their scores, discuss with their children to find out the problems, and improve their academic scores as soon as possible.

The online examination process of online examination module is shown in Fig. 1.

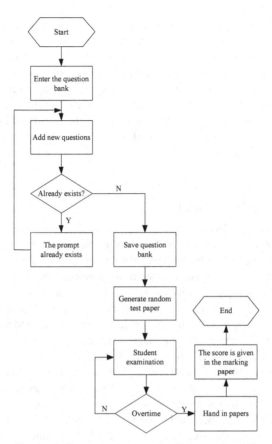

Fig. 1. Online exam process of online exam module

2.2.2 Design Course Resource Management Module

The course resource management module is an important functional module to realize distance education teaching. It mainly completes education output by uploading learning materials, downloading learning materials to complete education input, and resource management to complete the management of teaching resources.

Uploading learning materials means that teachers upload teaching courses, course analysis, and exercise solutions to the system database in various ways, such as electronic courseware, video and audio, for students to download remotely. The user clicks the browse button to find the path of the file to be uploaded, and then clicks to start uploading. After the upload is successful, the user will be prompted with a message. This can realize the function of single file upload and multiple file upload at the same time.

Downloading learning materials refers to listing the electronic courseware, teaching plan, syllabus and other teaching documents uploaded by teachers one by one in the course materials listed in the resource library, which are downloaded by students according to the current course progress and their own needs. The download process is relatively simple, you just need to click download directly to complete.

Resource management refers to the gradual increase of teaching resources with the development of teaching courses. In order to improve the quality and efficiency of the server database, it is necessary to screen and optimize the relevant teaching resources, clean up the resources that have not been downloaded for a long time, and reclaim the storage space.

2.2.3 Design Online Q&A Module

The online question answering module is mainly divided into four sub function modules: question base management, question search, online question and question answer.

The sub module of question bank management refers to that more and more questions are submitted to the system by students with the development of teachers' answering work. For some typical representative questions, the teacher or administrator will keep the questions, and further add research and analysis results to clear up the answers and questions, and do some optimization work on the display interface to remind students to pay attention to them; for some problems that have little access, teachers or administrators will delete the questions according to the actual situation.

The question search sub-module is mainly for students to search the questions that have been asked in the question library, find out the questions they are concerned about, and at the same time inquire related analysis and answers. The user can enter the question number in the question number single-line text box, or enter the question title in the question title multi-line text box. After inputting, click the query button to view the successful query page.

The online questioning sub-module is mainly for students to initiate a new question and wait for the teacher's answer when they cannot find the answer to the relevant question in the question search.

In problem solving sub module, the teacher to students at a certain time period the question list, select some typical or suitable teaching progress to solve the problem, and associated directly with the answers to answer questions, the students in the "search" project can directly search for the answer.

2.2.4 Design Client Module

The client module is designed based on Flash AS3.0, and the module uses the event listener mechanism. In the development process of the system, the client part mainly uses Flash cs5 to complete [9]. There is no corresponding component when using Flash cs5. At this time, you need to manually call soap and xml classes to communicate with the Web Service. To use soap and xml to connect to the Web Service, you need to construct the access request in soap format by yourself to bypass the security sandbox restrictions of Flashplayer. The format of SOAP is shown in Fig. 2.

1. POST /WebService/test.asmx HTTP/1.1
2. Host: 192.168.33.106
3. Content-Type: text/xml; charset=utf-8
4. Content-Length: length
5. SOAPAction: "http://92.168.33.106/say"

Fig. 2. Schematic diagram of the format of SOAP

When using the URL Request Header of flash AS3.0 to construct soap request header, post, host and content length are not supported. At the same time, it is unnecessary to set the content type and soapaction. Add the relevant information through the Request Heade URL Request Headers. Push method, as shown in Fig. 3.

1.var r:URL Request=new URL Request("http://
www.roading.net/WebService/Test .asmx?op=say");
2.r.method=URL RequestMethod.POST;
3.r.request Headers.push (newURL Request Header ("Content-
Type", "text/xml;charset=utf-8"));
4.r.requestHeaders.push(newURL Request Header
("SOAPAction", "http:// 192.168. 33.106isay"));

Fig. 3. Diagram of information joining process

Then the corresponding Web Service method can be accessed through the constructed URL Request object R.

The data obtained after the access will be stored in the data attribute of r in the form of xm1, and the relevant results can be obtained by accessing the data attribute.

The protocol used to connect to Flash Media Server 3 is RTMP: Real Time Messaging Protocol. The latest RTMP is RTMPE (E stands for encryption).

The first thing to determine when using the RMTP protocol to access the FMS3 server is the RMTP address to be accessed. This address consists of three parts, as follows:
rmtp:// 192.168.3 3 .106/deux.

This address consists of protocol name, server address and application name. The application program on FMS3 is different from the general application program. Its application program is only the name of a directory corresponding to the relevant location. As long as the directory exists, FMS3 can complete most of the media functions (connection control and other functions still need to be completed by script).

Flash client connects to FMS3 server mainly using the connect method of NetConnection object, and uses RMTP address as the connection parameter. After the connection is successfully established, the video stream can be obtained on the connection, or the video stream can be published.

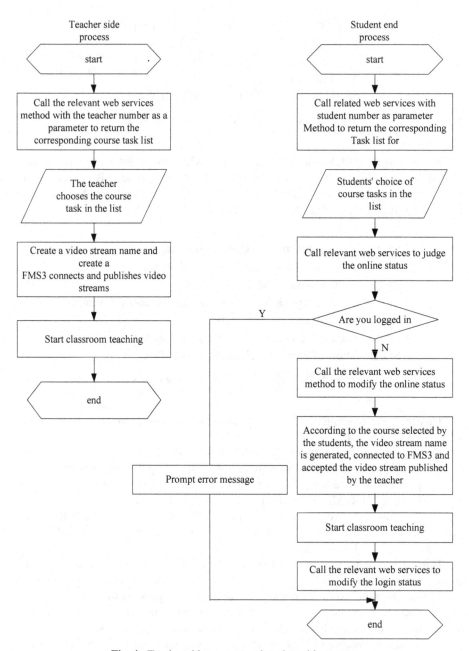

Fig. 4. Teacher side process and student side process

2.2.5 Design Video Teaching Modules

In the video teaching module, identity authentication and other functions are completed by the login page. The client focuses on the implementation of the corresponding course video teaching tasks, and mainly uses the methods provided when data and verification judgment are needed. When the teacher completes the video setting and publishes the video stream, the teacher and student can carry on the video teaching. In this process, the server can count the number and identity of connected users for class roll call and other functions. The main functions of the student side of the video teaching module are basically the same as the teacher side. However, due to the large number of students, the system needs to prevent malicious users from repeatedly logging in or non authenticated users logging into the classroom, which will have adverse effects on the classroom order.

Among them, the teacher-side process and the student-side process are shown in Fig. 4.

2.2.6 Design Personal Information Management Module

In the personal information management module, after the educational administrators add students and teachers to the system, the corresponding students and teachers can query and modify their own information. The query and modification process of the two users is basically similar. Taking student users as an example, students need to use the student number information when they query their own information. At the same time, in order to prevent users from modifying the information of other users, we should only extract the student number from the information stored in when the user logs in, and query. When modifying students' personal information, we should pay attention to whether the original information has been changed, so as to avoid unnecessary operation. When updating the information, the information generated when the user logs in shall also prevail, so as to avoid modifying other user information. When the student user enters the personal information page, the information generated during login is extracted first, and then the information to be displayed in the web page is returned by querying the database. If the information is wrong or there is no information, it will jump to the login page directly to prevent users from maliciously tampering with the information. When the student user clicks the Modify button, the information submitted by the user is compared with the original data. If the information has not changed, no operation will be done; if there is a change. Then the new student information will be updated to the database.

3 Experimental Verification

3.1 Experimental Design

In order to prove the effective performance of the remote online teaching assistance system based on human-computer interaction, experiments are conducted to verify it. The experimental environment data is shown in Table 2.

Table 2. Experimental environment data

Serial number	To configure	Project	Data
1	Hardware configuration	CPU	Intel(R) Core(TM)2 Duo GPU E8400@3.OO GHz
		Memory	2 GB DDR3 1066 MHz
		Hard disk	320GB SATA
		Graphics card	GeForce GTX 460
		Quantity	3台
2	Software configuration	Operating system	Microsoft Windows 7
		Browser	Microsoft IE 6, Microsoft IE 7, Microsoft IE 8, Mozilla Firefox Sogou high speed browser, Tencent TT browser

The experimental network topology is shown in Fig. 5.

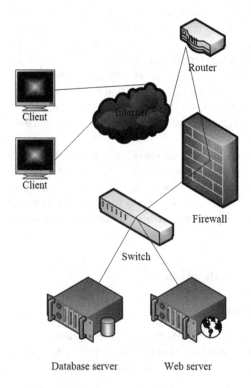

Fig. 5. Experimental network topology

In the environment shown in Table 2 and Fig. 5, the performance verification of the remote online teaching assistance system based on human-computer interaction is carried out, and the system performance data is obtained as experimental data. Select some key application scenarios for testing, including randomly selecting test questions to generate test papers, score calculation time, query score time, test paper answer query, question search time test, etc.

3.2 Result Analysis

The experimental data of the average response time of the remote online teaching aid system based on human-computer interaction is shown in Table 3.

Table 3. Experimental data of system average response time

Test component	Connection times/times	Average response time (ms)
Test paper generation	100	2.756
Score calculation	100	1.792
Student performance query	200	3.201
Class results query	50	2.067
Time answer query	100	1.593
Problem search	200	1.285

From the experimental data of the average response time of the system shown in Table 3, it can be seen that when 100 students connect to the system for online exams, the average response time of the test system is about 3 s, and the average response time of online question search is about 1 s., To meet the requirements of user applications.

The experimental results of system security test are shown in Table 4.

Table 4. System security test results

Test components	Test times/time	Times of being broken
Student landing	1000	2
Teachers landing	1000	1
Administrator login	2000	0

According to the experimental results of system security test in Table 4, when students log in for 1000 tests, teachers log in for 1000 tests, and management log in for 2000 tests, the number of times they are broken is 2, 1, and 0, respectively. Therefore, the security of the system is relatively high.

Table 5. Experimental results of system database connectivity test

Test components	Connection times/times	Connection failure times/time
Student score query	10000	22
Class grade inquiry	10000	11
Time answer query	20000	9
Student information inquiry	20000	9
Teacher information query	20000	9

The system database connectivity test results are shown in Table 5.

According to the experimental results of database connectivity test in Table 5, the number of connection failures is 22, 11, 9, 6 and 9 respectively in the test of student score query, class score query, time answer query, student information query and teacher information query test, and the successful connection power is 99.78%, 99.89%, 99.91%, 99.94% and 99.91%, respectively. It is proved that the success rate of database connection is high after the application of this system.

The system uses the LoadRunner test tool for stress testing, setting 30 Vusers, and each User repeatedly visits the system page and performs 6 clicks to view operations. The operation was repeated 2031844 times during the 9-min run, and a total of 2031844 successful return results were returned. In the end, it succeeded 21,901,245 times, an average of 1,9004.8 per second, and failed once. After the stress test, the result proves that the system can support hundreds of users to click simultaneously.

4 Conclusion

In this paper, a new remote online teaching aid system is designed based on human-computer interaction. Through the processor, network camera and microphone constitute the camera module of the system, so as to complete the construction of the hardware environment, and then by the online examination module, course resource management module, online question-answering module, client module, video teaching module, personal information management module constitute the system software environment. The experiments show that the system has short average response time, strong database connectivity and high security, and its performance can meet the user's requirements, which has great significance for the development of distance teaching application.

References

1. Goldenberg, A., Cohen-Chen, S., Goyer, J.P., et al.: Testing the impact and durability of a group malleability intervention in the context of the Israeli-Palestinian conflict. Proc. Natl. Acad. USA **115**(4), 696–701 (2018)
2. Castan, D.O.C., Gomes-Junior, F.G., Marcos-Filho, J.: Vigor-S, a new system for evaluating the physiological potential of maize seeds. Agric. **75**(2), 167–172 (2018)

3. Makioka, Y., Tsukahara, T., Ijichi, T., et al.: Oral supplementation of Bifidobacterium longum strain BR-108 alters cecal microbiota by stimulating gut immune system in mice irrespectively of viability. Biosci. Biotechnol. Biochem. **82**(3), 1–8 (2018)
4. Xiaodong, S., Heguo, Z., Dashan, Z., et al.: Reaction mechanisms and tensile properties of the composites fabricated by Al-B2O3 system. J. Wuhan Univ. Technol.-Mater. Sci. Ed. **34**(5), 1024–1029 (2019)
5. Wei, G., Yu-Heng, Q.: Design and development of vehicle reversing brake assist system. Auto. Sci.-Tech. **4**(12), 1–12 (2018)
6. Fu, W.-N., Liu, S., Srivastava, G.: Optimization of big data scheduling in social networks. Entropy **21**(9), 902–918 (2019)
7. Liu, S., Matt, G., Marco, Z., et al. (eds.): E-Learning, E-Education, and Online Training, pp. 1–34. Springer International Publishing, New York (2018). https://doi.org/10.1007/978-3-319-13293-8
8. El-Senousey, H.K., Chen, B., Wang, J.Y., et al.: In ovo injection of ascorbic acid modulates antioxidant defense system and immune gene expression in newly hatched local Chinese yellow broiler chicks. Poult **97**(2), 425–429 (2018)
9. Sousa Junior, V.R.D., Sabino, L.A., Moura D.J.D., et al.: Application of computational fluid dynamics on a study in swine facilities with mechanical ventilation system. Agric. (Piracicaba, Braz.) **75**(3), 173–183 (2018)

Towards the Automatic Generation of Pedagogical Conversational Agents from Lecture Slides

Matthias Wölfel[✉]

Faculty of Computer Science and Business Information Systems, Karlsruhe University of Applied Sciences, Karlsruhe, Germany
matthias.woelfel@hs-karlsruhe.de

Abstract. Although corresponding technological and didactical models have been known for decades, the digitization of teaching has hardly advanced beyond simple non-interactive formats (e.g. downloadable slides are provided within a learning management system). The COVID-19 crisis is changing this situation dramatically, creating a high demand for highly interactive formats and fostering exchange between conversation partners about the course content. Systems are required that are able to communicate with students verbally, to answer their questions, and to check the students' knowledge. While technological advances have made such systems possible in principle, the game stopper is the large amount of manual work and knowledge that must be put into designing such a system and feeding it the right content.

In this publication, we present a first system to overcome the aforementioned drawback by automatically generating a corresponding dialog system from slide-based presentations, such as PowerPoint, OpenOffice, or Keynote, which can be dynamically adapted to the respective students and their needs. Our first experiments confirm the proof of concept and reveal that such a system can be very handy for both respective groups, learners and lecturers, alike. The limitations of the developed system, however, also reminds us that many challenges need to be addressed to improve the feasibility and quality of such systems, in particular in the understanding of semantic knowledge.

Keywords: Intelligent dialog systems · Voice assistants · Ontology-based information extraction · Natural language processing · Learning analytics

1 Introduction

New challenges due to the COVID-19 crisis as well as the increasing popularity of remote access to education by distance learning courses result in the abandonment of classroom teaching. Online learning is convenient, flexible, (possibly) cost-effective, tailorable to specific needs, immediate, and unrestricted. However, the shift into virtual space leads to an imbalance in communication and exchange between learners and lectures as well as between learners. Moving teaching from—real word—lecture halls to

© ICST Institute for Computer Sciences, Social Informatics and Telecommunications Engineering 2021
Published by Springer Nature Switzerland AG 2021. All Rights Reserved
W. Fu et al. (Eds.): ICMTEL 2021, LNICST 388, pp. 216–229, 2021.
https://doi.org/10.1007/978-3-030-82565-2_18

- **video lectures** offer *no real-time return channel of any kind and is, in general, a solo act (one screen per user)*
- **webinars** cause *hardly any interaction* between learners and the lecturer—and if there is any it is quite artificial due to time delays or modality change (lecturer speaks, learners write)
- **learning platforms** are impersonal, lack human-like communication, and offer mostly *close-ended questions* (e.g. dichotomous, multiple-choice, rank order)

Because, in many cases and for various reasons, allies for discussing relevant teaching content are not available alternative solutions are required to jump in. Handcrafting such systems, however, even though in those cases where templates are already available, requires significant time and effort. Thereby the deployment of pedagogical conversational agents in educational context and training settings remains limited even though the technology is readily available and proven to be beneficial. For instance Rus et al. found that intelligent tutoring systems are more effective at improving learning outcomes if they use natural language interaction in comparison to those systems that do not incorporate natural language [23].

Many approaches in technologically supported teaching fail because it requires additional efforts in *time* (content needs to be prepared or revised), *skills* (new tools need to be learned), and *didactics* (other media requires different approaches) for the already busy lecturers. To overcome this drawback Winkler and Söllner proposed a method that helps educators to create smart personal assistants for their learning environments [28]. Their goal is to empower educators to develop their own agents without deep technological knowledge. While the former arguments about the high entry barrier hold for all kinds of technological teaching support, this barrier is particularly high for dialog-based approaches as the required skills to design and develop such systems are quite demanding: to hold a conversation with learners of any kind in natural language, to understand and answer questions, to simulate the dialogue moves of human tutors, and to follow ideal pedagogical strategies. The few systems using dialog-based approaches to support teaching are created manually rely on techniques within the field of *artificial intelligence* (AI) and *natural language processing* (NLP). Those "agents can guide the learner on what to do next, deliver didactic instruction, hold collaborative conversations, and model ideal behavior, strategies, reflections, and social interactions" [12]. Those systems have been proven useful to augment common educational practice, which is often limited to classical lecture formats and the provision of documents, by an interactive component in natural language. In this way, learners can enter into a dialogue with the language assistant at any time, who answers questions in real-time, provides references to further sources, and rate given answers. To make such systems accessible for a broader audience we propose to *replace the time-consuming process of creating the dialog content and structure manually with an automated process relying on semantically prepared lecture slides* as a content provider. The effort for the lecturer, therefore, can be reduced to a minimum.

2 Literatur Review

AI-based systems have a rather long history of providing additional services to students. While some services augment the lecture by providing transcriptions [10, 29] or translations [18] of what the lecturer has said, other services analyze learning behavior, learning activities, and attitudes during the learning process. Ideally, this can lead to a guided learning process that can adapt, in real-time, to the particular skills and requirements of each individual learner [11]. Apart from the limited amount of empirical evidence regarding the effectiveness of these AI-based learning-teaching systems, limited autonomy and little interactivity of learners with the available systems can be observed [25]. To improve natural interactions within those tools, conversational assistants and task-oriented dialog systems have been introduced [34]. Today, conversational assistants, in the field of education, enable learners to access data and services and to exchange information by simulating human-like conversations in the form of a natural language dialogue about a specific topic [9].

The use of natural language user interfaces for learning systems seems to be particularly promising as the field of NLP (which includes the methods of speech recognition, speech synthesis, and natural language understanding) has developed rapidly in recent years and is becoming an established interface for non-pedagogical use cases within the target group. According to a recent survey by Forsa Politikund Sozialforschung GmbH, this is over 95% in the target group in Germany [24], 22% of all German citizens used voice assistants in 2019. In the US more than 33% of the total population use voice assistants and 20% of the population use smart speakers.

Examples in higher education where voice assistants are used include Amazon Alexa with frequently asked questions about a course, room booking systems, and campus signposts [1]. Also in practical tests at our university, simple chat offers, with which e.g. free workrooms, timetable contents, or the daily canteen offer can be determined, have proven to be an excellent information channel with high demand by students. While the given examples so far demonstrate the use of voice assistants to manage to get around on campus and to handle administrative tasks we now turn to conversational assistants that support coursework. A literature review on pedagogical conversational agents is given in [14]: In their descriptive analysis, the distribution of publications per year shows an increasing interest in recent years, and 'messenger-like' conversational agents are published more than twice as often as 'embodied' conversational agents. Further, Hobert and von Wolff [14] conclude that more often agents target non-formal over formal learning situations. As explained by Hobert and Berens [13], there is a trend towards the use of mobile voice assistants in education.

However, besides all progress, voice assistants lack an adequate generalization of existing research results and comprehensive evaluation studies and process models. These are important, however, because the success of new technologies depends on how easy technical innovations are to use, how great their personal added value is, and how well they can be integrated into familiar routines. Graesser [12] describes a system that simulates human tutoring conversation patterns as well as alternative patterns that follow ideal pedagogies. They argue that alternative strategies to the simulation of human patterns are superior as human tutoring is not always ideal. This opens a whole new discussion about the use of pedagogical conversational agents that need to be addressed in the future.

While hand-drafted conversational agents are in use, there is a lack of procedures that can generate conversational agents for different knowledge areas (domains) on the basis of un/semi-structured and slim information—such as lecture slides. One exception is the work by Kelsey et al. [16] who presented a framework to develop dialog-based tutors that interact naturally with learners. Their approach combines automatically generated domain-specific content with a generalized domain-independent framework. While domain-independent semantic language comprehension is still a long way off, there exist very good solutions for certain narrow areas (domains). Despite the disruptive advances in AI systems through deep learning, the dialogs and dialog structures of the voice assistants are still mostly created manually. This is due to the fact that corresponding sample dialogs with intents and entities are usually not available or only to a limited extent. Current research efforts are often focused on the aspect of *intent recognition* in dialogs rather than on the overall system [6]. Advances in dialog control based on semantic data have been achieved throughout the years.

3 Requirement Analysis

Our proposed system offers interactive, natural-language possibilities to convey learning content in a way that was previously only possible in the context of human-to-human training or by hand-crafted conversational dialog systems. Little is known, therefore, about the general requirements of learners on such a system, a first orientation is given by user stories for students, and educators as presented in [28]. The success of the voice assistant does not only depend on its technical implementation but also on its expectation, acceptance, and final use of the learners. Therefore, we conducted a brief survey among our students to get some insights into what is required and expected by students. Most respondents use chatbots several times a year, all have tried chatbots before. Interestingly, none of the asked students loves to chat with bots, but they are accepted as a means to fulfill particular goals just like normal messengers. The majority of respondents (83%) use messengers daily, all use it occasionally. Some (8%) exchange remote information through this channel exclusively. The use of messengers is based on different motivations, for instance, 41% prefer written over spoken language.

Students seem to *prefer writing over speaking as text input*. In line with the previous finding output in *written language is preferred over spoken output*. However, voice output is rated more popular than voice input. As it makes no difference in learning outcomes when students express their contributions in spoken or written form [7] both channels can be offered as an input device to fulfill personal preferences. In contrast findings by Lachert et al. suggest that explaining orally or written has an effect [15]. However, if this difference is caused by social presence is an open question and thus it stays unclear if this difference exists also for conversational tutors (in particular for those without embodiment). The popularity of written text in our questionnaire might lie in the fact that the given information from the *assistant should be accompanied by images and graphics*. Videos are less popular and equations should be presented only if required by the content of the lecture.

Asked about the 'character' students stated that the assistant should behave like a tutor (50%), or like a friend (25%), however not like a lecturer/teacher. The assistant should motivate (66%) but never praise (0%), be friendly in any case (83%) but rarely be funny (25%). The assistant should answer briefly to questions and thereafter ask whether further information is desired (66%), however, asking directly whether a topic was understood is not welcome by most users (33%).

The basic functionalities of the assistant should include answering questions about the content of the lecture (75%), replaying definitions (66%), and referring to relevant slides (66%). Advanced functionalities should include suggesting possible topics of discussion about teaching content (66%), examining content with evaluation and feedback (58%), and pointing out additional slide content (50%). Functionalities that are considered less relevant include linking to further literature (basic 25%, advanced 35%), to check contents without evaluation but with subsequent display of the correct answer (basic 25%, advanced 8%), small talk (basic 33%, advanced 8%), and to publish information about the lecturer/professor (25% each).

4 System Components

In this section, we present the system architecture and its components. Due to space constraints, we do not describe all elements of the system in detail but concentrate on the components which vary from or extend common conversational system architectures [27]. Figure 1 presents our system overview including *data sources* (on the left), *components* (in the center), and the *human-machine interfaces* (on the right). The grey boxes are those components described in more detail.

4.1 Knowledge Extractor

Building a dialog requires knowledge on how to design conversational user interfaces [21] and in-domain knowledge. While the former has to be woven into our system by applying generic patterns, the in-domain knowledge needs to be provided from external data sources. The extraction of relevant information and its underlying semantic meaning from a given source is by far the largest challenge in the semi-automatic generation of a dialog structure. The use of AI-based NLU components is absolutely necessary for this conversion process because semantic patterns have to be used together with pre-stored knowledge components.

In particular *contextualized word representations* [22] such as *keywords extraction* [33] and *named entity recognition* [19] needs to be detected automatically. Besides the detection of keywords and named entity the relationship between them is also important; e.g. 'conversational user interfaces' are a subtopic of 'natural user interfaces'.

As it is an unsolved problem by today's technology to automatically convert an unstructured text into a meaningful dialog structure we decided to use both: *structured data*, using slide templates designed particularly to provide a parseable semantic structure and large amounts of *unstructured data*. This hybrid approach allows to combines to good effect the *pedagogical knowledge*, available in a formalized ontology, and *large general text data* ('big data') when generating the dialog. Additional domain

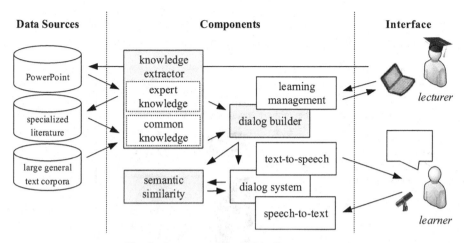

Fig. 1. System overview with all components.

knowledge (specific to the respective subject area) can be added from non-semantically annotated lecture materials (scripts, recommended textbooks if available in digital form) to extend and finetune the general knowledge base. Each layer in the ontology represents a particular view of the learning process: The *pedagogical* view is given by the structure of the slides, the *domain-specific* view defines the vocabulary and terminology, the *course-specific* view reflects the concrete realization of the learning material. The *learner-specific* aspect including age, gender, previous knowledge, and learning success. Therefore, those aspects are not represented within the provided learning material but need to be considered in the design of possible learning paths within the generated dialog structure.

Annotation of Slides

Since many lecturers prefer to use slides instead of blackboards when giving their presentations, extracting the content of the slides can be a very valuable source of information to be processed automatically. In contrast to second-hand sources, such as textbooks written by others, the lecture slides reflect exactly the outline and structure of the course, its content, and its lingua. Another advantage of lecture slides over textbooks is their stringent organization in a particular format which is quite similar to one another. These structures can be used in order to provide additional services such as the semantic ranking of lecture slides [26] or to generate concept maps [2]. The structure and information given in regular lecture slides, however, are not sufficient to find good mappings between specific text passages and the given ontology to generate useful dialogues. To support the parsing process we prepared PowerPoint slides to represent the defined ontology. Annotations include 'Chapter', 'Topic', 'Subtopic', 'Keywords', 'Abbreviation', 'Definition', 'Example', 'Idea', 'Goal', 'Quote', 'Attention', 'Equation', 'Image', 'Index', and 'Slide Number'. Each item by itself is representing a list and thus can include more elements. If required, the given ontology can be expanded, however, the inclusion needs to be specially treated in the dialog builder. An example of an annotated PowerPoint slide is given in Fig. 2.

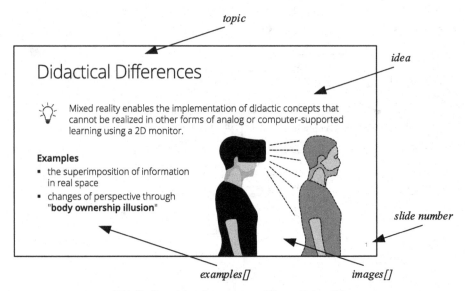

Fig. 2. Example of an annotated PowerPoint slide.

In order to make the application easy to use for lecturers, we developed semantically annotated presentation slide templates, which pre-define didactically adequate learning paths (as macro learning paths) for the lecturers through their set of slides, which gets reflected in the dialogue structure. Note that if the slide templates are created and used consistently no additional labeling is required in the production step of the slides. Therefore, no extra step is required here and no plugin to PowerPoint is required. To prepare our slides accordingly we had to edit the shape names within PowerPoint follow these simple steps:

1. click on the shape (textbox)
2. select *Format* tab
3. click on *Selection Pane*
4. rename the shape to defined the label (ID) for information extraction

The information given in those specifically prepared slides can now easily extracted and stored as a JSON-object and written into a database. To extract the information from PPTX files we used the python-pptx module which lets you access the different shape names and content. Because some relevant pieces of information such as font type or font style cannot be extracted using this tool we had to develop our own extension. The change of font type or style can be a good indicator to identify keywords as well as named entities.

Particular challenges in the parsing process appear if topics are spread over more than one slide or more than one topic (e.g. two definitions) is covered in a single slide. Thus, *intra-slide* and *inter-slides* relationships have to be considered:

- *index pages*—showing an overview of following slides, can be useful to structure subtopics but contains no content itself
- *combining continuous slides*—important topic may cover several continuous slides who might share the same title with or without potential numbering; e.g. 'Interface Design', 'Interface Design II', and 'Interface Design III'. Content coming from these slides should be considered as the same item in the content structure.
- *redundancy*—various slides might contain the same topic including the same, or even worse, contradicting information.
- *subtopic borders within slides*—some slides provide more than one topic at the same time e.g. in a comparison between two approaches. Content coming from those slides have to be considered as separate items in the content structure.

Up to this point, no user intervention is necessary. However, because not all information is already given within the slide context itself—in particular for slides containing images—we decided to allow to override or extend the given information by looking for JSON-expressions within the comments section of each slide. For instance, not any given acronym or domain-specific terminology may be reflected in the slides. The user has the possibility to modify, revise, and add content and questions not presented within the visual elements of the slides. For instance, to add keywords you can write in the comment section:

```
{
    "keywords": [
        "natural language understanding",
        "natural language processing"
    ]
}
```

Note that only JSON-formated text is parsed in the notes section while the continuous text is ignored in the parsing process. Therefore, the notes section can be used as usual.

4.2 Dialog Builder

To generate a useful dialog structure from the extracted data it is required to define transformation rules for each specific data type. Dependent on the data type the generated dialog structure has to offer prompts, hints, or forced-choice dialogue patterns and should be integrated into a more conversational dialog structure. Regardless of the defined data type, it is required to have various deviations in the dialogue to make the interactions seem more natural. In particular, the dialog system must be able to respond to several forms of spoken or written inquiries ranging from asking for the definition of a 'term' or for 'examples', and should also be able to answer questions that require higher levels of knowledge and understanding. Another challenge—specific for the task of a conversational tutor—in designing the dialog structure is the integrating of diagrams, images, and other visual media in addition to pure text.

Certain aspects of dialogue formulations within a teaching context are largely domain-independent such as chit-chat or based on phrases e.g. to ask for a definition.

We developed these elements of the dialogues as generic templates which were then filled according to our database. This library of templates can be easily extended to fit the particular needs of a data type and grow over time to get more variation for the data types already defined.

As a starting point to build our dialog system we used the open-source software RASA [3]. According to our defined rules, the dialog builder is generating a dialog syntax that follows the structure as given in the listing from which the dialog can be trained (note that our system works for German, but for better comprehensibility for the non-German speaking audience we show the dialog in English here):

```
nlu :
- intent : query_topics
examples : |
- [define]{"entity": "topic_attribute", "value":"
  definitions" }
- i look for [definition]{"entity": "topic_attribute","
  value": "definitions" }
- do you know [speech processing](topic_name) ?
[...]
- synonym : define
examples : |
- define
- specify
- determine
[...]
- lookup : topic name
examples : |
- intuitive interface
- sensor knowledge
- conversational user interface
[...]
```

4.3 Semantic Similarity

While most of the required functionalities are readily contained in any dialog system to build a pedagogical conversational agent, the evaluation of given 'free text' answers from learners needs to be treated otherwise. To grade the quality of 'free text' answers semantic textual similarity needs to be calculated. Literature has commonly reported that pre-trained text embedding models can be used as effective feature extractors and achieve good performance on calculating semantic textual similarities. Therefore, for the time being, we have not used any kind of transfer learning to adapt to the content of the slides or to tune the hyperparameters. To compare the semantic similarity between the given answer and the reference, we directly assess the similarity of the sentence embeddings produced by the transformer model as described in [31]. The similarity between the two sentence embeddings was calculated using the cosine similarity and converted into an angular distance by arccos. For more detail see [4].

5 Features of the Pedagogical Conversational Tutor

In this section, we describe some of the features currently implemented in the assistant. While some of the features such as small talk and user feedback are content-independent other features rely on the provided lecture slides such as listing, searching, and suggesting topics, asking for definitions, or being tested about the lecture context. Additional content might be favorable but is neither content independent nor given on the slides, this might include additional information of the lecturer such as curriculum vitae, opening hours, telephone numbers, etc. Due to space constraints, we only describe topics suggestions and self-test here and leave out descriptions for small talk, user feedback, and additional information.

5.1 List, Search, Suggest Topics, and Similar Content

While listening and searching for topics is a straight forward task after the DB has been generated from the slide content, suggesting topics based on a given topic needs more attention. We handle this by relying on different measures including the ontology defined by topic and sub-topic as well as the distance between slides (assuming that similar topics appear close in the slide order).

5.2 Self Test of Lecture Content

We have investigated two forms of self-tests: multiple choice/fill-in-the-blank text (close-ended questions) and free-text answers (open-ended questions). Note that both types of questions investigated here are limited to represent knowledge embedded in a very small-sized text fitting on a single slide and often represent only a single sentence.

Multiple-Choice & Fill-in-the-Blank Text

For multiple-choice, the task is to collect answers from the choices offered in a list. It is frequently used in educational testing and easy to grade automatically. CH and Saha present a systematic review of systems to automatically generate multiple-choice questions from text [5]. In the case to generate multiple-choice questions from annotated slides we have to perform four essential steps (excluding preand post-processing): *sentence selection*, *key selection*, *distractor generation*, and *question formation*. The *sentence selection* step finds relevant sentences from which questions are formed. For each selected sentence the *key* (or *target word*), which is the correct answer to the question, has to be determined in the *key selection* step. The set of *distractors* contains possible wrong answers along with the correct answer in order to befuddle the examinee. The *question formation* is the task of transforming the declarative sentence into its interrogative form.

While sentence selection and question formation will be covered later, as it is also relevant in free-text answers, we will briefly discuss key selection and distractor generation here. Obviously, for multiple-choice as well as fill-in-the-blank text tasks the selected word or word sequence that will be blanked out is of utmost importance. In the literature methods based on frequency count, part-of-speech, semantic information, and pattern matching is addressed. We regard a word or word sequence as key if a high semantic similarity was given in the 'Topic' as well as in the selected sentence. To find distractors is not as straight forward. For numerical questions, similar numbers can be generated, but for a word or word sequence, a more semantically driven approach is required. Wherever possible, in those cases where the found key matching a 'Subtopic', it is possible to rely on domain ontology, by drawing distractors from 'Subtopic' within the same 'Topic'. In those cases where this is not possible only open-ended questions have been formulated by the system.

Free-Text Answers

For free-text answers, the task is to collect answers which are freely formulated. It shares some steps in common with the automatic generation of close-ended questions, namely *sentence selection* and *question formation*, but has no need for *key selection* and *distractor generation*. While multiple-choice answers and grading can readily be integrated into a dialog structure, free-text answers need an extra processing step as described in Sect. 4.3. The similarity score can then be handed back to the dialog system and respective answers based on the score can be rendered; e.g. for a similarity score of 95% for a given definition you get a "you met the definition very well" while for a score of 30% you get a "maybe you should review the definition".

Sentence Selection

Not each sentence in a given text is worth to be rendered as a question. Only those sentences containing questionable facts should be selected. While the selection process for general question selection is non-trivial and different methods such as sentence length, parts-of-speech, semantic information, or the number of occurrence of a particular word, have been proposed, we regard a sentence worth to be rendered as a question based on semantic similarity and occurrence between the words used in 'Topic' and 'Definition' or 'Idea'. The sentence or sentences in the same tag showing a high correlation are selected.

Question Formulation

The selected sentence has to be rendered as a question to be useful for multiple-choice or free-text answers. Of course, the formulated question depends on the type of answer and has to be treated differently for multiple-choice or free-text. However, both types rely most of the time on rule-or pattern-based methods including appropriate 'wh-word' selection (who, what, why, when, where; including also how and how much), subject-verb-object and their relationship, dependency-based patterns, and syntactic transformation. More information on how to generate questions can be found in [20].

6   Observations and Limitations

We introduced a first working prototype of a pedagogical conversational agent to be generated from annotated lecture slides. The development has revealed that there are a couple of difficult problems that need to be addressed in order to provide a tool that can be easily applied as outlined in the introduction. Nevertheless, with the working prototype, it was already possible to demonstrate the proof of concept. A dialog structure given 577 semantically annotated slides for the university course 'Intuitive and Perceptual Interfaces' for computer science in media bachelor students in their third year of study at the Karlsruhe University of Applied Sciences have been semi-automatically parsed and converted into the dialog structure. No post-processing of any kind has been used to improve the system.

The generated pedagogical conversational agent has been used for the evaluation. In total 19 students (12 male, 7 female, age between 18 and 27) familiar with the content of the course tried the prototype. It could be observed that the participants were generous to small mistakes and serious deficiencies in the offered possibilities in the dialog or the given answers. At first, though this finding might contradict Graesser who observed that "many students expect the computers to be accurate rather than polite" in a conversation [12]. However, by analyzing the emerged problems within the conversation we found that the accuracy of finding the intend was not very good but if the intend was resolved correctly the accuracy of the resulting answer was quite high. In those cases where the intent could not be resolved, its incorrectness was sometimes even completely ignored and something else was tried or it lead to amusement rather than frustration. It is important to note that our findings might be biased as the involved students had a strong background in computer science and some had already prior knowledge in the theory of conversational user interfaces. While all students seem to be in favor of such a system, some had concerns about data security and were reluctant if they would actually use the system in production; e.g. one student stated "It has to show a real benefit and has to offer more than simply the slide content in a new format."

It has been shown that having the instructor visible on the screen has a very limited effect on the learning outcome (although eye contact seems to be helpful) [8]. Therefore, it has been decided that the agent uses no visual representation of a scholar such as a portrait, talking head, or avatar that generate speech, actions, facial expressions, and gestures to give the system some kind of body [17]. Even though forms of visual embodiment are missing and just a dialog are offered, the system got recognized as a personality, rather than a technology. In those cases where the dialog system was recognized as a personality the conversation tended to be more emotional; e.g. "Hey, could you give me some examples. Please!" instead of "show example". Users placed more emphasis on the linguistic interpersonal content and less on the technical function. In those cases where the dialog system was perceived more as a technology the dialog was more rationally and followed the structure of syntax and keywords; e.g. just "example" even without the verb show, and lacked any form of politeness. With an increased time of using the system, the behavior of the user became significantly freer, more relaxed, and more playful. At first, the users frequently explore which answers are given for different question formulations. Often they interact with the system at first only by keywords, later on, they switch to complete questions up to a complete, free dialog in natural language.

It is worth noting that the quality of the dialog depends heavily on the provided quality and quantity of the slides. Carelessness in the conception and creation of the lecture slides is directly reflected in the generated dialogue. Inconsistency, contradictions, or wrong labels in the slides result in inconsistent dialogs which might even have a stronger negative impact as in its original form of presentation. No measures have been applied so far to check the quality and consistency of the provided slides.

Results by Zellou and Cohn indicate that social and functional factors influence dialog structure within humans and between humans and a dialog system [32]. Therefore, conversational content should have a particular structure to flow naturally and the dialogue should be guided by the given answers of the dialog partner. It would be favorable if the dialogue would reflect the style of a tutor and personality. So far, these capabilities have not been integrated. Besides optimizing the dialog in the future it could be investigated how to create a more emotional dialog in written form; e.g. by reflecting voice characteristics in the textual representation [30].

The system presented here has to be validated and optimized in further research. To support this process the developed software solution, Powerpoint templates, and pre-trained models will be published under a Creative Commons license on GitHub.

References

1. Amazon: Alexa in higher education (2020). https://aws.amazon.com/de/education/alexa-edu/higher-education/
2. Atapattu, T., Falkner, K., Falkner, N.: A comprehensive text analysis of lecture slides to generate concept maps. Comput. Educ. **115**, 96–113 (2017)
3. Bocklisch, T., Faulkner, J., Pawlowski, N., Nichol, A.: Rasa: open source language understanding and dialogue management. arXiv preprint arXiv:1712.05181 (2017)
4. Cer, D.M., et al.: Universal sentence encoder. arXiv abs/1803.11175 (2018)
5. Ch, D.R., Saha, S.K.: Automatic multiple choice question generation from text: a survey. IEEE Trans. Learn. Technol. **13**(1), 14–25 (2020). https://doi.org/10.1109/TLT.2018.2889100
6. Damonte, M., Goel, R., Chung, T.: Practical semantic parsing for spoken language understanding. arXiv preprint arXiv:1903.04521 (2019)
7. D'Mello, S.K., Dowell, N., Graesser, A.: Does it really matter whether students' contributions are spoken versus typed in an intelligent tutoring system with natural language? J. Exp. Psychol. Appl. **17**(1), 1 (2011)
8. Fiorella, L., Stull, A.T., Kuhlmann, S., Mayer, R.E.: Instructor presence in video lectures: the role of dynamic drawings, eye contact, and instructor visibility. J. Educ. Psychol. **111**(7), 1162 (2019)
9. Følstad, A., Skjuve, M., Brandtzaeg, P.B.: Different chatbots for different purposes: towards a typology of chatbots to understand interaction design. In: Bodrunova, S., et al. (eds) INSCI 2018. LNCS, vol. 11551, pp. 145–156. Springer, Cham (2019). https://doi.org/10.1007/978-3-030-17705-8_13
10. Fügen, C., et al.: Advances in lecture recognition: the ISL RT-06s evaluation system. In: Ninth International Conference on Spoken Language Processing (2006)
11. Gašević, D., Dawson, S., Rogers, T., Gasevic, D.: Learning analytics should not promote one size fits all: the effects of instructional conditions in predicting academic success. Internet High. Educ. **28**, 68–84 (2016)
12. Graesser, A.C.: Conversations with autotutor help students learn. Int. J. Artif. Intell. Educ. **26**(1), 124–132 (2016)
13. Hobert, S., Berens, F.: Small talk conversations and the long-term use of chatbots in educational settings – experiences from a field study. In: Følstad, A., et al. (eds.) CONVERSATIONS 2019. LNCS, vol. 11970, pp. 260–272. Springer, Cham (2020). https://doi.org/10.1007/978-3-030-39540-7_18

14. Hobert, S., Meyer von Wolff, R.: Say hello to your new automated tutor–a structured literature review on pedagogical conversational agents (2019)
15. Jacob, L., Lachner, A., Scheiter, K.: Learning by explaining orally or in written form? Text complexity matters. Learn. Instr. **68**, 101344 (2020)
16. Kelsey, E., Ray, F., Brown, D., Robson, R.: Design of a domain-independent, interactive, dialogue-based tutor for use within the GIFT framework. In: Generalized Intelligent Framework for Tutoring (GIFT) Users Symposium (Giftsym3), pp. 161–168 (2015)
17. Kim, K., Boelling, L., Haesler, S., Bailenson, J., Bruder, G., Welch, G.F.: Does a digital assistant need a body? The influence of visual embodiment and social behavior on the perception of intelligent virtual agents in ar. In: 2018 IEEE International Symposium on Mixed and Augmented Reality (ISMAR), pp. 105–114. IEEE (2018)
18. Kolss, M., Wolfel, M., Kraft, F., Niehues, J., Paulik, M., Waibel, A.: Simultaneous german-English lecture translation. In: International Workshop on Spoken Language Translation (IWSLT) 2008 (2008)
19. Lample, G., Ballesteros, M., Subramanian, S., Kawakami, K., Dyer, C.: Neural architectures for named entity recognition. arXiv preprint arXiv:1603.01360 (2016)
20. Monz, C.: Machine learning for query formulation in question answering. Nat. Lang. Eng. **17**(4), 425–454 (2011)
21. Pearl, C.: Designing Voice user Interfaces: Principles of Conversational Experiences. O'Reilly Media, Inc., Sebastopol (2016)
22. Peters, M.E., Neumann, M., Iyyer, M., Gardner, M., Clark, C., Lee, K., Zettlemoyer, L.: Deep contextualized word representations. arXiv preprint arXiv:1802.05365 (2018)
23. Rus, V., D'Mello, S., Hu, X., Graesser, A.: Recent advances in intelligent systems with conversational dialogue. AI Mag. **34**, 42–54 (2013)
24. Schlobinski, P., Siever, T.: Sprachliche kommunikation in der digitalen welt. Eine repräsentative Umfrage, durchgeführt von forsa (1619–1021) (2018)
25. Seufert, S., Meier, C., Soellner, M., Rietsche, R.: A pedagogical perspective on big data and learning analytics: a conceptual model for digital learning support. Technol. Knowl. Learn. **24**(4), 599–619 (2019)
26. Wang, Y., Sumiya, K.: Semantic ranking of lecture slides based on conceptual relationship and presentational structure. Procedia Comput. Sci. **1**(2), 2801–2810 (2010)
27. Wei, C., Yu, Z., Fong, S.: How to build a chatbot: chatbot framework and its capabilities. In: Proceedings of the 2018 10th International Conference on Machine Learning and Computing, pp. 369–373 (2018)
28. Winkler, R., Söllner, M.: Towards empowering educators to create their own smart personal assistants. In: Proceedings of the 53rd Hawaii International Conference on System Sciences (2020)
29. Wölfel, M.: Robust automatic transcription of lectures. KIT Scientific Publishing (2009)
30. Wölfel, M., Schlippe, T., Stitz, A.: Voice driven type design. In: 2015 International Conference on Speech Technology and Human-Computer Dialogue (SpeD), pp. 1–9. IEEE (2015)
31. Yang, Y., et al.: Multilingual universal sentence encoder for semantic retrieval (2019)
32. Zellou, G., Cohn, M.: Social and functional pressures in vocal alignment: differences for human and voice-AI interlocutors (2020)
33. Zhang, Y., Tuo, M., Yin, Q., Qi, L., Wang, X., Liu, T.: Keywords extraction with deep neural network model. Neurocomputing **383**, 113–121 (2020)
34. Zhang, Z., Takanobu, R., Zhu, Q., Huang, M., Zhu, X.: Recent advances and challenges in task-oriented dialog systems. Sci. China Technol. Sci., 1–17 (2020)

Research on the Fusion Pattern Recognition System Based on the Concept of Production Education Integration and Application of Generative Countermeasure Network

Conggang Lv[✉]

Jiangxi Tourism and Commerce Vocational College, Nancang 330039, China

Abstract. In order to highlight the practical application value of network data and information fusion behavior under the background of industry-education integration, a fusion pattern recognition system that applies generative confrontation network under the concept of industry-education integration is designed. First, the cyclic neural network is used to generate independent text information packets. While establishing the generation of the confrontation network framework, various reinforcement learning parameters are adjusted to realize the construction of the hardware execution environment of the recognition system. On this basis, build an embedded network framework, with the help of EEPROM chip and LD3320 chip circuit, to supervise the fusion process of network data information identification and implementation behavior, and realize the construction of the system's software execution environment. Combined with the related hardware equipment structure, complete the research on the fusion pattern recognition system of the application generation confrontation network under the concept of integration of production and education. Comparative experiment results show that with the application of the above system, the mean value of network data information fusion time is reduced from 17.9 s to 11.2 s, while the maximum amount of information processed by a single fusion process reaches $9.3 \times 1012T$ which can be used in the context of the integration of production and education Effectively highlight the practical application capabilities of network data information fusion behavior.

Keywords: Industry education integration · Confrontation network · Fusion pattern recognition · Network text · Learning parameters · Embedded framework · Chip circuit

1 Introduction

The integration of industry and education refers to that vocational schools actively set up professional industries according to their specialties, closely combine industry and teaching, support and promote each other, and turn the school into an industrial business entity integrating talent training, scientific research and scientific and technological services, thus forming a school running mode in which schools and enterprises complement

© ICST Institute for Computer Sciences, Social Informatics and Telecommunications Engineering 2021
Published by Springer Nature Switzerland AG 2021. All Rights Reserved
W. Fu et al. (Eds.): ICMTEL 2021, LNICST 388, pp. 230–242, 2021.
https://doi.org/10.1007/978-3-030-82565-2_19

each other. The integration of industry and education is the deep cooperation between industry and education, and the deep cooperation between colleges and enterprises to improve the quality of talent training. The school running mode of "combination of production and education, integration of school and enterprise" is a new development road for vocational schools. However, due to the actual situation of each school is different, the characteristics of each profession is different, so the specific approach is not the same.

The basis of the combination of production and education is "production", that is, it must be based on real product production. With such a foundation and atmosphere for professional practical teaching, students can learn the true skills and teachers can teach the true level. Such "production" cannot be simply factory production. It must be closely integrated with teaching. Its purpose is to "teaching". When the combination of production and education is relatively mature, it will gradually develop into "production, learning, and research". After realizing the integration of production and education, the school has truly formed the ability of "production, learning, and research". The vocational school has adapted to the needs of the market, and the formation of development capabilities has been implemented, and there is a foundation for strengthening and improving.

According to the existing conditions and management conditions, it is more possible to introduce enterprises with more advanced management and technology in the society, and are willing to join the school enterprise cooperation. Through the use of the school's equipment, product production, the introduction of teaching content in the production process, the school and enterprise jointly formulate the implementation teaching and production plan of the combination of production and teaching, so that teachers can learn technology and students can join in the production, so that production can produce benefits, school and enterprise win-win, symbiosis and common prosperity.

For to improve the effect of production and education integration, a fusion pattern recognition system based on generative countermeasure network is designed.

2   Convergence Mode of Generating Confrontation Network

2.1   Text Generation Based on Recurrent Neural Network

This research is based on the sequence model to achieve text generation. This process refers to modeling along the one-dimensional dimension of the text tag sequence to construct a language model and then generate text. Common forms of sequence models include recurrent neural networks, sequence-to-sequence models, attention sequence models, etc.

For many years, recurrent neural networks with long-term and long-term memory units have shown excellent performance from natural language generation to handwriting generation. Recurrent neural network belongs to the category of deep learning, and it is also a common sequential model. It has achieved good results in many tasks of natural language processing. As shown in Fig. 1, the basic recurrent neural network is a network model for output inference in the form of shared parameters in the sequence dimension. The recurrent neural network can be expanded on the time axis. Through this expansion, the model can be understood as a deep network with the number of layers as the sequence length, and the particularity lies in the weight sharing among the layers. The main idea behind the recurrent neural network is to apply the temporal information of linear data structure [1, 2]. In the original neural network, the default assumption is that each input data is completely unrelated, but in many tasks, this is an unreasonable assumption and important information is lost. The basic structure of the recurrent neural network is shown in Fig. 1.

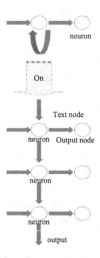

Fig. 1. The idea of cyclic neural network text generation

2.2   Generation of Countermeasure Network Framework

Generative confrontation network is not a complete model, but a network training framework. The structural design of the generative adversarial network is clever and simple. The original framework has only two components: the generator and the discriminator. Among them, the generative model used by the generator is not limited, but the training goal of the generator is always to fit the generated sample distribution as close as possible to the real sample distribution. When there is no discriminator, a loss function that measures the gap between the generated sample and the real sample needs to be defined in advance. The training of the generator needs to rely on multiple rounds of iteration to adjust the parameters and continuously minimize the loss function. But this method has a big problem, because the artificially defined loss function usually has limited characterization ability and can only one-sidedly describe the difference between the real sample distribution and the generated sample distribution [3]. There are two main problems in applying generative adversarial networks directly to sequence generation tasks including text generation. First of all, the generative confrontation network is designed to generate continuous-valued data, but it is difficult to directly generate discrete symbol sequences from continuous-valued data.

Facing the continuous value data task, the generator changes from random sampling to sampling controlled by generator parameters in the training process. The overall loss of the model is determined by both the discriminator parameters and the generator parameters. The loss gradient can be used to fine tune the parameters of the generator, so that the generator can produce more real data. However, if the data to be generated is composed of discrete tags, the small change of generator parameters will not sample new tags, that is, the sequence results sampled in the discrete space do not change, so the guidance signal given by the discriminator to the generator will lose its inherent directivity. The emergence of discriminator in Generative countermeasure network is to solve this problem. The training goal of discriminator is to maximize the probability of true sample judging as true and minimize the probability of generating sample judging as true, that is to find the best segmentation method between generated sample distribution and real sample distribution. Ideally, a fully trained discriminator is equivalent to a strong loss function [4]. At this time, the training goal of the generator is transformed from minimizing the difference between the generated sample and the real sample to weakening the discriminator's ability as much as possible. The overall structure of the framework for generating countermeasure network is shown in Fig. 2.

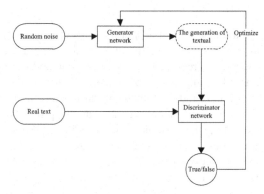

Fig. 2. Overall structure of the framework for generating countermeasure network

2.3   Reinforcement Learning Parameter Adjustment

There are some problems in the generation of discrete data such as text. The image data generation with good effect of the original generation countermeasure network belongs to the typical continuous data generation task, so the parameters in the model can be directly optimized, and finally the false image is generated. The image data are expressed in the form of real value tensor in computer. If it is a black-and-white image, it can be encoded as a two-dimensional matrix composed of gray values. If it is a multi-channel image such as a color image, it can be encoded as a three-dimensional tensor. In either case, the elements in the tensor are in the real number space, and their values have fixed meanings, which represent the properties of a certain dimension of the image. If the real values of tensors are directly aggregated together, they naturally represent an image. In short, the original image can be restored from tensor representation without "sampling" operation.

The principle of reinforcement learning parameter adjustment is shown in Fig. 3.

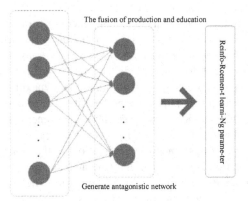

Fig. 3. Reinforcement learning parameter adjustment principle

Simulation and generation of sequential data is an important problem in unsupervised learning. Text generation can be classified into this problem. For a long time, recurrent neural network (CNN) has been regarded as an effective method to deal with sequence problems. Most of the deep learning text generation models are based on recurrent neural networks. Both feature matching and reinforcement learning face similar difficulties, that is, the reward signal is sparse [5, 6]. In order to alleviate the problem of signal sparsity, layered technology has become the most direct way of thinking. Some people think that text generation is naturally generated at the level of grammatical structure, because real text samples have such levels as semantic structure and part of speech. According to the characteristics of hierarchical structure, the whole character sequence generation problem is decomposed into a combination of several partial character sequence generation problems, which can build a more easy to learn model for complex problems.

3   Pattern Recognition System Based on the Concept of Integration of Production and Education

3.1   Embedded Network Framework

The traditional recognition framework of the embedded network is shown in Fig. 4. The whole system is mainly composed of several main modules such as MCU main control chip, dedicated network identification chip, identification list and counter network information collection.

(1) Core controller: the main control chip used to control the special network information identification chip, which can be programmed to achieve relevant functions. The system uses the way of serial port to USB to communicate with the upper computer. Its main types are 51 single-chip microcomputer, STM series, arm series, etc. this system uses 51 single-chip microcomputer as the core control unit.

(2) Data acquisition: a module used to collect data signals, and the collected data information analog signals are transformed into digital signals after preprocessing such as endpoint detection, denoising, etc. The purpose is to extract features of digital signals and match patterns to obtain the final recognition results.

(3) Recognition list: as the most characteristic module of offline information recognition. Because it is different from online recognition, it has a huge database of data recognition, which can be called through the network. While offline identification is to temporarily store the recognition command in the recognition list, and match the identification results of the identification chip, so as to get the recognition result with the highest matching degree and feed back to the user.

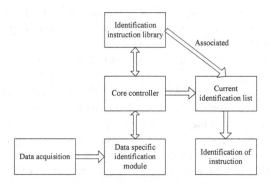

Fig. 4. Embedded network framework

There are differences between learning signals and reinforcement. The guidance signal in reinforcement learning is also called reinforcement signal. Reinforcement signal is provided by environment, which is a dynamic evaluation of action. Reinforcement signals in reinforcement learning are usually scalar. This training method does not directly tell the intelligent system what the correct action is or how to produce the correct action. Compared with supervised learning, the system obtains less information from the external environment each time, so it must rely on more rounds of attempts to learn. In this way, the intelligent system can continuously improve the action strategy to adapt to the environment [7, 8].

In the field of text generation, the traditional method is based on the recurrent neural network to complete the word-by-word generation of the text. Although this method of predicting the next word based on the generated sequence is reasonable in theory, it will be affected by gradient dispersion in actual engineering. Can't play the best role. At the same time, text generation models based solely on cyclic neural networks have the problem of not being able to judge complete sequence information, and prone to problems such as word repetition. Therefore, other technical means should be used to generate models on the basis of cyclic neural networks. Make improvements. If the word-by-word generation is changed from a classification problem at each time point to a decision problem that hopes to obtain the greatest expected return at the current time point, then the text generation problem can be solved using reinforcement learning techniques.

3.2 EEPROM Chip

Due to the disadvantages of off-line nonspecific countermeasure network fusion pattern recognition system, such as limited recognition instructions and limited storage space, users can only have limited command interaction when using it, and when changing instructions, they need to write the program code in ROM register of single chip micro-computer. The process is complex, which makes the interaction very troublesome, and it is also in the actual operation Problems that need to be avoided and improved in the process. Therefore, the EEPROM external register module is added, and the contents of the register can be directly rewritten by the upper computer, so that the recognition command can truly realize the function of dynamic free addition. It not only solves the problem of complex changing instructions, but also avoids the problem of limited recognition command. As long as the register is written into the register through PC according to certain protocol, it can be written in real time To identify. EEPROM chip structure is shown in Fig. 5.

AT24C02, as a two-wire serial EEPROM, is a low working voltage 2K-bit serial electrically erasable read-only memory [9]. The internal organization is 256 bytes, each with 8 bits. Considering that in the recognition process, the recognition instruction needs to cover the length of a sentence, this article has also improved this by changing the 8-bit byte to 16 bytes, and the internal organization has been reduced from 256 to 128. Bytes to lengthen the content of each identification. The main features of the chip are:

(1) Working voltage: 1.8 V–5.5 V;
(2) Input/output pins are compatible with 5 V;
(3) Application in internal structure: 128 * 16 (2k);
(4) Two wire serial interface;
(5) The input pin is filtered by Schmidt trigger to suppress noise;
(6) Two way data transmission protocol;
(7) Compatible with 400 kHz (2.5 V);
(8) Support hardware write protection;
(9) High reliability: read and write times: 1000000 times, data storage: 100 years.

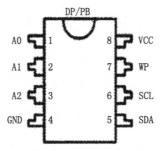

Fig. 5. EEPROM chip structure

3.3 LD3320 Chip Circuit

As one of the most important modules in the hardware platform, the process of reading and writing the function register is mainly between the speech recognition chip ld3320 and the main control chip. The register of ld3320 supports the serial spi read-write method of software and hardware, parallel read-write of software simulation and hardware parallel read-write. This design uses the parallel software simulation timing. The timing of parallel writing is shown in Fig. 6, and that of parallel reading is shown in Fig. 7.

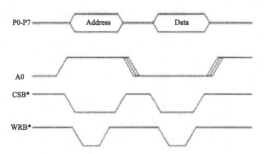

Fig. 6. Parallel write timing

When the read-write address is ready, in the parallel read-write sequence, make Ao equal to 1, pull CSB down and WRB up to write address respectively; when Ao is equal to 0, make CSB pull down and RD pull up to read in data. One of the main disadvantages of the existing text generation methods is that the binary feedback signal of the discriminator is sparse, because it can only be calculated when the whole text sample is completed.

In addition, the scalar guiding signal for the entire text is obviously insufficient in information, because it can no longer retain relevant information about the intermediate grammatical structure and semantics of the generated text, so the generator cannot be targeted for learning. All generative models based on generative adversarial networks face the problems of unstable training and mode collapse [10]. The two major issues in text generation tasks are also content to be considered. How to stably implement training and

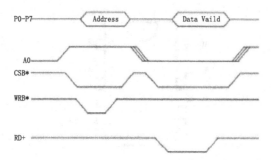

Fig. 7. Parallel read timing

how to obtain diverse texts. There is no perfect solution at the model level. Researchers still need to carefully adjust the hyperparameters to alleviate it. These questions.

It should be noted that in this read-write mode, the MD pin of MCU needs to be pulled down. At this time, the related components of ld3320 will have a long time delay, which will affect the operation of writing data to the 0×37 register, and the chip will also be interfered at this time, resulting in abnormal operation. In the process of identification, the register of 0×37 is the entrance of the control chip, which starts the operation of chip identification and the whole identification process. Ld3320 chip circuit is shown in Fig. 8.

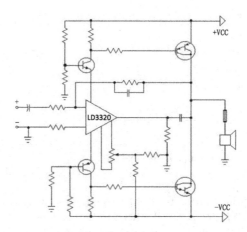

Fig. 8. LD3320 chip circuit

Layering is still one of the most promising techniques for signal sparsity. The typical method of hierarchical technology is to define several low-level subtasks. The learning content of each subtask is obtained by macro strategy, and then the subtasks learn micro strategies separately to complete the tasks assigned to them by macro strategies. The macro policy to solve the problem can be defined manually or acquired by learning. When domain knowledge for specific tasks is used in the construction of hierarchy, this method is very effective, but it can not flexibly adapt to other tasks.

The most direct way to build a text generation system is to use a recurrent neural network as a generator. Recurrent neural network is one of the most suitable models for sequence generation tasks in deep learning technology. It has the characteristics of simple structure and relatively fast inference speed. At the same time, in this task, the cyclic neural network has the characteristics of high randomness. As a new generative model training framework, the generative confrontation network uses the discriminator model to guide the generator model to optimize. Generative confrontation networks have achieved considerable success in real-valued data generation tasks. However, when the target task is to generate discrete tag sequences, generating adversarial networks has great limitations. An important reason is that the discrete output of the generator model makes it difficult to pass the gradient update of the discriminator model to the generator model. In addition, the discriminator model can only evaluate a completely generated tag sequence. For a partially generated sequence, it is very difficult for the original generation adversarial network framework to balance the current score and future scores when generating the entire sequence.

4 Comparative Experimental Analysis

In order to verify the practical application value of the pattern recognition system based on the concept of production education integration, the following comparative experiments are designed.

Debug the generated confrontation network to the application state as shown in Fig. 9. While ensuring that other experimental conditions remain unchanged, the experimental group host and the control group host are respectively connected to the network application environment. Among them, the experimental group host is equipped with a new recognition system, and the control group host is equipped with a traditional recognition system. In the same experimental environment, record the actual changes of various experimental indicators.

Fig. 9. Operation interface of generating countermeasure network

Make network information input equal to 1.0×10^9T, 2.0×10^9T, 3.0×10^9T, 4.0×10^9T, 5.0×10^9T, 6.0×10^9T, 7.0×10^9T, 8.0×10^9T, 9.0×10^9T, and record under different information input conditions, the specific changes of the actual mean fusion time are shown in Table 1.

Table 1. Comparison table of mean value of network data information fusion time

Network information input/($\times 10^9$T)	Actual fusion time/(S)	
	Test group	Control group
1.0	9.7	17.9
2.0	9.9	
3.0	10.4	
4.0	10.5	
5.0	10.6	
6.0	10.8	
7.0	11.0	
8.0	11.1	
9.0	11.2	

Analysis Table 1 shows that with the increase of network information input, the average fusion time of experimental group keeps increasing trend, and the global maximum value reaches 11.2 s, which is 1.5 s higher than the initial value of 9.7 s. The mean time of network data fusion in the control group remained stable throughout the experiment, which was 6.7 s higher than the maximum value of 11.2 s in the experimental group. To sum up, with the application of the pattern recognition system of application generation antagonism network fusion under the concept of industry education integration, the average time of network data information fusion has obviously decreased, which meets the practical needs of maintaining the application ability of information fusion behavior.

It is stipulated that every 15 min is regarded as a unit duration. Table 2 records the actual changes in the amount of information processed by the experimental group and the control group during a single fusion within 4 unit durations.

It can be seen from Table 2 that the amount of information processed by single fusion in the experimental group keeps a steady upward trend, and the global maximum value reaches 9.3×10^{12}t. In the control group, the amount of information processed by single fusion increased continuously, and gradually stabilized. The global maximum value reached 4.1×10^{12}t, which decreased by 4.7×10^{12}t compared with the extreme value of the experimental group. To sum up, with the application of pattern recognition system of application generation antagonism network fusion under the concept of industry education integration, the amount of information processed by single fusion has increased significantly, which can fundamentally improve the practical application value of network data information fusion behavior.

Table 2. Comparison of single fusion processing information

Experimental group	Experiment time/(min)	Information quantity of single fusion processing/($\times 10^{12}$T)	
		Test group	Control group
1	5	8.6	2.7
	10	8.6	2.8
	15	8.6	2.9
2	20	8.9	3.3
	25	8.9	3.4
	30	8.9	3.5
3	35	9.1	3.9
	40	9.1	4.0
	45	9.1	4.1
4	50	9.3	4.1
	55	9.3	4.1
	60	9.3	4.1

5 Conclusion

In order to highlight the practical application value of network data and information fusion behavior under the background of industry-education fusion, this research uses generative confrontation network to design a fusion pattern recognition system, and the effectiveness of this method is proved through experiments.

References

1. Du, Q., Liu, Q. Conditional generative adversarial network based on image semantic annotation of cloud model. Pattern Recognit. Artif. Intell. **31**(4), 379–388 (2018)
2. Liang, H., Hao, L., Song, J., et al.: The data visualization and pattern recognition method based on the fusion of incremental learning and Lasso. Chin. High Technol. Lett. **28**(1), 39–51 (2018)
3. Xie, C., Wang, Y., Lin, Z., et al.: Monte Carlo noise removal algorithm based on adversarial generative network. Pattern Recognit. Artif. Intell. **31**(11), 85–98 (2018)
4. Chen, Y., Li, Y., Yu, L., et al.: A system of convolutional neural networks based handwritten number recognition. Microelectron. Comput. **35**(2), 71–74 (2018)
5. Liu, S., Matt, G., Marco, Z., et al. (eds.): E-Learning, E-Education, and Online Training. Springer, Cham (2018). https://doi.org/10.1007/978-3-319-93719-9. 15(01):1–15
6. Liu, S., Li, Z., Zhang, Y., et al.: Introduction of key problems in long-distance learning and training. Mob. Netw. Appl. **24**(1), 1–4 (2019)
7. Fu, W., Liu, S., Srivastava, G.: Optimization of big data scheduling in social networks. Entropy **21**(9), 902–918 (2019)

8. Xie, Z., Jiang, P., Yu, X., et al.: Hyperspectral face recognition system based on VGGNet and multi-band recurrent network. J. Comput. Appl. **39**(2), 388–391 (2019)
9. Liu, Y., Yao, L., Wu, Y., et al.: Target point tracks association and error correction with optical satellite in geostationary orbit and automatic identification system. J. Electron. Inf. Technol. **40**(7), 1546–1552 (2018)
10. Chen, T., Zeng, J., Xie, C., et al.: Intelligent identification system of disease and insect pests based on deep learning. China Plant Prot. **39**(4), 28–36 (2019)

Design of Multimedia Learning Resource Recommendation System Based on Recurrent Neural Network

Zijin Xiao[✉], Ying Li, and Hai Zhou

College of Science, Engineering, Agriculture and Medicine, Gansu Radio and Television University, Lanzhou 730030, China
fddsf222@aliyun.com

Abstract. The existing learning resource recommendation system has the defect that the average absolute error of the recommendation result is large due to the limitation of its own adaptation range. For this reason, this research designed a multimedia learning resource recommendation system based on recurrent neural network. Introduce the recurrent neural network to design the architecture of the multimedia learning resource recommendation system, and design the system functional modules based on this, including the learner's demand retrieval representation module, learner preference representation module, recurrent neural network training module, database module and system management module. The simulation experiment results show that compared with the existing system, under the Gowalla data set, the average absolute error coefficient of the recommended results of this paper is reduced by 0.356; under the Yelp data set, the average absolute error coefficient of the recommended results of this paper is reduced 0.404. The above results fully show that the recommendation effect of this system is better.

Keywords: Recurrent neural network · Multimedia learning resources · Resource recommendation · Demand retrieval · Learner preference

1 Introduction

The booming development of the Internet not only brings a variety of fast and convenient to people's life, study, work, etc., but also makes people's life and the way of communication have changed greatly, and people are more and more inseparable from the Internet in every aspect of daily life. In this process, multimedia learning resources also show exponential growth [1]. Such a large number of learning resource data has brought great troubles to both learners and Internet learning resource services. For learners, in the face of such a large amount of multimedia learning resource data, it becomes very difficult to retrieve items that are relevant or interesting to them.

Massive and sufficient multimedia learning resources are the advantages of online learning. However, the excessive accumulation of online learning resources also brings

W. Fu et al. (Eds.): ICMTEL 2021, LNICST 388, pp. 243–254, 2021.
https://doi.org/10.1007/978-3-030-82565-2_20

difficulties in screening high-quality resources, which in disguise causes the plight of shortage of high-quality resources [2]. Therefore, the contradiction between the redundancy of online learning resources and the personalized learning needs of online learners makes the waste and utilization of multimedia learning resources increasingly prominent. It has become an important topic in the field of learning system research to select suitable learning resources for learners. In this context, recommendation system as a tool to provide personalized learning services, due to its high efficiency of resource retrieval, has attracted the attention of researchers, and is widely used in the field of education.

The existing recommendation system of learning resources has the defect of large average absolute error due to the limitation of its adaptive scope. Recursive neural network is an artificial neural network with tree hierarchical structure and network nodes recurse input information according to their connection order, which is one of the branches of deep learning algorithms [3]. Recursive neural networks, which have variable topology and weight sharing, are widely used in machine learning tasks containing structural relations and have been widely used in natural language processing. The aim of this study is to reduce the average absolute error of the recommendation of the design system and provide more accurate and effective recommendation service of multimedia learning resources for learners through the application of recursive neural network.

Therefore, this paper designs a new multimedia learning resource recommendation system based on recursive neural network. This system introduces the recursive neural network into the multimedia learning resource recommendation system architecture, and designs the learner demand retrieval representation module, the learner preference representation module, the recursive neural network training module, the database module and the system management module. The simulation experiment proves that the system has the advantage of small mean absolute error.

2 Design of Multimedia Learning Resource Recommendation System

In order to meet the needs of today's learners, a recurrent neural network is introduced to design a multimedia learning resource recommendation system. Its architecture is shown in Fig. 1.

Based on the system architecture shown in Fig. 1, the system functional modules are designed. The specific design process is as follows.

2.1 The Module of Learners' Needs Retrieval and Representation

In the records generated by the learner's browsing system, the sequence of multimedia learning resources interacting with the learner is recorded. The interactive behaviors generated by these multimedia learning resources and the learner are often of different types. For example, every learner has behaviors such as clicking, browsing, collecting, downloading, etc. [4]. This research intuitively and reasonably assumes that the different interactive behaviors of learners and multimedia learning resources represent different

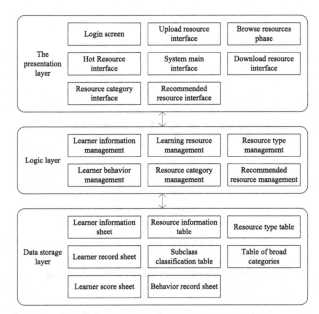

Fig. 1. Architecture of multimedia learning resource recommendation system

behavioral characteristics of learners. The purpose of the recurrent neural network algorithm is to obtain the expression of potential learner characteristics from the learner's demand retrieval. Therefore, an embedding layer of learner behavior characteristics is designed.

Specifically, the conventional process of processing discrete features by recurrent neural network is used to transform the ID of multimedia learning resources into the form of one hot coding. The dimension of one hot coding vector is the number of multimedia learning resources in the data set, which is a high-dimensional sparse vector. The embedding layer is essentially a full connection layer, which maps the one hot coding of learning resource ID from high-dimensional sparse vector to low-dimensional dense vector, which is conducive to feature extraction and abstraction of neural network. Based on this, after getting the dense embedding vectors of learning resources, the average pooling strategy is used to aggregate the learning resources of different interaction types in the history behavior records of learners, which are used as the feature vectors of different types of behaviors of learners, and these behavior feature vectors are connected to form the input layer of multi-layer perceptron.

The learner's demand retrieval program is shown in Fig. 2.

In order to better abstract the learner's demand retrieval feature into a vectorized expression, the vector representation of the potential learner's demand retrieval can be obtained from the learner's behavior feature combination vector through the fully connected hidden layer [5].

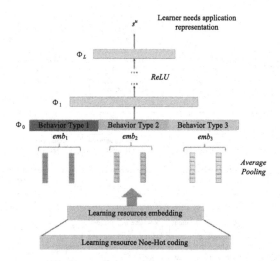

Fig. 2. Program diagram of learners' needs retrieval

As shown in Fig. 2, $emb_1, emb_2, \cdots, emb_n$ refers to embedding vectors of different behavior characteristics in learners' demand retrieval, and the input layer and hidden layer of recurrent neural network are represented as

$$
\begin{cases}
z_0 = \Phi_0(emb_1, \cdots, emb_n) = [emb_1; \cdots; emb_n] \\
\quad z_1 = \Phi_0(z_0) = \sigma(W_1 z_0 + b_1) \\
\qquad \cdots \\
\quad z_L = \Phi_L(z_{L-1}) = \sigma(W_L z_{L-1} + b_L)
\end{cases}
\tag{1}
$$

In formula (1), z_0 represents the output expression of the input layer, which connects different types of user behavior feature vectors $emb_1, \cdots, emb_n$ to form the output of the hidden layer; $z_1 \cdots z_L$ represents the output expression of the hidden layer 1 to L; W_i and b_i respectively Represents the weight matrix and bias of the i layer; σ represents the activation function of the fully connected layer, and its expression is:

$$
ReLU(x) = \max(0, x)
\tag{2}
$$

As the activation function of neurons, relu function is proved not to lead to supersaturation. At the same time, it supports sparse activation, which is very suitable for sparse data, so that the recurrent neural network algorithm is not over fitted. The output z_L of the last layer of relu layer is the vectorized representation s^u of learners' requirements retrieval which is obtained by recurrent neural network algorithm.

2.2 Learner Preference Representation Module

Learners' recent behavior reflects the user's recent needs or intentions. Modeling learners' short-term behavior is an important task to better understand learners' preferences. Therefore, self attention mechanism is used to model the nearest learning resource sequence in the learners' demand retrieval sequence to capture the learners' interest in short-term learning resource demand [6]. Self attention mechanism is a special case of attention mechanism. Different from the basic attention mechanism, it improves attention expression by matching a single sequence with itself.

In order to construct the temporal characteristics of the learner's demand retrieval behavior, the sequence position code is added to the learner's demand retrieval behavior sequence [7]. First, the user's demand retrieval behavior is sorted by timestamp, and then the timestamp is discretized into a time series number, and these sequences are coded using a triangular coding method. The coding formula is as follows:

$$PE_i(t) = \begin{cases} PE_{2i}(t) = \sin\left(\dfrac{t}{10000^{\frac{2i}{d}}}\right) \\ PE_{2i+1}(t) = \cos\left(\dfrac{t}{10000^{\frac{2i}{d}}}\right) \end{cases} \quad (3)$$

In formula (3), $PE_i(t)$ represents the element value of the i dimension of the $PE(t)$ vector of the time series position code; t represents the discretized time series; d represents the dimension of the position code, which is the same as the dimension of the multimedia learning resource embedding vector.

Considering the embedded expression vector sequence $X_u = [x_1^u, x_2^u, \cdots, x_t^u]$ of learners' needs retrieval sequence, the size of the observation window of attention mechanism is set to H, that is, the nearest H vectors in the learners' demand retrieval sequence are intercepted as the input of neural network, that is, the subsequence x_H^u with X_u length of H is selected as the input sequence of learners' short-term preference expression:

$$X_H^u = \left[x_{t-H+1}^u, x_{t-H+2}^u, \cdots, x_t^u\right] \quad (4)$$

In Eq. (4), $X_H^u \in R^{H \times d}$ and d denote the dimension of vector embedded vector.

Specifically, the learning resource vector in the learner demand retrieval sequence is added to the time-series position encoding vector at the corresponding time to form a new learner demand retrieval sequence, namely:

$$\tilde{X}_H^u = \left[\tilde{x}_{t-H+1}^u, \tilde{x}_{t-H+2}^u, \cdots, \tilde{x}_t^u\right] \quad (5)$$

Then, $\tilde{X}_H^u$ nonlinear mapping transformation is performed to obtain the query matrix and key value matrix of the attention mechanism. The mapping transformation formula is as follows:

$$\begin{cases} Q = \sigma\left(\tilde{X}_H^u W_Q\right) \\ K = \sigma\left(\tilde{X}_H^u W_K\right) \end{cases} \quad (6)$$

In formula (6), W_Q and W_K respectively represent the weight matrix in the query matrix and the key matrix mapping transformation; $\sigma(\cdot)$ represents the nonlinear activation function, and this study uses the ReLU function as the activation function. After that, the attention weight matrix can be obtained by calculating the attention weight:

$$M_H^u = soft\max\left(\frac{QK^T}{\sqrt{d}}\right) \quad (7)$$

In Eq. (7), $\sqrt{d}$ represents the scaling factor of inner product calculation.

The short-term preference of learners can be obtained by the above formula:

$$a^u = \frac{1}{H} \sum_{h=1}^{H} Att_h \tag{8}$$

In formula (8), it represents the attention expression matrix of the learner's search sequence.

2.3   Recurrent Neural Network Training Module

Based on the learner's demand retrieval vectorized representation s^u and the learner's short-term preference representation a^u, the two are connected in vectors, and then a fully connected hidden layer is used to obtain the fusion feature expression of the learner's long-term historical behavior and short-term preference. The hidden layer The output is expressed as:

$$h = \sigma\left(W_T\left[s^u; a^u\right] + b_T\right) \tag{9}$$

In Eq. (9), W_T and b_T are the weight matrix and offset vector of the hidden layer respectively.

The fusion feature expression h is used as the input vector of the output layer, and the output layer uses softmax activation function to get the output vector expression of recurrent neural network

$$\hat{y} = soft\max(W_o h + b_o) \tag{10}$$

In formula (10), W_o and b_o are the weight matrix and bias vector of the output layer, respectively.

Considering the learner's needs, the retrieval behavior is an implicit feedback behavior. In the neural network training, the learner's next interactive learning resource is used as a positive sample, and other non-interactive multimedia learning resources are used as a negative sample, so that the recurrent neural network will take the next Requirement retrieval modeling is a multi-classification task, using multi-class cross entropy as the objective function of neural network minimization:

$$Loss = -\sum_{i=1}^{|V|} y_i \log(\hat{y}_i) + (1 - y_i) \log(1 - \hat{y}_i) \tag{11}$$

In formula (11), $\hat{y}_i$ is the element value of the i dimension of the output vector $\hat{y}$ of the recurrent neural network, which represents the probability distribution vector of the learner's next learning goal. The element value $\hat{y}_i$ of each dimension of the vector represents the possible probability of learning resource v_i appearing in the next click of learners in the current sequence, which can be regarded as the recommendation basis for the next click learning resource. y_i represents whether the learner has real interaction with learning resource v_i. when the learner interacts with learning resource v_i, then

$y_i = 1$, otherwise $y_i = 0$. In the probability distribution $\hat{y}_i$ of the output vector, the Top-k recommendation of the next click multimedia learning resources can be obtained by selecting the first K maximum values.

Input the learners' demand retrieval statements into the recursive neural network algorithm, and the output result is the recommendation result of multimedia learning resources [8].

2.4 Database Module

The background of multimedia learning resource recommendation system mainly uses MySQL database for data processing. It mainly designs the learner information table, multimedia learning resource information table, multimedia learning resource type table, learner resource rating table, learning record table, large category classification table, small class classification table and learner behavior table. The specific design of these tables is introduced below.

(1) Learner information table
The learner information table stores learner-related data, such as user name, password, date of birth, gender, and major. The specific table structure is shown in Table 1.

Table 1. Learner information table

Field Chinese name	English field	Types of
User number	userID	int
Username	userName	varchar(20)
Real name	realName	varchar(20)
Password	password	varchar(20)
Gender	sex	char(2)
Date of birth	birthday	datetime
Profession	career	varchar(15)
Telephone	phone	varchar(12)
Mailbox	email	varchar(30)

(2) Information table of multimedia learning resources

The multimedia learning resource information table stores the relevant data of learning resources, such as the name of learning resources, the type of learning resources, the classification number of major categories of learning resources, the classification numbers of small categories of learning resources and the description of learning resources. The specific table structure is shown in Table 2.

Table 2. Multimedia learning resource information table

Field Chinese name	English field	Types of
Resource number	resourceID	int
Resource Name	resourceName	varchar(20)
Resource type	resourceTypeID	int
release time	releasetime	datetime
Opening Hours	openingtime	datetime
Belonging to the course	courseName	varchar(20)
Uploader number	authorID	int
description	discration	varchar(200)
Category number	subjectID	int
Subclass classification number	subsubjectID	int
Storage path	path	varchar(200)

2.5 System Management Module

The system management module is mainly divided into four parts: multimedia learning resource category management, multimedia learning resource management, learner management and recommendation management.

(a) Category management of multimedia learning resources. The category management of multimedia learning resources is mainly to classify learning resources into major and sub-categories. Pedagogy, philosophy, literature, economics, science, law, medicine, history, engineering and management are regarded as major categories. Divide the major categories into several sub-categories. For example, take computer, electrical, economic management, architecture, finance, English, diplomacy and psychology as subcategories. The learner can select the corresponding category for quick query according to the category of the learning resource. According to the different types of learning resources, the learning resources are divided into course resources, case resources, e-books, exam certification, material resources and other resources. Learners can choose the type of learning resources needed according to their own needs;

(b) Multimedia learning resource management. The functions of multimedia learning resource management include uploading new learning resources, filling in the name, resource type, large category classification category, small category classification category of the learning resource to be uploaded and the introduction of the resource [9, 10]. After the successful upload of learning resources, the administrator also needs to check whether the resources meet the requirements. If the learning resource information is not correct, you can modify and delete the learning resource;

(c) Learner management. The functions realized by learner management include learner registration, login, downloading learning resources, online browsing learning resources, collecting learning resources, scoring and commenting learning resources. The information registered by the learner includes user name, password, age, major and other information. At the same time, the system has recommendations of popular resources and the latest resources to facilitate learners' learning of learning resources;

(d) Recommendation management. The function of recommendation management is to recommend the interesting learning resources for different learners. The recursive neural network algorithm is applied to the multimedia learning resource recommendation system, which provides the multimedia learning resource recommendation service for learners.

Through the design of the above system architecture and functional modules, the operation of the multimedia learning resource recommendation system is realized, and learning resources more in line with their needs are provided for learners.

3 System Application Performance Test

In order to verify the application performance of the multimedia learning resource recommendation system based on recurrent neural network, MATLAB software is used to design simulation experiments. The specific experimental process is as follows.

3.1 Experimental Data Set Preparation

Select Gowalla dataset and Yelp dataset as experimental data. Each check-in record in the data set contains a timestamp, a user ID, the user's social relationship and ResourceID. The statistical overview of the two data sets is shown in Table 3.

Table 3. Statistical overview of data sets

Data set	Gowalla	Yelp
User	43074	30887
Resource	46234	18995
Check-ins	1720082	860888
Density	0.0500%	0.1399%

In order to filter noise data, for Gowalla dataset, users with less than 20 signatures and multimedia learning resources with less than 20 visits are deleted. For yelp dataset, users with less than 10 signatures and multimedia learning resources accessed less than 10 times are deleted.

3.2 Experimental Environment Construction

Each node of the recurrent neural network can have data input. For the nodes of the i level, the calculation method of the system state is as follows:

$$h^{(i)} = f\left(U^T h_c^{(i)} + W^T X + b\right) \tag{12}$$

In formula (12), $h^{(i)}$ and $h_c^{(i)}$ are the system states of the node and all its parent nodes. When there are multiple parent nodes, the system state can be combined into a matrix. If the node has no input, no calculation is performed. It is an excitation function or encapsulated feedforward neural network, the latter corresponds to gating algorithms and some deep algorithms.

The experimental recurrent neural network environment is shown in Fig. 3.

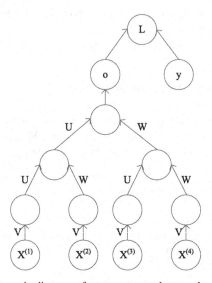

Fig. 3. Schematic diagram of recurrent neural network environment

In Fig. 3, U, W and V are weight coefficients, X is input data, o is output information, y is error, and L is candidate information.

3.3 Selection of Experimental Evaluation Index

The mean absolute error MAE was chosen as the evaluation index. At present, almost all the researches on recommendation choose Mae as the evaluation standard. Mae determines whether the recommendation is accurate by comparing the deviation degree. Deviation degree refers to the error between the recommendation results and the actual needs of users. The lower the MAE value is, the smaller the recommendation error is, the more accurate the recommendation is; on the contrary, the higher the MAE value, the greater the recommendation error and the worse the recommendation effect.

The average absolute error formula is defined as follows:

$$MAE_i = \frac{\sum_{j=1}^{n} |x_i - y_i|}{n} \tag{13}$$

In formula (13), n represents the total number of resources required by the user; x_i represents the system's demand score for resource i; y_i represents the user's real demand score for resource i.

3.4 Analysis of Experimental Results

According to the prepared experimental data and experimental environment, the multimedia learning resource recommendation experiment is carried out, and the average absolute error data of the recommendation is shown in Table 4.

Table 4. Recommended mean absolute error data table

(1) Gowalla data set		
Number of experiments/time	Recommended average absolute error coefficient	
	Existing systems	Text system
1	0.98	0.56
2	0.98	0.50
3	0.85	0.54
4	0.78	0.51
5	0.80	0.50
Average value	0.878	0.522
(2)Yelp data set		
Number of experiments/time	Recommended average absolute error coefficient	
	Existing systems	Text system
1	0.89	0.50
2	0.84	0.49
3	0.87	0.45
4	0.94	0.50
5	0.90	0.48
Average value	0.888	0.484

According to the data in Table 4, compared with the existing system, the average absolute error of the system in this paper is reduced by 0.356 and 0.404 in the Gowalla and Yelp data sets, which fully shows that the recommendation effect of the system in this paper is better.

4 Conclusion

In this paper, a new multimedia learning resource recommendation system based on recursive neural network is designed. This system introduces the recursive neural network into the multimedia learning resource recommendation system architecture, and designs the learner demand retrieval representation module, the learner preference representation module, the recursive neural network training module, the database module and the system management module. The system greatly reduces the average absolute error of the system recommendation, can provide more accurate multimedia learning resources for learners, and also provides more effective support for improving the utilization of learning resources.

References

1. Zhu, H., Hao, J., Niu, Y., et al.: Molecular targets of Chinese herbs: a clinical study of metastatic colorectal cancer based on network pharmacology **8**(1), 7238–7238 (2018)
2. Lee, T., Lee, I.: AraGWAB: network-based boosting of genome-wide association studies in Arabidopsis Thaliana **15**(6), 2925–2925
3. Tanabe, K., Liu, J., Kato, D., et al.: LC–MS/MS-based quantitative study of the acyl group- and site-selectivity of human sirtuins to acylated nucleosomes **37**(2), 2656–2656 (2018)
4. Radner, J.M., Ferrer, M.J.S., Dominique, M.M., et al.: Practical considerations for transitioning early childhood interventions to scale: lessons from the Saving Brains portfolio. Ann. N. Y. Acad. Sci **1419**(1), 230–248 (2018)
5. Liu, S., Li, Z.J., Zhang, Y.D., et al.: Introduction of key problems in long-distance learning and training. Mob. Netw. Appl. **24**(1), 1–4 (2019)
6. Liu, S., Lu, M.Y., Li, H.S., et al.: Prediction of gene expression patterns with generalized linear regression model. Front. Genet. **10**, 120 (2019)
7. Liu, S., Matt, G., Marco, Z., et al. (eds.): E-Learning, E-Education, and Online Training, pp. 1–374. Springer, Cham (20s18). https://doi.org/10.1007/978-3-319-93719-9
8. Liu, Q., Dong, Z., Wang, E.: Cut based method for comparing complex networks. Sci. Rep. **8**(17), 5134s (2018)
9. Wang, J., Cao, H., Zhang, J.Z.H., et al.: Computational protein design with deep learning neural networks. Sci. Rep. **45**(19), 6349 (2018)
10. Roffman, D., Hart, G., Girardi, M., et al.: Predicting non-melanoma skin cancer via a multi-parameterized artificial neural network. Sci. Rep. **28**(13), 1701 (2018)

Human/Medical Based Data Processing and Systems

Research on Constructing Regional Telemedicine Imaging Diagnosis Center Based on Ctirix Technology

Jinshun Ding[1(✉)], Yu Ren[1], Kefeng Xu[1], and Yixin Wang[2]

[1] Changshu Meili Hospital, Changshu 215500, Jiangsu, China
[2] Changshu No. 2 People's Hospital, Changshu 215500, Jiangsu, China

Abstract. Medical informatization is an important direction of medical development, and regional medical information sharing is the overall trend of medical development. Content Establish the integration of information in the radiology department of the community health center and the imaging department of the secondary hospital in the medical union. Solve the problem of ineffective sharing of clinical imaging information data caused by different systems and servers in the region. It can optimize the rapid viewing of clinical data and historical case data of referral patients in the region to achieve an efficient and fast tracking of the entire treatment process of patients And the image information of the disease development. It mainly adopts CITRIX virtualization technology, which has the advantages of small occupied bandwidth, high security, convenient deployment, remote management, convenient maintenance, stable connection, and high reliability. Through Citrix technology, the clinical data sets of the branch hospitals are effectively centralized, and a relatively unified data system is established, which is stored, managed and transferred to a standardized data model to form a data set, and integrates internal data in the region to effectively serve clinical images.

Keywords: Citrix technology · Virtualized storage · Regional imaging

1 Introduction

Medical informatization is an important direction of my country's medical reform, and it is a key step to promote the vertical integration of medical care and form a medical consortium. Regional medical information sharing is the overall trend of medical development [1]. Establish information integration between the radiology department of the community health center and the imaging department of the secondary hospital in the medical union [2, 3]. In order to adapt to the social and economic development of the city, in 1999, the Changshu Municipal People's Government approved the adjustment of the existing layout of the health centers in the three towns along the river, and cancelled the "Changshu Zhenmen Health Center" and "Changshu Zhao City Health Center" and merged them into "Changshu Meili Central Health Center" was renamed "Changshu Meili Central Health Center Zhenmen Branch" and "Changshu Meili Central Health

W. Fu et al. (Eds.): ICMTEL 2021, LNICST 388, pp. 257–266, 2021.
https://doi.org/10.1007/978-3-030-82565-2_21

Center Zhaoshi Branch". After the merger of Meili People's Hospital and Meili Town Community Health Service Center, Meili People's Hospital, as a regional medical center of the Municipal Second Hospital Medical Community, will organize and implement various tasks in accordance with the spirit of the Changshu Medical Reform Office document to achieve medical and Pay equal attention to public health and develop together [4]. Among them, the General Hospital has paid close attention to the improvement of medical service technology and capacity, and advanced to the second-class general hospital in management and technology to drive the comprehensive development of the second branch and public health; Zhaoshi branch focuses on exploring the integration of medical care; Zhenmen branch focuses on Do a good job in the exploration of medical rehabilitation business; it will take three years to build a basic-level Grade 2 A general hospital with powerful functions, complete services and guaranteed quality.

2   Research Status

Image storage and transmission system (PACS) is an important part of hospital informatization, which mainly solves related problems such as digital acquisition of medical images, high-quality storage of image files, and unified management of text materials [5–7]. In order to solve the problems of difficult and expensive medical treatment for patients and the construction of personal medical files, the sharing of medical information and the regionalization of medical treatment will be a major trend in the future [8, 9]. Realize information sharing between regions, improve the efficiency of daily diagnosis of medical institutions in the region, and provide a strong guarantee for scientific analysis and comprehensive diagnosis [10–12].

Some application problems of current medical image storage and transmission systems are affected by the network, security and stability. Hospitals have generally established image storage and transmission systems to archive, store and communicate hospital image data. However, with the continuous improvement of the accuracy of digital diagnostic equipment and the increasing number of patients, there are obviously many problems and deficiencies in the use of traditional image storage and transmission systems [13]. The operating systems, databases and storage devices used by the major image storage and transmission system software vendors are not the same, which makes each image storage and transmission system not only completely heterogeneous in software and hardware, but also lack of interoperability [14–16]. Because the image storage and transmission system storage platforms of hospitals and communities are inconsistent, and the storage interface is also chaotic, it is difficult to realize the sharing of image storage and transmission system information between hospitals. Moreover, the funds of township hospitals and community health centers are relatively limited. It is very difficult to purchase expensive PACS independently. It is often the report writing software provided by the manufacturer when the equipment is purchased. It cannot be integrated with other systems [17]. It is often caused by incorrect input of patient information. Misdiagnosed. In addition, the platforms of township hospitals and community health centers are limited, unable to recruit experienced imaging doctors, and often can only perform routine examinations. Patients then go to secondary and tertiary hospitals for diagnosis, and the quality of printed film is relatively low [18, 19]. If the image storage and transmission system area is to be shared, data must be shared from the medical digital imaging and communication interface. This will lead to a large number of changes in the application of the image storage and transmission system. With the development of regional health informatization, image storage and communication and interoperability have gradually expanded to between medical and health institutions in the entire region, interconnecting the PACS of multiple medical institutions in the region, and making the image information generated by each medical institution be The image information platform system that shares and exchanges medical needs and resource optimization principles in the region is called regional PACS [20].

By building a regional PACS, patients can be examined at any medical institution in the region, and networked hospitals can share image information, apply for online consultations, analyze and discuss the condition, so as to further clarify the diagnosis and guide the determination of treatment plans. Realize the sharing of information such as imaging resources, expert diagnosis resources, equipment resources, and medical research results, and reduce the number of repeated examinations for patients, and reduce the cost of diagnosis and treatment for patients.

3 Status Analysis and Research Purpose

3.1 Status Analysis

Ctirix technology to support the realization of unified clinical information applications, improve the security and disaster recovery capabilities of the information system, establish an imaging information and clinical communication system between the branch and the Meili People's Hospital, to ensure the practicability and operability of the combined system To respond to the development plan of Meili People's Hospital, and to solve the current situation of basic-level branch hospitals that are difficult to recruit or quickly train suitable imaging talents due to factors such as their location and medical technology level. In order to solve the shortcomings of technical talents in branch hospitals, remote consultation medical services have been brought into people's vision and become a breakthrough in the grassroots service of superior radiotherapy talents. This research combines the practice of community medical treatment to study the PACS system of the medical consortium.

3.2 Research Purpose

(1) Solve the problem that clinical imaging information data cannot be effectively shared due to different system servers in multiple branches and community service stations in the region; It can optimize the rapid viewing of clinical data and historical case data of referred patients in the region to facilitate efficiently and quickly trace the patient's entire treatment process and disease development; Integrate basic clinical data in the Meili area, so as to more efficiently and conveniently trace the patient's entire treatment process and disease changes in the future.

(2) Using the existing hardware equipment of Meili People's Hospital, combining the actual situation of the imaging system of each branch in the region, using Citrix virtualization technology, the imaging servers of the three hospitals are effectively integrated, effectively reducing the hospital's operating costs.

(3) Use information technology to further strengthen the telemedicine image service capabilities in the region, solve the limitations of the metropolitan area network in different regions, effectively solve the shortage of branch resources and talents, and provide better and more professional treatment for the treatment of primary patients Program.

4 Technical Architecture

4.1 Model Design of Regional Imaging System

(1) The regional PACS architecture diagram is shown in Fig. 1. Patient information can be directly called by all parties from the main PACS database after being entered by the system. After the patient completes the imaging examination, the community radiologist can quickly access, browse and process the imaging data through the computer. Community doctors follow the unified diagnostic template of the radiology department of the upper-level hospital of the medical consortium, and carry out standardized editing of diagnostic reports, which can reduce the input workload, shorten the report generation cycle, and improve work efficiency. Set up different permissions, community radiologists write initial diagnosis reports, which are reviewed by radiologists from higher-level hospitals (associate chief physicians and above), and the system retains traces of the modified content. The reviewed report can be submitted and uploaded after being signed and confirmed by the physician The main server stores the backup, which is then printed and distributed by the community radiology department. The printed report can no longer be modified, and it can be accessed as a read-only reference.

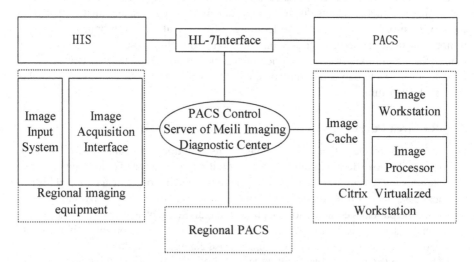

Fig. 1. PACS architecture diagram based on Citrix virtualization area

(2) Citrix virtualization construction. Take advantage of the existing server resources of Meili People's Hospital, build Citrix related servers and establish efficient links and business relationships between the branches and run data through the health metropolitan area network to realize hospitals such as patients, departments, equipment, and hospital images Unified management of operations. Citrix technology installs and publishes various applications centrally by setting up application servers (groups). The client maintains communication with the server by installing simple ICA software, so that the required applications are completely executed on the server, and then The client obtains the interface results locally, so that the user can efficiently access the upper-level Windows, UNIX or Internet programs and data through various network connection methods (WAN, LAN, Internet, etc.) no matter where they are or what equipment they use.

The application server software (MetaFrameTM) separates the execution and operation logic of the application from the display interface, so that the application can be executed 100% on the server, and the interface is displayed on the client.

The ICA (Independent Computing Architecture) protocol greatly reduces the amount of network transmission. Normally, it only occupies a width of about 10K per second, which can save more than 40% to 60% of the frequency band.

ICA client software Through this software, any form of client can log in to the application server, access the required applications and data, and seamlessly integrate server resources and local resources.

(3) Data storage technology, with Meili People's Hospital in Changshu as the center and secondary hospitals in the region as branch points. The clinical data sets of the two branches are effectively centralized through Citrix technology to establish a relatively unified data system. Centralized storage, management and transfer to a standardized data model to form a data set, effectively integrating regional internal data to serve clinical images. See Fig. 2.

Data storage The storage of image data is also in DICOM format, and the international standard DICOM3.0 interface is used between components. In view of the large data of medical imaging information, massive data storage and management are required, and a single centralized storage has certain risks. In this case, PACS image data adopts a combination of distributed and centralized management to establish PACS1 and PACS2 storage paths. PACS1 is transmitted to the local data storage, and PACS2 is transmitted to the database of the second-level hospital in the medical association, managed with Oracle 11 g software, and set up based on the mainstream J2EE technology platform. The community radiology image data is regularly stored in CDR in DICOM mode. Therefore, this system has the following advantages: prevent data loss; avoid unilateral database failure and affect the work of the community radiology department; multiple stored data can be interchanged.

(4) Network architecture construction, using the existing hardware equipment of Meili People's Hospital and combining the actual situation of the imaging system of each branch in the area, PACS is an open system based on network communication and transmission. The network of this center adopts the VPN network connection established by the Health Commission. The network transmission protocol standard is TCP/IP.DICOM. The backbone adopts Gigabit switched fast Ethernet, which is directly transmitted to each work terminal through 100Mb Ethernet. The image

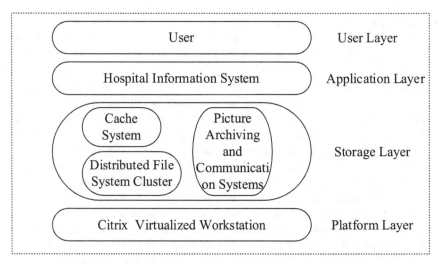

Fig. 2. Medical image storage architecture based on Citrix

retrieval time is controlled in Within 10 s. Radiologists can access the images within ≤3.5 s.

4.2 Citrix Virtualization Technology

CITRIX virtualization is composed of many core components, mainly including: virtual controller, virtual agent CITRIX online plug-in, scheduler component, etc. With the cooperation of these components, virtualization can operate normally. First, the user requests to obtain the desktop. The client can be any thin client equipped with a virtual connection protocol. When the terminal is started, an authentication message will pop up. At this time, as long as the user enters the correct authentication information, it will be obtained on the server. Virtual system consistent with office system. After the user is authenticated, the system delivery controller will dynamically configure the virtual system, use the built-in scheduler (Provi-sioning), deliver on-demand according to the network, combine user-customized applications, OS, and settings together, and use files Stream delivery to the hosting environment, waiting for users to connect. The following are the advantages of CITRIX virtualization:

1 Reduce bandwidth occupation In K/3 applications, the effective bandwidth of the client terminal and the middle layer connection needs to be above 20 KB. The bandwidth occupation is much smaller than that of direct registration, which greatly saves the cost of leased lines for enterprises.
2 The security is high. Citrix itself provides encrypted transmission, combined with VPN and other technologies, it can provide a higher level of security technology guarantee.

3 Reduce maintenance work. The client no longer needs to install the client, just install the Citrix client. The client upgrade, patching and other maintenance are concentrated on the Citrix server, which greatly reduces the workload and maintenance, and shortens The maintenance cycle.

4 Realize remote management. Through remote management, remote maintenance and management of Citrix servers or further internal servers can solve many problems that do not require on-site support, greatly reducing service costs and greatly reducing response time.

5 The connection is stable. The Citrix connection is very stable. Even if it is disconnected, the information of the disconnection point will be retained, and the disconnection point will be returned directly after the next successful connection.

6 High reliability. In high-end multi-user applications, multiple Citrix servers can be used. Through network load balancing, instead of polling, resources such as CPU, memory, and applications are dynamically allocated on demand to achieve high performance and high performance reliability.

5 Function Introduction

(1) Centralized reporting function of regional radiological imaging examinations Community residents can perform imaging examinations at the community health service center. The image diagnosis is submitted to the imaging diagnosis center of this hospital, which provides diagnosis services. The image diagnosis report is printed by the community center and delivered to the patient. This measure not only realizes the integration of the resources of the imaging department and the imaging diagnosis center of the community health service center, but also improves the imaging diagnosis level of the community health service center, thereby eliminating the suffering of patients. See Fig. 3.

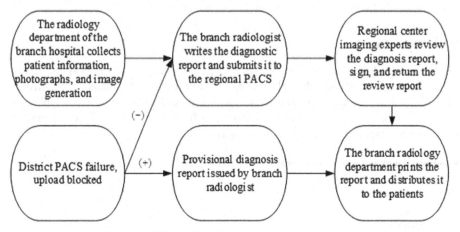

Fig. 3. PACS workflow in the medical consortium area

(2) Homogeneous service process The regional PACS system was established, and the imaging diagnosis report work in the area was coordinated in the report and diagnosis workstation of the hospital, and the reports and images to be processed by the hospital and each community were displayed on the same interface. The business unity of the community health service center provides the same quality service process in the joint body at the level of diagnosis and treatment and quality control.

(3) Remote reservation through the construction of the imaging center system, the community can make reservations for equipment in the central hospital. That is, when a patient is in a community medical institution, the community medical equipment cannot complete the examination. The community doctor can directly call the registration appointment system or examination appointment system interface of the diagnosis center in the local doctor station system to complete the corresponding appointment, that is, make an appointment for registration or examination. If the equipment is occupied in advance, patients will see the doctor on time according to the appointment arrangement. Remote appointment not only improves business efficiency, but also facilitates patient visits.

(4) The construction of a regional medical consortium for quality control and reading will realize centralized storage and centralized diagnosis of examination images in each community. In order to standardize the business operations of community filming technicians, improve image quality, obtain better diagnostic results, and complete radiation quality control management for community hospitals. At the same time, the quality control and reading function in the medical complex can on the one hand find out the work quality and equipment performance of the photographer, typesetting person and equipment through the evaluation; Control level management.

(5) The regional PACS project makes full use of the advantages of centralized storage of digital image information, and implements a regional electronic film process, thereby reducing the investment of medical institutions at all levels in film printing, storage, and verification.

6 Summary

With Changshu Meili People's Hospital as the center and the secondary hospitals in the region as branch points, the clinical data sets of the two branch hospitals are effectively centralized through Citrix technology, and a relatively unified data system is established to centrally store, manage and transfer. A data set is formed in a standardized data model to effectively integrate regional internal data to serve clinical images.

Funding. Guiding project of Suzhou Science and Technology Bureau, Research on the construction of Meili regional telemedicine imaging diagnosis center based on Ctirix technology. (No. SYSD2020022).

References

1. Surahmat, Tenggono, A.: Analysis of server virtualization service performance using Citrix Xenserver. J. Phys: Conf. Ser. 1500, 012098 (7pp.) (2020)

2. Dordevic, B., Timcenko, V., Savic, S., Davidovic, N.: Comparing hypervisor virtualization performance with the example of citrix hypervisor (XenServer) and Microsoft Hyper-V. In: 2020 19th International Symposium INFOTEH-JAHORINA (INFOTEH), p. 6 (2020)
3. Liu, X., Huo, X.-L., Qiu, Z., Chen, M.-R.: Scheme of cloud desktop based on citrix. In: Zhou, Q., Gan, Y., Jing, W., Song, X., Wang, Y., Lu, Z. (eds.) ICPCSEE 2018. CCIS, vol. 901, pp. 415–425. Springer, Singapore (2018). https://doi.org/10.1007/978-981-13-2203-7_32
4. James, C., Frantzis, J., Ripps, L., Fenton, P.: Total centralisation and optimisation of an oncology management suite via Citrix. J. Phys: Conf. Ser. **489**, 012092 (4 pp.) (2014)
5. Zhao, J., Wang, C., Sun, R., Wang, B.: A Citrix XenApp and web based system for product design and management. Appl. Mech. Mater. **163**, 121–124 (2012)
6. Hui, D., Jin-yun, F., Hong-chao, Z., Zhen-lin, C.: Design and implementation of remote software sharing system based on Citrix. Comput. Eng. **35**(1), 49–51, 54 (2009)
7. David, F.: Benchmarking epic's thick client on Citrix. In: 32nd International. Conference Computer Measurement Group (2006)
8. Li, J.-Y., et al.: The implementation of a GPU-accelerated virtual desktop infrastructure platform. In: Proceedings - 2017 International Conference on Green Informatics, ICGI 2017, p 85–92, 21 November
9. Wang, F., Sun, X., Li, S., Wang, Y., Xiao, B., Chang, S.: The implementation of virtualization technology in EAST data system. Fusion Eng. Des. **89**(5), 766–769 (2014)
10. Suliman, I.I.: Estimates of patient radiation doses in digital radiography using DICOM information at a large teaching hospital in Oman. J. Digit. Imaging **33**(1), 64–70 (2019). https://doi.org/10.1007/s10278-019-00199-y
11. Yanjie, Q., Zehui, Y., Lin, K.: Fusion of multi-voltage digital radiography images based on support value transform. In: Proceedings - 2019 6th International Conference on Information Science and Control Engineering, ICISCE 2019, pp. 302–308, December 2019
12. Wang, Y., Ding, J., Fang, W., Cao, J.: Segmentation-assisted diagnosis of pulmonary nodule recognition based on adaptive particle swarm image algorithm. In: Ning, H. (ed.) CyberDI. CCIS, vol. 1138, pp. 504–512. Springer, Singapore (2019). https://doi.org/10.1007/978-981-15-1925-3_36
13. Chen, X., Zhao, D., Zhong, W.: Auxiliary recognition of alzheimer's disease based on gaussian probability brain image segmentation model. In: Ning, H. (ed.) CyberDI. CCIS, vol. 1138, pp. 513–520. Springer, Singapore (2019). https://doi.org/10.1007/978-981-15-1925-3_37
14. Li, D., Dong, M., Tang, Y., Ota, K.: A novel disk I/O scheduling framework of virtualized storage system. Clust. Comput. **22**(1), 2395–2405 (2018). https://doi.org/10.1007/s10586-017-1363-9
15. Arulraj, L.: Department of Computer Sciences, University of Wisconsin, Madison, United States. In: Arpaci-Dusseau, A.C., Arpaci-Dusseau, R.H.: Improving virtualized storage performance with Sky, pp. 112–128, 8 April 2017, VEE 2017
16. Alatorre, G., Singh, A., Mandagere, N., Butler, E., Gopisetty, S., Song, Y.: Intelligent information lifecycle management in virtualized storage environments. In: 2014 Annual SRII Global Conference (SRII), pp. 9–18 (2014)
17. Noorshams, Q., Rentschler, A., Kounev, S., Reussner, R.: A generic approach for architecture-level performance modeling and prediction of virtualized storage systems. In: ICPE 2013 - Proceedings of the 2013 ACM/SPEC International Conference on Performance Engineering, pp. 339–342 (2013)
18. Josephson, W.K., Bongo, L.A., Li, K., Flynn, D.: DFS: a file system for virtualized flash storage. In: Proceedings of FAST 2010: 8th USENIX Conference on File and Storage Technologies, pp. 85–99 (2019)

19. Tai, J., Liu, D., Yang, Z., Zhu, X., Lo, J., Mi, N.: Improving flash resource utilization at minimal management cost in virtualized flash-based storage systems. IEEE Trans. Cloud Comput. **5**(3), 537–549 (2017)
20. Park, H., Yoo, S., Hong, C.-H., Yoo, C.: Storage SLA guarantee with novel SSD I/O scheduler in virtualized data centers. IEEE Trans. Parallel Distrib. Syst. **27**(8), 2422–2434 (2016)

Research on Multi-agency Data Fusion Mode Under Regional Medical Integration

Yixin Wang[1], Weiqing Fang[1], Wei Zhu[1(✉)], and Jinshun Ding[2]

[1] Changshu No.2 People's Hospital, Changshu 215500, Jiangsu, China
[2] Changshu Meili Hospital, Changshu 215500, Jiangsu, China

Abstract. 2020 is not only the stage of intensive implementation of medical informatization related policies, but also a key year for the further development of regionalization of medical informatization projects. The medical community data sharing technology using multi-source heterogeneous data fusion solves the problem of different hospitals, different procedures, different database structures, and information islands in each hospital. Through ETL technology, using the SSIS tool in Microsoft SQL Server, a relatively standard data system is built for the original information system of each hospital in the medical community group to centrally convert, clean and transfer to a standardized data model to form a data set: Patient Master Index (EMPI), Master Data Management (MDM), etc., to solve the problem of reducing repeated statistics and discrepancies in various hospitals, improve data quality, complete interconnection and data sharing.

Keywords: Data sharing · Data fusion · ETL technology

1 Introduction

2020 is not only the stage of intensive implementation of policies related to medical informatization, but also a key year for the further development of regionalization of medical informatization projects [1]. In accordance with the overall planning of the supporting implementation measures for the pilot program for further deepening the comprehensive reform of public medical institutions in Changshu City (Changbanfa [2018] No. 124), the city's second hospital regional medical community was established to promote the sharing of regional medical resources and provide the overall capabilities and capabilities of the medical service system. Performance. The medical community data sharing technology using multi-source heterogeneous data fusion solves the problem of different hospitals, different procedures, different database structures, and information islands in each hospital [2–4]. In order to carry forward the advantages of medical regional integration of the Second People's Hospital of Changshu City, fully tap and play the value of data, integrate the clinical data accumulated for many years into the clinical data center (CDR), and plan to carry out a number of community service centers and central health centers [4–6]. The data resource integration of the hospital realizes the data resource sharing between the general hospital and community hospitals.

W. Fu et al. (Eds.): ICMTEL 2021, LNICST 388, pp. 267–277, 2021.
https://doi.org/10.1007/978-3-030-82565-2_22

2   Research Status

The ultimate goal of regional medical-oriented clinical data exchange is to solve the two problems of information integration and data standardization. In order to solve the various challenges faced by information system integration, promote the information sharing and coordination of medical information systems, and provide integration solutions between different subsystems, the North American Association of Radiological Medicine and the American Association of Medical and Health Information and Management Systems established Medical in 1988 Institutional integration [7]. In North America, organizations such as RSNA, HIMSS, and the American Heart Association were responsible [8, 9]. The first five-year plan was formulated in 1999. The main participants include RSNA, HIMSS, California healthcare institute (CHI), etc. In Europe, IHE is under the responsibility of the European Society of Radiology and the association of the medical imaging industry [10]. The participants mainly include the Hospital Information System Exhibition Organization, the French Radiological Society, the German-Italian Radiological Society, and the Italian Radiological Society. In Asia, countries such as Japan, South Korea, and Taiwan have participated in the IHE project. Taiwan has conducted several IHE connection tests before this [11].

In China, there is still very little research and application of IHE, but it has gradually entered this field. IHE China was established in Shanghai in 2007 [12, 13]. In order to promote the popularization and promotion of IHE in China, the University of Shanghai for Science and Technology undertakes the technical preparation and organization of the test, and the first test was conducted in 2007. In 2008, the China Medical Equipment Association also started testing work and conducted the first test in Beijing Tiantan Hospital, including Mindray, General Medical, Siemens and other domestic and foreign manufacturers [14].

In terms of clinical data exchange standardization, in the process of medical informationization, countries such as the United Kingdom, the United States, and France have invested a lot of manpower and material resources in standardization work [15, 16]. Many standards have been widely recognized and applied. For example, the international code of diseases (ICD) standard coding is used in the classification of diseases and treatments; ICD-9, ICD-10 and other standard codes are used in diseases and surgical operations; Adopt systemized nomenclature of human and veterinary medicine (SNOMED) coding system in the electronic medical record system [17–19]. In addition, there are the US medical and health information transmission and exchange standards (health level seven, HL7), digital imaging and communications in medicine (digital imaging and communications in medicine, DICOM), and laboratory information system and inspection equipment interface standards [20].

3   Research Purpose

3.1   Purpose of Research and Application

(1)   Solve the problem that the clinical information data cannot be effectively shared due to the different hospital systems in the medical community; it can optimize the continuity of the clinical data of the referred patients in the region and quickly view the historical case data for efficiency, Quickly trace the patient's entire treatment process and disease development; integrate the clinical basic data unit in the medical community, so as to more efficiently and conveniently trace the patient's entire treatment process and disease changes in the future [21, 22].

(2)   Using the data center experience that has been initially established in Changshu Second People's Hospital, combining the actual situation of each hospital system in the medical community, using the sharing technology of multi-source heterogeneous data fusion, they have accumulated a large number of years. Standardized storage and classification of clinical data and operational data are used to improve the medical quality and performance during the daily operation of the hospital, and to make full use of existing data to improve the level of diagnosis and treatment in the hospital [23].

(3)   Use shared data technology to further strengthen the quality of operational indicators and data between hospitals in the medical community, integrate data, and provide a basis for decision-making.

3.2   Characteristics of Multi-agency Data Fusion Model

(1)   Overall characteristics
      System construction considers the protection and utilization of existing IT investment, based on the existing business system, without affecting the original system, to achieve seamless data and business connection between functions and the existing business system. The specific performance is: ease of use: implement the principle of end-user-oriented, establish a friendly user interface, make user operation simple and intuitive; security: security is a necessary condition for effectiveness and usability, and data cannot be lost due to various reasons. Or it may be illegally modified to affect or even stop the development of hospital medical services. In addition to hardware configuration measures, the security of the medical information system should also be addressed in many aspects such as system operation mode, software settings, rules and regulations; flexibility: the system must change accordingly with changes in health policies and regulations, and full consideration must be given to the system's Flexibility, reasonable arrangement of system structure.

(2)   Data characteristics
      Data input: It must be formatted data, and use selective input as much as possible to input it quickly and efficiently; Data statistics: Data statistics functions for all selected items must be provided, so that users can freely choose and count freely; Data backup: With data backup function, it can be divided into automatic timing backup, automatic remote backup and manual operation backup; data authority: data use authority function must be provided; data security: the system should

provide a complete user authority data access system, and database backup and different Provide scientific and reasonable security measures for machine backup and recovery. See Fig. 1.

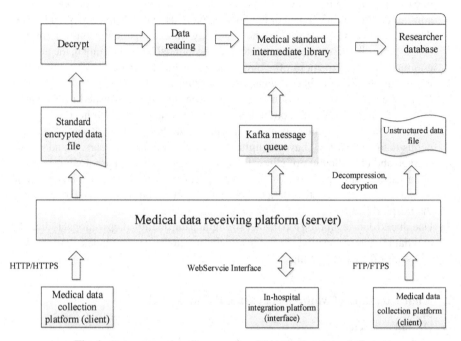

Fig. 1. Data processing diagram of multi-institution data platform

(3) Function parameters

Clinical Data Center (CDR): the data accessed by the clinical data center, and the organization of the access data is distinguished; hospital operation management: the system needs to increase the organization selection function, which is convenient for querying the indicators of the headquarters and community hospitals; switching institutions The function requires the authority control function, which can be conveniently and quickly set up the authority; the main patient index EMPI: to identify patients from multiple institutions, through the integration of EMPI numbers, it is convenient for other systems to identify and display patients with different card numbers; patient 360 view: Yes The medical information of multiple institutions is integrated to facilitate better diagnosis and treatment by medical workers.

4 Architecture Design

4.1 The Overall System Architecture is Divided into Five Levels

(1) Basic business layer: including HIS, LIS, PACS and other business systems that have been built by the member units of the medical community and various community service centers. See Fig. 2.

(2) Platform data layer: build a hospital-wide integrated data center, including business replication database and ODS, clinical data center (CDR), master data (MDM), data warehouse (DW), the main focus of this layer construction includes data The scientific organization of the domain model, the storage of high-quality data after cleaning and conversion, the theme design of the data warehouse, and the design of the data mart (including the data cube) model, etc.

(3) Platform service layer: Build the core service components of the hospital data center. These services provide services for hospital data integration, data statistical analysis, and platform construction for application layer data applications, including UI engine, patient main index EMPI, etc.

(4) Platform application layer: The platform application layer is to provide hospital platform users with key application systems based on the hospital data center and provide application support for other application systems. The project mainly includes patient views, hospital operation management, scientific research applications, etc.

(5) Platform portal layer: establish single sign-on services to break the physical location constraints of the platform, including manager portals, doctor portals, patient portals, researchers portals, and public portals.

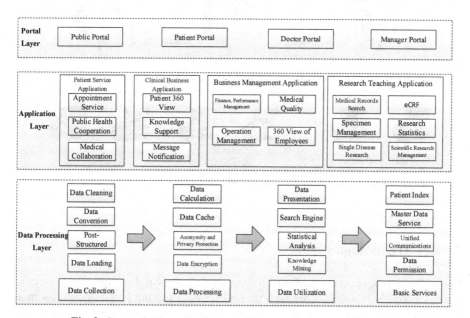

Fig. 2. Layered schematic diagram of the overall system architecture

4.2 Network Data Structure

Take Changshu Second People's Hospital as the center, as shown in Fig. 3, each in the region as branch points, through ETL technology to effectively centralize the clinical data sets of each hospital, and establish a relatively standard data system for centralized conversion, cleaning and transfer A data set is formed in a standardized data model to effectively integrate regional internal data to serve the clinic.

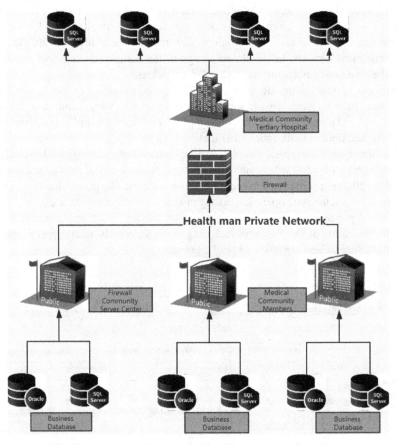

Fig. 3. Schematic diagram of regional center network structure

5 Key Technologies

Using the current experience of establishing a small clinical data center in Changshu Second People's Hospital, a research method for data sharing based on multi-source heterogeneous data fusion under the medical community has been established to solve the different database structures of different procedures in different hospitals within the medical community. The problem of information isolation in various hospital systems. Through ETL technology, using the SSIS tool in Microsoft SQL Server, the original information system of each hospital in the medical community group, including hospital management information system (HIS), electronic medical record information system (EMR), nursing information system (NIS), Laboratory information system (LIS), medical image cataloging (PACS), etc. for data extraction, combined with the his table structure to establish a relatively standard data system, centralized conversion, cleaning, and transfer to a standardized data model to form a data set: Patient main index (EMPI), Master Data Management (MDM), etc., to solve the problem of reducing repeated statistics and disagreements in various hospitals, and propose to target the five-level application level of hospital electronic medical records, standardize integration to build the big data of the medical community, and unify statistics Caliber, improve data quality, complete interconnection and data sharing.

5.1 Data Model

(1) The data model should include the main business areas of the hospital and support at least the following data queries. See Table 1, Table 2, and Table 3.

Table 1. Data model business areas

Field	Patient Management Domain	Cost	Laboratory Domain
Structure	Basic patient information Registered information Admission and admission registration information Diagnostic information Admission information	Outpatient settlement master record Outpatient settlement details Inpatient settlement master record Inpatient settlement details	Application registration information Specimen information Clinical examination and biochemical report Microbiology report Pathology report

(2) Data consolidation, including at least the following key dictionaries, hospital identification, update time, import time, and time stamp. See Table 4.

5.2 Main Patient Index

The Patient Master Index Service (EMPI) uses unique algorithms and technologies to create, search, and maintain the patient's basic information index throughout the hospital, which can intelligently assist medical staff in effectively searching for patients. Medical institutions use the main index (EMPI) to identify, match, merge, and cancel duplicate data, purify patient records, and use the main index to obtain a complete and single patient view. EMPI will create a unique identifier for each patient and establish a mapping between the identifiers of the medical records in the relevant system.

Table 2. Data model business areas

Field	Observation Domain	Medical Record Domain	Care Domain	Surgical Domain
Structure	Observation report Vital signs observation information Allergy information observation information	Medical Record Home Medical record diagnosis Medical record surgery	Medical order execution record Care delivery record	Surgical registration Operation record Surgical diagnosis Surgical anesthesia information Postoperative recovery information Surgery participants

Table 3. Data model business areas

Field	Medical Order Domain		Medical Record Field
Structure	Outpatient drug prescription Outpatient examination prescription Outpatient inspection prescription Outpatient treatment prescription Outpatient surgery prescription	Inpatient Drug Order Hospital checkup Inpatient examination order Hospital surgery doctor's order Hospital care order Hospital blood transfusion order Hospitalization Hospital Meal Order	Medical record master data Medical record segment data Medical record style data Full-text index of medical records Unstructured medical record data Hospital outpatient medical records

5.3 Master Data Management

Master data management MDM (Master Data Management) mainly stores dictionary data stored in the hospital business system, as well as national standards, industry standards, landmarks, hospital departments, service units, service personnel, service items and other custom data elements used in the hospital business.

Table 4. Key dictionaries for data consolidation

Serial number	Column name	Data type	length primary	key	Column description
1	HospitalNo	nvarchar(30)	30	√	Medical institution code
2	HospitalName	nvarchar(60)	60		Medical institution name
3	PatientlD	nvarchar(30)	30	√	Patient identification
4	MedicalRecordNo	nvarchar(30)	30		Medical record number
5	PatientName	nvarchar(60)	60		Patient name
6	PY	nvarchar(60)	60		pinyin
7	Wb	nvarchar(60)	60		Wubi

6 Summary

(1) The medical community data sharing technology using multi-source heterogeneous data fusion solves the problem of different hospitals, different procedures, different database structures, and each hospital system information island.

(2) Medical community data collection uses ETL technology to collect, and the scalability of the system can be realized through the database engine. Keep all data in the database at all times, avoid data loading and export, thereby ensuring efficiency and improving system monitorability. It is also possible to optimize the distribution of data in parallel, and use the inherent functions of the database to optimize disk I/O.

(3) It is proposed to organize the clinical data of patients with patients as the main line, and store the clinical data of patients in a comprehensive, standard and unified manner, which provides a unified platform support for the sharing of clinical data of the medical community, and provides some applications of clinical data Also laid a solid foundation.

(4) Through data sharing technology based on multi-source heterogeneous data fusion, extract clinical quality-related data, improve the medical quality and performance during the daily operation of the hospital, and improve the level of diagnosis and treatment in the hospital.

(5) Through medical community research and practical application, the mature medical community data sharing technology and information big data company will be promoted to other regional medical communities to better serve clinical and hospital management.

Funding. 2019 Changshu City Science and Technology Development Plan (Social Development) Project, Research and application of sharing technology based on multi-source heterogeneous data fusion under the medical community applied to clinical-related data quality (No.CS201913).

References

1. Wang, G., Liu, X., Wu, G., Guo, Y., Ma, S.: Research on data fusion method based on rough set theory and BP neural network. In: ICCEA 2020, pp. 269–272, March 2020
2. Gao, J., Li, P., Chen, Z., Zhang, J.: A survey on deep learning for multimodal data fusion. Neural Comput. **32**(5), 829–864 (2020)
3. Lin, D.: Research on key technologies of regional synergy emergency system based on medical data center. Proc. Comput. Sci. **154**, 732–737 (2019)
4. Jiemin, Z.: Analyzing the models of medical data center on cloud computing. In: 2015 10th International Conference on Computer Science & Education (ICCSE), pp. 76–9 (2015)
5. Apao, N.J., Feliscuzo, L.S., Romana, C.L.C.S.: Developing a patient information and descriptive analytics system for data actors of university of bohol medical and rehabilitation center: Towards policy making. In: ACM International Conference Proceeding Series, DSIT 2019, pp. 42–48, 19 July 2019
6. Yang, Y., et al.: A new medical imaging sharing service network based on professional medical imaging center. Progress in Biomedical Optics and Imaging, vol. 10954, p. 109540U (2019)
7. Jiemin, Z., Jinsheng, L.: The model of district medical data center. In: 2010 International Conference on Computer Application and System Modeling (ICCASM 2010), pp. 471–474 (2010)
8. Biswas, N., Sarkar, A., Mondal, K.C.: Efficient incremental loading in ETL processing for real-time data integration. Innovations in Systems and Software Engineering, vol. 16, no. 1, pp. 53–61, 1 March 2020
9. Oliveira, B., Oliveira, Ó., Santos, V., Belo, O.: ETL development using patterns: a service-oriented approach. In: The 21st International Conference on Enterprise Information Systems, ICEIS 2019, vol. 1, pp. 204–210 (2019)
10. Wojciechowski, A., Wrembel, R.: On case-based reasoning for ETL process repairs: Making cases fine-grained. In: Communications in Computer and Information Science, CCIS, vol. 1243, pp. 235–249 (2020)
11. Muddasir, N.M., Raghuveer, K.: A novel approach to handle huge data for refreshment anomalies in near real-time ETL applications. In: Soft Computing: Theories and Applications. SoCTA 2019. Advances in Intelligent Systems and Computing (1154), pp. 545–54 (2020)
12. Mandal, S., Jha, R.R.: Exploring the importance of collaborative assets to hospital-supplier integration in healthcare supply chains. Int. J. Prod. Res. **56**(7), 2666–2683 (2018)
13. Greenroyd, F.L., Price, A., Demian, P., Hayward, R., Sharma, S.: Modeling and simulating hospital operations in a 3D environment. In: Proceedings - Winter Simulation Conference, WSC 2017, pp. 2952–2963, 28 June 2017
14. Mandal, S., Jha, R.R.: Exploring the importance of collaborative assets to hospital-supplier integration in healthcare supply chains. Int. J. Prod. Res. **56**(7), 2666–2683 (2018)
15. Tsumoto, S., Hirano, S., Kimura, T., Iwata, H.: From hospital big data to clinical process: a granular computing approach. In: 2018 IEEE International Conference on Big Data (Big Data), pp. 2669–78 (2018)
16. Usama, M., et al.: Deep feature learning for disease risk assessment based on convolutional neural network with intra-layer recurrent connection by using hospital big data. IEEE Access **6**, 67927–67939 (2018)

17. Kazancigil, M.A.: Innovations in medical apps and the integration of their data into the big data repositories of hospital information systems for improved diagnosis and treatment in healthcare. Smart Innovation, Systems and Technologies, vol. 189, pp. 183–192. Human Centred Intelligent Systems - Proceedings of KES-HCIS 2020 Conference (2021). https://doi.org/10.1007/978-981-15-5784-2_15

18. Tao, J.: Application of the big data processing technology in the hospital informatization construction. Lecture Notes in Electrical Engineering, vol. 551 LNEE, pp. 1589–1595, 2020, Frontier Computing - Theory, Technologies and Applications, FC (2019)

19. Liu, Z., Pu, J.: Analysis and research on intelligent manufacturing medical product design and intelligent hospital system dynamics based on machine learning under big data, Enterprise Information Systems (2019)

20. Sirisawat, P., Hasachoo, N., Kaewket, T.: Investigation and prioritization of performance indicators for inventory management in the university hospital. In: 2019 IEEE International Conference on Industrial Engineering and Engineering Management (IEEM), p. 691–695 (2019)

21. da Silva Etges, A.P.B., et al.: Proposition of a shared and value-oriented work structure for hospital-based health technology assessment and enterprise risk management processes. Int. J. Tech. Assessment Health Care **35**(3), 195–203 (2019)

22. Canha, M., Loureiro, R., Marques, C.G.: The impact of the introduction of logistics management systems in an organization: a case study in a hospital center. In: 2018 13th Iberian Conference on Information Systems and Technologies (CISTI), p. 4 (2018)

23. Xinlei, C., Xiaogang, R., Yue, W., Jiufeng, Y.: Design and realization of a compre-hensive management system for severe mental disorders based on FLUX mode. J. Med. Imaging Health Inform. ASP **10**(2), 522–527 (2020)

Research on Brain Image Segmentation Based on FCM Algorithm Optimization

Xinlei Chen[✉], Dongming Zhao, Wei Zhong, and Jiufeng Ye

Suzhou Guangji Hospital, Suzhou 215000, Jiangsu, China

Abstract. Brain disease is becoming a threat to human health. Many countries begin to pay attention to the research of brain science. If brain diseases are predicted in advance, diagnosed accurately and treated with comprehensive intervention, the life expectancy of patients will be greatly improved. There are many explorations and applications in the field of computer-aided disease diagnosis, which can significantly improve the efficiency of disease diagnosis. Medical image processing is one of the medical imaging technology. It can help doctors improve the diagnosis quality by processing and analyzing the medical image data by computer. An improved FCM clustering method Sagakfcm algorithm is proposed for brain tissue segmentation in MRI images. Sagakfcm model fully combines the advantages of simulated annealing algorithm and genetic algorithm, so as to obtain the best initial clustering center, reduce the iteration times of fuzzy c-means algorithm, avoid the initial clustering falling into local optimum, and accelerate the operation speed. The algorithm combines Gaussian kernel function to improve the robustness of FCM algorithm.

Keywords: Brain disease · Image segmentation · Image processing

1 Introduction

As the pace of social life has increased significantly, the pressure on all aspects has increased sharply, and the eutrophication of people's diet has also brought a great burden to the body. The subsequent brain diseases often cause disability and death. With an increasing trend every year, brain diseases have increasingly become a threat to human health, and many countries have begun to pay attention to brain science research. According to incomplete statistics, about 20% of the world's total population is suffering from chronic mental illness. Some common brain diseases in our lives, such as Alzheimer disease (AD) and Parkinson's Diseases, autism, depression, etc. belong to this category of diseases. Brain diseases are more threatening to people's lives than other diseases [1]. According to a research report from a foreign disease prevention and control center, if people's brain diseases are predicted in advance, early and accurate diagnosis, and comprehensive intervention and treatment, then the life expectancy of the patient will be greatly improved. With the development of medical imaging technology in recent years, with the help of accurate deep analysis and induction of brain tissue images, results with

© ICST Institute for Computer Sciences, Social Informatics and Telecommunications Engineering 2021
Published by Springer Nature Switzerland AG 2021. All Rights Reserved
W. Fu et al. (Eds.): ICMTEL 2021, LNICST 388, pp. 278–289, 2021.
https://doi.org/10.1007/978-3-030-82565-2_23

imaging characteristics that are closely related to brain diseases can be found, which is of great significance for the prevention and treatment of brain diseases [2, 3].

Due to the unique and complex brain of human beings, human beings have become the spirit of all things. The human brain has evolved and developed about 5 million years ago, and the maturity of the human brain has gone through millions of years. The brain is connected by tens of billions of neurons, and there are about trillions of synaptic connections between neurons, forming a complex information processing network system. Each neuron contains millions of proteins that perform different functions, so that the brain provides the most important advanced brain functions for humans. With the advancement and development of science and technology, people are gradually aware of the role of the brain, and more and more attention has been paid to human exploration of the mystery of the brain [4]. The study of the brain has become the most esoteric subject in science and the most difficult scientific fortress to overcome. One of the ultimate goals of the research of the Brain Project is to predict brain diseases in advance, which is a major challenge in the health field facing all mankind. The latest statistics show that there are nearly one billion patients with brain diseases in the world, and the annual economic burden caused by this item is about one trillion US dollars. In my country, due to the continuous deterioration of the environment, the aging of the population, the increasingly accelerated social rhythm and the intensified social competition, brain developmental health, mental illness, and neurodegenerative diseases affect the health of people of all ages in our country.

Computer-aided Diagnosis (CAD) is a product of the combination of medical diagnosis and artificial intelligence (AI). There are many explorations and applications in the field of computer-aided disease diagnosis, which can significantly improve the diagnosis of diseases [5]. effectiveness. With the development of modern medicine, a large number of different types of information are often generated during patient visits, including symptoms, signs, laboratory examination results, physical diagnosis results, etc. How to accurately and fully utilize this information has become a problem that must be addressed in clinical work. The computer-aided diagnosis system has opened up an effective way to make full use of various clinical information related to diagnosis [6].

At present, the auxiliary diagnosis of brain diseases is mainly performed by clinicians by observing brain images to perform feature extraction and judgment based on experience. Doctors need to view a large number of pictures for analysis. This not only greatly increases the workload of clinicians, but also because of doctors' experience and technical level. Different, it is easy to cause missed diagnosis or misdiagnosis. With the aid of modern medical imaging technology for auxiliary diagnosis, it has a positive effect on the prevention and treatment of brain diseases.

In order to better recognize images of patients with brain diseases, first use segmentation algorithms on brain tissue images to segment the parts that need to be observed, and then extract appropriate features for areas with research needs and lesion features, and finally extract the features Information induction and identification. Accurate segmentation, proper selection of features and classifiers can improve recognition accuracy, which is of great significance to patients and doctors.

2   Research Status

Since the brain science plan was put forward in the 1990s, with the advancement of diagnostic technology and molecular biology technology, mankind has had a breakthrough understanding of this complex and mysterious organ of the brain. At present, many research units at home and abroad focus on intelligent diagnosis of brain imaging. For example, overseas Harvard Medical School, Stanford University, University of Washington, Northwestern University Molecular Imaging Center, Duke University, Massachusetts General Hospital, etc., as well as medical imaging of Chinese Academy of Sciences, Tsinghua University, Huazhong University of Science and Technology, Nanjing University, Southeast University and other units in China The laboratories have achieved certain results [7, 8].

Xiong Zhiqi, a brain scientist at the Chinese Academy of Sciences, proposed that early diagnosis and early intervention of brain diseases are the key means to treat brain diseases. He Yongqi thought about multi-modal neuroimaging technology and brain connectionomics methods to explore the altered patterns of brain structure and functional connection in the dementia stage and dementia stage of Alzheimer's disease. Li Haijiao and others use multi-modal magnetic resonance imaging for joint exercises to provide information on brain tissue anatomy, function, and metabolism [9].

Based on the clinical data of 128 patients with cerebral infarction admitted from March 2009 to February 2011, Huang Yuanbing screened and classified OCSP based on their clinical signs and main symptoms. Zhang Daoqiang and others proposed to use a multi-modal correlation vector regression machine to predict the value of clinical variables through the learning of multi-modal features [10]. Fei et al. adopted a brain-connected network classification method based on discriminative subgraph mining. Ke Shanhong and others applied FCM (Fuzzy means clustering) algorithm and its kernel method version KFCM (Kernel-basedFCM) to segmentation of MR images [11–15]. Maitra et al. used the improved orthogonal wavelet transform Slantlet transform and proposed a new image feature extraction algorithm based on the wavelet transform. El-Dahshan et al. adopted a three-step joint algorithm and introduced an artificial neural network (Artificial-Neural Network, ANN). Chaplot et al. used the Daubechies-4 wavelet transform to extract the approximate coefficients and detail coefficients of the image, and input the features obtained from the wavelet transform into the Self-Organizing Map (SOM) [16, 17]. The experimental data showed that the result of the SOM clusterer could reach 94%. However, the disadvantage is that after image feature extraction, there is a lack of information screening, which leads to a feature dimension of 4761, a sharp increase in calculation load, and a reduction in calculation performance. For MRI images, Wu proposed to use a forward neural network as a classifier [18–20].

3   Introduction to the Image Processing Process

Medical image processing is one of the medical imaging technologies. It uses computers to process and analyze medical image data to help doctors improve the quality of diagnosis.

For medical imaging of the brain, only from the superficial perspective, only the external planar imaging of the brain tissue can be seen. The detailed information inside the tissue is difficult to find through direct observation with the naked eye. At this time, it is necessary to perform brain imaging. The series of processing and analysis, and the general steps related to it are as follows see Fig. 1.

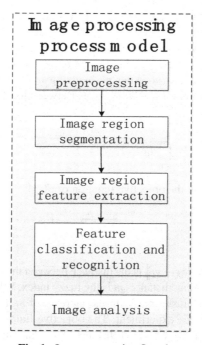

Fig. 1. Image processing flowchart

(1) Image preprocessing;
(2) Segmentation of the region of interest in the image;
(3) Perform feature extraction on the acquired region;
(4) Input the features into the relevant classifier to complete the classification and recognition of the target area;
(5) Analyze the image according to the results; in the brain image analysis process, the image is preprocessed to reduce the interference of the offset field on the segmentation. In the process of medical image processing, segmentation is a step that cannot be ignored. It is the premise of other image processing. Segmentation is actually to separate the target area in the image from the background area according to the needs of the user. The feature extraction process is the process of extracting information from other features such as color feature, shape feature or texture of the segmented region of interest. The process of image recognition is to take the extracted data information as input, and then divide the data with the same characteristics into the same category, so as to achieve the purpose of image recognition.

4 Key Technologies for Segmentation

4.1 Principle of FCM Algorithm

The FCM algorithm is obtained by Bezdek improving the Hard C-Means (HCM) clustering method proposed by Dunn in 1973. The FCM clustering algorithm divides the feature points in the feature space $X = \{x_1, x_2, \ldots, x_n\}$ into c categories ($2 \leq c \leq n$), the cluster center of each category is $v_i \in R$, and the cluster center matrix is $V = \{v_1, v_2, \ldots, x_c\}$, the membership of the i-th category of any feature point $c_i \in R$ is $V = \{v_1, v_2, \ldots, x_c\}$, U is its fuzzy membership matrix. After normalizing it, the sum of the membership degrees of the data set is equal to 1, u_{ij} introduces Between [0,1], that is, u_{ij} satisfies the following conditions:

$$\sum_{i=1}^{c} u_{ij} = 1, \ \forall j = 1, \ldots, n \tag{4-1}$$

The generalized form of the objective function of FCM:

$$J_{FCM} = \sum_{i=1}^{c} \sum_{j=1}^{n} u_{ij}^{m} d_{ij}^{2} \tag{4-2}$$

In formula (4-2), $d_{ij} = \|x_j - v_i\|$ is the distance between the i cluster center and the j th data point For the Euclidean distance, m is the fuzzy index. When $m \in [1, \infty)$, $m = 1$, it means hard C-means clustering. With the increase of m, the result is more fuzzy, Usually $m = 2$ is used in the experiment. The objective function can be expressed as the sum of the squares of the weighted distances from all sample points in the data set to each cluster center. The best classification result is that the sample points are divided into the class with the smallest difference from it, so the clustering goal of the FCM algorithm is to find the minimum value of the cost function J_{FCM}. That is to find the optimal clustering center and the optimal membership matrix to minimize the cost function J_{FCM}. Under the constraints of Eq. (4-1), the minimum value of Eq. (4-2) is solved and solved by Lagrange multiplier method. Construct a new objective function:

$$\bar{J}_{FCM} = J_{FCM} + \lambda \left(1 - \sum_{j=1}^{c} u_{ij}\right) = \sum_{i=1}^{c} \sum_{j=1}^{n} u_{ij}^{m} d_{ij}^{2} + \lambda 1 - \left(\sum_{j=1}^{c} u_{ij}\right) \tag{4-3}$$

(1) The degree of membership is solved. According to formula (4-3), the objective function $\bar{J}_{FCM}$ is derived from the degree of membership u_{ij} to obtain 0:

$$\frac{\partial \bar{J}}{\partial u_{ki}} = \sum_{i=1}^{c} \sum_{j=1}^{n} m u_{ij}^{m-1} d_{ij}^{2} - \lambda = 0 \tag{4-4}$$

From the above formula:

$$\mathbf{u}_{ij} = \left(\frac{\lambda}{m d_{ij}^{2}}\right)^{\frac{1}{m-1}} \tag{4-5}$$

Because of $\sum\limits_{k=1}^{c} u_{kj} = 1, \ \forall j = 1, \ldots, n$, there is

$$\sum_{k=1}^{c} \left(\frac{\lambda}{md_{ij}^2} \right)^{\frac{1}{m-1}} = 1 \tag{4-6}$$

From the above formula:

$$\lambda^{\frac{1}{m-1}} = \frac{1}{\sum\limits_{i=1}^{c} \left(\frac{1}{md_{kg}^2} \right)^{\left(\frac{1}{m-1} \right)}} \tag{4-7}$$

Incorporate formula (4-7) into formula (4-5) to obtain the degree of membership:

$$u_{ij} = \frac{\frac{1}{\sum\limits_{k=1}^{c} \left(\frac{1}{md_{kj}^2} \right)^{\left(\frac{1}{m-1} \right)}}}{(md_{ij}^2)^{\frac{1}{m-1}}} = \left[\sum_{k=1}^{c} \left(\frac{d_{ij}^2}{d_{kj}^2} \right)^{\frac{1}{m-1}} \right]^{-1} \tag{4-8}$$

(2) Find the clustering center v_i, according to formula (4-3), the objective function $\overline{J}_{FCM}$ to the clustering center v_i, find the partial derivative 0:

$$v_i = \frac{\sum\limits_{j=1}^{n} u_{ij}^m x_j}{\sum\limits_{j=1}^{n} u_{ij}^m} \tag{4-9}$$

Although the traditional FCM algorithm has good stability, the segmentation effect is poor. The algorithm in this paper has obvious advantages in both stability and segmentation effect, which is about 0.02 higher than other algorithms, which can affect the subsequent recognition effect.

4.2 Based on KFCM Simulated Annealing Genetic Algorithm

The traditional FCM algorithm ignores the spatial information of neighboring pixels when segmenting an image, and is susceptible to noise interference during segmentation, making the segmentation result unsatisfactory. WU and Yang proposed an improved FCM algorithm, in which the kernel function is used for distance measurement for the first time. Compared with the traditional Euclidean measure, the robustness of the algorithm is enhanced.

Simulated Annealing Genetic Algorithm: Based on the simulation statistics of the annealing process of high-temperature objects in physics, the Simulated Annealing Algorithm (SA) is finally derived. Because this algorithm is very similar to the process of solving random problems, it is widely used Solve the global optimal solution and achieved good results. In addition to accepting the global optimal solution, the simulated annealing algorithm (SA) uses the Metropolis criterion to accept the non-local optimal solution to a limited extent, and repeats the Metropolis process, so that the probability of acceptance is gradually oriented to 0, so as to ensure that it will not fall into the local optimal solution. The algorithm finally converges to all the optimal solutions with probability 1, but because the search process of the algorithm is random, sometimes the algorithm cannot search the whole world, and it may also jump out of the optimal solution. Genetic algorithm is easy to fall into the problem of local optimization when searching for local optimization, but its ability to search for the whole world is relatively strong. If the two algorithms are combined to complement each other, the algorithm can be more effective and converge to the global optimal solution. Genetic simulated annealing algorithm is an improved algorithm that combines the advantages of traditional genetic algorithm (GA) and simulated annealing algorithm. In principle, this algorithm has many similarities with traditional genetic algorithm. Like the traditional genetic algorithm, the implementation process of the simulated annealing genetic algorithm is to first initialize the population and individuals, calculate the fitness value of the individual according to the fitness function, and then perform operations such as selection, crossover, and mutation to generate new individuals, and then be independent Perform the operation of the simulated annealing algorithm on a single individual among them, and then evaluate the fitness of the simulated annealing to generate new individuals, and iterate this process repeatedly until the end conditions are met, and the output is confirmed as the current optimal individual. Simulated annealing genetic algorithm has the advantages of genetic algorithm and simulated annealing algorithm, so the algorithm model effectively avoids the premature problem of traditional genetic algorithm in the optimization process. In this paper, the simulated annealing genetic algorithm is used for cluster analysis, and the initial clustering center is optimized by the simulated annealing genetic algorithm. According to different situations, the coding method and fitness function suitable for the situation are designed and used to solve the corresponding fitness. Value, so that the global optimal solution can be solved efficiently and quickly.

4.3 KFCM Segmentation Based on Simulated Annealing Genetic Algorithm

4.3.1 Chromosome Coding and Population Initialization

Due to the uncertainty of the initial cluster centers in the clustering process, the simulated annealing genetic algorithm used in this paper is required to initialize the initial cluster centers. There are many ways to encode chromosomes in genetic algorithms. Choosing an appropriate encoding method will affect the subsequent calculation methods of genetic operators such as crossover, mutation, and fitness, and ultimately affect the evolution speed and results of the entire genetic operator, so choose the appropriate one. Genetic operators are very important. Commonly used genetic operators include binary encoding methods, symbol encoding, real number encoding, etc. Binary encoding is simple to operate, but has poor local search capabilities, it is difficult to achieve the optimal goal, and it takes a long time; symbol encoding is different from general Using numbers for encoding, using letters instead of numbers for chromosome encoding, requires higher design requirements for subsequent operators; real number encoding is encoding in the form of real number solution space, and there is no limit to the length range of chromosomes, and each gene corresponds to A number, the advantage is that the search space is large, it is easy to search for the optimal solution, and it does not need to be decoded frequently. This article will choose the real number encoding method for encoding. For n data samples, the dimension is d, and each chromosome $V_i = \{v_1, v_2, \ldots, v_c\}$, If there are c cluster centers, it can be expressed as the length $l = c \times d$. A chromosome can look like this:

$$V_i = \left\{ \underbrace{a_{11}a_{12}\ldots a_{1d}}_{v_1} \underbrace{a_{31}a_{22}\ldots a_{2d}}_{v_2} \cdots \underbrace{a_{c1}a_{c2}\ldots a_{cd}}_{c_c} \right\} \tag{4-10}$$

For the gene values of all individuals in the initial population, in actual operation, they are represented by randomly generated numbers, and these numbers are required to conform to a uniform distribution.

4.3.2 Calculation of Fitness

The performance of genetic algorithm depends on the selection of fitness function to a certain extent. According to the fitness value determined by the fitness function, it will directly affect the adaptability of the population to the environment. It is precisely because of it that the survival of the fittest of the population will occur. Therefore, the choice of fitness function is very important. Usually in practical applications we will Objective function to calculate fitness function. Suppose the objective function is $J_{KFCM} = f(x)$, and generally speaking, the minimum value of the objective function is the optimal solution of the problem, and to calculate the maximum fitness value of the population, we need According to the following fitness function $Fit(f(x)) = 1/(1+f(x))$ In addition, the selection of fitness function should try to avoid the phenomenon of premature in the early stage of algorithm iteration. The purpose of this is to ensure the diversity and diversity of individual populations. The formula of the fitness function used in this article is:

$$Fit(f(x)) = \frac{1}{1 + \sum\limits_{i=1}^{c} \sum\limits_{k=1}^{n} u_{ik}^m \|\Phi(x_k) - \Phi(v_i)\|^2} \tag{4-11}$$

4.3.3 Simulated Annealing Genetic KFCM Algorithm Flow

In order to avoid repetition, the implementation of the following algorithm is based on the above chromosome coding, initial population and fitness. The algorithm flow chart is shown in Fig. 2:

(1) Initialize various control parameters: population number $Gsize$, evolutionary algebra $Gmax$, crossover probability Pc, mutation probability Pm, annealing initial temperature, temperature cooling coefficient K, termination temperature Ta;

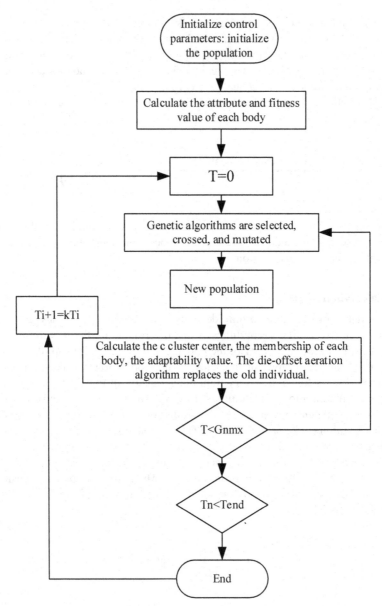

Fig. 2. Algorithm flow chart

(2) Initialize the genetic algebra $t = 0$, the fuzzy coefficient $m = 0$, and set their initial values to 0, randomly generate c cluster center matrices and use these cluster center matrices to form an initial population representation for $V_i = \{v_1, v_2, \ldots, v_c\}$;

(3) Calculate the membership matrix U and fitness Fit $(f(x))$ of each body in the population $S(t)$ using formula (4-9) in the KFCM algorithm $\bar{f} = \frac{1}{Gsize} \sum_{k=1}^{Gsize} f(k)$, if $\left| \overline{f(t)} - \overline{f(t-1)} \right| < \varepsilon$.

The average fitness value changes very little from the average fitness value before evolution. When $t = G\max$ (that is, the set evolutionary algebra is reached), select the individual with the highest fitness S in the population and turn to (9); Otherwise, go to (4);

(4) Perform a selection operation on the t generation population according to the selection operator, and get M individuals to form a subpopulation $S^*(t)$;

(5) Perform crossover operations on the individuals in the subpopulation $S^*(t)$ according to the probability of the size of Pc to obtain a new population $S^{**}(t)$;

(6) Perform a mutation operation on individuals of the population $S^{**}(t)$ with the mutation probability Pm according to the mutation operator to obtain the population $S^{***}(t)$:

(7) According to the simulated annealing operator, call the simulated annealing algorithm on the individuals of the population $S^{***}(t)$ to obtain the new population $S^{****}(t)$;

(8) Calculate the fitness of all individuals in $S(t)+S^{***}(t)$, and eliminate M individuals with smaller fitness values to form a new generation of population $S(t+1)$; $t = t + 1$; return (3);

(9) If $T_i < T_{end}$, calculate the individual $V_i = \{v_1, v_2, \ldots, v_c\}$ chromosome length len, determine the initial cluster number as $c = len$;

(10) Call the KFCM algorithm with c and $V_i = \{v_1, v_2, \ldots, v_c\}$ as the initial values, so as to get the final. The clustering center and membership matrix of.

5 Summary

This study proposes an improved FCM clustering method—SAGAKFCM algorithm, which is used to segment brain tissue in MRI images. The SAGAKFCM model fully combines the strong local search ability of the simulated annealing algorithm and the global search ability of the genetic algorithm, thereby obtaining the best initial clustering center, reducing the number of iterations of the fuzzy C-means algorithm, and avoiding the initial clustering from falling into the local maximum. Excellent, speed up the calculation speed. The algorithm combines the Gaussian kernel function to improve the robustness of the FCM algorithm. Under the influence of different intensities of noise, the segmentation time of this algorithm is 1–3 times less than the traditional FCM algorithm, ARKFCM algorithm, and FCMLSM algorithm. The segmentation accuracy index SA is about 0.02 larger than that of ARKFCM and FCMLSM. And the algorithm can obviously overcome the influence of noise on the segmentation result. Comparing various algorithms to segment brain white matter and gray matter in clinical brain images can also find the advantages of this algorithm, which provides a very reliable reference basis for segmenting real brain MRI images.

Funding. Science and Technology Demonstration Project of Suzhou Science and Technology Bureau, Big Data Analysis Processing and Clinical Application Research of Psychiatry (No. SS201706).

Guiding project of Suzhou Science and Technology Bureau, Research on Auxiliary Recognition of Alzheimer's Disease Based on Gaussian Probability Brain Image Segmentation Model (No.SYSD2019146).

References

1. Fuchs, A.III. Shape and Size of Neurons. Neurocytology, Springer International Pub-lishing (2015). https://doi.org/10.1007/978-3-319-06856-5
2. Sandeep, C., Patnaik, L.M., Jagannathan, L.M.: Classification of magnetic resonance brain images using wavelets as input to support vector machine and neural network. Biomed. Sig. Process. Control 1(1), 86–92 (2006). https://doi.org/10.1016/j.bspc.2006.05.002
3. Zhang, Y., Wu, L., Wang, S.: Magnetic resonance brain image classification by an improved artificial bee colony algorithm. Progress Electromagnet. Res. 116(2011), 65–79 (2011)
4. Jayachandran, A., Dhanasekaran, R.: Brain tumor detection and classification of MR images using texture features and fuzzy SVM classifier. Res. J. Appl. Eng. Technol. 6(12), 2264–2269 (2013)
5. Sumitra, N., Saxena, R.: Brain tumor classification using back propagation neural network. Int. J. Image, Graph. Sig. Process. 5(2), 45–50 (2013). https://doi.org/10.5815/ijigsp.2013.02.07
6. Nanthagopal, A.P., Sukanesh, R.: Wavelet statistical texture features-based segmentation and classification of brain computed tomography images. IET Image Proc. 7(1), 25–32 (2013)
7. Saritha, M., Joseph, K.P., Mathew, A.T.: Classification of MRI brain images using combined wavelet entropy based spider web plots and probabilistic neural network. Pattern Recogn. Lett. 34(16), 2151–2156 (2013)
8. Sudeb, D., Manish, C., Malay, K.K.: Brain Mr Image Classification Using Multiscale Geometric Analysis of Ripplet. 137(1), 1–17 (2013)
9. Padma, A., Sukanesh, R.: Segmentation and classification of brain CT images using combined wavelet statistical texture features. Arab. J. Sci. Eng. 39(2), 767–776 (2013). https://doi.org/10.1007/s13369-013-0649-3
10. Manoochehri, M., Kolahan, F.: Integration of artificial neural network and simulated annealing algorithm to optimize deep drawing process. Int. J. Adv. Manuf. Technol. 73(1–4), 241–249 (2014). https://doi.org/10.1007/s00170-014-5788-5
11. Rabeh, A.B., Benzarti, F., Amiri, H.: Segmentation of brain MRI using active contour model. Int. J. Imaging Syst. Technol. (2017)
12. Ng, C.R., et al.: Double segmentation method for brain region using FCM and graph cut for CT scan images. In: IEEE International Conference on Signal & Image Processing Applications IEEE (2016)
13. Du, B.J.M.H, Kardan, M., Spann, M.: Texture feature performance for image segmentation. Pattern Recogn. 23(3), 291–309 (1990)
14. Haralick, R.M., Shanmugam, K., Dinstein, I.: textural features for image classification. IEEE Trans. Syst. Man Cybern. SMC-3(6), 610–621 (1973). https://doi.org/10.1109/TSMC.1973.4309314
15. Rachmadi, M.F., del Maria, C., Valdés-Hernández, M.L., Agan, F., Di Perri, C., Komura, T.: Segmentation of white matter hyperintensities using convolutional neural networks with global spatial information in routine clinical brain MRI with none or mild vascular pathology. Comput. Med. Imaging Graph. 66, 28–43 (2018). https://doi.org/10.1016/j.compmedimag.2018.02.002

16. Wells, W.M., Colchester, A., Delp, S. (eds.): MICCAI 1998. LNCS, vol. 1496. Springer, Heidelberg (1998). https://doi.org/10.1007/BFb0056181
17. Aslam, A., Ekram Khan, M.M., Beg, S.: Improved edge detection algorithm for brain tumor segmentation. Procedia Comput. Sci. **58**, 430–437 (2015). https://doi.org/10.1016/j.procs.2015.08.057
18. Upadhyay, A., Kanchan, K., Goyal, P.G., Yerramilli, A., Gorai, A.K.: Development of a fuzzy pattern recognition model for air quality assessment of Howrah City. Aerosol Air Qual. Res. **14**(6), 1639–1652 (2014). https://doi.org/10.4209/aaqr.2013.04.0118
19. Xinlei, C., Ren Xiaogang, W., Yue, Y.J.: Design and realization of a comprehensive management system for severe mental disorders based on FLUX mode. J. Med. Imag. Health Inf. **10**(2), 522–527 (2020). https://doi.org/10.1166/jmihi.2020.2898
20. Gore, J.C.: Principles and practice of functional MRI of the human brain. J. Clin. Invest. **112**(1), 4–9 (2003). https://doi.org/10.1172/JCI200319010

Facial Expression Recognition via ResNet-18

Bin Li[1], Runda Li[2], and Dimas Lima[3]([envelope])

[1] School of Computer Science and Technology, Henan Polytechnic University, Jiaozuo 454000, Henan, People's Republic of China
libin@home.hpu.edu.cn
[2] Nanjing Foreign Language School, Nanjing, Jiangsu, China
[3] Department of Electrical Engineering, Federal University of Santa Catarina, Florianópolis, Brazil
dimaslima@ieee.org

Abstract. As an important part of human-computer interaction, facial expression recognition has become a hot research topic in the fields of computer vision, pattern recognition, artificial intelligence, etc., and plays an important role in our daily life. With the development of deep learning and convolutional neural network, the research of facial expression recognition has also made great progress. Moreover, in the current face emotion recognition research, there are problems such as poor generalization ability of network model. The extraction of traditional facial expression recognition features is complex and the effect is not ideal. In order to improve the effect of facial expression recognition, we propose a feature extraction method for deep residual network, and use deep residual network ResNet-18 to extract the features of the data set. Through the experimental simulation of the specified data set, it can be proved that this model is superior to state-of-the-art methods model.

Keywords: Deep residual network · Facial expression recognition · ResNet-18

1 Introduction

With the rapid development of computer technology and neural network technology, people have a higher and higher demand for intelligent automation. We hope that the computer can acquire the changes of facial expressions [1] just like the communication between people. Only in this way can we achieve real intelligence and better human-computer interaction. So, in order to interpret human emotions, computers are required to have accurate facial expression recognition. Facial expression recognition is to separate the specific facial state from the given static image or dynamic video sequence, so as to determine the psychological emotion of the object to be recognized. On the other hand, facial expressions are a form of non-verbal communication and are the main means by which people express information. By looking at the changes in facial expressions, we

---

B. Li and R. Li—Those two authors contributed equally to this paper, and should be regarded as co-first authors.

© ICST Institute for Computer Sciences, Social Informatics and Telecommunications Engineering 2021
Published by Springer Nature Switzerland AG 2021. All Rights Reserved
W. Fu et al. (Eds.): ICMTEL 2021, LNICST 388, pp. 290–303, 2021.
https://doi.org/10.1007/978-3-030-82565-2_24

can better identify the emotional changes in the other person. Face recognition is also an important research field in computer vision. Accurate facial expression recognition will be helpful to human-computer interaction, security monitoring, auxiliary medical treatment, auxiliary driving and other work smoothly.

The purpose of facial expression recognition is to analyze a given facial expression and then classify the corresponding emotions. According to the basic facial emotions defined by American psychologists Ekman and Friesen in 1971, we can divide facial emotions into seven kinds: happy, sad, fearful, angry, surprised, disgusted and neutral.

Facial expression recognition can be divided into four stages: image acquisition, image preprocessing, feature extraction and classification recognition. The core of traditional facial expression recognition algorithms is feature extraction and classifier design. Artificial features include local binary mode (LBP), gradient histogram, etc., and classifier design includes neural network, support vector machine (SVM), K-nearest neighbor algorithm, etc. The problem is the facial expression of this kind of method of preprocessing. Feature extraction and classifier's generalization ability will influence the final classification results. Photo angle, light and shade, color of skin can cause different expression recognition difficulty. Thus, it needs for a specific case for image preprocessing and feature extraction and work more difficult. In recent years, convolutional neural network has developed rapidly, and its biggest advantage is that it can automatically learn the best features for specific tasks. Facial features such as local binary pattern (LBP), Active Shape Mode (ASM) and other features can be learned through deep learning network, and even higher-level abstract features can be learned automatically which is not available with traditional algorithms.

However, through reading recent literature, it can be found that most methods for extracting facial expression features are prone to lose the original emotional information. For example, Ali, et al. [2] proposed the use of support vector machine (SVM) method. Evans [3] presented to use Haar wavelet transform (HWT) method. In addition, the generalization and robustness of the network model are poor. When the operating environment on which the network model depends slightly changes, the network model is likely to get stuck in the recognition process, which directly affects the speed and accuracy of facial emotion recognition. Lu [4] used biorthogonal wavelet entropy as feature extractor, and employed fuzzy SVM as classifier. Phillips [5] employed Jaya algorithm to classify facial emotion recognition. Yang [6] utilized cat swarm optimization to recognize facial emotions. Li [7] chose to use biogeography-based optimization (BBO) for the same task.

The main content of this paper is to study the recognition of facial expressions, and propose an image facial expression recognition algorithm based on deep learning, and realize the recognition of image sequence facial expressions on the basis of static expression recognition. The main contributions of this paper are as follows: Study the input image pretreatment operation to improve the recognition rate of facial expressions; ResNet-18 is used as the backbone network for static facial expression recognition algorithm. Compared with other algorithms, the experimental results show that the recognition rate of this algorithm is improved to some extent.

2 Dataset

In order to make the experimental process easier to implement and the experimental results more comparable, the data set adopted in this paper is a new data set composed of a face model. The reference data set captures the facial expressions of objects of different ages, occupations, and races, including images of seven facial emotions: happy, sad, fearful, angry, surprised, disgusted, and neutral. Figure 1 displays samples of our dataset.

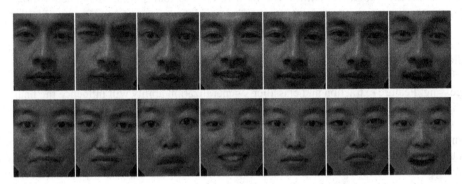

Fig. 1. Samples of our dataset [4]

3 Methodology

3.1 Convolution

The main function of convolutional layer is to extract key features from the input image and compress the image into a form that is easier to process, so as to obtain good prediction. In functional analysis, convolution is a definition of a function [8–10]. It is a mathematical operator that generates a third function by two functions f and g, representing the area of the overlap between the functions f and g after flipping and shifting. The calculation formula of convolution is as follows:

$$h(x) = f(x) * g(x) = \int_{-\infty}^{+\infty} f(t)g(x-t)dt \tag{1}$$

As is shown in (1), the output of the system at a certain time is the result of the superposition of multiple inputs. $f(x)$ and $g(x)$ are two integrable functions. And $h(x)$ is the result of the convolution operation [11]. In the image analysis, $f(x)$ can be understood as the original pixel points, all the original pixel points added up to be the original graph. $g(x)$ can be called the action point, and all the action points are collectively called the convolution kernel. After all the action points on the convolution kernel act on the original pixels in turn, the output result of linear superposition is the output of the final convolution, which is called destination pixel [12].

Convolutional neural network is a process of extracting features, selecting features and then classifying them. Some specified features of the original image can be extracted by mathematical operation with the convolution kernel [13]. The extracted features are different with different convolution kernels. The extracted features are the same, and different convolution kernels have different effects.

3.1.1 Standard Convolution

Each image can be regarded as a matrix composed of pixel values, and features can be extracted from the image through convolution. In the convolutional layer, the unit used for the convolution operation is called the convolution kernel [14–16]. Its parameters are what we want to learn, and the size should be smaller than the input image. In the process of convolution, each kernel carries out convolution computation with the input image [17], slides the convolution kernel on the image, multiplies the pixel value on the image with the corresponding value on the convolution kernel, and adds up all the multiplied values and finally slide each part of the image [18].

The Fig. 2 shows a two-dimensional convolution process with a 3×3 kernel and a stride of 1.When the convolution kernel is scanned on the input image, the value of the corresponding position in the input image is multiplied by the convolution kernel one by one, and the final sum is summarized to obtain the convolution result of the position [19]. By constantly moving the convolution kernel, the convolution results at each position can be calculated. For each point, we can take this point and convolve it with the 3 by 3 points around it.

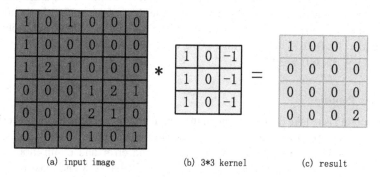

(a) input image   (b) 3*3 kernel   (c) result

Fig. 2. Standard convolutional process

3.2 Pooling

Pooling is used to reduce the dimension of the data. In CNN, after convolution, the feature dimension of the output of the convolutional layer is usually reduced by Pooling, the size of the matrix generated by the convolutional layer is reduced, and the over-fitting phenomenon can be prevented while the network parameters are reduced [20–22]. In short, pooling is to remove the redundant information, retain the key information, reduce the impact of noise, and make each feature more robust. The common pooling operations are Max pooling and Average pooling.

3.2.1 Average Pooling

Averaging pooling means averaging the characteristic points in the neighborhood. There are two errors in feature extraction of pooling method: first, the limitation of neighborhood size leads to the increase of estimated variance; Second, parameter error of convolutional layer causes deviation of the estimated mean value. The average pooling of image can reduce the first error and retain more background information of the image.

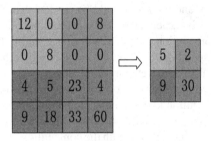

Fig. 3. Average pooling process

In Fig. 3, the input is a 4 × 4 matrix and the stride is 2. The kernel that performs the average pooling is a 2 × 2 matrix. We break up the 4 × 4 input into different areas and color these areas. For a 2 × 2 output, each element of the output is the average element value in its corresponding color region. The Average pooling result is obtained from Average (12, 0, 0, 8) = 5, Average (0, 0, 8, 0) = 2, Average (4, 5, 9,18) = 9, and Average (23, 4, 33, 60) = 30.

3.2.2 Max Pooling

The max pooling is to take the maximum of the characteristic points in the neighborhood. Features of Max pooling selection have better recognition and provide nonlinear features. In addition, maximum pooling can reduce the second error and retain more texture information [23–25]. The advantage of Max pooling is that only the maximum value (features) in the area is retained and other values are ignored to reduce the impact of noise and improve the robustness of the model. In addition, the hyper-parameters required for Max pooling are only filter size F and filter stepping length S, and no other parameters need to be obtained by model training, so the calculation amount is very small. If there are multiple channels, the Max Pooling operation is performed separately for each channel.

In Fig. 4, the input is a 4 × 4 matrix and the stride is 2. The kernel that performs the max pooling is a 2 × 2 matrix. We break up the 4 × 4 input into different areas and color these areas. For a 2 × 2 output, each element of the output is the maximum element value in its corresponding color region. The max pooling result is obtained from Max(12, 0, 0, 8) = 12, Max(0, 8, 0, 0) = 8, Max(4, 5, 9, 18) = 18, and Max(23, 4, 33, 60) = 60.

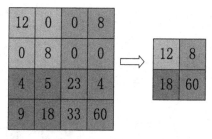

Fig. 4. Max Pooling Process

3.3 Batch Normalization

Due to the activation of the input value in deep neural network before nonlinear transform as the network depth deepening or in the process of training, its distribution deviates or changes gradually, the training convergence is slow and gradually approaches the upper and lower limits of the value interval of the nonlinear function, such as the sigmoid function, the activation input value Wx+ B is a large negative or positive value, so it leads to lower when back propagation neural network gradient disappear, this is a fundamental reason for the slow convergence is more and more deep neural network training, BN through certain means of standardization, this input neurons in each layer of the neural network value forced back to the distribution of the mean to 0 variance 1 standard normal distribution, distribution of more and more partial forced back to the standard distribution, in order to activate the input value falls in the area of nonlinear function is more sensitive to input, this will lead to small changes in input change a loss function, mean let gradient get bigger, so avoid gradient disappeared, and gradient bigger means learning convergence speed is fast. The large step towards the optimal value of loss function can accelerate the training speed greatly [25–27].

BN can prevent gradient explosion or dispersion, improve the robustness of the model to different hyperparameters (learning rate, initialization) during training, and keep most activation functions away from its saturated region. All of these properties of BN can help us to have a fast and robust training network. The real reason why BN can work is that BN changes the optimization problem again, making the optimization space very smooth.

In the process of image preprocessing, we usually standardize the image, which can accelerate the convergence of the network. As shown in the Fig. 5, regarding the Conv1, the distribution of the input is to satisfy a certain characteristic matrix, but, for Conv2, the feature map input may not satisfy a certain distribution, here to meet a certain distribution does not mean a certain feature map data to satisfy the distribution, the data of the feature map corresponding to the whole training sample set should meet the distribution. The purpose of Batch Normalization is to make feature map meet the distribution law of mean value 0 and variance 1.

As shown in the following formula, one layer has n dimensional input: $a = (a_1 \cdots a_n)$. μ_A is the average of the values of a. $\sigma_A{}^2$ is the variance of a. And ε is a small constant that prevents the denominator from being zero. O_i is the result by Batch

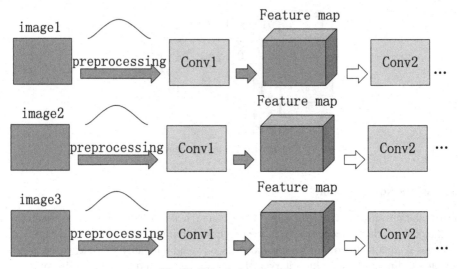

Fig. 5. Convolution example

Normalization process. C in (5) is used to adjust the variance size of the numerical distribution, and D is to adjust the location of the numerical mean. These two parameters are learned in the back propagation process, and the default value of C and D is 1 and 0.

$$\mu_A \leftarrow \frac{1}{n}\sum_{i=1}^{n} a_i \tag{2}$$

$$\sigma_A^2 \leftarrow \frac{1}{n}\sum_{i=1}^{n} (a_i - \mu_A)^2 \tag{3}$$

$$\widehat{a_i} \leftarrow \frac{a_i - \mu_A}{\sqrt{\sigma_A^2 + \varepsilon}} \tag{4}$$

$$O_i \leftarrow C\widehat{a_i} + D = BN_{C,D}(a_i) \tag{5}$$

The training sample set corresponding feature map data to satisfy the distribution, to calculate the feature map of the entire training set and then standardizing, for a large data set is obviously not possible, so we calculate a Batch data feature map and then standardize, The larger the batch is, the closer it is to the distribution of the entire data set, the better the effect is. As is shown in (2), μ_A represents the mean value of the feature map, and each element of μ_A vector represents the mean value of a dimension (channel). σ_A^2 represents the variance of the feature map, and each element of σ_A^2 vector represents the variance value of a dimension (channel). Then according to μ_A and σ_A^2 and through Eq. (4), do the standardized calculation to get the final value.

The Fig. 6 shows the calculation process of the Batch Normalization with a batch size of 2, the feature1 and feature2 are feature matrix obtained by a series of convolution and pooling of image1 and image2 respectively. The channel of feature is 2, then $a^{(1)}$ represents the data of Channel 1 of all features of the batch ($a^{(1)} = \{1, 1, 1, 2, 0, -1, 2, 2\}$), Similarly, $a^{(2)}$ represents the data of Channel2 of all features

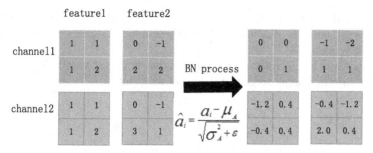

Fig. 6. Batch normalization process

of the batch ($a^{(2)} = \{-1, 1, 0, 1, 0, -1, 3, 1\}$). Then calculate the mean and variance of $a^{(1)}$ and $a^{(2)}$ respectively to get μ_A and σ_A^2 ($\mu_A = \begin{pmatrix} 1 \\ 0.5 \end{pmatrix}$, $\sigma_A^2 = \begin{pmatrix} 1 \\ 1.5 \end{pmatrix}$).

The value of each channel is then calculated according to Eq. (4). In the process of training the network, the data is trained from one batch to one batch. In the course of the training we're going to keep counting the mean and the variance of each batch, and using the method of moving average to record the mean and the variance of the statistics, and after we've trained, we can approximate the mean and the variance of the statistics that we're going to be equal to the mean and the variance of our entire training set. Then, in our validation and prediction, we use the mean and variance of the mean and variance that we count to standardize the process.

3.4 Rectified Linear Unit

$$\sigma_{\text{ReLU}}(z) = \max(0, z) \tag{6}$$

ReLU is an activation function. Why the activation function was introduced? The output of each layer is the linear function of the upper input, no matter how many layers of the neural network, the output is the linear combination of the input, and no hidden layer effect. Therefore, the introduction of the nonlinear function as the activation function [28–30], so that the deep neural network is intentional, no longer is a linear combination of input, which can approach any function. The original idea is the Sigmoid function or the Tanh function, which has a bounded output and can easily be entered as the next layer. In the ReLU [31], less than 0 is directly placed in 0, which is greater than 0 as input. This is the realization of the nonlinear transformation. The partial gradient of greater than 0 is 1. So the gradient of the activation function is always 1 for the information that needs to be passed from the input [32]. Even if continuous multiplication is not smaller, ReLU solves the problem of gradient disappearing [33], which is a powerful way to help train rapid convergence. According to the definition of ReLU, information can only be propagated in the region of ReLU greater than 0 (forward and backward), which brings another advantage is the sparseness [34], reducing the interdependence of the parameters and reducing the occurrence of the overfitting problem. The sparse ability not only helps the performance of the network, but also from the perspective of the neuroscience, the activation rate of the neurons is low [35], which is also a simulated simulation. In addition, the activation function such as Sigmoid has exponential operation in Forward propagation and when calculating the error gradient in Back propagation, the derivative involves the division [36, 37]. While ReLU activation function saves a lot of calculation in the whole process [38].

As is shown in Fig. 7, when the input is less than 0, the output is 0. When the input is greater than 0, the output value is the value of the input.

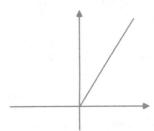

Fig. 7. Rectified linear unit

3.5 ResNet-18

As the number of layers in the network deepens, gradient disappearance or gradient explosion will occur. In other words, as the number of layers increases, the gradient of back propagation in the network will become unstable with continuous multiplication and become particularly large or small. It can be solved by data standardization, weight initialized, and Batch Normalization. However, with the deepening of layers, there is also a degradation problem, that is, deeper networks have higher training set errors, which can be solved by the residual structure in ResNet-18 [39, 40].

When we simply stack the network directly to a long length, the features inside the network have reached their best at a certain layer, and the remaining layers should not make any changes to the features and automatically learn the form of identity mapping. Compared with the shallow network, deeper networks should not have worse effects, but this is not the case for the degradation of network. What we need to do is to make the deep network achieve at least the performance of shallow networks under the network degradation, and make the layer behind the deep network achieve the identity mapping. Therefore, the residual structure is proposed to help the identity mapping of networks.

Due to the existence of many residual modules, the connections of some neural layers are weakened and reduced, and the linear transmission of the interlayer is realized instead of blindly pursuing nonlinear relations. The model itself can "tolerate" deeper neural networks. In terms of performance, additional residual modules will not degrade the performance of the Big NN.

As is shown in Fig. 8, the straight line forward is the residual mapping, and the curved line is the identity mapping, so the final output is $y = F(x) + x$. $F(x)$ is obtained from the input after a series of convolution, BN operations, and activation of the function. And x is the value of the input. The downsample uses the 1 * 1 convolution kernel, which makes the latitudes equal.

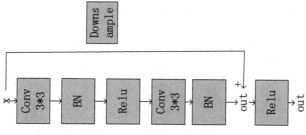

Fig. 8. Basic block

As is shown in Fig. 9, the ResNet-18 first goes through a 7 * 7 convolutional layer, then through a 3 * 3 maximum pooled subsampling, then through a series of residual structures, and finally through average pooled subsampling and full connection layer [41].

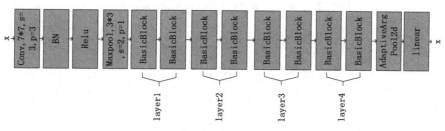

Fig. 9. ResNet-18

4 Experiment Result and Discussions

4.1 Statistical Analysis

The sensitivity analysis is shown in Table 1. The data is closely related to the facial muscles that correspond to expressions, with lip funneler and nose wrinkles making their early facial expressions similar, and expressions such as jaw drop and the upper lid raiser also make expressions based on the same muscle movement characteristics look similar.

Table 1 shows the sensitivity analysis of the seven emotion classes running for 10 times. According to the data from Table 1, the sensitivity of each expression is as follows: $95.20 \pm 2.35\%$, $95.70 \pm 2.16\%$, $94.90 \pm 1.66\%$, $93.60 \pm 2.88\%$, $95.30 \pm 2.67\%$, $93.20 \pm 3.58\%$, $95.70 \pm 1.34\%$. From this we can get: the expression of Disgust is the most sensitive and easy to recognize, followed by the expression of Surprise, and the third is the expression of Neutral. According to Table 2, the overall average accuracy of the system after 10 runs is $94.80 \pm 1.43\%$.

Table 1. Statistical analysis on the sensitivities of each class

	Anger	Disgust	Fear	Happy	Neutral	Sadness	Surprise
Run 1	97.00	92.00	94.00	89.00	97.00	95.00	95.00
Run 2	97.00	97.00	97.00	97.00	97.00	97.00	98.00
Run 3	92.00	92.00	96.00	93.00	98.00	87.00	97.00
Run 4	97.00	96.00	97.00	97.00	97.00	96.00	96.00
Run 5	97.00	96.00	95.00	96.00	93.00	96.00	94.00
Run 6	96.00	98.00	94.00	92.00	90.00	96.00	95.00
Run 7	95.00	95.00	96.00	94.00	96.00	95.00	97.00
Run 8	93.00	96.00	95.00	92.00	92.00	90.00	95.00
Run 9	91.00	97.00	92.00	90.00	96.00	89.00	94.00
Run 10	97.00	98.00	93.00	96.00	97.00	91.00	96.00
Average	95.20 ± 2.35	95.70 ± 2.16	94.90 ± 1.66	93.60 ± 2.88	95.30 ± 2.67	93.20 ± 3.58	95.70 ± 1.34

Table 2. Statistical analysis on the overall accuracies

Run	OA
1	94.14
2	97.14
3	93.57
4	96.57
5	95.29
6	94.43
7	95.43
8	93.29
9	92.71
10	95.43
Average	94.80 ± 1.43

4.2 Comparison with State-of-the-Art Approaches

The OA of the "ResNet-18" method used in this experiment was compared with that of the other three methods, which were HWT [3], CSO [6] and BBO [7]. The results are shown in Table 3: OA of HWT [3] is 78.37 ± 1.50%; OA of CSO [6] is 89.49 ± 0.76%; OA of BBO [7] is 93.79 ± 1.24%. We can clearly see that the method of "ResNet-18" has the highest accuracy (94.80 ± 1.43%), followed by BBO [7], and the third highest accuracy is CSO [6], while the lowest accuracy is HWT [3].

It can be seen from Table 1 that the highest OA obtained by "ResNet-18" method mainly depends on: (i) the ability of CNN to extract image features; (ii) the excellent training ability of ResNet-18. And the next best method is BBO [7], which comes from the theory of biogeography and is a swarm intelligence optimization algorithm based on the general rules of migration and variation of different populations of different organisms in different habitats. The third best method is CSO [6], which mainly combines the seeking mode and the tracing mode in the algorithm through mixture ratio to achieve global optimization.

We should note that there are currently several variants of ResNet, such as Wide Residual Network (WRN), ResNeXt and MobileNet. In the future research, we will test their performances.

Table 3. Comparison with State-of-the-art methods

Method	OA
HWT [3]	78.37 ± 1.50
CSO [6]	89.49 ± 0.76
BBO [7]	93.79 ± 1.24
ResNet-18 (Ours)	94.80 ± 1.43

5   Conclusion

In this content, we propose an improved facial emotion recognition system. We use ResNet-18 for feature extraction. The facial emotion recognition system has achieved good recognition effect. In the future research, we will continue to focus on the research of facial emotion recognition and try to collect more emotional images than in this experiment, so as to optimize and propose a better algorithm to train the hyperparameter of the neural network, such as the weights and biases. And we will also try such optimization algorithms based on ResNet-18 to improve the performance of neural network.

References

1. Oji-Mmuo, C.N., Speer, R.R., Gardner, F.C., Marvin, M.M., Hozella, A.C., Doheny, K.K.: Prenatal opioid exposure heightens sympathetic arousal and facial expressions of pain/distress in term neonates at 24–48 hours post birth. J. Maternal-Fetal Neonatal Med. **33**, 3879–3886 (2020)
2. Ali, H., Hariharan, M., Yaacob, S., Adom, A.H.: Facial Emotion recognition based on higher-order spectra using support vector machines. J. Med. Imaging Health Inf. **5**, 1272–1277 (2015)
3. Evans, F.: Haar wavelet transform based facial emotion recognition. Adv. Comput. Sci. Res. **61**, 342–346 (2017)
4. Lu, H.M.: Facial emotion recognition based on biorthogonal wavelet entropy, fuzzy support vector machine, and stratified cross validation. IEEE Access **4**, 8375–8385 (2016)
5. Phillips, P.: Intelligent facial emotion recognition based on stationary wavelet entropy and Jaya algorithm. Neurocomputing **272**, 668–676 (2018)

6. Wang, S.-H., Yang, W., Dong, Z., Phillips, P., Zhang, Y.-D.: Facial emotion recognition via discrete wavelet transform, principal component analysis, and cat swarm optimization. In: Sun, Yi., Lu, H., Zhang, L., Yang, J., Huang, H. (eds.) IScIDE 2017. LNCS, vol. 10559, pp. 203–214. Springer, Cham (2017). https://doi.org/10.1007/978-3-319-67777-4_18

7. Li, X.: Facial emotion recognition via stationary wavelet entropy and biogeography-based optimization. EAI Endorsed Trans. e-Learn. **6**, Article ID: e4 (2020)

8. Lv, Y.-D.: Alcoholism detection by data augmentation and convolutional neural network with stochastic pooling. J. Med. Syst. **42**, Article ID: 2 (2018)

9. Tang, C.: Twelve-layer deep convolutional neural network with stochastic pooling for tea category classification on GPU platform. Multimed. Tools Appl. **77**, 22821–22839 (2018)

10. Pan, C.: Abnormal breast identification by nine-layer convolutional neural network with parametric rectified linear unit and rank-based stochastic pooling. J. Comput. Sci. **27**, 57–68 (2018)

11. Hasebe, T., Ueda, Y.: Unimodality for free multiplicative convolution with free normal distributions on the unit circle. J. Oper. Theory **85**, 21–43 (2021)

12. Belinschi, S.T., Bercovici, H., Liu, W.H.: The atoms of operator-valued free convolutions. J. Oper. Theory **85**, 303–320 (2021)

13. Kumar, S., Mahadevappa, M., Dutta, P.K.: Lensless in-line holographic microscopy with light source of low spatio-temporal coherence. IEEE J. Sel. Top. Quantum Electron. **27**, 8, Article ID: 6800608 (2021)

14. Fujioka, T., Yashima, Y., Oyama, J., Mori, M., Kubota, K., Katsuta, L., et al.: Deep-learning approach with convolutional neural network for classification of maximum intensity projections of dynamic contrast-enhanced breast magnetic resonance imaging. Magn. Reson. Imaging **75**, 1–8 (2021)

15. Hou, X.-X.: Seven-layer deep neural network based on sparse autoencoder for voxelwise detection of cerebral microbleed. Multimed. Tools Appl. **77**, 10521–10538 (2018)

16. Pan, C.: Multiple sclerosis identification by convolutional neural network with dropout and parametric ReLU. J. Comput. Sci. **28**, 1–10 (2018)

17. Bercovici, H., Dykema, K., Nica, A.: Dan-virgil voiculescu at seventy. J. Oper. Theory **85**, 5–20 (2021)

18. Egger, H., Schmidt, K., Shashkov, V.: Multistep and Runge-Kutta convolution quadrature methods for coupled dynamical systems. J. Comput. Appl. Math. **387**, 14, Article ID: 112618 (2021)

19. Erbay, H.A., Erbay, S., Erkip, A.: A semi-discrete numerical method for convolution-type unidirectional wave equations. J. Comput. Appl. Math. **387**, 13, Article ID: 112496 (2021)

20. Katsagounos, I., Thomakos, D.D., Litsiou, K., Nikolopoulos, K.: Superforecasting reality check: evidence from a small pool of experts and expedited identification. Eur. J. Oper. Res. **289**, 107–117 (2021)

21. Huang, C.: Multiple sclerosis identification by 14-layer convolutional neural network with batch normalization, dropout, and stochastic pooling. Front. Neurosci. **12**, Article ID: 818 (2018)

22. Zhao, G.: Polarimetric synthetic aperture radar image segmentation by convolutional neural network using graphical processing units. J. Real-Time Image Proc. **15**, 631–642 (2018)

23. Muhammad, K.: Image based fruit category classification by 13-layer deep convolutional neural network and data augmentation. Multimed. Tools Appl. **78**, 3613–3632 (2019)

24. Wang, S.-H., Sun, J.: Cerebral micro-bleeding identification based on a nine-layer convolutional neural network with stochastic pooling. Concurr. Comput. Pract. Exp. **32**, e5130 (2020)

25. Sangaiah, A.K.: Alcoholism identification via convolutional neural network based on parametric ReLU, dropout, and batch normalization. Neural Comput. Appl. **32**, 665–680 (2020)

26. Choi, S.H., Jung, S.H.: Stable acquisition of fine-grained segments using batch normalization and focal loss with L1 regularization in U-Net structure. Int. J. Fuzzy Logic Intell. Syst. **20**, 59–68 (2020)
27. Wang, S.-H.: DenseNet-201-based deep neural network with composite learning factor and precomputation for multiple sclerosis classification. ACM Trans. Multimed. Comput. Commun. Appl. **16**, Article no. 60 (2020)
28. Olimov, B., Karshiev, S., Jang, E., Din, S., Paul, A., Kim, J.: Weight initialization based-rectified linear unit activation function to improve the performance of a convolutional neural network model. Concurr. Comput. Pract. Exp. **11** (2021). (Article; Early Access). https://doi.org/10.1002/cpe.6143
29. Zhang, Y.-D.: Advances in multimodal data fusion in neuroimaging: overview, challenges, and novel orientation. Inf. Fusion **64**, 149–187 (2020)
30. Wang, S.-H.: Covid-19 classification by FGCNet with deep feature fusion from graph convolutional network and convolutional neural network. Inf. Fusion **67**, 208–229 (2021)
31. Yaliniz, G., Ikizler-Cinbis, N.: Using independently recurrent networks for reinforcement learning based unsupervised video summarization. Multimed. Tools Appl. **80** (2021). (Article; Early Access). https://doi.org/10.1007/s11042-020-10293-x
32. Kawahara, D., Tang, X.Y., Lee, C.K., Nagata, Y., Watanabe, Y.: Predicting the local response of metastatic brain tumor to gamma knife radiosurgery by radiomics with a machine learning method. Front. Oncol. **10**, 8, Article ID: 569461 (2021)
33. Dubey, S.R., Chakraborty, S.: Average biased ReLU based CNN descriptor for improved face retrieval. Multimed. Tools Appl., 26 (2021)
34. Yamaguchi, M., Iwamoto, G., Nishimura, Y., Tamukoh, H., Morie, T.: An energy-efficient time-domain analog CMOS BinaryConnect neural network processor based on a pulse-width modulation approach. IEEE Access **9**, 2644–2654 (2021)
35. Farrell, M.H., Liang, T.Y., Misra, S.: Deep neural networks for estimation and inference. Econometrica **89**, 181–213 (2021)
36. Tripathi, D., Edla, D.R., Kuppili, V., Bablani, A.: Evolutionary extreme learning machine with novel activation function for credit scoring. Eng. Appl. Artif. Intell. **96**, 10, Article ID: 103980 (2020)
37. Satapathy, S.C.: A five-layer deep convolutional neural network with stochastic pooling for chest CT-based COVID-19 diagnosis. Mach. Vis. Appl. **32**, Article ID: 14 (2021)
38. Moon, S.: ReLU network with bounded width is a universal approximator in view of an approximate identity. Appl. Sci. **11**, 11, Article ID: 427 (2021)
39. Bernardo, P.P., Gerum, C., Frischknecht, A., Lubeck, K., Bringmann, O.: UltraTrail: a configurable ultralow-power TC-ResNet AI accelerator for efficient keyword spotting. IEEE Trans. Comput. Aided Des. Integr. Circuits Syst. **39**, 4240–4251 (2020)
40. Alotaibi, B., Alotaibi, M.: A hybrid deep ResNet and inception model for hyperspectral image classification. PFG J. Photogramm. Remote Sens. Geoinf. Sci. **88**, 463–476 (2020)
41. Hammad, M., Plawiak, P., Wang, K.Q., Acharya, U.R.: ResNet-attention model for human authentication using ECG signals. Expert Syst., 17, Article ID: e12547 (2020)

Comparison of AWS and AZURE for COVID-19 Information Retrieval

Hemil Patel, Roopakala Mankaveettil[✉], Reshmi Kanakuzhiyil Rajan,
Nagamaisamma Challa, Rajeshwar Maryala, Saitheja Parsha,
and Pavan Kumar Bayyarapu

University of Leicester, Leicester L1 7RH, UK
rm635@student.le.ac.uk

Abstract. This paper deals with the most well-known and widely used technology which is cloud computing . There are some significant techniques which are needed for the implementation of the cloud computing. These techniques have also been discussed in this report. The cloud service is provided in three cloud computing model and each model will be chosen by the cloud user based on their requirement. These cloud service models has also been discussed in this report. A Covid19 information retrieval system for tracking the disease spread has been developed. This information system web application will be hosted in the AWS and Azure Cloud platform. The significant differences between the AWS and Azure cloud platform will also be discussed based on the pros and cons of each cloud platform .

Keywords: Azure · Aws · Cloud services

1 Cloud Computing

Cloud computing refers to the delivery of computer services in the cloud in other words computing services can be found through the internet. The various services in cloud computing include; storage, servers networking, software, analytics, and artificial intelligence. The services offered in the cloud bring about faster innovation, economical raise, and flexible resources. To access the services one needs to incur charges. The charges include buying data bundles or sometimes the services might require one to buy them. Organizations and individuals turn to cud computing because of the many advantages it has to offer. Cloud computing has different ways of deploying services including; Public clouds, they are owned by the third-party services providers who deliver servers and storage through the internet. Private cloud refers to services used by specific people i.e. sine business owners. A hybrid cloud is a combination of public and private clouds that are connected to enable them to communicate.

2 Cloud Computing Techniques

Cloud computing has various techniques which include;

© ICST Institute for Computer Sciences, Social Informatics and Telecommunications Engineering 2021
Published by Springer Nature Switzerland AG 2021. All Rights Reserved
W. Fu et al. (Eds.): ICMTEL 2021, LNICST 388, pp. 304–320, 2021.
https://doi.org/10.1007/978-3-030-82565-2_25

2.1 Virtualization

This entails giving out of various applications to different users. The purpose of this technology gets to provide the simplest version of the cloud software being offered. This process is often used for flexible applications and processes that need instant running. Virtualization technique is classified into many types;

- **Hardware Virtualization:** The virtual machine has to have some connection for it to work. The connection can be on a hardware device or a hardware server. In the event that the virtual machine is straightforwardly introduced on equipment workers, at that point it is called Hardware virtualization since it is anything but difficult to control a Virtual Machine than an actual worker.
- **Operating System Virtualization:** The virtual machine can be connected to a guest server or an operating system rather than being connected to a hardware server If the virtual machine is introduced in a visitor worker rather than the equipment framework, at that point it is called an Operating framework Virtualization. It expanded the testing circumstance of different programming on different OS stages,
- **Server Virtualization:** The machine can also be connected to a server other than being connected to either a hardware or an operating system server. On the off chance that the virtual machine is introduced on the framework it is called Server Virtualization. It is separated into various assets and used for load adjusting onrequest premise.
- **Storage Virtualization:** Data needs to be stored after collection.. In case of any loss of data with storage virtualization it is easy to restore and back up the data. The way toward gathering actual capacity from various organization stockpiling gadgets is called Storage Virtualization. It is predominantly utilized for back-up and recuperation.
- **Application Virtualization:** Under this technique of cloud computing abstracts the application layer for separating it from the operating system. By providing a level of isolation, this application allows for an application to run in an encapsulated form without being dependent upon the operating system. This technique of cloud computing is used for delivering SaaS services.

2.2 Service-Oriented Architecture

This application can divide the serves into two the daily procedure and the business functions. It is a component that gives the cloud applications a space to adjust to fit business needs. SOA is divided into two; software as a service and quality as a service. The quality of service identifies the behavior and function of certain services. The software as a service gives a new mode of delivery to the services providers.

2.3 Utility Computing

This model defines the services that are paid for to enable use. It is pay –per-utilize model. It only offers the computational services if it is there are some benefits in place. This model helps in cutting costs and the initial investment. As the enrolling necessities for a business change, the charging in like manner changes properly, without increasing any additional cost. If the client usage has reduced, by then charging cost moreover diminishes fittingly.

2.4 Grid Computing

This is the process of connecting more than one server to come up with one major role. Grid computing breaks down big robles into small problems and sends them to the servers that put them in grids. It is often used in e-commerce, it is used to share resources. It involves making use of unused computers and then solve hard problems.

2.5 Infrastructure as a Service (IAAS)

It is a readily available resource or infrastructure that is managed and provisioned over the internet. IAAS demand one to pay for it to use. It saves on cost since one pays for what is to be used. It also saves on cost since one doesn't have to buy servers and data infrastructure. All the resource is offered as a separate service and one needs to only buy the one service that is needed. Organizations use IAAS to; Test and improvement.

Gatherings can promptly set up and crush test and improvement conditions, setting up new applications available to be purchased to the public faster. IaaS makes scaling dev-test conditions all over rapid and viable.

Web facilitating.
Running locales using IaaS can be more moderate than ordinary web encouraging.

Capacity and reinforcement.
Affiliations sidestep the capital expense for limit and unpredictability of limit the board, which ordinarily requires talented staff to administer data and meet legitimate and reliable necessities.

2.6 Software as a Service (SAAS)

It is a method of giving software applications through the internet. It allows users to connect and use the software through the internet. It provides complete software that provides solutions to users. An organization rents certain software, and the users connect to it through the internet. All the resources are located in the data center. The service agreement gives a platform for the service provider to manage hardware and software.

2.7 (Platform as a Service) PAAS

It is an environment in the cloud that helps one deliver everything from the cloud-based applications. PaaS fuses structure – laborers, amassing, and frameworks organization – yet likewise middleware, progression gadgets, business understanding (BI) organizations, data base organization systems and that is just a hint of something larger. PaaS is expected to help the absolute web application life cycle: building, testing, sending, directing, and reviving.

PaaS grants you to dodge the expense and complexity of buying and administering programming licenses, the shrouded application structure, and middleware and holder orchestrators.

3   Differences Between AZURE and AWS

Amazon Web Services is a cloud service that is from amazon that provides services on different platforms. This platform is used to deploy and create applications in the cloud. Services are designed to work with each other.

Azure was launched and it is the biggest cloud service provider offering commercial services. It offers functionalities and cloud services that are integrated into the environment to achieve scalability and scalability (Table 1).

Table 1. Main differences

AWS	AZURE
The users in AWS can configure its images	Azure needs to choose a virtual hard disk to develop a VM which is configured by a third party
AWS offers temporary storage which begins every time it is opened and destroyed when is it stopped	Azure offers storage that is temporarily but it is blocked
It provides a virtual private cloud that the user utilizes to isolate the networks	It provides a virtual network that the user uses to develop isolated networks
AWS supports the hybrid clouds	Azure supports both public and private cloud providers
AWS charges per hour	Azure charges per minute
AWS has a lot of features and it is flexible enough	Azure is easier o use with a user who is more informed about windows

3.1   The Design of the Two Runnable Systems

The main of this section is to design a cloud computing platform using AWS and Azure platforms. The systems that are designed in this case will be used in the storage and retrieval of the system information for the cloud platform. The system that is created is aimed at storing information for covid 19 patients. The information that is stored and can easily be retrieved from the clouds system, includes the positive cases that are recorded daily and the number of recovered cases that are recorded in each country.

Fig. 1. .

The system is designed as shown below using the azure and the AWS cloud platforms (Figs. 1 and 2).

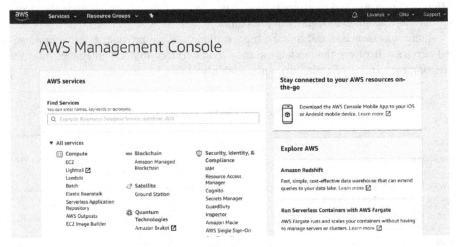

Fig. 2. .

Explore the Amazon management console (Fig. 3).

Fig. 3. .

Lambda function (Fig. 4).

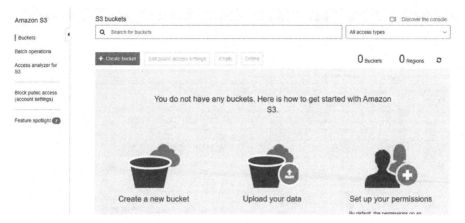

Fig. 4. .

Choose S3 functions if applicable (Fig. 5).

Fig. 5. .

View the services that Amazon cloud offers (Fig. 6).

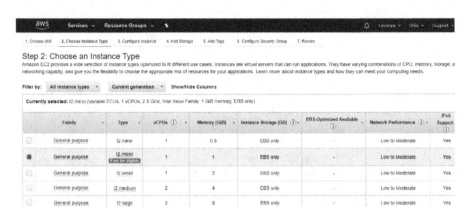

Fig. 6. .

Select an instance from the services provided (Fig. 7).

Fig. 7. .

Choose an Amazon cloud image (Fig. 8).

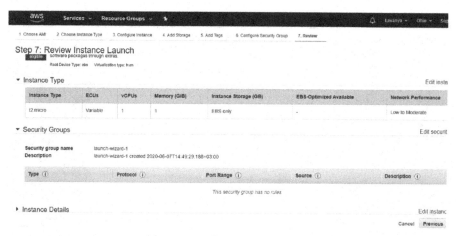

Fig. 8. .

Review the selected Amazon instance (Fig. 9).

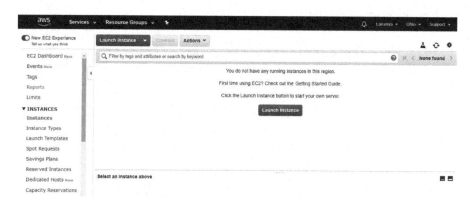

Fig. 9. .

Launch Amazon instance (Fig. 10).

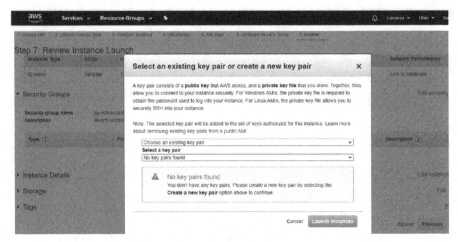

Fig. 10. .

3.1.1 Azure Implementation.

1. First, login to your account.

2. Once you are logged in, click on "Storage Account" service.

3.   After that, click on the add button

4   Under the Resource group field, select your desired resource group, or create a new resource group.

5.   Next enter a name for your storage account.

Instance details

The default deployment model is Resource Manager, which supports the latest Azure features. You may choose to deploy using the classic deployment model instead. Choose classic deployment model

Storage account name * ⓘ	covidwebsite	✓

6. Select a location for your storage account and after that set the Account kind field to Storage V2(*general purpose-v2*).

7. Now click on the "Review + create" button.

Review + create

8. Now, here is your storage account details.

9. Now open "static website" manager from the side bar.

10. Enable the static website option.

11. Enter your index document name and after that click on the save button.

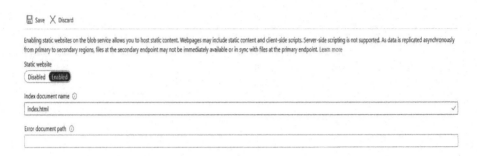

12. Now copy the primary endpoint for later.
    EndPoint: https://covidwebsite.z13.web.core.windows.net/

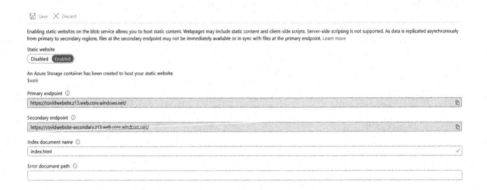

13. Open container manager.

14. Now select "$web" from the container listing.

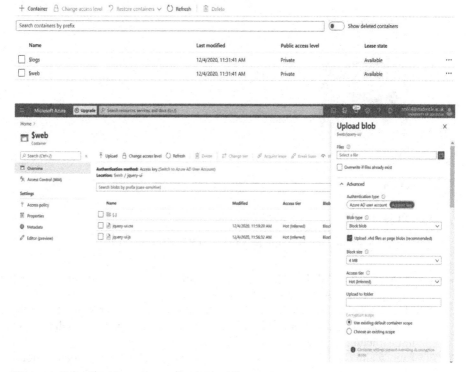

15. Click on the upload button to upload your files.

16. Now you just need to select your files and then click on upload button.
17. Here is your website link: https://covidwebsite.z13.web.core.windows.net/

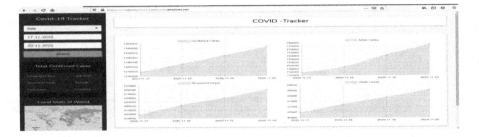

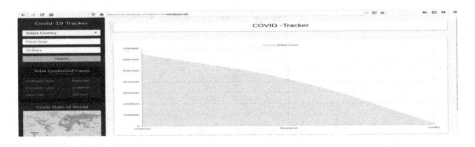

4 AWS

4.1 Pros of AWS

Following are the key benefits of AWS cloud platform

1. There is a detailed documentation and videos for using the features of AWS are provided on the AWS website.
2. This cloud platform is very cost effective for the companies ranging from start-ups to the large organizations. This is less expensive when compared to the on-premise infrastructure services.
3. Auto-scaling feature is very much useful for changing needs. The organizations need not worry about the guessing of scaling the resources based on the business changes.

4. Security of AWS services are said to be the best. Since AWS services are used by the many big organizations and government organizations, AWS gains huge trust and it is considered as a secured cloud service platform.
5. The performance and productivity of the business can be improved by using the backup and recovery services of AWS cloud platform.
6. AWS cloud services have commitment towards innovation and providing many new services.
7. AWS is the global cloud service provider (Arunkumar 2019).

4.2 Cons of AWS

1. Though the AWS cloud services are well designed still there are some issues related with the services.
2. There are some security issues when the users configure some option which is faced by every cloud provider.
3. The cloud services of AWS is specific to the country. The users of all the countries cannot access the same cloud services.
4. AWS sometimes allow the access of data by other companies without the concern of the data owner.
5. Sometime bill shocks are experienced by the users. This can be avoided by setting the "enable monitoring" and get the notification when the usage exceeds the threshold set by the user (Cog Editor 2020).

5 Azure

5.1 Pros of Azure

1. 1. Azure provides high availability of services which is ranging from low percentage of 90 and high percentage of 99.95. In an entire year, there will be only 4.5 h of downtime.
2. This provides high security by using multi factor authentication and various password strategies.
3. Azure offers very good scalability features.
4. This is very cost-effective solution for many organizations.
5. Redundancy of data makes the easier service and data access.
6. Allows the organizations to configure the hybrid infrastructure.
7. This provides a wide range of artificial intelligence services (Gaille 2018).

5.2 Cons of Azure

1. The users need to understand the Azure customization options before configuring based on the requirement.
2. There is less contribution in documentation.
3. This needs effort in improving the technical support.
4. There are only less open source features.

6 In Conclusion

Pandemic caused some issues for cloud providers like Microsoft, Google and Amazon Web Services as the market goes down all over the world, but the clouds provides flexibility for enterprises that struggles to maintain their normal operations. Both Microsoft Azure and Amazon AWS web service can be used for Covid-19 data retrieval. AWS has created data lakes to help health workers and scientists to analyse and defend spreading of Covid-19, even then the facilities that offered by Microsoft Azure like high reliability and availability for the services that offered to the consumers and Azure seems cost effective cloud service with attractive pay-as-you-go pricing packages makes Azure more convenient for users.

References

Gruman, G.: What cloud computing means. InfoWorld (2008)

Regalado, A.: Who Coined 'Cloud Computing'?. MIT Technology Review (2011). Retrieved 31 July 2013

Baburajan, R.: The Rising Cloud Storage Market Opportunity Strengthens Vendors (2011). It.tmcnet.com.

Gartner, M.P., Malinverno, P., Thoo, E.: Gartner Reference Model for Integration PaaS (2017)

Kumar, G.: A review on data protection of cloud computing security, benefits, risks and suggestions (PDF). United Int. J. Res. Technol. 1(2), 26 (2019). Retrieved 9

Lawson, L.: IT Business Edge (2012). Retrieved 6 July 2015

Oestreich, K.: Converged Infrastructure. CTO Forum. Thectoforum.com. Archived from the original (2015)

Simpson, T., Novak, J.: Hands-on Virtual Computing. ISBN **1337515744**, 451 (2017)

Vaughan-Nichols, S.J.: Microsoft developer reveals Linux is now more used on Azure than Windows Server (2019)

Heyong Wang, W., He, F.-K.W.: Enterprise cloud service architectures. Inf. Technol. Manage. **13**(4), 445–454 (2012). https://doi.org/10.1007/s10799-012-0139-4

Expression Recognition Algorithm Based on Infrared Image

Ying Cui[1] and Shi Qiu[2]([⊠])

[1] College of Equipment Management and Support, Engineering
University of PAP, Xi'an 710086, China
[2] Key Laboratory of Spectral Imaging Technology CAS, Xi'an Institute of Optics and Precision
Mechanics, Chinese Academy of Sciences, Xi'an 710119, China

Abstract. It's important to recognize facial expressions in social communication. To solve the problem that facial expression recognition by visible light is vulnerable to interference, we built a model from the perspective of thermal infrared. Based on the distribution characteristics of thermal infrared, the face region is firstly located by building a multi-projection model toward color. Then, the level set function of the local Gaussian fitting model was optimized, the regular term was removed, and the larger iteration step size was selected to achieve accurate face segmentation on the premise of segmentation accuracy. Finally, based on the structure of traditional deep learning network, the characteristics of DPN and CBAM network are given full play to realize expression recognition by thermal infrared images.

Keywords: Infrared image · Face · Multi-projection · Level set · Identify

1 Introduction

Facial expression recognition is the main means of analyzing inner activity, which is of great significance in social and medical fields. At present, facial expression recognition is mainly based on visible images. Sarode [1] uses computers to recognize facial expressions. Berretti [2] extracted SIFT features to achieve expression matching. Jain [3] recognizes facial expressions based on the shape change model. Moore [4] used Local Binary Patterns to recognize expressions from multiple perspectives. Guo [5] classifies facial expressions through videos. Lajevardi [6] selected representative features to carry out the study. Liu [7] constructed a deep network to classify facial expressions. Luo [8] extracted PCA and LBP features and used SVM to classify facial expressions. Owusu [9] established a neural-AdaBoost to extract facial features hierarchically. Saeed [10] uses geometrical features to recognize the expression of a single frame image. Yu [11] constructed multiple deep networks to recognize static image expressions. Lopes [12] constructed convolutional networks to recognize expression. Chen [13] researched on multi-feature fusion based on video sequences to realize expression recognition. Elaiwat [14] established a spatio-temporal RBM to realize expression recognition. Xie

W. Fu et al. (Eds.): ICMTEL 2021, LNICST 388, pp. 321–330, 2021.
https://doi.org/10.1007/978-3-030-82565-2_26

[15] established the FRR-CNN network for expression recognition. Meng [16] proposed Identity-aware convolutional neural network for facial expression recognition. Zhang [17] analyzed the relationship between characters from facial expressions. Li [18] fused CNN with the attention model to realize expression recognition of a covered face. Georgescu [19] integrated depth features with handcrafted features to realize expression recognition. Shao [20] established 3D-CNN to realize expression classification. Wang [21] realized expression recognition based on figure posture and facial image. Li [22] introduced the attention mechanism to realize expression recognition. Visible light imaging is consistent with human perception and can objectively reflect the characteristics of objects. Although many studies have been carried out based on visible-light images, the following problems still exist: 1) It is easily disturbed by the external environment and focus on the face is hard. 2) The established model has limited utilization characteristics.

Given the above problems, based on the characteristics of thermal infrared imaging, we use the infrared images to carry out research. 1) The face extraction model was established, and the area of the face was focused. 2) Build an expression recognition model to analyze facial expressions.

2   Algorithm

To meet the needs of getting facial expression accurately, the algorithm in this paper builds a face extraction model based on the acquisition of thermal infrared images, focuses the face area, and then proposes an expression recognition network to realize expression recognition based on the existing deep learning framework. The specific flow chart is shown in Fig. 1.

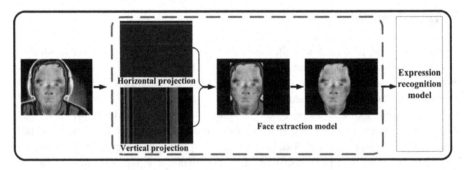

Fig. 1. Algorithm flow chart

2.1   Face Extraction Model

The infrared images can directly display the heat distribution [23]. The human body produces heat, which makes people with different skin tones tend to be red in the infrared image. Based on this feature, facial detection of different skin tones can be realized. We can build a model to measure the similarity of colors:

$$D_{(SR,SG,SB)}(x, y) = |C_R(x, y) - SR| + |C_G(x, y) - SG| + |C_B(x, y) - SB| \quad (1)$$

where $C_R(x,y)$, $C_G(x,y)$ and $C_B(x,y)$ are pixel values of R, G, and B of the infrared image respectively, and (SR, SG, SB) is the target pixel value.

The facial region is continuous and tends to be red, so we construct the horizontal projection M_X and the vertical projection M_Y to determine the face region indirectly.

$$\begin{cases} M_X = \min\big(D_{(SR,SG,SB)}(x, 1), \cdots, D_{(SR,SG,SB)}(x, n), \cdots, D_{(SR,SG,SB)}(x, H)\big) \\ M_Y = \min\big(D_{(SR,SG,SB)}(1, y), \cdots, D_{(SR,SG,SB)}(n, y), \cdots, D_{(SR,SG,SB)}(W, y)\big) \end{cases} \quad (2)$$

where $(SR, SG, SB) = (255, 0, 0)$. Then measure the difference between horizontal and vertical projections:

$$E(x, y) = \begin{cases} 0\left(\begin{array}{l} abs(M_X(x, y) - M_Y(x, y)) > T_1 || M_X(x, y) \rightarrow (0, 0, 0) \\ || M_Y(x, y) \rightarrow (0, 0, 0) || I(x, y) \rightarrow (0, 0, 0) \end{array}\right) \\ I(x, y) \; others \end{cases} \quad (3)$$

Then determine the area where the face is, and then carry out the operation in this area.

According to the infrared imaging principle, the parts with poor heat dissipation are hair, behind ears, clothing, etc. [24]. The transition zone between face, clothing, and hair presents an obvious continuous red transition zone due to friction heating. Based on this feature, the facial contour can be extracted effectively.

Signed distance function is often used in traditional level sets [25]:

$$u(x, y, t) = \begin{cases} d\big[(x, y), C\big] \\ -d\big[(x, y), C\big] \end{cases} \quad (4)$$

where C is the evolution curve, $d[(x,y),C]$ is the distance function from the point(x,y) to curve C. Since the gradient of the level set is collinear with the normal, but the direction is opposite, the value of the point in a certain region is defined as negative inside and positive outside. The gradient modulus of the signed distance function is identical to 1, which ensures that the change of $u(x,y,t)$ is uniform everywhere and the numerical calculation is stable.

According to the curve evolution theory, the evolution equation of the level set function is:

$$\frac{\partial u}{\partial t} = \beta |\nabla u| \quad (5)$$

where β is the normal rate and t is the evolution time. After many iterations, the level set function deviates from the inner negative and outer positive characteristic of the signed distance function, thus destroying the stability of the iteration. When $|\nabla u| \gg 1$, the level set function will be rush or ravines, cause the energy function into local minimum; When $|\nabla u| \ll 1$, the level set function is too flat, boundary fitting is very difficult.

Local Gaussian Distribution Fitting (LGDF) model [26] is a classic segmentation algorithm based on the level set active contour model, and its energy generic function is:

$$E(\varphi, u_1, u_2, \sigma_1, \sigma_2) = A(\varphi) + B(\varphi, u_1, u_2, \sigma_1, \sigma_2) \tag{6}$$

$$\begin{cases} A(\varphi) = \alpha \int_\Omega \frac{1}{2}(|\nabla\varphi| - 1)^2 dx + \beta \int_\Omega \delta(\varphi)|\nabla\varphi| dx \\ B(\varphi, u_1, u_2, \sigma_1, \sigma_2) = \lambda \iint C(\varphi, u_1, \sigma_1) H(\varphi(y)) dy dx \\ \quad + (1 - \lambda) \iint C(\varphi, u_2, \sigma_2)(1 - H(\varphi(y))) dy dx \\ C(\varphi, u, \sigma) = K(x - y)\left(\log \sigma(x) + \frac{(I(y) - u(x))^2}{2\sigma^2(x)}\right) \end{cases} \tag{7}$$

where $A(\varphi)$ is the regular term, $K(x-y)$ is the Gaussian window, u_1 and u_2 are the local mean values inside and outside the contour, σ_1 and σ_2 are the local variances inside and outside the contour. The level set function is guaranteed to remain a signed distance function and to be smooth during evolution. $B(\varphi, u_1, u_2, \sigma_1, \sigma_2)$ is controlled by the local binomial fitting term $C(\varphi, u, \sigma)$.

LGDF model uses the mean value and variance to describe the local pixel distribution, which can effectively solve the segmentation problems of uneven grayscale and low contrast images, but at the same time, it also increases the calculation cost.

Aiming at the deficiency of the signed distance function, we built parameterized level set according to mathematical theory:

$$\varphi(x, \mathbf{W}) = 1 - \prod_{i=1}^{N}\left(1 - r_{ij}(x)\right) \tag{8}$$

$$r_{ij}(x) = \frac{1}{1 + \exp\left(\sum_{k=0}^{n} w_{ijk}x_k\right)} \tag{9}$$

where $\mathbf{W} = [w_{ijk}]$ is the target contour, and the updating process of parameter w_{ijk} is the contour evolution process. $r_{ij}(x)$ determined by w_{ijk} is used to represent the half-space, and the level set function is composed of polyhedra so that $\varphi(x, \mathbf{W}) \in [0,1]$ is guaranteed. The level set of $\varphi(x, \mathbf{W}) = 0.5$ is used as the boundary between foreground and background. When $\varphi(x, \mathbf{W}) > 0.5$, the level set function belongs to the foreground region, when $\varphi(x, \mathbf{W}) < 0.5$, the level set function belongs to the background region, so $\varphi(x, \mathbf{W})$ replaces the regular term. $\mathbf{W}$ adopts the interactive method, The user initializes φ by defining N faces in the region of interest in the image, and the polyhedron is approximately a half-sphere.

When $\varphi(x, \mathbf{W})$ is introduced into LGDF, the level set energy functional is:

$$P(\mathbf{W}) = \lambda \iint C(\varphi, u_1, \sigma_1)\varphi(x, \mathbf{W}) dy dx$$
$$+ (1 - \lambda) \iint C(\varphi, u_2, \sigma_2)(1 - \varphi(x, \mathbf{W})) dy dx \tag{10}$$

$$\begin{cases} u(x) = \frac{\int K(y-x)I(y)H(\varphi-0.5)dy}{\int K(y-x)H(\varphi-0.5)dy} \\ \sigma^2(x) = \frac{\int K(x-y)\left(I(y-u(x))^2\right)H(\varphi-0.5)dy}{\int K(x-y)H(\varphi-0.5)dy} \end{cases} \tag{11}$$

The evolution process of φ requires neither the regular term nor initialization, which simplifies the energy functional and reduces the calculation cost.

Image segmentation using gradient descent flow:

$$\frac{\partial \varepsilon}{\partial w_{ijk}} = (\lambda_1 e_1 - \lambda_2 e_2)\frac{\partial \varphi}{\partial w_{ijk}} \tag{12}$$

$$\begin{cases} e_n(x) = \int K(x-y)C(\varphi,u,\sigma)dy \\ \frac{\partial \varphi}{\partial w_{ijk}} = x_k\left[r_{ij}(x)\right]\prod_{l=1}^{M}\left(1-r_{ij}(x)\right)\prod_{r\neq i,r=1}^{N}\left(1-\prod_{j=1}^{M}\left(1-r_{ij}(x)\right)\right) \end{cases} \tag{13}$$

In the iteration process, the discriminant parameter vector W is constantly updated:

$$w_{ijk} \rightarrow \tau\frac{\partial P}{\partial w_{ijk}} - w_{ijk} \tag{14}$$

where τ is the step, when $P(W)$ is the smallest, the parameter is optimal. Therefore, this algorithm is not restricted by the CFL standard and can choose the larger τ to accelerate convergence.

2.2 Expression Recognition Model

While the ResNet network does a good job of refining features, Densenet supports deeper detail exploration. DPN network combines the advantages of RESNET and DENSENET models. DPN network has a highly coupled two-channel link structure, which can effectively solve the problem of gradient disappearance in deep network training. By combining the channel selection mechanism with the spatial orientation selection mechanism, CPAM can achieve multi-directional convolution to obtain better results.

For this reason, we combined the two to construct a C-DPN model and normalized the size of the face image was sent into the Block. Both blocks have transitions. The Transition layer structure reduces the amount of data. There are 4 blocks in the C-DPN network, and the number of M-blocks in each Block determines the network depth, which can realize data partition. Rich feature information is extracted from the matrix through the Block, and the data dimension reduction is realized through the adaptive average pooling layer to reduce the computation. Adding the Dropout layer in front of the full connection layer can further reduce the feature redundancy, speed up the computing speed, and solve the overfitting problem to some extent. Finally, the feature matrix is expanded through the full connection layer, and the weight is obtained to realize expression state classification. Its network structure is shown in Fig. 2.

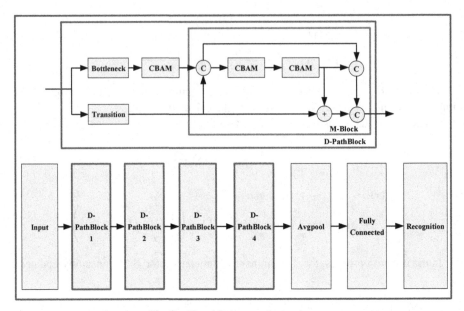

Fig. 2. Algorithm network structure

3   Experiment and Result Analysis

The database was composed of 150 frames of an image taken by a thermal infrared camera with 7 groups of different expressions, and the facial boundaries in the database were manually marked as the gold standard. The experimental equipment is a PC, equipped with Win7 operating system and VC++ software writing platform.

3.1   Algorithm Renderings

To measure the contour extraction effect of the algorithm, we introduce DC (Dice coefficient) to measure the detection accuracy [27]:

$$DC(\Omega_s, \Omega_r) = \frac{2Area(\Omega_s \cap \Omega_r)}{Area\Omega_s + Area\Omega_r} \tag{15}$$

where Ω_s is the manually marked result, as the gold standard. Ω_r is the algorithm extracting effect. The closer the DC value is to 1, the better.

Compared with the traditional LGDF, MSLCV, and our algorithm, the results are shown in Table 1. The segmentation performance, number of iterations, and calculation time of the proposed algorithm are all optimal. This is because the parameterized level set function constructed in this paper replaces the regular term in LGDF and MSLCV algorithm to improve the segmentation performance. The algorithm needs no initialization and has strong robustness. The iteration step τ is not limited by CFL and can be increased to reduce the number of iterations without reducing the segmentation accuracy, which accelerates the curve evolution to the real contour.

Table 1. Comparison of algorithm effects

Image sequence	DC		
	LGDF	MSLCV	Ours
Angry	0.86	0.87	0.89
Disgust	0.84	0.88	0.91
Fear	0.80	0.82	0.86
Happy	0.87	0.89	0.92
Normal	0.86	0.88	0.90
Sadness	0.84	0.86	0.89
Surprise	0.86	0.87	0.90
Image sequence	Number of iterations		
	LGDF	MSLCV	Ours
Angry	564	124	61
Disgust	682	171	76
Fear	721	214	92
Happy	506	101	50
Normal	410	80	45
Sadness	680	160	72
Surprise	701	201	86
Image sequence	Computing time/s		
	LGDF	MSLCV	Ours
Angry	45.8	24.1	12.5
Disgust	48.7	26.5	14.6
Fear	52.4	27.8	18.4
Happy	43.2	31.6	20.6
Normal	40.3	35.5	24.5
Sadness	47.6	37.6	26.6
Surprise	50.1	39.5	30.4

In order to display the algorithm performance, we demonstrate the segmentation effect of 7 groups of data. It can be seen from Table 2 that the temperature of the skin is higher than that of the hair and clothing. The algorithm proposed in this paper takes full advantage of the characteristics of thermal infrared imaging to build a multi-projection model with color orientation, which can meet the requirements of facial localization at different scales. The improved LGDF model can accurately segment the facial region.

3.2 Facial Expression Recognition Algorithm

UF1 (Unweighted F1-score), UAR (Unweighted Average Recall) and ROC (Receiver Operating characteristic Curve) were used to measure the evaluation effect.

Table 2. Algorithm renderings

	Angry	Disgust	Fear	Happy	Normal	Sadness	Surprise
Orininal							
Facial positioning							
Facial segmentation							

$$UF1 = \frac{1}{C} \sum_{C} \frac{2TP}{TP + FP + FN} \tag{16}$$

$$UAR = \frac{1}{C} \sum_{c} \frac{TP}{N} \tag{17}$$

where C represents the total number of types, and TP, FP, and FN represent the proportion of calculated results.

By comparing our algorithm with the current mainstream algorithm, the results are shown in Table 3, and the recognition effect of counting angry expressions is shown in Fig. 3. Adaboost [9] algorithm uses multi-scale thought focusing feature to achieve feature extraction. Multiple deep network [11] algorithm builds the depth model from multiple angles, which enhances the robustness of the model. The FRR-CNN [15] integrates the two network structures to improve the accuracy of detection. D-H-F [19] integrates depth features with traditional features to realize expression recognition. The algorithm proposed in this paper gives full play to the advantages of DPN and CBAM, extracts image features and realizes expression recognition, and achieves good results.

Table 3. Comparison of algorithm effects

	AdaBoost	Multiple deep network	FRR-CNN	D-H-F	Ours
UF1	0.63	0.66	0.68	0.70	0.73
UAR	0.65	0.69	0.70	0.74	0.76

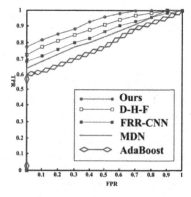

Fig. 3. Recognition effect of angry expressions

4 Conclusion

Because of the need to analyze facial expressions in social communication and the inaccuracy of facial expression analysis caused by the interference of visible light imaging, a new facial expression analysis algorithm based on the thermal infrared image was proposed. A color-oriented multi-projection model was established to locate the face region, the LGDF level set algorithm was optimized, and the parameterized level set framework was constructed to achieve fast and accurate face image segmentation. Taking full advantage of the network, the expression recognition model is built to analyze the expression. Follow-up studies on facial expression analysis and social relationship prediction will be carried out.

Acknowledgement. This work is supported by Postdoctoral Science Foundation of China under Grant No. 2020M682144. The Open Project Program of the State Key Lab of CAD&CG (Grant No. A2026), Zhejiang University.

References

1. Sarode, N., Bhatia, S.: Facial expression recognition. Int. J. comput. Sci. Eng. **2**(5), 1552–1557 (2010)
2. Berretti, S., Del Bimbo, A., Pala, P., Amor, B.B., Daoudi, M.: A set of selected SIFT features for 3D facial expression recognition. In: 2010 20th International Conference on Pattern Recognition pp. 4125–4128. IEEE (2010)
3. Jain, S., Hu, C., Aggarwal, J.K.: Facial expression recognition with temporal modeling of shapes. In: 2011 IEEE International Conference on Computer Vision Workshops (ICCV Workshops) pp. 1642–164. IEEE (2011)
4. Moore, S., Bowden, R.: Local binary patterns for multi-view facial expression recognition. Comput. Vis. Image Underst. **115**(4), 541–558 (2011)
5. Guo, Y., Zhao, G., Pietikäinen, M.: Dynamic facial expression recognition using longitudinal facial expression atlases. In: European Conference on Computer Vision pp. 631–644. Springer, Heidelberg (2012). https://doi.org/10.1007/978-3-642-33709-3_45

6. Lajevardi, S.M., Hussain, Z.M.: Automatic facial expression recognition: feature extraction and selection. SIViP **6**(1), 159–169 (2012)

7. Liu, M., Li, S., Shan, S., Chen, X.: Au-aware deep networks for facial expression recognition. In: 2013 10th IEEE International Conference and Workshops on Automatic Face and Gesture Recognition (FG) pp. 1–6. IEEE (2013)

8. Luo, Y., Wu, C.M., Zhang, Y.: Facial expression recognition based on fusion feature of PCA and LBP with SVM. Optik-Int. J. Light and Electron Opt. **124**(17), 2767–2770 (2013)

9. Owusu, E., Zhan, Y., Mao, Q.R.: A neural-AdaBoost based facial expression recognition system. Expert Syst. Appl. **41**(7), 3383–3390 (2014)

10. Saeed, A., Al-Hamadi, A., Niese, R., Elzobi, M.: Frame-based facial expression recognition using geometrical features. Adv. Hum. Comput .Interact. **2014**, 1–13 (2014)

11. Yu, Z., Zhang, C.: Image based static facial expression recognition with multiple deep network learning. In: Proceedings of the 2015 ACM on International Conference on Multimodal Interaction pp. 435–442 (2015)

12. Lopes, A.T., De Aguiar, E., Oliveira-Santos, T.: A facial expression recognition system using convolutional networks. In: 2015 28th SIBGRAPI Conference on Graphics, Patterns and Images pp. 273–280. IEEE (2015)

13. Chen, J., Chen, Z., Chi, Z., Fu, H.: Facial expression recognition in video with multiple feature fusion. IEEE Trans. Affect. Comput. **9**(1), 38–50 (2016)

14. Elaiwat, S., Bennamoun, M., Boussaïd, F.: A spatio-temporal RBM-based model for facial expression recognition. Pattern Recogn. **49**, 152–161 (2016)

15. Xie, S., Hu, H.: Facial expression recognition with FRR-CNN. Electron. Lett. **53**(4), 235–237 (2017)

16. Meng, Z., Liu, P., Cai, J., Han, S., Tong, Y.: Identity-aware convolutional neural network for facial expression recognition. In: 2017 12th IEEE International Conference on Automatic Face & Gesture Recognition (FG 2017) pp. 558–565. IEEE (2017)

17. Zhang, Z., Luo, P., Loy, C.C., Tang, X.: From facial expression recognition to interpersonal relation prediction. Int. J. Comput. Vis. **126**(5), 550–569 (2018)

18. Li, Y., Zeng, J., Shan, S., Chen, X.: Occlusion aware facial expression recognition using CNN with attention mechanism. IEEE Trans. Image Process. **28**(5), 2439–2450 (2018)

19. Georgescu, M.I., Ionescu, R.T., Popescu, M.: Local learning with deep and handcrafted features for facial expression recognition. IEEE Access **7**, 64827–64836 (2019)

20. Shao, J., Qian, Y.: Three convolutional neural network models for facial expression recognition in the wild. Neurocomputing **355**, 82–92 (2019)

21. Wang, K., Peng, X., Yang, J., Meng, D., Qiao, Y.: Region attention networks for pose and occlusion robust facial expression recognition. IEEE Trans. Image Process. **29**, 4057–4069 (2020)

22. Li, J., Jin, K., Zhou, D., Kubota, N., Ju, Z.: Attention mechanism-based CNN for facial expression recognition. Neurocomputing **411**, 340–350 (2020)

23. Baker, E.A., Lautz, L.K., McKenzie, J.M., Aubry-Wake, C.: Improving the accuracy of time-lapse thermal infrared imaging for hydrologic applications. J. Hydrol. **571**, 60–70 (2019)

24. Raccuglia, M., Heyde, C., Lloyd, A., Hodder, S., Havenith, G.: The use of infrared thermal imaging to measure spatial and temporal sweat retention in clothing. Int. J. Biometeorol. **63**(7), 885–894 (2019). https://doi.org/10.1007/s00484-019-01701-5

25. Vercruysse, D., Sapra, N.V., Su, L., Trivedi, R.: Analytical level set fabrication constraints for inverse design. Sci. Rep. **9**(1), 1–7 (2019)

26. Li, Y., Cao, G., Yu, Q., Li, X.: Active contours driven by non-local Gaussian distribution fitting energy for image segmentation. Appl. Intell. **48**(12), 4855–4870 (2018). https://doi.org/10.1007/s10489-018-1243-x

27. Qiu, S., Luo, J., Yang, S., Zhang, M., Zhang, W.: A moving target extraction algorithm based on the fusion of infrared and visible images. Infrared Phys. Technol. **98**, 285–291 (2019)

The Study About the Emotional State and Physical Activity of Adolescents During the COVID-19 Epidemic

Runda Li[1], Yutong Wu[1], Wenxuan Zhanggu[1], Chihao Xu[1], Yuhan Gu[1], Shihan Yao[1], Hangxiao Li[1], Yuwei Shi[1], Yaojun Yang[1], Zhuoyang Zhen[1], Baijun Zhang[1], Chengyu Ye[1], Zimeng Li[1], Shumeng Shi[1], Xinyan Wang[1], Jingyang Chen[1], and Jiaxi Lei[2(✉)]

[1] Nanjing Foreign Language School, Nanjing, Jiangsu, China
[2] Department of Psychiatry, Nanjing Brain Hospital, Nanjing Medical University, 264 Guangzhou Road, Nanjing 210029, China

Abstract. To investigate the relationship between emotional status and physical activity in adolescents during the epidemic period of Corona Virus Disease 2019. 600 junior and senior high school students from three municipal middle schools were randomly selected as the research objects. The self-evaluation of anxiety and depression and the evaluation of physical activity were carried out in the form of questionnaire survey. A total of 600 questionnaires were put in and 562 were recovered. The scores of SDS and SAS were 49.30 ± 7.02, and 53.42 ± 5.37 respectively. According to different age groups, there was significant difference in SAS among the three groups in different age groups ($P < 0.05$). The total score of PA was (3.24 ± 0.98). According to different age groups, there were significant differences in PA total score, MVPA activities, physical education activities, weekend activities and one week total activities among the three groups ($P < 0.05$). The total score of anxiety was negatively correlated with the total score of PA ($r = -0.54$, $P = 0.024$), MVPA ($r = -0.38$, $P = 0.049$) and physical education ($r = -0.62$, $P = 0.016$), and the total score of one week was negatively correlated ($r = -0.44$, $P = 0.041$). During the period of Corona Virus Disease 2019 epidemic, the anxiety level of adolescents increases with age, while the physical activity status decreases gradually, and is negatively correlated with anxiety. It is necessary to strengthen sports activities and protect emotional health in this special period.

Keywords: Adolescents · Emotional state · Physical activity

1 Introduction

COVID-19 (Corona Virus Disease 2019) has outbreak since December 2019. By the end of September 30th this year, more than 33.78 million cases have been confirmed and about one million people have died all round the world. The spread of the epidemic, convenient access to information, and unknown feature of the virus have aggravated public panic

W. Fu et al. (Eds.): ICMTEL 2021, LNICST 388, pp. 331–337, 2021.
https://doi.org/10.1007/978-3-030-82565-2_27

and anxiety. Previous studies showed that adolescents who is exposed in major disasters is more sensitive to suffer from psychotic illness than their peers, including anxiety and depression, which may in turn lead to more serious consequences [1]. Therefore, a better understanding and effective intervention of the psychological status of adolescents in this special period can reduce adverse impacts on adolescent's education and social functions. These may avoid depression and anxiety disorders developing into adulthood.

Regular and continuous physical exercise can lead to positive mental health outcomes and provide a buffer against illness [2]. Previous studies showed that even short-term exercise can alleviate the adverse impacts of stressful event on emotion such as trauma, reduce acute and chronic stress, and improve overall mental health. During the COVID-19 epidemic, physical exercises of adolescents decrease due to factors social isolation. Furthermore, because of academic pressure, regular physical classes are often occupied by other cultural courses, which is deemed valuable for future education.

In this study, we investigated the mental status and physical activity of middle school students aged 15–17 during COVID-19 epidemic period, and analyzed the relationship between them. Through clarify the emotional state of teenagers in this special period, and the influence of physical activity on them, it maybe provide the basis for the education department to formulate relevant measures.

2   Methods

2.1   Objects

During the novel corona-virus pneumonia epidemic period, from June 2020 to September, a total of 600 students who aged 15–17 years old coming from Junior high school were evaluated. All samples were assessed for emotion scale, including Self-Rating Anxiety Scale (SAS), Self-rating Depression Scale (SDS) and Physical Activity Questionnaire for Adolescents. In order to eliminate the interference of college entrance examination on the results, students of 18 years old were not included.

2.2   Clinical Assessment

2.2.1   Physical Exercise Assessment

Physical Activity Questionnaire for Adolescents (PAQ-A) was adopted for assessment physical exercise. The original PAQ-A was compiled by University of Saskatchewan, and it was put into use after being edited according to a Chinese norm. Compared with similar exercise scales, it can distinguish sex and age differences sensitively, and reflect the overall physical activity (PA) and moderate to vigorous physical activity (MVPA) of adolescents in the past 7 days truthfully. The questions are clear and easy to understand, and can be completed within 8–10 min, which avoids recall bias. A 5-point system was adopted as the rank variable to facilitate statistics. The good reliability of validity making it as an effective tool for assessing physical activity of adolescents. The total score is the average score of eight questions. The higher the total score is, the higher the level of physical activity [3–6].

2.2.2   Emotion Scale

Self-Rating Anxiety Scale (SAS) and Self-rating Depression Scale (SDS) were adopted for assessment. Formulated by Zung in 1971, SAS is mainly used for assessing subjective feelings of anxiety of the subjects and the changes during the treatment. This scale consists of 20 item scales, with each item had a 4-level score according to the frequency of symptom occurrence, with frequency options explained to students: no or very little time (this situation lasts less than 1 d in the past 1 week), a few time (this situation lasts 1 to 2 d in the past 1 week), considerable time (this situation lasts 3 to 4 d in the past 1 week), and most or all of the time (this situation lasts 5 to 7 d in the past 1 week). After the scoring, the 20 items were converted into standard scores and the anxiety standard score (rounded) = raw score (sum of all item scores) $\times$ 1.25. As shown by the Chinese norm results: $\geq$50 scores represents the existence of anxiety; 50–59 scores represents mild anxiety; 60–69 scores represents moderate anxiety; $\geq$70 scores represent severe anxiety. Self-rating Depression Scale also consists of 20 items with 4-level score. It is originated from the Depression Scale formulated by W.K. Zung in 1965, with form of scale structure and specific assessment method which are similar to that of SAS. 53–62 scores represent mild depression, 63–72 scores represents moderate depression and $\geq$73 scores represents major depression [7, 8].

2.2.3   Statistical Analysis

SPSS21.0 statistical software was used for data processing. Measurement data were expressed as mean value $\pm$ standard deviation ($\bar{X} \pm s$). One-way ANOVA was conducted. Pearson correlation analysis was used to test the correlation between variables. The level of significance was set at $p < 0.05$.

3   Results

3.1   Participant Characteristics

The research data were collected by on-the-spot distribution and self-administered questionnaires. Questionnaires were distributed in three municipal middle schools. The investigators were trained to introduce the significance of this questionnaire survey through the importance of WeChat official account. Those who have questions about the answers to the questions can be instructed and help by investigator at the scene. According to the time taken to fill the questionnaire in pre-survey, the researcher excluded the people who finish it within 10min from the analysis. In this questionnaire survey, totally 600 questionnaires were distributed, and 562 questionnaires were recovered, with a collection rate of 93.67%; 38 questionnaires were not filled out or finished within a too short time, thus, deemed as invalid. Among them, there were 260 males and 302 females, aged 15–17 years old, with an average of 15.1 $\pm$ 1.82 years old.

3.2   Emotion Scale

The scores of Self-rating Depression Scale (SDS) for students were 49.30 $\pm$ 7.02, with 12 students with mild depression (14.05%); The scores of Self-rating Anxiety Scale

(SAS) were 53.42 ± 5.37, with 306 students with anxieties (54.44%), of which, 196 students had mild anxiety (34.88%), 98 students had moderate anxiety (17.44%) and 12 students had severe anxiety (2.14%). According to different age groups, there is no significant difference in SDS of the three groups (p > 0.05), and significant differences exist in SAS of the three groups with different ages (p < 0.05), which is of statistical significance. Among them, the anxiety score of the group aged 16 (52.80 ± 5.39) is significantly higher than that of the group aged 15 (41.37 ± 6.42), and the anxiety score of the group aged 17 (54.74 ± 5.92) is significantly higher than that the group aged 15, while there is no significant difference between the group aged 16 and the group aged 17. For details, see Table 1.

Table 1. The comparison of anxiety and depression scores in different age groups

Age group (proportion)	SAS	SDA
15 years old (30%)	41.37 ± 6.42	48.32 ± 4.74
16 years old (35%)	52.80 ± 5.39[*]	49.67 ± 5.42
17 years old (45%)	54.74 ± 5.92[*]	50.03 ± 8.09
P	0.012	0.534

SAS: Self-rating Anxiety Scale; SDS: Self-rating Depression Scale.

For the one-way analysis of variance, there is no significant difference in SDS of the three groups ($p >$ 0.05), and significant differences exist in SAS of the three groups with different ages (p < 0.05). [*]$p < 0.05$ in inter group comparison, compared with 15-year-old group.

3.3 Physical Exercise Status at Different Age Groups

As shown by the PAQ-A scores of students, the total PA score was 3.24 ± 0.98, among the scores of each factor, MVPA activities was 1.41 ± 1.02, physical education activities was 3.26 ± 1.37, the activities during lunch break was 1.72 ± 1.00, after-school activities was 3.62 ± 1.40, evening activities was 2.42 ± 1.06, total evaluation of the week was 3.42 ± 0.80, and daily total evaluation was 3.12 ± 0.46. According to different age groups, the total score of PA, MVPA activities, physical education activities, weekend activities and total activities of the week among three groups had the significant difference (p < 0.05), and they were statistically significant; Three groups in different age groups were not statistically significant in the activities during lunch break, after-school activities, evening activities and daily total evaluation (p > 0.05); Wherein, the scores of PA score (2.62 ± 0.56), MVPA activities (1.21 ± 0.03), physical education activities (3.21 ± 0.71), weekend activities (2.64 ± 1.02) and total evaluation of the week (3.37 ± 1.03) of the group aged 16 was significantly lower than the group aged 15 (3.64 ± 0.41, 1.59 ± 0.31, 4.34 ± 0.82, 2.72 ± 1.16 and 3.75 ± 1.06). The scores of PA score (2.55 ± 0.71), MVPA activities (1.04 ± 0.21), physical education activities (3.04 ± 0.56), weekend activities (2.04 ± 1.18) and total evaluation of the week (3.21 ± 1.04) of the group aged 17 was significantly lower than the group aged 15, but there was no significant difference between the group aged 16 and the group aged 17. For details, see Table 2.

Table 2. Scores of Physical Activity Questionnaire for Adolescents (PAQ-A) at different age groups

Age group	Total PA score	MVPA	Physical education activities	Activities during lunch break	After-school activities	Evening activities	Weekend activity	Total evaluation of the week	Total evaluation each day
15	3.64 ± 0.41	1.59 ± 0.31	4.34 ± 0.82	1.77 ± 1.0	3.66 ± 1.21	2.93 ± 1.73	2.72 ± 1.16	3.75 ± 1.06	3.18 ± 0.86
16	2.62 ± 0.56*	1.21 ± 0.03*	3.21 ± 0.71*	1.42 ± 1.2	3.41 ± 1.02	3.01 ± 1.22	2.64 ± 1.02*	3.37 ± 1.03*	3.10 ± 0.84
17	2.55 ± 0.71*	1.04 ± 0.21*	3.04 ± 0.56*	1.31 ± 1.2	2.98 ± 2.1	3.03 ± 0.95	2.04 ± 1.18*	3.21 ± 1.04*	3.12 ± 0.90
P	0.002	0.01	< 0.001	0.32	0.57	0.94	0.042	0.04	0.78

PA: Overall physical activity level, MVPA: Physical activity with the moderate to high intensity; For the one-way analysis of variance, $^*P < 0.05$ in inter group comparison, compared with 15-year-old group.

3.4 Correlation Between SAS and Physical Exercise

Pearson correlation analysis was used to test the correlation between the self-rating anxiety and all PAQ-A factors of physical exercise of adolescents. The result showed that the total anxiety score of adolescents had the significant negative correlation (r = −0.44, P = 0.041) with the total PA score of PAQ-A (r = −0.54 P = 0.024), MVPA (r = −0.38, P = 0.049), physical education activities (r = −0.62, P = 0.016) and total evaluation of the week.

4 Discussion

The age between 15 and 18 belongs to the late adolescence, which is an important stage of life. In the process of entering adulthood, the adolescent begins to develop a sense of identity and independence, and the personality shaping is becoming more and more perfect, which will bring much pressure for the expectation of academic performance and change of social role. Meanwhile, the environmental pressure and negative social events occurred in the childhood and early adolescence, such as trauma and disaster, jointly form the mental health crisis of this age group. In the recent one year, the COVID-19 epidemic has spread all over the world, and the death toll is increasing. The exaggeration of the media and the panic of the masses all have an impact on the young people, a special susceptible group, which is probably to cause common mental disorders. Therefore, we take middle school students in a city as the research object to explore possible intervention measures for adolescence facing major disasters.

Consistent with the previous research results, our data showed that the anxiety level of the adolescents increased with the ages in the period of COVID-19. Although all depression scores in SDS did not exceed the normal value, but it has shown the trend to break through the upper bound of normal value, which showed the unstable emotions of the adolescents in this special period. Worldwide, the prevalence of mental disorders (anxiety and depression, etc.) increases significantly in late adolescence. The research showed that 5.6% of the adolescents aged 13–18 suffered from depression and anxiety; persistent depression and anxiety are associated with serious complications such as poor academic performance and social adaptation, adult depression, and suicide [9]. If the adolescents suffered from depression and anxiety in the late stage, the incidence of various behavior problems and somatic symptoms within 10 years after being an adult is 2–3 times than those who had no similar symptoms in the late adolescence, including poor health, migraine, emotional disturbance, poor social adaptation, alcohol addiction and smoking [10]. The suicide risk of the patients who once suffered from the anxiety and depression in the late adolescence is 70 times higher than that of their peers [11]. According to the latest statistics, the suicide rate of Chinese adolescents ranks No. 1 in the world [12]. In China, nearly 0.1 million adolescents commit suicide every year, two people succeed in suicide every minute on average and another 8 people attempt the incomplete suicide [13]. Therefore, paying attention to the psychological status of adolescents in special period, early identification of emotional disorders, and effective intervention can reduce the impact on adolescents' academic and social functions, and cut down the possibility of depression and anxiety disorder continuing to develop into adulthood.

Our research investigated the physical activities of the adolescents aged 15–17, and the results showed that with the age increase, the physical activity was decreasing, and it was negatively correlated to the anxiety emotions. In the late adolescence, the adolescents studied in the middle school or high school, and the schoolwork pressure became more significant with the age increase. It was very common to reduce or occupy PE class schedule, especially in senior high school. Physical education time is used for other courses closely related to higher education, which leads to a significant reduction in actual exercise time. In addition, the COVID-19 epidemic led to the social isolation and closure of public spaces, believed to reduce the possibility of sports. Young people take advantage of the time of online class and contact with computer, which further aggravates the lack of sports. A global survey shows that between the ages of 10 and 19, teenagers' exercise activity decreases by 7% a year [14]. However, one large number of longitudinal and experimental evidence suggested that the regular physical activities can bring positive mental health outcomes and provide a buffer for the disease. The short-term physical exercise can also improve the negative interference effect of the stressful events on the emotion. The physical exercise can significantly reduce the incidence of self-injury in patients with emotional disorders. The clinical meta-analysis showed that the exercise is an effective mean to prevent and treat the depression, anxiety and other unhealthy emotions, and the effect is more significant in the adolescents [15].

Therefore, due to the potential risk of mental disorders in late adolescence, which may become the basis of early adult onset, regular physical exercise can protect emotional health and cognitive function. It is necessary to intervene relevant laws and regulations and other supporting policies to promote the continuous and effective exercise in this group, which has important public health significance.

References

1. Saltz, S.B., et al.: Cyberbullying linked with depression, emotional abuse. Presented at American Psychiatric Association Annual Meeting, San Diego, 20–24 May 2017 (2017)
2. Schuch, F.B., Vancampfort, D., Firth, J., et al.: Physical activity and incident depression: a meta-analysis of prospective cohort studies. Am. J. Psychiatry **175**(7), 631–648 (2018)
3. Voss, C., Dean, P.H., Gardner, R.F., et al.: Validity and reliability of the Physical Activity Questionnaire for Children (PAQ-C) and Adolescents (PAQ-A) in individuals with congenital heart disease. PLoS One **12**(4), e0175806 (2017). https://doi.org/10.1371/journal.pone.017 5806
4. Wyszyńska, J., Matłosz, P., Podgórska-Bednarz, J., et al.: Adaptation and validation of the Physical Activity Questionnaire for Adolescents (PAQ-A) among Polish adolescents: cross-sectional study. BMJ Open **9**(11), e030567 (2019). https://doi.org/10.1136/bmjopen-2019-030567
5. Bervoets, L., Van Noten, C., Van Roosbroeck, S., et al.: Reliability and validity of the Dutch Physical Activity Questionnaires for Children (PAQ-C) and Adolescents (PAQ-A). Arch. Public Health **72**(1), 47 (2014). https://doi.org/10.1186/2049-3258-72-47
6. Martínez-Gómez, D., Martínez-de-Haro, V., Pozo, T., et al.: Reliability and validity of the PAQ-A questionnaire to assess physical activity in Spanish adolescents. Rev. Esp. Salud Publica **83**(3), 427–439 (2009). https://doi.org/10.1590/s1135-57272009000300008
7. Knight, R.G., Waal-Manning, H.J., Spears, G.F.: Some norms and reliability data for the State-Trait Anxiety Inventory and the Zung Self-Rating Depression scale. Br. J. Clin. Psychol. **22**(Pt 4), 245–249 (1983)
8. Samakouri, M., Bouhos, G., Kadoglou, M., et al.: Standardization of the Greek version of Zung's Self-rating Anxiety Scale (SAS). Psychiatriki **23**(3), 212–220 (2012)
9. Borschmann, R., Becker, D., Coffey, C., et al.: 20-year outcomes in adolescents who self-harm: a population-based cohort study. Lancet Child Adolesc. Health **1**(3), 195–202 (2017)
10. Naicker, K., Galambos, N.L., Zeng, Y., et al.: Social, demographic, and health outcomes in the 10 years following adolescent depression. J. Adolesc. Health **52**(5), 533–538 (2013)
11. Hawton, K., Saunders, K.E., O'Connor, R.C.: Self-harm and suicide in adolescents. Lancet **379**(9834), 2373–2382 (2012)
12. Jiang, H., Niu, L., Hahne, J., et al.: Changing of suicide rates in China, 2002–2015. J. Affect. Disord. **240**, 165–170 (2018)
13. Xu, Y., Wang, C., Shi, M.: Identifying Chinese adolescents with a high suicide attempt risk. Psychiatry Res. **269**, 474–480 (2018)
14. Beauchamp, M.R., Puterman, E., Lubans, D.R.: Physical inactivity and mental health in late adolescence. JAMA Psychiat. **75**(6), 543–544 (2018)
15. Helgadóttir, B., Hallgren, M., Ekblom, Ö.: Training fast or slow? Exercise for depression: a randomized controlled trial. Prev. Med. **91**, 123–131 (2016)

Remote Consultation Information Mobile Phone Intelligent Display System Under Augmented Reality and Human-Computer Interaction

Ying Bao$^{(\boxtimes)}$

The First Affiliated Hospital of Soochow University, Suzhou 215000, China
baoying2172@tom.com

Abstract. The current mobile phone intelligent display system lacks the matching operation of display mode before the display driving operation, which leads to the large average variance of display results. Therefore, this research designs a new intelligent display system of remote consultation information based on augmented reality and human-computer interaction technology. The research and design is mainly for software design. Firstly, two-dimensional display matching algorithm is applied to complete the matching operation of display mode. At the same time, Linux is used as the system framework to be compatible with different modules. In the system, augmented reality and UI human-computer interaction module are established to increase the system functions. GPRS technology is used as the carrier in remote transmission. Finally, a new display driven algorithm is designed. In order to verify the feasibility of the intelligent display system on mobile phone, a comparative experiment was designed to display the remote consultation information, and the power consumption and mean square deviation of different systems were analyzed. The experimental results show that the power consumption and mean square deviation of the system are low, which fully proves the feasibility of the system.

Keywords: GPRS technology · Augmented reality · Display drive · Human-computer interaction · Consultation information · Mobile phone display

1 Introduction

The rapid development of electronic technology, computer technology and communication technology has brought convenience to people's life and created new opportunities for the development of medical system [1–3]. The proposal of telemedicine improves the efficiency of medical resources, and mobile phone can be used as one of the ports of telemedicine. At the same time, it has a wide range of applications and has a high prospect.

The mobile phone display terminal has higher requirements for image clarity. However, the image quality of the current mobile phone display system is difficult to meet the requirements, and there are still major limitations [4, 5]. In the early display system, the

© ICST Institute for Computer Sciences, Social Informatics and Telecommunications Engineering 2021
Published by Springer Nature Switzerland AG 2021. All Rights Reserved
W. Fu et al. (Eds.): ICMTEL 2021, LNICST 388, pp. 338–348, 2021.
https://doi.org/10.1007/978-3-030-82565-2_28

single-chip microcomputer was usually used as the control chip of the display system at home and abroad, and the ARM embedded microprocessor was used as the control chip of the display system in the later period. The application of micro-processing technology has significantly improved the display quality of the display system, and can also realize more complex display driving operations. Therefore, the researchers used the CPLD algorithm for display drive calculations. However, as far as current research is concerned, researchers lack relevant considerations for display mode matching, which affects the results of driving calculations, and there is still room for improvement in image quality [6, 7].

Under the above background, this research designs a new remote consultation information mobile intelligent display system with the support of augmented reality and human-computer interaction technology, and verifies the application advantages of low power consumption and average variance through simulation experiments, which can enhance the effect of remote consultation information mobile intelligent display.

2 System Design

As this system is an intelligent display system applied to mobile phone, the software design is focused on.

2.1 Display Pattern Matching Algorithm

In the core calculation of the system in this paper, a two-dimensional display matching algorithm with a wide range of application scenarios is designed to perform matching operations on remote consultation displays under different conditions. First, the string is formalized. A string is defined as a sequence of characters on a limited character set. Suppose there are two strings T and P, the length of the string T is n, the length of the string P is m, where $m \leq n$, the string T is called the string to be matched or the text string, and the matched string P is Called a pattern string. If $0 \leq k \leq n - m$, the string should meet the following conditions:

$$T[k...k + m] = P[0...m - 1] \tag{1}$$

When the formula (1) is satisfied, the pattern string P is said to have an exact match in text T. the exact matching position is k. in a long string, a shorter string is found. In depth matching, BF algorithm is used to compare the first character $T[1]$ and $P[1]$ in text string T and pattern string P. If they are exactly the same, continue to compare the second characters $T[2]$ and $P[2]$ in the text string T and pattern string P until $T[M]$ and $P[M]$ are matched. In the case of mismatching, the characters in the text string T are moved and compared with the pattern string P until the matching result is obtained. At the same time, $T[k + 1...k + M] = P[1...M]$ is satisfied. If the above formula is satisfied, the matching is successful, otherwise it is the matching failure. The two-dimensional display string is obtained by matching algorithm.

2.2 Linux System Framework

In order to achieve multi-functional compatibility, the system framework adopts the embedded Linux system framework. This support module has many, at the same time the system compatibility is better, the running speed is high and has the good network performance [8]. Support for more processors, such as some mainframes and embedded systems, while improving the support for existing processors. The use of a preemptive kernel greatly improves the response speed of interactive operations. According to the embedded framework, the partition information of Nand Flash needs to be set up to facilitate the initialization of the system at startup. The Nand Flash partition setting code is shown in Fig. 1.

```
static struct mtd_partition smdk_default_nand_part[]={
[0]={
    .name=' bootloader",
    .size=SZ_128K+SZ_65K,
    .offset=0,
}
[1]={
    .neme=" parameter" ,
    .offset=SZ_128K+SZ_64K,
    .size=SZ 64K,
}
[2]={
    .name=" kernel"
    .offset=SZ_128K*2,
    .size+SZ_4M+(SZ_1M-SZ_128K*2)
},
```

Fig. 1. Code of NAND flash partition setting

After the system partition of the MTC is determined, the system partition is checked. Set S3C2410 in drivers/MTD/NAND/S3 c2410. C file_ nand_ init_ Chip - > of chip() function ecc.mode = NAND_ ECC_ Soft to NAND_ ECC_ None. The reason is that using mtdecc function in yaffs file system can easily cause the system to read wrong data.

2.3 Augmented Reality Driven Development

Drivers of different functions can be developed directly in the embedded Linux system [9]. During development, the automatic configuration and initialization subroutines must be executed first, which is responsible for detecting whether the hardware device to be driven exists and whether it can work normally [10]. If the device is normal, initialize the device and its related state. This part of the driver is only called once during initialization. Secondly, it serves the subroutine requested by I/O, which is also called the upper part of the driver. This part of the call is the result of a system call. When this part of the program is executed, the system still thinks that it belongs to the same process as the process that called sleep(), but changed from the user mode to the core mode, so functions related to the process operating environment can be called in it. Then implement interrupt operation to the subroutine.

In the Linux framework, the interrupt service subroutine of the device driver is not invoked directly from the interrupt vector table. Instead, the hardware interrupt is received by the Linux framework, and the interrupt service subroutine is called by the system. Interrupt process can be generated in any process to run the program, so when the interrupt service program is called, it can not rely on the state of any process, and can not call any function related to the process running environment.

Use Linux framework to transplant the open source visual processing library OpenCV to realize augmented reality. OpenCV provides basic structures such as arrays, sequences, matrices, trees, etc., as well as many advanced mathematical calculation functions such as differential equation solving, Fourier analysis, integral operations, special functions, as well as various image processing operations and target tracking, camera calibration, three-dimensional Reconstruction and other advanced vision functions. Use armv41-tools-2.95.2 cross-compiler to compile OpenCV during transplantation, and modify the source code according to C99 until the compilation is completed.

2.4   Remote Consultation Information Transmission

In the remote consultation information display system designed in this paper, GPRS technology is used as the carrier to improve the quality of information transmission. The structure of information received by mobile phone in this system is shown in Fig. 2.

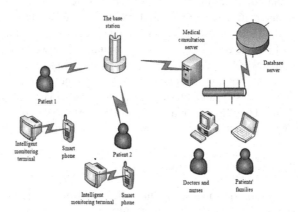

Fig. 2. Smart phone consultation information transmission architecture

In the transmission architecture, firstly, the patient data collected by the relevant intelligent monitoring equipment is used for transmission, including other forms of patient medical information. The data is transmitted to the base station, processed by the database server, and then sent to the mobile phone. After the above display data matching operation, the relevant display data is obtained.

2.5 UI Human-Computer Interaction Establishment

The design of mobile phone UI is relatively simple than that of computer, but it is an extension tool of computer Internet. Conceptually speaking, multi-channel interaction mode refers to the combination of two or more input and output modes, such as voice and video. Sometimes, due to the low input efficiency, the cognitive load of users will be increased during the operation. Therefore, the multi-channel interaction mode of handheld devices can improve the efficiency and naturalness of interaction.

For different types of interfaces, the usability elements are different, and the interaction characteristics are also different. For example, there are two significant differences between the physical user interface and the sound user interface, real and virtual. The combination of the two achieves effective integration and makes the interface of mobile phone products more usable. The interface design of the machine product needs to consider the product interface related to its use, and there should be no interactive "fault" phenomenon, which fundamentally solves the technical and operational obstacles of the product. The research on the usability of multi-channel user interface is to take the user as the core and pursue the natural interface of "human-machine harmony".

Multi channel user interface has the following basic characteristics: first, multiple sensory and effect channels; second, three-dimensional and directly manipulated interface; third, allowing imprecise interaction; fourth, mutual bidirectional interface; fifth, the implicit interaction. Therefore, it is necessary to ensure that the user interface can be changed at any time, so that the interaction channel is more diversified. Therefore, the development of multi-channel interface technology will improve the efficiency and naturalness of human-computer interaction to a certain extent.

The update of interactive technology and mobile phone interface technology has caused changes in the shape of the mobile phone interface, which cannot be changed if only the increase of mobile phone functions. As digital and networked homes become a reality, mobile phones enter people's living and working spaces in small and invisible forms. Driven by information technology, mobile phone products will be able to communicate better wirelessly, and interface systems will also The realization of multi-channel and multimedia intelligence and efficiency will further promote communication and exchange between people.

2.6 High Quality Display Driver Algorithm

The display-driven algorithm flow used in this article is shown in Fig. 3.

First, the input image transmitted by remote information is converted from the actual RGB space to the YUV space, where Y represents brightness information, and U and V represent color information. Then calculate the average brightness Y_{av} and the maximum brightness Y_{max}. The key of this algorithm is to calculate the key two straight lines, and generate a new brightness component Y' according to the model. Finally, the YUV space is converted to the RGB space to obtain the processed image.

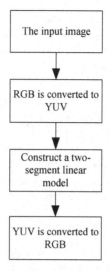

Fig. 3. Algorithm flow chart

Because the power consumption is limited by using two linear operations, only one operation is needed, and the complexity of hardware is reduced. The processing speed is improved, which makes the algorithm suitable for real-time scene processing. In this algorithm, the high brightness part of the image details are processed to limit the power consumption, and the low brightness part is reserved. Therefore, the visual effect of the image is improved while the power consumption is limited. In YUV space, luminance component and chroma component are separated. Therefore, there is no mutual confusion and influence between brightness and chroma. In the process of low-power image processing, the brightness information should and should only be changed, and the chroma information should not be changed. On the other hand, the power consumption can be reduced by processing y channel. The YUV space converted by RGB is as follows:

$$\begin{cases} Y = 0.257R + 0.504G + 0.098B + 16 \\ U = -0.148R - 0.291G + 0.439B + 128 \\ V = 0.439 - 0.368G - 0.071B + 128 \end{cases} \quad (2)$$

In formula (2), R, G, and B represent the gray levels of the three primary color channels, Y represents the luminance component, and U and V represent the chrominance component. In the process of low-power high-quality image processing, Y_{av} is an important parameter. In order to improve the visual effect of the processed image, it is not necessary to process all the pixel units in the original image. For example, low brightness part of the image details will not lead to an increase in power consumption. If this part of image details are not processed, the visual effect of this part is maintained. Therefore, the algorithm proposed in this paper does not deal with low brightness partial pixel cells. However, the key point is to find a watershed brightness. The pixel unit with brightness lower than the brightness is not processed, and the pixel unit with brightness higher than the brightness is processed with low power consumption. If the watershed brightness is too high, the visual effect of the processed image is good and the power consumption is reduced. Otherwise, the visual effect becomes worse and the power consumption limitation is increased. Through a lot of research, Y_{av} is selected as the watershed brightness value, as shown in the following formula:

$$Y_{av} = \frac{1}{W \times H} \sum_{i=0}^{W-1} \sum_{j=0}^{H-1} Y(i,j) \qquad (3)$$

In formula (3), W represents the horizontal resolution of the image, H represents the vertical resolution, $Y(i,j)$ represents the brightness value of the pixel unit in the i column and the j row, and Y_{av} represents the average brightness of the original image. Under the two-section straight line theory, the new brightness Y' obtained is as follows:

$$Y' = Y - Y_{offset} \qquad (4)$$

In formula (4), Y_{offset} represents the intermediate value between Y_{av} and Y_{max}. The other two components U and V in YUV space remain unchanged, and YUV is transformed into RGB, The results are as follows:

$$\begin{cases} R' = 1.164\left(Y' - 16\right) + 1.596(V - 128) \\ G' = 1.164\left(Y' - 16\right) - 0.813(V - 128) - 0.391(U - 128) \\ B' = 1.164\left(Y' - 16\right) + 2.018(U - 128) \end{cases} \qquad (5)$$

At this point, the design of the display drive operation of the mobile phone is completed.

3   Analysis of Experimental Demonstration

In order to verify the feasibility of the mobile phone intelligent display system designed in this paper, remote consultation application is added to the mobile phone used in this paper, and then the patient information in a hospital is displayed by this system, the traditional consultation information mobile phone intelligent display system based on virtual reality, and the consultation information mobile phone intelligent display system based on ZigBee Results the advantages and disadvantages of different systems were judged.

3.1   Experimental Mobile Terminal

The mobile phone equipped with intelligent display system of mobile phone is selected as honor Play4t, the main screen size of the mobile phone is 6.39 in., the main screen resolution is 1560×720 pixels, the rear camera is 48 million pixels + 2 million pixels, the front camera is 8 million pixels, the electromagnetic capacity is 4000 MAH, the battery type is non removable battery, the number of cores of the mobile phone is 8 cores, the CPU model is hyskirin 710A, the CPU frequency is 2.0GHz, the mobile phone memory is 6GB, and the mobile phone carrying system is an droid 10.

3.2 Experimental Evaluation Method

In this experiment, we compare the advantages and disadvantages between this system and the traditional system mainly by comparing the power consumption and the mean square error of the display. The calculation method of power consumption PD is as follows:

$$PD = (1/N) \cdot \sum_{i=0}^{W} \sum_{j=0}^{H} \left[\omega_r R^2(i,j) + \omega_g G^2(i,j) + \omega_b B^2(i,j) \right] \qquad (6)$$

In formula (6), N represents the number of displayed image pixels, W represents the horizontal resolution of the image, H represents the vertical resolution of the image, $R(i,j)$, $G(i,j)$ and $B(i,j)$ represent the gray scale of pixel units in column i and row j in channel R, G and B respectively, and ω_r, ω_g and ω_b represent the power consumption coefficients in each channel. The mean square error MSE is calculated as follows:

$$MSE = \frac{1}{W \times H} \sum_{i=0}^{W} \sum_{j=0}^{H} sqrt \left[R^{'}(i,j) - R(i,j) \right]^2$$
$$+ \left[G^{'}(i,j) - G(i,j) \right]^2 + \left[B^{'}(i,j) - B(i,j) \right]^2 \qquad (7)$$

In formula (7), $R^{'}(i,j)$, $G^{'}(i,j)$, $B^{'}(i,j)$ represents the gray levels of pixel units in the i column and j row of channels R, G, and B in the original image. The smaller the MSE, the smaller the difference between the image displayed in the mobile phone and the image of the transmission source, and the better the visual effect.

3.3 Experimental Result

In the experiment, the patient's relevant diagnostic information is sent remotely and sent to the intelligent display system on the mobile phone, and the corresponding image is obtained. Figure 4 shows the ECG image of the patient obtained in this system.

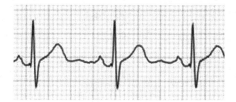

Fig. 4. Patient ECG image

The image in Fig. 4 is clear and can clearly reflect the patient's ECG image information, and the feedback to the remote consultation information is more obvious. The patient's X-ray diagnosis information is shown in Fig. 5.

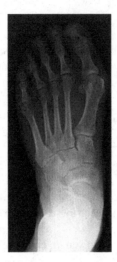

Fig. 5. X-ray images of patients

Figure 5 shows the patient's bone and joint clearly, and Figs. 4 and 5 prove that the mobile phone intelligent display system designed in this paper can meet the display of remote consultation information. The comparison results of power consumption between this system and traditional system in displaying the same sample information are shown in Table 1.

Table 1. System display power consumption

Sample number	System 1 power consumption (mW)	System 2 power consumption (mW)	System 3 power consumption (mW)
Sample No.1	181.71	215.64	238.71
Sample No.2	192.15	241.33	231.51
Sample No.3	181.43	211.56	246.75
Sample No.4	182.51	246.35	244.81
Sample No.5	218.73	399.34	359.77
Sample No.6	244.59	481.21	505.33
Sample No.7	247.64	501.41	521.79
Sample No.8	241.14	511.15	504.21

In Table 1, system 1 is the intelligent display system designed in this paper, system 2 is the traditional consultation information mobile intelligent display system based on virtual reality, and system 3 is the traditional consultation information mobile intelligent display system based on ZigBee. Among the samples used, samples 1–4 are ECG images, sample 5 is X-ray examination images of patients, and samples 6–8 are MRI images of patients. In Table 1, the smart display system in this article consumes less power under the same sample.

The mean square error values of different systems in the display are shown in Table 2.

Table 2. Average error of system display image

Sample number	System 1 power consumption MSE	System 2 power consumption MSE	System 3 power consumption MSE
Sample No.1	2.7	2.73	2.75
Sample No.2	2.34	2.41	2.44
Sample No.3	2.47	2.55	2.53
Sample No.4	2.48	2.49	2.52
Sample No.5	4.51	7.45	8.69
Sample No.6	6.11	10.34	12.15
Sample No.7	6.52	12.11	15.61
Sample No.8	6.66	11.58	15.74

As can be seen in Table 2, when displaying ECG images of patients, the difference of mean square error among the three systems is not big. In the subsequent display of X-ray examination and nuclear magnetic resonance imaging, the mean square error of system two and system three has great changes, and the mean square error of system one has obvious advantages over system two and system three The experiment proves that the intelligent display system of remote consultation information mobile terminal designed in this paper is feasible.

The reason for this result is that this system uses augmented reality and human-computer interaction technology to increase the interactive functionality of the system, and uses Linux as the system framework to be compatible with different modules, and GPRS technology as the driver carrier, so as to fundamentally reduce the mean square error of the display results.

4 Conclusion

Based on augmented reality and human-computer interaction technology, a new mobile intelligent display system for remote consultation information is designed. Experiments show that the system reduces the power consumption of display and improves the quality of display image. However, the designed system is only used in mobile phones under Android operating system, and it does not support mobile phones with other operating systems. Future research will try to improve the compatibility of the system.

References

1. Nusbaum, N.J., Peratrovich, J.: Some thoughts on implementing remote telehealth. South. Med. J. **111**(9), 542–543 (2018)
2. Navneet, A., Ashish, S., Premlal, M.V., Puneet, S.: Telemedicine and virtual consultation: the Indian perspective. Natl Med. J. India **31**(4), 245–218 (2018)
3. Graziane, J.A., Gopalan, P., Cahalane, J.: Telepsychiatry consultation for medical and surgical inpatient units. Psychosomatics **59**(1), 62–66 (2018)
4. Pancer, Z., Moore, M., Wenham, J.T., Burridge, M.: The challenge of generalist care in remote Australia: beyond aeromedical retrieval. Aust. J. Rural Health. **26**(3), 188–193 (2018)
5. Whetten, J., van der Goes, D.N., Tran, H., Moffett, M., et al.: Cost-effectiveness of access to critical cerebral emergency support services (ACCESS): a neuro-emergent telemedicine consultation program. J. Med. Econ. **21**(4), 398–405 (2018)
6. Tuo, J., Sun, W., Peng, D.: Research on multi-point temperature detection and time display system. IOP Conf. Ser.: Mater. Sci. Eng. **452**(4), 102–116 (2018)
7. Liu, S., Lu, M., Li, H., et al.: Prediction of gene expression patterns with generalized linear regression model. Front. Genet. **15**(10), 120 (2019)
8. Fu, W., Liu, S., Gautam, S.: Optimization of big data scheduling in social networks. Entropy **21**(9), 902–918 (2019)
9. Liu, S., Li, Z., Zhang, Y.D., et al.: Introduction of key problems in long distance learning and training. Mobile Networks Appl. **24**(1), 1–4 (2019)
10. Xu, M.C., Li, C.L., Lei, Z.C.: Wide color gamut liquid crystal display system Chin. J. Liq. Cryst. Displays **10**(16), 606–614 (2018)

Design of Real Information Collection Model of Physical Fitness for the Elderly Based on Internet of Things Technology

Wei-Ping Cao[1]([⊠]) and Yu-Shuo Tan[2]

[1] West Normal University Physical Culture Institute, Chengdu 637099, China
[2] Shijiazhuang Posts and Telecommunications Technical College, Shijiazhuang 050021, China

Abstract. In order to optimize the efficiency of traditional physical information collection, this research designed a physical fitness information collection model for the elderly based on the Internet of Things technology. In the Internet of Things environment, select the collection node and install sensor equipment, and use the Internet of Things technology to drive the collection program. From the three aspects of human body structure, physical fitness health parameters and fitness action posture, the collection content of physical fitness information for the elderly is determined. Then call the sensor equipment, with the support of the Internet of Things technology, through the analog-to-digital conversion and filter storage to obtain the real-state information collection results. Through comparison with traditional collection methods, it is found that the collection accuracy of the model in this paper is higher and the collection time required is shorter, so the collection efficiency of the model in this paper has been effectively improved.

Keywords: Internet of Things technology · Sports fitness · Real state information · Information collection · Sensor equipment

1 Introduction

Physical fitness highlights the physical exercise as the main means of attention to people's physical growth and development and physical development. Through the selection and study of fitness and sports, we can cultivate people's sports fitness hobbies and sports expertise, so as to obtain scientific fitness methods, develop a civilized and healthy lifestyle, and make people have the adaptability to adhere to physical fitness in different environments. The most important role of physical exercise is to improve people's health in an all-round way. The specific performance is as follows: prevent cardiovascular disease, improve the function of respiratory system, improve the function of digestive system, reduce the risk of diabetes and prevent bone fracture. With the promotion of national fitness fever, the audience group of sports fitness is gradually expanding, and the elderly also join the ranks of sports fitness.

Unlike young people, the physique and body organs of the elderly are gradually failing, and the exercise intensity they can withstand is limited to a certain extent. In

W. Fu et al. (Eds.): ICMTEL 2021, LNICST 388, pp. 349–361, 2021.
https://doi.org/10.1007/978-3-030-82565-2_29

order to avoid a series of physical problems caused by improper exercise or excessive exercise intensity for the elderly during physical fitness exercise, it is necessary to use high-tech means to collect and monitor physical fitness information.

Data acquisition refers to the automatic acquisition of non electric quantity or electric quantity signal from analog and digital units to be tested, such as sensors and other devices to be tested, and then sent to the upper computer for analysis and processing. Most of the collected data are instantaneous values, that is, a characteristic value in a certain period of time.

According to the relevant research results at home and abroad, the typical data acquisition methods include metadata based data acquisition method, compressed sensing based data acquisition method and LabVIEW based data acquisition method [1, 2]. However, there is a problem of low collection efficiency when the traditional information collection methods are applied to the real state information collection of the elderly sports fitness. Therefore, based on the traditional methods, this paper applies the Internet of things technology.

The Internet of Things technology is the third revolution in the information technology industry. The Internet of Things refers to the connection of any object to the network through information sensing equipment according to an agreed protocol, and the object exchanges and communicates through information media to realize intelligent identification, positioning, tracking, supervision and other functions. There are two key technologies in IoT applications, namely sensor technology and embedded technology. In this study, the Internet of things technology is applied to the elderly sports fitness real information collection, to provide hardware equipment and technical support for data collection, in order to improve the efficiency of elderly sports fitness real information collection. The experimental verification shows that the acquisition model designed in this study has higher accuracy and shorter acquisition time, which fully proves that the model has higher application advantages.

2 Design of Information Collection Model of Physical Fitness for the Elderly

First select the appropriate development technology based on the understanding of the model design principles, then clarify the functions of the entire system, and finally determine the overall process plan of the system. The physical fitness information collection model for the elderly should follow the principles of reliability, advancement, operability and maintenance, integrity and openness [3]. Under the above-mentioned design principles, the design and development of the model are realized from multiple aspects such as signal sensing, analog-to-digital conversion and data processing. The sequence diagram of the data acquisition program is shown in Fig. 1.

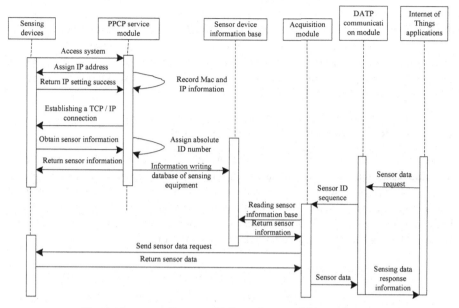

Fig. 1. Sequence diagram of information acquisition program

2.1 Build an IoT Network Environment

Internet of things is a network based on the Internet, traditional telecommunication network and other information carriers, which enables all the ordinary objects that can perform independent functions to realize interconnection and interworking. According to the location of each measurement point in the Internet of things, the structure of IOT network can be divided into three topologies: star, tree and net. The specific results are shown in Fig. 2.

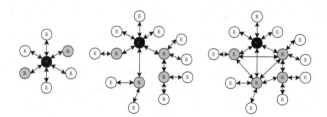

Fig. 2. Topological structure diagram of IoT network

In Fig. 2, C is the coordinator, R is the router, and E is the terminal device. As can be seen from Fig. 2, the star structure is a single hop network composed of a coordinator and multiple terminal devices. There is only communication between the coordinator and each terminal device, and the communication between each terminal device is forwarded by the coordinator. The tree structure is composed of a coordinator and multiple star structures. In addition to point-to-point direct communication between devices and parent or child nodes, other devices can only complete message transmission through tree routing [4]. However, the mesh structure is based on tree network. The difference is that the network structure allows all nodes with routing function to be directly interconnected. The routing table in the router cooperates to realize the network routing of messages, which reduces the message delay at the cost of more storage space and enhances the reliability.

2.2   Install Real Information Collection Equipment

Before installing the real-state information acquisition equipment, it is necessary to determine the basic content of the real-state information collection and select the installation node of the collection device. The movement of human body comes from the movement of bones, so the two-dimensional stick human body model is selected to build the human body structure. A total of 13 line segments and 15 joint points are used to represent these features. The names of the marked points are shown in Fig. 3.

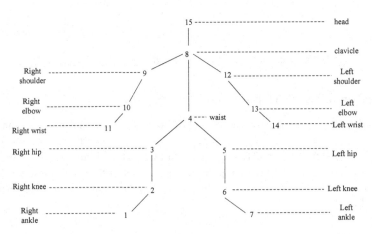

Fig. 3. Two-dimensional stick-shaped human body structure diagram

Location of the marking points corresponding to the human body is shown in Fig. 4.

Through the data characteristics of each human body structure sports fitness movement, determine the type of corresponding node installation acquisition equipment and the corresponding data collection content [5]. Through the analysis, it is found that the acquisition equipment to be installed includes acceleration collector, temperature collector, pressure collector, health data collector, etc. The overall design of acquisition node is shown in Fig. 5.

Fig. 4. Human position map corresponding to the installation node of the acquisition device

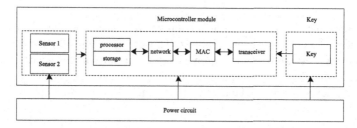

Fig. 5. Block diagram of acquisition node design

In Fig. 5, the sensor module consists of sensor and peripheral circuit. The sensor collects analog signal and converts it into digital signal through on-chip A/D conversion circuit, and the single-chip microcomputer can read the data. The microcontroller module reads the data and sends it out by radio frequency, using the protocol specifications of application layer, MAC layer, network layer and physical layer, and the data is transmitted in the specified format; the key is mainly responsible for function selection; the power supply circuit supplies power to the node.

Design a three-axis acceleration sensor circuit, as shown in Fig. 6.

Since the selected chips belong to the same series of products, the chip packaging and peripheral circuits can be used in common. As an analog acceleration sensor, the voltage signals of the three axes output in the circuit need to be filtered by capacitors C16, C18, C19 and then input to the MCU AD conversion module. The ACC_X output from pin 12 is connected to the AD of the MCU STM32. The PC0 pin of the conversion module, the ACC_YY output from pin 10 is connected to the PC1 pin of the MCU, and the ACC_Z output from the pin 8 is connected to the PC2 pin of the MCU. The reference voltage of the AD conversion module of MCUSTM32 is the regulated voltage of 3.3 V [6]. The capacitor C10 in the circuit is a de-pro-capacitor, and its function is to ensure the stability of the chip's supply voltage.

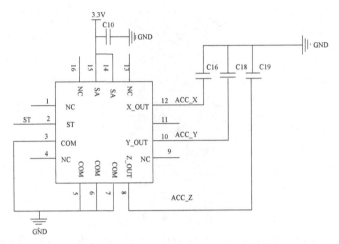

Fig. 6. Circuit diagram of acceleration sensor

The temperature sensor uses infrared temperature measurement technology. Due to the movement of charged particles, all objects whose temperature is higher than absolute zero continuously emit infrared radiation energy to the surrounding space. The energy wavelength is mainly concentrated in the 0.6–15 um band. The relationship between the radiation energy density and temperature is in accordance with Stephen Boltzmann radiation law

$$E = \varepsilon\sigma T^2 \tag{1}$$

In the formula, E is the total radiant energy of an object with a temperature of T, σ is the Stephen Boltzmann constant, and ε is the emissivity. As long as the temperature and emissivity of the object are known, the radiant power emitted by it can be calculated. Conversely, if the radiant power of the object is measured, the temperature of the object can be determined. The output signal of the infrared sensor is the result of the combined effect of the measured target temperature T_o and the sensor's own temperature T_a:

$$V_{ir}(T_a, T_o) = A(T_o - T_a) \tag{2}$$

Where the unit of temperature is Kelvin and A is the instrument constant, which is related to the design structure of the sensor. In the same way, the operation principle and structure of other sensors can be designed.

2.3 Use IoT Technology to Drive the Acquisition Program

When the sensor equipment is installed, the microcontroller is used to realize the call control of multiple sensors and the driving of acquisition program. Microcontroller is the core of acquisition node and collection node, which is responsible for sensor parameter configuration, protocol program initialization, operation, data reading and sending [7]. In the collection node, it is responsible for the initialization and operation of protocol program, the establishment and binding of network, and the reception of data. The received data is processed and sent to PC serial port debugging software through serial port. The connection between the sensor and the microcontroller structure is shown in Table 1.

Table 1. Comparison table of acquisition sensor and microcontroller interface

Sensor number	Name of external sensor and power supply	Microcontroller pin
1	BUTTON1	P0.1
2	ADXL_MISO	P0.2
3	ADXL_MOSI	P0.3
4	ADXL_CSN	P0.4
5	ADXL_SCLK	P0.5
6	INT1	P0.6
7	TMP_DATA	P0.7
8	INT2	P2.0
9	LED1	P1.0
10	LED2	P1.1
11	TMP_SCK	P1.2
12	TMP_CS	P1.3
13	DEBUG_CSN	P1.4
14	DEBUG_SCLK	P1.5
15	DEBUG_MOSI	P1.6
16	DEBUG_MISO	P1.7
17	DEBUG_DD	P2.1
18	DEBUG_DC	P2.2
19	RESET	RESET_N

2.4 Determine the Content of Physical Fitness Information Collection for the Elderly

2.4.1 Body Structure Information

Human motion analysis pays attention to the kinematics and dynamics information of the human joints, and has no requirements for the appearance of the human body. Therefore, a simple and efficient bone model can meet the needs. The human body can be divided into 14 parts: head, left upper arm, left forearm, left hand, right upper arm, right forearm, right hand, torso, left thigh, left calf, left foot, right thigh, right calf and right foot. Each part of the human body can be regarded as a rigid body, and each rigid body is connected by joint points. According to the position of the connection point, it can be divided into 14 joints: neck, left wrist, left elbow, left shoulder, right wrist, right elbow, right shoulder, waist, left Marrow, left knee, left heel, right marrow, right knee and right knee joints. The most basic movement of each joint is the rotational movement around the x, y and z axes, which are called rolling, pitching and yaw, respectively. There are 34 degrees of freedom in rotation. In order to simplify the motion of human joints, the following conventions are made for the motion analysis of each joint: the rotation of the ankle joint in three directions only analyzes the pitch motion; the hip joint and the shoulder joint have three degrees of freedom, but these two joints are biased during walking and running. The pendulum direction movement is small, so only the rolling and pitching movement is analyzed; the rotation movement of the wrist joint is not analyzed [8]. However, due to differences in genes and growth environments, there will be subtle differences in human body structure. Therefore, in the process of human body data collection, specific collections are mainly based on the size of each joint and the length of bones.

2.4.2 Sports Fitness Health Information

The physical health information of the elderly includes body temperature information, pulse information, heart rate information, blood oxygen information, ECG information and blood pressure information. The temperature information is mainly collected from the temperature sensor to read and convert the data. The conversion formula between the read-out data and the temperature information is as follows:

$$T = (\text{Data H: Data L}) \times 0.02 \times 273.15 \tag{3}$$

In the formula (3), Data H: Data L is the result of the read data. Pulse is the arterial pulse. In each cardiac cycle, the cyclic expansion and return of arterial vessels due to the alternation of ventricular contraction and relaxation is called pulse, and pulse is the fluctuation caused by heart contraction, so under normal circumstances, the pulse is exactly the same as the heart rate. A typical pulse waveform is shown in Fig. 7.

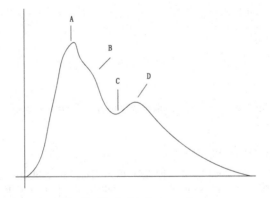

Fig. 7. Typical pulse waveform

In Fig. 7, a, B, C and d represent the main wave, tidal wave, and the trough and peak of the heavy pulse respectively, which constitute a pulse wave period. The photoelectric sensor is based on Lambert Beer law. According to Lambert Beer law, when a beam of monochromatic light passes through a uniform non scattering light absorbing material vertically, the absorptivity of the absorbing material for a certain monochromatic light is directly proportional to its concentration. The formula of this relationship is expressed as follows:

$$I = I_0 e^{-\mu CL} \tag{4}$$

In the formula (4), I and I_0 are the intensity of the emitted light and the incident light respectively, μ is the light absorption coefficient of the medium, C is the solution concentration, and L is the optical path length. Reading the reading in the photoelectric sensor can get the result of the pulse data collection during the physical exercise of the elderly. In addition, the heart rate information is collected using the electrocardiogram method, which extracts the heart rate from the electrocardiogram signal.

In order to measure ECG signal, it is necessary to place signal electrodes and reference electrodes at different positions on the human body surface, which are usually placed on both sides of the chest, left and right hand or hands and feet. The electrode is connected with the positive and negative electrodes of the electrocardiograph through the lead wire, and the heart rate value is obtained from the lead ECG. In the same way, we can get the results of sports fitness health information collection according to the corresponding sensor equipment.

2.4.3 Sports Fitness Action Posture Information

According to the guide electrode and placement position used in the measurement, the detected EMG signal can be divided into needle electrode EMG signal and surface electrode EMG signal. The former uses needle electrode as the guide electrode and inserts it into the muscle., The potential information detected directly in the vicinity of the active muscle fiber, the latter is based on the surface electrode as the guiding electrode, and the electrical activity of the muscle measured when it is placed on the skin surface is integrated on the detection surface [9]. Using IoT sensor equipment combined with the muscle power of the elderly in the physical fitness process, the electrical signals of each joint, sole and skin are obtained, and the current physical fitness strength and posture are analyzed.

2.4.4 Analog Signal Conversion

The process of analog-to-digital conversion is the process of analog signal acquisition, which includes three basic steps: sampling, quantization and coding. The sample data set is composed of continuous analog signals in time according to a certain time interval, and it is transformed into discrete signals in time angle. This process is called signal sampling. The value of the continuous signal at any time is known, but after sampling, in addition to the value of the sampling time, other signals are lost. The larger the sampling period, the more serious the loss of information. Therefore, in actual data collection, a certain sampling frequency must be guaranteed [10]. Quantization is a process of approximating analog quantities with finite word length digital quantities, that is, the process of digitizing analog quantities. Encoding is to convert the quantized number into binary digits for the computer to receive and process. After the three-step conversion, the analog signal becomes a digital signal that is discrete in time and quantized in amplitude. These three steps are all done by the A/D converter. Figure 8 is a schematic diagram of signal analog-to-digital conversion.

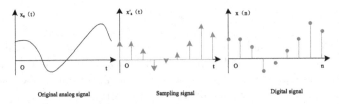

Original analog signal   Sampling signal   Digital signal

Fig. 8. Schematic diagram of analog to digital signal conversion

2.5   Real-State Information Collection, Transmission and Filtering Storage

The physical fitness information data of the elderly collected by the sensor device is uploaded using the Internet of things technology. When uploading, the MAC address of the device is carried. After receiving the data, first judge whether the main switch of the data point storage state of the device is on according to the MAC address of the device. If it is, the value of each key in a frame of JSON data is extracted, Determine whether its storage state is true. If it is true, continue to judge whether the data type of the data is the same as that stored in the database. Only when the above three conditions are met can the data be stored.

3   Comparative Experiment Analysis

Based on the Internet of things technology, the real-time information collection model of the elderly sports fitness is established. Through the steps of establishing ZigBee network, collecting and analyzing the sensor measurement data, the data is finally sent to the computer through the serial port to display, which can make the user conveniently observe in real time. In this process, we should set up serial assistant, connect sensor and acquisition board, host computer coordinator and PC. PC can output the address of terminal node, collected temperature, pulse, acceleration information and analyze the result through serial port.

Figure 9 shows the actual collection results of sports fitness acceleration information for the elderly under this model.

A total of 10 elderly people were selected as the research objects in the experiment. The same test object was measured five times, and the average value was obtained as the information collection result of the object. In order to form an experimental contrast. Using professional data measurement equipment to measure the real-time sports data of physical fitness, and taking it as the control standard of the collection results. In addition, the traditional information collection method is also set as the comparison method in

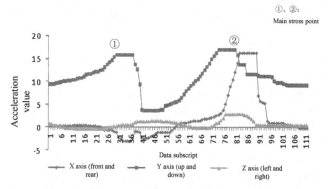

Fig. 9. Real state acquisition results of acceleration information of sports fitness

the experiment. After the operation of the collection model and the comparison with the standard data, the test and comparison results about the collection accuracy are shown in Table 2.

Table 2. Comparison results of acquisition accuracy test

Sample number		1	2	3	4	5
Standard data	Temperature (K)	35.9	35.8	35.2	36.1	35.9
	Pulse (beats/min)	120	111	116	108	112
	Acceleration (m^2/s)	16	22	14	21	17
Traditional models collect data	Temperature (K)	35.6	35.7	35.1	35.9	35.7
	Pulse (beats/min)	118	109	114	106	111
	Acceleration (m^2/s)	15	19	13	18	16
Data acquisition of the model in this paper	Temperature (K)	35.9	35.8	35.2	36.0	35.9
	Pulse (beats/min)	120	110	115	108	112
	Acceleration (m^2/s)	16	21	15	21	17
Sample number		6	7	8	9	10
Standard data	Temperature (K)	36.3	36.5	36.0	36.1	36.6
	Pulse (beats/min)	117	121	115	105	113
	Acceleration (m^2/s)	19	21	20	16	19
Traditional models collect data	Temperature (K)	35.9	36.1	35.5	35.8	36.2
	Pulse (beats/min)	120	118	117	101	110
	Acceleration (m^2/s)	17	19	21	14	16
Data acquisition of the model in this paper	Temperature (K)	36.3	36.5	36.0	36.1	36.6
	Pulse (beats/min)	116	120	115	105	113
	Acceleration (m^2/s)	19	21	19	16	18

It can be seen from the data in Table 2 that the data collection results obtained by the model in this paper are closer to the standard data, that is, the accuracy of the design model is higher. In addition, in the operating environment of the model, the start and end time of the collection program is called to obtain the time consumption of physical fitness information collection. After data calculation and comparison, it is found that the time cost of the model in this paper is less. Comprehensive time-consuming and collection accuracy test results show that the information collection efficiency of the physical fitness information collection model for the elderly based on the Internet of Things technology has improved.

To sum up, the real information collection model of the elderly sports fitness based on the Internet of things technology designed in this paper can not only accurately obtain the health information and movement posture information of the elderly in the process of exercise, but also greatly improve the collection efficiency.

4 Conclusion

This study designed a real information collection model of the elderly sports fitness based on the Internet of things technology, which can accurately obtain the health information and movement posture information of the elderly in the process of exercise, and the collection efficiency has been improved, and the real information collection function of the elderly sports fitness has been effectively realized. When the model is applied to the motion monitoring of the elderly, the alarm can be raised according to the results. In the future research, we can make further intelligent analysis of the elderly fitness data combined with medical knowledge, so as to customize more perfect PC program and mobile phone program, and further improve the effectiveness and applicability of the collection model.

References

1. Shiraishi, M., Ashiya, H., Konno, A., et al.: Development of real-time collection, integration, and sharing technology for infrastructure damage information. J. Disaster Res. **14**(2), 333–347 (2019)
2. Sun, P., Tian, Z., Wang, Z., et al.: PRSS: a prejudiced random sensing strategy for energy-efficient information collection in the Internet of Things. IEEE Internet Things J. **6**(2), 2717–2728 (2019)
3. Brusseau, E., Bernard, A., Meynier, C., et al.: Specific ultrasound data acquisition for tissue motion and strain estimation: initial results. Ultrasound Med. Biol. **17**(4), 859–867 (2018)
4. Lukyanenko, R., Parsons, J., Wiersma, Y.F., et al.: Expecting the unexpected: effects of data collection design choices on the quality of crowdsourced user-generated content. MIS Q. **43**(2), 623–647 (2019)
5. Guo, J., Yang, L., Bie, R., et al.: An XGBoost-based physical fitness evaluation model using advanced feature selection and Bayesian hyper-parameter optimization for wearable running monitoring. Comput. Netw. **151**(14), 166–180 (2019)
6. Li, X., Pak, C., Bi, K.: Analysis of the development trends and innovation characteristics of Internet of Things technology – based on patentometrics and bibliometrics. Technol. Anal. Strat. Manag. **32**(4), 1–15 (2019)

7. Liu, S., Li, Z.J., Zhang, Y.D., et al.: Introduction of key problems in long-distance learning and training. Mob. Netw. Appl. **24**(1), 1–4 (2019)
8. Liu, S., Lu, M.Y., Li, H.S., et al.: Prediction of gene expression patterns with generalized linear regression model. Front. Genet. **10**, 120 (2019)
9. Fu, W.N., Liu, S., Srivastava, G.: Optimization of big data scheduling in social networks. Entropy **21**(9), 902–918 (2019)
10. Zhou, C., Luo, H., Fang, W., et al.: Cyber-physical-system-based safety monitoring for blind hoisting with the internet of things: a case study. Autom. Constr. **97**(1), 138–150 (2019)

Track and Field Head Posture Error Correction System Based on Deep Reinforcement Learning

Liu Er-wei[✉]

School of Road Bridge and Architecture, Chongqing Vocational College of Transportation, Chongqing 402247, China

Abstract. The problem that track and field athletes generally have non-standard postures in their playing actions, a track and field head posture error correction system based on deep reinforcement learning is designed. By optimizing the system configuration, improving the recognition accuracy, using deep reinforcement learning technology to obtain 3D deep dynamic image data of track and field sports, converting the data into quaternion format, storing the data file in VBH format, and shaping the data through deep reinforcement learning technology a dynamic three-dimensional model is used to judge whether the track and field posture is standard using the Euclidean distance comparison method. Using the powerful learning ability of deep reinforcement learning, a series of non-linear operations are performed on the input face image, the abstract features in the image are extracted layer by layer, and then the extracted features are used for classification and recognition and error correction. Finally, through actual research, the standardization of the track and field head attitude error correction system based on deep reinforcement learning is proved. The experimental results show that this method effectively improves the accuracy of attitude estimation.

Keywords: Deep strong chemistry · Track and field · Head posture · Error correction

1 Introduction

In track and field competition, the standard posture of track and field athletes not only determines the stable play of track and field ability, but also determines the probability of injury of track and field athletes. The traditional track and field sports posture can only rely on the naked eye of the coach to correct it, but in most cases, a coach is facing a group of track and field players, so that the wrong posture of the team members cannot be corrected in time, so that most of the track and field athletes generally have non-standard movement posture [1, 2]. Therefore, it is proposed to combine the dynamic three-dimensional model with track and field teaching to reduce the pressure of coach teaching and promote the standardization of track and field sports posture. Two problems need to be solved in practical application of head pose estimation: to solve the influence of illumination, occlusion, background and other factors on the recognition accuracy,

W. Fu et al. (Eds.): ICMTEL 2021, LNICST 388, pp. 362–372, 2021.
https://doi.org/10.1007/978-3-030-82565-2_30

simplify the calculation steps, and improve the speed and accuracy of the system. As deep reinforcement learning has achieved rich results in the field of image processing, and has mature applications in the field of character recognition, face recognition and so on. Therefore, it has important research value to solve the problems of head posture in practical application [2]. In traditional methods, neural network is used to design track and field head posture error correction system and deep learning is used to design track and field head posture error correction system. However, these two systems have the problem of non-standard play posture. In order to solve this problem, this paper proposes a head posture estimation method based on deep reinforcement learning, and applies this method to the track and field head posture error correction system. This method has the following two advantages: the designed deep reinforcement learning structure uses convolution kernels of different scales to extract features from the original face image, which enriches the image feature expression while retaining the original image information, and better Constructing the corresponding relationship model between face pose and head pose has good robustness to interference factors such as illumination and occlusion. The designed deep reinforcement learning structure can effectively reduce the cost of system calculations, making the system more time-sensitive and accurate.

2 Head Posture Error Correction System in Track and Field

2.1 Hardware Configuration Optimization of Head Posture Error Correction System in Track and Field

In the process of designing the track and field head posture error correction system, it is necessary to consider the head posture characteristics of human body for multi-path recognition, which mainly involves the four fields of track and field head pose image feature analysis, processing, feature extraction and pattern recognition. The head posture image of track and field is a local representation method of human motion, which is accumulated from the first frame of head posture image of track and field to the current frame of the motion video sequence, which covers the specific area of the head posture image of the whole track and field, which is the area where the movement occurs. The specific feature mining process of head posture error in track and field is shown in the Fig. 1 below.

Before head posture feature detection in track and field, the acquired image information needs to be preprocessed to filter the noise and provide accurate data for subsequent recognition [3]. The step of detecting human head posture features in track and field is to extract relevant feature points from complex human motion regions. Under occlusion conditions, clear human images can be obtained through morphological processing. Further select the appropriate human body representation method and extract useful motion information from the human body sequence to determine which type of motion the current exercise belongs to.

Starting from the general recognition process, using depth information, the multi-path recognition and monitoring system of human head posture features in track and field is composed of five parts, which are upper computer monitoring system, posture sensor and STM32 sensor. The system is written with VC++ 6.0, and the main frequency of the computer is 1 GHz, the memory is 256 M, and the video memory is 32 m, After

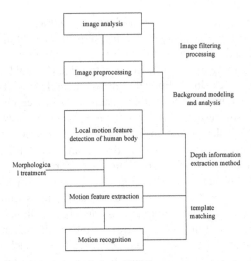

Fig. 1. Mining the characteristics of head posture errors in track and field

the completion of the system, it is handed over to Bailey optical instruments Co., Ltd. for testing, which meets the requirements of the project [4]. The system structure is mainly composed of lpc1788 microprocessor, LCD display control panel, flash, reset module, clock module, power module and wireless transceiver module. The specific hardware structure design is shown in the Fig. 2.

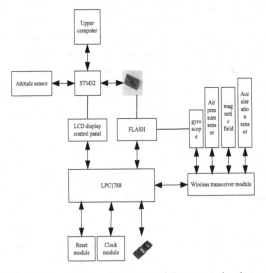

Fig. 2. The main block diagram of the system hardware

It can be seen from the figure that the LPC1788 microprocessor is composed of a 32-bit core high-speed microprocessor of the ARMCortex-M3 model. The maximum operating frequency can reach 150 MHz. The external resources are very rich, including 128 MB of FLASH memory, one for static The external storage controller, LCD display controller, etc., which store external information, and the microprocessor, as the main controller of the human-machine interface, is mainly responsible for controlling each module and realizing the communication function. The controller uses a 6-inch LCD screen with a high resolution of 565RGB mode and a 40-pin digital interface [5]. The LCD display controller is built into the interface, which includes the data bus for image transmission and necessary control signals such as LCD DCLK, LCD ENAB M [6]. Using the touch screen to display the control screen can achieve simple operation in the Internet of Things environment. The display and refresh are displayed on the screen. The system needs to have enough memory space to store complete data. For this reason, need to expand the memory capacity in the design [7]. Based on the original design idea, the wireless module adds the power amplifier function, which can amplify the maximum output power of the wireless module through the power amplifier circuit, and receive the increased signal strength through the LAN circuit, which can effectively increase the communication distance of the wireless module.

2.2 Software Processing Algorithm of Head Posture Error Correction System in Track and Field

Combining deep reinforcement learning methods to optimize the software processing algorithm of the track and field head posture error correction system. Since the training data contains the true value of the head position and head posture, a set of true head position and head orientation vectors can be marked during training. The specific marking points of the head position are different. Based on this, the head posture and marking values of the track and field are standardized, as follows (Fig. 3):

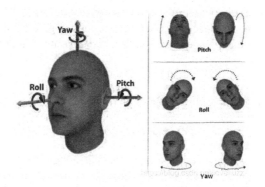

Fig. 3. Head posture and marked value of track and field

In the figure: Q_1—nose tip position, Q_2—A point along the head toward the vector starting from the nose tip point; Q_3—The center point of the sample sub domain image, S_1—sample sub domain sampling range, S_2 and S_3 random rectangle for calculating decision function. Using the labeled head position and head orientation vector, F_1 and

F_3 are saved in the sampling sub domain of depth data. Assuming that $\boldsymbol{\theta}n$ is a Gaussian random distribution of three variables, the labeled true value of set P can be expressed as follows:

$$p(\boldsymbol{\theta}_n) = N(\overline{\theta}_n, \Sigma_n) * \begin{cases} F_3, F_2, F_1 \\ S_3, S_2, S_1 \\ Q_3, Q_2, Q_1 \end{cases} \tag{1}$$

Thus, the corresponding differential entropy can be calculated for $n \in \{1, 2\}$:

$$H(P)_n = \frac{1}{2}p(\theta_n)\Big((2\pi e)^3|\Sigma_n|\Big) \propto |\Sigma_n|N(\overline{\theta}_n, \Sigma_n) \tag{2}$$

The regression metric function is the sum of the entropy of all parameters:

$$H_x(P) = H(P)_n \sum_n a_n p(\theta_n) g_{1c}(\phi)(|\Sigma_n|) \tag{3}$$

In the formula, a_n is the weighting coefficient of parameter correlation, and Σn is the variance matrix. The regression measurement function is substituted into the information gain $g_{1c}(\phi)$ to maximize it, even if the covariance of the Gaussian distribution calculated by all the label vectors θn of the child nodes is minimized, the uncertainty of the regression can be reduced. Mark the category probability as $p(c = k|P)$, and save the distribution of continuous head pose parameters $p(\theta_1)$ and $p(\theta_2)$, where k is the feature category. The calculation of the distribution is carried out by using the image blocks that reach the sub-domain of the training sample, which will be used in the calculation of head pose estimation in the following part [8]. In order to make the relationship between the calculation objects more general and reduce the estimation variance. The selection of the best decision function comes from a set of randomly generated decision function sets $\phi'' = \{\phi\}$. All sample subdomain image blocks arriving at this node must be evaluated by all decision functions in this set, so that the information gain of this node is split The maximized decision function is used as the split decision function of the current node:

$$\phi^* = \arg H_x(P) \max g_{1G}(\phi) \tag{4}$$

The information gain is further defined

$$g_{1G}(\phi) = H(P) - \omega_L H(P_L(\phi)) - \omega_R H(P_R(\phi)) \tag{5}$$

Where ω_L and ω_R are the ratios of the image blocks arriving at the left/right sub nodes to the total training sample set; $H(P)$ is an entropy like metric function of the image block set P in the sample sub domain [9]. In the training process, according to the optimal decision function saved by the node, the data enters into the left/right sub node, and the whole training process goes on iteratively. The stop condition of iteration is that the maximum tree depth specified in the decision tree is reached, or the number of remaining training samples is lower than the specified minimum value. The remaining points after filtering are finally created the cloth is used to estimate the nose tip position θ_1, that is, by adding the average deviation $\overline{\theta}_1$ to the center $\theta(P)$ of the image block, the distribution of the nasal tip position is obtained. According to the statistical average diameter of the human head, all the votes are clustered and analyzed, and further optimized by meanshift to remove those outliers. The multi-path recognition of head posture features of track and field sports is carried out. The specific head posture recognition process is shown in the Fig. 4.

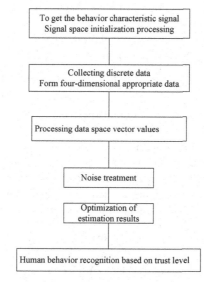

Fig. 4. Head posture recognition steps of track and field

According to the recognition process shown in the figure, the trust level of each component of the data space can be set, and each level can be de-aired to obtain the optimal feature data. The sum of the Gaussian distribution of the head cluster is a new multivariate Gaussian distribution, the mean value as the estimated value of the head posture, the covariance is used as the estimated confidence to calculate and identify the wrong head posture of the athlete.

2.3 Correction of Head Posture Errors in Track and Field

In order to extract multiple features that can predict the deflection angle of the head in the input image, different convolution kernels are needed for convolution operation [10]. The convolution operation can be expressed as follows:

$$x^j = x^i \min(0, a^j + \sum u^{\tilde{q} \neq xi})$$
$$y^j = y^i \max(0, b^j + \sum u^{\tilde{q} \neq xi})$$

(6)

Among them, x^i and y^i respectively represent the i input feature map and the j output feature map; $u^{\tilde{q} \neq xi}$ is the convolution kernel between the q input feature map and the j output feature map, a^j represents convolution, and b^j is The offset term of the j output graph. In order to avoid insufficient expression ability of the linear model, it is usually necessary to perform a nonlinear operation on the feature map obtained after convolution to prevent overfitting. Use unsaturated nonlinear functions for hidden layer neurons. Due to the principle of local correlation of image, through down sampling the image, the dimension of the feature map is reduced while retaining the useful information of the image. The operation of single feature map mainly includes average pooling down sampling and maximum pooling down sampling. Average pooling down sampling takes the average value in the neighborhood as the output, and the maximum pooling down sampling takes the maximum value in the neighborhood as the output. The depth learning principle is used to sample the head pose features.

$$z_{j,k}^i = \max_{0 \leq m, n \in s} \left\{ y^j x_{j \cdot s} + m, x^j k * s + n^i \right\} \tag{7}$$

Among them, $x_{j \cdot s}$ represents the j output spectrum in the down-sampling process, and each neuron is sampled from the s × s local area in the i input spectrum, and m and n respectively represent the step size of the down-sampling frame movement. Soft Max regression is expanded on the basis of logistic regression, mainly to solve multi-classification problems, and is a supervised learning algorithm. The last layer of the network is the Soft Max function, which is used in conjunction with deep reinforcement learning to distinguish the angle category of the input image.

$$F_i = \frac{z_{j,k}^i \exp(y^j)}{b_j \sum_{j=1}^{n} \exp(x^j)} \tag{8}$$

Where: $b_j = \sum_{i=1}^{128} x_i \cdot w_{i,j} + b_j$ is a linear combination of 128 features, and the optimization goal of the whole network is to minimize. After obtaining the three-dimensional movement posture data of track and field athletes by deep reinforcement learning technology, these data can be effectively stored and used to drive the dynamic three-dimensional model movement. The storage format of action data is very important. The commonly used storage formats of dynamic 3D model data include rotation matrix, Euler angle and quaternion. The comparison of the three data formats is shown in the table. Based on this, the rotation matrix, Euler angle and quaternion of head posture are standardized. The details are as follows (Table 1):

According to the application comparison of the data storage format in the above table, the quaternion has more advantages than the other two storage formats. Therefore, the 3D dynamic data collected from the deep reinforcement learning is converted in quaternion format. After the data conversion, BVH format is used to store the files. BVH is a common format of action data file, which has the function of import and export, and it is easy to edit and change, and it is convenient to recognize and correct the small posture of head features. Because the dynamic 3D model is established to standardize the standard of track and field posture, a method of comparing the posture of track and field is needed to compare the standard of track and field posture in the model. This time, the European distance comparison method is adopted. The method is to form a threshold value by comparing the track and field posture with the distance of

Table 1. Head posture rotation matrix, Euler angle, quaternion specification parameters

Function	Rotation matrix	Quaternion	Euler angle
Can it be converted into 3D coordinate rotation point	It can't be converted to 3D coordinate rotation point directly, but it needs to be converted to matrix first	can	It can't be converted to 3D coordinate rotation point directly, but it needs to be converted to matrix first
Can rotation be connected	Generally not	can	Generally not
Can interpolation be done	No	can	can
Conversion difficulty	Hard	Easy	Hard
Memory usage	6 numbers	8 numbers	9 numbers
Is the representation of a given mode unique	yes	There are many expressions in the same direction	yes
Can the stored data be used illegally	Illegal use of data may occur	can't	Due to errors, illegal use of data may occur

each joint in the standard sports posture in the model. The smaller the threshold is, the more regional the track and field posture standard is. The formula is as follows:

$$D = F_i \text{sqrt}(x_1 - x_2) + (y_1 - y_2) + (z_1 - z_2) \tag{9}$$

In formula (1), D represents the absolute distance between two track and field posture joints, and the three-dimensional coordinates of the two points are $A(x_1, y_1, z_1)$, $B(x_2, y_2, z_2)$ respectively. Then the two track and field posture thresholds T are:

$$T = \text{sqrt}D \sum A - B \tag{10}$$

The threshold T is the absolute distance of all joints in two track and field postures. When the T value is larger, it means that the posture of track and field is not standardized, so as to standardize the posture standardization of track and field, and ensure the effective correction of head posture error.

3 Analysis of Results

In order to verify the operation effect of the track and field head posture error correction system based on deep reinforcement learning, experiments were carried out. The experiments were mainly carried out on the CAS-PEAL data set. CAS-PEAL is a data set commonly used for head pose estimation. On this data set, the head pose is divided into 7 discrete angles $\{-45°, -30°, -15°, 0°, 15°, 30°, 45°\}$ in the yaw direction and

3 discrete angles in the pitch direction $\{-30°, 0°, 30°\}$. For each picture, use a head gesture recognizer to locate the face area of the picture, intercept the face picture and normalize it to 32*32. Some sample pictures in CAS-PEAL are shown in the Fig. 5:

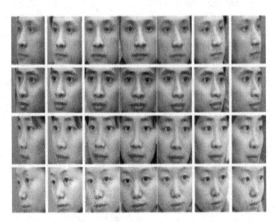

Fig. 5. Head pose image sample

The experiment was carried out on a subset of CAS-PEAL dataset with object number $401 \sim 600$. There are a total of $4200(21 * 200)$ images on the data subset, and 4166 face images are detected by head pose recognizer. The experimental data set is divided into three data subsets, one of which is used for testing and the other two for training. In this way, all training pictures and test pictures are not crossed. Repeat the experiment three times to make each subset participate in the test. The experimental results are the average of the three test results. On the experimental data set, the experimental results are shown in the table. (Among them, VoD and kVoD use the track and field head posture error correction system based on neural network and the track and field head posture error correction system based on deep learning) (Table 2).

Table 2. Accuracy test results of head posture recognition system in track and field.

	VoD	kVoD	The system of this paper
Error value	4.2	3.9	0.8
Time consuming (min)	8.2	5.6	1.0

Based on the analysis of the detection results in the above table, it can be seen that compared with the traditional two systems, the track and field head posture error correction system based on deep reinforcement learning proposed in this paper has relatively higher recognition accuracy for head posture errors in the actual application process. The time-consuming is shorter. The experimental results show that as the number of objects in the experimental data set increases, the more representative information is contained in the data set. Under the same network structure, the classification accuracy of the test images gradually increases, and the average absolute error slowing shrieking. Further compare the correction effects of the three systems under the noise interference environment and record them, as shown in the Fig. 6 below:

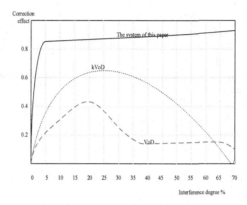

Fig. 6. Comparative detection of system correction effect.

Based on the analysis of the above detection results, compared with the traditional two systems, the head posture error correction system based on deep reinforcement learning proposed in this paper has a better correction effect on the head posture error of athletes in the actual application process, and the system operation is always stable in the case of interference. The experimental results show that compared with the existing correction system, the system has a better effect on correcting the head posture error of athletes. The system has good robustness and accuracy, and can better meet the requirements of practical application.

4   Concluding Remarks

A head pose estimation method based on deep reinforcement learning is proposed. Extracting features through the deep network and classifying and predicting them can significantly reduce the error of attitude estimation on the CAS-PEAL data set, and achieve better experimental results. But the generalization ability of this method depends on the diversity of training data and the complexity of the network structure. The next step is to integrate multiple data sets to train a more complex network structure, and increase the generalization ability of the network structure on the premise of ensuring a lower attitude angle error.

References

1. Burch, A.: From passion to patent: raytheon track-and-field coach inspires STEM in sports [pipelining: attractive programs for women]. IEEE Women Eng. Mag. **12**(1), 28 (2018)

2. Gurioli, L., Di Muro, A., Vlastélic, I., et al.: Integrating field, textural, and geochemical monitoring to track eruption triggers and dynamics: a case study from Piton de la Fournaise. Solid Earth **9**(2), 431–455 (2018)
3. Wu, G., Chen, F., Pan, X., et al.: Using the visual intervention influence of pavement markings for rutting mitigation–part I: preliminary experiments and field tests. Int. J. Pavement Eng. **20**(5–6), 734–746 (2019)
4. Zmitri, M., Fourati, H., Vuillerme, N.: Human activities and postures recognition: from inertial measurements to quaternion-based approaches. Sensors **19**(19), 4058–4059 (2019)
5. Long, T., Liang, Z., Liu, Q.: Advanced technology of high-resolution radar: target detection, tracking, imaging, and recognition. Sci. China Inf. Sci. **62**(04), 1–26 (2019). https://doi.org/10.1007/s11432-018-9811-0
6. Xu, Y., Hou, Z., Liang, J., et al.: Action recognition using weighted fusion of depth images and skeleton's key frames. Jisuanji Fuzhu Sheji Yu Tuxingxue Xuebao/J. Comput. Aided Des. Comput. Graph. **30**(7), 1313 (2018)
7. Wang, B., Liu, D., Wang, W., et al.: A hybrid approach for UAV flight data estimation and prediction based on flight mode recognition. Microelectron. Reliab. **84**, 253–262 (2018)
8. Liu, S., Bai, W., Zeng, N., et al.: A fast fractal based compression for MRI images. IEEE Access **7**, 62412–62420 (2019)
9. Fu, W., Liu, S., Srivastava, G.: Optimization of big data scheduling in social networks. Entropy **21**(9), 902 (2019)
10. Liu, S., Liu, D., Srivastava, G., Połap, D., Woźniak, M.: Overview and methods of correlation filter algorithms in object tracking. Complex Intell. Syst. (2020). https://doi.org/10.1007/s40747-020-00161-4

Visual Imaging Method of 3D Virtual Scene Based on VR Technology

Zhao Bing[1](✉) and Zhou Qian[2]

[1] Elites Partners Corporation, Beijing 100027, China
[2] Guizhou Power Grid Corporation, Guiyang 550002, China

Abstract. The traditional 3D virtual scene visualization imaging method has low accuracy and serious center offset in the imaging process. Therefore, a visualization imaging method of 3D virtual scene based on virtual reality technology is designed. In order to reduce the complexity of the imaging scene and reduce the texture interval, texture mapping is used to improve the overall interaction performance of VR technology. In order to improve the reality of the scene, a 3D virtual viewpoint structure is designed by optimizing dynamic collision detection with octree. The visualization of 3D virtual scene is completed by mapping calculation. In order to verify the effectiveness of the design method, an experiment is designed. The results show that the coordinates of the center point obtained by this method are closer to the actual coordinates, indicating that the imaging process is more in line with the actual situation and the imaging accuracy is higher.

Keywords: VR technology · 3D virtual scene · Visualization imaging

1 Introduction

The visual imaging technology of virtual scenes is an important means to realize the interaction between humans and computers and complex data. Its core theory is to realize the real reproduction of virtual scenes or virtual environments and interact with them. The current visual imaging technology of virtual scenes It has been widely used in industrial manufacturing, medical diagnosis, science fiction scene design, virtual combat environment simulation, seismic inversion, oil and gas exploration and many other fields [1]. In the medical field, foreign scholars integrate binocular vision positioning technology and brain tumor resection, stereo vision image acquisition sensor is used to track the operation area, and reconstruct the three-dimensional contour of the local surface through calculation, which greatly reduces the difficulty of operation; while the binocular vision three-dimensional reconstruction technology is used in gastrointestinal appearance inspection to improve the accuracy of operation matching. Chinese scholars have studied the independent litchi picking system. The system uses binocular vision technology, image processing uses fuzzy c-means method to segment the stem and fruit, accurately judge the position of picking point, and then guide the manipulator to pick litchi. Binocular vision is applied to the terminal guidance of autonomous underwater

W. Fu et al. (Eds.): ICMTEL 2021, LNICST 388, pp. 373–384, 2021.
https://doi.org/10.1007/978-3-030-82565-2_31

vehicle (auk). Because the shooting environment is underwater, the nonlinear transformation matrix caused by underwater refraction phenomenon is linearized to approximate, which reduces the range of epipolar variation and achieves high accuracy positioning. Harbin University of technology applies binocular vision to the soccer robot to realize the full autonomous navigation of the soccer robot. The difference is that two cameras are installed: one camera is fixed on the top of the robot, and the other camera that can rotate horizontally is installed on the middle and lower part of the robot. In this way, the detection range is larger, so that the ranging accuracy and processing speed of the robot in the field of vision can match The best way is to adjust the posture in time when encountering obstacles in the process of competition. In the visual imaging technology of virtual scene, the model construction and model rendering of virtual scene are the key links. At present, there are two methods to solve the problem of visual modeling of virtual scene in the world. One is the modeling and rendering of virtual scene based on geometric model based on computer graphics, which is also called virtual scene modeling and rendering based on computer graphics; The other is to use the image acquisition and analysis of 3D environment to build virtual scene, which is based on image [2]. In order to meet the high-precision requirements for visual imaging of virtual scenes such as seismic inversion and oil and gas exploration, many effective imaging methods have been proposed. However, the traditional imaging method has low accuracy and serious imaging shift. Therefore, a visual imaging method of 3D virtual scene based on VR technology is designed.

2 3D Virtual Scene Visualization Imaging Method Based on VR Technology

2.1 Reduce Scene Complexity

In the construction of 3D scene model based on VRML, virtual reality technology is used to describe the roaming virtual environment, which requires a large number of solid surface triangles. Due to the limitation of hardware conditions supporting roaming, the real-time interaction will be stuck or even overloaded, resulting in failure. Therefore, the complexity of the scene must be reduced to improve the overall interactive performance [3]. This article uses texture mapping technology to control the complexity of the scene. Texture refers to the surface details of an object, which is mainly divided into color texture and geometric texture. For example, the non-three-dimensional patterns on indoor furnishings belong to the color texture; the geometric texture includes some three-dimensional folds. The texture mapping is carried out between image space, object space and texture space, as shown in the following Fig. 1.

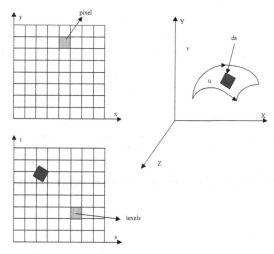

Fig. 1. Mapping process of texture in space

Texture mapping is to map a two-dimensional texture image in a two-dimensional array to a three-dimensional solid surface, and change the light intensity distribution of the surface through a modification process. On the indoor wooden floor model, photos or pictures can be used as texture for mapping, which can save the polygonal surface of the wooden stripes, and the detailed feature description of the wooden floor will not be distorted [4]. The surface area DS corresponding to the pixel on the object surface is mapped to the texture region. The results of partial subtraction are shown in the Table 1 below.

Table 1. 3D virtual scene reduction result table.

Object name	File name	Original file size	Number of original file lines	File size after modification	The number of lines in the modified file
wall	Kz	23.6KB	1065	10.3KB	1065
Interior furnishings	Kz	123.6KB	2640	78KB	1883
Outdoor light	Sxll	724KB	11365	613KB	5610

In the above table, the main reductions made include: removing the spaces caused by shrinkage in the wall, making the supporting parts of the indoor furnishings into prototype nodes, and changing the large amount of repeated parts into prototype nodes in the indoor light. So far, the complexity of the scene has been reduced.

2.1.1 Optimize Dynamic Collision Detection

In VR environment, it is necessary to render the interior space decoration scene. In this process, real-time interactive collision processing will occur to enhance the authenticity of the system for interior decoration scene display [5]. Collision processing mainly includes collision detection, collision determination and collision response. Collision detection is mainly used to determine whether the moving object will collide with other objects when moving an object in three-dimensional space. When it is judged as the relevant information of collision, the operation is determined according to the specific collision situation between two objects [6]. The system in this paper adopts the octree space division technology, and octree is a very effective management method in 3D scene management. The space division process of the octree is shown in the following Fig. 2.

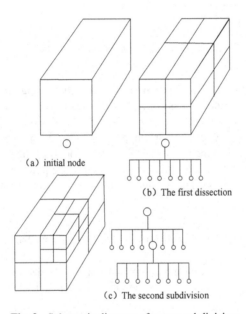

(a) initial node

(b) The first dissection

(c) The second subdivision

Fig. 2. Schematic diagram of octree subdivision

Assuming that the indoor scene is simplified to a cuboid box, the cuboid is equally divided into 8 small cuboids with all the same shape, and the scene polygons are traversed to determine the positional relationship between the polygons and the small cuboid in the scene, and add it to the node representing the small cuboid In the polygon list, view the number of polygon faces in each non-empty small cuboid. These small cuboids are used as the non leaf nodes of the octree, and are divided recursively. The point in three-dimensional space is represented by non-homogeneous coordinate

(wx, wy, wz, w), which is not unique. To transform a point in space from one coordinate system to another coordinate system, a homogeneous transformation formula must be applied:

$$T = \begin{bmatrix} m_{00} & m_{01} & m_{02} & m_{03} \\ m_{10} & m_{11} & m_{12} & m_{13} \\ m_{20} & m_{21} & m_{22} & m_{23} \\ m_{30} & m_{31} & m_{32} & m_{33} \end{bmatrix} \tag{1}$$

Until the division reaches a certain depth or the number of polygons contained in the sub-node space is within a given threshold range. If a child node obtained by the division is empty, set it as a leaf node and stop the division [7]. In the process of subdivision, if a polygon exists in two or more small box boxes, the polygon can be divided according to the normal parts in different node cuboids, and the small polygon obtained from the segmentation can be added to the polygon list of corresponding node cuboids to increase the number of polygons in the scene. Aiming at the loose octree data structure in the system, this paper completes the intersection query through the octree scene manager, roughly judges the intersection of objects in the local space where the cuboid of the target node is located, and excludes most objects that will not collide. Create collision geometry and implement the corresponding algorithm. Optimally name all objects that need to collide, and manually add judgment conditions in the background code.

2.2 Synthesis of 3D Virtual Viewpoint Structure

The traditional two-dimensional virtual viewpoint synthesis method only uses the horizontal disparity map to perform virtual synthesis of the viewpoint images adjacent to the reference image in the horizontal direction. In the three-dimensional virtual viewpoint synthesis method mentioned in this chapter, it is necessary to use both horizontal and vertical disparity maps to generate The virtual viewpoint image adjacent to the reference image horizontally, vertically and diagonally [8]. The structure diagram of 3D virtual viewpoint synthesis synthesized in this paper is as follows: (Fig. 3).

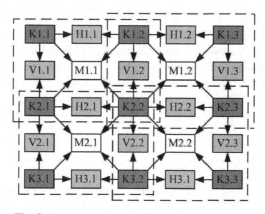

Fig. 3. Structure of 3D virtual viewpoint synthesis

This figure takes a 3×3 multi-viewpoint image array to generate a 5×5 multi-viewpoint image array as an example. The figure divides the multi-viewpoint images into four categories: K, H, V and M. Among them, the K-type images are actually collected The images of class H and class V are obtained by virtual synthesis of two horizontally and vertically adjacent images of class K respectively. The M class image is located in the center of the 2×2 K class image sub-array, and the four K class images are simultaneously Perform virtual synthesis to obtain [9]. The virtual synthesis order of this method is calculated by 2×2 class k image subarray from top to bottom and from left to right. The class k image in the above figure is divided into four subarrays. When each subarray is virtual synthesized, the order of each virtual viewpoint image is h, V and m. It can be seen from the above figure that there is an overlap area between adjacent sub-arrays, and this overlap relationship is manifested in the sharing of the disparity map of the overlap area during the virtual synthesis of M-type images. Due to the huge amount of calculation to generate the disparity map, in order to avoid repeated calculations, this chapter will cache the shared disparity map.

In order to generate horizontal and vertical parallax maps, the method of generating the corresponding initial virtual view image from the right view is as follows: define the right view and right parallax map with the size of $C \times R$ pixel as $I_R(i, j)$ and $D_R(i, j)$ respectively, where $i = 0, 1, ..., C-1$ and $j = 0, 1, ..., R-1$ are the location coordinates of the pixel and the parallax value in the right view and the right parallax map, and the coordinate origin is located in the lower left corner of each image. The corresponding generated initial virtual viewpoint image I_{VR} can be expressed as:

$$I_{VR}(i + \alpha \times D_R(i, j), j) = I_R(i, j) \tag{2}$$

In the above formula, α represents the ratio of the distance between the virtual viewpoint to the right viewpoint and the distance between the left and right viewpoints. In the same way, the initial virtual viewpoint image corresponding to the left view can be calculated by using the left view and the left disparity map. The calculation formula is:

$$I_{VL}(i - (1 - \alpha) \times D_L(i, j), j) = I_L(i, j) \tag{3}$$

Where I_L and D_L are the left view and the left parallax map respectively, and I_{VL} represents the initial virtual viewpoint image generated by the left view [10]. Since the disparity map cannot accurately extract the edges of objects located in different depth planes, in the generated initial virtual viewpoint image, there are pixels of other depth planes at the edge of the same depth plane, and these pixels are mostly located around the holes in the image. This chapter enlarges the image hole by 1 pixel to eliminate the influence of these confused pixels on image quality. The method to merge the two initial virtual viewpoint images generated separately into one image is:

$$I_{VH} = (1 - \alpha) \times I_{VL} + \alpha \times I_{VR} \tag{4}$$

Where: I_{VH} is the merged virtual viewpoint image. For the small holes still existing in the merged image, the hierarchical interpolation method is used in this paper. The specific method is as follows: the unfilled pixels are classified according to the number of filled pixels around them. The more the number is, the more priority is given. In the processing, the average value of all the filled pixels within the range of 7×7 is taken as the pixel value of the point.

2.3 Visual imaging of 3D virtual scene

In the three-dimensional virtual viewpoint synthesis structure diagram, the virtual viewpoint image in the oblique direction of each subarray is not on the connecting line of any two horizontal or vertical adjacent reference images. Therefore, the initial virtual viewpoint image in oblique direction cannot be generated only by relying on one parallax map of the reference image. To solve this problem, this chapter proposes a method to obtain the initial virtual view image by using the horizontal and vertical parallax map of the reference image at the same time. The method of generating the corresponding initial virtual view image from the upper right view is as follows: firstly, the vertical disparity map of the upper right view and the vertical parallax map of the upper right view are used the specific formula is as follows:

$$I_{VRTM}(I + \alpha_H \times D_{RTH}(i,j), j) = I_{RT}(i,j) \tag{5}$$

Where: I_{RT} represents the upper right view, D_{RTH} represents the horizontal disparity map of the upper right view, I_{VRTM} is the generated middle view, and α_H is the ratio of the horizontal distance between the virtual viewpoint to the upper right viewpoint and the left and right viewpoints. Then, use the obtained intermediate disparity map to map the intermediate view to generate an initial virtual viewpoint image:

$$I_{VRT}(i, j + \alpha_V \times D_{VRTM}(i,j)) = I_{VRTM}(i,j) \tag{6}$$

Where: I_{VRT} is the initial virtual viewpoint image generated by the upper right view, and α_V is the ratio of the vertical distance from the virtual viewpoint to the upper right view and the distance between the upper and lower viewpoints. In the process of merging the generated initial virtual view images, this chapter first merges the initial virtual view images generated by two reference images on the same horizontal line, and then merges the generated two images to generate the final virtual view image. The specific formula is as follows:

$$I_{V1} = (1 - \alpha_H) \times I_{VLT} + \alpha_H \times I_{VRT}$$
$$I_{V2} = (1 - \alpha_H) \times I_{VLB} + \alpha_H \times I_{VRB} \tag{7}$$
$$I_{VM} = \alpha_V \times I_{V1} + (1 - \alpha_V) \times I_{V2}$$

In the formula: I_{V1} and I_{V2} are the combined images obtained from the two initial virtual viewpoint images located above and below the sub-array respectively, and I_{VM} is the final synthesized virtual viewpoint image. So far, the research on the visualization and imaging method of 3D virtual scene based on VR technology is completed.

3 Experiment

3.1 Experiment preparation

In the experiment, a series of simulation images are generated by using the generated simulation platform, and the imaging accuracy of the system is detected. The measurement target of the system is the three-dimensional coordinate value of space points. The measurement of typical entity models such as point, line, plane, surface, cube, etc., the entity to be tested is added with different mark types and different levels of noise to study their positioning accuracy respectively. The definitions of points, lines, and polygons in OpenGL are not exactly the same as those in mathematics. On the one hand, the coordinates of geometric figures in OpenGL will cause minor errors due to errors in computer floating point operations; on the other hand, the display of graphics is also subject to The display resolution is limited. Here we use experiments to study the rendering accuracy of geometric primitives in OpenGL. In the experiment, 9×9 sub-images in the sub-image array are extracted as experimental data, as shown in the Fig. 4 below.

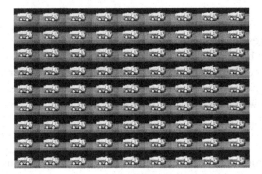

Fig. 4. Two dimensional multi view image array actually collected

Take the odd-numbered row and odd-numbered column images in the above array as reference images, and use other position images as unknown viewpoint images for virtual synthesis, and calculate the peak signal-to-noise ratio (PSNR) of the synthesis result and the corresponding actual viewpoint image. The following figure shows the subjective effect of some virtual viewpoint images and corresponding actual viewpoint images: (Fig. 5).

Fig. 5. Subjective effect

In the experiment, the hardware environment is Hisense computer, with Intel (R) Pentium III 996 MHz, 768 m ram, and the card is video quadro2 MXR/ex; the software environment is Windows XP Professional, Visual C++ 6.0, and the display resolution is $1024 \times 768 \times 32$bit. In the process of experiment, we designed some common marks,

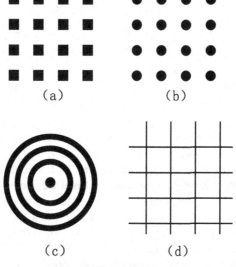

Fig. 6. Simulation mark

such as square point, circle point, stripe and grid. The following is the specific effect of the mark map, as shown in the following Fig. 6.

The accuracy of the generated simulation image is tested. Under different resolutions and imaging functions, the points and lines in any position and direction are verified. At the same time, Gaussian noise and impulse noise of 60dB are added to the image to study the influence of noise on target point positioning.

In this paper, the PSNR of the horizontal virtual view image relative to the actual view image is shown in the Table 2 below.

Table 2. PSNR (dB) of the virtual viewpoint image in the horizontal direction.

Specific location	Column 2	Column 4	Column 6	Column 8
Line 1	29.3	28.0	29.1	29.4
Line 3	30.4	28.3	30.1	30.4
Line 5	30.4	28.9	30.4	30.7
Line 7	29.1	28.7	30.2	29.4
Line 9	28.3	27.3	30.7	29.3

The PSNR of the virtual viewpoint image in the vertical direction relative to the actual viewpoint image is shown in the following Table 3.

Table 3. PSNR (DB) of virtual viewpoint image in vertical direction.

Specific location	Column 2	Column 4	Column 6	Column 8
Line 1	28.5	27.9	26.6	27.5
Line 3	28.5	29.1	26.4	28.3
Line 5	27.3	28.5	28.4	29.8
Line 7	29.5	28.4	26.9	28.4
Line 9	29.5	28.5	19.3	29.0

The PSNR of the virtual viewpoint image in the diagonal direction relative to the actual viewpoint image is shown in the following Table 4.

It can be seen from the above three tables that the horizontal and vertical virtual view images have higher PSNR than the oblique virtual view images, but the subjective quality of the oblique virtual view images is not significantly worse than that of the horizontal and vertical directions. The main reason for this phenomenon is that the images used in this chapter are real scene images, and the distance between adjacent shooting viewpoints Distance is not exactly equal, Therefore, there is a slight error between the virtual synthesized viewpoint position and the corresponding actual acquisition viewpoint position. This error only affects the PSNR calculation result and will not cause

Table 4. PSNR of the virtual viewpoint image in the diagonal direction (dB).

Specific location	Column 2	Column 4	Column 6	Column 8
Line 2	23.4	22.8	23.3	24.5
Line 4	23.5	24.1	24.2	24.0
Line 6	22.1	23.0	22.9	23.4
Line 8	22.0	22.8	23.5	23.4

the deterioration of the display effect, and the error has greater influence on the virtual viewpoint image in the diagonal direction. The impact on the horizontal and vertical directions.

3.1.1 Analysis of experimental results

Under the above experimental conditions, the imaging centers of the two imaging methods are determined, and the results obtained are shown in the following Table 5.

Table 5. Comparison of center point coordinates.

Number of imaging experiments	The coordinates of the center point in this method	Traditional method center point coordinates
1	(150,150)	(137,126)
2	(150,150)	(141,150)
3	(149,149)	(159,162)
4	(200,100)	(157,132)
5	(151,159)	(134,159)
6	(149,153)	(132,161)
7	(150,150)	(173,159)

In this paper, the actual coordinates of the imaging center point are set as (150, 150). According to the coordinate results of the imaging center point in the table above, the coordinates of the center point obtained by the 3D virtual scene visualization imaging method based on VR technology are closer to the actual coordinates, which shows that the method in this paper has higher accuracy in the imaging process and is more in line with the actual situation.

4 Concluding remarks

With the in-depth development of industrial manufacturing, medical diagnosis, science fiction scene design, virtual combat environment simulation, seismic inversion, oil and gas exploration and many other fields, the visualization imaging of virtual scene has become a global hot topic. Because the current imaging methods can not meet the application requirements of various fields, a virtual scene visualization imaging method based on common focus is proposed The visual imaging results of the pseudo complex surface interface model verify the effectiveness and feasibility of the proposed method, and provide effective guidance for the further development of oil and gas exploration, seismic simulation and other fields.

References

1. Hu, C., Wang, L., Li, Z., et al.: Inverse synthetic aperture radar imaging using a fully convolutional neural Network. IEEE Geosci. Remote Sens. Lett. **17**(7), 1203–1207 (2020)
2. Martel, J.N.P., Müller, L.K., Carey, S.J., Dudek, P., Wetzstein, G.: Neural sensors: learning pixel exposures for HDR imaging and video compressive sensing with programmable sensors. IEEE Trans. Pattern. Anal. Mach. Intell. **13**(02), 1–14 (2020)
3. Xiaokang, Z., Qiuyu, Z., Peng, R.: Research on panoramic imaging system based on VR miniature satellite. Electron. Measur. Tech. **41**(05), 33–37 (2018)
4. Yang, S., Wang, Y., Shi, B., et al.: Construction of anatomical and pathological simulation laboratory based on VR and 3D prisnting technology. J. Zhengzhou. Railway. Vocational Tech. Coll. **30**(01), 31–33 (2018)
5. Guo, W.: The application of 3D laser virtual reality technology in the reconstruction of ancient buildings. Laser. J. **39**(12), 102–105 (2018)
6. Chen, Z., Liu, Q., Yin, W., et al.: Visualization of petroleum hydrocarbon content in latosol based on hyperspectral imaging technology. Spectrosc. Spectral. Anal. **38**(09), 2916–2922 (2018)
7. Liu, S., Lu, M., Li, H., et al.: Prediction of gene expression patterns with generalized linear regression model. Front. Genet. **10**, 120 (2019)
8. Fu, W., Liu, S., Srivastava, G.: Optimization of big data scheduling in social networks. Entropy **21**(9), 902 (2019)
9. Xiuju, X.: 3D visualization technology of collapse column advanced detection by mine transient electromagnetic method. China. Coal. **44**(10), 60–64 (2018)
10. Liu, S., Bai, W., Zeng, N., et al.: A fast fractal based compression for MRI images. IEEE. Access. **7**, 62412–62420 (2019)
11. Bagi, R., Mohanty, S., Dutta, T., et al.: Leveraging smart devices for scene text preserved image stylization: a deep gaming approach. IEEE Multimedia **12**(05), 1–12 (2020)
12. Xu, X., Ma, Y., Sun, W.: Towards real scene super-resolution with raw images. In: IEEE/CVF Conference on Computer Vision and Pattern Recognition (CVPR) (2020)

Human Centered Computing in Digital Persona Generation

Nisha Ramachandra$^{(\boxtimes)}$, Manish Ahuja, Raghotham M. Rao,
and Neville Dubash

Accenture Labs, Accenture, Bengaluru, India
{nisha.ramachandra,manish.a.ahuja,raghotham.m.rao,
neville.dubash}@accenture.com

Abstract. Deepfake (or as we call it Digital Persona) has been very popularly used to create synthetic media in which a person in an existing image or video is replaced with someone else who is not present in that media. It refers to manipulated videos, or other digital representations produced by sophisticated artificial intelligence (AI), that yield fabricated images and sounds that appear to be real.

Deepfakes generally have been used for the purpose of defaming someone, where the user experience is not much of a concern. However, our work demonstrates using this technique for a good purpose. We created a digital persona of a renowned deceased artist with the aim to bring an enriching human experience through conversing with the persona projected on a 3d holographic stage in a museum. The digital persona responds in the voice of deceased artist to any questions asked by visitors related to his art journey and artwork. To ensure that the end results would have the audience immersed or awed with the outcome a.k.a. the digital persona, we adopted the human centered computing methodology which aims at radically changing the standard computing techniques of software development. In this work, the key elements of human centered computing include: a. Technology b. Cognitive Psychology and Ergonomics c. Social and Organizational Psychology d. Design and Arts e. Interaction f. Analysis for design of systems with a human focus from beginning to the end. We present the usage, details and outcomes of the mentioned focus areas in our design of developing deepfakes for good. We also present results of a social experiment conducted with children during their interaction with digital persona.

Keywords: Conversational deepfake · Human centered computing · Cognitive Psychology and Ergonomics · Social and Organizational Psychology · Design and Arts · Interaction · Analysis

1 Introduction

Deepfake means creating fake personas using deep learning methods. Deepfakes leverage powerful techniques from machine learning and artificial intelligence to

© ICST Institute for Computer Sciences, Social Informatics and Telecommunications Engineering 2021
Published by Springer Nature Switzerland AG 2021. All Rights Reserved
W. Fu et al. (Eds.): ICMTEL 2021, LNICST 388, pp. 385–401, 2021.
https://doi.org/10.1007/978-3-030-82565-2_32

manipulate or generate visual and audio content with a high potential to deceive [25].

A synthetic media is created by morphing the face. Speech synthesis techniques can also be applied to generate fake voice. Researchers have developed new software that uses machine learning to let users edit the text transcript of a video to add, delete or change the words coming right out of somebody's mouth [17]. Deepfakes have largely been used to create fake celebrity pornographic videos, fake news, hoaxes and financial fraud. In the above mentioned use cases, impersonation is the main objective and not the user centered design.

However, when used ethically, deepfakes can also be used for good. There can be many useful applications of deepfakes such as creation of visual storytelling in the field of education and films, creating real enough medical images to train AI in the medical field [23] and to originate a conversation to guide the end user towards positive thinking.

In such cases, the creator of the fake needs to consider the end user experience as a part of the design requirements. There is no existing framework for deepfake creation which can act as guide to generate an impressive deepfake within ethical limits.

We have applied the deepfake technology in the field of art to create a digital persona of a renowned deceased artist to help increase the awareness of Indian artworks. The goal of the digital persona creation is to enable learners during art and culture training sessions to better understand concepts from famous creators, curators and personalities.

The requirements of the digital persona were to interact with the users and create an effect of users having conversation with a real person by engaging the users in talks related to Indian art and art works through the life of the digital persona. To create this digital persona, we adapted the techniques of face superimposition [28] and speech synthesis [18] based on deep learning, natural language understanding for conversation and emotion detection [14] to measure the end user involvement during interactions. However, we believe that to create an "ideal" deepfake which is to be perceived as very realistic, it needs to be: a. immersive, b. expressive, c. responsive, d. proactive and e. adaptive; the definitions of which, used in our context are as below.

Immersive: There should be no visual flaw in creation of the deepfake for the end users to identify it as fake. The digital experience of the fake being projected on a screen should keep the end user engaged and focused.
Expressive: The digital persona should effectively and eloquently converse with the end user with appropriate expressions.
Responsive: The digital persona should correctly respond to the questions asked by the end user and reply diplomatically to any unfamiliar questions.
Proactive: If during the interaction, the end user deviates from the talks related to art works, the digital persona should proactively guide the end user to the art related topics.
Adaptive: Based on the involvement level and end user expression, the digital persona should understand the user mood and be flexible during the conversations.

To ensure adherence to the above listed characteristics, we conclude that, just the usage of the technology is insufficient for developing the digital persona and we propose to adapt the human centered computing design principles along with ethical guidelines.

This paper is structured as follows. In Sect. 2, we talk about the related work. In Sect. 3, we talk about the approach in depth by mentioning the implementation of each of the elements of human centered computing in detail. We discuss the outcome and social experiment results in Sects. 4 and 6 and conclude in Sect. 7.

2   Related Work

Generating good quality deepfakes is very well explored using deep learning techniques. The Dali museum in USA had already implemented digital persona of legendary artist Salvador Dali [6], however our approach goes beyond the Dali experience as our solution approach is conversational and employs human centric design principles. We also used speech generation using deep learning techniques and entire experience is not on a screen but is a 3D holographic projection. The basic architecture of all the deepfake generation techniques is same and uses the autoencoder with common encoder weights [15]. There are numerous enhancements over the basic deepfake architecture that people use for getting better results such as adding a discriminative network to the basic autoencoder architecture for training a generative discriminative network [16], where the decoder network of autoencoder acts as the generator network. The generator and discriminator network are then jointly trained to compete, resulting in better quality fakes. Other variations include learning with attention mechanism, adding multiple face extraction methods such as MTCNN and S3FD [12], adding perceptual loss [24,28].

Just like image synthesis, speech synthesis that can depict a person saying things is also very well explored. The speech synthesis algorithms use various parameters like intonation, tone, stress, rhythm, frequency spectrum etc. to generate voice from text. Deep learning is also used to train models using recorded speech data. Wavenet by Deepmind [30] and Tacotron by Google [36] are two such examples. While, multiple methods for creating good quality deepfakes through technology exists, to the best of our knowledge, there are no standard guidelines of using a well-defined framework/approach for creating the deepfakes with an immersive experience. There are no reference materials which talk about the various aspects of interface, interaction, design process and putting together the knowledge of people and technology in the creation of deepfake a.k.a. the digital persona. Based on our work, we have presented the design approach implemented, which we believe, is a well defined methodology and could be the baseline for any future works.

3   Approach

While deepfake technology can and has been used for unethical and illegal purposes, it can also be used ethically for social good too in the sample use cases mentioned in the Introduction section. For implementation in the social good scenario, it is important to consider the aspects of the deployment environment and study the user interactions during deployment.

The proposed approach focuses on leveraging the human centered computing design [20] to create a realistic digital persona using deepfake technology along with adherence to compliance and ethics. We believe that an "ideal" software development design to create the digital persona should: (i) foster engagement and satisfaction (ii) support multimodal approach by taking into account human feedback for an enhanced experience (iii) respect individual user behavior during interaction (iv) reflect the aim of creating the digital persona and (v) be ethically compliant to reflect trustworthiness and avoid misuse. Keeping these principles in mind, we present the immersive software development design approach implemented for the creation of the digital persona in our use case of creating the deepfake to enable art education (see Fig. 1).

Fig. 1. Immersive software development design for creation of digital persona with multimodal inputs

3.1   Technology

Technology represents the software techniques used in generating the digital persona. We implemented 1. Face superimposition through deep learning to create the synthetic video 2. Speech synthesis using deep learning to create the synthetic audio and 3. Natural Language Understanding and Natural Language Processing for Dialog Management 4. Real time Emotion analytics through facial analysis. All these components are provided as an input to the adaptation engine. The way these technology elements interact and intervene is shown in Fig. 2.

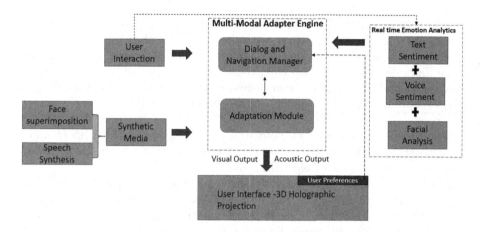

Fig. 2. Technology landscape depicting the interactions

Deepfakes are synthetic videos created using deep learning techniques where an individual's face is inserted into an existing video to appear as if the individual performed actions that occurred in the original video (Face Superimposition). In the generated video, the computer generated speech can also be integrated for a fake audio. The recent advances in speech synthesis leverage deep learning techniques to generate natural sounding speech.

In our implementation we created the synthetic video and audio and merged them together. The media file output was then marked with a digital signature to ensure appropriate usage. Several such deepfake media files (.mp4 format) were created based on the conversation topics.

To enable seamless user interaction with the persona during the conversation, we implemented the dialog and navigation manager to provide appropriate responses to user queries. The responses were in the form of the appropriate deepfake media files created. User preference on the topic of conversation was also provided to the dialog manager through the user interface. Real time emotion analytics was also implemented to analyze user reaction during the conversation and accordingly adapt the conversation to suit the user's mood. Emotions were aggregated based on the inputs of voice sentiment, text sentiment and facial emotions. For text sentiment, user's speech during the conversation was converted to text and then sentiment analysis was applied on the generated text.

Thus, based on inputs from the dialog manager, user preference and real time user emotions, the adaptation engine provided an appropriate deepfake video as an output which was projected to the user as a 3D Holographic projection [37].

Face Superimposition. For face superimposition, many freely available software's like deepfakes webβ [3], FaceSwap [15], FaceSwap-GAN [16] and DeepFaceLab [12] can be explored. For our design implementation, we picked up DeepFaceLab. For the implementation of deepfake in our work, we had to ensure the face superimposition works even if there is lot of movement.

The way in which all these software create fakes is through the trick of training two autoencoder networks, with shared weights of encoder network (i.e. a common encoder) and separate decoders for source and target face as shown in the Fig. 3. For the generation part, these architectures simply pass the latent representation of source face obtained from common encoder to the target face decoder as shown in Fig. 4, thereby converting the source face to target face in the process.

The faces that are passed as input to the common encoder for both training and generation are the aligned faces, that can be got through the use of any of the common face alignment algorithms like MTCNN, S3FD etc.

Other enhancement can also be added to make the output quality better. For example, jointly training a discriminator network along with the above encoder decoder network. Here the decoder network acts as generator and these are known as GAN based deepfakes. We can also try to increase the facial mask size to cover more of forehead for replacement.

In our case of creating the digital persona of the deceased artist, we had to superimpose the artist's face [Face A] on the face of an actor [Face B]. To ensure the face superimposition looks visually perfect, we realized based on our experiments that the actor needed to have the same facial structure, skin tone, hairstyle and beard.

The other guidelines for perfection include:

1. Sufficient Face A training data with a certain criterion: To collect the training data, various videos from YouTube featuring the artist were collected with the artist front facing the camera and without any obstructions on the face
2. In these video collections, the artist had to be of the same age and the lighting in the videos had to be consistent. Also, in the videos, the artist must be front facing the camera in most of the frames. With the mentioned criteria, we could collect around 10 min of video which lead to an extraction of around 9000 image frames.
3. Sufficient FaceB training data with a certain criterion: To get the training data, we had to video shoot the actor for a duration of around 10 min. During the shoot, we had to ensure the actor is both front facing and side facing the camera. The actor also had to exhibit varied expressions and the lighting during the shoot had to be only in the front.
4. Preprocessing of training data: Once the videos of the artist [Face A] from YouTube were collected, we had to remove the frames consisting of other people using a video cutter. The cut portions of the video were stitched back together before using it as input to the DeepFaceLab software.

Training

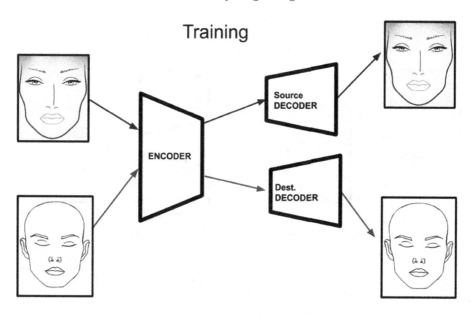

Fig. 3. Autoencoder architecture for deepfake training

Speech Synthesis. Since the person whose digital persona is to be created is deceased, we also had to synthesize his voice. To implement the voice synthesis, we explored the following software: a. sprocket-Kobyashi [26] b. ParallelWave-GAN [9] c. Tacotron2 [34] d. Transfer Learning from Speaker Verification to Multispeaker Text-To-Speech Synthesis [22] e. Neural Voice Cloning With Few Samples [8] and f. Deep Voice 3 [13,31].

The challenge we had with implementing speech synthesis was that we had limited samples of the artist's voice. Most of the software's listed above needed around 20 h of training data. With the challenge of low resource domain, we discovered that, with Deep Voice 3 we could retrain on target speaker data by training with 20 to 30 min of voice data from any other speaker. Therefore, from three prerecorded interview videos of the artist (available in YouTube), audio in .mp3 format was extracted and then 283 samples of audio files comprising of 5 s, 6 s, 9 s & 10 s were generated. In total, we could gather around 29 min of voice data that only contained artist's speech discarding other ambient noise. Along with the audio samples, corresponding text had to be extracted from each sample for training. We used Google's speech recognition API to extract text. However, the text output was not 100% due to the speaking style of the artist. Therefore, we had to manually curate the text data by listening to each audio sample. This was a time intensive task because audio samples had to be listened multiple times to record corresponding text accurately.

Post creating the speech synthesized audio, we merged the audio with the deepfake video created as described in the previous section. During the creation of the deepfake video, we ensured that the actor spoke as per the decided

Generation

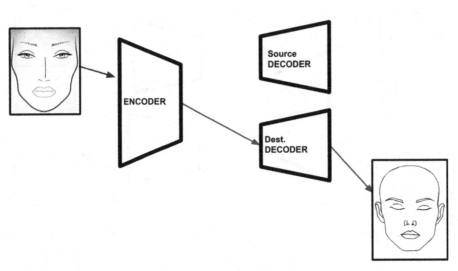

Fig. 4. Generating deepfakes after training

conversation topics. Thus, during merging of the deepfake video (synthesized video) and fake audio (synthesized audio), lip synchronization was taken care of.

Conversation AI. As mentioned earlier, the requirement of the digital persona was to have a conversation with the end user about Indian art and artworks. To enable this, any natural language processing or natural language understanding technologies [21] can be implemented to understand the user's intent and respond in the most useful way. We implemented Microsoft speech recognition service and Miscrosoft LUIS bot [4] API in conjunction with an adapter engine. The conversation was designed in a question-answer format. For the conversation with the persona, we configured 69 intents with 1244 utterances and Luis provided a 96.5% accuracy of predicting the intents correctly. In the engine, the intent response of Luis was mapped to a specific deepfake video. Thus, for any question asked by the user, a specific deepfake video of the digital person answering the question was provided as a response. The response video (output media file in mp4 format) was then projected on the 3D-holographic stage.

Emotion Analytics. Emotion Analytics software collects data and performs analysis on how people communicate verbally and non verbally to understand the mood or emotions of the person at an interval of time [27]. To avoid monotonous conversation between the digital persona and the end user, emotion analytics was implemented in the design approach. Various emotions of the user were detected as an aggregate of the outcome of voice sentiment, text sentiment and facial emotions. Based on the involvement level and emotion detection, the aim was to change the conversation to suit the end user's mood. Involvement refers to the measure of user engagement during the conversation with the digital persona. For example, if the detected involvement level drops to less than 50%, the conversation must change to a different topic to lighten the mood or grab the attention of the user through a different dialog response.

We used microsoft azure's facial emotion detection and text sentiment analysis api's [2, 7] for capturing facial and text emotions and used an open source implementation for capturing voice sentiments [5]. We then observed each short interaction with the digital persona and manually labelled it as high or low involvement. These api's collectively returns 18 real valued features, each between 0 and 1 representing strength of emotion. Text emotion analysis returns 3 features depicting positive, negative or neutral text emotions, facial emotion detects 8 features depicting anger, contempt, disgust, fear, happiness, neutral, sadness or surprise facial emotions and audio emotions returns 7 features depicting joy, surprise, neutral, anger, disgust, sadness or fear audio emotions. We collected around 700 such data points and used them to train a rbf kernel SVM [11]. We then use the trained SVM for predicting user's emotions. We take consent from users and constantly monitor them through a camera feed which is fed to three emotion detection APIs. The output from these api's are then passed to SVM classifier which then predicts high or low involvement along with prediction score.

Below is the snippet of sample data used to train the SVM classifier in Table 1.

3.2   Cognitive Psychology and Ergonomics

Cognitive psychology often uses computers to study human mental phenomena for the sake of developing general theories about human mental behavior. Cognitive ergonomics studies mental phenomena and applies theoretical knowledge in order to solve the practical problems related to using computers [1]. Cognitive ergonomics is based on psychological phenomena, such as knowledge, perception, and planning. It focuses on making systems simple and easy to use by analyzing human perception and mental processing.

By understanding cognitive psychology and ergonomics, we can build systems by (i) understanding user behavior and needs (ii) measuring user satisfaction (iii) planning content by: understanding how information is organized and presented to the users (iv) facilitating actions which are easy to access and use (v) focusing on accessibility as to how a disabled person can use the system (vi) collecting user feedback and improving the system functionality. To build the digital persona with the above stated pointers in mind and formalize a design approach, we had to understand the deployment environment - how will user interact with the persona? What will likely be of interest to them? And how the digital persona should adapt to support user's needs? To choose a design approach, we also had to think of the relevant criteria to assess and evaluate the approach for design

Table 1. Sample data used for training the SVM classifier

Text			Facial								Audio							Label
.82	0.01	0.17	0	0	0	0.05	0.62	0.28	0	0.05	0.7	0	0.23	0.07	0	0	0	High
0.72	0.02	0.26	0	0.05	0.06	0	0.19	0.6	0.02	0.08	0.6	0	0.32	0.08	0	0	0	High
0.2	0.7	0.1	0	0	0.1	0	.3	.5	0	.1	0	.1	.8	0	0	.06	.04	Low
.1	.2	.7	0	0	0	.1	.7	.2	0	0	.3	0	.5	.2	0	0	0	High
.3	.2	.5	0.7	0	0	.2	0	.1	0	0	0	0.1	.7	0	0.2	0	0	Low
.9	0	.1	0	0	0	0	.3	.6	0	0.1	.8	0	0	.1	0	0	0.1	High
0	.19	.81	0	0	0	0	0	.9	0.1	0	0	.9	.1	0	0	0	0	High
.1	.8	.1	0	0	0.3	0	0	.7	0	0	.1	0.4	.4	0	0	0.1	0	Low
.63	.3	.07	0	0.1	0	0	.6	.3	0	0	0	0.2	.6	0	0	0	0.2	High
0	.42	.58	0.3	0	0	0	0	.68	0.02	0	0	0	.8	.2	0	0	0	Low

representation and how well the approach answers different design questions by also allowing room for improvement.

Post our design thinking sessions and evaluating various storyboards, we chose to implement the digital deepfake person as a holographic projection [19]. There were 3 options for a holographic experience – a holographic table, holographic wall and a holographic stage. If a holographic table had to be used, the persona had to be projected only up to 3 ft. Because of this limitation, we did not consider this option. We further evaluated the options of a holographic wall and a holographic stage. The holographic stage setup gave us the flexibility of having a stage where we could place art artifacts on top of the stage for a more immersive effect. Also, the stage provided an auditorium environment which would enable large number of visitors experience the interaction with the digital persona of the deceased artist. The distance of the projection was designed to ensure people sitting on wheelchairs also could watch the experience without interruption. Since the distance was selected considering the accessibility, we had to choose to perform deepfake by not only taking video of the actor till the chest but the entire body. Implementing holographic projection of the entire length of the body was also visually more appealing than projecting it till the chest.

Conversation with the digital persona was designed to be related to the artist, Indian art and art works. The natural language understanding and natural language processing techniques were built in with multilingual feature to support both the global and local visitors in the museum. Accurate natural language understanding (NLU) is also a challenge due to speech recognition errors occurring due to noisy environment, speaker accent, speaker interruption, self correction etc. To minimize the errors, a moderator was needed to have a controlled environment and a noise reduction handheld mic with master/slave configuration was provided to the users so that there could be only one single user interacting with the persona at any given point in time. To facilitate user feedback and adapt to individual user's attention span, emotion analytics was implemented as described in Sect. 3.1.

3.3 Social and Organization Psychology

While cognitive psychology and ergonomics is about studying human behavior in a single user environment, social and organization psychology is concerned with the study of interpersonal, group, intergroup and interorganizational behavior. It deals with how interactions can be understood and modified with various types of interventions.

For applying social and organization psychology in creating the digital persona, we had to get views of the deployment environment from our internal team as well as the team in the museum. The museum team also needed to have the infrastructure visualized for the holographic projections. A pilot was also conducted with mock visitors to the museum and get their views on how they would feel about the interaction with the persona and what genre of questions would they likely ask the persona during their interaction to learn about the artist and Indian art. Group behavior which involved interactions among individuals post their experience in the pilot was also studied. In terms of organization psychology, the teams to build the digital persona was dynamic multi team environment. Thus, task design played an important key role in team effectiveness. The development environment was set to have openness and transparency among all key stakeholders and ensured no individual team worked in silos.

3.4 Design and Arts

Another traditional idea within human centered computing is formalizing the Arts as a source of inspiration. Certainly, artistic research can have an epistemic value and artworks can inspire reflection even in software engineering [35].

According to Solder Pold's book of Interface Aesthetics [32], he recognizes three types of works dealing with alternative realism of the interface which can be combined in the same artwork - a. Artworks dealing with Functional realism b. Artworks dealing with Media realism and c. Artworks dealing with Illusionistic realism.

In the creation of the holographic digital persona, artworks dealing with illusionistic realism is applied where interfaces are designed by maximizing reality towards immersive simulation. Applying this artwork design will enable users to become immersed in the illusionistic world presented. During storyboarding, sketches and visualization of the artist's projection on the holographic stage was made even before the implementation of the persona. This ensured early feedback and agreement of the outcome with the involved stakeholders. Sketches were made keeping in mind the considerations of the physical features, dress, style, props, shoe wear etc. Also, to maximize the immersive simulation in the outcome, post production tools to provide the digital visual effects were used.

3.5 Ethics

Since the intention is to apply deepfake for good, it must be created ethically as well. The challenge is how do we call a fake as genuine? If we follow the rules of fairness, accountability and transparency, we can address some of the concerns related to the fakes. Accountability and transparency mean to report, explain the algorithmic decision making, secure training data, as well as mitigate any negative social impact. To minimize negative social impact, secure communication channels need to be used and the deepfakes need to be deployed in a controlled environment with authorized access to play the deepfake video. Transparency can be achieved by making the data and code available along with the decisions taken during the system development. For example, the decisions taken for choosing a particular software for face superimposition and speech synthesis, decision taken on the parameter values for the face superimposition and speech synthesis etc.

Fingerprinting can be used with encryption while creating the video in order to ensure authorized use during deployment. Permissions and consent need to be taken from source artist or from the rightful heir in the artist's family of whose fake we want to create. To ensure fairness, we must evaluate that the person chosen to be source of the fake does not provide an impression of gender and racial bias when the outcome of the deepfake video is consumed by the end users.

Ingenuity in AI and technology development must be tempered with integrity, values, governance, policy and legal consequences for misconduct. These are issues that need collectively informed public solutions with input from industry, consumer and government regulators [33]. The questions we need to answer are: a. Have we taken consent from both the parties (actor and the artist) b. Does the message put forth though the deepfake is trustworthy and is reliable source of information? c. Does the actor and the message put forth have no indications of any gender or racial bias? d. Can we confidently showcase the deepfake created in public or is it only for private viewing? e. Do we have enough reasoning to explain the creation of the deepfake f. Can the deepfake creation process be auditable? g. Are there any existing guidelines or regulatory compliance followed for creating deepfake for good?

The deepfake should be ethical by design itself. An industry wide commitment to basic legal standards, significant regulation and technological ethics need to be implemented to address immediate harms of any bad design. For example, from regulatory point of view, the content distribution platforms should be put under certain stricter legal obligations to control the deepfake content dissemination.

4   Outcome

We applied our digital persona generation approach to generate the 3 dimensional holographic persona of M.F. Husain (known as Picasso of India) with an aim to generate interest in art education for children.

We implemented two versions of the same. One, the online version that allows users to interact with persona through a web browser. Here is the link of a short demo video for the online version.

The other is the visually appealing 3 dimensional holographic version of M.F. Husain. Here is the link of how the experience would look when the video is projected on the 3d holographic stage. When viewed by naked eye, the live experience is immersive. However, the 3 dimensional aspects do not come out well in the video link presented above since it is shot using a camera and whole experience looks 2 dimensional as the depth can't be realized.

In both the versions, the persona converses with users on his life and artworks to invoke interest in the field of art. It also speaks in the voice of M.F. Husain. The experience is as if the deceased artist himself speaks to you.

The key outcomes of the generated persona are:

1. Visual appeal - We and the team at the museum found interacting with the 3 dimensional holographic digital persona more engaging as compared to interaction using 2d screen [29]. Also, since the persona converses in the voice of deceased artist, the experience is as if artist himself came to life.
2. Conversational - The persona answers around 1244 variations of questions asked by visitors related to his life and artwork. For example, questions related to persona's favourite painting, painting style, childhood, entry in the field of art, art journey etc. It can also answer tactfully to diplomatic questions to keep conversation light and funny.

5 Discussion

We have presented so far, the human centered computing design approach implemented for the creation of the digital persona. For our business implementation scenario of creating the digital persona of an artist to enable art education, the system was designed as multimodal with inputs and outputs in more than one modality. It was designed to be proactive where the digital persona understood the cultural and social context to provide an appropriate response. Affective computing was implemented to recognize, interpret and process the human interactions.

Clients or businesses who wish to use generative AI techniques to create digital personas for good, face gap in lack of reference framework, agility, adaptability and compliance issues. They need an understanding of digital persona creation to bring in the best experience for the end user. We believe, adapting the human centered design principals described in the above sections will help business to rapidly develop digital persona while being compliance aligned to provide material business impact and create sustainable value.

In future, we plan to improve the feedback loop by improvising on the text sentiment analysis and voice tone analysis on the conversation between the user and the persona.

6 Experiment Results

To evaluate the impact of our framework on learning experience of kids, we conducted a small social experiment post the deployment of the digital persona at the museum. The social experiment was conducted between two groups of

10 kids each, between the age group of 9–14 years. We wanted to check if this experience of interacting with a 3d Holographic digital persona would bring in improvement in retention of memory and enhance creativity among kids. Not only the experiment results showed a positive impact on both the factors, but also the kids who were exposed to this experience were motivated to visit the museum again.

The details of the social experiment is as follows: Both the groups were taken to museum and were taught about legendary Indian artist M.F Husain. Both the groups were given placards of 20 questions that they can ask and were encouraged to ask about Husain's life, family, artwork, interest, favorite paintings. The kids were also told that there could be a test from these 20 questions after few days (so that they can ask more questions). First group learned about M.F Husain through the traditional way in which a museum guide walked them through the museum while telling about Husain's paintings, life and interests. Kids were also allowed and encouraged to ask questions. Second group interacted with digital persona of M.F Husain and was also accompanied by a museum guide. We observed that the second group retained the learning better than first group, they also rated their experience higher than the first group. The total number of questions asked by first and second groups respectively was 14 and 17. Each group was asked to rate their experience on a scale of 1 to 4, i.e. how satisfied they were on learning about Husain from four choices 4) Extremely Satisfied 3) Satisfied 2) Dissatisfied 1) Extremely Dissatisfied. First group average score was 3 and second group average was 3.67.

After 3 days, all students were given a test of 14 short questions. All of which were parts of the elaborate answers provided to them for 20 questions. First group answered 34% correctly, while second group answered 43% correctly. Each kid was also asked the same questions that they had asked in their previous visit. While first group correctly remembered 6 answers out of 14 questions asked i.e. 43%, second group remembered 10 answers out of 17 questions asked i.e. 59%. All the kids were also asked if they would like to have the experience again, only six from first group answered in a yes, while eight kids from second group wanted to interact with Husain's persona again.

7   Conclusion

For a richer and immersive experience, any software system should employ the human centered computing design approach. Human centered computing involves creation of theoretical frameworks, design and implementation of technical approaches and systems in many areas which include – a. Systems for problem-solving by people interacting in distributed environments b. Multimedia and multimodal interfaces c. Intelligent interfaces and user modelling d. Information visualization and adaptation of content to accommodate different capabilities, modalities, bandwidth, latency etc. [10].

In this paper, we showed the human centered computing design approach implemented for the creation of a digital persona adhering to the characteristics of being expressive, responsive, proactive and adaptive. While implementing the approach, it is observed that sociology, psychology and cognitive science play important roles apart from just the use of technology in presenting the digital persona for an engaged and immersive experience. We provided the outcome of our approach for creating digital persona of a renowned deceased artist M.F. Husain. We also conducted and presented the results of a social experiment which showed that our implementation allows children visiting the museum to explore artists and art forms in completely new ways. This framework allows us to create human centric digital personas in an affordable manner. These digital personas can be used in various other industries as well to improve customer experience.

References

1. Cognitive ergonomics and user interface design (2008). http://members.upc.nl/g.haan24/articles/chapter1.html. Accessed 7 Feb 2020
2. An AI service that analyses faces in images (2020). https://azure.microsoft.com/en-in/services/cognitive-services/face/. Accessed 17 May 2020
3. Create your own deepfakes online (2020). https://deepfakesweb.com/. Accessed 5 Feb 2020
4. Language understanding (LUIS) (2020). https://www.luis.ai/home. Accessed 15 June 2020
5. Real-time multimodal emotion recognition (2020). https://github.com/maelfabien/Multimodal-Emotion-Recognition. Accessed 29 July 2020
6. The Salvador Dali museum (2020). https://thedali.org/. Accessed 17 July 2020
7. Text analytics API documentation (2020). https://docs.microsoft.com/en-us/azure/cognitive-services/text-analytics/. Accessed 22 July 2020
8. Arik, S.Ö., Chen, J., Peng, K., Ping, W., Zhou, Y.: Neural voice cloning with a few samples. CoRR abs/1802.06006 (2018). http://arxiv.org/abs/1802.06006
9. kan bayashi: Unofficial parallel wavegan (+ MelGAN) implementation with Pytorch (2020). https://github.com/kan-bayashi/ParallelWaveGAN. Accessed 24 Feb 2020
10. CISE - IIS - About (2020). http://www.nsf.gov/cise/iis/about.jsp. Accessed 12 Jan 2020
11. Cortes, C., Vapnik, V.: Support-vector networks. Mach. Learn. **20**(3), 273–297 (1995)
12. DeepFaceLab is the leading software for creating deepfakes (2020). https://github.com/iperov/DeepFaceLab. Accessed 11 Jan 2020
13. Pytorch implementation of convolutional neural networks-based text-to-speech synthesis models (2019). https://github.com/r9y9/deepvoice3_pytorch. Accessed 21 Feb 2020
14. Egger, M., Ley, M., Hanke, S.: Emotion recognition from physiological signal analysis: a review. Electron. Notes Theor. Comput. Sci. **343**, 35–55 (2019). https://doi.org/10.1016/j.entcs.2019.04.009. http://www.sciencedirect.com/science/article/pii/S157106611930009X. The Proceedings of AmI, The 2018 European Conference on Ambient Intelligence (2018)
15. Faceswap: Deepfakes software for all (2020). https://github.com/deepfakes/faceswap. Accessed 29 Jan 2020

16. A denoising autoencoder, adversarial losses and attention mechanisms for face swapping (2019). https://github.com/shaoanlu/faceswap-GAN. Accessed 19 Jan 2020

17. Fried, O., et al.: Text-based editing of talking-head video. ACM Trans. Graph. **38**(4), July 2019. https://doi.org/10.1145/3306346.3323028

18. You can now speak using someone else's voice with deep learning, July 2019. https://towardsdatascience.com/you-can-now-speak-using-someone-elses-voice-with-deep-learning-8be24368fa2b. Accessed 16 Feb 2020

19. Holography (2020). https://en.wikipedia.org/wiki/Holography. Accessed 4 Feb 2020

20. Jaimes, A., Sebe, N., Gatica-Perez, D.: Human-centered computing: a multimedia perspective. In: Proceedings of the 14th ACM International Conference on Multimedia, MM 2006, New York, NY, USA, pp. 855–864. Association for Computing Machinery (2006). https://doi.org/10.1145/1180639.1180829

21. These five platforms will make your bots language-intelligent (2016). https://chatbotsmagazine.com/these-five-platforms-will-makeyour-bots-language-intelligent-634556750abd. Accessed 5 Jan 2020

22. Jia, Y., et al.: Transfer learning from speaker verification to multispeaker text-to-speech synthesis. CoRR abs/1806.04558 (2018). http://arxiv.org/abs/1806.04558

23. Kazeminia, S., et al.: GANs for medical image analysis. Artif. Intell. Med. **109** (2020). https://doi.org/10.1016/j.artmed.2020.101938. http://www.sciencedirect.com/science/article/pii/S0933365719311510

24. VGGFace implementation with Keras framework (2020). https://github.com/rcmalli/keras-vggface. Accessed 4 Jan 2020

25. Kietzmann, J., Lee, L.W., McCarthy, I.P., Kietzmann, T.C.: DeepFakes: trick or treat? Bus. Horizons **63**(2), 135–146 (2020). https://doi.org/10.1016/j.bushor.2019.11.006. http://www.sciencedirect.com/science/article/pii/S0007681319301600

26. Kobayashi, K., Toda, T.: sprocket: Open-source voice conversion software, pp. 203–210, June 2018. https://doi.org/10.29007/s4t1

27. Emotion analytics (2018). https://searchcustomerexperience.techtarget.com/definition/emotions-analytics-EA. Accessed 14 Jan 2020

28. Nguyen, T., Nguyen, C., Nguyen, T., Nguyen, D., Nahavandi, S.: Deep learning for deepfakes creation and detection, September 2019

29. 10x your employee engagement with immersive learning experiences (2019). https://www.jolt.io/blog/10x-your-employee-engagement-with-great-learning-experiences. Accessed 27 June 2020

30. van den Oord, A., et al.: WaveNet: a generative model for raw audio. arXiv (2016). https://arxiv.org/abs/1609.03499

31. Ping, W., et al.: Deep voice 3: scaling text-to-speech with convolutional sequence learning (2017)

32. Pold, S.: Interface realisms: the interface as aesthetic form. Postmod. Cult. **15**, January 2005. https://doi.org/10.1353/pmc.2005.0013

33. Sanders, N., Wood, J.: The Humachine: Humankind, Machines, and the Future of Enterprise. Taylor & Francis, Abingdon (2019). https://books.google.co.in/books?id=OVauDwAAQBAJ

34. Shen, J., et al.: Natural TTS synthesis by conditioning WaveNet on MEL spectrogram predictions, pp. 4779–4783, April 2018. https://doi.org/10.1109/ICASSP.2018.8461368

35. Tomáis, E.: How the arts can help tangible interaction design: a critical reorientation. Informatics **4**, 31 (2017). https://doi.org/10.3390/informatics4030031
36. Wang, Y., et al.: Tacotron: a fully end-to-end text-to-speech synthesis model, March 2017
37. Liang, W.: The 3D holographic projection technology based on three-dimensional computer graphics, pp. 403–406, July 2012. https://doi.org/10.1109/ICALIP.2012. 6376651

Content-Based Image Retrieval Using Local Derivative Laplacian Co-occurrence Pattern

Prashant Srivastava[1]([✉]), Manish Khare[2], and Ashish Khare[3]

[1] NIIT University, Neemrana, Rajasthan, India
prashant.jk087@gmail.com
[2] Dhirubhai Ambani Institute of Information and Communication Technology, Gandhinagar, Gujarat, India
mkharejk@gmail.com
[3] Department of Electronics and Communication, University of Allahabad, Prayagraj, Uttar Pradesh, India
ashishkhare@hotmail.com

Abstract. For accessing images from huge repository in an easy manner, the images are required to be properly indexed. Content-Based Image Retrieval (CBIR) is a field which deals with finding solutions to such problems. This paper proposes a new multiresolution descriptor namely, Local Derivative Laplacian Co-occurrence Pattern (LDLCP) for CBIR. Gray level image is subjected to four-level Laplacian of Gaussian filtering in order to perform multiresolution processing of image. Local Derivative Pattern descriptors of resulting four-level filtered image is computed to extract local information from the image. Finally, the Gray-Level Co-occurrence Matrix is used for constructing feature vector. Corel-1K and Corel-5K datasets have been used to test the proposed descriptor and its performance is measured using precision and recall metrics.

Keywords: CBIR · Image retrieval · Laplacian of Gaussian · Local Derivative Pattern · Gray-Level Co-occurrence pattern

1 Introduction

Capturing the images is quite easy nowadays resulting in huge repository of different types of images. For an easy access, proper organization of images is very important. To solve such problems, image retrieval systems play an important role. Image retrieval systems are categorized broadly into two classes-Text-Based Image Retrieval (TBIR) systems and Content-Based Image Retrieval systems (CBIR). TBIR systems use keywords to retrieve relevant images from dataset. But such systems are not considered to be very efficient as manual annotation of huge repository of images is needed, and retrieval of visually similar images is difficult. In CBIR systems, the image itself is provided in the form of query from which features are extracted. This results in construction of a feature vector of that particular image which is then matched with other images in the repository. Based on similarity measurement, visually similar images get retrieved [1].

© ICST Institute for Computer Sciences, Social Informatics and Telecommunications Engineering 2021
Published by Springer Nature Switzerland AG 2021. All Rights Reserved
W. Fu et al. (Eds.): ICMTEL 2021, LNICST 388, pp. 402–412, 2021.
https://doi.org/10.1007/978-3-030-82565-2_33

The primary features, which include colour, texture, and shape, have been extensively used for constructing feature vector. Many feature descriptors [2, 3] have been used to extract colour features from image. For extracting texture features Gabor transform [4] and local patterns [5–8] have been extensively used. Similarly, shape features have been extracted using polygonal structures and moments to construct feature vector [9].

Construction of feature vector using single feature proved to be insufficient due to complex structure of image. This limitation shifted the trend of CBIR techniques towards combination of primary features [10]. The combination of features has been mostly exploited on single resolution of image. An image consists of varying level of details and for extracting such details, single resolution processing of image proves to be insufficient. This drawback is overcome by making use of multiresolution processing of image which analyzes and interprets an image at multiple scales. Processing of images at more than one resolution has an important advantage of detecting those features at a particular level which were left undetected at previous level [11]. This paper proposes a multiresolution feature vector Local Derivative Laplacian Co-occurrence Pattern (LDLCP). It exploits multiple resolutions of image to extract local information by computing Local Derivative Pattern descriptor of Laplacian of Gaussian of image using three different filters of size 3×3, 5×5, and 7×7 and different values of standard deviation. Construction of feature vector has been performed using Gray-Level Cooccurrence Matrix (GLCM). The proposed descriptor efficiently extracts directional local information at multiple resolutions of image.

The remaining sections of the paper is organized as follows- Sect. 2 discusses Related work, Sect. 3 discusses briefly about LDP, LoG, and GLCM. The Proposed Method is discussed in Sect. 4. Section 5 describes Experiments and Results and finally, Sect. 6 concluding the paper.

2 Related Work

Image feature descriptors play a significant role in extraction of discriminating features. Local feature descriptors such as LBP [5], LTP [6], and LDP [7] have been extensively used for feature extraction. While these feature descriptors extract low level features, there are many features descriptor such as HID [12] which extract high level features from the image along with low level features. These feature descriptors have been mostly exploited using single resolution of an image for feature extraction. Processing an image using only single resolution for feature extraction proves to be insufficient as image contains complex details. For overcoming this limitation, feature descriptors which utilize multiple resolutions of image to extract features have been introduced. Srivastava and Khare [13] proposed a multiresolution descriptor which combined Local Spatial Binary Pattern and Gaussian filtering technique for construction of feature vector. The method proposed in [14] computed wavelet coefficients of LBP descriptor image. Another descriptor Wavelet Correlogram which combined wavelet transform and colour correlogram for image retrieval is proposed in [15]. Multiresolution feature descriptors extract features by utilizing multiple resolutions of image. This proves to be advantageous as features which were left undetected in previous levels get detected at another level. This paper proposes a novel multiresolution feature descriptor, Local Derivative Laplacian Co-occurrence Pattern (LDLCP).

3   Laplacian of Gaussian, Local Derivative Pattern, and Gray-Level Co-occurrence Pattern

3.1   Laplacian of Gaussian

Laplacian is a measure of second derivative of an image. Laplacian is used for detecting edges in an image. The Laplacian $L(x, y)$ of an image having intensity value I can be mathematically expressed as-

$$L(x, y) = \frac{\partial^2 I}{\partial x^2} + \frac{\partial^2 I}{\partial y^2} \tag{1}$$

However, the original form of Laplacian is not used for detecting edges in the image because of its sensitivity to noise. The segmentation operation becomes complicated because the magnitude of Laplacian generates double edges. Due to this, it is unable to detect edge direction. In order to overcome this drawback, the image is first blurred using Gaussian filter. The degree of blurring is determined by standard deviation σ. The equation that combines both these filters is called Laplacian of Gaussian and is mathematically expressed as-

$$LoG = -\frac{1}{\pi \sigma^4}[1 - \frac{x^2 + y^2}{2\sigma^2}]e^{\frac{x^2+y^2}{2\sigma^2}} \tag{2}$$

LoG filtering has a number of important applications apart from removing noise from image. One of the most important applications is multiresolution processing of image. The multiresolution processing of image is performed through convolution operation between kernels of different size and image thereby resulting in a series of images at different resolutions. These images can be further used for extracting features to construct feature vector for retrieval.

3.2   Local Derivative Pattern

Local Derivative Pattern (LDP) is a local feature descriptor which encodes higher-order derivative information in different directions unlike LBP which encodes $(n-1)^{th}$ order derivative direction variations on the basis of binary coding function [7]. It extracts information in multiple direction which represent various distinctive relationships. LDP extracts more discriminative information as it encodes more distinguishing relationships among intensity values in a local region.

3.3 Gray-Level Cooccurrence Matrix

GLCM computes how frequently pixel pairs located adjacently having specific values and at specific directions occur in an image [16]. Such information are not provided by other features such as histogram.

3.4 Advantages of Local Derivative Laplacian Cooccurrence Pattern

Advantages of the proposed descriptor can be summarized as follows-

1. Multiresolution processing of image extracts features at more than one scale. Due to this, undetected features at a particular scale are detected at another scale.
2. The proposed descriptor extracts local information from image through LDP which encodes higher-order derivative information unlike LBP
3. LoG filtering of image at multiple levels help in removal of noise which may cause local pattern descriptors to vary.
4. Although LoG filtering extracts features at multiple scales of image, it fails to extract directional information. LDP descriptor extracts local information at four different orientations (0^0, 45^0, 90^0, and 135^0). Combination of LoG with LDP perform extraction of local directional information at more than one level of resolution of image.
5. Construction of vector through GLCM provides spatial distribution details which are not provided by other features such as histogram.

4   The Proposed Method

The proposed method consists of the following steps –

1. Application of Laplacian of Gaussian on gray scale image.
2. Computation of Local Derivative Pattern descriptor of resulting filtered image.
3. Construction of GLCM of LDP descriptors.
4. Similarity Measurement.

4.1   Laplacian of Gaussian (LoG) Filtering

Application of LoG filters results in multiresolution processing of gray scale image. Image decomposition into multiple resolutions gather varying discriminative details. LoG filter is applied on grayscale image by performing convolution operation between grayscale image and LoG filter. In the proposed method, in case of level 1, the kernel size is considered 3×3, and standard deviation value as 1; for level 2, size of kernel is considered as 5×5, and standard deviation value as 1.25; for level 3, size of kernel is considered as 7×7, and standard deviation value as 1.5; and for level 4, size of kernel is considered as 9×9, and standard deviation value as 1.75.

4.2 Computation of LDP Descriptors

The next step of the proposed method is computation of second order LDP descriptor of resulting filtered images. The resulting descriptor are then stored in four separate matrices. Second order LDP extracts local information at multiple orientations.

4.3 Construction of Gray-Level Co-occurrence Matrix (GLCM)

GLCM of resulting second order LDP descriptors is constructed in the next step. GLCM acts as feature vector to retrieve visually similar images. In the proposed method, GLCM for 0^0 angle and distance 1 has been considered for constructing feature vector and rescaled to size 8×8.

4.4 Similarity Measurement

Similarity measurement serve the purpose of retrieving images that are visually similar to the query image. Let $(f_{Q1}, f_{Q2}, ...f_{Qn})$ be the set of query images and let $(f_{DB1}, f_{DB2}, ...f_{DBn})$ be the set of database images. Then, the similarity between query image and database image is computed using the following formula-

$$Similarity(S) = \sum_{i=1}^{n} \left| \frac{f_{DBi} - f_{Qi}}{1 + f_{DBi} + f_{Qi}} \right|, \; i = 1, 2, \ldots, n \tag{3}$$

5 Experiment and Results

To carry out the experiment using the proposed method, images from the two datasets, namely Corel-1K [18] and Corel-5K [19] datasets are considered. There are of 1000 images in Corel-1K dataset which are divided into 10 categories, each containing 100 images. Corel-5K datasets consist of 5000 of images divided into 50 categories, each containing 100 images. In case of Corel-1K dataset, the size of each image is either 256×384 or 384×256. In case of Corel-5K dataset, the size of each image is either 127×187 or 187×127.

In order to ease the computation process, the resizing of each image of Corel-1K dataset has been done to size 256×256 and to size 128×128 of Corel-5K dataset. For experimentation purpose, each image in the dataset is considered as query image.

5.1 Performance Evaluation

Precision and recall metrics have been used to evaluate the proposed method. Precision metric is defined as the ratio of total number of relevant images retrieved to the total number of images retrieved. The mathematical expression of precision can be expressed as

$$P = \frac{I_R}{T_R} \tag{4}$$

where I_R denotes total number of relevant images retrieved and T_R denotes total number of images retrieved. Recall metric is defined as the ratio of total number of relevant images retrieved to the total number of relevant images in the database. The mathematical expression of recall can be expressed as

$$R = \frac{I_R}{C_R} \tag{5}$$

where I_R denotes total number of relevant images retrieved and C_R denotes total number of relevant images in the database. In this experiment, $T_R = 10$ and $C_R = 100$.

5.2 Retrieval Results

Application of LoG with different values of standard deviation and filter size produce four smoothed images. LDP descriptors of resulting smoothed images is computed which results in four LDP matrices. The construction of feature vector is performed by computing GLCM of each of these matrices separately. In order to perform similarity measurement, each of these feature vectors are used separately resulting in four sets of similar images. Union of these sets of similar images results in final sets of similar images. The computation of recall is done by counting total number of relevant images in the dataset. In order to compute precision value, counting of top n matches is performed for each set, followed by computing union of these sets for producing final set. For the computation of precision, top n matches in the final set are considered. The relevant image set of previous level along with the relevant image set of that level is considered to obtain relevant image set for the current level.

For four levels of resolution, average precision and recall values can be observed in Table 1 and Table 2 for Corel-1K and Corel-5K datasets. The plot between average values of precision and dataset, and recall and dataset for four levels of resolution is shown in Fig. 2 for Corel-1K and Corel-5K datasets. There is a surge in the precision and recall values as the level of resolution increases, which can be observed from Table 1, Table 2, and Fig. 1. The proposed method exploits more than one resolution of image because of which the features that are not detected at a particular level get detected at another level of resolution. This phenomenon results in surge in precision and recall values.

Table 1. Average Recall and Precision values of the Proposed Method for Corel-1K dataset.

Level of resolution	Recall (%)	Precision (%)
Level 1	35.79	57.89
Level 2	41.31	70.52
Level 3	44.33	75.79
Level 4	46.13	78.80

Table 2. Average Recall and Precision values of the Proposed Method for Corel-5K dataset.

Level of resolution	Recall (%)	Precision (%)
Level 1	14.83	34.18
Level 2	18.57	43.59
Level 3	20.87	49.14
Level 4	22.69	53.16

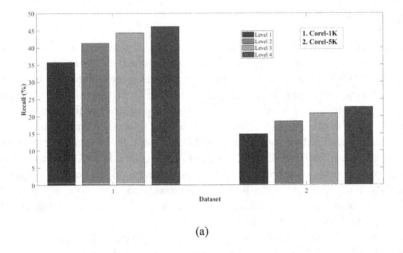

(a)

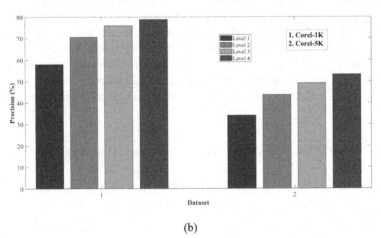

(b)

Fig. 1. (a) Average Recall vs. Dataset (b) Average Precision vs. Dataset

5.3 Performance Comparison

For testing the efficiency of the proposed descriptor LDLCP, its performance has been compared with some of the such as Srivastava et al. [9], Srivastava and Khare [13], Zeng et al. [17], Tiwari et al. [2], Vipparthi and Nagar [8], in terms of precision. These methods combine multiple features at single resolution of image. Single resolution processing does not prove to be efficient for extracting discriminating details present in the image. Hence, these methods fail to produce high retrieval accuracy. The proposed descriptor constructs feature vector by extracting local information at more than one scale of image. Therefore, the proposed descriptor produces better retrieval accuracy in terms of precision metric than some of the other state-of-the-art CBIR methods. Table 3 and Table 4 show with other CBIR techniques in terms of precision on Corel-1K and Corel-5K datasets respectively. Figure 2 demonstrates performance comparison in terms of precision on Corel-1K and Corel-5K datasets. The results shown in Table 3, Table 4, and Fig. 2 clearly demonstrate the effectiveness of the proposed method in comparison to other CBIR techniques in terms of precision metric.

Table 3. Performance comparison of the Proposed Method with other state-of-the-art methods on Corel-1K dataset

Method	Precision (%)
Srivastava et al. [9]	53.70
Srivastava and Khare [17]	76.46
Tiwari et al. [2]	71.78
Proposed method	**78.80**

Table 4. Performance comparison of the Proposed Method with other state-of-the-art methods on Corel-5K dataset

Method	Precision (%)
Srivastava and Khare [9]	32.18
Zeng et al. [17]	51.80
Vipparthi and Nagar [8]	42.40
Proposed method	**53.16**

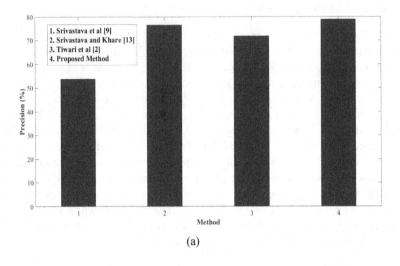

(a)

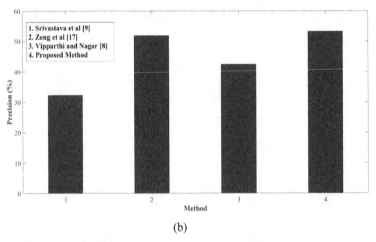

(b)

Fig. 2. Performance comparison of the Proposed Method with other state-of-the-art CBIR techniques in terms of precision on (a) Corel-1K dataset (b) Corel-5K dataset

6 Conclusion

A novel descriptor Local Derivative Laplacian Co-occurrence Pattern (LDLCP) is proposed in this paper. The proposed descriptor integrates multiresolution processing of image with local pattern descriptor for constructing feature vector to perform retrieval. Multiresolution processing of gray scale image was performed using Laplacian of Gaussian (LoG) filter followed by extraction of local information from the filtered image using Local Derivative Pattern (LDP). Finally, the construction of feature vector was carried out using GLCM. A significant advantage of the proposed descriptor is that it exploits image at more than one scale to extract features so that the features that do not get detected at one level get detected at another level. The proposed descriptor utilizes second order Local Derivative Pattern which efficiently extracts local information at different orientations. Performance measurement of the proposed method was carried out using precision and recall metrics. The proposed method has better performance than some of the other CBIR methods as demonstrated by experimental results. Use of other multiresolution techniques such as contourlet transform along with efficient local feature descriptors to improve retrieval accuracy can further improve the performance of the proposed method. Also, incorporating intelligent techniques such as deep learning can help in extracting semantic features.

References

1. Dutta, R., Joshi, D., Li, J., Wang, J.Z.: Image retrieval: ideas, influences, and trends of the new age. ACM Comput. Surv. **40**(2), 5:1–5:60 (2008)
2. Tiwari, A.K., Kanhangad, V., Pachori, R.B.: Histogram refinement for texture descriptor based image retrieval. Sig. Process. Image Commun. **53**, 73–85 (2017)
3. Huang, J., Kumar, S.R., Mitra, M., Zhu, W., Zabih, R.: Image indexing using color correlograms. In: IEEE Computer Society Conference on Computer Vision and Pattern Recognition Proceedings, pp. 762–768 (1997)
4. Manjunath, B.S., Ma, W.Y.: Texture features for browsing and retrieval of image data. IEEE Trans. Pattern Anal. Mach. Intell. **18**(8), 837–842 (1996)
5. Ojala, T., Pietikäinen, M., Harwood, D.: A comparative study of texture measures with classification based on featured distributions. Pattern Recogn. **29**(1), 51–59 (1996)
6. Tan, X., Triggs, B.: Enhanced local texture feature sets for face recognition under difficult lighting conditions. IEEE Trans. Image Process. **19**(6), 1635–1650 (2010)
7. Zhang, B., Gao, Y., Zhao, S., Liu, J.: Local derivative pattern versus local binary pattern: face recognition with high-order local pattern descriptor. IEEE Trans. Image Process. **19**(2), 533–544 (2009)
8. Vipparthi, S.K., Nagar, S.K.: Expert image retrieval system using directional local motif XoR patterns. Expert Syst. Appl. **41**(17), 8016–8026 (2014)
9. Srivastava, P., Binh, N.T., Khare, A.: Content-based image retrieval using moments of local ternary pattern. Mob. Netw. Appl. **19**(5), 618–625 (2014)
10. Wang, X., Yu, Y., Yang, H.: An effective image retrieval scheme using color, texture and shape features. Comput. Stand. Interfaces **33**(1) 59–68 (2011)
11. Mallat, S.G.: A theory for multiresolution signal decomposition: the wavelet representation. IEEE Trans. Pattern Anal. Mach. Intell. **11**(7), 674–693 (1989)
12. Zhang, M., Zhang, K., Feng, Q., Wang, J., Jun, K., Lu, Y.: A novel image retrieval method based on hybrid information descriptors. J. Vis. Commun. Image Represent. **25**(7), 1574–1587 (2014)
13. Srivastava, P., Khare, A.: Content-based image retrieval using multiscale local spatial binary Gaussian co-occurrence pattern. In: Intelligent Communication and Computational Technologies Proceedings, pp. 85–95. Springer, Singapore (2018)
14. Khare, M., Srivastava, P., Gwak, J., Khare, A.: A multiresolution approach for content-based image retrieval using wavelet transform of local binary pattern. In: Asian Conference on Intelligent Information and Database Systems Proceedings, pp. 529–538. Springer, Cham (2018)
15. Moghaddam, H.A., Khajoie, T.T., Rouhi, A.H., Tarzjan, M.S.: Wavelet correlogram: a new approach for image indexing and retrieval. Pattern Recogn. **38**(12), 2506–2518 (2005)

16. Haralick, R.M., Shanmugam, K., Dinstein, I.H.: Textural features for image classification. IEEE Trans. Syst. Man Cybern. **6**, 610–621 (1973)
17. Zeng, S., Huang, R., Wang, H., Kang, Z.: Image retrieval using spatiograms of colors quantized by Gaussian mixture models. Neurocomputing **171**, 673–684 (2016)
18. http://wang.ist.psu.edu/docs/related/ Accessed Apr 2014
19. http://www.ci.gxnu.edu.cn/cbir/ Accessed Jun 2015

Multi-spectral Image Filtering Algorithm Based on Convolutional Neural Network

Dan Luo[1][✉] and Rong Hu[2]

[1] Chengdu College of University of Electronic Science and Technology of China, Chengdu 641402, China
[2] School of Intelligence Technology, Geely University, Chengdu 641402, China

Abstract. In order to solve the problem of long processing time and poor processing effect of traditional methods, a multispectral image filtering algorithm based on convolutional neural network is proposed. Based on convolution neural network, the spectrum image features are defined, and the image SNR is registered. Based on Fourier transform, the improved algorithm of multi spectrum superposition is used to realize the mean filtering of multi spectrum image. The experimental results show that this method has higher stability and effectiveness in the actual operation process, and the image filtering time is shorter. The experimental results prove the effectiveness of the algorithm.

Keywords: Convolutional neural network · Multispectral image · Image filtering · Coarse grain index · Edge point

1 Introduction

In the process of image formation, transmission, reception and processing, due to the actual performance of the transmission medium and the limitation of the performance of the receiving equipment, there are inevitably external and internal interferences, which will generate various noises. Therefore, it is necessary to filter the image [1–3].

At present, there are many research results about filtering image noise at home and abroad. The performance of the proposed filters is better than that of the traditional filters, but they all filter all the input samples without selection or distinction. Filtering each pixel without selection or distinction will inevitably lose some original information of the image. In the process of traditional FFT (fast Fourier transform), the coordinate transformation is easy to produce large interpolation error, which reduces the registration accuracy. And it needs several iterations, so the computational efficiency is low. It is obvious that the traditional method is difficult to have both registration ratio and computational efficiency. In addition, reference [4] proposes a median filtering method for quantum images, which uses the iterative comparison method to sort the target pixels and get the median. This paper introduces the quantum circuits of various basic modules needed to realize median filtering, and then focuses on the quantum realization method of median computing. Finally, the overall circuit framework of quantum image median

W. Fu et al. (Eds.): ICMTEL 2021, LNICST 388, pp. 413–424, 2021.
https://doi.org/10.1007/978-3-030-82565-2_34

filtering is given. The experimental results show that the method can effectively filter the noise in the image, but there is a problem of long image processing time.

Aiming at the problems of traditional methods, this paper proposes an improved algorithm based on the multi-resolution spectrum superposition of image. The algorithm does not need iteration, and has the advantage of faster image processing speed, and can achieve large magnification image registration. This paper first introduces the basic concepts of capacity measurement, multi-spectral singularity index and multi-fractal spectrum in multi-fractal analysis, and then gives the estimation method of multi-fractal spectrum based on kernel estimation method, and finally proposes a method based on multi-fractal spectrum analysis Image filtering algorithm, and the experimental results of the algorithm are given. The experimental results show that, compared with the traditional method, it has higher stability and effectiveness in the actual operation process, and the image filtering processing time is shorter, which fully verifies the practical application value of this method.

2   Multispectral Image Filtering Algorithm

2.1   Definition of Spectral Image Features Based on Convolutional Neural Network

Convolution neural network is mainly used to study the morphological structure of mixed images. Because the information on the image is not transmitted on a single channel, the image signal can not be regarded as a set of sinusoidal frequencies. According to the features of the mixed image, the spatial object is found. Since these objects contain geometric shape, color and brightness features, they can be used to analyze image information. Convolution neural network has strong generalization ability, which can be used for regular control and fault diagnosis of the algorithm. In order to better construct the image filtering fusion simulation model, convolution neural network is constructed by the following steps:

Convolutional neural network is a three-layer feedforward neural network with a hidden layer, with 3 input nodes and 1 output node. Convolutional neural network is also called radial neural network. Its initial weight has nothing to do with subsequent operations and is only determined by the structural characteristics of the network. The 3 input nodes of the default convolutional neural network are I_a, I_b, I_c and 1 output node is I_w. The structure details are shown in Fig. 1.

The core of the convolutional neural network learning method is the determination of the output weight by the network center. For the image filtering fusion simulation model, the sample set is relatively limited and the input and output nodes are few. The clustering self-organizing dynamic learning method is most suitable. The clustering self-organizing dynamic learning method has a small amount of calculation and short time to find the network center. The clustering self-organizing dynamic learning method can obtain the output weight in the shortest time, and the solution process is easier. Convolutional neural network is a theory based on the principle of mean filtering and the parallel processing method of image structural elements. It can achieve feature extraction by transforming the morphology of the target image.

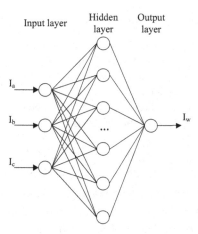

Fig. 1. Structure of convolution neural network

Based on this, the high-performance implementation method of image frequency domain filtering using multi spectrum is studied. The algorithm structure of image frequency domain filtering and the implementation of multiple spectrum are optimized, and a high-performance image frequency domain filtering algorithm based on multi spectrum is designed [5]. The traditional frequency domain filtering algorithm needs to be implemented in the multi spectrum Fourier transform inverse part and zero frequency point moving part, only the corresponding operation of the filter parameters outside the multi spectrum, so as to reduce the resource consumption of the multi spectrum and provide more resources to improve the processing speed of the real-time processing part [6–8]. In the aspect of multi spectrum implementation, based on the analysis of data dependence and resource affordability, an efficient implementation architecture is built, which reduces the total processing time of frequency domain filtering algorithm. Based on this, the multispectral image processing method based on convolution neural network is defined.

Definition 1: Let $f(x)$ be the function of $f : R \rightarrow R$, if there is:

$$|f(x) - P(x - x_0)| < C|x - x_0|^a \tag{1}$$

Where, $a > 0$, P is the closed sphere of polynomial $x \in B$ whose degree does not exceed a, and C is a constant greater than 0, such that:

$$a(x) = \sup\left(a : f \in C_x^a\right) \tag{2}$$

Therefore, the multispectral index a can well describe the local characteristics of the function $f(x)$.

Based on the above definition, the definition of multispectral image filtering algorithm can better ensure the accuracy of the algorithm.

2.2 Multi-spectral Image Registration Signal-To-Noise Ratio

Image signal-to-noise ratio (SNR) is the ratio of power spectrum of image signal to noise, which can be approximately equal to the peak signal-to-noise ratio (PSNR) of $10 \times$ LG (2552 /MSE). However, in the image registration based on frequency domain method, whether the two kinds of images can be accurately registered depends on whether the maximum position of the inverse Fourier transform image of the cross power spectrum is accurate. Based on this, the registration SNR is defined:

$$\text{SNR}_{\text{match}} = \frac{E_{\text{peak}}}{E_{\text{no peak}}} = \frac{\iint_{\text{peak}} |p(x, y)|^2 dxdy}{\iint_{\text{no}_p\text{eak}} |p(x, y)|^2 dxdy} \tag{3}$$

Where, E_{peak} and $E_{\text{no\_peak}}$ respectively represent the peak energy and non-peak energy in the cross power spectrum, and $p(x, y)$ is the inverse Fourier transform value of the cross power spectrum. And prove that the formula satisfies:

$$\text{SNR}_{\text{match}} \approx k \frac{E_{\text{signal}}}{E_{\text{noise}}} = k \frac{\iint |f(x, y)|^2 dxdy}{\iint |n(x, y)|^2 dxdy} = k \times \text{SNR} \tag{4}$$

Where E_{signal}, E_{noise} is the energy of signal and noise respectively; $f(x, y)$ and $n(x, y)$ are the original image and noise function values respectively, and k is a constant. Under normal conditions, the maximum value of registration signal-to-noise ratio corresponds to the correct registration parameters. However, when the noise is stronger than the signal, the mismatch will occur. Therefore, it is particularly important to distinguish the types of noise and remove or weaken them [9]. The larger the SNR, the higher the SNR. The SNR is inversely proportional to the noise power. Therefore, the spectrum noise caused by the image scaling, rotation and interpolation in the registration process can be minimized to improve the image registration accuracy. Based on this, the image clustering fusion standard is analyzed, as shown in Table 1.

Table 1. Multi-spectral image filtering standards

Positive and negative value range of image filtering	Fusion parameters	Multi spectrum image filtering processing function
$Y \in (0, 0.35]$	λ_1	$f_1 = \sum\limits_{0}^{Y=0.35} \frac{i \cdot \sqrt{\lambda_1}}{ds}$
$Y \in (0.35, 0.70]$	λ_2	$f_2 = \sum\limits_{0.35}^{Y=0.70} \frac{i \cdot \sqrt{\lambda_2}}{ds}$
$Y \in (0.70, 1.05]$	λ_3	$f_3 = \sum\limits_{0.70}^{Y=1.05} \frac{i \cdot \sqrt{\lambda_3}}{ds}$

Using the histogram estimation method to estimate a strictly stationary process can usually obtain satisfactory estimation results, but for non-stationary processes and composite processes, especially when the multispectral image is not a concave function, the histogram method The estimated result will cause the loss of some detailed information. Taking into account the limit relationship of image features, if $p(x, y)$ is the gray value of the local blurred pixel of the image, combine the principle of median filtering to segment the image contour of the blurred area and record it For the gray values and characteristic corner points in the grid image, the standard gray values of the horizontal and vertical coordinates of the three-dimensional point image of the local area are set as:

$$F = \text{SNR}_{\text{match}}\, p(x, y) \times \frac{v(y)}{v(x)} \tag{5}$$

According to the principle of edge constraint, the local filtering frequency of image blurred area is calculated

$$K(x, y) = \frac{F}{L(a, b) - p(x, y)} \tag{6}$$

Furthermore, wavelet analysis and feature detection are performed on the global gray value of the image. According to the detection results, local feature fusion processing is performed to improve the recognition and repair effect of the image features of the blurred area. The specific identification steps are shown in Fig. 2.

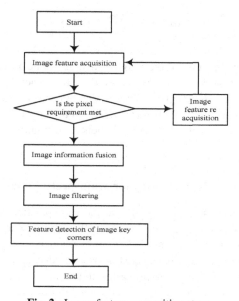

Fig. 2. Image feature recognition steps

Usually, the partial blurring of the image is mostly caused by noise. Therefore, in order to better realize the effective processing of the partial blur area of the image, the interference noise collected in the process of fuzzy image feature recognition is reduced. In order to ensure the denoising effect, denoise the gray value of the superimposed light source. By collecting and filtering the value of the strong light point in the image, the characteristic value m of the wave frequency of the sharp change in the gray value and the amplitude z of the speckle superposition are obtained. The specific algorithm for:

$$E = \sum_{n}^{m} F(n) - 1 \sum_{n-1}^{m} m \exp \frac{1}{2(m-z)} \lim_{n \to \infty} w * \gamma (n-1)^{n-1} \tag{7}$$

Where, γ is the light spot wave oscillator, w is the phase angle of the light spot area. If the detection area element value is g, ξ is the independent statistical quantity of image denoising information. Based on the above algorithm, the requirements of noise reduction for local fuzzy features of multi-dimensional color image can be realized, and the noise reduction effect can be improved to the greatest extent. In order to better optimize and improve the automatic filtering algorithm of image local fuzzy features. The size of selected structural elements should be kept moderate. If the size is too large, the image details will be lost. The selected structural elements can cover the noise and retain the image details. When the size of the structure elements is selected, the image can be filtered. Mean filtering is to replace the gray value of the original image $f(a, b)$ with the average value of each point in the image to remove the suddenly changed points. K is $i \times j$ rectangle template, $\frac{1}{h}$ is template coefficient, and $g(c, d)$ is gray value of pixel after filtering:

$$g(a, b) = \sum_{(c,d) \in K}^{n} g(c, d) \tag{8}$$

Each pixel in the mixed image is the weighted average value of each pixel value in the neighbor, which is easy to cause the image edge to be lost. Therefore, the most suitable structural element is $N \times N$ rectangle, and the gradient image is used as a guide to ensure that the structural element is filtered from the center of the image. The intensity gradient will change with the size of the structural element, and finally the optimal structural element changes are obtained. Kind of form.

2.3 Implementation of Mean Filtering for Multispectral Images

The grid interpolation error is calculated, and the superposition of double and triple spectrum is calculated respectively to determine the optimal parameter value, which represents the minimum grid spacing. When multi frequency spectrum superposition is used, the outermost spectrum is selected as $\alpha = 1$, that is, the original spectrum. Using multi grid can significantly improve the interpolation accuracy with log polar grid. Therefore, based on Fourier transform and using multi spectrum superposition, an improved algorithm can be obtained. For a given target image A and structure element λ, the corrosion process of convolutional neural network can be described. The structure element λ is moved freely on the image, so that all pixels B constitute the set of structure elements and image maximum correlation points. The set is the corrosion of λ to A, which can be recorded as follows:

$$A \ominus \lambda = g(a, b)\{B | \lambda \subseteq A\} \tag{9}$$

The expansion in the convolutional neural network is the dual operation of the corrosion process. The corrosion is regarded as each set of congruent structure element λ in image A shrinking into one pixel, then expansion is to expand each pixel in A. Using the convolutional neural network to open the operation, the image A can be used to corrode the structural element λ, and the image A can be used to expand the corrosion result, which can eliminate the pollution points on the image, which are noise points. According to the above average filtering principle, the opening and closing operation method in the convolutional neural network is introduced, and the mixed image noise is filtered out under the premise of keeping the original signal as much as possible. The principle of opening and closing operation is as follows:

$$OCF(t) = (t \cdot \lambda_1)\lambda_2 \tag{10}$$

Where, λ_1 and λ_2 represent the structural elements in the two kinds of mixed images respectively. The size structure of λ_1 is the smallest, which can save many details of the mixed image, and the size of λ_2 size structure is related to λ_1. The open operation in λ_1 size structure can effectively filter out noise, but some noise will be amplified in the first corrosion process of open operation, so it is necessary to use size structure λ_2 for closed operation. Since the size of some structural elements in the mixed image is larger than λ_1 and λ_2, the noise can not be completely removed in the open operation of λ_1 size structure. Therefore, in λ_2 closed operation, the size of this part should be greater than λ_1. Generally, the λ_1 size structure should be 5×5 or 7×7, which will not destroy too many details of the mixed image. After closed operation, the noise can be effectively removed while keeping the details of the mixed image as much as possible. The difference between the pixel value after open and close operation and the original pixel is as follows:

$$\begin{aligned} S_1 &= t - t \cdot \lambda_3 OCF(t) \\ S_2 &= t \cdot \lambda_3 - tOCF(t) \end{aligned} \tag{11}$$

In the formula: λ_3 represents a structural element with a size of 3×3; t is the original signal. Set a threshold R and compare S_1, S_2 and R. The noise pollution detection for the pixels of the mixed image is shown in the formula:

$$r(a, b) = \begin{cases} 1, & \pi(S_1 \geq R, S_2 = 0) \\ -1, & (S_1 = 0, S_2 \geq R) \\ 0, & (\text{others}) \end{cases} \tag{12}$$

In the formula, if the value of $r(a, b)$ is 1 or -1, then the pixel is noise; if the value of $r(a, b)$ is 0, the pixel is normal. The selection of filter enhancement block is a key factor for the successful application of this algorithm. If the number of enhanced blocks in each block's 8-neighborhood is Num_{Nai}, then the neighborhood priority B_{pri} of each block is defined as:

$$B_{\text{Pin}} = \begin{cases} 1 & Num_{\lambda n} \geqslant 5 \\ 2 & 5 > Num_{\lambda n} \geqslant 2 \\ 3 & \text{others} \end{cases} \tag{13}$$

In the formula: the value of B_{pri} is 1, 2, and 3 corresponding to the block neighborhood priority of high, medium and low respectively. If it is the first iteration, that is, all blocks are unenhanced blocks, the enhanced block to be filtered is uniquely determined by the block quality level; if it is not enhanced in the first iteration, the selection of the block to be enhanced not only depends on the block quality $Q_b(x, y)$, but also Also consider the neighborhood enhancement priority BPri of the block. Let Setc be the set of blocks to be enhanced, initially empty. The specific process of selecting the block to be enhanced is:

1) If it is the first iteration, add all blocks with $Q_b(x, y) = 1$ to SETC and end. Otherwise, go to step 2);
2) The bpri values of all blocks with the highest quality level are calculated;
3) If there are blocks of $Q_b(x, y)$, add all blocks of $B_{Pri} = 1$ to SETC and end. Otherwise, go to step 4);
4) If there are blocks of $B_{Pri} = 2$, add all blocks of $B_{Pri} = 2$ to SETC and end. Otherwise, go to step 5);
5) If there are blocks of $B_{Pri} = 3$, add all blocks of $B_{Pri} = 3$ to SETC.

In order to make the frequency spectrum of the higher-quality block more fully diffuse to the lower-quality block, the outer block is taken as 64×64. The enhancement block is taken as the inner block, and the corresponding outer block is selected, and the block spectrum matched filter is filtered and enhanced in the frequency domain. With the support of the convolutional neural network, the number of series filtering is reduced, and the multi-filter fusion of the image is completed under the impact of a few high-voltage filtering. This process requires that each input node must be filtered once before proceeding to the fusion center, which greatly increases the information entropy value compared with the traditional form. The improved image multi-filter fusion form, combined with the convolutional neural network, retains the advantages of the original form, and suppresses the noise while solving the phenomenon of edge information loss. The improved image multi-filter fusion form is shown in Fig. 3.

This process can ensure that the evaluation results are completely accurate and the reliability of high-quality blocks in the evaluation results. In this way, the calculation of multi-spectral image filtering characteristics can ensure the accuracy and effectiveness of the image filtering algorithm in the use process.

3   Analysis of Experimental Results

In order to verify the operation effect of the multi-spectral image filtering algorithm based on the convolutional neural network, an experiment was performed compared with the traditional algorithm. In order to ensure that the experimental results are true and effective, the experimental environment and experimental parameters are uniformly set.

The hardware platform is xilinxxc7v2000tfhg1761-2 multispectral chip. The target clock period is 10 ns, that is, the maximum frequency is 100 MHz, the clock uncertainty is 1.25 ns, and the estimated clock cycle is 8.42 ns. According to the estimated multifractal

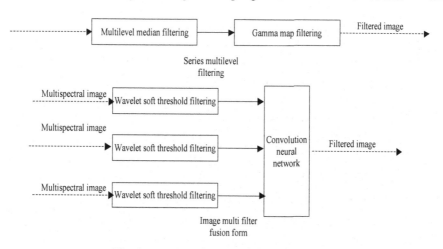

Fig. 3. Steps of multispectral image filtering.

spectrum, image pixels are classified: if the multifractal spectrum of a pixel is $f_g(A) = 1.0$, then the pixel is called a smooth edge point; if the multifractal spectrum B of a pixel is $f_g(a) = t(1.0 < t < 2.0)$, the pixel is called a class T singular edge point, and smooth edge points and singular edge points constitute the edge of the image to be detected. The contrast experiment platform is a Lenovo e4302370m32-bit processor, the main frequency is 2.40 GHz, the version is 2012bo series notebook computer, the processor is Intel Core 134 gb installed memory. The operation software is matlab software, the hardware design tool is xilinxhls advanced comprehensive tool, the version used is 14.3.

Matlab model and SPAS/DYEMCT software are used to build a simulation experiment detection platform. The experimental equipment chose the HPLC-Corei5 processor with 64GB of memory. Suppose the pixel value of the initial collected image sample is 300×300, the local filter transformation scale is 0.3–0.6, the decomposition coefficient of the image gray value is 1.51, the signal-to-noise ratio is -15 dB, the adaptive template size is 30×30, and the image is blurred The training sample value is 1500. Randomly select 200 BMP format color images including landscapes, people, buildings, etc., and cut all images into 512×512 size uniformly, and set the R, G, and B channels of the 200 original images to 0.05 bpp, 0.10 bpp, 0.15 bpp, 0.20 The embedding rate of bpp and 0.25 bpp simulates encrypted information to generate a color carrier. Randomly select 100 from 200 images for training, and the remaining 100 for testing. Based on this, the experimental parameters are set, as shown in Table 2.

Under the above-mentioned experimental environment and parameters, the operation effect of traditional image filtering algorithm and the operation effect of filtering algorithm proposed in this paper are compared and recorded, and drawn into a graph. For the convenience of recording, the algorithm in this paper is recorded as B during the experiment, and the traditional algorithm is recorded as A. First judge the noise filtering effect during the operation of the two algorithms, and the result is shown in Fig. 4.

In the experimental detection process, the higher the signal-to-noise ratio removal rate, the higher the automatic filtering effect of the algorithm, that is, the better the running effect. According to the detection curve of Fig. 4, it can be seen that the detection curve of

Table 2. Experimental parameter setting.

Name	Experimental parameters
High speed sampling resolution	32
A/D sampling speed	1000 Hz
Analog spectrum channel	32CH
Input filter analog	±1000 mV
Basic error	±0.2%
Image size	200 × 150 × 300 mm

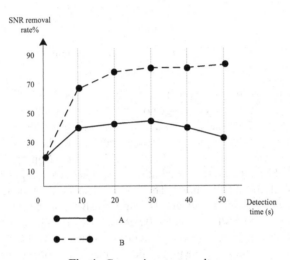

Fig. 4. Comparison test results.

algorithm B is much higher than that of algorithm A, and As the detection time increases, the overall detection results of Algorithm A gradually show a downward trend, while the overall detection curve of Algorithm A still tends to rise steadily. According to the detection results, compared with the traditional automatic filtering algorithm, the multi-spectral image filtering algorithm based on convolutional neural network proposed in this paper has higher stability and effectiveness in the actual operation process, and fully meets the research requirements.

In order to further verify the effectiveness of the method in this paper, the image filtering processing time is used as an experimental indicator to compare the image processing effect of the method in reference [4] and the method in this paper. The comparison result is shown in Fig. 5.

The analysis of Fig. 5 shows that the image filtering processing time of this method is significantly lower than that of the traditional method, and the image filtering processing time of this method is always less than 2.5 s, which indicates that the image filtering processing is realized based on multi-resolution spectrum superposition in this paper.

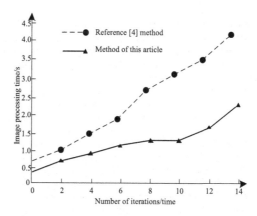

Fig. 5. Comparison of image filtering processing time of different methods

The algorithm does not need iteration, and has the advantage of faster image processing speed, thus improving the image filtering processing efficiency.

4 Conclusion

This paper proposes a multi-spectral image filtering algorithm based on convolutional neural network. The experimental results show that the edge of the image detected by this algorithm has certain advantages, eliminating the need for binary processing in some algorithms, and effectively improving Improve the image processing efficiency and accuracy. This is because the algorithm defines the spectrum image features through convolution neural network, and registers the signal-to-noise ratio of the image, which provides the basis for the mean filtering processing of multispectral images and improves the image processing effect.

References

1. Qi, X.P., et al.: The clinical spectrum of multiple endocrine neoplasia type 2A with cutaneous lichen amyloidosis in Ethnic Han Chinese. Cancer Invest. **36**(5), 1–11 (2018)
2. Xiaobo, Y., Liu, B., Shihai, W.: An analysis on the negative effect of multiple-faults for spectrum-based fault localization. Qual. Control Trans. **7**(4), 2327–2347 (2019)
3. Liu, B., et al.: Tri-band absorption enhancement in monolayer graphene in visible spectrum due to multiple plasmon resonances in metal–insulator–metal nanostructure. Appl. Phys. Express **11**(7), 072201.1–072201.4 (2018)
4. Zhao, Y., Guo, J., Li, P.: A median filtering scheme for quantum images. J. Electron. Inf. Technol. **43**(1), 204–211 (2021)
5. Mahmoud, H.M.: A spectrum of series–parallel graphs with multiple edge evolution. Probab. Eng. Inform. Sci. **33**(4), 487–499 (2019)
6. Liu, S., et al.: Overview and methods of correlation filter algorithms in object tracking. Complex Intell. Syst. (3) (2020)
7. Liu, S., et al.: A fast fractal based compression for MRI images. IEEE Access **7**, 62412–62420 (2019)

8. Liu, S., et al.: Introduction of key problems in long-distance learning and training. Mob. Netw. Appl. **24**(1), 1–4 (2019)

9. Zhang, N., et al.: Differentiate aquaporin-4 antibody negative neuromyelitis optica spectrum disorders from multiple sclerosis by multimodal advanced MRI techniques. Multiple Sclerosis Related Disord. **41**(5), 102–115 (2020)

Interactive Virtual Reality Indoor Space Roaming System Based on 3D Vision

Jing He[✉]

School of Road Bridge and Architecture, Chongqing Vocational College of Transportation, Chongqing 402247, China

Abstract. Due to the low performance of traditional virtual reality roaming systems, three-dimensional vision technology is used to optimize the design of interactive virtual reality indoor space roaming systems from the three aspects of hardware, software, and database. The optimization of the hardware system is mainly aimed at the connection structure of the rover and the interactive module. Collect all relevant data of indoor space and system operation, and store them in a certain format to get the design results of the system database. With the support of hardware equipment and database, the function of interactive virtual reality indoor space roaming is realized through the steps of creating virtual scene of indoor space, determining the roaming mode of 3D virtual reality and the path planning of indoor space roaming. Through the system test experiment, it is concluded that compared with the traditional roaming system, the designed interactive virtual reality indoor space roaming system has a higher success rate and better interactivity.

Keywords: 3D vision · Interactive · Virtual reality · Interior space · Roaming system

1 Introduction

Virtual reality is a higher level of multimedia technology development, and a higher level of integration and penetration of these technologies. It can give users more real experience and provide great convenience for people to explore the macro and micro world. Due to various reasons, it is not convenient to directly observe the movement law of things. In essence, virtual reality is an advanced computer user interface. It provides users with various intuitive and natural real-time perceptual interactive means such as vision, hearing and touch, so as to maximize the convenience of users' operation, so as to reduce the burden of users and improve the working efficiency of the whole system. One of the most basic functions of virtual reality applications is the roaming function of the virtual environment. The virtual roaming system is a simulation of imaginary or real space. It takes the real environment as a reference and virtualizes the scene in the space. It enables visitors to roam or look around. Visitors can also make corresponding behaviors to make the environment have a certain Artistic characteristics [1]. Users can

W. Fu et al. (Eds.): ICMTEL 2021, LNICST 388, pp. 425–435, 2021.
https://doi.org/10.1007/978-3-030-82565-2_35

plan and operate the landscape and various facilities through the network, observe the corresponding virtual objects in the process, and get the feeling of being on the scene. Virtual roaming system is based on geography, virtual reality, multimedia, broadband and other technologies, combined with the content of attributes and geospatial information, and constructs a realistic virtual campus environment. Users can access the landscape in the space through the computer network, and use the terminal computer to carry out roaming and corresponding search in the virtual space environment and query.

The establishment of the current indoor roaming system is actually the application of virtual reality technology to the field of indoor space. For traditional indoor roaming systems, an object-oriented approach is generally adopted, combined with virtual reality and other related knowledge to simulate indoor scenes. The system still has shortcomings in terms of human-computer interaction and code reuse, especially in terms of code reuse, it does not fully realize code reuse, and the interactivity is not strong [2]. The 3D entities in the existing indoor roaming system are static and developed in advance. Although the whole indoor scene can be observed from different directions by controlling the mouse and keyboard, it is impossible to dynamically add other 3D models to the scene after the scene is created, and the location, size and other attributes of these models cannot be changed there are also limitations in the rapid construction and reuse of three-dimensional model, so the whole application system still has deficiencies in flexibility control and later expansion.

In order to solve the problems in the above-mentioned traditional methods, three-dimensional vision technology is used to realize the optimized design of the interactive virtual reality indoor space roaming system. Design the hardware system through the connection structure of the rover and the interactive module, store all the relevant data of the indoor space and system operation, design the system database, use the 3D vision technology to create the indoor space virtual scene, determine the 3D space virtual reality roaming method and indoor Complete the system software design by steps such as space roaming path planning. The design of an interactive virtual reality indoor space roaming system based on three-dimensional vision is completed through hardware, software, and database. Finally, simulation experiments verify the effectiveness of the system designed in this paper.

2 Hardware System Design of Virtual Reality Indoor Space Roaming

The system must be able to represent the three-dimensional model of indoor space terrain undulations, scene buildings and other objects. It is very realistic in terms of form, lighting, texture, etc., so that participants can roam in the constructed lifelike virtual environment. In order to meet this requirement, The overall design must follow the principles of reality, interactivity, imagination and efficiency [3]. In order to ensure that the whole roaming system can run smoothly on the computer and achieve realistic scene rendering effect, according to the design ideas and design principles, the overall framework of the roaming system can be obtained, as shown in Fig. 1.

As can be seen from Fig. 1, each function in the system is relatively independent and interrelated through the data interface. In order to ensure the optimal design effect

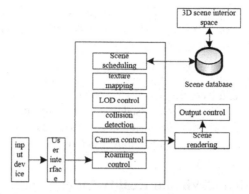

Fig. 1. The overall structure of the indoor space roaming system

of roaming system, the specific optimization design is carried out from three aspects of hardware, database and software.

The parts of the hardware system that need to be optimized include rover, interactive communication mechanism and so on. For different scenes and different roaming methods, you can choose roamers. For example, you can use trackball-based roamers for general roaming; when you are in a large-scale terrain scene, you can use terrain rovers; if you want to simulate real vehicles, Such as cars, airplanes, etc., you need to consider driving realistic scenarios at this time, you can use driving rover [4–6]. These rovers use real-time correction of the scene camera observation matrix to achieve smooth roaming. In the design of the rover, we mainly focus on the correctness and suitability of visual motion, that is, how to move the observer to the specified position and posture smoothly and accurately. The roaming operation is mainly controlled by three parameters: viewpoint, observation point and up direction.

The commonly used rover is the trackball rover, and its interaction is realized by mouse movement and the positioning of the trackball. This article implements the rotation function of the rover based on the principle of trackball, as shown in Fig. 2.

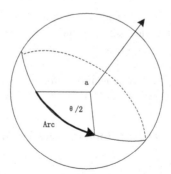

Fig. 2. Working principle of trackball Rover

The left mouse button realizes rotation, the middle mouse button realizes translation, and the movement direction of the mouse is the translation direction, and the mouse wheel and right button realize the scene zoom function.

In order to optimize the interaction of roaming system, the hybrid network structure is selected. This communication network structure combines the advantages of centralized directory structure of central control network and point-to-point structure of distributed network. In the network, some nodes are used to store the information of adjacent nodes. The whole network is divided into several autonomous subnets according to these nodes, and different subnets adopt pure point-to-point structure.

3   Database Design of Virtual Reality Indoor Space Roaming System

While describing a large-scale virtual environment based on real terrain data, virtual scene often involves the specific structure and detailed state of each entity in the virtual scene. Therefore, the relationship between the virtual entity model and the spatial model in each scene should be determined according to the geometry model of the virtual scene. The establishment of the scene database adopts the tree structure hierarchy to organize and manage the scene data, which can easily realize the hierarchical structure management of the model when modeling. The data mainly involved in the system includes user data, scene and model data, model information data, and user communication information data. The entity relationship of the virtual scene module in the entity relationship diagram can be obtained according to the attributes of each data and the relationship between them, thereby establishing a database table. In this roaming system design, the database table is divided into user information table, user communication data table, roaming data table, scene data table and other parts.

4   Software Function Design of Virtual Reality Indoor Space Roaming System

In this process, the virtual reality indoor space roaming system can establish the 3D scene model, and meet the function of view selection and view control. The design follows the idea: take the indoor space of a building as the environment, select several representative scenes from it, use 3D vision technology to model, use 3D texture mapping to draw the scene, and finally interact in the system development environment Control, so as to realize the design of the virtual reality indoor space roaming system function.

4.1   3D Vision Technology to Create Indoor Space Virtual Scene

In order to create an environment that enables users to feel immersed and immersed in it, one of the necessary conditions is that all objects in the objective world can be vividly displayed in the virtual reality system as required. It is not only required that the displayed object models are very similar to the real objects in appearance, but also that they are very realistic in terms of shape, illumination, texture, etc. The modeling of virtual environment is the foundation of the whole virtual reality system, including three-dimensional visual modeling and three-dimensional auditory modeling. Among them, visual modeling includes geometric modeling, motion modeling, physical modeling, object behavior modeling and model segmentation.

4.1.1 Collect Indoor Spatial Data

Define the constraint relationship between two monocular virtual cameras A and B. Firstly, define the distance D between two monocular virtual cameras and the angle of sight θ to give a three-dimensional virtual camera model. According to the principle of binocular parallax forming three-dimensional vision, the distance between the two viewpoints of the binocular camera is calculated, that is, the observation parallax is:

$$D = |P_{ea} - P_{eb}| \tag{1}$$

In the formula, P_{ea} and P_{eb} are used to describe the viewpoint of camera A and B respectively. Then calculate the angle of the camera's line of sight, you can get:

$$\sin\left(\frac{\theta}{2}\right) = \frac{|P_{ea} - P_{eb}| - |P_{ta} - P_{eb}|}{2|P_{ea} - P_{tb}|} \tag{2}$$

Where P_{ta} and P_{tb} represent the implementation direction of camera A and B respectively [7]. The line of sight length of the two cameras is the same, so the following relationship should be satisfied:

$$|P_{ta} - P_{ea}| = |P_{tb} - P_{eb}| \tag{3}$$

The three-dimensional vision camera equipment built above is used to collect image data in the indoor space.

4.1.2 Camera Calibration

One of the basic tasks of stereo vision is to use the photo taken by the camera to process the image to obtain the distance of the object from the camera and some three-dimensional information of the object. The computer establishes the model of the relationship between the image and the object. After this model is completed, the point in the object can be obtained from a certain point in the image. This model is called the camera imaging geometric model. There are many parameters in the model. These parameters are called the camera's internal and external parameters. In most cases, the parameters of the camera can only be obtained through experiments, which is called camera calibration. Therefore, the purpose of camera calibration is to determine the camera position, attribute parameters and establish the imaging geometry model, so as to determine the corresponding relationship between the object point in the space coordinate system and its image point on the image plane. Camera calibration needs to determine the internal geometric and optical characteristics of the camera, as well as the three-dimensional position and direction of the camera coordinate system relative to a world coordinate system.

4.1.3 Image Preprocessing and Feature Extraction

In the case of image shooting, due to various reasons, the image contains noise or even distortion. In order to improve the image effect and make the image clearer, it is necessary to eliminate these noise factors which are not conducive to image clarity. This kind of processing is the image preprocessing. After the preprocessing, the image can also be conducive to the future work, such as image feature extraction, etc. Processing, weakening or eliminating some unnecessary information in the image, making the image more conducive to computer recognition. Image preprocessing technology includes image contrast enhancement, weakening or noise elimination [8]. The image contains a lot of information. Some information is useless or not very important. In order to simplify the future work, useful and important information should be extracted from the image, and this information should be distinguished from other objects. The process is feature extraction. The extracted features usually include point features, linear features, and regional features. The point features are relatively small, such as corner points. After feature extraction, more point features can be extracted, but because they are small-scale features, Therefore, the amount of information is very small, and some constraints or some matching strategies need to be added in the next stereo matching; while the regional features are just the opposite. Regional features are relatively large features. After feature extraction, the extracted regional features are compared. The regional feature is a large-scale feature, which contains more information, which is conducive to future matching work.

4.1.4 Stereo Matching

Stereo matching means that the camera uses a certain algorithm to find the corresponding points in the two photos taken by the camera at the same time. Stereo matching is a key technology in binocular vision, because the camera is easy to shoot objects in two different perspectives. Affected by factors such as illumination, image shooting angle, noise and distortion, and camera characteristics. Therefore, it is very difficult to accurately match images with so many disadvantageous factors. The effectiveness of stereo matching method depends on the solution of three problems, that is, selecting the correct matching features, finding the essential attributes between features and establishing a stable algorithm that can correctly match the selected features.

4.1.5 Viewpoint Control and Conversion

The basic control operations of viewpoint, such as translation, rotation and scaling, are based on matrix transformation. The viewpoint coordinates can be obtained by multiplying the original vertex coordinates by the corresponding viewpoint transformation model viewpoint matrix. The attributes of the viewpoint mainly include the position coordinate (VPx, VPy, VPz) and the sight direction (VLx, VLy, VLz). By changing the attribute parameters of the viewpoint, the position of the viewpoint and the viewing direction of the viewpoint can be controlled, so as to realize the free control of the viewpoint. The principle of scene model flipping during viewpoint transformation is shown in Fig. 3.

As can be seen from the figure, in general, the angle between the line of sight direction and the axis is large, and the vector changes little. In the graph, the angle between the

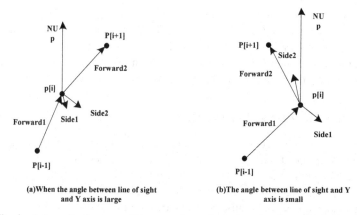

Fig. 3. Schematic diagram of the scene inversion when the viewpoint is changed

line of sight direction and the axis is small. As the current path point, the vector changes greatly, that is, the angle between the vector and the vector is obtuse angle, so the direction of the vector finally obtained is opposite to that of the previous state. Therefore, the line of sight after the viewpoint transformation is opposite in the direction, and the scene is flipped.

4.1.6 3D Scene Display of Indoor Space

The material settings are mainly realized through the material editor tool in 3ds max. The material editor is used to select and manage materials and maps. The common parameters that affect the material of the model mainly include the basic parameters of shading, Blinn, expansion and mapping, etc. in order to better express the attributes and characteristics of objects, different parameters should be used together. In the actual setting of the object properties, since the values of the parameters cannot be determined, a gradual fine-tuning method can be used until the external characteristics of the actual object are similar. At the same time, the color difference of the computer itself needs to be considered. In addition, it is necessary to set the lighting effects in the three-dimensional indoor space scene. The lighting is an integral part of a complete three-dimensional scene. The authenticity of the three-dimensional scene is inseparable from the illumination of the light. The model in the scene is visible, and the materials attached to the model are displayed correctly, so as to show the characteristics of objects in the real world, which greatly ensures the reality of the scene [9]. There are skylight, target spotlight, target parallel light, floodlight and so on. Finally, the lightingmap rendering and baking method is selected to obtain clear texture texture, and finally get the 3D scene of virtual reality interior space.

4.2 Determine the Three-Dimensional Virtual Reality Roaming Method

There are two ways to roam in 3D space: interactive roaming and automatic roaming. Interactive roaming can control the viewpoint through mouse, keyboard and other input devices, so as to realize human-computer interaction. Automatic roaming only needs to set the starting point and ending point of roaming, and the viewpoint moves according to the designed motion mode. During the process, the roaming picture can be output without inputting any parameters. Interactive roaming realizes users' free operation, while automatic roaming realizes browsing of given path.

4.3 Roaming Path Planning in Indoor Space

To calculate the collision between the viewpoint and each surface of an object is actually to calculate the relationship between the distance between the viewpoint and the triangular patch and the step size. For example, if the vertex coordinates of the triangle are (x_1, y_1, z_1), (x_2, y_2, z_2) and (x_3, y_3, z_3), then the plane where the triangle is located should be calculated first. Generally, the plane equation is defined as:

$$Ax + By + Cz + D = 0 \tag{4}$$

Among them, D represents the distance from the origin to the plane. The specific calculation process is as follows:

$$\begin{cases} p_1 = (x_1 - x_2)i + (y_1 - y_2)j + (z_1 - z_2) \\ p_2 = (x_1 - x_3)i + (y_1 - y_3)j + (z_1 - z_3) \\ n = Normalize(p_1 \times p_2) \\ d = n \cdot (x_1 i + y_1 j + z_1 k) \end{cases} \tag{5}$$

Where p_1 and p_2 are vectors of vertex 1 pointing to vertex 2 and vertex 3 respectively, n is the normal vector of the plane where the triangle vertex is located, and d is the distance from the triangle patch to the origin. The positional relationship between the camera sphere and the triangular patch mainly includes three situations: intersection, in front of the triangular patch and behind the triangular patch. When calculating the plane of the triangle, the distance from the current camera's position coordinate to the plane is needed to determine the position relationship between the camera and the plane, and to determine whether there is a current collision.

4.4 Realize the Function of Interactive Virtual Reality Indoor Space Roaming

In order to realize the interactive roaming function of virtual reality indoor space roaming, interactive scripts are added to the built 3D visual scene. Bind the camera to the virtual character to set the character's movement speed, add gravity and other parameters, and modify the virtual character's action name to add scripts. Modify the name of the button and add scripts, such as music playback, camera selection, character actions, animation playback, etc. [10]. Double click the object in the indoor space environment, click the action button on the right side of the window to open the "distance trigger", set the trigger distance, select the trigger object as the virtual character, click "trigger action script on entry" to pop up the script editor, then select "insert statement", find the animation command, and finally click to play the rigid body animation and write the script. In this way, the command to trigger the cultural relic animation distance is completed.

The interactive roaming function of indoor space roaming requires keyboard and mouse control. The keyboard roaming commands include: turn left, turn right, forward, back, rise, fall, look up, look down, move left, move right, move acceleration, move deceleration, Rotation acceleration, rotation deceleration, zoom in and zoom out. Finally, under the control of each peripheral device, the switching of the roaming mode is realized, and then the roaming function of the interactive virtual reality indoor space is realized.

5   System Testing

To test the roaming function of the designed interactive virtual reality indoor space roaming system based on 3D vision, the system test experiment is designed.

5.1   System Development Tools and Test Environment

In order to allow this system to run on an ordinary machine, this computer configuration was selected during the test. In the system test environment, the processor device used Intel (R) core (TM) i5 M430 2.27 ghz dual core, and the hard disk space was 500 GB, the graphics card is 512 discrete graphics cards, the virtual reality simulation software is VR, and the development tool for system interaction functions is VC++. In addition, the 3D indoor space scene creation environment uses the 3DS MAX software. The software function design results of the interactive virtual reality indoor space roaming system based on 3D vision are converted into program codes that can be directly recognized by the computer, and the running interface of the roaming system is displayed. The running scene interface of virtual reality indoor space roaming system is shown in Fig. 4.

Fig. 4. Virtual reality indoor space roaming system interface

5.2   Select Interior Space Sample

In order to ensure the credibility of the system test results, multiple indoor spaces were selected as experimental samples during the test. The experimental samples selected in this experiment included museums, residential buildings, large shopping malls, etc., and each sample was numbered as the experimental number.

5.3 System Testing Process

This system test experiment is mainly to test the roaming function of the system, which is mainly aimed at different functional modules, such as the completeness of 3D scene construction, collision detection accuracy, and the execution level of roaming control commands. In order to form an experimental comparison, a traditional roaming system (document [2] system) is set up as a comparison system in the system test experiment, and it is developed and operated in the same environment.

5.4 System Function Test

The calculation method of the success rate of the function operation is the ratio of the number of commands that the function runs successfully to the total number of commands. The test comparison results of each function module of the comprehensive system test are shown in Table 1.

Table 1. System function test results

Test function module	Number of test commands/piece	Number of successful commands of traditional system	Design system successfully run the number of commands/piece
3D scene construction	300	258	277
Perspective shift	300	265	289
collision detection	300	244	278
Keyboard control roaming direction	300	273	294
Mouse control roaming direction	300	268	291

Based on the test results obtained in Table 3, it can be seen that the number of successful commands of the traditional roaming system can reach up to 273, and the average success rate of its functions is 87.2%, while the number of successful commands of the designed system can reach up to 294. Its average function operation success rate is 95.3%.

6 Conclusion

The interactive virtual reality indoor space roaming system truly realizes the interaction between people and the virtual scene, giving users a real feeling of being on the scene and immersed in it. Users can simply click the mouse to carry out a variety of sightseeing modes, such as bird's-eye view, overlooking, first and third person autonomous roaming, etc., to display the internal spatial structure of the indoor environment and observe various objects in the space closely; by using the virtual reality system, people can visit different indoor spaces without going out of the house, and get real experience; and thoroughly break the space, the space, the space and the objects in the space can be fully displayed The limitation of time has certain practical significance.

This paper designs an interactive virtual reality indoor space roaming system based on 3D vision from three aspects of hardware, software and database. The hardware system is designed for the connection structure between the walkthrough and the interactive module, and all the relevant data collected from the indoor space and the system operation are stored. The system database is designed. The system software design is completed through the steps of creating the indoor space virtual scene, determining the 3D space virtual reality roaming mode and indoor space roaming path planning through 3D vision technology. Finally, the effectiveness of the interactive virtual reality indoor space roaming system based on 3D vision is verified by simulation experiments.

References

1. Li, H., Duan, D., Zhang, Z.: Implementation Of medical pendant interactive system based on virtual reality technology. IOP Conf. Series Mater. Sci. Eng. **711**(1), 012033 (5pp) (2020)
2. Lijun, C., Jing, L., Nan, L.: A virtual reality based study of indoor fire evacuation after active or passive spatial exploration. Comput. Hum. Behav. **90**, 37–45 (2018). S0747563218304163
3. Shamim, B., et al.: Where do satellite cells orbit? An endomysium space odyssey. J. Physiol. **596**(10), 1791–1792 (2018)
4. Jiang, B., et al.: Fusion of machine vision technology and AlexNet-CNNs deep learning network for the detection of postharvest apple pesticide residues. Artif. Intell. Agric. **1**, 1–8 (2019)
5. Donghui, C., et al.: Virtual reality technology applied in digitalization of cultural heritage. Clust. Comput. **22**(4), 1–12 (2017)
6. Chen, T.N., Yin, X.T., Li, X.G.: Application of 3D virtual reality technology with multi-modality fusion in resection of glioma located in central sulcus region. Zhonghua Yi Xue Za Zhi **98**(17), 1302–1305 (2018)
7. Baker, S., et al.: Evaluating the use of interactive virtual reality technology with older adults living in residential aged care. Inf. Process. Manage **57**(3), 102105.1–102105.13 (2020)
8. Liu, S., et al.: A fast fractal based compression for MRI images. IEEE Access **7**, 62412–62420 (2019)
9. Fu, W., Liu, S., Srivastava, G.: Optimization of big data scheduling in social networks. Entropy **21**(9), 902 (2019)
10. Liu, S., et al.: Overview and methods of correlation filter algorithms in object tracking. Complex Intell. Syst. (2020).https://doi.org/10.1007/s40747-020-00161-4

Multi-viewpoint Rendering Optimization of Indoor Scene Based on Binocular Vision

He Jing[✉]

School of Road Bridge and Architecture, Chongqing Vocational College of Transportation, Chongqing 402247, China

Abstract. The traditional multi-viewpoint rendering method for indoor scenes has poor lighting and shadow effects, resulting in too dark or bright indoor scene multi-viewpoint rendering. Therefore, an optimization method for indoor scene multi-viewpoint rendering based on binocular vision is proposed. This research plans light and shadow effects based on the visual relationship between point light sources and indoor scenes; sets rendering points based on binocular vision; and renders indoor scenes with multiple viewpoint angles. The simulation experiment results show that compared with the traditional rendering method, the light and shadow effect of the studied method is excellent, and the rendered indoor scene is suitable for light and dark.

Keywords: Binocular vision · Indoor scene · Multi-viewpoint rendering · Optimization method

1 Introduction

As an important factor affecting the brightness of indoor scenes, light plays a decisive role in the optimization of rendering of indoor scenes. The applicable light environment of indoor scenes, along with the development and upgrading of construction sites, has also formed its own unique system. However, with the continuous improvement of urban living standards, the use efficiency of point light source lamps is getting higher and higher, and the lighting intensity and type are different. Literature [1] studied the optimization of multi-viewpoint rendering of indoor scenes based on perception. For the input 3D indoor scene model, a novel viewpoint perception measurement function based on geometric information, structural information and aesthetic information was first defined; and then a The multi-view overall optimization model; then the simulated annealing algorithm is used to optimize the user-specified number of multi-view sets, and finally the image is rendered. The experimental results show that for the problem of multi-view rendering optimization of indoor scenes, the proposed method can be adaptively obtained A series of comprehensive and beautiful rendering pictures. Literature [2] studies the optimization of semantic segmentation network for indoor scenes based on rgb-d images. The network processes the original data by training separately and gradually fusing, and adds a strengthening supervision module in the decoding stage to

W. Fu et al. (Eds.): ICMTEL 2021, LNICST 388, pp. 436–447, 2021.
https://doi.org/10.1007/978-3-030-82565-2_36

effectively improve the accuracy of semantic segmentation. At the same time, the anti residual decoding method and jump structure are introduced to reduce the information loss. Reference [3] studies the method of building indoor and outdoor scenes based on BIM and GIS. Taking IFC and citygml as the research objects, IFC Standard building scene organization model is transformed into citygml standard through geometric reconstruction and multi-level LOD semantic mapping, and the visual rendering performance is optimized by model simplification and case processing. Finally, through the transformation of the terrain, the visual expression of the building indoor environment in the three-dimensional geographical environment is realized.

But the above three methods of rendering optimization, for the preset effect of point light disturbance is not ideal, so according to this problem in conventional methods, this paper proposes a multi view rendering optimization of indoor scene based on binocular vision. Binocular vision simulates the principle of human vision, which is a technical means of using computer to perceive distance passively. Observe an object from two or more points, obtain images under different vision, and calculate the offset distance between pixels according to the matching relationship of pixels between images, so as to obtain the three-dimensional information of indoor scene. Taking binocular vision as the innovation point, the original multi view rendering method of indoor scene is optimized.

2 Multi-Viewpoint Rendering Optimization Method of Indoor Scene Based on Binocular Vision

2.1 Get the Visual Relationship Between the Point Light Source and the Indoor Scene, and Plan the Lighting Effect

As a kind of light, point light source has two kinds of lighting characteristics: strong light and weak light. Under the strong light point light source, the indoor environment will be bright and dark, but under the weak light, the effect is not obvious. Under the action of strong light of point light source, every side of indoor objects is affected, giving people a strong visual experience. Therefore, it is necessary to obtain the visual relationship between the point light source and the indoor scene. The visual relationship between light source and space is very close. Only by controlling the effect of light and shadow can the residents feel the color difference of the building space. Therefore, according to the relevant data such as the intensity of the point light source, the disturbance area range of the point light source is determined

$$c_i = \sin(\alpha + \beta) \sum_{i=1,j=1}^{n} \pi r_j d_i \tag{1}$$

In the formula: α represents the illumination angle of the point light source; β represents the light scattering angle; i represents the light source position; j represents the illumination position; r_j represents the area radius; d_i represents the flash distance. According to the disturbance area of the above-mentioned point light source, the disturbance position of the indoor scene is determined, and the visual relationship between the two can be expressed by the visual mapping function:

$$\Delta_T = \frac{\gamma a \ln(s - s')}{q c_i m_j k} \tag{2}$$

In the above, γ is the optical path of point light source; a is the optical path path; s is the positive relationship; s' is the relationship error; q is the light intensity; m_j is the spatial range of the indoor scene affected; k is the indoor opening degree. According to the above formula, the visual relationship between the point light source and the indoor scene is obtained, and the multi-viewpoint light and shadow rendering effect of the indoor scene is guaranteed. The visual relationship between weak light environment and indoor scene is established, and the light and shadow effect of indoor scene is planned according to the new visual relationship. Figure 1 below is the visual relationship curve.

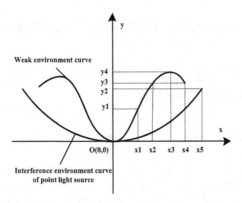

Fig. 1. Diagram of visual relation curve

According to the above figure, there is a corresponding relationship between the interference of the light source and the spatial structure, so the low-light environment established corresponds to the indoor scene. The final result of the relationship is:

$$\Delta_R = \sqrt{\frac{h x_a - 1}{\Delta_T \oplus g(\varepsilon + 1)}}^{-e} \tag{3}$$

In the formula: h is the weak light environment parameter; x_a is the curve node position; $\oplus$ is the mapping symbol; g is the corresponding relationship; ε is the visual relationship parameter, and its value range is [0, 1]. According to the calculation results of the above formula, plan the light and shadow effects of indoor scenes under low light conditions. Since the low-light environment is quiet and soft, it is necessary to consider the light scattering ability of indoor materials and household items under low-light conditions. Therefore, according to the basic characteristics of these coefficients, the light and shadow effect parameters in the indoor low-light environment are calculated. The calculation formula of the parameters is:

$$p = \arctan \frac{2\Delta_R(C - b)}{\omega D} \tag{4}$$

In the formula: C represents the light projection area; b represents the projection edge range; D represents the building space coverage area; ω represents the reflection coefficient [4]. According to the above calculation process, the lighting effect of indoor scene is planned.

2.2 Set Rendering Points Based on Binocular Vision

According to the known camera parameters, such as the overall dimension, corner type, corner coordinates under the coordinate system and the coordinates of these corners, corresponding to the coordinates in the actual environment, the internal and external parameters of the camera are calculated by using the least square method. The data parameters to be calibrated are shown in Table 1 below.

Table 1. Camera data parameter list.

Camera parameters	Expression
Internal parameters	$\begin{bmatrix} u & \gamma & m \\ 0 & v & n \\ 0 & 0 & 1 \end{bmatrix}$
Radial distortion, tangential distortion	s1, s2; p1, p2
External parameters	$W = \begin{bmatrix} w_1 & w_2 & w_3 \\ w_4 & w_5 & w_6 \\ w_7 & w_8 & w_9 \end{bmatrix} O = \begin{bmatrix} o_1 \\ o_2 \\ o_3 \end{bmatrix}$

In the above table, u, v, and γ are the scale factors of the camera on the x axis, y axis, and z axis. It should be noted that γ is the non-vertical factor; m and n are the optical centers of the two cameras. They are The internal parameters of the camera. W represents the rotation matrix, and O represents the translation vector [5]. According to the parameters in the above table, set the coordinate of the spatial point in the world coordinate system as $\delta = (x, y, z)^O$, and the corresponding projection coordinate as $\zeta = (m, n)^O$. $\delta' = (x, y, z)^O$ and $\zeta' = (m, n)^O$ are obtained after sorting, so there is a matrix formula:

$$\lambda\delta' = B[W, o]\zeta' = \begin{bmatrix} u & \gamma & m \\ 0 & v & n \\ 0 & 0 & 1 \end{bmatrix}[W, o]\zeta' \tag{5}$$

In the formula: B is the internal parameter matrix of the camera. In order to reduce the calculation error, let the value of z in the calibration angle $\delta = (x, y, z)^O$ be 0:

$$\lambda \begin{bmatrix} m \\ n \\ 1 \end{bmatrix} = B[w_1, w_2, w_3, o] \begin{bmatrix} x \\ y \\ 0 \\ 1 \end{bmatrix} = B[w_1, w_2, o] \begin{bmatrix} x \\ y \\ 1 \end{bmatrix} \tag{6}$$

In the formula: w_1, w_2 and w_3 are 3×1 column vectors; $[k_1, k_2, k_3]$ represents the camera rotation matrix. Suppose there is $\delta = [x, y]^O$, then there is $\delta' = [x, y, 1]^O$. At this time, the above formula can be simplified:

$$\lambda \zeta' = \eta \delta' \tag{7}$$

In the formula: $\lambda = B[w_1, w_2, o]$ is the homography matrix, which represents the corner points extracted from the indoor scene and the mapping of its corresponding pixel points in the coordinate system [6]. Let the data in the matrix be η_1, η_2, η_3, because w_1 and w_2 are orthogonal:

$$\begin{cases} \eta_1^O B^{-O} B^{-E} \eta_2 = 0 \\ \eta_1^O B^{-O} B^{-E} \eta_1 = \eta_2^O B^{-O} B^{-E} \eta_2 \end{cases} \tag{8}$$

B^{-O} and B^{-E} in the above formula are the projection matrices of the quadratic curve in the image coordinate system. According to the properties of the quadratic curve, let $D = B^{-O} B^{-E}$, the symmetric matrix of the camera can be obtained as:

$$D = \begin{pmatrix} D_{11} & D_{12} & D_{13} \\ D_{21} & D_{22} & D_{23} \\ D_{31} & D_{32} & D_{33} \end{pmatrix}$$

$$= \begin{pmatrix} \frac{1}{u^2} & -\frac{\gamma}{u^2 v} & \frac{m\gamma - nv}{u^2 v} \\ -\frac{\gamma}{u^2 v} & -\frac{1}{v^2} + \frac{\gamma^2}{u^2 v} & -\frac{1}{v^2} - \frac{\gamma[m\gamma - nv]}{u^2 v^2} \\ \frac{m\gamma - nv}{u^2 v} & -\frac{m}{v^2} - \frac{\gamma[m\gamma - nv]}{u^2 v^2} & \frac{[m\gamma - nv]^2}{u^2 v^2} + \frac{m^2}{v^2} + 1 \end{pmatrix} \tag{9}$$

Take the j column vector of matrix η, then there exists $\eta_j = [\eta_{j1}, \eta_{j2}, \eta_{j3}]^O$, and assume a 6-dimensional vector $\omega = [D_{11}, D_{12}, D_{22}, D_{13}, D_{23}, D_{33}]^{-O}$, then $\eta_j^O = D\eta_s = m_{js}^O \omega$ can be obtained. According to the matrix constraint conditions obtained by the above formula, we can know that:

$$\begin{bmatrix} m_{12}^O \\ (m_{11} - m_{12})^O \end{bmatrix} \omega = 0, \quad \begin{bmatrix} m_{12}^O \\ (m_{11} - m_{12})^D \end{bmatrix} = p \tag{10}$$

Then $p\omega = 0$. When the number of collected images meets the requirements, p is a 6×6 matrix; if p is a full-rank matrix, ω can get a unique solution. At this time, the internal and external parameters of the camera can be calculated:

$$
\begin{cases}
\eta = D_{33} - \left[D_{13}^2 + m(D_{12}D_{13} - D_{11}D_{23}) \right]/D_{11} \\
u = \sqrt{\eta/D_{11}} \\
v = \sqrt{\eta D_{11}/(D_{11}D_{22} - D_{12}^2)} \\
\gamma = -D_{12}u^2 v/\eta \\
m = (D_{12}D_{13} - D_{11}D_{23})/\left(D_{11}D_{22} - D_{12}^2 \right) \\
n = \gamma m/u - D_{13}u^2/\eta
\end{cases}
\tag{11}
$$

Through the above calculation process, the parameters are obtained to realize the setting of rendering point based on binocular vision [7].

2.3 Multi-viewpoint Rendering of Indoor Scenes

Considering the projection relationship between the object's point position and the panoramic image point position, the set rendering viewpoint is corrected. Due to the multi angle binocular vision shooting, the photo center will not be in the same position, resulting in the different perspective deformation state of the same scene in the overlapping area of the two groups of images, resulting in the compression of panoramic image information and distortion. Therefore, under the premise of keeping the parameters unchanged, the image viewpoint is corrected by using the translation concept, as shown in Fig. 2 [8].

In this image, c represents the origin of the viewpoint; c_1 and c_2 represent the optical center of the image sequence; L represents the projection distance; and A_1 and A_2 represent a certain point of the two groups of processed images. Make the optical center of image sequence coincide with the established coordinate system, and meet the following requirements:

$$
\sigma_i = x_i y_i
\tag{12}
$$

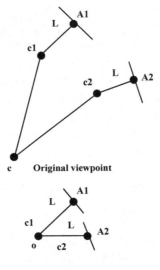

Fig. 2. Schematic diagram of image viewpoint correction process

In the formula: σ_i represents any point on the i th image and the three-dimensional coordinates in the camera coordinate system; y_i represents any point on the i image and the coordinates in the established three-dimensional coordinate system. i represents the camera coordinate system of the i image, compared to the rotation matrix of the three-dimensional coordinates. After the viewpoint is corrected, the mapping of the image plane to the spherical surface is calculated [9]. Assuming that the coordinate of any point i on the image is (x_0, y_0, z_0) and the coordinate of the mapping point c' is $\left(x'_0, y'_0, z'_0\right)$, according to the spherical three-dimensional European coordinate conversion, the stitching function of the panorama is obtained:

$$
\begin{cases}
x'_0 = \theta \sin \kappa \cdot \dfrac{y}{\theta} \cos \kappa \cdot \dfrac{x}{\theta} \\[2mm]
y'_0 = -\theta \sin \kappa \cdot \dfrac{y}{\theta} \sin \kappa \cdot \dfrac{x}{\theta} \\[2mm]
z'_0 = \theta \cos \kappa \cdot \dfrac{x}{\theta}
\end{cases} \tag{13}
$$

In the formula: κ is the positive angle between the plane projection vector and the horizontal axis in the 3D coordinate system; θ is the reverse angle. According to the above formula, the point cloud data of the image is obtained. Then the virtual 3D panoramic environment frame model is established, and the frame components are filled by using image simulation and rendering technology. However, the rendered 3D model does not have the characteristic points of the virtual object, so the surface of the designed model is required to be covered with texture. The process is divided into four stages. Firstly, the virtual item frame built and rendered is filled and rendered, and then the algorithm is used to draw the covering pattern on the surface of the object, and then other components with a single structure are filled, and the overall virtual item is plumped according to the frame structure. By analogy, according to the research content of the first two sections, a complete indoor scene panoramic image is rendered from a multi-viewpoint angle [10]. The key steps in the rendering algorithm are as follows:

```
{
Private enum
WavePosition/(Left = 1, Right = 2, Neutral = 3)/
Private enum
WaveGestureState/(Left = 1, Right = 2, Neutral = 3)
Private struct WaveGestureTracker/
Public int IterationCount;
Public WaveGestureState State/
Public Long Timestamp;
Public WavePosition StartPosition;
Public WavePosition CurrentPosition;
}
```

The above steps record the recognition status of multi view rendering, so as to realize the multi view rendering optimization of indoor scene based on binocular vision.

3 Experimental Study

In order to verify the effectiveness of this method, a simulation experiment is carried out. The proposed method is taken as group A, the method of literature [1] is taken as group B, the method of literature [2] is taken as group C, and the method of literature [3] is taken as Group D. under the same indoor scene test conditions, the differences between different methods are detected, and the test results of day and night are consistent, which will not affect the experimental results.

3.1 Experiment Preparation

The test platform is built. The computer model is rxt2060. The running memory of the computer is 8 GB, the hard disk capacity is 1t, and the video memory capacity is

6 GB, which meets the requirements of this experiment. Insert 3DMAX software and CAD software to facilitate rendering work. Randomly select an indoor building under construction as the experimental object, use landscape scanner to scan the indoor scene of the building in an all-round way, and establish the 3D indoor model of the building according to the scanning results. Table 2 below shows the basic parameters of the experimental scene.

Table 2. Basic parameters of the experimental scene.

Serial number	Information	Parameter
1	House type	Three rooms and two halls
2	South and north windows	2 group/2 group
3	East and West windows	2 group/2 group
4	Gross floor area	141.63 m^3
5	Horizontal height	3.28 m
6	Number of floors	22 layer
7	Interior decoration	Light color, dark color

Different methods are used to render indoor scenes from different viewpoints, and the lighting effects and rendering shading differences between different test groups are compared.

3.2 Light and Shadow Effect Test

Taking a clear day and night as the test background conditions, through different light environments, compare the light and shadow effects obtained by the four test groups before rendering, as shown in Fig. 3 below.

According to the test results in the figure, in the 24-h light shadow relationship acquisition, only the light shadow coefficient of experimental group A has a strong change, and the light shadow coefficient can reach more than 0.9, which shows that the proposed method captures a stronger light shadow relationship. Although the light and shadow coefficients of control group B, group C and group D were all within 0.8, they were not as good as experimental group A in general. It can be seen that the light and shadow relationship of the three test groups was not complete, and they focused more on the rainy weather with insufficient sunshine.

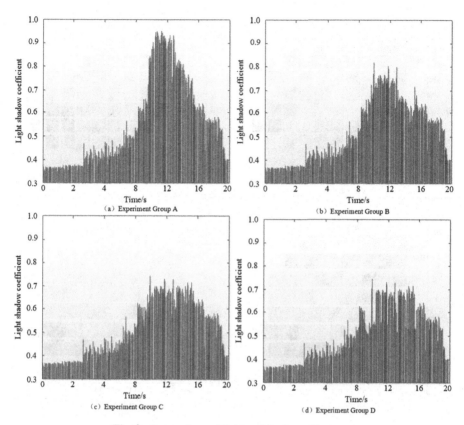

Fig. 3. Comparison of light and shadow effects test

3.3 Rendering Effect Test

The second stage is the rendering effect test. Due to the large differences in the test results of the first stage, it can be seen that the rendering capabilities of the four methods are different. The following Fig. 4 shows the rendering effect test results.

According to the comparison results of the rendering effect test in Fig. 4, it can be seen that the experimental group A has a good rendering effect of the indoor scene with a good light and shadow effect. However, the rendering of indoor scenes is too dim due to poor lighting and shadow effects in experimental group B and experimental group C. At the same time, the light and shadow effect of experimental group D is the worst, so the rendering effect is severely differentiated.

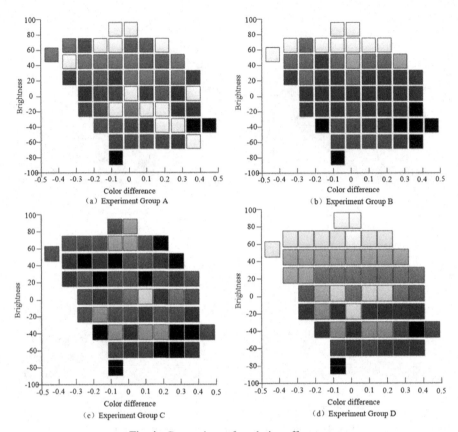

Fig. 4. Comparison of rendering effect test

4   Concluding Remarks

With the help of binocular vision, the optimization design has achieved good results. However, there are still two deficiencies in this study: one is that the calculation is too complex; the other is that the scale of the experiment is not expanded. Therefore, in the future research, we can design a simple algorithm to improve the efficiency of the rendering method, and expand the experiment to add persuasion to the test results.

References

1. Mengyu, J., Ligang, L.: Multi view rendering optimization of indoor scene based on perception. J Univ. Sci. Technol. China **48**(2), 140–147 (2018)
2. Ziyu, W., Yingmin, Z., Yongbin, C., et al.: Optimization of indoor scene semantic segmentation network based on rgb-d image. Automation Information Eng **2**, 27–32 (2020)
3. An, Z., Li, F., Wan, G., et al.: Construction method of indoor and outdoor scene based on BIM and GIS. Digital design 1, 2020, 009 (001):151–153.
4. Chen, X., Li, P.: Analysis of the light and shadow in the modern architecture's expression. China Illuminating Eng. J **29**(01), 82–86 (2018)

5. Fu, P., Chen, X., Wu, L.: Research on absolute positioning of binocular vision based on corner. J. Electr. Measur. Instrument **32**(03), 1–8 (2018)
6. Liu, Y., Wang, Z., Liu, Y., et al.: Reversing obstacle detection based on binocular vision image. J. Chongqing Jiaotong Univ. 37(3), 92–98 (2018)
7. Sun, S., Sun, S.: Precision matching simulation of binocular stereo vision target. Comput. Simul. **35**(11), 413–416 (2018)
8. Liu, S., Liu, D., Srivastava, G., Połap, D., Woźniak, M.: Overview and methods of correlation filter algorithms in object tracking. Complex Intelligent Syst (2020). https://doi.org/10.1007/s40747-020-00161-4
9. Fu, W., Liu, S., Srivastava, G.: Optimization of big data scheduling in social networks[J]. Entropy **21**(9), 902 (2019)
10. Liu, S., Bai, W., Zeng, N., et al.: A fast fractal based compression for MRI images[J]. IEEE Access **7**, 62412–62420 (2019)

A New Confidence Propagation Algorithm for Regional Image Based on Deep Learning

Jia Qian[1]([✉]), Li-li Wang[2], and Hai-yue Huang[3]

[1] Press Department, Anhui University of Arts, Hefei 230002, China
[2] Anhui University of Arts, Hefei 230002, China
[3] Press Office of the Propaganda Department of CPC Anhui Provincial Committee, Hefei 230002, China

Abstract. In order to improve the accuracy of regional image confidence propagation calculation, a regional image confidence propagation algorithm based on deep learning is designed. Firstly, the relevant information is collected, and then the data similarity is calculated. Finally, the regional image confidence propagation algorithm based on deep learning is calculated. The experimental results show that the regional image confidence propagation algorithm based on deep learning improves the calculation accuracy and reduces the calculation time.

Keywords: Deep learning · Regional image · Confidence · Communication

CLC No.: TP 183 document identification code: A

1 Introduction

At present, the research on the confidence of regional image is particularly important. Confidence, also known as reliability, or confidence level and confidence coefficient, means that when sampling to estimate population parameters, due to the randomness of the sample, the conclusion is always uncertain [1]. The span of confidence interval is a positive function of confidence level, that is, the greater the degree of assurance required, a wider confidence interval is bound to be obtained, which correspondingly reduces the accuracy of estimation [2].

Document [3] proposed a deep learning algorithm based on convolution neural network for automatic classification of lung nodules, and realized the division and extraction of regional features. [4] has applied deep learning algorithm to image segmentation and achieved some results. [5] pointed out that the traditional method of line fault detection in floatation mainly focuses on extracting specific foam features for segmentation, such as color and shape. Because the same segmentation algorithm can not be applied to all cases, it often leads to low accuracy and efficiency. An automatic flotation condition recognition method based on convolution neural network (CNN), transfer learning and support vector machine (SVM) is proposed. More specifically, CNN acts as a trainable feature extractor to handle bubble images, and SVM acts as an identifier to detect faults.

W. Fu et al. (Eds.): ICMTEL 2021, LNICST 388, pp. 448–461, 2021.
https://doi.org/10.1007/978-3-030-82565-2_37

Compared with the existing identification methods, the CNN-SVM model can automatically extract the characteristics of bubble images and perform high-precision fault detection.

In order to improve the accuracy of region image confidence propagation analysis, a region image confidence propagation algorithm based on deep learning is designed. Deep learning is a new branch of machine learning. Its purpose is to simulate the human brain to establish a neural network. It can use multiple information processing layers to process image, text, sound and other information, such as human brain [6]. By simulating the nervous system of the human brain, we use a hierarchical model to extract more abstract features from data layer by layer. Such multi-layer nonlinear information processing can be applied to image recognition, pattern recognition and feature extraction. Low level features can form high-level features. We turn such hierarchical structure into deep structure, which shows that deep learning is applied to confidence propagation. It is of great significance in multicast algorithm.

2 Regional Image Information Collection

Before calculating the confidence propagation of regional image, collecting regional image information and mining data, we first use the hybrid structure of deep learning algorithm to pre train the abnormal data, clean and dimensionless the relevant data sources, and get a standardized data matrix and standardized dimension vector [7, 8]. The processing formula is as follows:

$$x_e = \frac{v - s_g}{\sqrt{s_j D(k)}} \tag{1}$$

In formula (1), x_e represents the inherent modal function in the state space of the data source, s_j represents the weight vector of the data, $D(k)$ is the steady-state probability of the overall data, v is the multivariable time series of the data, and s_g is the cleaned data source.

On this basis, the query function [9] is used for further mining, and the process is as follows:

The initial population was constructed by using the cluster centers.

Step 1: randomly extract g network data from complex network data to form sample set $g_m = \{m_1, m_2, \ldots, m_3\}$;

Step 2: randomly select a network data v from the sample set as the first cluster center, and select the network data o with the largest distance from v as the second cluster center;

Step 3: use deep learning algorithm to calculate the distance between the remaining data in the network, and set the nearest value as $D_j = \min\{d_v, d_{v2}\}$;

Step 4: obtain the abnormal network data information corresponding to the nearest distance above;

Step 5: repeat the above steps until all network abnormal data clustering is finished;

Step 6: according to the above process, V cluster center is regarded as the suitable population, and the calculation is repeated until the initial population with B individuals is generated.

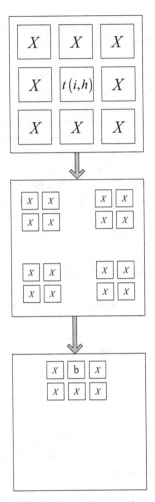

Fig. 1. Correction matrix

Step 7: the query function is the key to active learning. Therefore, the maximum uncertainty equation is a simple application of the query function to query the initial population. The information entropy is used to calculate the uncertainty of the classifier, that is, the greater the information content, the greater the uncertainty. The formula is as follows:

$$H(x) = -\sum_{y \in Y} P\left(\frac{y}{x}\right) \lg P\left(\frac{y}{x}\right) \qquad (2)$$

In formula (2), x is an example, y is a classifier sample, P is a classifier prior probability, and H is an uncertain function, namely information entropy function [10–12]. Examples of the most uncertain and optimal amount of information are selected as follows:

$$u = \arg \max_{x \in U} H(x) \qquad (3)$$

In formula (3), u is the most uncertain equation and U is the sample set where x is located. Outliers are subject independent samples, which will reduce the accuracy of classifier and bring noise to training [13–16]. Therefore, outliers should be removed from the training set. Therefore, the following correction matrix is proposed (Fig. 1):

The above figure shows the schematic diagram of correction matrix. If data point $q(i, h) = 0$ takes four diagonals of points as correction matrix, and then uses the matrix to correct it. If the number of non-zero points in the four points in the matrix is greater than 2, then judge $q(i, h) = 1$, and determine the corresponding another 0, the top point value of 1 matrix is 0, otherwise, the opposite is true.

Step 8: after preprocessing the correction matrix, two complementary data are obtained, and then the two images are superimposed. Since outliers will appear after stacking, k-nearest neighbor (KNN) density is used to remove outliers. The density measurement formula is as follows:

$$A(x) = \frac{1}{k} \sum_{s_i \in s(x)} similarity(x, S_i) \tag{4}$$

In formula (4), k is the number of samples with the greatest similarity to x. To sum up, the selected most informative examples are manually labeled and added to the training for iterative training model [17].

Through the above process, the regional image information mining and collection is completed.

3 Regional Image Similarity Calculation

In order to calculate the regional image similarity and analyze the data similarity information, the decision tree model is used to decompose the data similarity. The standardized dimension vector [15, 18, 19] of standard data is calculated to provide the basis for data analysis in the next step. The calculation formula is as follows:

$$y_0 = y_i \times \begin{bmatrix} y_1 \\ y_2 \\ y_m \end{bmatrix} \tag{5}$$

In formula (5), y_1, y_2 and y_m represent the main elements contained in y_0, and y_i is the main element of data.

According to the above-mentioned standardized data information, the prediction variables and determinants of abnormal data are defined, and the principal component is extracted. The following formula is used to extract the principal component of data. The calculation formula is as follows:

$$F_I = \frac{p \otimes x_0 y}{Y_i} \tag{6}$$

In formula (6), p represents the frequently occurring data, $x_0 y$ represents the frequently occurring data eigenvalue vector, and Y represents the time complexity of decomposition.

After extracting the principal components, the regression equation of the data is established, and the expression is as follows:

$$(x_b, x_n) = X_u \times \frac{a_1 + a_2 + a_3 + a_n}{t} \tag{7}$$

In formula (7), (x_b, x_n) is the linear regression coefficient of data, a_1, a_2, a_3 and a_n represent frequently occurring data, and X_u and t represent the correlation between data variables.

According to the above definition, the establishment of linear regression equation of data is completed [20]. On this basis, using depth learning algorithm, the mixed feature recognition and data classification of data are analyzed according to the classification attributes of network data. Assume that the attribute set of the data is X, singular value decomposed into:

$$X = ND * \frac{t}{v_i} \tag{8}$$

In formula (8), X represents the verification information of the data ontology mapping, ND represents the feature vector of the data, and $\frac{t}{v_i}$ represents the weighted value of the distributed feature quantity of the data.

The feature value of the data is extracted as the training subset, and the deep learning algorithm is used to analyze the similarity of the information [21–23]. The network data information is reconstructed. The average information feature expression after spatial data reconstruction is as follows:

$$I(Q, H) = \sum_d a(z)(l, h) \tag{9}$$

In formula (9), $I(Q, H)$ is the ontology concept set of data, $\sum_d a$ is the redundant data set, z is the joint distribution probability of data, and (l, h) is the abnormal data information.

According to the difference of different data attributes in clustering, the accurate probability density function is obtained as follows:

$$G = P_A^K (1 - F) \tag{10}$$

In formula (10), G is the similarity coefficient of data at sampling time, P_A^K is the information distribution density, and $1 - F$ is the calculation parameter of similarity between data and data.

According to the above formula, complete the calculation of data similarity. On this basis, deep learning common models are used to classify the relevant data. Automatic encoder is used to learn the representation (encoding) of a group of data, which is usually used to reduce the dimension. The simple description of automatic encoder is to encode first and then decode. The automatic encoding assumes that the output data are the same as the input data, and adjusts the parameters of the encoding automatically in the learning process to obtain the weight of each layer. Recently, automatic encoder has been widely

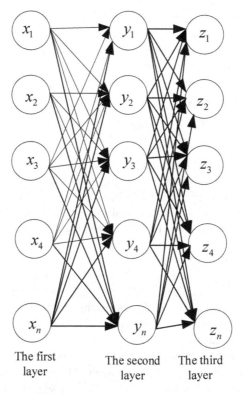

Fig. 2. Automatic encoder structure

used in learning data generation model. As shown in the figure is a simple automatic encoder (Fig. 2):

Among them, there are n cells in the first layer, m cells in the second hidden layer. The input X is the binary vector of n dimension, and the G-dimensional hidden layer represents h through the hidden layer. In general, nonlinear sigmoid functions are used to map in the coding stage [24]:

$$Y = S(WX + b) \qquad (11)$$

In formula (11), S represents a non-linear function. Similarly, in decoding, the vector needs to be reconstructed by a similar function.

$$X' = S\left(W^T Y + b'\right) \qquad (12)$$

In formula (12), X' represents the output of reconstruction, which can also be called the re representation of X. The symbol T is the matrix transposition, W is the weight, and b' is the bias. During the training process, the parameters can be adjusted by minimizing the error. The formula of error should be based on the assumption of reconstruction data distribution:

$$L(X', X) = X' - X^2 \qquad (13)$$

At this time, when the hidden layer is linear, the effect of the first layer to the hidden layer in the automatic encoder is the same as that of PCA. When the hidden layer is nonlinear, the results of the hidden layer can be stacked into many layers, and the input distribution of the automatic encoder becomes multimodal [19, 20, 25]. When input X is a probability vector or a binary vector, the error function is defined as:

$$L(X', X) = - \sum_{n}^{i=1} [x_i \log x_i' + (1 - x_i) \log(1 - x_i')] \tag{14}$$

The training process of automatic encoder is as follows:

Firstly, the unsupervised learning method is used to learn the features of unlabeled sample data. Because when training labeled data, the parameters can be adjusted according to the error between the output and the real value, which is different from automatic encoder. Therefore, in the training process of the automatic encoder, the difference between the output data and the input data is adjusted to minimize the error through encoding and decoding two stages.

Second, layer by layer training, through the encoder to learn features, and then to the next layer of training. According to the minimum reconstruction error in the first step, we think that the output is basically consistent with the original input. When the parameters of the first layer are fixed, we also start to train the second layer to get the parameters of the second layer.

Third, the automatic encoder is supervised to fine tune. Through the above two steps of training, we can get the final automatic encoder. At this time, we need to connect a classifier to classify the data. We can connect the SVM classifier, input the results of the second step into SVM, and then use the labeled data for supervised fine tuning. After the fine-tuning is completed, it can be applied to the real scene for classification.

4 Implementation of Confidence Spread Calculation of Regional Image

The message of belief propagation algorithm is transmitted between data points, so it has a lot of computation. Therefore, the idea of segmentation is introduced to transmit messages between the segmented regions, and a region based belief propagation algorithm is proposed [26]. The first mock exam can reduce the time complexity of the belief propagation algorithm, and the constraint of the same model in the segmentation area can eliminate the influence of distorted data points on the result. [27, 28] can also improve the ability of the belief propagation algorithm to process data. Since the purpose of belief propagation algorithm is to minimize the global energy function and obtain the optimal data distribution, in order to realize the confidence propagation algorithm based on the segmentation region, this paper first defines the region based global energy function.

Therefore, this paper uses the plane template set to replace the search space, in order to take the optimal distribution of the plane template instead of the optimal distribution. The global energy function based on region is defined as follows:

$$E(f) = \sum_{m} \lambda(s_i, s_j)/g \tag{15}$$

In formula (15), g is the set of adjacent segmentation region pairs, and $\sum_m \lambda(s_i, s_j)$ is the label of the plane template allocated by the segmentation area in the template set.

In order to minimize the global energy function formula and obtain the optimal template distribution, the message and confidence transfer functions are further modified. The modification process is as follows (Fig. 3):

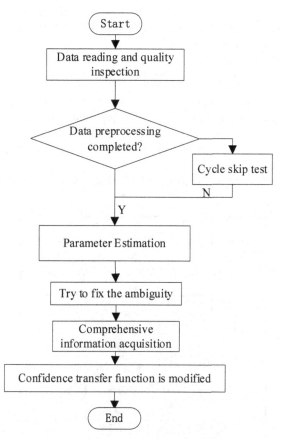

Fig. 3. Modifying process of confidence transfer function

At the same time, the smoothing term in the global energy function is calculated based on the data points in the segmented region, and the data items are calculated based on all the data points in the segmented region, so it is necessary to redefine the inter region smoothing cost and the intra region matching cost.

Message and confidence transmission can be defined as message iterative transmission based on segmented region:

$$k = \min_o /k + o/p \qquad (16)$$

In formula (16), p represents the label set corresponding to the template in the parallax plane template set, o represents the adjacent region set of the segmented region,

k represents the set of other adjacent segmentation regions, and min represents the label
of the plane template assigned by the segmentation area in the template set.

After T iteration, the transmitted message tends to be stable. At this time, the confidence level under different parallax plane templates of each segmentation region tends to be stable, and the iteration stops. Sample and the most representative sample, define a confidence measure function. Using the sample confidence value provided by this function, the most representative examples that need to be labeled manually and the examples with the highest correct rate added to the next round of self-training can be obtained. The confidence formula is as follows:

$$Confidence\ (p_{n1}, p_{nz}) = |p_{n_1} - p_{n2}| \tag{17}$$

In formula (17), n_1 and $n2$ are two nodes of the output layer, p_{n1} and p_{nz} indicate positive and negative polarity respectively, that is, node probability. Therefore, the definition of confidence function is intuitive and reasonable. The higher the value, the greater the confidence value of the classifier, that is, the greater the probability that the output is correct classification.

The simplified diagram of confidence transmission is as follows (Fig. 4):

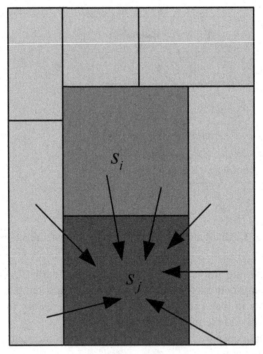

Fig. 4. Simplified graph of confidence transmission

In this case, the confidence degree of segmentation region S_i can be expressed as follows:

$$f^*(s_i) = \arg \min_{f(x_i) \in F} b_{s_i}(f(s_i)) \tag{18}$$

In formula (18), s divides the region, and after obtaining the best plane template label of each segmentation region, the difference value of data points in each region is calculated according to the plane template equation corresponding to the template set.

The most representative examples are selected from the query function (which combines density measurement and information function), and the annotation data is added to the training set to update the classifier performance. At the same time, the confidence measure function selects some of the most credible examples to label automatically, and adds them to the next training cycle. In the next training cycle, the training data can be enriched by adding high confidence samples and expert manually marked samples. The training process is iterative until the iteration criteria are met. In the testing stage, the original test corpus in the target language is translated into the source language by machine translation, and then the classification results are calculated by trained classifiers (Fig. 5).

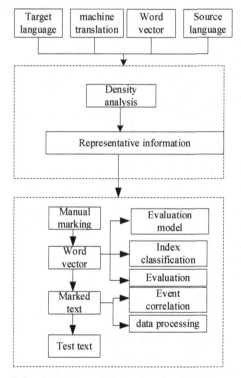

Fig. 5. Regional image information classification process

Through the above process, the confidence propagation calculation of regional image is completed.

5 Experimental Comparison

In order to verify the effectiveness of the regional image confidence propagation algorithm based on deep learning, the experimental comparison is carried out, and in order to ensure the rigor of the experiment, the research method is compared with the convolution neural network based feature map deep learning in literature [3] and the support vector machine based fault detection in flotation process in literature [5], and the accuracy and calculation time of the three methods are compared.

5.1 Comparison of Computational Accuracy

Data set 1 and data set 2 are calculated respectively, and the calculation accuracy of this research method is compared with that of literature [3] and literature [5]. Accuracy is an index to measure the accuracy of data transmission within the specified time. The accuracy formula is as follows

$$\gamma = \frac{\alpha}{\beta} \times 100\% \tag{19}$$

Where, γ is the precision, α is the error code in transmission, and β is the total number of transmitted codes (Figs. 6 and 7):

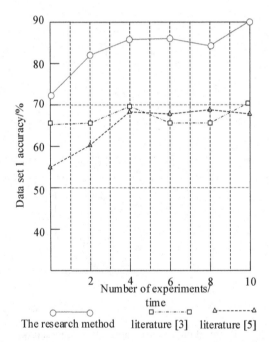

Fig. 6. Comparison of computational accuracy of Data Set 1

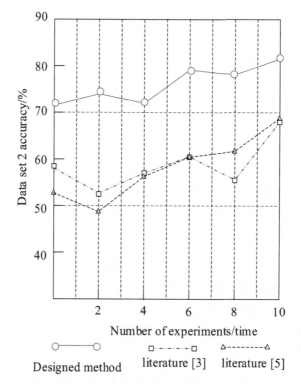

Fig. 7. Comparison of computational accuracy in Data Set 2

It can be seen from the analysis of the above figure that the calculation accuracy of the regional image confidence propagation algorithm based on deep learning is higher, and the data accuracy can be guaranteed at more than 72% in both data sets, which is higher than the methods in literature [3] and literature [5]. This is because this method uses the deep learning algorithm to calculate the similarity of regional information, and improves the calculation accuracy.

5.2 Time Comparison

The results of comparison between the algorithm in this paper and the methods in literature [3] and [5] are shown in the following figure: the calculation time is to test the calculation time of three methods for each group of data with 10 groups of data in dataset 1 as samples.

As shown in Fig. 8, the algorithm of confidence propagation of regional image based on deep learning in this study consumes less time. It is an ideal state within 5 min, and can meet the needs in the actual application process. Compared with the method in literature [3] and [5], it takes more time to calculate. Therefore, the effectiveness of this method is proved.

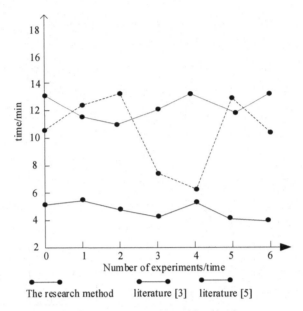

Fig. 8. Comparison of identification time

6 Conclusions

A region image confidence propagation algorithm based on deep learning is designed, and the effectiveness of the method is verified by experiments. However, due to the limitation of research time, there are still some shortcomings in the method of this study. In the follow-up study, we need to further optimize the method of this study.

References

1. Tom, Y., Devamanyu, H., Soujanya, P., et al.: Recent trends in deep learning based natural language processing [review article]. IEEE Comput. Intell. Mag. **13**(3), 55–75 (2018)
2. Sun, X., Wu, P., Hoi, S.C.H.: Face detection using deep learning: an improved faster RCNN approach. Neurocomputing **299**(19), 42–50 (2018)
3. Supriya, S., Subaji, M.: Deep learning the features maps for automated tumor grading of lung nodule structures using convolutional neural networks. Intell. Decis. Technol. **14**(1), 1–18 (2020)
4. Dreizin, D., Zhou, Y., Zhang, Y., et al.: Performance of a deep learning algorithm for automated segmentation and quantification of traumatic pelvic hematomas on CT. J. Digit. Imaging **33**(1), 1–9 (2019)
5. Li, Z.M., Gui, W.H., Zhu, J.Y.: Fault detection in flotation processes based on deep learning and support vector machine. J. Cent. South Univ. **26**(9), 2504–2515 (2019)
6. Altaheri, H., Alsulaiman, M., Muhammad, G.: Date fruit classification for robotic harvesting in a natural environment using deep learning. IEEE Access **7**(1), 117115–117133 (2019)
7. Hu, D., Zhang, Y., He, L., et al.: Low-complexity deep-learning-based DOA estimation for hybrid massive MIMO systems with uniform circular arrays. IEEE Wirel. Commun. Lett. **9**(1), 83–86 (2020)

8. Pathirage, C.S.N., Li, J., Li, L., et al.: Development and application of a deep learning-based sparse autoencoder framework for structural damage identification. Struct. Health Monit. **18**(1), 103–122 (2019)

9. Bao, Y., Tang, Z., Li, H., et al.: Computer vision and deep learning-based data anomaly detection method for structural health monitoring. Struct. Health Monit. **18**(2), 401–421 (2019)

10. Ho, K.K., Gwak, J.: Toward deep learning approaches for learning structure motifs and classifying biological sequences from RNA A-to-I editing events. IEEE Access **7**(99), 127464–127474 (2019)

11. Liu, S., Liu, D., Srivastava, G., et al.: Overview and methods of correlation filter algorithms in object tracking. Complex Intell. Syst. (2020). https://doi.org/10.1007/s40747-020-00161-4

12. Fu, W., Liu, S., Srivastava, G.: Optimization of big data scheduling in social networks. Entropy **21**(9), 902 (2019)

13. Liu, S., Glowatz, M., Zappatore, M., et al. (eds.): e-Learning, e-Education, and Online Training, pp. 1–374. Springer International Publishing, Cham (2018). https://doi.org/10.1007/978-3-319-93719-9

14. Atmane, K., Hongbin, M., Qing, F.: Convolutional neural network based on extreme learning machine for maritime ships recognition in infrared images. Sensors **18**(5), 1490 (2018)

15. Park, Y., Yang, H.S.: Convolutional neural network based on an extreme learning machine for image classification. Neurocomputing **339**, 66–76 (2019)

16. Liu, B., Xie, Y., Yuan, J.: A deep learning assisted node-classified redundant decoding algorithm for BCH codes. IEEE Trans. Commun. **PP**(99), 1 (2020)

17. Sourati, J., Gholipour, A., Dy, J.G., et al.: Intelligent labeling based on fisher information for medical image segmentation using deep learning. IEEE Trans. Med. Imaging **38**, 2642–2653 (2019)

18. Qian, T., Zhu, H., et al.: High temperature dielectric properties measurement system at 915? MHz based on deep learning. Int. J. RF Microw. Comput.-Aided Eng. **29**(11), e21948 (2019)

19. Horisaki, R., Takagi, R., Tanida, J.: Deep-learning-generated holography. Appl. Opt. **57**(14), 3859 (2018)

20. Peixoto, S.A., Medeiros, A.G., Hassan, M.M., et al.: Floor of log: a novel intelligent algorithm for 3D lung segmentation in computer tomography images. Multimedia Syst. (2), 1–13 (2020)

21. Yang, Y., Yang, Z., Yu, J., et al.: Fast calculation of probabilistic power flow: a model-based deep learning approach. IEEE Trans. Smart Grid **PP**(99), 1 (2019)

22. Geetha, A., Gomathi, N.: A robust grey wolf-based deep learning for brain tumour detection in MR images. Biomed. Eng./Biomedizinische Technik **65**(2), 191–207 (2020)

23. Li, X., Huang, H., Zhao, H., et al.: Learning a convolutional neural network for propagation-based stereo image segmentation. Vis. Comput. **36**(1), 39–52 (2020)

24. Duan, S., Yu, S., Chen, Y., et al.: On kernel method-based connectionist models and supervised deep learning without backpropagation. Neural Comput. **32**(1), 1–39 (2019)

25. Yabin, G., Zehan, T., Huanxin, C., et al.: Deep learning-based fault diagnosis of variable refrigerant flow air-conditioning system for building energy saving. Appl. Energy **225**, 732–745 (2018)

26. Park, E., Moon, Y.J., Lim, D., et al.: De-noising SDO/HMI solar magnetograms by image translation method based on deep learning. Astrophys. J. Lett. **891**(1), L4 (2020). (9pp)

27. Kriegeskorte, N., Golan, T.: Neural network models and deep learning. Curr. Biol. **29**(7), R225–R240 (2019)

28. Gautam, A., Singh, V.: CLR-based deep convolutional spiking neural network with validation based stopping for time series classification. Appl. Intell. **50**(3), 830–848 (2020)

Feature Extraction Method of EEG Signal Based on Synchroextracting Transform

Lin Han[1], Liang Lu[3], Haoran Dong[1], Shuangbo Xie[1], Gang Yu[1], Tao Shen[1], Mingxu Sun[1], Tianyi Wang[2], and Xuqun Pei[4(✉)]

[1] University of Jinan, Jinan 250022, China
[2] University of Sheffield, Sheffield S10 2TN, UK
[3] Jinan Minzu Hospital, Jinan 250012, China
[4] Jinan Central Hospital, Jinan 250013, China

Abstract. Brain-Computer Interface (BCI) can convert the electrical activity signal of the cerebral cortex into a computer or other machine language to directly control external equipment. Aiming at the problem of low recognition accuracy of visual stimulation Electroencephalogram (EEG) signals. This paper adopts a method of EEG signal feature extraction based on Synchroextracting Transform (SET). The mean value filter method is used to remove the noise in EEG signal, and the time-frequency energy of EEG signal is taken as the characteristic parameter. Finally, the signal characteristics are input into the SVM model as characteristic parameters. The experimental results show that SET can extract the characteristic energy of EEG signal well and improve the resolution of signal.

Keywords: Synchroextracting Transform · Genetic algorithm · Support vector machine · Brain-Computer Interface

1 Introduction

BCI as an interactive system with the outside world, can realize the communication between human Brain and the outside environment by collecting human Brain electrical signals and transforming them into programs that can be read by instruments after recognition and classification [1]. There are several ways to collect neural movements in the brain, EEG has the advantages of convenient collection, simple equipment, low risk and non-invasiveness. It has become one of the most effective ways to collect data. Since the 21st century, BCI technology has gradually matured. A large number of research results have emerged which can help patients with damaged nerve pathways such as stroke to restore the

Supported by focus on research and development plan in Shandong province (2019JZZY021005).

ability of their limbs to interact with the outside world and improve the quality of life. Its application fields also start from the initial medical diagnosis and medical treatment extends to recreational facilities and even military fields.

The research and development of BCI technology have also promoted the rapid development of many intersecting fields such as artificial intelligence, signal processing, and chip technology. Products related to BCI technology will emerge from the laboratory stage and be used in all areas of society.

Visual Evoked Potential (VEP) is a type of brain electrical evoked potential which refers to changes in the nerve potential in the cortex-occipital area when the brain is stimulated by simple flashes or images with alternating colors. As a characteristic signal reflecting brain activity, visually evoked EEG does not require any training. It has the advantages of high information transmission ability, strong anti-interference ability. In experiment, it is widely used in laboratory EEG signal measurement. When extracting features of EEG signals generated by VEP, it is necessary to find EEG features under different stimuli. The BCI technology includes signal acquisition, preprocessing, feature extraction and classification.

At present, traditional feature extraction methods include Short-time Fourier Transform (STFT), Wavelet Transform (WT) and Canonical Correlation Analysis (CCA). Guler et al. [2] designed five classifiers that used wavelet transform to classify different EEG signals. Lin et al. [3] obtained the EEG signals of VEP under moving conditions, and analyzed the signals using the CCA method, which proved the robustness of CCA to EEG signals. Zhou et al. [4] designed a dynamically optimized steady-state VEP BCI system and added post-processing on the basis of the CCA algorithm, thereby reducing frequency changes between different subjects and improving accuracy.

Although the traditional feature extraction method can reflect the EEG signals of different characteristics, the resolution is low and the accuracy is poor. Based on the above problems, this article uses SET [5] to extract different EEG signals various characteristics. The method of mean filtering is used to remove various interferences from EEG signals, and SVM was used to classify them.

2   Research Methods

2.1   Data Set Description

The data used in this paper are collected from the visual evoked Oddball BRAIN-machine interface experimental paradigm [6]. During the experiment, the subjects need to concentrate on looking at the display screen. The experimental paradigm is a 6×6 matrix composed of letters and numbers. Based on the EEG characteristics induced by visual stimuli, it recognizes the characters the subject is looking at and completes the task of spelling words. The character matrix used in the experiment is shown in Fig. 1.

Fig. 1. The flicker interface used in the experiment.

2.2   Data Preprocessing

The EEG signal is a non-stationary and extremely weak physiological signal. All the collected EEG signals are easily interfered by external noise, which will cause the real EEG signal to be submerged. Therefore, before the identification of the EEG signal, the original signal needs to get rid of the noise. This article uses mean filtering to remove noise from EEG signals.

The results of the original EEG signals after mean filtering is shown in Fig. 2.

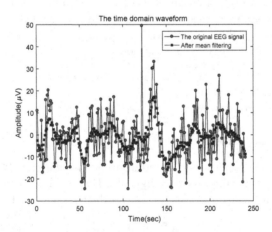

Fig. 2. EEG signal after mean filtering.

3 EEG Signal Feature Extraction and Classification

3.1 Short-Time Fourier Transform

After removing various noises, we need to perform feature extraction to extract the feature vectors of EEG signals under different stimuli. Fourier transform is to convert difficult-to-process time-domain signals into easy-to-analyze frequency-domain signals, and then use some tools to process the frequency-domain signals. But for some unstable signals, for example, the EEG signal, its frequency domain signal changes with time. For this changing signal, the Fourier transform cannot solve it. At this time, the STFT [7] is introduced, the complete signal was cut into time intervals consistent with the set window length through window function, so as to obtain the energy values of different time periods. The formula of the STFT is:

$$G(t, \omega) = \int \left[x(\tau)g(\tau - t)e^{-i\omega\tau}d\tau \right] \tag{1}$$

Among them, $x(\tau)$ is the signal function, $g(\tau)$ is the window function, and ω is the fundamental frequency in the signal function.

3.2 Synchroextracting Transform

When performing STFT, there will be constraints of Heisenberg's uncertainty principle, we cannot observe the signal in time and frequency direction at the same time with arbitrary accuracy, that is, time resolution High, will inevitably lead to poor frequency resolution. Therefore, we use the method of synchronous extraction and transformation for time-frequency analysis of the signal.

Under different stimuli, the energy of the collected EEG signals is different. By comparing the difference in energy value, the characteristics of the EEG signals under different stimuli can be obtained and the EEG signals are extracted after short-term fourier transform. The energy will be dispersed and the specific value of energy cannot be accurately obtained. SET can extract the energy at the center of gravity of the frequency, improve the resolution of the frequency and make the obtained characteristic value more optimized.

In the SET algorithm, the most important thing is to obtain the instantaneous frequency estimation operator through STFT, proceed as follows:

(1) Improve the frequency domain expression of the STFT, multiply it by a rotation factor $e^{i\omega t}$ to improve it, and convert it to its time domain expression. The formula is shown below:

$$G_e(t, \omega) = \int_{-\infty}^{+\infty} x(\tau)g(\tau - t)e^{-i(\tau - t)\omega}d\tau \tag{2}$$

Among them, $e^{i\omega t}$ is the rotation factor.

(2) For a harmonic signal:

$$x(t) = Ae^{i\omega_j t} \tag{3}$$

the partial derivative of its time domain expression can be obtained:

$$\omega_0(t, \omega) = -i\frac{\partial_t G_e(t, \omega)}{G_e(t, \omega)} \tag{4}$$

Among them, $\omega_0(t, \omega)$ is the estimated instantaneous frequency.

(3) As a non-stationary signal, the EEG signal is assumed to be expressed as:

$$x(\tau) = A(t)e^{i\left(\rho(t)+\phi'(t)(\tau-t)\right)} \tag{5}$$

By substituting its STFT into the formula (5). The equation is:

$$\omega_0(t, \omega) = -i\frac{\partial_t G_e(t, \omega)}{G_e(t, \omega)} = \varphi'(t) \tag{6}$$

Among them, $A(t)$ is the non-stationary signal.

(4) For a weak frequency modulation signal, the frequency estimation operator can accurately estimate the instantaneous frequency of the signal, and its expression is:

$$Te(t, \omega) = G_e(t, \omega)\delta\left(\omega - \omega_0(t, \omega)\right) \tag{7}$$

Among them, $\omega_0(t, \omega)$ is the estimated instantaneous frequency. SET is to construct an extraction operator to extract only the energy on the time-frequency ridgeline in the STFT, and ignore the rest of the energy to improve the resolution of the signal.

3.3   Support Vector Machine

SVM is a classifier, which is widely used in the human-machine interface recognition system of the two-class classification model, and it has good robustness and effectiveness [8]. The SVM algorithm obtains the maximum interval from the training samples by constructing the optimal hyperplane, thereby separating two or more training data sets and classifying the test data sets.

In the face of complex classification, when the data set is linearly inseparable in a finite-dimensional space, using kernel functions can put data into a high enough dimensional space. In this paper, radial basis function is chosen as kernel function. The formula is:

$$k\left(x_i, x_j\right) = \exp\left(-g\left\|x_i - x_j\right\|^2\right) \tag{8}$$

Among them, $k\left(x_i, x_j\right)$ is the mapping function, and g is the kernel function parameter.

4   Analysis and Results

According to the characteristics of event-related potentials, EEG signals generate a positive potential waveform after stimulation, namely, P300 potential.

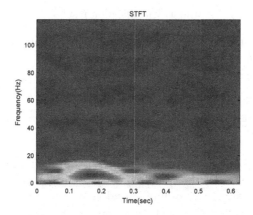

Fig. 3. Energy spectrum of EEG data after STFT.

The noise and artifact are removed by mean filtering and the P300 potential is extracted by SET. The energy spectrum of P300 potential after STFT is shown in Fig. 3. Due to serious energy divergence, the specific location of the stimulus potential cannot be seen.

When EEG signals use SET, the maximum energy near each potential can be extracted, and the P300 potential can be clearly seen from the figure, effectively extracting the required features is shown in Fig. 4.

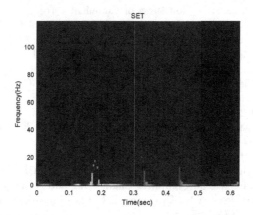

Fig. 4. Energy spectrum of EEG data after SET.

Compared with STFT, SET is more suitable for extracting the characteristics of EEG signal. After feature extraction, the classifier is used for classification. Each subject needs a total of 40 data sets, 20 data sets containing P300 signals, and 20 data sets without P300. Randomly use 24 groups as the training set and 16 groups as the test set. Table 1 shows the classifier accuracy.

Table 1. Classification results.

Experimenter	Contains P300 signal data set	Forecast data set	Accuracy (%)
A	10	9	90
B	9	8	88.9

5   Conclusion

In order to make up for the shortcoming of the traditional STFT algorithm, this article uses SET to extract the time-frequency coefficient on the time-frequency baseline as the characteristic parameter and ignore the energy around the ridge line. Data analysis results show that the proposed method has better resolution and noise robustness than the traditional time-frequency analysis method for EEG signals.

References

1. Zakaria, H., Ahmad, M.: The effect of sampling rate on the extraction of VEP features using wavelet transform. In: 2019 International Seminar on Intelligent Technology and Its Applications, pp. 343–347. IEEE (2019)
2. Guler, I., Ubeyli, E.D.: Adaptive neuro-fuzzy inference system for classification of EEG signals using wavelet coefficients. J. Neurosci. Methods **148**(2), 113–121 (2005)
3. Lin, Y., Wang, Y., Jung, T.: A mobile SSVEP-based brain-computer interface for freely moving humans: the robustness of canonical correlation analysis to motion artifacts. In: 2013 35th Annual International Conference of the IEEE Engineering in Medicine and Biology Society (EMBC), pp. 1350–1353 (2013)
4. Yin, E., Zhou, Z., Jiang, J., et al.: A dynamically optimized SSVEP brain-computer interface (BCI) speller. IEEE Trans. Biomed. Eng. **62**(6), 1447–1456 (2015)
5. Blankertz, B., Mller, K.R., Krusienski, D.J., et al.: The BCI competition III: validating alternative approaches to actual BCI problems. IEEE Trans. Neural Syst. Rehabil. Eng. **14**(2), 153–159 (2006)
6. Yu, G., Yu, M., Xu, C.: Synchroextracting transform. IEEE Trans. Ind. Electron. **64**(10), 8042–8054 (2017)
7. Lu, Y., Jiang, H., Liu, W.: Classification of EEG signal by STFT-CNN framework: identification of right-/left-hand motor imagination in BCI systems. In: The 7th International Conference on Computer Engineering and Networks, pp. 1–8 (2017)
8. Neshov, N.N., Manolova, A.H., Draganov, I.R., et al.: Classification of mental tasks from EEG signals using spectral analysis, PCA and SVM. Cybern. Inf. Technol. **18**(1), 81–92 (2018)

Human Cross-Border Alarm Detection Method Based on OpenPose

Hang Yu[1], Qinjun Zhao[1(✉)], Yong Zhang[1], and Shengjun Shi[2]

[1] University of Jinan, Jinan 250022, China
[2] Harbin Institute of Technology Robotics Group Co., Ltd, Harbin 150000, China
cse_zhaoqj@ujn.edu.cn

Abstract. Cross border detection is often used to monitor the behavior of people in specific places where people often entry and exit, people may cross some unsafe or forbidden borders, thus causing dangerous behaviors, such as large power plant or electrical equipment room. In order to prevent the occurrence of dangerous behaviors, this paper proposed a method for human cross-border alarm detection. First, the camera captures the image of the scene, and design the unsafe bounding line. Second, detect the human and its foot based on OpenPose. Third, when a cross-border behavior occurs, judge whether there is an intersection between the boundary line and the line formed by human feet in two images to send an alarm signal. This method effectively saves costs, replaces artificial ways and improves detection efficiency at the same time, and can make an alarm in time when humans cross an unsafe boundary.

Keywords: Cross-border · Detection · OpenPose · Kalman filter

1 Introduce

Human cross-border detection is often used in places with high insecurity factors, such as large power plant, electrical equipment room, etc. There may be multiple entrances and exits that can be crossed in these places, some of which are dangerous and prohibited. In order to prevent the occurrence of some dangerous behaviors, managers need to monitor people's behaviors through the monitoring system for a long time, and promptly alarm the occurrence of unsafe behaviors. However, through this method of human supervision, not only the cost of supervision is high, but also it is not possible to control all the information in real time, so the efficiency is low [1].

With the development of computer vision technology, it has become a new and effective method to analyze surveillance video by computer, capture human in the video and make judgments. The basic methods of domestic and foreign scholars on human cross-border detection include human detection and cross-border judgment. In the human detection part, [2] proposes to separate humans and backgrounds through Gaussian background modeling methods to detect humans in motion, the deep convolutional network model that has developed rapidly in recent years also has a very good effect on human

W. Fu et al. (Eds.): ICMTEL 2021, LNICST 388, pp. 469–475, 2021.
https://doi.org/10.1007/978-3-030-82565-2_39

detection [3]. The cross-border judgment part mainly analyzes the geometric positions of humans and the boundary line to judge whether humans have cross-border behaviors [4]. In order to realize the simplicity and efficiency of human's cross-border detection application, this paper combines OpenPose and Kalman filter to propose a method that can detect humans in video surveillance in real time and react to the cross-border behavior.

2 Detection and Judgment

2.1 OpenPose

Compared with the method of separating people and background through image processing and modeling to realize the recognition of moving humans, this paper uses the OpenPose model proposed by [5] to realize a more effective and fast human detection method. OpenPose is an open source library which present a real-time approach to detect the 2D pose of multiple people in an image. By using OpenPose, not only the position of the human in the image can be obtained, but also the key points of the human body can be detected. In the part of cross-border detection, it's clear that judging the geometric position of the human foot and the boundary line is more accurate and reliable than judging the geometric position of the entire pedestrian and the boundary line.

OpenPose first initializes and fine-tunes the input image through the first 10 layers of the VGG-19 network to generate a feature map F. The feature map F is calculated through two CNN network branches. Branch 1 is used to predict the confidence of the key points of the human body in the image, and branch 2 predicts the PAFs (Part Affinity Fields) of the key points. The architecture is shown in Fig. 1.

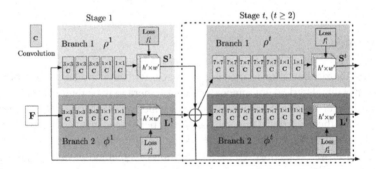

Fig. 1. Architecture of the two-branch CNN

The calculation equation of the confidence maps S^t and the PAFs L^t is as follows:

$$S^t = \rho^t(F, S^{t-1}, L^{t-1}) \quad \forall t \geq 2 \tag{1}$$

$$L^t = \varphi^t(F, S^{t-1}, L^{t-1}) \quad \forall t \geq 2 \tag{2}$$

When using formula (1) and (2) to predict key points, ρ^t and φ^t are the CNNs for inference as Stage t. Each iteration of the algorithm takes the S and T generated in the previous iteration and the original feature map F as input. In order to guide the network to iteratively predict confidence maps of body parts in the first branch and PAFs in the second branch, there are two loss functions at the end of each stage:

$$f_S^t = \sum_{j=1}^{J} \sum_{P} W(P) \bullet ||S_j^t(P) - S_j^*(P)||_2^2 \tag{3}$$

$$f_L^t = \sum_{c=1}^{C} \sum_{P} W(P) \bullet ||L_c^t(P) - L_c^*(P)||_2^2 \tag{4}$$

where S_j^* is the groudtruth part confidence map, L_c^* is the groudtruth part affinity vector field, W is a binary mask which is used to avoid penalizing the true positive predictions.

After multiple iterations, the Hungarian algorithm is finally used to integrate and connect the key points and output the skeleton structure of the human body. As shown in Fig. 2.

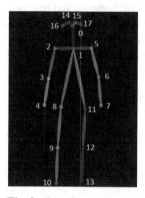

Fig. 2. OpenPose detection

2.2 Judgment

After the 18 key points of the human body are detected in the previous section, the human body needs to be tracked to achieve cross-border tracking. The Kalman filter algorithm is used here. First, draw a rectangular bounding box based on the detected key points of the human body. The bounding box contains the position, height and width of the human body. Second, send the information to the Kalman filter, and the person ID is assigned and traced.

Kalman filter use the bounding box information in the current frame to predict the bounding box information in the next frame, and the prediction can be modified according to the actual boundary box information to achieve the optimal effect [6]. The algorithm is as follows:

Predict:

$$x^k = Ax_{k-1} + Bu_{k-1} \tag{5}$$

$$P_k = AP_{k-1}A^T + Q \tag{6}$$

Update:

$$x^k = P_k H^T (HP_k H^T + R)^{-1} \tag{7}$$

$$x_k = x_k + K_k(z_k - Hx_k) \tag{8}$$

$$P_k = (I - K_k H)P_k \tag{9}$$

where x_k is the state of the target at k time, u_k is the external input, P_k is the error matrix, Q and R are the noise covariance matrices, H is the observation matrix, K_k is the Kalman gain coefficient.

When the different foot points of the target in two images have been caught, connect the foot points using straight lines. Suppose the first point is (x_1, y_1), the second point is (x_2, y_2), use (x_3, y_3) and (x_4, y_4) to represent the ends of the boundary lines. If the result d in the following equation is not zero, then calculate the results of d1, d2, d3, d4, if d1 and d2 are opposite, d3 and d4 are opposite, so there is an intersection between the two lines.

$$d = (x_2 - x_1) * (y_4 - y_3) - (y_2 - y_1) * (x_4 - x_3) \tag{10}$$

$$d1 = (x_4 - x_1) * (y_2 - y_1) - (y_4 - y_1) * (x_2 - x_1) \tag{11}$$

$$d2 = (x_3 - x_1) * (y_2 - y_1) - (y_3 - y_1) * (x_2 - x_1) \tag{12}$$

$$d3 = (x_1 - x_3) * (y_4 - y_3) - (y_1 - y_3) * (x_4 - x_3) \tag{13}$$

$$d4 = (x_2 - x_3) * (y_4 - y_3) - (y_2 - y_3) * (x_4 - x_3) \tag{14}$$

If a person crosses the boundary line, the two lines will have an intersection, then the system can detect that a person is crossing the boundary. As shown in Fig. 3.

2.3 Overall Framework

To summarize, achieve human crossing detection, OpenPose model is used to detect the person's key points in the image at first, and draw the bounding box according to the key points. Then Kalman filter is used to track and assign different human IDs based on the bounding box. Finally, the system judges that someone has crossed the boundary based on the intersection between the line generated by human movement and the boundary line and reacts. The overall framework is shown in Table 1.

Fig. 3. Intersection occurs when human crossing border

Table 1. Overall framework.

Load Model: OpenPose
Input: image from video stream
Repeat:
detect key points of human's body with OpenPose
draw bounding box of human
track human body with Kalman filter
if (human is detected in the image)
record human ID and location
then
compare current information with the next image
if (human illegally crossing borders)
system alarm
end
Until: end of video

3 Experiments and Results

An irregular boundary box is designed as the test object in the experiment, the bounding box can be regular or not irregular, in fact, it depends on your actual demand. Some sides are not allowed to pass, and we mark them with red lines. Besides, one side which we mark it with green line is allowed through. In order to verify the effectiveness of the method, a variety of human behaviors are tested in the experiment, as shown in Fig. 4.

In the experiment, the weight of the OpenPose model used was provided in [5]. The experiment was run on the Intel (R) Core (TM) 9400H CPU, Ubuntu 18.04 operating system. We tested dozens of behaviors and compared their effects on a variety of models, by combining the use of Kalman filter, the final experiment achieved good detection results, and the experimental results are shown in Table 2.

(a)Human dose not crossing border, state is normal

(b)Human crossing legal border, state is normal

(c)Human crossing illegal border, state is alarm

Fig. 4. Three kinds of human state in testing

Table 2. Test result

Method	Detect accuracy
G-RMI[7]+KF	89%
SSD[8]+KF	91%
Ours (OpenPose+KF)	95%

4   Conclusion

In this paper, the human cross-border detection method based on OpenPose and Kalman filter is proposed. Compared with other methods, this method is simple and does not require complex image processing. Experiments have shown that it has high detection accuracy and meets the needs of real-time engineering.

Acknowledgment. Supported by the National Key R & D Program of China (2018AAA0101703) and the key research and development project of Shandong province (2019GNC106093).

References

1. Lei, Y., Shao-yun, W., Li-ran, L., et al.: A pedestrian detection method in intelligent video monitoring system. Comput. Mod. (11), 69 (2019)
2. Raheja, J.L., Deora, S., Chaudhary, A.: Cross border intruder detection in hilly terrain in dark environment. Optik **127**(2), 535–538 (2016)
3. Li, G., Yang, Y., Qu, X.: Deep learning approaches on pedestrian detection in hazy weather. IEEE Trans. Ind. Electron. **67**, 8889–8899 (2019)
4. Dong, G., Song, C.-L.: Video-based pedestrian crossing detection system in mines. Ind. Mine Autom. (02), 29–34 (2017)
5. Cao, Z., Simon, T., Wei, S.E., et al.: Realtime multi-person 2D pose estimation using part affinity fields. In: Proceedings of the IEEE Conference on Computer Vision and Pattern Recognition, pp. 7291–7299 (2017)
6. Li, Q., Li, R., Ji, K., et al.: Kalman filter and its application. In: 2015 8th International Conference on Intelligent Networks and Intelligent Systems (ICINIS), pp. 74–77. IEEE (2015)
7. Papandreou, G., et al.: Towards accurate multi-person pose estimation in the wild, pp. 3711–3719 (2017). https://doi.org/10.1109/CVPR.2017.395.
8. Liu, W., et al.: SSD: single shot multibox detector. In: Leibe, B., Matas, J., Sebe, N., Welling, M. (eds.) ECCV 2016. LNCS, vol. 9905, pp. 21–37. Springer, Cham (2016). https://doi.org/10.1007/978-3-319-46448-0_2

Design and Implementation of Disconnector Condition Monitoring System Based on Attitude Sensor

Yueyu Du[1] and Shubo Qiu[2(✉)]

[1] Jinan Energy Engineering Group Co., Ltd., Jinan 250011, China
[2] School of Electronic and Information Engineering, Qilu
University of Technology, Jinan 250353, China

Abstract. In order to meet the new requirements of substation for the status monitoring of disconnector switch, a disconnector status monitoring system based on MPU9250 was designed. It realizes the double confirmation of status monitoring of disconnector switch in substation. A status determination algorithm of disconnector switch was proposed.

Keywords: Disconnector · Double confirmation · MPU9250

1 Introduction

The state of disconnector switch in domestic power system is generally judged by the remote signal, which is confirmed by operator observation. There are many problems with this approach. Therefore, it is particularly important to develop an effective and reliable state monitoring method for disconnector switches. In paper, the research condition of breaking-closing position monitoring technology for intelligent disconnecting switches is summarized [1].

By researching the attitude estimation and control of 4-axis rotorcraft [2–4], we introduce the attitude sensor commonly used in 4-axis rotorcraft to opening and closing state monitoring system of the disconnector switch. In order to accurately distinguish the disconnecting state of the real time disconnector switch, anopening and closing state monitoring system based on attitude sensor is designed, which providessafety guarantee for power system operation.

2 Hardware Structure

The system includes the attitude sensor installed on the disconnector switch, the receiving device used to receive attitude information and the process attitude data to judge the disconnector switch's opening and closing state. The upper computer used to display the opening and closing state in real time and record the opening and closing record. The system's topology is shown in Fig. 1.

© ICST Institute for Computer Sciences, Social Informatics and Telecommunications Engineering 2021
Published by Springer Nature Switzerland AG 2021. All Rights Reserved
W. Fu et al. (Eds.): ICMTEL 2021, LNICST 388, pp. 476–482, 2021.
https://doi.org/10.1007/978-3-030-82565-2_40

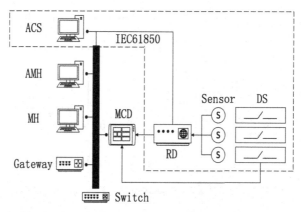

Fig. 1. The framework of disconnector switch status monitoring system

2.1 Function of Attitude Sensor

The attitude sensor MPU9250 is installed on the main shaft of the actuator of the disconnector switch to collect the rotation angle of the main shaft. The switching state of the disconnector is judged by the angle, and the angle data, acceleration, angular acceleration and other data are uploaded to the receiving device through the Modbus-RTU communication protocol. Data is processed based on Kalman filting algorithm [5, 6] and the unscented Kalmam filter algorithm is used for data fusion [7]. Based on the relevant information, the receiving device judges the switching state of the disconnector and controls the output of the corresponding switching quantity. The relevant data is uploaded to the monitoring host and auxiliary control system through the IEC61850 protocol [8, 9].

2.2 Receiving Device Hardware Design

The receiving device obtains sensor data through the RS485 interface, and judges the state of the disconnector switch through the calculation algorithm and logical judgment algorithm. The judgment result is uploaded to the monitoring system through RS485 or IEC61850 and the corresponding hard contact is opened. The hardware diagram of receiving device is shown in Fig. 2.

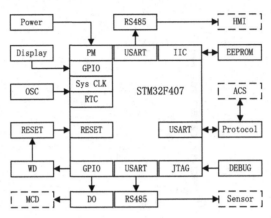

Fig. 2. Hardware diagram of receiving device.

3   State Determination Algorithm of Disconnector

3.1   The State of Disconnector Switch Judgment

The attitude sensor collects the angle of the disconnector in real time. During the deployment, the sensor needs to be calibrated according to the disconnecting and closing position of the disconnector switch. If the initial state of the disconnector switch is on, the sensor is calibrated to $0°$. The Angle margin between the opening and closing positions of the isolator is defined as Δ. The attitude sensor is defined to measure the angle at the beginning of the motion as θ_s and the angle at the end of the motion as θ_f after being awakened. The state judgment method of the disconnector switch is shown in formula 1.

$$\theta_o - \Delta \leq \theta_f - \theta_s \leq \theta_o + \Delta \tag{1}$$

When the angle measured by the attitude sensor satisfies formula 2, the state of the disconnector switch can be determined as off to on.

$$-\theta_o - \Delta \leq \theta_f - \theta_s \leq -\theta_o + \Delta \tag{2}$$

When the angle measured by the attitude sensor satisfies formula 3, the state of the disconnector switch can be determined as opening abnormal state.

$$\Delta < \theta_f - \theta_s < \theta_o - \Delta \tag{3}$$

When the angle measured by the attitude sensor satisfies formula 4, the state of the disconnector switch can be determined as closing abnormal state.

$$-\theta_o + \Delta < \theta_f - \theta_s < -\Delta \tag{4}$$

3.2 State Judgment Logic

To judge the state of the disconnector switch, the receiving device shall determine the opening and closing position and state of the disconnector switch by analyzing the sensor data installed in A, B and C. According to the position and state judgment logic to the isolation switch on and off state to determine. The diagram of position judgment logic is shown in Fig. 3.

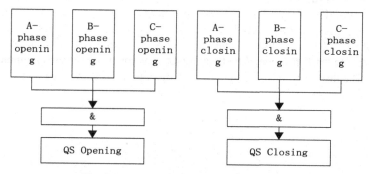

Fig. 3. Diagram of position judgment logic.

The position determination result is taken as the input parameter of the state determination result. The state judgment of the disconnector switch is realized according to the state determination logic. The diagram of state judgment logic is shown in Fig. 4.

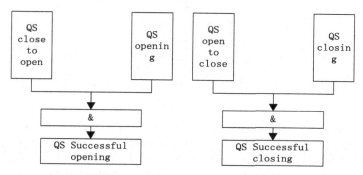

Fig. 4. Diagram of state judgment logic.

4 Software Design

The software of state monitoring system includes attitude sensor program and receiving device program. After the attitude sensor program is initialized, the sensor configuration is loaded and the attitude data is cyclically monitored to calculate the 3-axis acceleration, angular velocity, magnetic force value and temperature. The data is corrected and packaged in Modbus standard format. If a data request is received from the receiving device, it is sent to the receiving device. When a large angle change is detected, the transmission interrupt will be awakened and the data will be actively uploaded to the receiving device, while the data is actively uploaded to the receiving device. The flow chart of sensor programming is shown in Fig. 5. The receiving device program completes the initialization, loads the configuration information of the receiving device. It starts to query the data of each sensor. According to the sensor data received to judge the disconnector switch state and the state of the output of the corresponding hard contacts, the data is packaged into Modbus protocol standard packet. It sends to the IEC61850 protocol conversion module through the serial port, protocol conversion module according to the data point table to map the data to the IED model. The final implementation of IEC61850 communication function. The flow chart of receiving device programming is shown in Fig. 6.

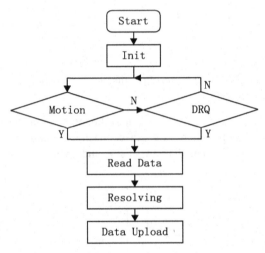

Fig. 5. Flow chart of sensor programming.

In order to verify the reliability of the system, repeated simulation tests are carried out for the system. The simulation test is the consistency test of switching state.

The consistency test method is to simulate the actual application process. The sensor is fixed on the main shaft of the disconnector switch operating mechanism. The opening and closing of the disconnector switch is simulated by rotating the main shaft of the operating mechanism. The system was simulated for 100 times in each of four states. The experimental results are shown in Table 1.

The consistency of disconnector switch is shown in Table 1. The accuracy of the opening and closing of four states reached 100% via 400 tests, which meets the practical application needs. It can be judged that the device can determine the disconnecting switch switching state stably and accurately.

Mentioned experimental data shows that the system can monitor the switching state of the disconnector stably and reliably in real time.

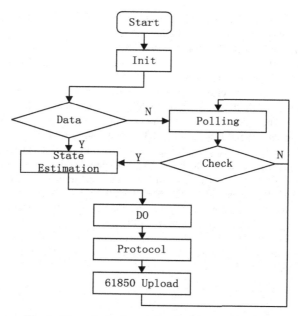

Fig. 6. Flow chart of receiving device programming.

Table 1. Opening and closing state to determine the consistency of the experimental results.

Path	Number of replicated tests	Number of correct tests	Number of errors	Consistency%
Closing in place	100	100	0	100
Closing abnormal	100	100	0	100
Opening in place	100	100	0	100
Opening abnormal	100	100	0	100

5 Conclusion

The state monitoring system designed in this paper can effectively realize the real-time monitoring of the state of the disconnector switch, which provides an effective criterion for double confirmation of disconnector switch in substation. The experimental results show that the system can effectively improve the monitoring accuracy of substation disconnector switch state. Mentioned research can support the intelligent development of substation.

References

1. Wang, B., Mao, W., Jiang, Y., et al.: Review on breaking-closing position monitoring method for intelligent disconnecting switches. IOP Conf. Ser. Earth Environ. Sci. **223**, 012026 (2019)

2. Rinaldi, F., Gargioli, A., Quagliotti, F.: PID and LQ regulation of a multirotor attitude: mathematical modelling, simulations and experimental results. J. Intell. Rob. Syst. **73**(1–4), 33–50 (2013). https://doi.org/10.1007/s10846-013-9911-x

3. Zhao, Z., Han, L., He, B., et al.: The research of four-rotor attitude simulator based on Matlab. Int. J. Autom. Control Eng. **4**(1), 14–18 (2015)

4. Si, S., Huaqing, M., Chun, L., et al.: Design and realization of attitude sensor estimation system. Comput. Measur. Control **019**(07), 1562–1564 (2011)

5. Peigang, J., Mingzhe, L.: Research on method of compensation of attitude sensor based on Kalman filtering algorithm. Manuf. Autom. **037**(12), 41–44 (2015)

6. Yangchun, L., Junling, X., Cheng, H., et al.: Attitude detection and data fusion based on sensor of MPU9250. J. Henan Univ. Sci. Technol. (Nat. Sci.) **036**(04), 16–18 (2015)

7. Xin, Z., Zhiyong, L., Zhiyi, Z., et al.: Design of attitude measurement system based on MEMS sensors. Comput. Meas. Control **023**(02), 362–365 (2015)

8. Xu, J., Xu, X., Du, H., et al.: Intelligent operation order management system of power network. Electr. Power Autom. Equip. **029**(11), 98–101 (2009)

9. Fei, D., Guangzhen, W., Huojun, Z., et al.: A detection platform of attitude sensor system used for double reconfirmation technology of disconnecting switch's opening and closing position. Electr. Power **052**(011), 153–158 (2019)

Author Index

Ahuja, Manish II-385
Alamir, Manal I-333
Alharth, Sadeem I-333
Alqurashi, Shahad I-333
Alqurashi, Tahani I-333
Ang, Li I-51
Anqi, Bi I-248

Bao, Ying II-79, II-338
Bayyarapu, Pavan Kumar II-304
Bi, Shuhui I-388, I-398, I-502, I-510
Bing, Zhao I-3, II-373

Can-song, Ding I-145
Cao, Wei-Ping I-39, II-349
Challa, Nagamaisamma II-304
Chen, Chonggao II-128, II-152
Chen, Jingyang II-331
Chen, Xindong I-273
Chen, Xinlei I-368, II-278
Chen, Xiyuan I-137, I-437, I-442, I-452,
    I-460, I-518, I-528
Cui, Ying II-321

Dan, Luo I-541
Da-xing, Chen I-91
Ding, Jinshun II-257, II-267
Ding, Yiqiong I-103, I-115
Dong, Haoran II-462
Du, Guangyue I-377
Du, Yueyu II-476
Dubash, Neville II-385

Er-wei, Liu II-362

Fan, Chao I-255
Fang, Jiajuan I-180, I-344
Fang, Weiqing II-267
Fei-feng, Wang I-91
Feng, Jidong I-470

Gao, Ruina II-21
Gao, Xingjun I-128
Gao, Ya II-43

Gao, Yalan II-21
Ge, Yijuan I-265
Geng, Renkang I-492
Geng, Yikun I-460
Gu, Yuhan II-331
Guan, Yuanyuan I-311, I-321
Guang, Xie I-77
Guan-hua, Fu I-91, I-145
Guo, Hang I-273, I-407, I-414

Han, Han I-39
Han, Lin II-462
Hao, Wei I-235
He, Jing II-425
He, Wei- na I-553
He, Wei-na I-566
Hou, Bo I-157, I-170
Hu, Rong II-413
Huang, Hai-yue II-448
Huang, Xi II-43
Huang, Yi I-191
Hui-jun, Wang I-51
Hussain, Samir I-485

Jia, Chenchong II-43
Jia, Xia I-91
Jiang, Hua I-281, II-62
Jiang, Rui II-62
Jiang, Xianwei II-21, II-43
Jing, He II-436
Jingya, Zheng II-178

Kai, Shen I-145
Khare, Ashish II-402
Khare, Manish II-402

Lei, Jiaxi II-331
Lei, Juan II-43
Li, Ang II-165
Li, Bin II-290
Li, Fukun I-502, I-510
Li, Hailei I-414
Li, Hangxiao II-331
Li, Huixia I-414

Li, Runda   II-290, II-331
Li, Shiqi   I-442
Li, Wei   I-427
Li, Xue   I-388
Li, Ying   II-203, II-243
Li, Yiping   I-202
Li, Yongbin   I-128
Li, Yu   I-255
Li, Zijian   I-128
Li, Zimeng   II-331
Liang, Tongwei   I-214
Lian-huan, Zhu   I-91, I-145
Liao, Jiehua   I-407
Lima, Dimas   II-290
Lin, Guozhi   I-103, I-115
Liu, Dong-dong   II-103
Liu, Dong-Dong   II-92
Liu, Er-wei   II-189
Liu, Tongqian   I-470
Liu, Yuan   I-235
Lu, Liang   II-462
Lu, Yanjing   I-180, I-344
Luo, Dan   II-413
Lv, Conggang   I-354, II-230

Ma, Chang-song   I-157, I-170
Ma, Gege   I-281, II-71
Ma, Liyao   I-388, I-492, I-502
Ma, Wanfeng   I-470
Ma, Zhen   I-137, I-437
Mankaveettil, Roopakala   II-304
Mao, Anmeng   I-476
Maryala, Rajeshwar   II-304

Ni, Yueli   I-265

Pan, Yuxia   I-64
Parsha, Saitheja   II-304
Patel, Hemil   I-485, II-304
Pei, Xuqun   II-462

Qian, Jia   II-117, II-448
Qian, Zhou   I-3, II-373
Qiao, Jia   I-476
Qiao, Yifei   II-43
Qiu, Shi   II-321
Qiu, Shubo   II-476

Rajan, Reshmi Kanakuzhiyil   II-304
Ramachandra, Nisha   II-385

Rao, Raghotham M.   II-385
Ren, Yu   II-257
Riaz, Usman   I-485
Rong, Hu   I-541

Shao, Xin   I-137
Shen, Tao   I-388, I-398, II-462
Sheng, Fangqing   I-281
Shi, Shengjun   I-223, II-469
Shi, Shumeng   II-331
Shi, Yuwei   II-331
Srivastava, Prashant   II-402
Su, Meiying   I-368
Sun, Bin   I-492
Sun, Mingxu   II-462

Tan, Yu-Shuo   I-39, II-349
Tang, Lai-feng   I-579, I-590
Tang, Wei   II-128, II-152
Tong, Le   I-288
Tong, Lei   I-298

Wang, Aihui   I-427
Wang, Bo   I-223
Wang, Fen   I-288, I-298
Wang, Hepeng   I-273
Wang, Hui-jun   II-165
Wang, Jing   I-39
Wang, Junwei   I-137, I-437
Wang, Lei   I-214
Wang, Li-li   II-117, II-448
Wang, Meng   I-502, I-510
Wang, Qiang   I-579, I-590
Wang, Tianyi   II-462
Wang, Xinyan   II-331
Wang, Ya-fei   I-553, I-566
Wang, Yixin   II-257, II-267
Wang, Yubin   I-191, I-202
Wang, Zhigang   I-273, I-407
Wei, Wei   I-145
Wei-yang, Zhu   I-145
Wen, Shengjun   I-214
Weng, Yuxiang   II-21
Wenhao, Ying   I-248
Wölfel, Matthias   II-216
Wu, Yutong   II-331

Xiao, Zijin   II-203, II-243
Xie, Guang   I-64
Xie, Shuangbo   II-462

Xu, Chihao   II-331
Xu, Kefeng   II-257
Xu, Yuan   I-470, I-492
Xu, Zheng   I-398

Yan, Jichao   II-142, II-178
Yang, Sun   I-91
Yang, Yaojun   II-331
Yao, Shihan   II-331
Ye, Chengyu   II-331
Ye, Jiufeng   II-278
Yu, Gang   II-462
Yu, Hang   II-469
Yu, Jiaohao   I-414
yu, Jun   I-427
Yu, Li   I-311, I-321
Yu, Min   I-273, I-407, I-414
Yuxia, Pan   I-77

Zhan, Qianyi   I-235
Zhang, Baijun   II-331
Zhang, Bo   I-502, I-510
Zhang, Li   I-14, I-27

Zhang, ShengWei   II-3, II-11
Zhang, Siyi   I-452
Zhang, Wen-Bin   I-39
Zhang, Xiaoling   I-265
Zhang, Xiaotian   I-518
Zhang, Yang   I-281
Zhang, Yong   I-223, I-476, II-469
Zhang, Yu   I-528
Zhanggu, Wenxuan   II-331
Zhao, Dongming   II-278
Zhao, Qinjun   I-223, I-398, II-469
Zhao, Ying   I-14, I-27
Zhen, Zhuoyang   II-331
Zheng, Jingya   II-142
Zhong, Wei   II-278
Zhou, Hai   II-203, II-243
Zhou, Qiang   I-128
Zhou, YunLei   II-3
Zhu, RongXin   II-11
Zhu, Rongxin   II-21
Zhu, Wei   II-267
Zhu, ZhaoSong   II-11
Zhu, Zhaosong   II-3

Printed in the United States
by Baker & Taylor Publisher Services